D0772555

Why Nietzsche Now?

Why Nietzsche Now?

Edited by Daniel O'Hara

INDIANA UNIVERSITY PRESS
Bloomington

First cloth edition published by Indiana University Press 1985
Copyright © 1981, 1985 by *boundary 2*, The State University of New York

All rights reserved

No part of this book may be reproduced or utilized in any form or by any
means, electronic or mechanical, including photocopying and recording, or
by any information storage and retrieval system, without permission in
writing from the publisher. The Association of American University Presses'
Resolution on Permissions constitutes the only exception to this prohibition.

Library of Congress Cataloging in Publication Data
Main entry under title:

Why Nietzsche now?

   1. Nietzsche, Friedrich Wilhelm, 1844–1900—
Addresses, essays, lectures.   I. O'Hara, Daniel T.,
1948–   .
B3317.W455   1985   193   84-48455
ISBN 0-253-36530-9

1 2 3 4 5   89 88 87 86 85

CONTENTS

223515

IV Critiques

Preface

Daniel O'Hara

Friedrich Nietzsche is not a serious writer. One may wonder, if this is really the case, why one would edit a collection of critical essays on the renewed impact of Nietzsche's influence in modern American culture. All of these essays, moreover, focus in one way or another upon the radical questions of value—about the worth or meaning of culture, religion, morality, science, art, the self, life itself—which everyone else understands Nietzsche to have raised in his work, and especially in *Thus Spoke Zarathustra.* What can one mean, then, by claiming that Nietzsche's not a serious writer? Let me try to explain my view and in the process I hope to give an account of this collection, which is intended to raise its own corollary question: "Why Nietzsche Now?" That is, by what right do these critics of Nietzsche bring *him* up again in our supposedly postmodern time?

Well, it is simply a fact of life in the disciplines of philosophy, cultural history, religious studies, and literary theory in America that Nietzsche has made another appearance. But unlike his earlier appearance before World War I as fierce ideologue of the aristocratic will or that after World War II as suffering precursor of an existential heroism, this most recent appearance by Nietzsche has been as the linguistic pathologist of the diverse signs of nihilism which are constitutive of the entire tradition of Western culture from the age of the

vii

Greeks to that of the Vietnam-era student revolutionaries and their current heirs in the academic and critical communities. For American scholars across the curriculum Nietzsche has recently come to stand for the new valorization of language and writing as the key to understanding nihilism that has been made possible and popular now by the revisionary readings and applications of Nietzsche found in the destructive hermeneutics of Martin Heidegger, in the deconstructive criticism of Jacques Derrida, and in Michel Foucault's genealogy of power in the scientific discourses of modern knowledge—psychiatric, medical, humanistic, penal, and so on.

This fact of intellectual life—Nietzsche's recent reappearance on the American scene as a post-structuralist strategist of textual power and diagnostician of decadence—inspires the various readings, comparative studies, and critiques of Nietzsche's works presented in this collection by leading scholar-critics of their generations from philosophy, religious studies, and critical theory. The essays by Heidegger, Miller, and Bové represent nearly in pure form the three major strains—hermeneutic/philosophical, deconstructive, and "archeological" or "genealogical"—which continue generally to inform the postmodern appropriation of Nietzsche and which are clearly blended together in the other essays included here. And for all three critical strains, Nietzsche is certainly not a serious writer.

For Heidegger, who represents the first strain, Nietzsche is indeed heroic—but it is the heroism of the philosophical buffoon who meant via *Zarathustra* especially to free us from the tradition of metaphysics only to end up reduplicating its structures of opposition by simply reversing Plato and celebrating sense over knowledge, will over reason, becoming over being, poetic language over rational dialectic. By saying this I don't mean to suggest that Heidegger is unsympathetic to Nietzsche. Rather, Heidegger identifies Nietzsche's problem as being his desire to become a poet in *Zarathustra,* and his failure to recall that the thinker and the poet are related but separate, distinct. Seduced by the dialectical play of philosophical structures and oppositions, as if it were the play of figures of speech, Nietzsche ends up repeating the very errors of the past he would overcome. The silence that results from this self-negation, however, Heidegger identifies as "a telling silence," the silence which stands at the origins of language and saying the unsaid: "Supremely thoughtful utterance . . . corresponds to the most profound essence of language, which has its origins in silence. As one in touch with telling silence, the thinker, in a way peculiar to him, rises to the rank of the poet; yet he remains eternally distinct from the poet, just as for his part, the poet remains eternally distinct from the thinker." Thus, for Heidegger and for the traditions of Nietzsche interpretation he inaugurates, Nietzsche functions as an heroic cautionary example, to be taken seriously precisely because one can only take his telling apocalyptic silence with a rueful originary laughter. Authentic philosophical seriousness, that is, fully resides in Kant, in Hegel, in Husserl, and, of course, in Heidegger himself; Nietzsche acts to help Heidegger become more himself. He is, in short, a comic educator as Schopenhauer was a tragic one for Nietzsche.

Similarly, for Hillis Miller, who represents the literary critical strain, Nietzsche is touched with the heroic; but even more than in Heidegger's case, Miller's Nietzsche is comical—with the comicalness reminiscent of the absent-minded professor whose words betray him—albeit in an exemplary ironic fashion:

> The inaccessible X is both outside Nietzsche's essay as its unnamable ground and also present inside it as what prevents it from being logical or systematic.
>
> Nietzsche both knows this and does not know it. He both forgets it and remembers. His essay forgets in one place what it remembers in another. . . . This dangerous incoherence is repeated by the reader of Nietzsche's essay ["On Truth and Lies in a Nonmoral Sense"].
>
> This impotence of both author and reader is the primary evidence of the presence of non-presence, everywhere in the text, of the unknown X, which it wrestles, unsuccessfully, to locate and name.

As Socrates argues in the *Phaedrus* against the partisans of sophistry who rely upon the material inscriptions of writing in a text for their sense instead of upon the representations of the truth implanted in the psyche by the authentic (because spoken) words of the genuine teacher; so Miller discovers a similar opposition in Nietzsche's text, but with an opposite evaluation. Writing, of whatever kind, including the proto-writing of speech, can play tricks with one's mind, the greatest of these performances being, of course, the Socratic dream of absolute presence. What Nietzsche's text both remembers and forgets, remembers to forget and forgets to remember, is precisely this play of inscriptions and signification which generates the opposition of presence and absence, genuine language and sophistry, transcendental signified and unnamable (because abysmal) ground of signification that Nietzsche *performs* in his text *as* a text. Thus Miller, following here Derrida, de Man, and in part Bloom, celebrates Nietzsche precisely for his uncanny self-betrayal, arising as it does from the endless dialectic of presence and absence, blindness and insight, or poetry and repression, which shapes his representative non-representational modern texts.

Finally, for Paul Bové, who speaks for the sociological strain in the recent history of Nietzsche interpretation, our hero expresses the sublime pathos, the pathetic sublimity of the alienated writer who both resists the temptation to re-imagine himself as a grand lawgiver in the style of Moses or Rousseau or Lenin by tracing the genealogy of this very figure; and who in fact surrenders to it, at times, against his announced intentions. That is, Nietzsche, for Bové, surrenders often to this dangerously seductive phantasmagoria of the modern intellectual. Thus, Bové retraces in his essay the way oppositional critics of Western culture compensate themselves and their kind in such fantastic solitary (and so falsely ideological or "regressive") visions.

> The genealogist is, as it were, a powerful synecdoche of this composite trope—powerful because he represents the sublime victory of the marginal intellectual over nihilism. That is, the genealogist is a domestic figure in Modernity. Akin in training and values to the leaders of the authorized disciplines of the hegemonic culture, the genealogist is a transformation of his enemy; he problematizes knowledge in a carnival of "truths." He is not outlandish, but subversive and different. Most importantly, his strength depends on his vision of himself as a predecessor of the perfect man. The genealogist promises that culture shall be formed once again by the intellectual warfare of ideas which will determine the "evolutionary" course of history. Like John crying in the wilderness, the genealogist pronounces a redeemer whose figure he himself is. . . . In Nietzsche's vision, the incarnation occurs *not* in an annunciation of the Word, but in a carnival staged repeatedly as a comic battle against knowledge and truth, and so against nihilism. The genealogist does not make himself god in his agonistic research; but, in each work's victory over ascetic nihilism, he appears an emanation of the perfect man—whose intuition fuels the genealogist's warfare to redeem man himself.

In light of these three strains—loosely speaking, Heideggerian, Derridean, Foucaultian—in postmodern critical appropriations of him, Nietzsche can only be seen as the prophet of our laughter: an innocence defined by its indetermination, its inexorable evasion of all human categories, including those of the heroic, the freely-playful, and the sublimely self-betraying. We laugh, therefore, with and at Nietzsche, as the herald neither of the poetic thinker, nor of the absent-minded deconstructor, nor of the genealogist of the humanistic concept of the always emerging "perfect man." Rather, it is as the prophet of an ironic perception of the worthlessness at the heart of *culture alone* that we laugh at and with him. For such a laughter and such a perception occasioning it speak of a Dionysian affirmation of nature, of the primordial innocence—without any definite content—of all becoming and (self-) overcoming, which forever comes round again at last: After all, isn't it the spirit of gravity in all its manifestations, however transcendent or abysmal, which Zarathustra, Nietzsche's stalking oracle, must attempt to *avoid* if he is to affirm the eternal recurrence of all things, "good" and "bad" included?

"You bold ones who surround me! You searchers, researchers, and whoever among you has embarked with cunning sails on unexplored seas. You who are glad of riddles! Guess me this riddle that I saw then, interpret me the vision of the loneliest. For it was a vision and a foreseeing. *What* did I see then in a parable? And *who* is it who must yet come one day? *Who* is the shepherd into whose throat the snake crawled thus? *Who* is the man into whose throat all that is heaviest and blackest will crawl thus? The shepherd, however, bit as my cry counseled him; he bit with a good bite. Far away he spewed the head of the snake—and he jumped up. No longer shepherd, no longer human—one changed, radiant, *laughing!* Never yet on earth has a human being laughed as he laughed! O my brothers, I heard a laughter that was no human laughter; and now a thirst gnaws at me, a longing that never grows still. My longing for this laughter gnaws at me; oh, how do I bear to go on living! And how could I bear to die now!" Thus spoke Zarathustra.

The rest of the fine essays in this collection work within the limits of this composite view of Nietzsche as an unserious writer whose very unseriousness must be accounted for and analyzed; or historically traced to and compared with such figures as Kant, Hegel, Schopenhauer or Pound, Joyce, James; or more simply read with appreciation and celebrated—or in large part critiqued as all too timely now in our postmodern age.

Yet in saying this, I don't mean to suggest that the other contributions are merely adumbrations of these three conceptual strains in current Nietzsche studies. Stanley Corngold's brilliant and original analysis of the self in Nietzsche's major period (1882-1888) or Joseph Riddel's playful mocking of Poundian poetics and Nietzschean transvaluations or Rodolph Gasché's critique of traditional notions of form via a reading of *Ecce Homo*—none of these or any of the other innovative essays can be reduced to a few discursive paradigms and their corrosive interplay. Having recognized this fact, however, one must also admit that Heidegger clearly and decisively informs Corngold, as Derrida does Riddel, or as both masters of suspicion inform Gasché—or, for that matter, Krell in his comic burrowings in the ontotheological tradition, Allison in his astringent revaluation of Nietzsche's views of Kant and Schopenhauer, or Silverman and Kuenzli in their destructive and deconstructive readings—respectively—of *Ecce Homo* and *Zarathustra*. And clearly, the sociological strain, the placement of Nietzsche's complex discursive structures within the cultural archive of the last two centuries, characterizes the contribution of Joseph Buttigieg, who relates Joyce to Nietzsche, of Cornel West, who sees Nietzsche as a precursor of postmodern, anti-foundational philosophy, and of

Gary Shapiro, who reads *The Antichrist* in the context of Renan's immense philological labors. Finally, McFadden also sees Nietzsche as a precursor, this time, as a precursor of black comedy; and Tracy Strong finds Nietzsche's life, works, and implicit political vision to be a sustained critique of the simplistic application of genealogical models to the study of cultural history.

But, as I have indicated already, such categorizations as are here deployed function to indicate alliances of interests, often partially realized by the individual contributors, which the collection brings out and highlights in a manner common to that of any collection. The essentially collective nature of research and critique thus stands in stark relief generally here, and could no more pointedly be illustrated than in Jonathan Arac's socially allusive analysis of Paul de Man's ironically Heideggerian/Derridan allegories of Nietzsche's subversive acts of (self-) reading. The collection itself also demonstrates this truism of scholarly disciplines, since it originates as a project and exists as a production, thanks essentially to the cooperation and support, intellectual and otherwise, of all the members of the group associated with *boundary 2: a journal of postmodern literature and culture,* and especially thanks to the help of the founding editor, William V. Spanos, who saved my editorial supervision of this collection more than once from needless obstacles and delays. The dangers of believing and acting (out) as if criticism were the intellectual equivalent of nineteenth-century *laissez-faire* enterprise are recorded in Charles Altieri's essay on Christopher Lasch's *The Culture of Narcissism* and Nietzsche's *Ecce Homo*—the latter is itself the inescapable enactment and critique of the bourgeois conception of the subject which defines the modern form of idealism as being also the experience of nihilism, an historical irony which Nietzsche learns at last to find divinely laughable. (This possibility of comic transcendence explains why *Ecce Homo* haunts this volume as much as nihilism does.) In short, then, this collection represents a concerted study of Nietzsche as the classic post-Enlightenment, impossible representation of the question of nihilism, whose specters shape all post-Nietzschean critics still.

Why Nietzsche Now?

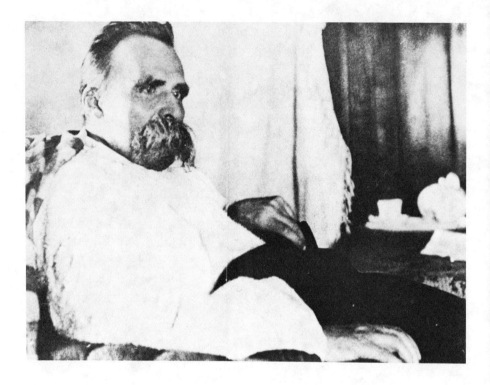

I Introduction

The Prophet of Our Laughter:
Or Nietzsche As—Educator?

Laughter is an affection arising from a strained expecta-
tion being suddenly reduced to nothing.
—Kant, *The Critique of Judgment*

Nietzsche, if I understand him, believed only in comic or
preposterous schemes of transumption, in which a future
laughter is introjected and a past tragedy is projected.
—Bloom, *Poetry and Repression*

One of the subtlest means for keeping up the deception
at least as long as possible and of successfully appearing
more stupid than one is—which in ordinary life is often
as desirable as an umbrella—is called *enthusiasm* . . .
—Nietzsche, *Beyond Good and Evil*

. . . . And with that I again return to the place from
which I set Out—*The Birth of Tragedy* was my first revaluation of all values: with that I again plant myself in
the soil out of which I draw all that I will and *can*—I, the

last disciple of the philosopher Dionysus—I, the teacher
of the eternal recurrence . . . .

—Nietzsche, *Twilight of the Idols*

I
The World Seen From Within

An 1885 entry in *The Will to Power* (Section 91) profiles succinctly the problematic form of modern writing as Nietzsche understands
it:

On German Pessimism

The eclipse, the pessimistic coloring, comes necessarily
in the wake of the Enlightenment. Around 1770 the decline of cheerfulness began to be noticed; women, with
that feminine instinct which always sides with virtue,
supposed that immorality was the cause. Galiani hit the
nail on the head: he cites Voltaire's verse:
Un monstre gai vaut mieux
Qu'un sentimental ennuyeux.
When I believe that I am a few centuries ahead in Enlightenment not only of Voltaire but even of Galiani,
who was far profounder—how far must I have got in the
increase of darkness! And this is really the case, and I be-
wared in time, with some sort of regret, of the German
and Christian narrowness and inconsequence of pessimism *à la* Schopenhauer or, worse, Leopardi, and
sought out the most quintessential forms (Asia). But in
order to endure this type of extreme pessimism (it can
be perceived here and there in my *Birth of Tragedy*) and
to live alone "without God and morality," I had to invent a counterpart for myself. Perhaps I know why man
alone laughs: he alone suffers so deeply that he *had* to
invent laughter. The unhappiest and most melancholy
animal is, as fitting, the most cheerful.[1]

Nietzsche deploys here a critical historical perspective (the Enlightenment
beginning and its decadent Romantic aftermath) on a significant issue of
his day (the question of German Pessimism). He does so in order to chart
in the text the emergence of his own eccentric sublimity (how the idea of
his Dionysian counterpart, Zarathustra, overtook him).[2]

All this is done in terms of an antithetical design of previous and
still possible influences (Galiani, Voltaire, Schopenhauer, and even Leopardi) that Nietzsche would go beyond. This design serves to highlight his

2

own Promethean difference from his dangerously belated time (as seen in the growing chiaroscuro effect that signals the increase in him of both masculine Enlightenment and feminine hysteria). The result of this solitary act of writing is a self-reflection that Nietzsche claims discloses to him the tragic nature of man's laughter (its awful recurrent necessity) and its therapeutic power of daimonic invention (*"Un gai monstre"* etc.). By means of this "tragic knowledge,"[3] Nietzsche would overcome his Romantic heritage.

The critical use of history to reduce the pretentions of the contemporary scene, and the coercive imposition of a sublime antithetical design on that abbreviated history recreate past origins in the interest of future aims, viz., Nietzsche's capacity to continue to write. Nietzsche represents this process of reading as the rediscovery of man's archetypal or daimonic imagination. As Nietzsche sees it, critical reduction, sublime re-creation, and mythic rediscovery mark the three phases of (self-) interpretation that compose the dialectic of modern irony—that self-conscious insight of the Western critical intelligence into its own historically formative, previously overlooked, and apparently universally representative defenses: "The unhappiest and most melancholy animal is, as fitting, the most cheerful."

The three inter-related questions that I want to ask about such irony are these: What are the conditions that made its emergence possible? What is the status of the "knowledge" gained from this "purely" textual economy? And, finally, what meaning are we to give to Nietzsche's reappearance recently as an authority whose example is appealed to by so many different kinds of literary and philosophical critics? In other words, by means of these questions, I hope to outline a critique of critical irony—to sketch an imaginative portrait of this clairvoyant suspect that will suggest its genealogy, expose its main features, and put its current influence into proper perspective. My attempt does not pretend to be exhaustive, and it is limited to the discourses of philosophy and literary criticism.

In the beginning, really, there is Kant. It is Kant in *The Critique of Judgment* (1790) who in his analysis of delight and terror as the founding moods of the beautiful and the sublime first points systematically to the indeterminate nature of aesthetic representation: "by an aesthetic idea I mean that representation of the imagination which induces much thought, yet without the possibility of any definite thought whatever, i.e., concept, being adequate to it, and which language, consequently, can never quite get on level terms with or render completely intelligible."[4] Kant's point, to put it simplistically, is that it is of the essence of such ideas—those notions inspired by one's aesthetic experience of the forms of man or nature—to be conceptual metaphors (i.e., unifying concepts produced by the play of differences between various metaphorical impressions) for something ungraspable by the rational understanding alone, namely, the mind's freedom. So when one makes a judgment about the meaning of aesthetic experiences one is engaging, strictly speaking, in a kind of private speculation that refers more to the relations of the individual mind's faculties (reason, imagination, understanding) to each other than to the operations of natural law "objectively" or inter-subjectively valid for all human minds and formulated in the rigorous concepts of a science.

To put it another way: Kant is suggesting that between the impressions of taste and the judgments of theory there lies a significant gap which the critic's assertions of meaning and value ironically bridges by representing it in other, largely imaginative terms.[5] The free-play of the mind's powers among themselves, inspired by the delight or terror of the aesthetic experience of the beautiful or the sublime, produces judgments that are essentially metaphorical: a transference from the realm of sensuous, iconic figures to the more abstract language of critical discourse on the basis of a subjective "intuition" of similarities amidst differences, a transference that requires or presupposes the methodical elaboration and resuscitation of "dead" metaphor.[6] The irony of this hermeneutical situation is that Kant makes such (conceptually "empty") aesthetic judgments the foundation of his own mediations between reason and understanding, knowledge and value, cognition and the rationally and morally valid motivations of action, with the mysterious power of the critical imagination occupying the middle ground as mediator:

> It is of note that the imagination, in a manner quite incomprehensible to us, is able on occasion, even after a long lapse of time, not alone to recall the signs for concepts, but also to reproduce the image and shape of an object out of a countless number of others of a different, or even of the very same, kind. And, further, if the mind is engaged upon comparisons, we may well suppose that it can in actual fact, though the process is unconscious, superimpose as it were one image upon another, and from the coincidence of a number of the same kind arrive at a mean contour which serves as a common standard for all.
>
> Say, for instance, a person has seen a thousand full-grown men. Now if he wishes to judge normal size determined upon a comparative estimate, then imagination (to my mind) allows a great number of these images (perhaps the whole thousand) to fall one upon the other, and, if I may be allowed to extend to the case the analogy of optical presentation, in the space where they come most together, and within the contour where the place is illuminated by the greatest concentration of

colour, one gets a perception of the *average size,* which alike in height and breadth is equally removed from the extreme limits of the greatest and smallest statures; and this is the stature of a beautiful man. . . .

This *normal idea* is not derived from proportions taken from experience *as definite rules:* rather it is according to this idea that rules for forming estimates first become possible. It is an intermediate between all singular intuitions of individuals, with their manifold variations—a floating image for the whole genus, which nature has set as an archetype underlying those of her products that belong to the same species, but which no single case she seems to have completely attained. . . . It only gives the form that constitutes the indispensable condition of all beauty, and, consequently, only *correctness* in the presentation of the genus. It is, as the famous *Dorphorus* of *Polycletus* was called, the *rule.* . . .[7]

(If one substitutes for the images of a thousand men falling upon one another those of a thousand poems so falling as in an anthology of poetry that one is skimming through, then one can begin to see witty origins of Arnold's "touchstone" approach.)

In any event, this "rule of metaphor"[8] establishes the preconditions of all judgment. It is like the trembling pool where Narcissus would gaze at his beloved: a self-reflecting phantasmagoria that would become, in its sublime variations, "a superhuman, mirror-resembling dream."[9] This situation, which is quite comical, holds true no matter what the critic's ideological orientation. Or so it would appear.

Nietzsche, despite his later and frequent denunciations of Kant for falling away from his own insight here and positing, illegitimately, the *ding an sich* as a limit-idea, was the first knowingly to apply Kant's view to the entire conceptual realm of philosophy and the whole field of human practice, as well as to that seemingly irreducible first idea of Schopenhauer's, the idea of the will itself. (Witness Nietzsche's early deconstruction of the metaphorical basis of our idea of "a leaf" in "On Truth and Lies in Non-Moral Sense.") Nietzsche says repeatedly in his works that all representation is aesthetic representation in the sense understood by Kant, all ideas are aesthetic ideas—rather indefinite conceptual metaphors glossing other metaphors from which the first set differs, within a particular genealogy of philosophical or literary judgments. Such difference produces an endless daisy-chain of interpretations that in this fashion constitutes "the language of the will"[10]—itself, of course, a wholly metaphorical conception: "The world seen from within, the world described and defined according to its 'intelligible character'—it would be 'will to power' and nothing else."[11]

The will to power, like Nietzsche's other ruling ideas, the superman and the eternal recurrence, are openly metaphorical conceptions that
bear witness to the state of relationships between the mind's and the
body's powers (the former being a mere refinement of the latter). It is the
form of the individual's dialectic of differences, his style of self-parody,
the "tragic culture" of his self-overcomings, his mood that matters:

> The meaning of knowing.—Non ridere, non lugere, neque
> detestari, sed intelligere! says Spinoza as simply and sub-
> limely as is his wont. Yet in the last analysis, what else is
> this intelligere than the form in which we come to feel
> the other three at once. One result of the different and
> mutually opposed desires to laugh, lament, and curse?
> Before knowledge is possible, each of these instincts
> must first have presented its one-sided view of the thing
> or event; after this comes the fight of these one-sided
> views, and occasionally this results in a mean, one grows
> calm, one finds all three sides right, and there is a kind
> of justice and a contract; for by virtue of justice and a
> contract all these instincts can maintain their existence
> and assert their rights against each other. Since only the
> last scenes of reconciliation and the final accounting at
> the end of this long process rise to our consciousness, we
> suppose that intelligere must be something conciliatory,
> just, and good—something that stands essentially op-
> posed to the instincts, while it is actually nothing but a
> certain behavior of the instincts toward one another.[12]

The difference between Kant and Nietzsche within the same tradition of
thinking, that is, aesthetic thinking, can be seen in Nietzsche's rhetoric: between Kant and Nietzsche, Hegel and Darwin (among other titans) had in-
tervened. As far as Nietzsche is concerned the "will to power" is the ultimate form that this "contract" between the "mutually opposed desires to
laugh, lament, and curse" can take, there being no other imaginable now.
  Nietzsche puts the consequences of this situation for the modern
writer most clearly in a note to himself written after his recovery from another bout of illness and the Lou-Salomé-Paul Ree affair, that is, at the
time when the idea of Zarathustra is about to overtake him and break him
up:

> I do not wish for life again. How have I borne it? Cre-
> atively. What makes one bear the sight of life. The view
> of the Superman who affirms life. I have tried to affirm
> it myself. . . .
>   It [such systematic affirmation] would have to

6

be something that was neither subject nor object, neither force nor matter, neither spirit nor psyche: but shall I not be told that such a thing will resemble nothing so much as a phantasmagoria? I, too, believe it will—all the better for that!

Of course, it must resemble that and everything else which exists or could exist, and not only a phantasmagoria. It must have that dominant family likeness by virtue of which all that is recognizes itself as related to it.[13]

The phantasmagoria of the critic, the competive inter-play of his aesthetic ideas produce, inevitably, a master-figure, a mask of the will as it were, what C. G. Jung calls a "god-image."[14] This idea of the creator establishes a certain economy of ruling figures that marks the fate of the individual imagination, foretelling whether it will continue to develop resemblances, affinities, that "dominant family likeness," or become fixated on one or two favorite sets: "The involuntary nature of image, of metaphor, is the most remarkable thing of all; one no longer has any idea what is image, what metaphor, everything presents itself as the readiest, the truest, the simplest means of expression. It really does seem, to allude to a saying of Zarathustra's, as if the things themselves approached and offered themselves as metaphors. . . . This is my experience of inspiration; I do not doubt that one has to go back thousands of years to find anyone who could say to me 'it is mine also.' "[15] In the final analysis, then, one is either a perfect decadent or a perpetual beginning: a Wilde or a Pater, a Hegel or a Kant, a Wagner or . . ?

II
The Shell's Music

An antithetical typology of god-images can be envisioned. In fact, Nietzsche envisioned just such an allegorical representation of the ironic situation of the modern writer—from the very beginning of his career up until the world was transfigured for him and, all too literally, he became "all the names in history." Nietzsche's example shows us that the opposi- tional critic of our culture can isolate and analyse the (too often) hidden or "unknown" god of a particular writer, a movement, a people—of him- self. In so doing, he can offer his prognosis. This unique kind of genealog- ical analysis forces the critic to discover his own antithetical will, his own difference, his own "god" (even if it be termed only the "machine" of lan- guage or the discourse of history and power).

The play of differences that arises from the contest between the various facets of the psyche and their competing affections *produces* the "god."

But how can we "find ourselves" again, and how can man "know himself"? . . . This is the most effective way: to let oneself look back on life with question, "What have I up to now truly loved, what has drawn my soul upward, mastered it, and blessed it, too?" Set up these things that you have honored before oneself, and, maybe, they will show you, in their being and their order, a law which is the fundamental law of your own self. Compare these objects, consider how one completes and broadens and transcends and explains another, how they form a ladder on which you have all the time been climbing to your self: for your true being lies not deeply hidden in you, but an infinite height above you . . . .[16]

In this passage from "Schopenhauer as Educator" Nietzsche claims that Schopenhauer taught him this lesson early on. Schopenhauer, like Wagner, is the means to Nietzsche's greater self-knowledge in this sense, to the more comprehensive reserve of his implication in the discursive formations of his time. As should be clear by now, Nietzsche's phantasmagoria enacts perfectly and so exhausts repeatedly the dialectical paradigm of modern irony discussed at the opening of this essay.

Nietzsche applies this kind of "analysis" (critical reduction, sublime recreation, mythic rediscovery) repeatedly to himself in what seems to be an endless battle of god-images, in which he always calls the overcoming diety, Dionysus, although throughout the career the lineaments of his god change again and again, coming to resemble those of Wagner less and less and those of Goethe more and more. For example, Nietzsche analyzes his first major attempt at discovering himself (*The Birth of Tragedy*) in the new preface he wrote for the 1886 edition of that work:

Already in the preface addressed to Richard Wagner, art, and not morality, is presented as the truly *metaphysical* activity of man. In the book itself the suggestive sentence is repeated several times, that the existence of the world is *justified* only as an aesthetic phenomenon. Indeed, the whole book knows only an artistic meaning and crypto-meaning behind all events—a "god," if you please, but certainly an entirely reckless and amoral artist-god who wants to experience, whether he is building or destroying, in the good and the bad, his own joy and glory—one who, creating worlds, frees himself from the *distress* of fullness and *overfullness* and from the *affliction* of the contradictions compressed in his soul. The world—at every moment the *attained* salvation of God, as the eternally changing, eternally new vision of the most deeply afflicted, discordant, and contradictory being who can find salvation only in *appearance:* you can call this whole artists' metaphysics arbitrary, idle, fantastic; what matters is that it betrays a spirit who will one day fight at any risk whatever the *moral* interpretation and significance of existence. Here, perhaps for the first time, a pessimism "beyond good and evil" is suggested. Here that "perversity of mind" gains speech and formulation against which Schopenhauer never wearied of hurling in advance his most irate curses and thunderbolts: a philosophy that dares to move, to demote morality into the realm of appearance—and not merely among "appearances" or phenomena (in the sense assigned to these words by Idealistic philosophers), but among "deceptions," as semblance, delusion, error, interpretation, contrivance, art.[17]

The young Nietzsche's god (as discovered by the mature Nietzsche in the interstices of the text) is a generalized image of the uncanny effects of Wagner's music on him, those "refinements of decay" that explode the logic of cause and effect, overturn the schemes of moral valuations, and produce the abyss of nightmare out of which emerges the genius of Romantic irony that is to incarnate itself in Nietzsche:

... Richard Wagner's overture to the *Meistrsinger* ... flows broad and full—and suddenly a moment of inexplicable hesitation, like a gap opening up between cause and effect, a pressure triggering dreams, almost nightmare—but already the old width and breadth are regained by the current of well-being, the most manifold well-being, of old and new happiness, very much including the artist's happiness with himself which he has no wish to hide, his amazed, happy sharing of the knowledge that the means he has employed here are masterly—new artistic devices, newly acquired, not yet tested, as he seems to let us know.[18]

Nietzsche refers here to what Yeats in "Poetry and Tradition" (1909) describes as the "secret" shared between the artist and his craft that the successful work can not help but betray by its overflowing rhythms and its excess of figures.[19] The "secret" being the experience of one's own growing sublimity.

The question that arises at this point is what kind of status can this "self-knowledge" have. Following Schopenhauer's lead, as the many different "living touchstones"[20] of perfection are recalled, their interplay

9

produces a distinctive style of justice that projects the shape of things to come, an inescapable justice of style. Just as the ruling conventions of a particular genre determine even the coming revolutions against that rule; just as a tradition of discourse sketches out in advance the possibilities of the new; so the dominant metaphors of the self, the god-images, those impossible possible philosopher's men, prophesize how one must become what one almost beholds. Like a shattered magic mirror whose many shards rush suddenly together as you bend to collect the fragments. . . .

In short, this "knowledge" is "tragic" in the sense that one writes in order to know that all knowledge is apparent. In a fragmentary note of the early 1870s, Nietzsche identifies himself as "the philosopher of tragic knowledge"[21] because like the great poets (and unlike the philosophers) he recognizes the "truth" that there is no Truth, just one's interpretations of those powerful illusions of art and culture that, despite their openly seductive fictionality, still transform men into either gods or swine.

This aristocratic, aesthetic nihilism informs all of Nietzsche's concern with the idea of the creator-philosopher, the artistic Socrates, the Homeric Plato, who, Moses-like, would shape a people out of the modern herd-men of his day by means of his new tablets of noble values beyond the Judeo-Christian "good and evil." That is, Nietzsche's is the politics of irony, the stammering prophecy of our anxious laughter, the ultimate philosophy of ideology.

In short, Nietzsche has more in common with the aesthetic humanism of Arnold and Pater, Valéry and Joyce, than the Mandarian brutalities of Mallarmé and Strinberg, or Kafka and Beckett. Nietzsche in his texts attempts to compose a new seductive music, special Dionysian measures that would lead the reader on and provoke in him a "crisis of identity" of the sort described in the passage from "Schopenhauer As Educator" quoted above. This "crisis" would force the reader, in Ezra Pound's telling phrase, to "gather the limbs of Osiris," that is, to recollect actively the pieces of the Self scattered across the modern cultural landscape and form them into a radically new whole that is as capricious as it is unified:

> Reckon into a single sum the spirit and goodness of all
> great souls: all of them together would not be capable of
> producing one of Zarathustra's discourses. The ladder
> upon which he climbs up and down is tremendous; he
> has seen further, willed further, *been able* further than
> any other human being. He contradicts with every word,
> this most affirmative of all spirits; all opposites are in
> him bound together in a new unity.[22]

As an example of Nietzsche's art of seduction at its best, take section 302 of *The Gay Science:*

The danger of the happiest.—To have refined senses, including the sense of taste; to be accustomed to the most exquisite things of the spirit as if they were simply the right and most convenient nourishment; to enjoy a strong, bold, audacious soul; to go through life with a calm eye and firm step, always prepared to risk all— festively, impelled by the longing for undiscovered worlds, seas, people and gods; to harken to all cheerful music as if it were a sign that bold men, soldiers, seafarers were probably seeking their brief rest and pleasure there—and in the most profound enjoyment of the moment, to be overcome by tears and the whole crimson melancholy of the happy: who would not wish that all this might be *his* possession, his state! This was the *happiness of Homer!* The state of him that gave the Greeks their gods—no, who invented his own gods for himself! But we should not overlook this: With this Homeric happiness in one's soul one is also more capable of suffering than any other creature under the sun. This is the only price for which one can buy the most precious shell that the waves of existence have ever yet washed on the shore. As its owner one becomes ever more refined in pain and ultimately too refined; any small dejection and nausea was quite enough in the end to spoil life for Homer. He had been unable to guess a foolish little riddle posed to him by some fishermen. Yes, little riddles are the danger that confronts those who are happiest.—[23]

The passage is divided into two major sections: the first part describes and analyzes the happiness of Homer, that "one great mood incarnate" of poetic divination; and the second part warns of the danger afflicting those who possess such happiness. Basically, Nietzsche says in this last part that all opposite values are entangled. They are just different perspectives on a single fate that one must understand and learn to love or else one runs the risk of letting the little riddles of life upset one's precarious balance.

The only catch is the puzzling figure of the shell. Why a shell? Perhaps, it is a metonomy meant to suggest, paradoxically enough, the pearl of great price in the religious tradition? (Or should that be an ironic synecdoche?) Or perhaps, it is a sublime symbol evoking the murderous myth of Venus in a subtle riposte to Kant's pronouncement in *The Critique of Judgment* that "many shells" are the "perfect" embodiments of disinterested beauty as he conceived of it.[24] But, perhaps, it is a transumptive allusion to Shelley's unbound Promethean conch? Hardly any of these, I think. Nietzsche's most characteristic figures are not semantically overdetermined. Rather, they are almost empty—hollows like this figure of the shell itself, a spiral labyrinth in which one thinks one hears textual "echoes" composing a riddling music suggestive of one's own "feary Father" and meant to captivate and provoke. Nietzsche's figures never mean the obvious things they seem to refer to. But they do not therefore represent some grandiose presumption. They just initiate one in the phenomenon they articulate. Could it be that Nietzsche is an educator in the same way Plato was? I think so.

The highest goal of Nietzsche's form of education, however, is the production of the creative genius and not the dialectical inquisitor: a Goethe, not a Socrates. Each age requires its own great heroes. Ours, a time when God is dead, decadence rules, and the last men blink and hop, hold office and decide the fate of millions—our time needs a new kind of hero. Not the warrior, although he must be a warrior in a certain sense. Not the priest, certainly, although he must be able to overcome himself like no saint of the desert ever could. Not simply a genealogist of the modern ironic imagination, although he must explore the past like Columbus plunged ahead after a new route to the Orient. What our world needs is the idea of the writer as a humane god, who can justify the past by enabling us to imagine a future that transcends this nihilistic present, one who can take all the guilt upon himself but none of the punishment. We need a Christ who refuses to take up his Cross—a Prometheus who breaks up (rather than curses) Jupiter—a scapegoat whose knowing smiling eyes tellingly reflect our most vicious resentments and transform this leaden weight alchemically into airy golden light. We need a master of touchstones:

> Anyone who manages to experience the history of humanity as a whole as *his own history* will feel in an enormously generalized way all the grief of an invalid who thinks of health, of an old man who thinks of the dreams of his youth, of a lover deprived of his beloved, of the martyr whose ideal is perishing, of the hero on the evening after a battle that has decided nothing but brought him wounds and the loss of his friend. But if one endured, if one *could* endure this immense sum of grief of all kinds while yet being the hero who, as the second day of battle breaks, welcomes the dawn and his fortune, being a person whose horizon encompasses thousands of years past and future, being the heir of all the nobility of all past spirit—an heir with a sense of obligation, the most aristocratic of old nobles and at the same time the first of a new nobility—the like of which no age has yet seen or dreamed of; if one could burden one's soul with all of this—the oldest, the newest, losses,

hopes, conquests, and the victories of humanity? If one could finally contain all this in one's soul and crowd it into a single feeling—this surely would have to result in a happiness that humanity has not known so far: the happiness of a god full of power and love, full of tears and laughter, a happiness that, like the sun in the evening, continually bestows its inexhaustible riches, pouring them into the sea, feeling richest, as the sun does, only when even the poorest fisherman is still rowing with golden oars! This godlike feeling would then be called—humaneness.[25]

Nietzsche's fullest attempt at such a romance of interpretation, at finding the philosopher's stone by imagining the mood of a god who would allow us to become the best that we can behold rather than forcing us to become the worst, is, of course, *Thus Spoke Zarathustra.*[26] Its art of the sublime would shape a new nobility.

III
Sublime Notation:
The Irony of Understanding Nietzsche

Do Nietzsche's texts on Homer and the Greeks (and all the rest), then, operate like a laboratory in Necropolis where the future is being pieced together out of the dead past in a present dominated by an interminable waiting for the lightning to strike and the final switch to be thrown? Or do they form a single gigantic transparent umbrella, which is designed to help one to sail over such tasteless displays so beneath one's own exalted frivolity? In short, are these texts "second nature," Nietzsche's will to power over the earth and so in earnest, or are they swishes of Becoming's veils, and so "pure" play? Who is right about Nietzsche, Heidegger or Derrida?[27] In essence, that is the issue that all of the essays collected here address, either directly or indirectly, as they attempt to answer the original question put to potential contributors almost two years ago: "Why Nietzsche Now?" The readings of Nietzsche's texts, the charting of his affinities with and differences from other thinkers and writers, and the subtle critiques of his ironic project included in the volume are the fruits of his joint effort to answer such a question concerning Nietzsche's uncanny reappearance.

The differences between Heidegger and Derrida over Nietzsche center on "How the True World At Last Became A Myth: History of An Error" from *The Twilight of the Idols,* Heidegger systematically interprets Nietzsche as the last metaphysician who in attempting to overturn Platonism merely reinscribed and preserved it in ironic form, since he allowed it to act as the negative from which he would print his affirmative, sensuous ideal.[28] As such, this philosophy only serves to indicate that "the over-turning of Platonism and the ultimate twist out of it imply a metamor-phosis of man,"[29] i.e., Nietzsche's transvaluation of all values is ultimately just another humanism. The question for Nietzsche, then, according to Heidegger, boils down to whether or not man will be able to transform himself into the *übermensch* who would rule all the earth thanks to his technological mastery. Nietzsche, too, has forgotten the "being-question."

Derrida focuses his critique of Heidegger in *Spurs* on the biggest hole in the latter's argument. Heidegger virtually ignores this passage from the notorious section:

> 2. The real world, unattainable for the moment, but promised to the wise, the pious, the virtuous man ('to the sinner who repents').
>
> (Progress of the idea: it grows more refined, more en-ticing, more incomprehensible—*it becomes a woman,* it becomes Christian. . .)[30]

Derrida argues that Nietzsche's writings, his "styles," have more to do with the wiles of the womanly woman who knows the truth about this history the way she knows the truth about man's fear of literal castration by woman—*viz.,* that it never, in fact, occurs where it counts—on the level of signification. So, for Derrida, Nietzsche is not in the least a metaphysician, despite himself, who is really interested in erecting a brooding logocentric tower of eloquence against the invading waves of becoming. Rather, Nietzsche is the first "self-conscious" deconstructor of the Western tradition who puts up the sail of his umbrella when the weather becomes inclement one way or another. That is, Nietzsche is a master of self-parody: "What if this totality [of Nietzsche's texts] would eventually be of the same sort as an 'I have forgotten my umbrella'?"[31]

So which Nietzsche is it? Is he, as Heidegger thinks, the tragic Oedipus-like philosopher who in celebrating the will to power as art over the Truth of the Ideas as morality has merely resurrected that which he would see buried for good? Did Nietzsche really mean to say, but failed to say, what Heidegger helps him to say, that the will to power "as the es-sence of reality is in itself that Being which wills itself by willing to be be-coming?"[32] Is Nietzsche like Yeats's Self at the conclusion of "A Dialogue of Self and Soul," an aristocrat of Form even as he sings the praises of the terrible democracy of flux? Or, perhaps, is Nietzsche the hermaphrodite of writing? Suppose, as Derrida contends, he is also "woman" in the sense elaborated in *Spurs:*

> There is no such thing as the essence of woman because woman averts, she is averted of herself. Out of the

14

depths, endless and unfathomable, she engulfs and distorts all vestige of essentiality, of identity, of property. And the philosophical discourse, blinded, flounders on these shoals and is hurled down these depthless depths to its ruin.[33]

The issue is this: either Nietzsche is the ultimate representative and overdetermined "symbol" of his epoch (that of the technological enframing of the earth), or he is the vestigial trace empty of all significance except that of a seductively winking subversion of the seductions of truth. Is he the philosopher of the will to dominate the earth via science and technology, despite his intentions to the contrary to transform this rabid will to knowledge and power into a will to power as art; or is he the playful deconstructive genealogist of the will to power in all its manifestations whatsoever, the potential creator of the humane future? In Nietzsche's own words, is he "décadent" or "beginning"? [34] Or, to remain faithful to his own grammar, and so in a sense to be "at once" both "decadent and beginning"? If this is so, what does this mean for those of us who now would appeal to or attempt to overcome his authority?

Nietzsche's life and work represent, to me, the ironic supplement of the consistently self-revising tradition of Western culture. It is as if as that culture breaks up and reproduces itself endlessly in all its many fragments, Nietzsche becomes, paradoxically enough, the *genius loci,* of that dispersion and imperialistic reproduction of the intellectual world.

I think Walter Pater describes best what I want to say about Nietzsche, when at the opening of a late, rather neglected "imaginary portrait," "Apollo in Picardy," he examines "a certain [late Medieval] manuscript volume taken from an old monastic library in France at the revolution":

> It presented a strange example of a cold and very reasonable spirit disturbed suddenly, thrown off its balance, as by a violent beam, a blaze of new light, revealing, as it glanced here and there, a hundred truths unguessed at before, yet a curse, as it turned out, to its receiver, in dividing hopelessly against itself the well-ordered kingdom of his thought. Twelfth volume of a dry enough treatise on mathematics, applied, still with no relaxation of strict method, to astronomy and music, it should have concluded that work, and therewith the second period of the life of its author, by drawing tight together the threads of a long intricate argument. In effect however, it began, or, in perturbed manner, and as with throes of childbirth, seemed the preparation for, an argument of an entirely new and disparate species, such as would de-

mand a new period of life also, if it might be, for its due expansion.

But with what confusion, what baffling inequalities! How afflicting to the mind's eye! It was a veritable "solar storm"—this illumination, which had burst at the last moment upon the strenuous, self-possessed, much-honoured monastic student, as he sat down peacefully to write the last formal chapters of his work ere he betook himself to its well-earned practical reward as superior, with lordship and mitre and ring, of the abbey whose music and calendar his mathematical knowledge had qualified him to reform. The very shape of Volume Twelve, pieced together of quite irregularly formed pages, was a solecism. It could never be bound. In truth, the man himself, and what passed with him in one particular space of time, had invaded a matter, which is nothing if not entirely abstract and impersonal. Indirectly the volume was the record of an episode, an interlude, an interpolated page of life, And whereas in the earlier volumes you found by way of illustration no more than the simplest indispensable diagrams, the scribe's hand had strayed here into hazy borders, long spaces of hieroglyph, and as it were veritable pictures of the theoretic elements of his subject. Soft wintry auroras seemed to play behind whole pages of crabbed textual writing, line and figure bending, breathing, flaming, into lovely "arrangements" that were like music made visible; till writing and writer changed suddenly, "to one thing constant never," after the known manner of madmen in such work. Finally, the whole matter broke off with an unfinished word, as a later hand testified, adding the date of the author's death, *"deliquio animi."*[35]

The "tradition" of Western culture is like this manuscript, and Nietzsche like this invading "veritable 'solar storm'—this illumination." And we? We must be the scholars of this solecism, the scribes whose hands trace those "Soft wintry auororas," and seductive mid-winter Springs that compose Nietzsche's sublime notation of "music made visible . . . after the known manner of madmen in such work." Or as Nietzsche himself puts it in *Zarathustra* with such prophetic poignancy: "Not only the reason of millenia—their insanity, too, breaks out in us."[36]

In other, less heated words of my own, it may be that Nietzsche is so "clever" an influence now, as he claims he would be in *Ecce Homo* with an urbane cynicism worthy of Pilate before Christ or Napolean before Goethe ("Voilà un homme! "), precisely because he knows that the ruling idea of his play of metaphors is "the crown of laughter,"[37] to be won at "a carnival in the grand style,"[38] a saturnalia of the dead God's "buffons" (comedians of our own ideals), which for Nietzsche is still to come: "Perhaps this is where we shall still discover the realm of our *invention,* that realm in which we, too, can still be original, say, as parodists of world history and God's buffons—perhaps, even if nothing else today has any future, our *laughter* may yet have a future."[39] Nietzsche's "redemption" from the terrible "it was" of time is the creative or daimonic will constituted in the act of writing, which, like those haunting crystalline structures of Adrian Leverkuhn's father in Thomas Mann's *Doctor Faustus* that mimic perfectly the ceaseless formations of life, translate the indecipherable moan of becoming into the productive articulation of a culture—into those smiles of Dionysus—that in themselves offer a prescription on how the history of the future must now begin to be written: " 'In my early days I had a teacher. . .' "[40] This is how one becomes what one is—with a vengeance.

Temple University

NOTES

1   *The Will to Power,* trans. Walter Kaufmann and R. J. Hollingdale (New York: Random House, 1967), pp. 55-56.

2   Given the context of Nietzsche's remarks here, it is as Kaufmann's note argues, highly probable that Zarathustra's being referred to here.

3   For a further discussion of this notion, see the first chapter of my *Tragic Knowledge: Yeats's Autobiography and Hermeneutics* (New York: Columbia Univ. Press, 1981).

4   *The Critique of Judgement,* trans. James Creed Meredith (Oxford at the Clarendon Press, 1928), pp. 175-76.

5   This is essentially Paul de Man's position on the nature of critical reflection in *Blindness and Insight: Essays in the Rhetoric of Contemporary Criticism* (New York: Oxford Univ. Press, 1971).

6   For a discussion of this issue as it relates to deconstructive criticism, see my essay "The Irony of Being Metaphorical," in *boundary 2* (Winter 1980).

7   Kant, pp. 77-79. This "rule" then produces the *represented differences* between impressions as the *sublime deviations* of genius.

8   For a discussion of this notion as it relates to Paul Ricoeur's dialectical hermeneutics, see my essay "The Irony of Being Metaphorical" in *boundary 2* (Winter 1980).

9   *The Collected Poems of W. B. Yeats* (New York: Macmillan, 1967), p. 176.

10   *On the Genealogy of Morals,* trans. Walter Kaufmann and R. J. Hollingdale (New York: Vintage Books, 1969), p. 103.

11   *A Nietzsche Reader,* ed. and trans. R. J. Hollingdale (New York: Penguin Classics, 1977), p. 229.

12   *The Gay Science,* trans. Walter Kaufmann (New York: Vintage Books, 1974), p. 261.

13   As quoted in J. P. Stern's *Friedrich Nietzsche* (New York: Penguin Modern Masters, 1979), p. 26.

14   For a discussion of this term, see the first chapter of my *Tragic Knowledge: Yeats's Autobiography and Hermeneutics.*

15   *Ecce Homo* trans. R. J. Hollingdale (New York: Penguin Classics, 1979), p. 103.

16   *The Philosophy of Nietzsche,* ed. Geoffrey Clive (New York: New American Library, 1965), pp. 329-30.

17   *The Birth of Tragedy and The Case of Wagner,* trans. Walter Kaufmann (New York: Vintage Books, 1967), "Attempt At Self-Criticism," pp. 22-23.

18   *Beyond Good and Evil,* trans. Walter Kaufmann (New York: Vintage Books, 1967), p. 173.

19   See *Essays and Introductions* (New York: Collier Books, 1962), pp. 136-38.

20   *Beyond Good and Evil,* p. 32.

21   *Philosophy and Truth: Selections From Nietzsche's Notebooks of the Early 1870's,* ed. and trans. Daniel Breazeale (New Jersey: Humanities Press, 1979), p. 33.

22   *Ecce Homo,* p. 106.

23   *The Gay Science,* pp. 242-43.

24   Kant, p. 46.

25   *The Gay Science,* p. 268.

26   For an examination of the romance of interpretation as a dominant 'post-modern' critical style, see my essay "The Romance of Interpretation" in *boundary 2* (Spring 1980).

27   By so phrasing my question I do not intend to short-change the meditations on Nietzsche accomplished by Paul de Man and now collected in *Allegories of Reading: Figural Language in Rousseau, Nietzsche, Rilke and Proust* (New Haven: Yale Univ. Press, 1979), which are discussed expertly elsewhere in this volume.

28   See David Farrell Krell's excellent translation of Heidegger's *Nietzsche, Volume I: The Will to Power As Art* (San Francisco: Harper and Row, 1979).

29   *Ibid.,* p. 208.

30   *Twilight of the Idols and The Anti-Christ,* trans. R. J. Hollingdale (New York: Penguin Classics, 1968), p. 40. For reasons of space, I have not quoted the entire section, and so I refer the reader to this edition.

31   Jacques Derrida, *Spurs: Nietzsche's,* trans. Barbara Harlow (Chicago: The Univ. of Chicago Press, 1979), p. 135.

32   Heidegger, p. 218.

33   Derrida, p. 51.

34   *Ecce Homo,* p. 38. Cf. Hegel, *The Phenomenology of Mind,* trans. J. B. Baillie (New York: Harper, 1968), p. 751, for a similar portrait of Spirit.

35   Walter Pater, *Miscellanous Studies* (London: Macmillan, 1910), pp. 143-45. This "imaginary portrait" goes on to record one of Apollo's Dionysian lapses.

36   *The Portable Nietzsche,* ed. and trans. Walter Kaufmann (New York: The Viking Press, 1954), "On the Gift-Giving Virtue," p. 189.

37   *Ibid.,* "On the Higher Man," p. 406.

38   *Beyond Good and Evil,* p. 150.

39   *Ibid.,* p. 150.

40   *Doctor Faustus: The Life of the German Composer Adrian Leverkuhn As Told by a Friend,* trans. H. T. Lowe-Porter (New York: Knopf, 1960), p. 412. On the question of Nietzsche's theory of music, see his letter to Carl Fuchs (August, 1888) in *Selected Letters,* ed. and trans. Christopher Middleton (Chicago: The Univ. of Chicago Press, 1969), pp. 308-10. See, also, the letter to Fuchs dated Winter, 1884-85, pp. 232-35. These and similar letters to Fuchs through the years provide the most succinct introduction to Nietzsche's idea of music, much more accessible than the early notes on the subject.

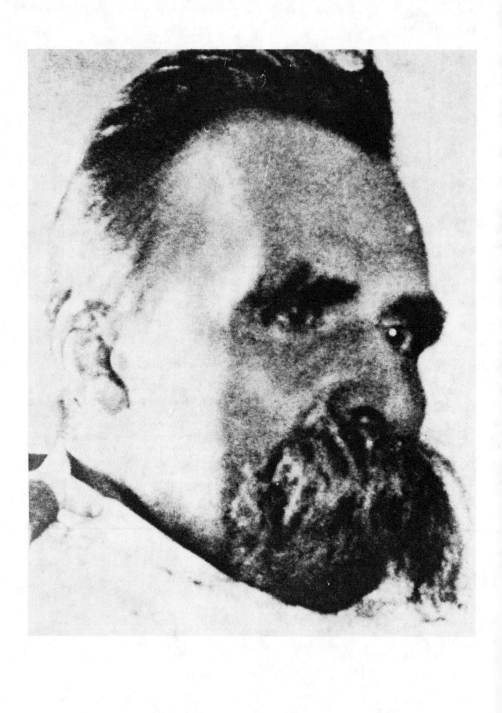

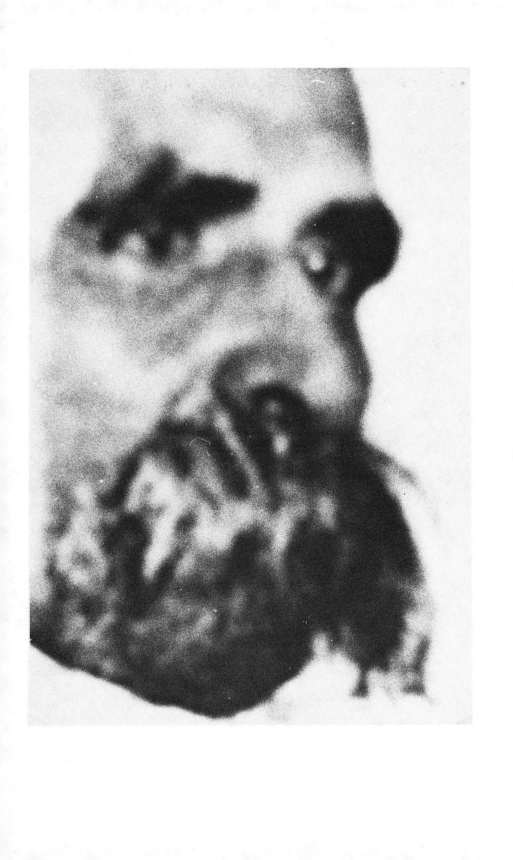

II Readings

Tragedy, Satyr-Play, and Telling Silence in Nietzsche's Thought of Eternal Recurrence*

Martin Heidegger

translated by David Farrell Krell

Nietzsche's work must first be brought before us if we are to confront it fruitfully. Therefore let the thinker's own words introduce the guiding thought of our lecture course:

> Everything in proximity to the hero becomes tragedy; everything in proximity to the demigod becomes satyr-play; and everything in proximity to God becomes . . . what? "world" perhaps? (*Beyond Good and Evil*, 1886, no. 150)

"Incipit tragoedia"

The thought of the eternal recurrence of the same, as the weightiest of thoughts, is also the hardest to bear. What happens when we actually think the thought? Nietzsche provides the answer in the title of the section which follows immediately upon his first communication of that most difficult thought and which forms the proper conclusion to *The*

Gay Science (first edition, 1882; no. 342): *"Incipit tragoedia."*—The tragedy begins. Which tragedy? The tragedy of beings as such. But what does Nietzsche understand by "tragedy"? Tragedy sings the tragic. We have to realize that Nietzsche defines the tragic purely in terms of the *beginning* of tragedy as he understands it. When the thought of eternal recurrence is thought, the tragic as such becomes the basic trait of beings. Viewed historically, this marks the beginning of the "tragic age for Europe" (*The Will to Power*, no. 37; cf. the *Grossoktav* edition, XVI, 448). What begins to happen here transpires in utter stillness; it remains concealed for a long time and to most men; nothing of this history goes into the history books. "It is the stillest words that bring on the storm. Thoughts that approach on doves' feet govern the world" (*Thus Spoke Zarathustra*, conclusion to Part Two)."—What does it matter that we more cautious and reserved ones do not for the nonce abandon the venerable belief that it is only the great thought that lends greatness to any deed or thing" (*Beyond Good and Evil*, no. 241). And finally: "The world revolves, not about the discoverers of new noises, but about the discoverers of new values. It revolves *inaudibly*" (*Thus Spoke Zarathustra*, Part Two, "Of Great Events").

Only the few, the select, only those who have ears for such inaudible revolutions will perceive the *"Incipit tragoedia."* But how does Nietzsche understand the essence of the tragic and of tragedy? We know that Nietzsche's first treatise, published in 1872, was devoted to the question of "the birth of tragedy." Experience of the tragic and meditation on its origin and essence are proper to the very basis of Nietzschean thought. Nietzsche's concept of the tragic grew increasingly clearer in step with the inner transformation and clarification of his thinking. But right from the outset he opposed the interpretation of Aristotle, according to which the tragic is said to accomplish κάθαρσις, the moral cleansing and elevation attained when fear and pity are aroused. "I have repeatedly put my finger on the vast misunderstanding of Aristotle, who believed he had found the tragic emotions in two *depressive* affects, namely, terror and pity" (*The Will to Power*, no. 851, from 1888). The tragic has absolutely no original relation to the moral. "Whoever takes tragedy *morally* still has a few rungs to climb" (*Grossoktav* ed., XII, 177, from 1881-82). The tragic pertains to the "aesthetic" domain. To clarify this we would have to give an account of Nietzsche's conception of art. Art is *"the* metaphysical activity" of "life"; it defines the way in which beings as a whole are, insofar as they are. The supreme art is the tragic; hence the tragic is proper to the metaphysical essence of beings.

The frightful does pertain to the tragic as such, but not as what arouses fear, in the sense that the tragic would allow one to circumvent the frightful by fleeing toward "resignation," by yearning for nothingness. On the contrary, the frightful is what is affirmed, indeed, affirmed in its unalterable affiliation with the beautiful. Tragedy prevails where the frightful is affirmed as the opposite that is intrinsically proper to the beautiful. Greatness and great heights subsist together with the depths and with what is frightful; the more originally the one is willed, the more surely the other will be attained. "Frightfulness is proper to greatness: let us not be deceived" (*The Will to Power*, no. 1028). Affirmation of the convergence of these opposites is tragic insight, the tragic attitude; it is what Nietzsche also calls the "heroic." *"What makes someone heroic?"* asks Nietzsche in *The Gay Science* (no. 268), and he replies, "Going out to meet one's supreme suffering and supreme hope alike." The word "alike" is decisive here: not playing off one against the other, still less averting his glance from both, but becoming master over his misfortune and good fortune as well, in that way not permitting his ostensible victory to make a fool of him.[1] "The *heroic* spirits are those who in the midst of tragic horror say to themselves, 'Yes'; they are hard enough to feel suffering as *pleasure*" (*The Will to Power*, no. 852). The tragic spirit incorporates contradictions and uncertainties (*Grossoktav* ed., XVI, 391; cf. XV, 65; XVI, 377; and XIV, 365 f.). The tragic holds sway only there where the "spirit" rules, so much so that it is only in the realm of knowledge and knowers that the supremely tragic occurs: "The supremely tragic motifs have remained untouched up to now: the poets have no knowledge based on experience of the hundred tragedies of knowers" (*Grossoktav* ed., XII, 246, from 1881-82). Beings themselves imply the pain, the destruction, and the "no" as proper to them. In *Ecce Homo*, at the place where he describes the gestation of the thought of eternal return of the same, Nietzsche says, ". . . the supreme formula of affirmation that can be achieved anywhere" (XV, 85). Why is the thought of eternal return supreme affirmation? Because it affirms the uttermost "no," annihilation and suffering, as proper to beings. Thus it is with this thought that the tragic spirit first comes into being, originally and integrally. *"Incipit tragoedia,"* Nietzsche says. But he adds, "INCIPIT ZARATHUSTRA" (*Twilight of the Idols*, VIII, 83).

Zarathustra is the initial and proper thinker of this thought of thoughts. *To be* the initial and proper thinker of the thought of the eternal return of the same *is the essence of Zarathustra*. The thought of the eternal return of the same is so much the hardest to bear that none of the prior, mediocre men can think it; they dare not even raise a claim to think it; and that holds for Nietzsche himself. In order to let the most difficult thought—i.e., the tragedy—begin, Nietzsche must therefore first poetically create the thinker of that thought. This happens in the work that begins to *come to be* one year following *The Gay Science,* that is to say, from 1883 on. For the report on the gestation of the thought of the eternal return of the same also says that this thought constitutes "the fundamental conception of the work [i.e., of *Thus Spoke Zarathustra*]." But the concluding section of *The Gay Science,* bearing the title *"Incipit tragoedia,"* runs as follows:

> *"Incipit tragoedia."*—When Zarathustra was thirty years old he left Lake Urmi and his homeland and went into the mountains. There he communed with his spirit and his solitude and for ten years did not weary of them. But finally something in his heart turned—and one morning he rose with the dawn, confronted the sun, and spoke in this way: "You magnificent star! What would become of your felicity if you did not have those you illumine? Ten years you've been coming up here to my cave: you would have had enough of your light and this path had it not been for me, my eagle, and my serpent. But every morning we waited for you, relieved you of what you didn't need, and blessed you for it. Look! I am glutted with my wisdom, like the bees that have gathered too much honey. I need hands that reach out, I want to give, to dispense, until the wise among men are happy again in their folly and the poor in their splendor. For that I must descend into the depths, just as you do evenings when you slip behind the sea and bring light to the very underworld, you overabundant star! Like you, I must *descend*, as men call it, to those I want to go down to. So bless me, then, tranquil Eye that can look without envy upon a happiness which is all-too-great! Bless the cup that wants to overflow until the waters stream from it golden, bearing to all parts reflections of your delight! Look! This cup wants to become empty again, and Zarathustra wants to become man again."—Thus began Zarathustra's downgoing.

The conclusion of *The Gay Science* constitutes the unaltered beginning of the first part of *Thus Spoke Zarathustra*, published during the following year; the sole change is that the name of the lake, "Urmi," is dropped and is replaced by the phrase, "the lake of his homeland." When Zarathustra's tragedy begins, so does his downgoing. The downgoing itself has a history. It is the history proper; it is not merely an end. Here Nietzsche shapes his work with an eye to his profound knowledge of great Greek tragedy. For Greek tragedy is not the "psychological" matter of preparing a "tragic conflict," of "unraveling the knots," and such. Rather, everything that one usually takes as constituting "the tragedy" has already occurred at the moment the tragedy begins. The "only thing" that happens in tragedy is the downgoing. The "only thing," we say, quite wrongly, for only now does the proper matter begin: without the "spirit" and the "thought," all deeds are nothing.

"The Convalescent"

... In the present section Zarathustra's animals speak to him about what they themselves symbolize: they speak of eternal return. They speak to Zarathustra, hovering in proximity to him, and remain present to his solitude until a particular moment when they leave him alone, cautiously stealing away. Their standing by him suggests that they are curious about him and are ever on the search for him; they want to know whether he is becoming the one he is, whether in his Becoming he finds his Being. But Zarathustra's Becoming commences with his downgoing. The downgoing itself comes to its end in Zarathustra's convalescence. Everything here is indicative of the most profound strife. Only when we grasp the various facets of the strife will we near the thought that is hardest to bear.

We shall place special emphasis on the characterization of the doctrine of eternal return, as befits the preliminary clarification we are now engaged in. Yet we must continue to keep to the style of the present work; we must grasp everything that happens in the way that it happens, in terms of Nietzsche's work itself. We must also understand the teaching, as taught, in connection with the questions of who Zarathustra is, how the teacher of that teaching is, and how the teaching defines the teacher. That is to say, precisely where the teaching is most purely expressed in doctrines, the teacher, the one who teaches and speaks, dare not be forgotten.

How do matters stand with Zarathustra at the beginning of the section entitled "The Convalescent"? What is happening here? Zarathustra has returned once again to his cave, home from his sea voyage. One morning soon after his arrival he leaps from his bed and calls out like a madman, gesturing frantically, "as though someone were still lying in his bed and refused to get up." Zarathustra speaks in a frightful voice in order to wake this other and to make sure that he will remain awake in the future. This other is his most abysmal thought, who, although he lies with him, still remains a stranger to Zarathustra; the other is his own ultimate recess which Zarathustra has not yet conducted to his supreme height and to the most fully wakeful of lives. The thought lies *beside* him in bed, has not yet become one with him, is not yet incorporated in him and hence is not yet something truly thought. So saying, we indicate what is now to happen: the full import and the whole might of the thought that is hardest to bear must now rise and come forth. Zarathustra screams at him, calls him a "sluggish worm." We easily discern the meaning of the image: the sluggish worm, lying as a stranger on the floor, is the counterimage to the ringed serpent who "wrings" his way to the heights, soaring there in vast circles, vigilant in friendship. When the invocation of the most abysmal thought begins, Zarathustra's animals grow fearful; they do not flee in terror, however, but come nearer, while all the other animals about them scatter. Eagle and serpent alone remain. It is a matter of bringing to the light of wakeful day, in purest solitude, what the animals symbolize.

Zarathustra invokes his ultimate recesses and so conducts himself to himself. He becomes what he is and confesses himself to be the one he is: "the advocate of life, and advocate of suffering, the advocate of the circle." Living, suffering, and circling are not three distinct matters. They belong together and form one: being as a whole, to which suffering, the abyss, belongs and which *is* inasmuch as, circling, it recurs. These three manifest their mutual affinity when they are gathered to the light of day, that is, when they are thought in their unity, by Zarathustra's supreme "Yes." In this supreme moment, when the thought is comprehended and is truly thought, Zarathustra cries, "Hail me!" But his "Hail me!" is at the same time a "Woe is me!"—for this is the victory that overcomes even itself as its greatest danger, the victory that grasps itself as downgoing.

Scarcely is it accomplished, when Zarathustra collapses. After he regains his senses he takes to his bed for seven days and seven nights. "But his animals did not abandon him, neither by day nor by night." Even so, Zarathustra remains in his solitude. The eagle, the proudest animal, flies off alone to fetch all sorts of nourishment. That means to say that Zarathustra does not waste away, that he continues to nourish his pride and to secure the certainty of his rank, even though he must lie prostrate, even though his wits do not bother about him now, so that he cannot even tell himself what he knows. Among other things, the eagle brings him "yellow and red berries," and we recall the earlier reference to "deep yellow and fiery red" (cf. Part Three, "On the Spirit of Gravity"). *Taken together,* these two colors conform to what Zarathustra wants to have in sight: the color of deepest falsehood, error, and semblance, and the color of supreme passion, of incandescent creation.

When interpreting the two colors we have to keep in mind the fact that "error" constitutes for will to power the necessary essence of *truth* and that it is therefore not at all to be valued negatively. "Deep yellow" may also be interpreted as the gold of the "golden flash of the serpent *vita*" (*The Will to Power*, no. 577), which is "the serpent of eternity." For the second interpretation "deep yellow" is the color of the eternal recurrence of the same, "fiery red" the color of will to power. For the first interpretation the two colors display the essential structure of will to power itself, inasmuch as truth as fixation and art as creation constitute the conditions of possibility for will to power.[2] In both cases the mutual affinity of the two colors points toward the essential unity of the Being of beings as thought by Nietzsche.

But after seven days "the animals felt that the time had come to talk with him." Zarathustra is now strong enough actually to think and to express himself about his most difficult thought, his ultimate recess. For what the eagle and serpent (the loneliest solitude) wish to talk about—the only thing they *can* talk about—is the thought of eternal return. In the dialogue between Zarathustra and his animals the thought of thoughts is now brought to language. It is not presented as a "theory"; only in conversation does it prove itself. For here the speakers themselves must venture forth into what is spoken: conversation alone brings to light the extent to which the speakers can or cannot advance, and the extent to which their conversation is only empty talk.

The two animals open the conversation. They inform Zarathustra that the world outside is like a garden that awaits him. They sense somehow that a new insight has come to him, an insight concerning the world as a whole. It must therefore be a pleasure to proceed to this newly constituted world, since all things are bathed in the light of the new insight and want to be integrated into the new dispensation. Insofar as they are so illuminated and integrated, things corroborate the insight in a profound way; they heal the one who up to now has been a seeker, they cure him of the disease of inquiry. That is what the animals mean when they say to Zarathustra, "All things yearn for you. . . . All things want to be doctors to you!" And Zarathustra? He listens to the animals' talk, indeed gladly, although he knows that they are only jabbering. But after such solitude the world *is* a garden, even when it is invoked by mere empty talk, in the sheer play of words and phrases. He knows that a cheerful loveliness and gentle humor settle over the frightful thing that being genuinely *is*; that being can conceal itself behind semblances in what is talked about. In truth, of course, the world is no garden, and for Zarathustra it dare not be one, especially if by "garden" we mean an enchanting haven for the flight from beings. Nietzsche's conception of the world does not provide the thinker with a sedate residence in which he can putter about unperturbed, like the philosopher of old, Epicurus, in his "garden." The world is not a cosmos present at hand in itself. The animals' allusion to the garden has the sense of rejecting any sedate residence; at the same time, indirectly, it has the task of referring us to the concept of world in the tragic insight. Here we must ponder an important note by Nietzsche (*Grossoktav* ed., XII, 368, from 1882-84):

> Solitude *for a time* necessary, in order that the creature be totally permeated—cured and hard. New form of community, asserting itself in a warlike manner. Otherwise the spirit grows soft. No "gardens" and no sheer "evasion in the face of the masses." War (but without gunpowder!) among different thoughts! and their armies!

31

The animals talk to Zarathustra about his new insight in seductive words that tempt him to sheer intoxication. But Zarathustra knows that in truth these words and tones are "rainbows and sham bridges connecting what is eternally distinct." Where things most reminiscent of other things are named in the conversation, when it sounds as though the *same* is being said, then and there comes the loveliest lie: "For the smallest gap is the hardest to bridge."

What is Zarathustra thinking about? Nothing else than the sole matter under discussion, the world, being as a whole. But what response did the dwarf give to this riddle?[3] The dwarf says that the paths of the gateway, running counter to one another, meet in the infinite; everything turns in a circle and is a circle. And what did Zarathustra call himself when he thought his most difficult thought out of his ultimate recess, a thought he did not take lightly, as the dwarf did? He called himself the "advocate of the circle." So the two of them, the dwarf and Zarathustra, say the same thing. Between them lies only "the smallest gap"—that in each case it is an other who speaks the same words. Otherwise that same word, "circle," is but a sham bridge between things eternally distinct. Thus one man's circle is not another man's circle. What now comes to light is that whenever the Being of beings as a whole is to be uttered the semblance of unanimity is greatest and correct understanding—which is decisive and determinative of rank—most difficult.

It is easy for anyone and everyone to say, "A being is," and "A being becomes." Everyone thinks that anybody can understand that. Meanwhile, talking this way, "man dances above and beyond all things." Man, drifting along as he usually does, oblivious to the true dimensions and proper stages of genuine thinking, needs that kind of dance, that kind of jabbering, and Zarathustra finds joy in it. But he also knows that it is an illusion, that this garden is not the world, that "the world is deep, and deeper than the day ever thought" (Part Three, "Before Sunrise").

Thus Zarathustra does not allow himself to be seduced by the animals' talk away from what he has known now for seven days and nights. He can find nothing reassuring in the fact that everyone confidently asserts—as though it were evident—that "everything turns in a circle," thereby to all appearances agreeing with him in their empty talk. But the animals reply, "To those who think as we do, all things themselves dance." We do not dance above and beyond the things, they seem to say, but see the things' own dance and sway: you can trust us. And now they tell how the world looks under the new sun of eternal recurrence:

> Everything goes, everything comes back; eternally rolls the Wheel of Being. Everything dies, everything blooms again; eternally runs the Year of Being.

32

Everything sunders, everything is joined anew; eternally the identical House of Being is built. Everything departs, everything greets again; eternally true to itself is the Ring of Being.

In every instant Being begins; around every Here the sphere of There rolls. The center is everywhere. Crooked is the path of eternity.

Thus speak Zarathustra's animals. And why shouldn't they, they who *are* only inasmuch as they soar in vast circles and form rings? Could the eternal return of the same be portrayed in more elegant words and more striking images than those employed here? How different this speech seems from the contemptuous grumblings of the dwarf! Nevertheless, the speeches of the dwarf and the animals betray a fatal resemblance. The dwarf says, "All truth," that is to say, what is truly in being, in its course and passage, "is crooked." The animals say, "Crooked is the path of eternity." Perhaps the animals' talk is only more effervescent, more agile and playful than—yet at bottom identical with—the talk of the dwarf, to whom Zarathustra objects that he makes things too easy for himself. Indeed, even the speech of his very own animals, who present his teaching to him in the fairest formulas, cannot deceive Zarathustra: " 'Oh, you rascally jesters and barrel organs,' answered Zarathustra, smiling again, 'how well you know what had to be fulfilled in seven days—'." But their knowing is not knowledge. If Zarathustra calls it that he is only being ironic and is really suggesting that they know nothing. They are barrel organs: they turn his words concerning the eternal return of the same, words obtained only after the hardest struggle, into a mere ditty; they crank it out, knowing what is essential about it as little as the dwarf does. For the dwarf vanishes when things take a serious turn and all becomes foreboding, when the shepherd has to bite off the head of the black snake. The dwarf experiences nothing of the fact that really to know the ring of rings means precisely this: to overcome from the outset and perpetually what is dark and horrid in the teaching as it is expressed, namely, the fact that if everything recurs all decision and every effort and will to make things better is a matter of indifference; that if everything turns in a circle nothing is worth the trouble; so that the result of the teaching is disgust, and ultimately the negation of life. In spite of their marvelous talk about the Ring of Being, Zarathustra's animals too seem to dance over and beyond what is essential. His animals too seem to want to treat the matter as men do: like the dwarf, they run away; or they too act as mere spectators, telling what results if everything revolves. They perch before beings and "have a look at" their eternal displacement, then describe it in the most resplendent images. They are not aware of what is going on there, not aware of what must be thought in the true thinking of being as a whole, namely, that such thinking is a cry of distress.

And even if the anguished cry is heard, what is it that usually happens? When the great man cries the little man hurries to the scene and takes pity. But everything that smacks of pity keeps to the periphery, stands on the sidelines. The little man's gregariousness accomplishes only one thing: his petty consolations diminish and falsify the suffering, delay and obstruct the true insight. Pity hasn't an inkling of the extent to which suffering and outrage crawl down the throat and choke a man until he has to cry out, nor does it know the extent to which this is "necessary to attain the best" in man. Precisely the knowledge that chokes us is that which must be known if being as a whole is to be thought.

This marks the essential and altogether unbridgeable difference between the usual kinds of spectation and cognition, on the one hand, and proper knowing, on the other. And it suggests what the dwarf failed to see when he misinterpreted eternal recurrence and turned it into a mere ditty, into empty talk. It should be apparent by now that nothing is said here about the content of the doctrine beyond what is said in the animals' ditty, that Zarathustra does not contrapose any other presentation to theirs, and that in the course of the conversation we are told *always and only by indirection* how the teaching is—or is not—to be understood. Nevertheless, the "how" does provide an essential directive for our understanding of the "what."

It is our job to pursue that directive more keenly and to ask: What is it that turns the doctrine into a ditty? The latter concedes that things do die, depart, and disintegrate; it also accepts everything destructive, negative, adverse, and outrageous; but at bottom these things are conceived of as eventually passing away in the world's circuitry, so that other things will come and everything shall take a turn for the better. Hence all is bound for perpetual compensation. Such compensation in fact makes everything indifferent: striving is flattened out into mere alternation. One now possesses a handy formula for the whole and abstains from all decision.

Looking back to the earlier section [section 6, "On the Vision and the Riddle"] we may now ask: In what way does the dwarf make the interpretation of the imagery, i.e., of the gateway and the two paths, too easy for himself? Zarathustra indicates the answer when he goes on to command, "Look at the gateway itself—the Moment!" What does that indication mean? The dwarf sees only the two paths that extend to infinity, and he thinks about them merely in the following way: If both paths run on to infinity ("eternity"), then that is where they meet; and since the circle closes by itself in infinity—far removed from me—all that recurs in sheer alternation within this system of compensations does so as a sequence, as a parade passing through the gateway. The dwarf understands nothing of what Zarathustra means when he says—bewilderingly enough—that the two paths "affront one another" at the gateway. But how is that possible, when each thing moves along behind its predecessor, as is manifest with *time* itself? For in time the not-yet-now becomes the now, and as soon becomes a no-longer-now, this as a perpetual and-so-on. The two paths, future and past, do not collide at all, but pursue one another.

And yet a collision does occur here. To be sure, it occurs only to one who does not remain a spectator but who *is himself* the Moment, performing actions directed toward the future and at the same time accepting and affirming the past, by no means letting it drop. Whoever stands in the Moment is turned in two ways: for him past and future *run up against* one another. He lets what runs counter to itself come to collision, though not to a standstill, by cultivating and sustaining the strife of what is given him as a task and what has been given him as his endowment.[4] To see the Moment means to stand in it. But the dwarf keeps to the outside, perches on the periphery.

What does all this say about the right way to think the thought of eternal recurrence? It says something essential: That which is to come is precisely a matter for decision, since the ring is not closed in some remote infinity but possesses its unbroken closure in the Moment, as the center of the striving; what recurs—if it recurs—is decided by the Moment and by the force with which the Moment can cope with the revulsion felt toward all antagonism. That is what is peculiar to, and hardest to bear in, the doctrine of eternal return, to wit, that eternity *is* in the Moment, that the Moment is not the fleeting "now," not an instant of time whizzing by a spectator, but the collision of future and past. Here the Moment comes to itself. It determines how everything recurs. Now, the most difficult is the greatest that must be grasped, and the greatest remains a sealed door to little men. But the little men too *are*; as beings they too recur forever. They cannot be put out of action; they pertain to that side of things that is dark and repulsive. If being as a whole is to be thought, the little men too wait upon their "Yes." That makes Zarathustra shudder.

And now that his most abysmal thought has been thought in the direction of that abyss, Zarathustra's animals "do not let him talk anymore." For when Zarathustra recognizes that the recurrence of the little man too is necessary, when he grapples with that "Yes" spoken to everything that over the years wearied and sickened him, to everything he wanted to repulse, when he conquers his illness with that "Yes" and so becomes a convalescent, his animals begin to speak again. Once more they repeat their message: the world is a garden. Again they call for Zarathustra to come out. But now they say more. They do not simply tell him to come out so that he can see and experience how all things are yearning for him. They call to him, that he should learn from the songbirds how to sing: "For singing does a convalescent good." The temptation to take the thought of eternal return merely as something obvious, to take it therefore at bottom as either contemptible mumbling or fascinating chatter, is overcome.

By now the dialogue between the animals and Zarathustra is moving upon a ground that has been transformed by the conversation itself. The animals are now speaking to a Zarathustra who has come to grips with his illness and overcome his disgust with the little man by achieving the insight that such things are necessary.

Now Zarathustra agrees with his animals. With their injunction to sing, the animals are telling him of that consolation he invented for himself during those seven days. But once again he warns against turning the injunction to sing into a call for ditties on the barrel organ or tunes on the same old lyre. What is being thought here? This, that the thought most difficult to bear, as the convalescent's conquering thought, must first of all be *sung*; that such singing, i.e., the poetizing of *Thus Spoke Zarathustra,* must itself become the convalescence; but also that such singing must be *singular*, that it dare not become a popular tune. Zarathustra therefore calls himself a poet as well as one who guesses riddles. Poet and riddler, but not in the sense that he is a poet and something else in addition, i.e., one who solves riddles. Both of these roles are thought in an original unity, thought therefore ultimately as some third thing. Hence poetry, if it is to fulfill its task, can never be a matter for barrel organs and readymade lyres. The lyre, viewed now as an instrument for the new singing and saying, has still to be created. The animals know that—after all, they are *his* animals. In the words they utter they gradually come closer to Zarathustra, the more so as Zarathustra comes closer to himself and to his task: "First make for yourself a proper lyre, a new lyre!" "For your animals know well who you are and who you must become, O Zarathustra: see, *you are the teacher of the eternal return*, for that is *your* destiny!"

But if Zarathustra is the first to have to teach that teaching, must he not, as the teacher, know it ahead of time, prior to anyone else; and must he not know it differently than those who are merely learning it? Indeed, he must know that by virtue of the teaching itself and in conformity with it "the great destiny" is also to be his greatest danger and disease. Only when the teacher comprehends himself *in terms of the teaching* as inevitably a victim, as one who must go down because he goes over, as a transition, only when the one who goes down gives himself his blessing as such a one, does he reach his end and goal. "Thus [i.e., in such wise] *ends* Zarathustra's downgoing," say the animals.

"Downgoing" here means two things: first, transition as departure; second, descent as acknowledgment of the abyss. This dual characterization of downgoing must at the same time be grasped in its temporality, on the basis of "eternity," correctly understood. The downgoing itself, thought with a view to eternity, is the Moment, but not as the fleeting "now," not as mere passing. Downgoing is indeed the briefest thing, hence the most transient, but it is at the same time what is most accomplished: in it the most luminous brightness of being as a whole scintillates as the Moment in which the whole of recurrence becomes comprehensible. The apposite imagery here is the ringed serpent, the living ring. In the image of the serpent the connection between eternity and the Moment is established for Nietzsche in its unity: the living ring of the serpent, i.e., eternal recurrence, and—the Moment. In one of his late sketches (*The Will to Power*, no. 577, from 1887) Nietzsche contraposes his concept of eternity to the extrinsic sense of that notion as the "eternally unchanging": "As opposed to the *value* of the eternally unchanging (note Spinoza's naiveté, and Descartes' as well), the value of the briefest and most transient, the seductive flash of gold on the belly of the serpent *vita*." In the end Zarathustra hears which eternity it is that his animals are proclaiming to him, the eternity of the Moment that embraces everything in itself at once: the downgoing.

When Zarathustra heard these words of his animals' "he lay still" and

> communed with his soul. But the serpent and the eagle,
> finding him thus, so silent, honored the vast stillness in
> his proximity and cautiously stole away.

In what way is Zarathustra now silent? He is silent inasmuch as he is communing with his soul alone, because he has found what defines him, has become who he is. He has also overcome outrage and repugnance by learning that the abyss belongs to the heights. To overcome outrage is not to put it out of action but to acknowledge its necessity. As long as it is merely repudiated in nausea, as long as our loathing is determined merely by nausea, the loathing remains dependent upon the loathsome. Only when loathing stems from love of the task, being transformed in such a way that, undergirded by an affirmation of the necessity of outrage, suffering, and destruction, it can pass over in silence; only in the silence of such loving passing-over, does the vast stillness extend, the proximity diffuse, about the one who in this way has become himself. Only now that the vast stillness pervades Zarathustra's spirit has he found his loneliest solitude, a solitude that has nothing more to do with a merely peripheral existence. And the animals of his solitude honor the stillness, that is to say, they perfect the solitude in its proper essence in that now they too "cautiously steal away." The eagle's pride and serpent's wits are now essential qualities of Zarathustra.

Zarathustra himself has become a hero, since he has incorporated the thought of eternal return in its full import, as the weightiest of thoughts. Now he is a knower. He knows that the greatest and smallest cohere and recur, so that even the greatest teaching, the ring of rings, itself must become a ditty for barrel organs, this always accompanying its true proclamation. Now he is one who at the same time goes out to meet his supreme suffering and supreme hope. We have already heard Nietzsche's answer to the question, *"What makes someone heroic?"* (V, 204), that is, what is it that makes a hero a hero? The response: "Going out to meet one's supreme suffering and supreme hope alike." But thanks to the motto of our own lecture course we also know that "everything in proximity to the hero becomes tragedy."

"Once I had created the Overman, I draped the great veil of Becoming about him and let the midday sun stand over him." (XII, 362). The veil of Becoming is recurrence, as the truth concerning being as a whole, and the midday sun is the Moment of the shortest shadow and the most luminous brightness, the image of eternity. When what is *"weightiest"* is assimilated to Dasein, *"Incipit tragoedia."* The two final sections of *The Gay Science*, which communicate the doctrine of eternal return for the first time, employ the two italicized phrases as their titles. The intrinsic connection between these two concluding sections becomes clear on the basis of *that* work which is designed to create poetically the figure who is to think the eternal return of the same.

Conclusion

The thinker inquires into being as a whole as such, into the world as such. Thus with his very first step he always thinks out beyond the world, and so at the same time back to it. He thinks in the direction of that *in the proximity of which* a world becomes world. Wherever that proximity is not constantly called by name, called aloud, wherever it is kept silent in the most interior questioning, it is thought most purely and profoundly. For what is kept in silence is genuinely preserved, and as preserved it is most intimate and actual. What to common sense looks like "atheism," and has to look like it, is at bottom the very opposite. In the same way, wherever the matters of death and the nothing are being treated, Being and Being alone is being thought most deeply, whereas those who ostensibly occupy themselves solely with "reality" are floundering in nothingness.

Supremely thoughtful utterance does not simply consist in growing taciturn when it is a matter of saying what is properly to be said; it consists in saying the matter in such a way that it is named in nonsaying: the utterance of thinking is a telling silence. Such utterance corresponds to the most profound essence of language, which has its origins in silence. As one in touch with telling silence, the thinker, in a way peculiar to him, rises to the rank of the poet; yet he remains eternally distinct from the poet, just as, for his part, the poet remains eternally distinct from the thinker.

Everything in proximity to the hero becomes tragedy; everything in proximity to the demigod becomes satyr-play; and everything in proximity to God becomes . . . what? "world" perhaps?

NOTES

1   On mastery of one's misfortune and good fortune or unhappiness and happiness, cf. Martin Heidegger, *Nietzsche, Vol. I: The Will to Power as Art*, trans. D. F. Krell (New York: Harper & Row, 1979), p. 159. On the entire question of beauty and the terrible or frightful, see sections 16-17 of that lecture course.

2   See Martin Heidegger, *Nietzsche*, vol. I, section 25. (*Trans.*)

3   Meant of course are the dwarf and the riddle of "On the Vision and the Riddle," in *Thus Spoke Zarathustra*, Part Three, discussed in detail by Heidegger in section 6 of the present lecture course (NI, 289-297). Zarathustra and the dwarf stand before the gateway "Moment" where the eternal paths of past and future collide. Do then these paths run counter to one another eternally? The dwarf, who does not stand in the gateway but merely gapes to his left and right, grumbles his contemptuous answer: "Everything straight lies. . . . All truth is crooked; time itself is a circle." Zarathustra is enraged, since the dwarf makes things too easy for himself. The riddle must be reformulated: What would it mean to *stand in* the gateway, to have time in one's face, then over the shoulder, time as the *moment* of eternity? (*Trans.*)

4   *Indem er den Widerstreit des Aufgegebenen und Mitgegebenen entfaltet und aushält. Aufgegebenen* could of course also have to do with surrender, but I am conjecturing that Heidegger here wants to juxtapose the task (cf. *Aufgabe*) that we project into and as the future to the endowment (cf. *Mitgabe, Mitgift*) of skills we bring to the task from our past. For here there often seems to be a disparity, a striving, and strife. (*Trans.*)

*Excerpted from Martin Heidegger, *Nietzsche, Vol. II: The Eternal Recurrence of the Same*, translated, with Notes and an Analysis, by David Farrell Krell (New York: Harper & Row, forthcoming), with the kind consent of the publishers. The excerpts are taken from the first, fourth, eighth, and final sections of Heidegger's 1937 lecture course (cf. NI, 255; 278-283; 302-316; and 471-472). They are arranged with three ends in view: first, to show Heidegger at work on a detailed piece of text-interpretation; second, to give at least some sense of the tendency of Heidegger's reading of Nietzsche as a whole; third, to focus on a theme of particular interest to readers who find themselves at one of those unmarked intersections of philosophy and literature. The texts are from *The Gay Science* and *Thus Spoke Zarathustra*. The theme is tragic insight in Nietzsche's thought of eternal recurrence. And the overall tendency? The title of the present piece—although the formulation is not Heidegger's as such—hopes to say something about the ultimate convergence of the *tragic theme* and the peculiar *task* of Heidegger's prolonged and intense confrontation with Nietzsche. (*Trans.*)

Dismembering and Disremembering
in Nietzsche's "On Truth and Lies
in a Nonmoral Sense"

J. Hillis Miller

In an essay in his early book, *Studies on Hysteria,* written with
Josef Breuer, Sigmund Freud interjects the following parenthesis:

> (I am making use here of a number of similes, all of
> which have a very limited resemblance to my subject and
> which, moreover, are incompatible with one another. I
> am aware that this is so, and I am in no danger of
> over-estimating their value. But my purpose in using
> them is to throw light from different directions on a
> highly complicated topic which has never yet been
> represented. I shall therefore venture to continue in the
> following pages to introduce similes in the same manner,
> though I know this is not free from objection.)[1]

This is a curious passage in a number of ways. None of his similes
(*Gleichnissen*),[2] says Freud, has more than "a very limited resemblance
(*eine recht begrenzte Ähnlichkeit*)" to what it names. What does this
mean? Limited in what way? By being a distorted picture, or by being an
allotropic trope, turning away from what it names and leading away from

c 1981 by Princeton University Press, from *The Linguistic Moment.*

it in its otherness? The similes, moreover, says Freud, are incompatible with one another. They cannot be reconciled in a single picture, however complicated a one. They are used in their heterogeneity "to throw light from different directions (*von verschiedenen Seiten her zu veranschau-lichen*)" on something, "a highly complicated topic (*ein höchst kompliziertes . . . Denkobjekt*)" which has never yet been "represented (*dargestelltes*)." Just because this topic has never yet been represented would not seem a sufficient reason for not representing it directly, giving a photograph of this hitherto unknown place, so to speak. It seems that this place cannot be represented in this way, perhaps because of its complexity, perhaps because it has never been "represented" before and so lacks a proper name in any language, perhaps because it could by no means, at any time or place, in any language, ever be represented except tropologically, that is, improperly. It can for some reason only be represented, at this time at least, in figures. Freud's figure for this is the projecting of light from different directions on a dark object or place, a midnight crossroads, by different light sources. Each of these perhaps reveals a new aspect of the place. Perhaps the figurative nature of the images, the fact that each bears only a limited resemblance to its object, will be cancelled out by the proliferation of images. A full multidimensional picture of the object would then be produced, like those superimposed slightly different images that make stereoscopic vision. Perhaps. In any case, all Freud's later work is commanded by this necessity of multiple figurative models, each replacing the last.

Why is it that Freud, for all his confidence, at the beginning of his career at least, in the objective existence of the pathogenic nucleus causing mental disorder, cannot avoid putting that existence in question, even in the *Studies on Hysteria?* He puts it in question by demonstrating repeatedly that it cannot be named literally, but only in figures that always break down and fail to figure adequately what they "represent." Why must Freud ultimately recognize that the center of the labyrinth of the mind is a place that can by no means, not even by figurative ones, be placed or named? The ultimate direction toward which Freud's exploration of his topographical figures in the *Studies on Hysteria* is leading is given not in this early book but in a more celebrated passage in *The Interpretation of Dreams.* Here Freud affirms that in a structure of this sort there is a center which can never by any means be reached or identified. This center is the source of the ramifying labyrinthine growth and yet it can never have any light shed on it:

> Even in the best interpreted dreams, there is often a
> place that must be left in the dark because in the process
> of interpreting, one notices a tangle (*ein Knäuel*) of
> dream-thoughts arising, which resists unravelling but has
> also made no further contributions (*keine weiteren*

Beiträge) to the dream-content. This is the dream's navel, the place where it straddles the unknown (*dem Unerkannten aufsitzt*). The dream-thoughts, to which interpretation leads one, are necessarily interminable (*ohne Abschluss*) and branch out on all sides into the netlike entanglement (*in die netzartige Verstrickung*) of our world of thought. Out of one of the denser places of this meshwork (*Geflechts*), the dream-wish rises like a mushroom out of its mycelium.[3]

The image here has at least a "limited resemblance" to that in the *Studies on Hysteria,* except that now Freud clearly recognizes that the center must necessarily remain unknown. It is impossible to give, whether literally or in figure. As a result, the dream-thoughts are a trap or netlike entanglement which can never be successfully unravelled. This is both because it branches out interminably in all directions and because its source can never be identified. That source is the origin of the net of dream-thoughts. Though it has made no further contributions to the dream-content beyond generating them in the first place, as mycelium generates mushroom, that initial contribution is enough to make the dream-thoughts an impenetrable and interminable entanglement. Within this net the interpreter may remain permanently trapped. Why is this so?

*

Friedrich Nietzsche, in "On Truth and Lies in a Nonmoral Sense," gives clear expression to the situation in which Freud finds himself. He also suggests reasons why that site cannot ever be clearly mapped. "Clear expression" must be qualified by saying that this clarity, for example in rational distinctions or in binary oppositions, is itself a trap for the unwary. In this it is like the entangling net of dream-thoughts in the passage from Freud's *On the Interpretation of Dreams.* Like Freud, Nietzsche cannot avoid becoming caught in the impasse he is attempting to describe. What seems at first so logical and rational in both cases breaks down into the illogical and irrational. It is a path to a blank wall the critic must in his own turn follow again if he goes far enough, not very far in fact.

In the case of the two passages from Freud I have cited, if the reader allows himself to apply to Freud's texts the mode of interpretation the texts themselves recommend,[4] he will not only find inconsistencies and contradictions. He will also come to recognize that Freud's apparent rational mastery of the use of figures to represent the psyche dissolves. It dissolves in such a way that his text ultimately comes to mean the opposite of what he seems to want it to mean. Instead of being based on a clear distinction between literal, scientific language and figurative representation, a distinction necessary to maintain the idea of the objective existence of the pathogenic nucleus in the ego, Freud's words circle around a gap which would be the clear recognition that the pathogenic nucleus is inaccessible except through the entanglements of figurative language. If this is the case, that nucleus is a permanently unknown X; it is neither thought, nor thing, nor word. This recognition the passage from *The Interpretation of Dreams* still to some degree evades by trying to claim that the blind spot of the unknowable at the center of each dream may be safely ignored by the masterful scientist presenting his theory of dreams. It may be ignored because it offers nothing further to the interpretation.

In Nietzsche's case the binary oppositions, on which "On Truth and Lies in a Nonmoral Sense" is built, ultimately collapse in such a way that the essay turns back on itself and no longer makes consistent sense. This selfsubversion exemplifies in its opacity precisely what the essay attempts to bring to clear understanding. The binary oppositions in question include the oppositions between scientist and artist, waking and sleeping, truth and lie, remembering and forgetting, motion and stillness, reason and emotion, inside and outside, image and concept, literal and figurative language.

The argument of Nietzsche's essay seems clear enough. He affirms that everything in the human world begins with an act of intuition or naming which is a metaphorical transposition of something outside human knowledge. This something remains necessarily unknown and unknowable. It is "the mysterious X (*das rätselhafte X*)."[5] On the basis of these "perceptual metaphors (*anschaulichen Metaphern*)" (Eng., p. 84; Ger., p. 314), and by a complex series of further transpositions, each "a stammering translation (*eine nachstammelnde Übersetzung*)" (Eng., p. 86; Ger., p. 316), each another false equivalence, man has built his complex conceptual, scientific, moral, and artistic structures: "To begin with, a nerve stimulus is transferred (*übertragen*) into an image (*ein Bild*): first metaphor. The image, in turn, is imitated (*nachgeformt*) in a sound: second metaphor. And each time there is a complete overleaping (*Überspringen*) of one sphere, right into the middle of an entirely new and different one" (Eng., p. 82; Ger., p. 312). Out of such unjustified leaps, in this process of "über" and "nach," the airy structure of the human world is made.

All the lines of causality, true equivalence, and necessary connection in such structures are cut by Nietzsche, so that their coherence is seen to be illusory, like a building made of fragments precariously balanced. Such a structure, in one of the metaphors of violence and mutilation which punctuate Nietzsche's essay, is said to be like a song concocted by a painter without hands to express what he sees but to which he cannot give a pictorial expression: "For between two absolutely different spheres, as between subject and object, there is no causality, no correctness, and no expression; there is, at most, an aesthetic relation (*Verhalten*): I mean a suggestive transference (*eine andeutende Übertragung*).... A painter without hands who wished to express in song the picture before his mind would, by means of this substitution (*Vertauschung*) of spheres, still reveal more about the essence of things than does the empirical world" (Eng., pp. 86-87; Ger., p. 317).

The difference between science and art, for Nietzsche, is that the structures of the former are rapidly frozen and codified, taken as true, while the structures of the latter are based on fresh intuitive metaphors motivated by emotion. Man cannot cease to form new metaphors. His instinct to form them is, Nietzsche says, "the fundamental human drive, which one cannot for a single instant dispense with, for one would thereby dispense with man himself" (Eng., pp. 88-89; Ger., p. 319). The human world, for Nietzsche as for Freud, in their different ways, is a labyrinth of figurative displacements around an unknown center. What Nietzsche names "metaphor," "illusion," "transposition," or "dissimulation" is originally a *catachresis*. It replaces the unknown X with a sign which is neither literal nor figurative. In this it undermines the distinction between the truth of literal language and the lie of figurative language which is the foundation of Nietzsche's construction of the labyrinth of his essay.

The image of the labyrinth appears in Nietzsche's language in this essay not as such but in closely related spatial forms. The edifice of concepts, for example, is "the construction of a pyramidal order according to castes and degrees, the creation of a new world of laws, privileges, subordinations, and clearly marked boundaries." This pyramid "displays the right regularity of a Roman columbarium," or it is like an astrological map dividing up the sky, or like a dice game, or like a spider web built on running water, or like a beehive made not of wax but of concepts that man has manufactured from himself (Eng., pp. 84-85; Germ., p. 315). The structure of metaphors solidified into concepts man has made is both as rigid and stonelike as the stratifications of a pyramid and yet as unreal as the astrological lines dividing the heavens. These imaginary lines have power, nevertheless, to conjure those ideas or things in themselves which seem to dwell behind every concept, for example in Platonism or in the long heritage of Platonic metaphysics. If the maze of concepts is as fixed as though it were of stone, at the same time it is as fragile, light, and resilient as a spiderweb. It may float on a stream or bend with the wind. For Nietzsche, as for W. B. Yeats, man is "lost amid the labyrinth that he has made/In art or politics,"[6] but it seems as if that labyrinth, constructed by man's extraordinary genius in architecture, is a safe habitation able "to bar that foul storm out" (Yeats, *op. cit.*, I. 111). This is true even though man's house of words has been made of the false equivalences of metaphor, according to the universal concept that "every concept arises from the equation of unequal things (*durch Gleichsetzen des Nichtgleichen*)" (Eng., p. 83; Ger., p. 313).

It seems as though the situation of man, the mazelike territory within which he dwells, and the boundary separating him from the mysterious X, the rushing stream on which he floats, has been accurately mapped at last. It might seem also that not only Nietzsche but man in general is safe. The image of the roaring stream may seem a little menacing, but the airy structure of concepts man has made will, it seems, protect him from the unknown. The X will be held at arm's length, where it is no danger, as in the image at the end of the essay of the Stoic philosopher protected by his cloak from the rain: "When a real storm cloud thunders above him, he wraps himself (*hüllt er sich*) in his cloak, and with slow steps he walks from beneath it" (Eng., p. 91; Ger., p. 322).

*

What of Nietzsche's own metaphors? Why is it that Nietzsche must use what he condemns? Why must he, like Freud or like Yeats, use a set of proliferating metaphors which are not quite congruent with one another? That he must use what he condemns is evident, since language, as Nietzsche sees it, is either made of overt metaphors or of those frozen and effaced tropes he calls concepts. Nietzsche's word for transposition, "Übertragung," carries in itself the metaphor of carrying over, as does the word "metaphor." Language is nothing but metaphors, hot or cold, overt or effaced, though it is difficult for someone impregnated with the coldness of the system of concepts within which he lives to believe "that even the concept—which is as bony, foursquare, and transposable (*versetzbar*) as a die—is nevertheless merely the *residue of a metaphor*" (Eng., p. 85; Ger., p. 315). Nietzsche's task, like Freud's, is to use metaphors of either sort in such a way as to reveal clearly the functioning of metaphors. "On Truth and Lies" is rich and suggestive in its proliferation of overt metaphors, such as the one describing the human condition as like that of a man "hanging in dreams on the back of a tiger" (Eng., p. 80; Ger., p. 311). It is also interest-bearing in its play of conceptual terms, that dicegame of concepts which involves, for example, all those words in "nach" and "über," to which attention has already been called, or the play among words beginning in "ver" which runs through the essay: *Verpflichtung; Verstellung; verwerflich; Verhalten; Vertauschung; verhullend; Vergesslichkeit; verbindlich; Vertragung; verloren; versetzbar; verleugnen,* and so on.

The examination of one of the best-known of Nietzsche's overt metaphors in this essay will show that he too is entangled in the situation he is attempting to clarify. He can by no effort survey that situation as if from above, in a species of aerial photography of the human predicament. Nietzsche's language is neither purely conceptual nor purely metaphorical, neither scientific nor artistic. It is an example of that perpetual casting of figurative constructions over the mysterious X which the figures attempt to describe. This torsion makes of the essay as a whole an extended example of what I call "the linguistic moment." It attempts the impossible task of defining in unambiguous signs the functioning of signs.

Among these signs for the act of signmaking the figure of the effaced coin has often been cited and commented upon:[7]

> What then is truth? A movable host of metaphors, metonymies, and anthropomorphisms: in short, a sum of human relations which have been poetically and rhetorically intensified, transferred (*übertragen*), and embellished, and which, after long usage, seem to a people to be fixed, canonical, and binding (*verbindlich*). Truths are illusions which we have forgotten (*vergessen*) are illusions; they are metaphors that have become worn out and have been drained of sensuous force, coins which have lost (*verloren*) their image (*ihr Bild*) and are now considered as metal and no longer as coins. (Eng., p. 84; Ger., p. 314)

All three forms of truth—truth of correspondence, truth of internal coherence, and truth of revelation—are implicated in this passage. They are put in question, and then dismantled. The passage, like the essay as a whole, moves among binary oppositions which are substituted metaphorically for one another, but which are in one way or another demolished as clear oppositions in that process of sideways displacement. Here movement is set against stillness, truth against illusion, bareness against the aesthetically enhanced, figurative against conceptual, metaphor against metonymy. What about "anthropomorphisms"? The opposition between the similarities of metaphor and the contiguities of metonymy is undone by the fact that both are anthropomorphisms. Both are products of that power man has to project himself toward the mysterious X or to put himself under it as its illusory foundation. Immanuel Kant calls this power *hypotyposis*.[8] Nietzsche calls it dissimulation (*Vertragung*), the old rhetoricians, *catachresis*. Man is the power of anthropomorphic substitution. For no instant can this power be suspended, for man would then no longer be himself. His essence is neither consciousness, nor "spirit," nor "selfhood," but the power of making false transpositions.

The metaphor of the coin seems at first pellucid. It is used, like the other metaphors in Nietzsche's essay, as a powerful instrument of demystification. It is used to penetrate through illusions or to wipe them away, as the images stamped on a coin are wiped away by time and use, in order to reveal what is really there underneath, the bare metal of the truth of things as they are. The metaphor, however, like all figures, is not innocent. It is guilty in more ways than one, guilty of a multiple crime. The figure comparing a coin to a metaphor has a long history.[9] Money is a good metaphor of metaphor because both are instruments of exchange and of establishing false equivalences. Both in different ways exchange this for that or turn this into that by means of transfers based on conventional or fictional equivalences, and there is much overlapping of rhetorical and economic terminology. If a metaphor is a transfer, property is transferred from this person to that by money, the universal solvent. As Wallace Stevens says, "money is a kind of poetry."[10]

What makes a coin valid or distinguishes true coin from counterfeit? This is the question of Nietzsche's essay, the question of verity. There are, it seems, two possible answers to this question. It may be the metal itself which gives the coin its value. The metal may be taken as having an intrinsic worth. It would then function as the measure of all other values. The money of a given country may be on the "gold standard" or on the "silver standard." Even its paper currency is upheld by a claim on its face to be backed by so much bullion. Such money is only a step beyond a barter economy, in the sense that the money, goods, or labor exchanged for one another are presumed to be equal in material value. The other possible validation of a coin is the image stamped on it. Such a coin is valid not because the metal has value in itself, but because it carries the king's image, for example, and behind that is guaranteed by the king's divine right to rule. In such a case paper money is as valid as metal coin. To indulge in coinage is treason, even if the counterfeit coins are of full weight, since what counts is the issuing authority, not the object itself, the substratum which is the bearer of the image of that authority.

To make a coin, then, is to coin a metaphor, or the two operations are metaphorically similar, so that there can be a free exchange between them. "To coin good metaphors," said Aristotle in the *Poetics,* "is the mark of genius" in a poet because it "involves an insight into the resemblances between objects that are superficially unlike."[11] When one looks more closely at Nietzsche's use of this metaphor, or indeed at the metaphor as used by anyone, it reveals itself to be odd or paradoxical. It is perhaps in some way a counterfeit coin of thought. It leads the mind astray into a false sense of rich implication and shining clarity. The oddness lies in the false ratio the metaphor sets up.

Nietzsche's statement begins with a conceptual formula taking the shape of a truthful equation: A is to B as C is to D. Truths, that is, illusions not known to be illusions, are to illusions known to be illusions as conceptual is to metaphorical, as coin mere metal is to coin stamped with an image, as forgetting is to remembering. To remember the metaphors, the poetic transpositon, enhancement, or aesthetic heightening, is like realizing one is face to face with pure blank metal. This is absurdly non-parallel. The failure in parallelism arises from the fact that the image of the removal of the illusory image revealing the bare metal has the form of a figure of unveiling. The bare metal seems to be what is "really there," the substantial truth beneath. Thinking of it this way depends on forgetting that actually the bare metal stands for the false world of concepts, of figures which are no longer recognized as figures. To see the bare metal as the truth one has to forget the forgetting, or to forget once more.

Nietzsche's formulation promises a confrontation with the "truth" in some one of its traditional senses. What is missing, in this stammering play of substitutions, is anything which corresponds to the unknown X underlying all the play. The mysterious X is not the bare metal. That is only effaced figure. Nor is it the images on the coin. They are only figures known to be figures. The ratio goes from figure to figure, not from figure to truth. The ratio has a missing term (A is to B as C is to X), as in the examples of *catachresis* given by Aristotle in the *Poetics,* 1457b, 26-31 (Butcher, ed. cit., pp. 78-79). This is just the point Nietzsche is making, namely that truth is only another name for illusion, for lie. The metaphor misleads the reader into thinking he can reach the "real" truth by way of Nietzsche's language. The metaphor leads him to believe he can reach the bare truth beneath, the bare coin, by an act of unveiling or the erasure of a forgetting (*aletheia*) through language. He has been led into error by forgetting that the metaphor of money is a metaphor. It is an image, like the face on a coin, not naked truth. He commits in a moment of inadvertence, of forgetting, the error the passage warns against. It warns against it and yet invites the reader to make it by taking the form of a truth statement. What is truth? The truth *is* so and so. This error is a version of that sin of the fetishism of money Marx denounces, for example in the *Grundrisse* or in Volume One of *Capital.* Such fetishism takes a conventional medium of exchange as a value in itself.

The reader of "On Truth and Lies" will commit that sin whether he takes the concepts of Nietzsche's essay or its figures as valid representations of the mysterious X. As the essay tells the reader, even the concepts of the essay are only a disguised form of figure. They are figures which have lost their faces, effaced themselves, as the Stoic philosopher, at the end of the essay, covers himself with his cloak. The Stoic hides his face. He becomes like a coin worn bare, which is appropriate, since the Stoic is pre-eminently the man of concepts. To coin metaphors or to coin metal into money are versions of the same activity, that activity of figuration without which man would not be himself. Either form of coinage brings both artistic language and scientific language, each with its appropriate internal contradictions, into existence at the same time.

The internal contradictions cause both the language on concepts and the language of metaphors, as for example Nietzsche uses them in this essay, to turn back on themselves in a reversal which is the most extreme form of what I am calling the linguistic moment. Insofar as the reader takes the metaphor literally and assumes that truth is an effaced coin, he is doing what the image tells him not to do. He is forgetting the aberrant ground of the figure, the way it is a stammering translation of something which remains unknown and unknowable. Insofar as the reader remembers it is a metaphor he remembers that has no truth value and so undoes the claim of the statement to tell him what the truth is, in however negative a fashion. Nietzsche gives an admirably succinct expression of this law of the torsion of truth upon itself in the notes written for a continuation of "On Truth and Lies": "Truth kills—what is more, it kills itself (insofar as it recognizes that its foundation is error)" (*Wahrheit tötet—ja tötet sich selbst* [*insofern sie erkennt, dass ihr Fundament der Irrtum ist*]).[12]

*

It should be clear now why the airy labyrinthine fabric man has constructed out of himself for himself is not a safe enclosure. It might seem at first that the building is safe. What does it matter that the unknown X remains unknown, that it remains the atopical in this topography, something without place? Man is safe as long as the labyrinth he has made in law, art, or science remains intact. This permanent displacement does not stay safely in its place, however. It displaces itself everywhere. It pervades the whole system and makes it unmappable, so that nothing within it remains where it ought to be, in its proper place. Everything moves, wobbles, or stammers, as it does also in any commentary on the system.

What, for example, of my use here of English translations? This use is commanded by the conventions of publication in the United States. If the metaphorical transpositions which are the basis of the human world are "properly" to be called stammering translations, what does this mean for a translation into English of Nietzsche's essay? It must be a further translation of what is already a translation. My subjection to an English translation is a dramatic example of the situation the essay describes. The essay is about figurative language, but it also uses figurative language throughout. The critic's ability to interpret it depends on his skill and tact with figures. Figures appear in two ways in the essay, one visible, the other effaced or visible only in a stammering, distorted form, like an inscription half worn away. One form of figure may be more or less successfully translated. This is the overt figure of speech, as when Nietzsche describes the human condition as being like a man hanging in dreams on the back of a tiger. The other form is the presence of "buried" metaphors in all Nietzsche's conceptual terms, as in the words in "über": "Übertragung," überspringen," and so on. Sometimes these "buried" figures correspond to those in the equivalent English words and sometimes not, but never exactly. "Translation" and "Übersetzung" are not quite the same figures, though they are similar. Translation in both cases is a form of carrying over, in fact of metaphor or transport, as both words suggest, but with a different nuance. "Setting over" is not quite the same as "carrying over." Reading Nietzsche's essay in English is something like the situation Nietzsche describes in one figure in his essay as typical of man in general, the situation of the deaf man trying to understand sounds from patterns in sand made by resonating sonorities (Eng., p. 82; Ger., p. 312).

If translation is always a form of stammering, so in its turn is the work of the critic.[13] Literary criticism is translation, but so is the text criticized. The latter is a stuttering transposition of what may not be articulated clearly, namely the atopical unknown X. The text reveals its non-equivalence with its "source" by the fact that it stammers. This stammering can be described as a forgetting. What the text remembers in one place it forgets in another. The situation of the critic is no different. He too is a translator. His materials are the words of a text which is itself a work of translation. It too is made as if by a painter without hands. The materials of the philosopher or poet, whether they are earlier texts or original "intuitions," in either case are transpositions of the unknown. By no process of reverse translation is it possible for the critic to reach back to the original text. The code of the sequence of translations cannot be cracked, only re-encrypted. What is expressed by any stage of that sequence, even the "first," has no existence as a thing to be located at any time or place. It can never be present to consciousness as an object to be given a literal name. It is nowhere at no time.

This non-thing or non-presence is neither the transcendental logos nor is it nothing. It is not open to sensation nor to perception. It is the inaccessible center of the labyrinth—neither mind, nor matter, nor distant spirit, nor word. It is wholly silent. At the same time it is already present within any labyrinth man has made as the hostile guest who is found inside the house. It is what ruins art, politics, philosophy, love, poetry. It makes them incoherent, self-dismantling, like the text of Nietzsche's essay. The inaccessible X is both outside Nietzsche's essay as its unnamable ground and also present inside it as what prevents it from being logical or systematic.

Nietzsche both knows this and does not know it. He both forgets it and remembers. His essay forgets in one place what it remembers in another. What it untwists in one place it twists up in another, like a knotted loop that cannot be wholly untangled. An example of this is the way the clear opposition at the end of the essay between the Stoic philosopher, protected by his cloak, and the artist, exposed to danger, is undercut by what has been said earlier. The opposition is undercut by the ironic echo of the passage in Aristophanes' *The Clouds* in which Socrates advises the novice philosopher Strepsiades to cover his head in order to meditate. There may also be an echo of the story in Plato's *Theaetetus* about the Thracian housemaid who laughed at Thales when he fell down a well while occupied in studying the heavens.[14] Even if these echoes are not noticed the reader may remember what Nietzsche has apparently forgotten, namely the way he has described anyone complacently enclosed (*verhüllend*) in his illusions as like a man asleep on the back of a tiger. As he says of the seeker after truth, in another part of the essay: "the scientific investigator (*der Forscher*) builds his hut right next to the tower of science (*Wissenchaft*) so that he will be able to work on it and to find shelter for himself beneath those bulwarks which presently exist. And he requires shelter, for there are frightful powers (*furchtbare Mächte*) which continuously break in upon him, powers which oppose scientific 'truth' with completely different kinds of 'truths' which bear on their shields the most varied sorts of emblems" (Eng., p. 88; Ger., p. 319).

These fearful forces have in fact already entered into the sage's hut, the scientist's tower, and the artist's fabrications. They have entered in the forms of ruinous selfcontradictions within all those forms of protective shielding. For Nietzsche, as for Yeats, it is impossible to bar the foul storm out because its violence has been incorporated into the structures intended to keep it out. However logical man tries to make the hierarchical system of concepts within which he lives, cutting everything neatly, like the sharp corners of a die, numbering everything, and fitting each thing into its proper pigeonhole, like coffins shelved in a Roman columbarium, this cutting and fitting reverses itself. The cutter is cut, as in all those images of grotesque mutilation which run through this essay and which describe man as about to be eaten by a tiger, or as like a deaf musician, or as like a painter without hands. He may be eaten. He has already been dismembered. This dismembering figures his disremembering, his inability to keep a total picture of his condition clearly present in his mind.

This dangerous incoherence is repeated by the reader of Nietzsche's essay. An interpretation of it can never be clear or complete. The laws of forgetting and of self-mutilation apply to any reader as well as to the author. Insofar as he thinks he has a clear, distinct, and coherent reading of the essay, he has forgotten some important part of it. He too is taking bare metal as valid coin, or, what is worse, taking bare metal as bare metal, as the naked truth behind illusion. This impotence of both author and reader is the primary evidence of the presence as non-presence, everywhere in the text, of the unknown X which it wrestles, unsuccessfully, to locate and name.

Yale University

NOTES

1   Sigmund Freud, *The Complete Psychological Works,* Standard Edition, trans. James Strachey *et al.,* II (London: The Hogarth Press, 1953-66), 291.

2   For the German original, see Sigmund Freud, *Gesammelte Werke,* I (London: Imago Publishing Co., Ltd., 1952), 295.

3   Standard Edition, V, 525; *Gesammelte Werke,* ed. cit., II-III, 530. See Samuel Weber's discussion of this passage in "Remarks on Freud's *Witz,*" *Glyph,* I, 1-27, esp. pp. 8 ff. I have followed Weber's alteration of Strachey's translation to bring it closer to Freud's German.

4   "But if we examine with a critical eye the account that the patient has given us without much trouble or resistance, we shall quite infallibly discover gaps and imperfections in it" (*Studies on Hysteria,* ed. cit., p. 293).

5   "On Truth and Lies in a Nonmoral Sense," *Philosophy and Truth: Selections from Nietzsche's Notebooks of the Early 1870's,* trans. Daniel Breazeale (Atlantic Highlands, New Jersey: Humanities Press, Inc., 1979), p. 83. I have occasionally altered this translation slightly to conform more closely to the original. For the German see Friedrich Nietzsche, "Über Wahrheit und Lüge im Aussermoralischen Sinn," *Werke in Drei Bänden,* ed. Karl Schlecta, III (Munich: Carl Hanser Verlag, 1966), 13. Further references to this essay will be to page numbers in these editions, identified as "Eng." and "Ger.," respectively.

6   "Nineteen Hundred and Nineteen," II. 70-71, *The Variorum Edition of the Poems of W. B. Yeats,* ed. Peter Allt and Russell K. Alspach (New York: Macmillan Publishing Co., Inc., 1957), p. 431.

7   For example by Jacques Derrida in "La mythologie blanche," *Marges* (Paris: Les Éditions de Minuit, 1972), pp. 257-58.

8   See paragraph 59, *Critique of Judgment,* trans. J. H. Bernard (New York: Hafner Publishing Company, 1951), pp. 196-200.

9   See, besides "La mythologie blanche," cited above, Marc Shell, *The Economy of Literature* (Baltimore and London: The Johns Hopkins Univ. Press, 1978), and *ibid.,* "Money and the Mind: the Economics of Translation in Goethe's Faust," *MLN,* XCV, 516-62.

10   Wallace Stevens, "Adagia," *Opus Posthumous* (New York; Alfred A. Knopf, 1957), p. 165.

11   Or, at any rate, that is what Aristotle says in Lane Cooper's translation (*Aristotle on the Art of Poetry,* trans. Lane Cooper [Ithaca, New York: Cornell Univ. Press, 1947], p. 74). S. H. Butcher translates the same passage simply as "to make good metaphors" (*Aristotle's Theory of Poetry and Fine Art* [New York: Dover Publications, Inc., 1951], p. 870). Butcher seems nearer to Aristotle, who said: "to gar eu metapherein to to homoion theorein estin." The metaphor of coining is counterfeit coin here, product of the translator's sleight of hand, however much it may be implicit in Aristotle's terminology describing poetry as a making.

12   Friedrich Nietzsche, *Das Philosophenbuch/Le Livre du philosophe,* bilingual ed., French trans. Angèle K. Marietti (Paris: Aubier-Flammarion, 1969), p. 202, my translation.

13   See Carol Jacobs, "Nietzsche: The Stammering Text," *The Dissimulating Harmony* (Baltimore and London: The Johns Hopkins Univ. Press, 1978), pp. 3-22.

14   Aristophanes, *The Clouds,* ll. 725 ff., trans. anonymous, *The Complete Greek Drama,* ed. Whitney J. Oates and Eugene O'Neill, Jr., II (New York: Random House, 1938), pp. 568-69. Plato, *Theaetetus,* 174 a-b, trans. F. M. Cornford, *Collected Dialogues,* ed. Edith Hamilton and Huntington Cairns (Princeton, New Jersey: Princeton Univ. Press, 1961), p. 879. For Martin Heidegger's comment on the passage in the *Theaetetus,* see *Die Frage nach dem Ding* (Tübingen: Max Niemeyer Verlag, 1975), p. 2; for a translation, see *What is a Thing?,* trans. W. B. Barton, Jr. and Vera Deutsch (Chicago: Henry Regnery Company, 1970), pp. 2-3.

The Question of the Self in Nietzsche during the Axial Period (1882-1888)[1]

Stanley Corngold

*To the memory of
Walter Kaufmann*

A philosopher must seek his way to
this right [to judge the value of life]
only from the most comprehensive—
perhaps most disturbing and destructive—
experiences.[2]

Jetzt—
zwischen zwei Nichtse
eingekrümmt,
ein Fragezeichen,
ein müdes Rätsel—
ein Rätsel für *Raubvögel* . . .
—sie werden dich schon "lösen,"
sie hungern schon nach deiner "Lösung,"
sie flattern schon um dich, ihr Rätsel,
um dich, Gehenkter! . . .

55

What has Nietzsche to say in his major texts of the axial period
(ca. 1882-1888)—in *The Gay Science, Thus Spoke Zarathustra, Beyond
Good and Evil, On the Genealogy of Morals* and *The Will to Power*—in
answer to the question, "What is the self? " Certainly the answer is not a
simple one. There are propositions which appear to deny the reality of the
self as plainly as the following: "The 'subject' is not something given, it is
something added and invented and projected behind what there is" (*WP*,
267). "We can set up a word at the point at which our ignorance
begins, . . . e.g. the word 'I' . . ." (*WP*, 267). "Through thought the ego is
posited; but hitherto one believed . . . that in 'I think' there was something
of immediate certainty, and that this 'I' was the given *cause* of
thought . . . . However habitual and indispensable this fiction may have
become by now—that in itself proves nothing against its imaginary
origin . . ." (*WP*, 267-68). " 'The subject' is the fiction that many similar
states in us are the effect of one substratum: but it is we who first created
the 'similarity' of these states; our adjusting them and making them similar
is the fact, not their similarity (—which ought rather to be denied—)" (*WP*,
269). "No subject 'atoms.' The sphere of a subject constantly growing or
decreasing, the center of the system constantly shifting . . . ."[4]

There are, however, propositions that affirm the reality of a self
as plainly as these: "At the bottom of us, really 'deep down,' there
is . . . some granite of spiritual *fatum*" (*BW*, 352). "Behind your thoughts
and feelings, my brother, there stands a mighty ruler, an unknown
sage—whose name is self" (*PN*, 146). "Whenever a cardinal problem is at
stake, there speaks an unchangeable 'this is I' " (*BW*, 352). "We are
unknown to ourselves, we men of knowledge—and with good reason. We
have never sought ourselves—how could it happen that we should ever *find*
ourselves . . . . Whatever else there is in life, so-called 'experiences'—which
of us has sufficient earnestness for them? . . ." (*BW*, 451). Here Nietzsche
puts us on the track of our genuine, our "creative" selves (*PN*, 147). If we
have missed ourselves, it is because we have not "had time" for, or "given
our hearts" to, the venture, and not because the self is a deception (*BW*,
451). Nietzsche's quarrel here is not with a theory of the self but with
weak theories of the self, e.g. as "pure spirit," as an indestructible monad,
as the agent of introspection, and so forth (*BW*, 193, 210, 213-14, 257, et
al.).

Faced with this contradiction we are tempted at first to produce a familiar distinction. These propositions need not be incompatible: the first group, after all, speaks negatively of a certain "subject"—the ego—but not of a certain "being"—the self (*BW*, 451). It would not be difficult to find concepts in Nietzsche creating apparently firm value-distinctions even within this sort of opposition. Thus if Nietzsche attacks a superficial, merely instrumental, "herd" *ego* (*GS*, 299; *BW*, 234, 399), he affirms a deep, creative, authentic self or *being* which founds (and eludes) the ego—a being linked to "the body" and to "the soul."[5]

In addition to the polarities: "superficial"/"profound"; "instrumental"/"creative"; "herd"/"authentic"; a considerable number of parallel pairs can be constructed—everything necessary, it seems, to distinguish conceptually the ego from the genuine self.[6]

But the opposition of concepts defining the shallow self to those defining the deep self will not hold up for long. We find, in examining the range of Nietzsche's work, a persistent fluctuation in the value of the qualities attached to the ego. Thus, typically, Nietzsche rejects a certain sort of Platonic critique of the surface as deception, as mere seeming—affirming, by litotes, the value of the surface (*BW*, 237, 241, 350, in al.). He also speaks of the intersubjective communicative factor (the "herd" factor) as the chief refiner of self-consciousness and language. Under the pressure of the need to communicate, "consciousness . . . has developed subtlety." "The ultimate result is an excess of this strength and art of communication," whose "heirs are those who are called artists."[7] If "consciousesss . . . [is] at first at the furthest distance from the biological center of the individual, . . . [it] deepens and intensifies itself, and continually draws nearer to that center" (*WP*, 274). We find it impossible, in the long run, to stabilize the predicates of the epiphenomenal self which Nietzsche allegedly attacks, and oppose them to those of the deep self, which Nietzsche appears to affirm.

What may help in our perplexity is the fact that Nietzsche has never meant to assuage our perplexity on this point, and has said so explicitly at the outset of *Beyond Good and Evil* (*BW*, 199).

The argument concerns the origin of our "will to truth" and turns on Nietzsche's surmise about what might underlie this will: a Who or a What?[8] We see recurring here in the form of a question the identical division we pointed to above. Nietzsche hesitates to say whether the self is properly cast as an ego or a being. This problem is then immediately placed on its ground: another problem has to be raised as primary, as having to precede the question of the self. This is the question of the *value* of this will to truth (of the self).

What is therefore more seriously at stake is the very intelligibility of such questions as: Is there a self? What is the self? as examples of any questions that may be asked (excepting, perhaps, rhetorical questions). The question of the self pushes toward its own enabling structure. Who, when such a question is asked, asks? The self? Which self? With what authority? Or does the question pose itself? "The problem of the value of truth," writes Nietzsche, "came before [was confronted by] us—or was it we who came before [were confronted by] the problem? Who of us is Oedipus here? Who the Sphinx? It is a rendezvous, it seems, of questions and question marks."9 Can the self be, finally, only this very question that comes *as if* to provoke an answer, to dispel an illusion or to fill in a void—but remains inexpungeably "the problem we *are* (*BW*, 352)? For "the genuine philosopher . . . risks *himself* constantly . . ." (*BW*, 315).

This passage from *Beyond Good and Evil* can be defined more sharply in the light of the "Introduction" to Heidegger's *Being and Time*—"The Formal Structure of the Question of Being."10 To make the comparison fitting, we have to make one substitution. For the term "the value of the will to truth"—the fundamental term in the passage from *Beyond Good and Evil*—we substitute the word "being" (*unser Sein*), which occupies a similar place in the argument of the first part of the "Preface" to *On the Genealogy of Morals* (II, 763). Here Nietzsche's formulation reads: "As one divinely preoccupied and immersed in himself into whose ear the bell has just boomed with all its strength the twelve beats of noon suddenly starts up and asks himself: 'what really was that which just struck?' so we sometimes rub our ears *afterward* and ask, utterly surprised and disconcerted, 'what really was that which we have just experienced?' and moreover: 'who *are* we really?' and, afterward as aforesaid, count the twelve trembling bell-strokes of our experience, our life, our *being*—and alas! miscount them.—So we are necessarily strangers to ourselves . . ." (*BW*, 451). This passage also turns on the question of the value of a certain form of the will to truth (—to self-knowledge);11 and it links the provenience of this question to the being of the self that evades it.

Now the key trope in both Nietzsche passages, making the substitution possible, is the at least potential metonymic reversal of questioner and question in "a rendezvous of questions and question marks." In the passage from the *Genealogy* we do not have a conscious ego that poses the question of its will to truth with any degree of sovereignty. Instead the ego—"utterly surprised and disconcerted"—is assailed by the question of its being. We shall see then that Nietzsche anticipates—and proleptically corrects—Heidegger's description in *Being and Time* of human existence (*Dasein*) as questioning-being.

Nietzsche's formulation of the problem of the self is, once again, that "we came before [were put into question by] the question of the value of truth"—or, by substitution, "we come before [are put into question by] the question of our being." Here, now, is Heidegger: "To work out the question of Being means to make a being—he who questions—perspicuous in his Being. Asking the question, as a mode of

58

being of a being, is itself essentially determined by what is asked about in it—Being. This being which we ourselves in each case are and which includes inquiry among the possibilities of its Being we formulate terminologically as *Dasein*. The explicit and lucid formulation of the question of the meaning of Being requires a prior suitable explication of a being (Dasein) with regard to its Being" (*MH*, 48).

What Nietzsche and Heidegger both tell us is that a fundamental mode of human being is constituted by a question. The question is inevitable. If man expressly formulates it, he does not invent it; he is the instance—indeed, the object—of that question. Man questions *because* the question of being is a constitutive mode of his being. Heidegger writes literally, "The asking (putting as a question) of this question is . . . a mode of *being* of a being . . ." (Das Fragen dieser Frage ist . . . *Seinsmodus* eines Seienden . . .).[12] Through that question a certain mode of being comes to light.

But now the difference between these two writers emerges and is crucial. The difference turns on the object of the question which constitutes the questioner—a question "itself essentially determined by what is asked about in it." For Heidegger the question is the meaning of Being; for Nietzsche, the question is of *our* being—the self. That man is asked the question of his being can mean for Nietzsche no more nor less than that the self exists as the question of its being and to this extent is "self-determined."[13]

Heidegger reads differently that being which is "asked about" in the question constituting *Dasein*. What is asked about is Being, and by this Being a mode of human being is "essentially determined." This is the strong form of the claim, which in this section of *Being and Time* is afterward neutralized and almost dissolved. Here is the less strong form: "['In the question of the meaning of Being,'] . . . there is . . . a notable 'relatedness backward or forward' of what is asked about (Being) to asking as a mode of being of a being" (*MH*, 49). The more nearly neutral form reads: "This only means that the being that has the character of Dasein has a relation to the question of Being itself, perhaps even a distinctive one. But have we not thereby demonstrated that a particular being has a priority with respect to Being and that the exemplary being that is to function as what is primarily *interrogated* is pregiven? . . ." (*MH*, 49). Finally the claim is dissolved: "In what we have discussed up to now neither has the priority of Dasein been demonstrated nor has anything been decided about its possible or even necessary function as the primary being to be interrogated" (*MH*, 49-50). Then the claim is reasserted in a "typically Heideggerian" manner—at once unassailable, if one is persuaded by the rhetoric of the author—its authority—and also vacuous, indeed, sophistic, if one is not. Heidegger writes: "But indeed something like a priority of Dasein has announced itself" (*MH*, 50).

The fault here is that the task at hand is to clarify the meaning of

Being that comes to light in being *announced* as the predicate of an insistently assertive question. Such a discussion has itself to be preceded by a clarification of the kind of visibility and evidence which belongs to Being thus *announced*. Heidegger begs the question.

We return to Nietzsche. The self is constituted not by the question of the meaning of Being but by the question of *its* being. This is precisely what Zarathustra says in the "speech" called "On the Afterworldly": "Verily, all being is hard to prove and hard to induce to speak" (Wahrlich, schwer zu beweisen ist alles Sein und schwer zum Reden zu bringen) (II, 298) (*PN*, 144). And Nietzsche continues on behalf of the question of the ego. "Tell me, my brothers, is not the strangest of all things proved most nearly?

"Indeed, the ego (*dies Ich*) and the ego's contradiction and confusion still speak most honestly of its being—this creating, willing, valuing ego, which is the measure and value of things. And this most honest being, the ego, speaks of the body and still wants the body, even when it poetizes and raves and flutters with broken wings. It learns to speak ever more honestly, this ego: and the more it learns, the more words and honors it finds for body and earth" (*PN*, 144).

Zarathustra's speech is so anti-metaphysical in its thrust, so bent on speaking on behalf of man and not his gods, so violent in closing off any path of access to truth and being that leads away from man, the body, and the earth, that in its urgency to anchor the human ego it forgets that in its being the ego is a question.

Nietzsche does not forget for long. Whatever claims he makes to a "perfect" being that "speaks of the meaning of the earth," he is inclined simultaneously to relativize in irony or else to contradict in the course of an allegorical narrative (*PN*, 145). The next speech of Zarathustra—"On the Despisers of the Body"—robs the earlier speech of any suggestion of finality. It introduces another ego, the "ego's ruler" (*des Ichs Beherrscher*) —the self (*das Selbst*) (II, 300). The status of the ego is made fully problematic, itself appropriately become a question; for the purpose of even the ego of Zarathustra—Nietzsche's fullest fiction—is to *break*, to *shatter*: "Who am *I*?" says Zarathustra. "I await the worthier one; I am not worthy even of being broken by it" (*PN*, 258). Zarathustra's speech on behalf of the self is worth quoting at length.

> But the awakened and knowing say: body am I entirely, and nothing else; and soul is only a word for something about the body.
> The body is a great reason, a plurality with one sense, a war and a peace, a herd and a shepherd. An instrument of your body is also your little reason, my brother, which you call "spirit"—a little instrument and

toy of your great reason.

"I," you say, and are proud of the word. But greater is that in which you do not wish to have faith—your body and its great reason: that does not say "I," but does "I."

What the sense feels, what the spirit knows, never has an end in itself. But sense and spirit would persuade you that they are the end of all things: that is how vain they are. Instruments and toys are sense and spirit: behind them still lies the self. The self also seeks with the eyes of the senses; it also listens with the ears of the spirit. Always the self listens and seeks: it compares, overpowers, conquers, destroys. It controls, and it is in control of the ego too.

Behind your thoughts and feelings, my brother, there stands a mighty ruler, an unknown sage—whose name is self. In your body he dwells; he is your body.

There is more reason in your body than in your best wisdom. And who knows why your body needs precisely your best wisdom?

Your self laughs at your ego and at its bold leaps. "What are these leaps and flights of thought to me?" it says to itself. "A detour to my end. I am the leading strings of the ego and the prompter of its concepts."

The self says to the ego, "Feel pain here!" Then the ego suffers and thinks how it might suffer no more—and that is why it is *made* to think.

The self says to the ego, "Feel pleasure here!" Then the ego is pleased and thinks how it might often be pleased again—and that is why it is *made* to think.

I want to speak to the despisers of the body. It is their respect that begets their contempt. What is it that created respect and contempt and worth and will? The creative self created respect and contempt; it created pleasure and pain. The creative body created the spirit as a hand for its will.

Even in your folly and contempt, you despisers of the body, you serve your self. I say unto you: your self itself wants to die and turns away from life. It is no longer capable of what it would do above all else: to create beyond itself. That is what it would do above all else, that is its fervent wish.

But now it is too late for it to do this: so your self wants to go under. O, despisers of the body. Your self wants to go under, and that is why you have become despisers of the body! For you are no longer able to create beyond yourselves. (*PN*, 146-47)

In our copying out, however, Nietzsche's text on the "creative self" that rules the ego, our argument appears to have returned to its beginning. How could there be a plainer statement on behalf of a substantial self anchored in the body, a "deep" self *not* to be confused with the epiphenomenal ego? Speaking in a certain Heideggerian manner, we could say, "Indeed something like a priority of the bodily self has announced itself."[14]

This would be mystifying; the meaning of Nietzsche's statement is limited by its context. In *Zarathustra* it frames Nietzsche's polemic against the "afterworldly" who figure as "despisers of the body," for the text speaks less on behalf of the body than it does *against* those "who are angry with life." It begins, "I want to speak of the despisers of the body," and concludes, "I shall not go your way, o despisers of the body! You are no bridge to the overman!" When the term of self is introduced, it is as a supplement to the body, a "name" that confers prestige on the body: "A mighty ruler . . . whose name is self . . . is your body." And when the body is anatomized for exact celebration, we see Nietzsche simply "using" for this task the very words of the metaphysical tradition which, elsewhere, he is at work venting of their meaning: "reason,"[15] "sense" [or "meaning"— "mit *einem* Sinne" (II, 300)], "society" in the pejorative term "herd," viz., "The body is a great reason, a plurality with one sense, a war and a peace, a herd and a shepherd."

This text is important, but it does not make a decisive contribution to Nietzsche's egology: it does not sustain its authority. As soon as the self has been defined as the body, the body is in turn translated back into the key-words of the metaphysical tradition. This is familiar as the strategy—and the pitfall—of Nietzsche's argument on behalf of the "will to truth" at the outset of *Beyond Good and Evil*. As that argument advances a little past the first aphorism, we see too that in "coming down" from the mystified "heights" of dogmatic metaphysics, Nietzsche has no place to go but to the body: "Most of the conscious thinking of a philosopher is secretly guided and forced into certain channels by his instincts" (*BW*, 201). But *the* body quickly imposes on Nietzsche a notion of plurality—"instincts" in the sentence above, and afterwards "drives," for example: "I do not believe that a 'drive to knowledge' is the father of philosophy; but rather that another drive has, here as elsewhere, employed understanding (and misunderstanding) as a mere instrument. But anyone who considers the basic drives of man to see to what extent they may have been at play just here as *inspiring* spirits . . . will find that all of them have done philosophy at some time—and that every single one of them would like only too well to represent just *itself* as the ultimate purpose of existence and the legitimate *master* of all the other drives. For every drive wants to be master—and it attempts to philosophize in that *spirit*" (*BW*, 203-04).

The "self" which, in *Zarathustra*, is "that mighty ruler ... the body," in *Beyond Good and Evil*, it appears, still has to search for itself, in the master drive. But this argument is plainly regressive (By what single decisive attribute could mastery be known?); and so Nietzsche promptly revises it: "[The philosopher's] morality bears decided and decisive witness to ... what *order of rank* the innermost drives of his nature stand in relation to each other" (*BW*, 204; ital. mine). The "master" has become an "order," a "structure"—and not a substantial term; and yet, at the same time, this instinctual "order of rank" is supposed to define "*who [the philosopher] is*" ... (*BW*, 204). As the answer to the question of the self plunges from the aporia of the Who/What to the seeming unity of instinctual life—to the body—that life splits into an agon, metaphorized—displaced, disseminated—in social strife but then swiftly reassembled into the Who of the personal subject of the mischievous "subject and ego superstition" (*BW*, 192). The question of whether the self is to be cast as a Who or a What is not resolved. At whatever point attributes of personality are dissolved, and the surviving "agent" termed an unknown structure or *being*, we tend to see that What dispersed, pluralized—but then also regathered into a Who, a cryptic personality. The problem of whether the self is properly understood as like an ego (Who) or a being (What) remains unresolved.

(The being of the self, meanwhile, in the moment of its pluralization, is, as we shall see, invariably represented by Nietzsche in images of "society."[16] The "soul," for example, in *Beyond Good and Evil*, is hypothesized as a "social structure of the drives and affects" [*BW*, 210]).

That the self is linked in these texts to the body is not in itself, then, an argument on behalf of a substantial self. The "move," in *Zarathustra*, is based on an act of vehement opposition to a traditional metaphysical-religious rhetoric exalting subject, soul, or ego. The argument against the body-despisers knows no better revenge than to adopt for its party some of the etiolated key-words of the adversary position. Nietzsche's tactic is to perform one more "herd-moral" inversion on the "original" herd-moral inversion of strong values by dogmatic philosophy. If there has to be a rhetoric of "spirit"—of reason and meaning—then these terms can be reconquered for the body. In the couple "a herd and a shepherd" Nietzsche makes a precise allusion having a self-reflexive function: it names the procedure of re-inverting inverted values. This procedure is also plain in the phrase from *Beyond Good and Evil* which we cited above. Considering that "the way is open for new versions of and refinements of the soul-hypothesis," Nietzsche offers one such new "scientific" hypothesis: "soul as social structure of the drives and affects"

(*BW,* 210). He inverts the terms of the original catastrophic frustration of instinct producing "the *internalization* of man" ("thus it was that man first developed what was later called his 'soul' "); and he annexes to the soul the currents of the body life (*BW,* 520).

This procedure, however, of reasoning by the trope of litotes— viz., the soul is not non-body—never, for obvious reasons, finds firm ground. The strategy which informs it can be implacably levelled against itself. Indeed this is what Nietzsche does again and again when, with a sort of throwaway gesture, he unsettles in other texts the phrase "a plurality with one sense" by asymmetrical polyvalent terms: "no subject 'atoms' . . . the center of the system constantly shifting . . ." (*WP,* 270). Or in the aphorism from *Beyond Good and Evil,* just following the definition of the soul as "social structure of the drives and affects," he amusingly redefines the *body* as "a social structure composed of many souls" (*BW,* 216). Typically, at this point of irony, circularity and dispersion of meaning, Nietzsche again arbitrarily asserts a center, a Who: "the complex state of delight of the person exercising volition . . . [includes] his feelings of delight as commander" [!] (*BW,* 216). This "Who" can be further dispersed, but Nietzsche means the process to be interminable: it is the way of the "world," as in the triumphant account concluding *The Will to Power*: ". . . a sea of forces flowing and rushing together, eternally changing, eternally flooding back . . . , out of the simplest forms striving toward the most complex . . . , most self-contradictory, and then again returning home to the simple out of this abundance, out of the play of contradictions back to the joy of concord . . ." (*WP,* 550).

We have returned once more to the problem of the intact bodily self that "announced itself" with apparent priority in Zarathustra's speeches. This is not a real problem. It "announced" itself in my account of Nietzsche's reflections on the self only because I meant to make it belong to a sequence illustrating the point that for Nietzsche, unlike Heidegger, "the belly of being does not speak to humans at all, except as a human" (*PN,* 144).

We should not leave this *Zarathustra* passage, however, without marking out a positive result. The passage does *assert* the priority of the self over the ego (however readily it can be shown that these terms do not point to exclusive and non-contradictory groups of attributes). This is a distinction about names which Nietzsche maintains throughout his work.[17] Occasionally he will use the term ego as an equivalent of self when he means to speak on behalf of the self—when, for example, he writes of the herd's suspiciousness of ego: "The delight in the herd is more ancient than the delight in the ego; and as long as the good conscience is identified with the herd, only the bad conscience says: I" (*PN,* 171-72). When he wishes to discredit belief in the subject, however, he will speak not against the "self" but rather against the ego, as in "the soul superstition which, in the form of the subject and ego superstition, has not even yet ceased to do mischief" (*BW*, 192). The name "self" enjoys special protection—and has indeed more than a nominal privilege: entities, as Wittgenstein said, are sublimated names.[18] The self points to something irreducible, something crucial, even if its degree of difference from the signified of the "ego" cannot be defined. But "is it not sufficient to assume *degrees* of apparentness . . ." (*BW*, 236; *ital.* mine)?

Reprise

We have seen that the question of the self in Nietzsche cannot be answered directly—apart, that is, from the question about the question(er) of the self. The question of the self is itself insistently problematic; one kind of answer—the one, perhaps, we want to hear—is one which, according to Nietzsche, we cannot accept or even hope for. Such an answer would be substantive; it would, for example, equate the self and a unified body. This would be the outcome of the supposition that the questioner of the self is the self which the question refers to (as its predicate nominative), that this questioner is a self-identical substance and, finally, that it is not itself a question. Such an answer could identify the substantial identity of the questioner: again, as the body, certain drives, a highest value. (But even "the body [has] despaired of the body," (*PN*, 143).

We do not have a significantly different state of affairs even when the supposition of the substantial identity of subject and nominative is modified to include duality and contradiction. The questioner-self might then be marked "deep" or "authentic" in diacritical opposition to a "superficial" or "instrumental" ego not "earnestly" involved in the questioning. Or indeed the question may be regarded—as Nietzsche sometimes regards it—as a "weak" question in a sense that his essays on slave morality make clear. Briefly, the very asking of the question, marks "the slowly arising democratic order of things: the originally noble and rare urge to ascribe value to oneself on one's own . . . [is] actually encouraged more and more" (*BW*, 399). "[B]ut just this need *for* what is noble is fundamentally different from the needs of the noble soul itself and actually the eloquent and dangerous mark of its lack" (*BW*, 418). " 'Truly high respect one can have only for those who do not *seek* themselves' " (here Nietzsche cites Goethe) (*BW*, 405).

This "lack" in the slave type provokes the "weak" answer to the question, the "weak" theory of the self; it validates the "slave," who invents the self as "a neutral substratum . . . *free* to express strength or not to do so, . . . the little changeling . . . , the neutral, independent 'subject' (*das indifferente, wahlfreie 'Subjekt')*" (II 791) (*BW*, 481-82). This theory pretends to reflect a meritorious attitude of "scientific" objectivity. In fact it is "interesting" for the weak to declare the self "free," "just as if the weakness of the weak . . . were a voluntary achievement, willed, chosen, a *deed*." To perceive, now, the sublime *self-deception* that interprets weakness as "freedom" is to advance, on behalf of the "master," a "strong" theory of the weak self and part of a theory of the strong self. This perception "divides" the substance of the weak questioner along the lines of his own self-dissimulation.

The "weak" theory of the self inclines to another form of the question, presupposing "the concept of 'immediate knowledge' " and tending to produce the speciously "definite" self-knowledge which Nietzsche calls *Selbst-Erkenntnis* (II, 748) (*BW*, 414-15). "There must be a kind of aversion in me" he writes, "to *believing* anything definite about myself" (*BW*, 415). "To become what one is, one must not have the faintest notion *what* one is" (*BW*, 710). (Even this invoked ignorance, of course, follows a repetition of the question of the self, is another "answer.")

No matter how we conceive the "value" of the question of the self, however, the distinction between "noble" and weak forms of the question cannot be maintained on the basis of a firm polarity of attributes distinguishing a more substantial questioner from a less substantial questioner—even providing for the "insistence" of the one self in the other. (Recall Nietzsche's hostility to polarities).[19] Nietzsche's deconstruction of this difference, is, as we have seen, persistent. In his account in *The Gay Science* of the refinement of consciousness, the furthering factor is intersubjective communicative utility (*GS*, 298). This very instrumental intent continues to operate even when consciousness puts into question its own usefulness to life.[20] The ego that is instrumental grows "deep" in the judgment that by "thinking" instrumentality it relativizes the force of this intersubjective intent. But "for us" "the falseness of a judgment is . . . not necessarily an objection to a judgment." Indeed "we are fundamentally inclined to claim that the falsest judgments . . . are the most indispensable to us [as 'life-promoting, life-preserving, species-preserving']" (*BW*, 201). Hence, if this judgment is true, it impairs its instrumentality to life and becomes false. If it is false, it continues to act as a communicative instrument, but it promotes life and is therefore true. Finally, however, "even what is here called [communicative] 'utility' is ultimately also a mere belief, something imaginary, and perhaps precisely the most calamitous stupidity of which we shall perish some day" (*GS*, 300). Hence "utility"—whether to the "herd" or to life—becomes a predicate assignable neither exclusively to the shallow nor to the deep side of the ego, and thus unsettles the polarity.

The crucial articulation in Nietzsche's chain of questions is a break toward a different level of reflexiveness. The question of the self is no longer to be read reflexively as the question of the character of the self who questions. The personality, "intelligence," steadfastness, etc., of the self who questions (its "character" as a self) is put into question in the question. The personal attributes of the self dissolve under the force of Nietzsche's surmise about "the perspective character of existence": "is [not] all existence essentially actively engaged in *interpretation*[?] ." "One may not ask: 'who then interprets?' . . . ."[21] The question of the self continues to reflect on itself as the question of its origin but does so as the rhetorical question, *What* (not Who) is the self?[22] As such it can provoke no answer except: whatever (not whoever) is the provenience of the question of the self. In a word, the self tends to become the question which asks itself.

In this case the substantial self proves marginal to the chain, as only a spent fiction having enabled the chain to generate new links. The chain advances as a *rhetorical* movement—or what we may at least call initially a rhetorical movement. For if we term it thus, we still understand the self-reflexiveness even of the question that is self-positing on the model of a certain symmetry and homology. This is the very model of the self-reflexiveness that we ascribed to the question that poses an answer in terms of the substantial properties of the questioning self. Just as we posited the meaning of the self—in the question, Who is the self?—as the substance of the questioner, the Who; here too we are positing the meaning of the self—in the question, What is the self?—as the "substance" of the "questioner": namely, as language itself. The interrogative sentence arises within questioning language. The "answer" to the question, What is the self? is the anonymous language of the very question.

Is there not, however, a model of self-reflexiveness other than the model of homology and symmetry? The question, again, is: What is the self, such that the question of the self could arise without a speaker? We answered: that event in language which produces the question. The self is the articulate energy of language which provokes the question of the self: it is questioning language.

But if we break with this model—as Nietzsche does—we ask in a renewed way about the being of this rhetorical fold. That event in language which asks, What is the self? need not be self-identical on the model of a self-identical meaning for the "name" "self." The verbal question could arise as the "asymmetrical" trace of a "questioning something" and still be self-reflexive—self-mirroring and self-skewing, setting its "origin," "its provenience," a being itself mirror-like, *en abyme.*[23] The verbal question is mirror-like: "the human intellect cannot avoid seeing itself in its own perspectives, and *only* in these. We cannot look around our own corner . . ." (*GS*, 336). The self to which the question alludes is itself mirror-like: "And do you know what 'the world' is to me? Shall I show it to you in my mirror?" (*WP*, 549-50). "The whole of life would be possible without, as it were, seeing itself in a mirror" (*GS*, 297). The self is a mirror in the sense of having always to face away from itself, to picture something other than itself, and to introduce the subtle skew of secondary representation. The question of the self, therefore, mirrors something itself mirror-like (the self) of which it is part but which is only partly like itself—in the manner of an indexical and not an iconic sign, that is, as an effect of the self and not as its double.[24]

What is signified by the word "self," then, need not be a "signified" at all, in the sense of possessing the conditions-of-being governing all signifieds. It may be neither a speaking subject nor a referent nor a content of thought, while mediating a discourse whose "subject" is an irreducible being.[25] That being may indeed withdraw in leaving the trace of the rhetorical question and produce (what one recent writer calls) "originary bewilderment." "Thus," writes Harold Alderman, "does Nietzsche make philosophy . . . whole by asking the philosopher to repeat the originary experience of bewilderment out of which thought is born."[26] The self would be an incommensurable being precisely in provoking a continuous withdrawal from itself. This falling away generates in language —or elsewhere—the question of, or openness toward, whatever the self has taken itself to be.

In introducing, however, terms cognate with bewilderment— "openness," "wonder," "unansweredness," "questioning-being"—we should not fail to stress that this all has an antithetical air—at first glance. Nietzsche repeatedly asserts, as in *Beyond Good and Evil*, that the strong self, the "noble human being," possesses "some fundamental certainty . . . about itself, something that cannot be sought, nor found, nor perhaps lost."[27] "The noble soul accepts this fact of its egoism without any question mark" (*BW*, 405). "At the bottom of us, really 'deep down,' there is . . . some granite of spiritual *fatum*, of predetermined decision and answer to predetermined selected questions" (*BW*, 352). If we are tempted to construe this "nobility" as a being that does not put itself into question, we will of course be producing an antinomy: What has happened to the self that is the question of itself?

Even the "noble" self thus self-possessed could still exist as a question—as a *fatum* that always needs to surpass itself, always requires, like an "answer," another mode of its being. It would sustain an openness to being, an unansweredness, with athletic poise, not needing, disinclined to ask the question of the self explicitly, yet "conscious" of the self as an affect.[28]

In the *Will to Power* Nietzsche describes "the subject" purely and simply in qualities that can be accomodated by the "noble soul": "No 'substance,' rather something that in itself strives after greater strength, and that wants to 'preserve' itself only indirectly (it wants to surpass itself)" (*WP*, 270). (This is the one exception, in the section entitled "Belief in the 'Ego': the subject," to the tone of commination.) The self is the question of the being whose trace is the explicit question but which otherwise comes to light.

The formula of the self "that wants to 'preserve' itself only indirectly (it wants to surpass itself)" fulfills the "requirements" of questioning-being. "We see ['certain solutions'] only as steps to self-knowledge" (*BW*, 352). All the experience of such a self is a preserving of itself as a question while appropriating "virtual answers."

Excursus: Mastery as an Aesthetic State

Questions are viable as they are "legitimate," i.e. able to provoke "answers." The self is viable only as it can provoke the experience of an answer, full of "significance and use" to its concerns (*GS*, 224). The "masterful" self sustains itself as a question (while not asking the explicit question of the self) by continually performing acts of interpretation, so that its experience brings an answer to it—indeed so that it have experience. "The spirit's power [is] retouching and falsifying the whole ['of "the external world"'] to suit itself. Its intent in all this is to incorporate new 'experiences'..." (*BW*, 350). "Whatever exists, having somehow come into being, is again and again reinterpreted to new ends, taken over, transformed and redirected by some power superior to it; all events in the organic world are a subduing, a *becoming master*, and all subduing and becoming master involves a fresh interpretation, an adaptation through which any previous 'meaning' and 'purpose' are necessarily obscured or even obliterated" (*BW*, 513).

This should not be read, however, as saying that mastery is mastery precisely according to the measure of felt disparity that must be overcome by my interpreting something to my usage "worlds apart [from] the cause of [its] origin..." (*BW*, 513). Mastery is not principally in the degree of recalcitrance overcome by the self in its commerce with contingencies, with "the world."[29] At the level of whole cultures, Nietzsche's early text "Of the Use and Disadvantage of History for Life" criticizes the dissolution of societies into warring "inwardness and convention." "That people to whom one attributes culture," he writes, "ought in all reality at least to be something that is a living unity and not be divided so miserably into something internal and external, content and form" (I, 233-4). Nietzsche's early argument against vehement "self-control" or "self-mastery" (*Selbstbeherrschung*) (II, 180) attacks a type of negating interpretation that issues from the fortress of the self:

> *Self-control*—Those moralists who command man first of all and above all to gain control of himself thus afflict him with a peculiar disease; namely, a constant irritability in the face of all natural stirrings and inclinations—
> ...Whatever may henceforth push, pull, attract, or impel such an irritable person from inside or outside, it will always seem to him as if his self-control were

endangered. No longer may he entrust himself to any instinct or free wingbeat; he stands in a fixed position with a gesture that wards off, armed against himself, with sharp and mistrustful eyes—the eternal guardian of his castle, since he has turned himself into a castle. Of course, he can achieve *greatness* this way. But he has certainly become insufferable for others, difficult for himself, and impoverished and cut off from the most beautiful fortuities of his soul. Also from all further *instruction*. For one must be able to lose oneself occasionally if one wants to learn something from things different from oneself.[30]

Self-"control" has a component of self-aimed aggression arising from the fear of self-loss. Its value increases where the danger of self-loss is already overwhelming. Then it exerts a counterpoising force, auxiliary to a being natively conflicted to an unbearably rich extent, assailed by an abundance of internalized "world," excessive "fortuities":

> In an age of disintegration that mixes races indiscriminately, human beings have in their bodies the heritage of multiple origins, that is, opposite, and often not merely opposite, drives and value standards that fight each other and rarely permit each other any rest. Such human beings of late cultures and refracted lights will on the average be weaker human beings; their most profound desire is that the war they *are* should come to an end. Happiness appears to them, in agreement with a tranquilizing (for example, Epicurean or Christian) medicine and way of thought, pre-eminently as the happiness of resting, of not being disturbed, of satiety, of finally attained unity, as a "sabbath of sabbaths," to speak with the holy rhetorician Augustine who was himself such a human being.
>
> But when the opposition and war in such a nature have the effect of one more charm and incentive of life—and if, moreover, in addition to his powerful and irreconcilable drives, a real mastery and subtlety in waging war against oneself, in other words, self-control, self-outwitting, has been inherited or cultivated, too— then those magical, incomprehensible, and unfathomable ones arise, those enigmatic men predestined for victory and *seduction*, whose most beautiful expression is found in Alcibiadies and Caesar . . . and among artists perhaps Leonardo da Vinci . . . . (*BW*, 301-02)

The function of interpretation and mastery here is again conciliatory, aiming to create an aesthetic mode of existence in which the world may appear as already interpreted, already mastered. Such conciliatory passages are by no means confined only to the early work: they are fundamental, recurrent and important to stress because they mitigate both the popular and esoteric view of the Nietzschean self as posited by an act of arbitrary violence. The providential mood of the Sanctus Januarius passages of *The Gay Science* strikes this basic note: an experience of the harmonious co-presence of sign and meaning:

> There is a certain high point in life; once we have reached that, we are, for all our freedom, once more in the greatest danger of spiritual unfreedom, and no matter how much we have faced up to the beautiful chaos of existence and denied it all providential reason and goodness, we still have to pass our hardest test. For it is only now that the idea of a personal providence confronts us with the most penetrating force, and the best advocate, the evidence of our eyes, speaks for it—now that we can see how palpably always everything that happens to us turns out for the best. Every day and every hour, life seems to have no other wish than to prove this proposition again and again. Whatever it is, bad weather or good, the loss of a friend, sickness, slander, the failure of some letter to arrive, the spraining of an ankle, a glance into a shop, a counter-argument, the opening of a book, a dream, a fraud—either immediately or very soon after it proves to be something that "must not be missing"; it has a profound significance and use precisely for *us* . . . .
>
> I think that . . . we should . . . rest content with the supposition that our own practical and theoretical skill in interpreting and arranging events has now reached its high point. Nor should we conceive too high an opinion of this dexterity of our wisdom when at times we are excessively surprised by the wonderful harmony created by the playing of our instrument—a harmony that sounds too good for us to dare to give the credit to ourselves. Indeed, now and then someone plays with us—good old chance; now and then chance guides our hand, and the wisest providence could not think up a more beautiful music than that which our foolish hand produces then. (*GS*, 223-24)

No discounting of course the restless sly play of interpretations upon this moment that seemed to require none (being of "immediately ... profound significance"): is this meaning produced by invisibly rapid dexterous movements of interpretive skill, or chance, or providence? But this text's claim to unitive experience cannot be so rapidly deconstructed, especially in light of Nietzsche's astonishing account of his inspired moods while writing *Zarathustra:*

> Has anyone at the end of the nineteenth century a clear idea of what poets of strong ages have called *inspiration*? If not, I will describe it.—If one had the slightest residue of superstition left in one's system, one could hardly reject altogether the idea that one is merely incarnation, merely mouthpiece, merely a medium of overpowering forces. The concept of revelation —in the sense that suddenly, with indescribable certainty and subtlety, something becomes *visible*, audible, something that shakes one to the last depths and throws one down—that merely describes the facts. One hears, one does not seek; one accepts, one does not ask who gives; like lightning, a thought flashes up, with necessity, without hesitation regarding its form—I never had any choice . . . .
>
> Everything happens involuntarily in the highest degree but as in a gale of a feeling of freedom, of absoluteness, of power, of divinity.—The involuntariness of image and metaphor is strangest of all; one no longer has any notion of what is an image or a metaphor: everything offers itself as the nearest, most obvious, simplest expression. It actually seems, to allude to something Zarathustra says, as if the things themselves approached and offered themselves as metaphors. ("Here all things come caressingly to your discourse and flatter you; for they want to ride on your back. On every metaphor you ride to every truth . . . . Here the words and word-shrines of all being open up before you; here all being wishes to become word, all becoming wishes to learn from you how to speak") . . . .[31]

For Nietzsche the world is a text—its component signs requiring interpretation.[32] But seen from "great health" the world's signs are more than signs: they are vehicles of the things they name, that "ride upon their backs" as the things that would ride on Zarathustra's back, and he on them—their vehicles—"to every truth." Active interpretation is at a minimum. Things proffer themselves astride their own names. They too are metaphors, they carry themselves and their meanings over into the discourse of the inspired self. The ability to see the world of things in a figurative text is a function of poetic rapture; *then* only: "It . . . happened —and verily, it happened for the first time—that his work pronounced *selfishness* blessed, the wholesome, healthy selfishness that wells from a powerful soul—from a powerful soul to which belongs the high body, beautiful, triumphant, refreshing, *around which everything becomes a mirror* . . ." (*Zarathustra*) (*PN*, 302; second ital. mine). The soul for which all things are mirrors *already* possesses these things in its "discourse."

Nietzsche's phrase for this blessed selfishness is *"selige Selbstsucht."* German readers will smile—or wince: *"selige Sehnsucht"* (blessed longing) is the title of a notorious lyric of Goethe concluding "The Book of the Singer" of the *Westöstlicher Divan* (*West-easterly Divan*). Goethe's poem, like Nietzsche's, speaks of a highly sexualized kind of extinction, playing on the sexual meaning of "dying"; a "self" dies (in orgasm) to become himself again—"stirbt und wird"—but he becomes himself through the other, his lover, his candleflame and his grave. Nietzsche's emulation of this poem is remarkable in substituting for the medium of this resurrection not another human being but another mode of self. Suppose the ego is whatever the self has taken itself to be (*Satzung*); the self, the openness from which this particular being has sprung (*Setzung*).[33] Then the love which Nietzsche celebrates is that of the ego for the self or "soul," "around which everything becomes a mirror."[34]

In an important sense *Zarathustra*, even more than *Ecce Homo*, is Nietzsche's book of self; it is nothing but a book of the self, of a higher selfishness: "The Wanderer" (Part III: Section 1) reads:

> And whatever may yet come to me as destiny and experience will include some wandering and mountain climbing: in the end, one experiences only oneself. The time is gone when mere accidents could still happen to me; and what could still come to me now that was not mine already? What returns, what finally comes home to me, is my own self and what of myself has long been in strange lands and scattered among all things and accidents. And one further thing I know: I stand before my final peak now and before that which has been saved up for me the longest. Alas, now I must face my hardest path! Alas, I have begun my loneliest walk! But whoever is of my kind cannot escape such an hour—the hour which says to him: "Only now are you going your way to greatness! . . . ."[35]

The phrase "You are going your way to greatness" is repeated twice. Zarathustra merits the charge of self-consecration in a degree that would not have allowed even Wordsworth to pass unalarmed.[36]

      We have dwelt on the point that the question of the self must be viable as an openness, an unansweredness to being; yet it must bend the world into virtual answers in order to preserve itself as a question. The self is an interpreting being (*"ein auslegendes Dasein,"* II, 249) that needs to interpret in order for that interpretation to interpret the self (*GS*, 336). Only in finding answers can it find the occasion to re-formulate itself, produce a new "articulation of self-consciousness."[37] The mood of the fullest answer, which thus fully identifies but does not close the question, is inspiration—and not the vacuity of nostalgia nor the agitation of coerciveness: "Learning to *see* . . . is almost what, unphilosophically speaking, is called a strong will: the essential feature is precisely *not* to 'will'—*to be able* to suspend decision" (*PN*, 511). The semiotic paraphrase of inspiration—the rapture of the historical sense—is the convergence of figure and thing.

Reprise (concluded)

      Nietzsche circumscribes the self as the question of the being whose trace is the explicit question of the self. This being is not "Being." Neither is it language without a maker. Nietzsche does not fabulate language as arising without an agent: nomination is the enterprise of the will to power; the genealogy of questions is a genealogy of morals and hence a "semiotics" of the self (*PN*, 501; *BW*, 203).

      The question of the being of the event which produces the question of the self is the question of the will to power. *"For Nietzsche,* writes Ludwig Giesz, *"the will to power and the self have the same structure."*[38] I cannot open up to this question except to note that Heidegger reads Nietzsche aberrantly in calling the will to power "the being of beings." In *The Will to Power* and elsewhere Nietzsche calls this will innumerable different "things": self-overcomer, creator, commander, even a fiction. But the intelligibility of "the being of beings" is itself only a project of the will to power, indeed a by-product of the fiction of the ego. In a passage of which Heidegger is well aware, but which he slights, Nietzsche writes:

> In its origin language belongs in the age of the most rudimentary form of psychology. We enter a realm of crude fetishism when we summon before consciousness the basic presuppositions of the metaphysics of language, in plain talk, the presuppositions of reason. Everywhere it sees a doer and doing; it believes in will as *the* cause; it believes in the ego, in the ego as being, in the ego as substance, and it projects this faith in the ego-substance upon all things—only thereby does it first

create the concept of "thing." Everywhere "being" is projected by thought, pushed underneath, as the cause: the concept of being follows, and is a derivative of, the concept of ego. (*PN*, 483)

It will hardly do to read this passage, as Heidegger does, as marking Nietzsche's scepticism toward the conventional psychological interpretation of will and hence as requiring that the matter be thought through fundamentally, but as not somehow protecting Nietzsche against misunderstanding Being as the being of beings.[39] For it is just this "error" which is sharply identified in the passage. (It is remarkable, incidentally, that the concept of self is not arraigned.) "[W]e [Germans] "—Nietzsche writes elsewhere—"hardly believe in the justification of the concept of 'Being' " (*GS*, 306). "Heraclitus will remain eternally right with his assertion that Being is an empty fiction."[40]

Toward a Conclusion

This discussion about what is alive in Nietzsche's reflections on the self takes whatever novelty it may have from the background of recent—apparently conclusive—discussion about the death of the self in Nietzsche.[41] Discussion on this matter has been foreclosed chiefly, I think, because of the general appeal of demonstrations of the vacuousness of the category of self (it has functioned productively as a heuristic term in discussions of Rousseau and Freud); because of the valorization of *The Will to Power*, following Heidegger's practice in his Nietzsche-book, as part of a general appreciation of marginal, "unspoken" and fragmentary texts; and, finally, because, for our reading taste, *Zarathustra* is hard to take. The result is that the mainly destructive commentary in *The Will to Power* on cognate-words for the ego is read comprehensively, as extending to all its cognate-words. Without reading *Zarathustra*, however, it cannot be appreciated that ego and subject are not the self. And when Zarathustra isn't read, what a woeful flattening out of "The Dionysian drama of 'The Destiny of the Soul' " ensues (*BW*, 458).

The claim, however, that Nietzsche speaks the self to death is untenable for a variety of reasons. One of these reasons emerges by our taking an elliptical route—by putting into question the seemingly powerful argument that a certain preponderance of irony in Nietzsche determines the loss of the self.

Certainly it is not easy to write about Nietzsche's irony with an easy assumption of authority: his texts are repercussive. Ernst Behler (while not commenting on the question of the self in Nietzsche) has made a useful preparatory classification of tonalities and types of irony in Nietzsche.[42] It would still be a daunting task to find the uniform principle or principles generating this diversity.

The first remarkable fact about irony in Nietzsche is the relative paucity of his explicit uses of this word, despite the apparent saturation of his work with ironic themes and moods. This may be a telling suppression or not: if so, then one can speculate (as does Behler) that the word is suppressed because of its association with a Romantic philosophical tradition including especially Fichte, Hegel, and Friedrich Schlegel. The first two names are almost always polemical targets for Nietzsche; on the other hand he seems not to have read Schlegel and nowhere mentions him, despite astonishing similarities of tonality, rhetoric, and philosophical thrust between them. But the association with Romantic literary practice of the word "irony" (like, incidentally, the word "mood" [*Stimmung*], with which Nietzsche happens also to associate the word "irony") probably determines the omission.

Without more than occasional mention of the word "irony" and without a decisive intertextual line leading from Nietzsche to earlier theorists of irony, interpreting Nietzsche's irony is then itself a matter for irony in the modern sense: i.e. free play. Behler speaks of at least five strains in Nietzsche's writing which can come under the head of irony: Nietzsche's theory of the necessity for elliptical communication (in effect Nietzsche translates the trope of *irony* [Latin: *dissimulatio*] as "mask"); his sense of the innumerable thicknesses, of the groundlessness, of personal identity, promoting a certain artistry of pose and feeling; Nietzsche's "romantic" irony: an endless self-reflexive play of antithetical positions; his sense of the "tragic" obligation of affirming inexorable suffering; finally, his sense of the "world-historical" irony of the individual blinded by his particular interests to the exigencies of nature and history. And Nietzsche implies countless other types. What is immediately valuable about this table of categories is the cumulative effect it makes: indeed Nietzsche's work (despite his frequently asseverated distaste for ironic [read, "decadent"] attitudes in others) appears to lend itself uniformly to one or another category of ironic subject-matter (not to speak of "tonality"), so that the work, it appears, can be called "pan-ironic."

The current discussion about the ubiquitousness of Nietzsche's irony, however, goes beyond accounting for various types of intended irony. It is not only that Nietzsche conceptualizes irony but he does so uncontrollably, even while "knowing" it. In this case he heralds more than the death of God ("our most enduring lie"); he also appears to herald the death of the little god—the human self (*GS*, 283). This death is a corollary of the fact that "his" texts engage us in unrelenting irony. These views on Nietzsche, if they are true, sustain each other mutually. In the absence of an organized intentional subject (an absence afflicting Nietzsche himself!), capable of acts of exact projection, texts cannot have a stable meaning (*Meinen*). Their various meanings or illusory feints at meaning subvert one another, more radically even than meanings deliberately projected as unstable, infinite irony. If Nietzsche saw better than any other writer the "merely" fictive character of the self, then he would have to be considered the most thoroughgoing of ironists. The converse of this hypothesis is also true.

Despite this flux, Nietzsche's writing might still be shown to possess a residual coherence in the patterned recurrence of distinctive metaphors, tropes or fictions: these might indeed be familiar metaphors of originary states, causes and effects, intact persons, whole epochs, cultures, and worlds. One could construct chains of such "metaphysical" tokens, choosing to forget that in other places Nietzsche exposes them as fraudulent—as the counterfeits, the "errors" of reason.[43]

But however solid and plausible such constructions may seem, they cannot stand for long; one cannot ignore Nietzsche's instruction on rhetoric. 1. Only rarely—in certain inspired states which we must take on faith—do metaphors literally bear the burden of things.[44] But without the presence of signified "things"—"contents of thought"—or of things in the world to supply the analogy, it is impossible to connect metaphorical figures of thought. 2. All metaphors have a genealogy, a "pre-history": it is a "question of origins" (*BW*, 453 in al.). As "semiotically compressed processes" they carry along—not things—but a textual history of the accommodations to which other metaphysicians have submitted them.[45] Nietzsche's text is only a moment in sign-chains criss-crossing the greater text of European writing.[46] They have no "author."[47] 3. Finally, much the most urgent obstacle to the appropriation of Nietzsche's metaphors is his critique internal to metaphor. The efficacity, the intelligibility of metaphor itself depends on the reduction of the strange (sign) to the familiar (meaning). "All thought, judgment, perception, considered as comparison," Nietzsche writes, "has as its precondition a *positing* of equality, and earlier still a *'making* equal' " (*WP*, 273-74). What, however, is the validity of such "equality"? Apart from its usefulness for life, it is, in Nietzsche's phrase, a "fiction of logic" (*BW*, 202). Metaphorical *comparisons*, where a human sense is involved, means "measuring reality against the purely invented world of the unconditional and self-identical . . . , a constant falsification of the world by means of numbers . . ." (*BW*, 202). The possibility of making comparisons is sustained by the myth of integral being. Not only (this demonstration proceeds) must we dispense, therefore, with the subject that integrates being on the strength of its own self-presence; but it would appear that nothing whatsoever of this subject remains to be salvaged. To reduce the self to a "mere metaphor" is in fact to make it the epiphenomenon of a self—dependent on some other self for the act of "equalization" without which it could not come into existence. This other self would itself be subject to another such deconstruction and so on . . . . The self—like all "philosophy"—is annihilated, lowered into "an abysmally deep ground" (*BW*, 419). And in the absence of a unitive self, writing becomes a boundless flux of fragmentary metaphors. The momentary "victory" of a metaphorical meaning comes from the mere assertion of an interpretive will blind to the irony of its inflicting upon the text an "authenticity" which the text cannot own.

There is, of course, a good deal in this argument which finds support in Nietzsche, but also a good deal that is contradicted. The extreme familiarity of the case (under the head of "deconstruction")—the fact that this demonstration of "wild" irony has been applied persuasively to Rousseau and Freud, to Romantic writers and to the "modern scriptor"—might, in fact, give one pause. How enfeebling if Nietzsche wrote with the same "intention" as every other modern writer and his distinction were at best only the "centrality" he enjoyed within the modern tradition—his special tenacity and vigilance in contributing to the dissolution of "man"! This is exactly the surmise that one might welcome as a provocation to read Nietzsche from beginning to end to see if the story is not differently nuanced.

The story *is* different. Not only does Nietzsche's discussion of the self, as we have seen, implicitly speak against a pan-ironic reading, but his explicit remarks about irony reshape this argument in important ways. On a closer view, the notion of a "pan-ironic" text proves a misleading, an unintelligible idea: it hides the fact that irony can take place only through "punctual" abrogations of irony. Something must be "taken seriously" for its ironical sublimation to matter. The movement of irony has to occur within a frame of rule-directed activity. The rules themselves cannot be "ironical," or else irony could not be discernable from chaos. Yet Nietzsche holds that irony is not chaos but rather a relation between form and chaos:

> The total character of the world . . . is in all eternity chaos—in the sense not of a lack of necessity but of a lack of order, arrangement, form, beauty, wisdom, and whatever other names there are for our aesthetic anthropomorphisms . . . . Judged from the point of view of our reason, unsuccessful attempts are by all odds the rule, the exceptions are not the secret aim . . . . None of our aesthetic and moral judgment apply to it . . . , it does not observe any laws either. (*GS*, 168)

"Pure" irony, like "an eye turned in no particular direction," would be indistinguishable from blind chaos: its chaos is not that of Dionysus but of "that lascivious ascetic discord that loves to turn reason against reason . . ." (*BW*, 555). In pure irony a frenzy of asceticism turns on the "universe" in which neither "heartlessness and unreason [n]or their opposite" prevails (*GS*, 168). This idea clearly does not have a solitary rule in Nietzsche: it figures in fact as the negative pendant of a "godlike feeling . . . —humaneness." Here "the historical sense" has turned to the human past and "manage[d] to experience the history of humanity as a whole as *his own* history . . . . If one *could* endure . . . the losses, hopes, conquests, and the victories of humanity; if one could finally contain all this in one soul and crowd it into a single feeling—this would surely have to result in a happiness that humanity has not known so far: the happiness of a god full of power and love . . ." (*GS*, 268). This unborn Faust of the historical sense conjures an ideal of the full self that endures the separate frenzies of Socrates and Dionysus.

Without now adding much discussion to this point, or indeed in further sentimentalizing it, I should like to state its direction apodictically. Nietzschean irony devalues the category of the ego—the so-called personal subject—as the agent or object of reflective cognition. "A thought comes when 'it' wishes," he writes, "and not when 'I' wish, so that it is a falsification of the facts of the case to say that the subject 'I' is the condition of the predicate 'think.' *It* thinks; but that this 'it' is precisely the famous old 'ego' is, to put it mildly, only a supposition, an assertion . . . ." A supposition that is not harmless, as we saw earlier, when, in the guise of a "weak" theory of the self, it was unmasked by another movement of ironic consciousness as an apology for "the weakness of the weak" (*BW*, 214).

Nietzsche's irony, on the other hand, does not discredit the category of self as the organization of ironical practice. I say "organization" and mean with this word to defer the self's irony. The self, while it has a questionable structure, can evidently speak ironically or not. Ironic practice in language is therefore not wild, not uncontrolled, because it is not the invariable symptom of a self. Indeed the terms self and irony are more often than not oppositional, with self dominant. It is the virtual absence of self in the "decadent" which issues into uncontrollable ironical expression. This irony is pejorative, privative in a sense exactly contrary to the sense in which the link of self and irony is asserted by "wild" readers. The strong self neither perceives nor furthers its dissolution in irony. For Nietzsche, irony as often marks fatigue, a superfoetation of the historical sense, of the sense of possibility stifling action; irony is Socratic lassitude; only the obliterated self speaks ironically. On the other hand a strong spirit of determinate irony speaks against all the unselfing tendencies of religion and culture. The "noble" personality has "faith in [it] self, pride in [it] self, a fundamental hostility and *irony* against 'selflessness' . . ." (*BW*, 395; ital. mine). Ironical practice in Nietzsche is consistent with a strong self grasped as an "abysmal" mirror-like structure of questioning-being reflecting itself—but not entirely or necessarily—in the explicit question of the self. When such a self does pose the *explicit* question of itself, it does so with a certain irony: "A matter that becomes clear ceases to concern us.—What was on the mind of that god who counseled: 'Know thyself!' Did he mean: 'Cease to concern yourself! Become objective!—And Socrates?—And 'scientific men'?—" (*BW*, 271). The question of the self is posed in order to put a stop to reflexive cognition. Though this may

79

be an ironical state of affairs, the question of the *self* is not posed ironically. Unless an answer is forthcoming there can be no meaning to the word "objective."

I stress that in writing "directly" on Nietzschean irony I do not pretend to a certainty which this notion cannot allow. Heidegger (and Derrida) are right in marking Nietzsche's "transformation of the very value of hierarchy itself"[48]—the category which enables a conventional account of irony as a play of distinct "positive" and "negative" moments. If irony functions Beyond Hierarchy it cannot be conceptualized.

Another Route

There may be a better way, an indirect way, of "doing justice" to Nietzsche's organization of ironies. This path leads us back to the crucial point in the argument for "wild" irony—Nietzsche's alleged dissolution of the self as a fiction or metaphor whose intelligibility is itself dependent on a fiction of logic.

The argument for "wild" irony follows Nietzsche in considering the "subject" as a fiction added to an act or event, an imputation (something shoved under as a support), a supplementary metaphor of origin. This is the way we are inclined to add a fiction, an underpinning or a conceptual supplement, say, to a lightning flash, saying "lightning" caused the lightning flash, and lightning is the "subject" of this event (*BW*, 481). *"The mistake lies in the fictitious insertion of a subject."*[49] This mistake is a characteristic of "first" thinking—which is less like thought than the production of fetishes.

Nietzsche, however, has more to say on the subject of "first" thinking" than to detect its skew, its poverty at the origin. He also writes about "first" thinking as normative—as "thinking as such." A crucial aphorism in the *Genealogy* describes all thought as springing out of a basic measuring of the self against another self, out of a fixing of interpersonal relation: of subordination, of indebtedness, etc. Thought is essentially a "setting prices, determining values, contriving equivalences" (*BW*, 506); thought doubles perceived likeness—makes *metaphors*. But this action, however described, flows out of or along with what Nietzsche calls "this *Selbstgefühl*" (II, 811)—"pride" but also "self-consciousness," "sentiment of self" (*BW*, 506). The self is not a fiction or an underpinning or a concept subsequently added to the essential act of thought marking difference and likeness.

A sense of self is inexpungeably present at the event of thought. To say that the self is (only) a metaphor—namely, the product of an act of likening, of equalizing—is to reverse the priorities established in the *Genealogy*. The self precedes, it is not itself the product (metaphor) of a primary act of making metaphors and comparisons.[50]

This section of the *Genealogy* thus simplifies the story of

80

originary thought. But it complicates it too by situating it in a rudimentary system of interpersonal exchange—in society. It might be possible to sidestep this difficulty by citing the letter of the text: "Buying and selling," writes Nietzsche, "together with their psychological appurtenances, are older even than the beginnings of any kind of social forms of organization and alliances . . ." (*BW*, 506). The kinds of comparison Nietzsche has discussed, strictly speaking, precede "social forms." Nonetheless, "the custom of comparing, measuring and calculating" exerts itself on "power against power"—the first man to think and hence to experience a *Selbstgefühl* does so in a social matrix—*primus inter pares imparesque.*

Now, we will wonder, where at the "beginning" is the Other? —in what way does it affect, in what way is it excluded from the self? The question is inevitable. We cited a phrase from *Beyond Good and Evil*: "the soul as social structure of the drives and affects" (*BW*, 506). In an unpublished note Nietzsche writes: "the ego is a plurality of forces—each one like a person (*personen-artigen Kräfte*)."[51] Such passages employing social metaphors for the self are abundant and compelling. In Zarathustra's speech on the self, the self figures *ab initio* at once as ruler and ruled ("shepherd and herd") (*PN*, 146). The Other is actively "inside" the self before the self has encountered other persons, in which matrix it discovers itself. The problem is not averted by repeated demonstrations in Nietzsche, through passages rarely cited in the "new Nietzsche,"[52] of the primacy of *self*-constitution. These texts are worth closer examination.

The "blond beasts exemplify that terrible artists' egoism that . . . knows *itself* justified to all eternity in its 'work.' " Their work is nothing less than the creation of the "state"—"an instinctive creation and imposition of forms; they are the most involuntary, unconscious artists there are—wherever they appear something new soon arises, a ruling structure that *lives*, in which parts and functions are delimited and co-ordinated, in which nothing whatever finds a place that has not first been assigned a 'meaning' in relation to the whole" (*BW*, 522-23; first ital. mine). [We are not, in talking about "unconscious" artists, impoverishing or eliminating their "egoism," their sense of self, since "consciousness does not really belong to man's individual existence but rather to his social or herd nature" (*GS*, 299). "Egoism," meanwhile, "belongs to the nature of a noble soul": it is a species of self-magnification (*BW*,405)] . This, then,"is how the 'state' began on earth." Social organization is secondary to an original state of affairs, consisting, on the one hand, of the strong self—"he who can command, he who is by nature 'master' "—and, on the other, an "unchecked and shapeless populace" (*BW*, 522).

Consider, again, the primacy awarded to the self as Nietzsche describes that "noble soul [which] accepts this fact of its eogism without any question mark: . . . perhaps it admits under certain circumstances . . . that there are some who have rights equal to its own; as soon as this matter of rank is settled it moves among these equals with their equal privileges, showing the same sureness of modesty and delicate reverence that characterize *its relations with itself*" (*BW*, 405; ital. mine).

Finally, in the celebrated creation in *Beyond Good and Evil* of the "noble" type, the self is constituted in an initial act of reflection. "The noble type of man experiences *itself* as determining values." The self arises within a feeling (the *Selbstgefühl* of the account of "thought as such" in the *Genealogy*). "Everything it knows as part of *itself* it honors; such a morality is *self*-glorification. In the foreground there is the feeling of fullness, of power that seeks to overflow, the happiness of high tension, the consciousness of wealth that would give and bestow . . . . The noble human being honors *himself* as one who is powerful . . . ." The value system organized on the polarity good/bad originates with an act of self-magnification. The "good" has priority over the "bad" as both logical and temporal primacy. "Bad" is discovered in the master's feeling of "contempt" which he attaches to beings (*die Wesen*, II, 730) perceived as "cowardly, anxious, . . . petty"; also to "the suspicious with their unfree glances . . ." (*BW*, 394-95; ital. mine).

The initial founding act that discovers the "good" is pre-social. Nothing in this account of the discovery of the good seems to require a social situation. The act of perceiving—properly, performing—the negation of the mood of abundance is, of course, secondary; and this is the act which creates social distinction and hence constitutes a society. This act occurs simultaneously as the felt "pathos of distance" (*BW*, 391). The "distance" between social classes is the expression of an inner division—the scene of the conversion of self-abundance into contempt.

The self is conceived in advance of a social situation; the self is not of social provenance. Since evaluative acts are self-reflexive—i.e. arising directly or indirectly from a centering on qualities of the self—social beings and acts, too, are to be judged with respect to a pre-social self. And yet even this direct account of origins is itself only the product of a certain foreground—what Nietzsche calls—"a frog perspective" (*BW*, 200). It is found in his essay but it is attached to a quite different version which turns it around.

We noted that "the ruling group" of masters discovers the good on the basis of "exalted proud states of the soul." But Nietzsche also describes this moment in non-positive terms. "The moral discrimination of values," he writes, "has originated . . . among a ruling group whose consciousness of its difference from the ruled group was accompanied by delight . . ." (*BW*, 394). Here "delight" figures not as a synonym for the strong mood of self-glorification on which the "good" is founded. It is instead a supplementary, epiphenomenal consciousness to what is basic—a "consciousness of its difference from the ruled group." Further on, Nietzsche adds, "when the ruling group determines what is 'good,' the exalted, proud states of the soul are experienced as conferring distinction and determining the order of rank . . . . The noble human being separates from himself those in whom the opposite of such exalted, proud states finds expression . . ." (*BW*, 394).

This account speaks not of an experience of self but of a "consciousness of difference," of states of mind which "confer distinction and determine the order of rank," of an act of "separation" from what is "opposite." These categories will make post-Saussurean readers think of the diacritical categories constituting a language without positive terms. "From the structuralist point of view" (as one writer puts it), "the sign is a negative entity: its being lies in what it is not, that is, in the systematic way in which it signifies its opposition to other words in the language."[53] The "noble" type no more has an abundant experience of the bedrock meaning of the self than does the reader solely by virtue of reading these words. Whatever sense the reader can make of such "experiences" depends on his power—better, the power of his language—to discriminate these signs from their opposite numbers (not "cowardly," not "anxious," not "petty"). Equally the "noble" type has an experience of difference, distinction, separation and opposition from what is not the self. This elides an immediate experience of the self, since the former experience can arrive at the self only after awarding a putative immediacy to what is Other, then perceiving (performing) its negation of this Other. This state of affairs puts the "self" (which does not yet exist) precisely in the position toward itself of a language-user, not a being capable of "immediate experience of the inner life"—an interpreter, not a "reader" of the "basic text of *homo natura*" (*der Grundtext homo natura*, II, 696) (*BW*, 351). We see that this account is diametrically opposite to the preceding account of the origin of the self given in this aphorism. The revelatory, disclosive act of negation is performed not on the self but on the Other as the occasion of an experience of difference. The "noble" type, the author of the moral polarity "good/bad," is revealed to be no less reactive than its posited opposite, the "slave" type, the author of the moral polarity "good/evil." Even "before" the noble self has been constituted, it contains a trace of the Other as the derivative of the other person (the "slave") encountered in an interpersonal exchange. The noble type would himself bear the marks of the "internal" aggressiveness which Nietzsche paraphrases as the property of the reactive slave type—*ressentiment* (and which Lacan has identified as a derivative of the "mirror phase").

We find ourselves in the interpretive situation which all readers of Nietzsche sooner or later encounter and which makes inevitable such words as aporia and irony. Nietzsche inscribes into his genetic fictions of polar valuations everything the reader needs in order to produce the topsy-turvy account, in which polar terms leap incessantly across the bar of their division. If the polarity is founded, as inevitably in such accounts, on an attribution of "firstness" to the (dominant) term, it soon emerges that that "firstness" is in fact based on its "difference," "distinction," "opposition" to what's "secondary."

Is there any way to arrest this endless circulation of ostensible priorities? What seems to be insufficiently appreciated is that the act of arrest is a precise metaphor for the critical act. Criticism—past ferreting antitheses—arrests the flux of meaning by an act undeniably arbitrary. It calls things off beyond the point where the author in the text has laid his emphasis. Nietzsche is one case, Kafka quite another. Nietzsche makes distinctions, in order (if only momentarily) to unify them in one will. Kafka means to dissolve every "arrest" into a violence as empty of authority as a grimace on the face of a dreamer.

We faced a similar problem earlier: it was impossible in a rigorous way to distinguish the properties of the ego from the self. Nonetheless the critic shows Nietzsche giving primacy to the self over the ego. That is chiefly because the self, unlike the ego, never designates the hypostasis of the subject or object within the closure of so-called "self-knowledge" (*Selbst-Erkenntnis*).[54]

The "primacy" of the self can be eroded by antithetical arguments produced from different standpoints. But the "self" remains indispensable, an insistently productive perspective within Nietzsche's "system"; the self promotes discourse in at least these four registers. It articulates the field of metaphysics: the self, as a being that has to become what it is, distinguishes being from becoming. It articulates the field of meta-psychology, allowing for the distinctions between depth/surface; authentic/herd, etc. It allows for distinctions in psychological kinetics (more grandly—the "Dionysian drama of 'The Destiny of the Soul' ") (*BW*, 458), viz. "The great tragedian, . . . like every other artist, arrives at the ultimate pinnacle of his greatness only when he comes to see himself and his art beneath him."[55] Finally, as we have seen, the self allows for distinctions which articulate the social field: the self is a synonym for the "noble" type, the "master," which "has some fundamental certainty . . . about itself, something that cannot be sought, nor found, nor perhaps lost" (*BW*, 458). It therefore enables the master to stand apart from the slave.

In the social field the self has primacy over the other encountered in interpersonal exchange, even as we grant the impossibility of maintaining a strict distinction: the Other is "always already" in the self. Still this difficulty can be grasped intelligibly. In Giesz's words: " 'The self' cannot be spoken of as something-at-hand in the world (*vorhandenes Weltding*), since it is always already a *relation to itself*. This circumstance first makes it possible to reach for social analogies for the strivings of human inwardness."[56] The social metaphor is irresistible because the concept of the self involves self-overcoming, a relation of mastery. The will to power is informed by an entire organization of wills—a social organization, with a history and a pre-history beset by a struggle for mastery. We do not hide the enigma, once again, of the appositeness of "mastery" for relations internal to a self that has yet to establish its mastery over another. But

84

here we stop. This sort of circularity has an indefatigable power to engage, tease, perplex, exhaust, and engage again.

For the highly self-conscious writer of *fiction*, whose first business is his rhetoric—his figures of speech including figures of argument—the recurrence of this "discussion" about the self- or non-self-origination of valuable features (language, reason, personality) will serve as a *pointe*. He knows it is unanswerable, it does not presuppose or produce for him the vexable, polemical attention of the philosophical attitude. Instead it is a founding figure of rhetoric: it can be manipulated, placed in odd places, used to produce more rhetoric, to tell a story, but it has no other truth. Here this crucial foundational argument has become only a trope. This is *not* the case for Nietzsche. It is the case for Kafka. Consider Kafka's "A Report to an Academy," the story of an "ape's" account of how it has emerged as a man. "Today I can see it clearly: without the most profound inward calm I could never have found my way out. And indeed perhaps I owe all that I have become to the calm that settled within me after my first few days in the ship. And again for that calmness it was the ship's crew I had to thank."[57] But the philosopher's (and critic's) first concern is different. It is not, for Nietzsche, the founding figures of rhetoric. The primal scene of the human world is a scene of primal arrest that individuates "the will as the most originary form of appearance, encompassing all becoming."[58] Nietzsche repeats this act when he asks the question, "And what created . . . value and will? " and answers, "the creative self" (*PN*, 147).

Ending

The self in Nietzsche is not a simple fiction, it is not a vacuous fiction, and it is not urgently in need of disabusing. (For the "fiction" of the "self" we can now write, simply, the self, since truth—i.e. words without actual or virtual quotation marks—is in each case fictions or metaphors that are not simple, not vacuous, and not urgently in need of disabusing.) In Nietzsche's hands the self is a generative word, a generative concept: "Individual philosophical concepts . . . grow up in connection and relationship with each other . . . ; they belong . . . to a system . . . . Something within them leads . . . them in a definite order, one after the other—[namely] the innate systematic structure and relationship of their concepts. Their thinking is in fact far less a discovery than a recognition, a remembering, a return and a homecoming to a remote, primordial and inclusive household of the soul, out of which those concepts grew originally . . ." (*BW*, 217).

"Self" is the name of such a concept—a concept whose different aspects are also named by such terms as "will to power," "ego," "mastery." Equally, in such names different concepts ("processes") are semiotically concentrated (*BW*, 516); and each prompts and informs a potentially endless reflection on its implications, an endless unpacking. The generativity of the concept self is not sheerly linguistic: the word "self" does not generate infinite reflection by virtue alone of the history of its textual juxtapositions. This history of the word articulates a reflection forced by experience. There is always abundant experience of an urgent state of the will requiring, issuing into, writing on the subject of the self. "The will to power *interprets* . . . : it defines, limits, determines degrees, variations of power. Mere variations of power could not feel themselves to be such: there must be present something that wants to grow and interprets the value of whatever else wants to grow" (*WP*, 342). Indeed, apart from such upheavals of the will, such "extreme states," "the milder, more middling and indeed the lower levels in perpetual play weave the texture of our character and our fate . . ." (I/1090). Indeed, by assuming "that really words exist only for *superlative* degrees of [inner] events and drives . . . we misread ourselves in this apparently clearest letter-script of our self (*Selbst*). *Our opinion about ourselves*, however, which we have found on this false track—the so-called 'ego'—continues to operate on our character and destiny" (*Morgenröte [The Dawn]* , I, 1090). This texture, torn by the abrupt intermittences of the will, forces an endless writing.

What movements in this Book of the Self recur? I hold to just three:

1. *Unity*. The strong self is one "thing"—not at once itself and something else. Like the biological cell, it is not strictly speaking "a separate entity":[59] "the marks of identity, distinguishing self from non-self, have long since been blurred" (*LC*, 8). Nonetheless, it is informed by "mechanisms for preserving individuality" (*LC*, 9), for "the discrimination between self and non-self" (*LC*, 21), able to generate "precise unequivocal directions about . . . how to establish that one is, beyond argument, one's self" (*LC*, 18). The self "desires to 'preserve' itself" "only indirectly," because it is not a "separate entity" but a relation of self-surpassing (*WP*, 270). Yet it keeps "a fundamental certainty about itself" without which, indeed, no violence to itself would not be admissable.

2. *Responsibility*. This concept of individuality secures a certain order of truth in defending against the implications of the contrary position, which is seductive: the self as sheerly Other. "What indeed *does* man know about himself" (*TF*, 175-76)? "We are unknown to ourselves, we men of knowledge" (*BW*, 451). The self as individual is *responsible*; it cannot be that I was elsewhere—my other self prevailing at the moment that I acted, that, therefore, the action is another's. "For what is freedom? That one has the will to assume responsibility for oneself" (*PN*, 452). The

self as individual cannot be another self, however desirable it is to be that other self. "The weak-willed . . . seek to *lay the blame for themselves somewhere else.*"[60] This moment contains Nietzsche's critique of "renunciation": the self cannot invent itself as more severe, more ascetic, more exclusive than it *is*.

Certain of himself, Nietzsche can make use of another self, other selves; " 'objectivity' . . . as the ability to *control* one's Pro and Con and to dispose of them, so that one knows how to employ a *variety* of perspectives and affective interpretations in the service of knowledge" (*BW*, 555). But the self is not its mask. "The ugliest man [is he] who has to decorate himself (historical sense) and always seeks a new garment." "There is a sort of actor's art of temporarily assuming an alien soul . . . . At the same time a sign of weakness and lack of unity . . . etc. Romanticism."[61] Nietzsche cannot become *an* authorial self, either, and guarantee consistency. His resolution in *Das Philosophenbuch* "to write . . . in an impersonal and cold manner" registers this insight: "Avoid all mention of 'us' and 'we' and 'I.' "[62] Nietzsche perceives (and enacts) the fact that the yield can be great short of *becoming* this second self.

In an early text Nietzsche wrote, social man is devoured by others: the solitary devours himself. This state of affairs exerts an exact epistemological constraint. The self in solitude would double itself in creating an interpreter (or itself), yet succeeds in projecting that second self as a center of thought, of reflection and of literary activity only at the instant it ceases to be itself. What is not the case cannot be invented as the case. The invention cannot adequately read the self. As interpreter it is only a certain mask of a mode of its being.[63] The self is most transparent as a state of exorbitant "freedom"—acutely unsettled, torn by inquiries— but that being is unidentifiable, cannot be situated, since it exists as a function of devouring and incorporating its witness.

3. *Passion.* In *The Middle Years* Henry James has the character Dencombe say, " 'A second chance—*that's* the delusion. There never was to be but one. We work in the dark—we do what we can—we give what we have. Our doubt is our passion and our passion is our task. The rest is the madness of art.' "[64] Nietzsche specifies this madness.

> That hidden and masterful something for which we long
> does not have a name, until finally it proves itself to be
> our task—this tyrant in us wreaks horrible revenge for
> every attempt we make to dodge or escape it, for every
> premature resignation, for every acceptance of equality
> with those among whom we do not belong, for every
> activity, however respectable, which distracts us from
> our main cause—indeed for every virtue which would
> protect us from the hardness of our inmost responsi-
> bility. (*PN*, 677)

And where should we find named this task, this self of Nietzsche? It is revealed *and* turned back on itself in *Beyond Good and Evil*:

> To translate man back into nature; to become master over the many vain and overly enthusiastic interpretations and connotations that have so far been scrawled and painted over that eternal basic text of *homo natura*: to see to it that man henceforth stands before man as even today, hardened in the discipline of science, he stands before the *rest* of nature, with intrepid Oedipus eyes and sealed Odysseus ears, deaf to the siren songs of old metaphysical bird catchers who have been piping at him all too long, "you are more, you are higher, you are of a different origin!"—that may be a strange and insane task, but it is a *task*—who would deny that? Why did we choose this insane task? Or, putting it differently: "why have knowledge at all?" (*BW*, 351-52)

Here we have closed our circle.

Princeton University

NOTES

1   The "axial period" is not a phrase often encountered in essays on Nietzsche; I mean by it what is usually meant by the phrase "the mature period." The period 1883-1887 is a familiar "cut" because these are the years of the publication of *Thus Spoke Zarathustra* [in *The Portable Nietzsche*, trans. and ed. by Walter Kaufmann (New York: Viking, 1954) (hereafter cited as *PN*)] and its "commentaries": *Beyond Good and Evil* (1886) and *The Genealogy of Morals* (1887) [both in *Basic Writings of Nietzsche*, trans. and ed. by Walter Kaufmann (New York: The Modern Library, 1966) (hereafter cited as *BW*)]. *Beyond Good and Evil* "says the same things as my *Zarathustra*," wrote Nietzsche to Overbeck, "but differently, very differently—" (*BW*, 182). And the *Genealogy* is also offered as a "supplement" and "clarification" of *Beyond Good and Evil* (*BW*, 439). Moreover, the entire third section of the *Genealogy* is devoted, according to Nietzsche, to an exemplary exegesis of a single aphorism from *Zarathustra* (*BW*, 459).

The period 1883-1888 is also a familiar cut since it is from the notebooks of these years that the notes are taken comprising *The Will to Power* [trans. by Walter Kaufmann and R. J. Hollingdale and ed. by Walter Kaufmann (New York: Vintage Books, 1968) (hereafter cited as *WP*)]. This period also includes the powerful work "The Case of Wagner" (published in 1888). I begin the "axial period" with 1882, however, so as to take in the whole of *The Gay Science* (first published in 1882, yet supplemented by a Fifth Book in 1887) [trans. by Walter Kaufmann (New York: Random House, 1974) (hereafter cited as *GS*)], which contains a number of aphorisms crucial for my discussion.

2   *BW*, 314.

3   Roman numerals refer to volume numbers, arabic numerals to page numbers, of *Friedrich Nietzsche: Werke in Drei Bänden*, ed. by Karl Schlechta (Munich: Carl Hanser Verlag, 1954-1956).

    A plain translation of this poem reads: "Now, contorted between two nothingnesses, a question mark, a weary riddle, a riddle for birds of prey: they will 'solve' ('dissolve') you all right, they are already hungry for your 'solution,' they are already flapping around you, their riddle, around you, hanged man! ... O Zarathustra ... *self-knower!* ... *hangman of your self!* ..." "Between Birds of Prey," from the *Dithyrambs to Dionysus*, composed before the end of 1888, first published in 1891.

4   *WP*, 270. All these passages which speak of the self as invented, posited, as un-self-stable—as imaginary, a fiction, a projection, a supplement—are taken from Book III, section 3, of *The Will to Power*, headed "Belief in the 'Ego.' The Subject." I take them from this source rather than the individual published works in which they are elaborated because of the irresistible impression made by so concentrated a strain of writing against the self in a demystifying way. Walter Kaufmann comments about this third section of *The Will to Power* that "some of the epistemological reflections ... [have] no close parallel in the works Nietzsche finished" (*WP*, xiv); but what is in fact remarkable (and cautionary) about this sub-section on "The Subject" is that *each* of these aphorisms can in fact be traced to more fully elaborated and nuanced versions in the published work. As a result this "attack" on belief in the subject is nowhere else encountered in so pure a state and will always be found modified by various types of argument on behalf of the self. The reader who relies on *The Will to Power* for Nietzsche's last testament and takes from it a position of radical epistemological nihilism will miss the intricacy of his published statement.

5   The "self ... is your body" (*PN*, 146). "[Zarathustra's] word pronounced selfishness blessed, the wholesome, healthy selfishness that wells from a powerful soul— ... to which belongs the high body ...—the supple, persuasive body, the dancer whose parable and epitome is the self-enjoying soul" (*PN*, 302). Further: "it is not at all necessary to get rid of 'the soul' ... and thus to renounce one of the most ancient and venerable hypotheses— ... But the way is open for new versions and refinements of the soul-hypothesis ..." (*BW*, 210).

6   Other attributes of the ego: it is a "fable, a fiction, a play on words" (*PN*, 495). Its individuality is merely exemplary: it instantiates what is general, indeed, *common* to the species (*GS*, 299). As the subject of "egoism," it is "interesting" and dangerous—but this is also how Nietzsche construes the "self."

    The self has few attributes. "Individual psychological observations," writes Ludwig Giesz, "never really treat the self, which precisely isn't general. The presupposition of science is that assertions of a categorical kind can be made [only] about an 'exemplary' individual," *Nietzsche: Existenzialismus und Wille zur Macht* (Stuttgart: Deutsche Verlagsanstalt, 1950), p. 45. As that which cannot be known, the self can be described as "there," a "granitic fate" (*BW*, 352), profoundly present and hidden, never lost and therefore never having to be sought (*BW*, 418). Or else it can be represented as insistently problematic, an eternal question. In both cases immediate self-knowledge is impossible (*BW*, 415). The self can be represented, however, by certain more or less inspired metaphors, as we shall see.

7   *G-S*, 297-300. In its main thrust, however, this passage derogates "the thinking that rises to *consciousness*" as "the most superficial and worst part" of all thinking (*BW*, 299). Consciousness is chiefly "superfluous" except for the purpose of communication; as a result it must adopt the "herd perspective" and debase the "incomparably personal, unique, and infinitely individual" character of our actions. (Cf. Kafka: "One cannot express that which one is, since that is precisely what one is; one can only communicate that which is not, i.e. the lie.") "Whatever becomes conscious," continues Nietzsche, "*becomes* by the same token shallow, thin, relatively stupid, general, sign, herd signal; all becoming conscious involves a great and thorough corruption, falsification, reduction to superficialities, and generalization (*BW*, 300)." This charge applies to *self*-consciousness as well: "The human being inventing signs is at the same time the human being who becomes ever more keenly conscious of himself. It was only as a social animal that man acquired self-consciousness . . ." (*BW*, 299). At the same time this process resembles (or at least precipitates) that famous process of "internalization" (*Verinnerlichung*) which, in the account given in *The Genealogy of Morals* (*BW*, 520-521), contributes to more depth, hope and interest in man than it does to his enfeeblement. Both texts were of course published in the same year—1887.

8   *BW*, 199. In consecutive episodes of *Thus Spoke Zarathustra*—"On Human Prudence" and "The Stillest Hour"—the vain man sighs, from a sense of modesty, "What am *I*!"; and Zarathustra, perceiving his own smallness next to the superman, says, "Who am *I*? I await the worthier one . . ." (*PN*, 255, 258). Clearly the choice of pronoun here makes a difference: in the first case it expresses an absolute abjectness of being; the "vain man" feels himself (though unawares) inferior to *anyone* who will praise him. In the second passage the redoubtable Zarathustra speaks as an ego ["A new pride my ego taught me" (*PN*, 144)] and as a self ["Instruments and toys are sense and spirit: behind them still lies the self" (*PN*, 146)]; but this identity is only something wanting to perish for a stronger being. The distinction here may not be precisely the one Nietzsche is pointing to in speaking of the "questioner" underlying the will to truth. But these passages support the view that Nietzsche's rhetorical distinction between "who" and "what" is significant.

9   *BW*, 199. Nietzsche's mythology of temptresses has its important distinctions in value: the Sphinx is not a Circe. To say the Sphinx is a Circe is to adopt the makeshift consolations of the "skeptic"—"a delicate creature," the product of "nervous exhaustion and sickliness." The skeptic cannot hear "Yes!" He will not "straighten what is crooked," he counsels waiting; "the uncertain has its charms, too," he says; "the sphinx, too, is a Circe; Circe, too, was a philosopher" (*BW*, 319-20). The encounter of Oedipus and the Sphinx, which is a metaphor of the encounter of the self and the question of its being, is in deadly earnest and in need of solution!

10   In *Martin Heidegger, Basic Writings*, ed. by David Farrell Krell (New York: Harper and Row, 1977), pp. 45-50. Heidegger had read Nietzsche by the time of writing *Being and Time* in the mid-1920s; his work mentions Nietzsche in connection with notions of Being-towards-death, conscience, and the "use and abuse" of "historiology" (hereafter cited as *MH*).

11   The next aphorism (*BW*, 452) speaks literally of "a *fundamental will* of knowledge."

12   *Sein und Zeit*, 10th ed. (Tübingen: Max Niemeyer Verlag, 1963), p. 7.

13   The self *wants* itself as a question. In *Zarathustra* (Part II: "On Immaculate Perception") Nietzsche writes, beautifully, "Wo ist Schönheit? Wo ich mit allem Willen *wollen* muß; wo ich lieben und untergehn will, daß ein Bild nicht nur Bild bleibe" (379) ["Where is beauty? Where I must will with all my will; where I want to love and perish that an image may not remain a mere image" (*PN*, 235)].

14   See pp. 9-10 *infra*.

15   In *The Gay Science* Nietzsche also identifies an unconscious reason, viz. "The development of language and the development of consciousness (*not* of reason but merely of the way reason enters consciousness) go hand in hand (299).

16   And, moreover in such varied and specifically imagined ways as to make Freud's "social" model of super-ego/ego seem thin and under-realized. See *in. al.* the aphorism from *The Will to Power* headed "The Body as a Political Structure" (*WP*, 348).

17   I discount compound words with the prefix "self" (*Selbst*), which have variable value. Thus Nietzsche will discredit a certain kind of introspection he calls *"Selbst-Erkenntnis"* (self-knowledge), *BW*, 414; see p. 11 *supra*) but value that *"Selbst-Bekenntnis"* (personal confession) which is "what every great philosophy so far has been . . . [:] a kind of involuntary and unconscious memoir" (*BW*, 203).

18   This privilege of the self that is decisively nominal but otherwise obscure lends such confident distinctions as the following their unwitting irony: "In Nietzsche the ego—sometimes called a grammatical fiction, sometimes called a mask—has lost its self-identity"[!]. Alphonso Lingis, "The Will to Power," in *The New Nietzsche*, ed. by David B. Allison (New York: Delta, 1977), p. 40.

19   "For one may doubt . . . whether there are any opposites at all, and secondly whether these popular valuations and opposite values on which the meta-physicians put their seal, are not perhaps merely foreground estimates, only provisional perspectives . . . . *[L]anguage*, here as elsewhere, will not get over its awkwardness, and will continue to talk of opposites where there are only degrees and many subtleties of gradation . . ." (*BW*, 200, 225). Cf. Kafka: "My repugnance for antitheses is certain . . . . They make for thoroughness, fullness, completeness, but only like a figure on the 'wheel of life' [a toy with a revolving wheel] ; we have chased our little idea around the circle. They are as undifferentiated as they are different . . ." (*The Diaries of Franz Kafka: 1910-1913*, ed. by Max Brod [New York: Schocken Books, 1948] , p. 157).

20   As, for example: "It is not too much to say that even a partial *diminution of utility*, an atrophying and degeneration, a loss of meaning and purposiveness, —in short, death—is among the conditions of an actual *progressus*, which always appears in the shape of a will and a way to greater power and is always carried through at the expense of numerous smaller powers" (*BW*, 514).

21   "For the interpretation itself is a form of the will to power, exists (but not as a 'being' but as a process, a becoming) as an affect" (*WP*, 302).

22   The question is rhetorical; it "cannot be decided . . .; for in the course of this analysis the human intellect cannot avoid seeing itself in its own perspectives, and *only* in these. We cannot look around our own corner . . ." (*GS*, 336).

23 The "mise en abyme" is the endless mirror effect shown, for example, on the Quaker Oats box of my childhood. The Quaker is depicted as holding up a box of oats on which he is depicted holding up a box of oats . . . . Valery's verbal equivalent is M. Teste's confession, "En voyant me voir . . . ."

24 Laurence Rickels writes in a Peircean vein: "A mirror-image is not a total or iconic image but an indexical image, and thus its relation to its object is based not on identity and simultaneity but on sequential difference and connectedness." In his unpublished doctoral dissertation: "The Iconic Imagination," Department of German, Princeton University, 1980.

25 I paraphrase here a phenomenological view of the linguistic sign. See Gerald L. Bruns, *Modern Poetry and the Idea of Language* (New Haven and London: Yale Univ. Press, 1974), p. 233.

    We have floated two theories of the "origin" of a linguistic event, once a personal speaker has been excluded. One theory calls this "origin" language itself; this is the structuralist position. In effect it replaces the concept of "origin" by that of an always present synchronic system. In a formulation by Paul Ricoeur, "the system of language has no more subject than it has reference. The system is anonymous. Or rather, it is neither personal nor anonymous, since the question 'Who is speaking?' has no longer a meaning. Nobody speaks; the dictionary is mute. The exclusion of the subject results from the closure of a system of signs, since this closure implies the exclusion of the question, 'Who is speaking?' It is rules of the chess game without the moves, without the players" ("Philosophy of Language and Phenomenology," an unpublished lecture delivered at the University of Texas at Austin, November 24, 1968, p. 8). Nietzsche does indeed "exclude" the question "Who is speaking" from the question of the self by mutating it as "What is the self?" This formulation excludes the self as speaking subject. On the other hand Nietzsche describes the self as "something that *wants* [aims] . . . to *surpass* itself" (*WP*, 270). He therefore lines up with (a version of) another theory of the "origin" of the linguistic event—the phenomenological.
    "What is the sentence for a phenomenological description? First," says Ricoeur, "it is an event. The dictionary is not an event, it is a system. I oppose here event and system" (as indeed Nietzsche does). "A sentence," Ricoeur continues, "is an event because somebody rises up and says something. Something happens, the sentence occurs and disappears. It is historical reality" (10). Moreover, it refers to an encompassing reality, to existence as a field of meaning. "In the sentence we experience language not as an object, not as a closed system, but as a mediation, that is to say, that through which we move towards reality, whatever it may be . . . . In the sentence and through the sentence language escapes itself towards what it says. It goes beyond itself and disappears into its intentional referent" (11-12).
    Some of this fits Nietzsche's account of the self; but the *décalage* is instructive. Indeed, the self's language transcends itself toward its "subject." The subject, however, is not "somebody"; the way in which it "says" its question is closer, in the phenomenological account, to the self's primary articulation of the existential field of meaning. The self, indeed, like "language" in the Husserlian view "is, in itself, a medium, a mediation, an exchange between the *telos* of logicity [rationality] and the origin in experience" ("Philosophy of Language and Linguistic Analysis," an unpublished lecture delivered at the University of Texas at Austin, November 22, 1968, p. 9). The question of the self articulates the self as an interpreter.

Thereafter interpretation involves the self whether or not it explicitly poses the question of itself. Its being *is* a question—the transcendental agent of its mutation from a "natural involvement" to a "signifying relation" with experience (13).

26   In *Nietzsche's Gift* (Athens, Ohio: Ohio Univ. Press, 1977), p. 165.

27   *BW*, 418. This suspension of the explicit question of the self is connected in Nietzsche to the entire complex of ideas that comes under the head of "active forgetfulness"—the condition of action and truth. See especially *BW*, 493-94, and the early essays "On Truth and Falsity in Their Ultramoral Sense," in *The Complete Works of Friedrich Nietzsche*, Vol. II, ed. Oscar Levy (New York: Macmillan, 1909-1911) (translation is unreliable) and "The Use and Abuse of History," Levy, Vol. V.

28   Again, "One may not ask: 'who then interprets?' for the interpretation itself is a form of the will to power, exists (but not as a 'being' but as a process, a becoming) as an affect" (*WP*, 302).

29   Nietzsche also asserts the opposite position, but in such a form that I lay my stress where I do. The (opposite) idea is found in *The Will to Power*, viz. "The will to power can manifest itself only against resistances; therefore, it seeks that which resists it" (*WP*, 346). The context of this remark is, however, "the primeval tendency of the protoplasm." The idea reappears in *The Twilight of the Idols*: "How is freedom measured in individuals and peoples? According to the resistance which must be overcome . . . to remain on top" (*PN*, 542). Here again the context disqualifies general authority: This is the case essentially "five steps from tyranny, close to the threshold of the danger of servitude"—in an extreme situation; and Nietzsche's language is infected by the mood of extremity: "The human being who has *become free*—spits on the contemptible type of well-being dreamed of by shopkeepers, Christians, cows, females, Englishmen, and other democrats" [sic] (*PN*, 542). It is wrong to assert, as does Gayatri Spivak, that the description of the will to power "as a search for what is resistant to itself" is "irreducible." "Translator's Preface," *Of Grammatology*, a translation of *De la Grammatologie* by Jacques Derrida (Baltimore and London: Johns Hopkins Univ. Press), p. xxvi. Yet this claim passes current as the cardinal axiom in "pan-ironic" readings of Nietzsche. See pp. xx-xx *supra.*

30   *GS*, 244-45. Maire Kurrik makes enlightening distinctions between unconscious negation and the consciousness of negativity in *Literature and Negation* (New York: Columbia Univ. Press, 1979).

31   *BW*, 756-57; inner quote: *PN*, 295-96.

32   "For Nietzsche knowledge is a (re)constructed text; the world is the lost original." Bernd Magnus, *Nietzsche's Existential Imperative* (Bloomington, Indiana, and London: Indiana Univ. Press, 1978), p. 27.

33   "Satzung" (statute, law) and "Setzung" (positing, stake) are central categories in Giesz's discussion of the will to power. Giesz writes of "the structure of the will to power . . . [as] defining at the same time the self-developing Self. This being 'becomes' by producing itself ['We, however, *want to become those we are*—human beings who are new, unique, incomparable, who give themselves

laws, who create themselves' (*GS*, 266)]. The Self produces itself by relating understandingly to itself (by orienting itself toward something more general). It relates to itself by relating to something else—to contexts of meaning, which it indeed respects as "statutes" (*Satzungen*) [but] which, however, finally owe their binding character, their 'objectivity,' once again, to the Self which 'created' them" (p. 14). Hence they are only the *Setzungen* of the Self. The fiction of the "stable ego" "accords" with what Nietzsche elsewhere calls "our inevitable need to preserve ourselves [:] to posit a crude world of stability, of 'things,' etc." (*WP*, 380). The ego is that "thing" of the inner life which "still speak[s] most honestly of its being"—the Self (*PN*, 144).

34   Nietzsche's "defiance" of Goethe should not be represented, of course, as innocent: Nietzsche was well aware of the text of Goethe which he parodies. Speaking against Wagner's assumption in *Parsifal* of the cause of chastity, Nietzsche writes of "all those well-constituted, joyful mortals who are far from regarding their unstable equilibrium between 'animal and angel' as necessarily an argument against existence—the subtlest and brightest among them have even found in it, like Goethe and Hafiz, *one more* stimulus to life" (*BW*, 535). See also *BW*, 300. *The West-Easterly Divan* is inspired by Goethe's reading of the Persian poet Hafiz.
       This example nuances Harold Bloom's comment, "Nietzsche . . . was the heir of Goethe in his strangely optimistic refusal to regard the poetical past as primarily an obstacle to fresh creation" (*The Anxiety of Influence* [New York: Oxford, 1973], p. 50). Goethe assimilates Hafiz, unafraid. Nietzsche's allusion to Goethe is oddly alienating: it inverts Goethe; it suggests that the condition of enduring Goethe is keeping distance. This is not so much taking Goethe's influence as stating that one will go one's own way.

35   *PN*, 264. Henry David Aiken comments shrewdly: "In *Zarathustra* . . . the ever-recurrent and combative *ego*, which elsewhere Nietzsche seems to be trying to impose upon the reader, is for once submerged in the creative life, or world, of the work itself. And for this reason, by what is only an apparent paradox, Nietzsche's whole self is able to disport itself more freely . . . [and] more powerfully than in his more explicitly didactic works." ("An Introduction to *Zarathustra*," in *Nietzsche: A Collection of Critical Essays*, ed. by Robert C. Solomon [New York: Anchor Books, 1973], p. 116).

36   And cost Blake more than a bowel complaint. In the 1814 "Preface" to *The Excursion* Wordsworth quotes lines revealing that to an extravagant degree the subject of his poem is *himself*—"our Minds, . . . the Mind of Man." Upon reading these lines Blake is supposed to have been afflicted by a bowel complaint that nearly killed him. Helen Darbishire, *The Poet Wordsworth* (Oxford: Clarendon Press, 1958), p. 139.

37   George Santayana, *Egotism in German Philosophy* (New York: Scribner's, 1940), p. 12.

38   *Nietzsche*, p. xiii.

39   *Nietzsche*, Vol. I: *The Will to Power as Art*, trans. by David Farrel Krell (New York: Harper and Row, 1979), p. 38.

40   *PN*, 481. Further: "To impose upon becoming the character of being—that is the supreme will to power" (*BW*, 330). The word "impose" certainly merits the quotes of "pervasive irony." See Spivak, "Translator's Preface," *Of Grammatology*, p. xxxv.

41   In speaking about "the death of the self in Nietzsche" and later, too, about Nietzsche's ubiquitous irony, "wilder" even than "unstable" irony (see pp. 21-25 *infra*.); in speaking about "wild" readers (see p. 50 ff. *infra*.), meaning no harm to those readers of Nietzsche who have seen his texts as an interminable semantic dissonance; in speaking, finally, about the "new" Nietzsche of post-structuralist French writers; I point to a phenomenon that has moved saliently out of texts into the general (university) discourse about Nietzsche. This reading of Nietzsche is now in circulation everywhere, with an energy that is hard to account for, even after we have identified several essays advancing this position.

Three essays on Nietzsche in Paul de Man's *Allegories of Reading* (New Haven and London: Yale Univ. Press, 1979), pp. 79-131, are important. The drift of these essays is suggested by de Man's published comment on the occasion of a Nietzsche symposium in 1974: "Irony . . . puts the notion of the self in question; . . . in Nietzsche we are dealing with a radically ironic rhetorical mode" [Nietzsche and Rhetoric," *Symposium* 28 (1974), 45].

De Man's "deconstruction of the subject" in his first essay, on "Genesis and Genealogy" in the *Birth of Tragedy*, proceeds by questioning Nietzsche's presentation of Dionysus as the "father" of all art, of all appearance. The analysis turns on the "voice" which speaks in the text on his behalf. This text is "empowered to decide on matters of truth and falsehood," but with what authority? The claim it advances on behalf of music as the representation of the will is plainly made "in bad faith." Furthermore, the will figures as a subject, a consciousness. How can this subject speak against the category of representative art all the time it is itself a theatrical representation of the will? Finally, the text is discordant on the question of whether Dionysus is true or illusory. Therefore, "the will has been discredited as a self." "The pan-tragic consciousness of the self" is "made to appear hollow when . . . exposed to the clarity of a new ironic light" (de Man, *Allegories of Reading*, p. 102).

The "new ironic light" is de Man's reading, which is ironic in more than one sense. De Man adduces for his argument a passage from Nietzsche's aphorisms written apropos of *The Birth of Tragedy*. Nietzsche writes, "Intelligence can exist only in a world in which mistakes can occur, in which such a thing as error can take place—a world of consciousness" (*Gesammelte Werke* III [*Musarion*], p. 239). Here is de Man's translation: "Intellegence can only exist in a world in which mistakes occur, in which *error reigns*—a world of consciousness" (my ital.). This allows him to conclude that "Dionysus, as music or as language, must now belong [. . .] to the teleological domain of the text and then he is *mere error* and mystification . . ." (*Allegories of Reading*, p. 100; my ital.).

De Man's second essay, "Rhetoric of Tropes," means "to put into question the prevalent scheme by which Nietzsche has been read. In this scheme "it seems as if Nietzsche had turned away from the problems of language to questions of the self" (p. 106). In fact, writes de Man, Nietzsche persistently uncovers the "figurality of all language," in which perspective "the idea of individuation, of the human subject as a privileged viewpoint, is a mere metaphor . . ." (p. 111). The "subject" is then identified with the "self."

In the third essay, "Rhetoric of Persuasion," the text which is explored opposes possibility and necessity and "no longer such spatial properties as inside and outside, or categories such as cause and effect, or experiences such a[s] pleasure and pain all of which figure prominently in the many sections in which consciousness or selfhood [*sic*] are the targets of Nietzsche's critique" (p. 121). This assertion—and much of the argument of the essay on the rhetoric of tropes—is made unintelligible by de Man's equation of subject or consciousness and self.

David Allison's "Introduction" to *The New Nietzsche*, an anthology of recent essays on Nietzsche mainly by French writers, is another text figuring in this discourse. In giving an account of Nietzsche's semiotics, Allison writes, typically: "Thus there is nothing [for Nietzsche] beyond language, to guide or subtend linguistic signification from without. Language makes sense because it can draw upon itself" (p. xvi). Here, now, is Nietzsche: "Words are acoustical signs for concepts; concepts, however, are more or less definite image signs for often recurring and associated sensations, for groups of sensations. To understand one another, it is not enough that we use the same words; one also has to use the same words for the same species of inner experiences; in the end one has to have one's experience in *common*" (*BW*, 406). Language makes sense because it can draw on inner experience.

Allison furthermore sees Nietzsche as deconstructing the "axiomatic system" of "Western thought as such" by exhibiting the *grammatical* necessity producing the terms of thought, viz. "Identity gives rise to the concepts of unity, plurality, specific difference, number, permanence, movement (space and time), subject and substance (self, ego, soul, God, particle)" (p. xxii). In fact Nietzsche maintains a specific *difference* between "ego" and "self," terming the latter a "plurality with *one* sense"!

Gayatri Spivak's "Translator's Introduction" to her translation of Jacques Derrida's *On Grammatology* belongs to this wave. Like Allison she also leans heavily on Nietzsche's early essay "On Truth and Falsehood in an Extra Moral Sense" (1873) and on Derrida's reading of Nietzsche as one who "contributed a great deal to the liberation of the signifier from its dependance or derivation with respect to the logos, and the related concept of truth or the primary signified . . ." (p. xxi). She writes, "The human being [for Nietzsche] has nothing more to go on than a collection of nerve stimuli" (p. xxii). Yet it is perfectly evident, by a process of trial transformation, that to substitute the words "collection of nerve stimuli" for the word "experience" in all the appropriate passages we have cited is to distort their sense and resonance. For Spivak, Nietzsche's conception of knowledge is of "an unending proliferation of interpretations whose only 'origin' [is] that shudder in the nerve strings . . ." (p. xxiii). (This "shudder" returns to Nietzsche's "nerve-stimulus" in his description of the structural moments of language formation). Is this true, however, for the being in whom " 'deep down' there is some granite of spiritual fatum" (*BW*, 352)? Nietzsche has *not* interpreted value-systems as infinite textuality and does not say that his distinction between master and slave modes of evaluation are capable of being "infinitely" reinterpreted or put "under erasure." Spivak writes, "The Nietzschean unconscious is that vast arena of the mind of which the so-called 'subject' knows nothing" (p. xxv). But Nietzsche wrote, "Indeed, the ego and the ego's contradiction and confusion still speak most honestly of its being" (*PN*, 144). Curiously, Spivak appears to want to repair this fault—without too much of the fanfare of awareness, yet with the assertive self-consciousness of a gender claim. She reintroduces the category of the self to account for Nietzsche's (the philosopher's) deliberate reversal of opposed perspectives: "The dissolving of opposites is the philosopher's gesture against that will to power which would mystify her [*sic*] very self" (p. xxviii).

Finally, central to the discourse of the "new" Nietzsche is, of course, Derrida's *Spurs*, for which—in a word—"Nietzsche is a bit lost in the web of the text, like a spider, unequal to what he has produced" (*The New Nietzsche*, p. 186).

42 "Nietzsches Auffassung der Ironie," *Nietzsche-Studien*, Vol. IV (Berlin and New York: Walter de Gruyter), pp. 1-35.

43   This exposure occurs principally in "The Four Great Errors" of *Twilight of the Idols* (*PN*, 492-501).

44   See pp. 17-18 *infra.*

45   "All concepts in which an entire process is semiotically concentrated elude definition" (*BW*, 516).

46   Nietzsche wrote in the early text *Human, All-Too-Human* (*Menschliches Allzumenschliches*), 1878-1879, "Immediate self-observation is insufficient by far for self-knowledge; we need history, because the past flows on in a hundred waves in us; indeed we ourselves are no more than what we experience in every moment of this flowing on (I, 823). The notion is developed in *The Gay Science* under the head of *"the historical sense"* (see p. 24 *supra.*) and further in *Beyond Good and Evil.* "The past of every form and way of life, of cultures that formerly lay right next to each other or one on top of the other, now flows into us 'modern souls' . . ." (*BW*, 341).

Such passages form the basis of Nietzsche's "defense," supposing he needed one, against Dilthey's charge that he lacked an historical sense and maintained that the royal road to human truth was introspection. The charge cannot stand. This "debate" is interestingly presented in J. Kamerbeek, "Dilthey versus Nietzsche." *Studia Philosophica, Jahrbuch der Schweizerischen Philoso-phischen Gesellschaft*, 10 (1950), 52-84.

47   "And if somebody asked, 'but to a fiction there surely belongs an author?'—couldn't one answer simply: *why?* Doesn't this 'belongs' perhaps belong to the fiction, too? Is it not permitted to be a bit ironical about the subject no less than the predicate and object?" (*BW*, 237).

48   Jacques Derrida, *Spurs/Eperons*, trans. by Barbara Harlow (Chicago and London: The Univ. of Chicago Press, 1979), p. 81.

49   *WM*, 337. Or again, " 'The subject' is the fiction that many similar states in us are the effect of one substratum: but it is *we* who first created the 'similarity' of these states . . ." (*WP*, 269; ital. mine).

50   *Pace* Spivak, "Translator's Preface": "The 'subject' is a unified concept and therefore the *result* of 'interpretation' (p. xxiv; ital. mine).

51   *Unschuld des Werdens II*, aphorism 359. Cited in Giesz, *Nietzsche*, p. 6.

52   See footnote 116, *supra.*

53   Gerald Bruns, "Modern Poetry," p. 233.

54   See, in ms., p. 23 *supra.*

55   *BW*, 535; *PN*, 674. Nietzsche's late work *Nietzsche contra Wagner* is pieced together from passages about Wagner in Nietzsche's earlier works, "perhaps clarified here and there, above all, shortened" ("Preface," *PN*, 662). In the section of *Nietzsche contra Wagner*—"Wagner as an Apostle of Chastity:"— Nietzsche reprints an earlier aphorism from the *Genealogy of Morals*: III, 3, but omits the sentence I have quoted. Why would Nietzsche not have wanted to re-assert in 1888 that the great artist "comes to see himself and his art beneath him?"

56   Giesz, *Nietzsche*, p. 6. As opposed to "the subject" which is "a created entity, a 'thing' like all others, a simplification with the object of defining the force which posits, invents, things . . ." (*WP*, 302).

57   *Selected Short Stories of Franz Kafka*, trans. by Willa and Edwin Muir (New York: Modern Library), pp. 173-74.

58   *Gesammelte Werke*, Vol. III (Munich: Musarion, 1920), p. 344. In these early jottings surrounding the composition of *The Birth of Tragedy*, Nietzsche speculates on an "innermost being," a world "core," which is "wholly indecipherable." This is that "power" out of whose "womb a visionary world is generated in the form of the 'will.'" This womb is the "origin of music . . . and lies beyond all individuation" (pp. 341-45). It is, therefore, quite incorrect of Paul de Man, who comments on this text, to assert that once the play of the will has been "shown to be . . . the endless tension of a nonidentity, a pattern of dissonance, . . . [it] contaminates the very source of the will, the will as source (*Allegories of Reading*, p. 99). It is furthermore untrue that the "unpublished fragments . . . deny this possibility," namely, that "this essence is able to function as origin" (*Allegories of Reading*, p. 101). The citation from Nietzsche reproduces the very imagery of filiation, indicating the identity of essence and origin.

59   Lewis Thomas, *The Lives of a Cell: Notes of a Biology Watcher* (Toronto, New York, London: Bantam Books, 1974), p. 3 (hereafter cited as *LC*). Writing about the self in Nietzsche apropos of problems of identity in the (biological) cell should not seem too strange in light of Nietzsche's reflections on the "Biology of the Drive to Knowledge" in *The Will to Power*. See, e.g., *WP*, 272.

60   Reference lost.

61   From Nietzsche's notebooks, cited in Beda Alleman, *Ironie und Dichtung* (Pfullingen: Günther Neske, 1956), p. 105.

62   Cited in *Allegories of Reading*, p. 94.

63   The point is roughly dramatized by what I hear as the difference between the positions of, say, *Human, All-Too-Human* (their lack of resonance) and those of the works of the axial period. The author of the 1396 aphorisms of *Human, All-Too-Human* is an idea born of, forced by Nietzsche's conviction in his solitude that he had better not admit to the solitude of his ego—to his iron restriction to the point of the ego.

64   *The Short Stories of Henry James*, ed. Clifton Fadiman (New York: The Modern Library, 1945), p. 315.

Nietzsche's Zerography: *Thus Spoke Zarathustra*

Rudolf E. Kuenzli

Nietzsche, the one who questions everything, the one who puts everything into doubt, his own work included, who calls his philosophy a school of suspicion, who describes himself as the philosopher of the "dangerous perhaps," who tempts us with his attempts and temptations (*Versuche und Versuchungen*), how do we read him? Nietzsche who has cast the strongest doubt on language itself, how are we to comprehend his language, and how do we use ours in commenting on his work? These questions Nietzsche raises for us are at the center of critical literary discourse today, a sure sign of the crisis in which literary theory finds itself. Nietzsche's deconstruction of his own text, his zerography, has become the model for critics who, having subdued their former rage for the organic whole, are now drawn to the holes, breaks, ruptures and discontinuities in the text.

I

More traditional philosophers may very well disagree with the misreading of Nietzsche as a zerographer. But they have to be aware of their own methods and strategies by which they manufacture their Nietzsche. A brief consideration of some of these.philosophical studies on Nietzsche may indicate at what price they establish definite meanings in Nietzsche's writings. These philosophers see in their interpretations of Nietzsche an opportunity to exercise their sense of charity, to save Nietzsche from himself, from his style, the "irridescent webs of myth and metaphor,"[1] and to rewrite him in unambiguous statements that produce a philosophical system. Danto's attempt at rewriting may serve as an example, when he states: "I believe it is exceedingly useful to see his analyses in terms of logical features which he was unable to make explicit, but toward which he was unmistakably groping. His language would have been less colorful had he known what he was trying to say."[2] In adhering to the principle of identity, the stability of meaning, the main strategy of these interpreters consists in explaining away Nietzsche's contradictions by various ways. Some commentators focus only on one work, in order to avoid contradictions with all the other works by Nietzsche. Karl Löwith's study *Nietzsches Philosophie der ewigen Wiederkehr des Gleichen* only focuses on *Thus Spoke Zarathustra,* since Löwith declares that work as Nietzsche's "testament" which contains Nietzsche's whole philosophy.[3] Steiner and Möbius use slightly different tactics in avoiding contradictions between Nietzsche's early and late works. They simply discredit and dismiss his late works as having been written by Nietzsche with only half his brain.[4] Arthur Drews and Eugen Fink attempt to avoid contradictions by dividing Nietzsche's works into three or four phases within each of which they find a stability of meaning.[5] Such an approach draws its support from Zarathustra's saying that he sees his life divided into the three phases of the camel, the lion and the child. Walter Kaufmann even claims that there are no real contradictions in Nietzsche's work if passages are read in context. Since Walter Kaufmann has probably been the most influential commentator and translator of Nietzsche in America, and since his view of Nietzsche has informed his own translations, we may examine his approach more closely. In the Preface to the fourth edition of his *Nietzsche, Philosopher, Psychologist, Antichrist* he reveals his intent in his Nietzsche enterprise: "It seemed needful to dissociate him from the Nazis and to show that he had been a great philosopher."[6] In order to present him as a great philosopher, Kaufmann had to ignore Nietzsche the stylist: "I had been reacting against the view that Nietzsche was primarily a great stylist, and the burden of my book had been to show that he was a great thinker."[7] In order to make Nietzsche's views coherent he was forced to liberate him from his wicked, treacherous style.[8]

But what remains of Nietzsche's writings if one ignores, brackets his style? This question is not only crucial in considering Kaufmann's interpretation of Nietzsche, but also that by Heidegger. Heidegger devoted fourteen hundred pages of commentary to the work of Nietzsche, not even a negligible effort in view of the forthcoming edition of all of Heidegger's writings. The question concerning the relationship between Heidegger and

Nietzsche is central, but a deep silence seems to surround it. In order to avoid contradictions, Heidegger completely ignores them and focuses his attention on what he calls Nietzsche's key work, "The Will to Power," which of course Nietzsche never wrote, but which Heidegger is able to construct. He argues, that Nietzsche's thought moved towards expressing "The Will to Power," implied it, but that his key thought, his only thought[9] was inexpressible to Nietzsche himself. *The Will to Power,* as published by Nietzsche's sister, serves Heidegger as "a basis for an attempt to follow the thinking process, and in this process to think Nietzsche's only thought. But we have to free ourselves from the beginning and everywhere from the presented order of the published book" (*N,* I, p. 486). Or he states: "We always distinguish very sharply between the subsequently published book entitled 'The Will to Power' and the hidden thinking process to the will to power, whose innermost law and structure we attempt to re-think" (*N,* I, p. 487). He bases his interpretation primarily on notes from 1887/88, since Heidegger claims that Nietzsche's thinking reached its greatest clarity in those two years just before his collapse (*N,* I, p. 486). What Heidegger seems to be doing is to write the work "The Will to Power," which Nietzsche never wrote. In composing this work Heidegger is able to make out of Nietzsche the last metaphysician, the most unrestrained Platonist of Western philosophy. In order to avoid contradictions and reach definite meanings Heidegger writes/rewrites "The Will to Power" and ignores Nietzsche's own form and style. He primarily concentrates on some of Nietzsche's notes and neglects the works that Nietzsche himself published by claiming that "What Nietzsche himself published during the period of his creativity remains always a foreground. . . . The genuine philosophy remains behind as 'post-humous material' " (*N,* I, p. 17). Heidegger's strategy, the "obliteration" of Nietzsche, as Lacoue-Labarthe calls it, may be seen as Heidegger's own effort at overcoming Nietzsche. Lacoue-Labarthe hypothesizes that Heidegger's commentary of Nietzsche against Nietzsche might very well stem from Heidegger's anxiety of influence: ". . . in the obstinance, above all, with which Heidegger unceasingly interprets Nietzsche *against himself* for ten years in order to subordinate him to metaphysics, are there not symptoms of a certain dread or fear (more than a distrust in any case) felt in the face of Nietzsche, in the face of a menace represented by Nietzsche? The menace would of course be the fact of a proximity."[10] Less diplomatically Laruelle calls for an immediate, thorough investigation of Heidegger's interpretation of Nietzsche, since he sees Heidegger as "the most dangerous of the classical interpreters of Nietzsche, whose old image he merely disguises."[11] The "old image" refers, of course, to that of Nietzsche the fascist. That Heidegger gave a political interpretation to Nietzsche's thought of the will to power is clear from his lectures entitled *What Is Called Thinking?* For Heidegger technology is the final fruit of a will to power that aims to subdue the world. Nietzsche's thought heralds "the moment when man is about to assume dominion of the earth as a whole."[12] Heidegger's two volumes on Nietzsche, published in 1961, are the lectures that he held at Freiburg from 1936 to 1940, intermittently having a Nazi spy in his seminars. In view of Laruelle's suggestion, how do we interpret Heidegger's recently published statement that these lectures on Nietzsche were his altercation (*Auseinandersetzung*) with Nazi socialism? [13] The question of Heidegger-Nietzsche is very central, also in view of Lacan, and should be addressed perhaps less diplomatically than it has been done by Derrida. Heidegger's Nietzsche interpretation obliterates, as do other philosophical misreadings, Nietzsche's multivalent, pluralistic style in order to establish a definite meaning, which then serves as a basis for a systematization of Nietzsche's doctrines.

In stark contrast to these thematic philosophical interpretations which construct Nietzsche's philosophic system, Bataille, Klossowski, and to a certain extent Blanchot and Derrida see in Nietzsche's writing only a labyrinth free of definite meaning. Georges Bataille rejects any logical commentary on Nietzsche's work. His only interpretation of Nietzsche is his own life, to act Nietzsche. Bataille's book on Nietzsche, written in the form of his own diary, attempts to recreate the play with language that Bataille sees in Nietzsche's works.[14] Pierre Klossowski shares Bataille's view of the dichotomy between the plurality of bodily impulses and language.[15] The rational order of language can never express the irrational, chaotic world of the impulses which, according to Bataille and Klossowski, are the true self. Their interpretation can find support in Nietzsche's essay "On Truth and Lie" where Nietzsche states: "The word is not made for intuitions; man is silenced when he sees them, or he talks in forbidden metaphors and in a very distorted grammar in order to creatively respond to the powerful, present intuition at least by destroying and disregarding the old tower of concepts."[16] Klossowski therefore sees in Nietzsche's "concepts" of "eternal recurrence," "will to power," "Dionysos," only simulacra. According to these critics, Nietzsche's best works are his non-written ones, his ten-year silence, his aphasia, the total escape from language. Bataille and Klossowski's misreading of Nietzsche's work as an undecipherable labyrinth stems from their concentration on the notes and fragments at the expense of the more coherent works that Nietzsche himself published.

Blanchot distinguishes two ways of writing in Nietzsche, one belonging to the philosophical, coherent discourse, the other to the fragmentary one. But he too stresses the fragmentary, discontinuous nature of Nietzsche's work, which does neither affirm nor deny, but which establishes a pluralism of meaning, a labyrinth. He even likens Nietzsche's writings to the fragments of Heraclitus. In his essay on "Nietzsche et l'écriture fragmentaire" Blanchot himself uses a kind of aphoristic form, a series of paragraphs presented as separate units by his use of indentation marks.[17] But unlike his description of the isolated fragments in Nietzsche his own units are quite continuous. Derrida probably presents the most extreme misreading of Nietzsche's works as a labyrinth of isolated fragments. In the first part of his essay entitled "La question du style" Derrida attempts to establish a thematic reading, a coherent codification of Nietzsche's views on women by gathering quotes from Nietzsche's works. Not being able to unite the heterogeneous statements concerning women Derrida writes: "One has to say, quite stupidly, that if one cannot assimilate—among themselves first—the aphorisms concerning women and the rest, this is also that Nietzsche did neither see it very clearly nor in a ... moment, and that such regular, rhythmical blindness, with which one can never come to terms, takes place in Nietzsche's text. Nietzsche is a little bit lost there."[18] He then offers the view that perhaps the whole work of Nietzsche consists of isolated, discontinuous sentences, such as the very unusual one Derrida found in Nietzsche's notes, all by itself and in quotation marks: " 'I forgot my umbrella.' "[19] Since Derrida reads Nietzsche's text primarily as a series of isolated notes he is able to suggest a simple reason for the heterogeneity in Nietzsche's writings: Nietzsche took notes on topics such as the women, eternal recurrence, will to power at different places and at different points in time.[20]

Is Nietzsche's work a labyrinth of isolated, contradictory statements, as Bataille, Klossowski, Blanchot and Derrida read it? Can the "true" Nietzsche only be found in the maze of his unpublished notes or in silence? Why do these commentators ignore the works that Nietzsche himself published? Derrida explicitly likens the style of his own essay to that of Nietzsche.[21] But he achieves his clear, understandable and at the same time indecipherable quality of his own text not by juxtaposing isolated, heterogeneous statements à la "I forgot my umbrella," but by quite different strategies that are far more related to Nietzsche's zerography than the ones Derrida discusses in his essay. He himself describes his zerography in the following way: "... a blaze of words: to consume the sign to ashes, but first and more violently dislocate the verbal unity, the integrity of the voice through the irritated verve, to wear down or to frighten ... the calm surface of 'words' by subjecting their body to a gymnastic ceremony."[22] The self-deconstructive process in Derrida's own writings seems to be much more closely related to Nietzsche than Derrida has been willing to reveal. Is Derrida's relative silence concerning Nietzsche another case of the anxiety of influence, or can we see Derrida in the light of Bataille, who acts Nietzsche in his own style, whose style is the only possible commentary on Nietzsche's work?

Having tried to present two types of misreading, the one that ignores Nietzsche's forms and rewrites his works according to the principle of identity, and the one that only considers the fragments, isolated notes, and forgotten umbrellas, I would finally like to very sketchily present my own misreading which is an examination of Nietzsche's zerography, the textual machinery by which he is able to put everything he states into doubt. "Zerography" seems to be at least in the English and French language a suitable term. The *OED* lists the Arabic word "çifr" as the common root for "zero" and "cipher." The relatedness and former interchangeability of "zero/cipher" is given in the following quote from the *OED:* "They accounted their weeks by thirteen days, marking the days with a zero or cipher." "Zero" is then a "cipher," a marking, a character. Zerography then is the writing process, the strategy by which the whole is deconstructed and rendered as a cipher, the signifier is liberated from the "primary signified."[23] Zerography then is the turning of the wheel, the circle, the loosening of the fixed meaning, the production of the pluralistic text. Pautrat describes Nietzsche's wheel, his writing of circles, his zerography in the following way:

> The exchange realized in such a way, from "life" to "interpretation," from "interpretation" to "impulse," to "force," from "force" to "difference," from "difference" to "the will to power," from "the will to power" to "Dionysos," and so forth (and in reverse order), in spite of their signifying difference and their determined, delimited or defined character, these "concepts"—these signifiers—do not have any proper meaning, no signified "essence" that would halt this course or this movement and stop the text in an anchoring point, similar to the truth in which the classical text found its rest, and its security.[24]

Bernard Pautrat, Sarah Kofman and Jean-Michel Rey, all students of Derrida, announced in their recent studies on Nietzsche a reading of Nietzsche's works "above any thematic cutting in order to present the signifying process."[25] But somewhat disappointingly, these studies do not analyze Nietzsche's zerography, his strategies, the signifying process, but only collect and discuss Nietzsche's own metalinguistic statements concerning the nature of language and style. Their very intriguing generalizations seem to be weakened by their sole reliance on Nietzsche's statements about style, and by their failure to analyze Nietzsche's own form of writing. In spite of their announcement they are still caught in a thematic reading by cutting up Nietzsche's texts and collecting the quotes pertaining to the topics of language and style.[26]

During the Nazi years, more than three decades before these recent studies by Derrida's students, Karl Jaspers wrote a remarkable book on Nietzsche in which he interpreted his total work as a self-deconstructive text. In Nietzsche's contradictions Jaspers sees the primary strategy of his zerography: "All statements seem to be annulled by other statements. *Self-contradiction* is the fundamental ingredient in Nietzsche's thought. For nearly every single one of Nietzsche's judgments, one can also find an opposite."[27] Jaspers therefore demands of Nietzsche's reader "to be forever dissatisfied until he has *also* found the contradiction, to search out contradictions in all their forms, and then, if possible, to gain direct experience of their necessity."[28] What Jaspers calls Nietzsche's philosophizing is not any more a set of doctrines, but a movement, the process of the reversal. In his study Jaspers takes up the themes and topics of the "philosophical" Nietzsche interpretations and empties their definitions of Nietzsche's ideas by quoting contradictions taken from all of Nietzsche's writings, including letters, fragments, and notes. We have to ask ourselves if Jaspers is not rewriting Nietzsche too, since he cuts up Nietzsche's work according to certain topics? Is he not still a prisoner of the thematic interpretation of Nietzsche? In focusing solely on Nietzsche's strategy of contradiction, and in cutting quotes from any formal context, Jaspers ignores the other aspects of Nietzsche's style of writing. We might also be tempted to ask: who performs the deconstructing? Nietzsche, the text, or Jaspers the reader, who certainly must depend on a reliable index to the complete works of Nietzsche in order to find the contradiction to each statement?

Can the reader recognize the self-deconstructive nature of Nietzsche's work only if he has total recall of all the contradictions in all of Nietzsche's writings? Is this the way we should read Nietzsche? Do not the works published by Nietzsche deconstruct themselves if we are willing to read them with, as Nietzsche recommends, a "cheerful belly," with "new ears for new music," with the understanding that Nietzsche's writings are "a kind of dancing? " Seldom was a writer so concerned about the process of reading and interpreting his texts. He calls philology, the field he was trained in, "the art of reading," "the art of ruminating, like a cow." Fearing that he would be misunderstood as a saint, as the bringer of truth, of new tables, he constantly admonished the readers to pay attention to his style of writing, to learn how to dance and to follow the shifts in tempo. After the long obliteration, bracketing of Nietzsche's form by his interpreters, we propose to finally attempt to describe Nietzsche's style.

II

We have seen that most of the commentators have focused their attention on Nietzsche's notes. We might suspect that they did so because they could quite easily reproduce their own self-reflection in these rearrangeable notes. The labyrinthians have found their labyrinth, the systematizers have found their system. These isolated notes have proven especially suitable for quoting. Marxists, Nazis, Atheists, Christians, existentialists, they all have found some of Nietzsche's notes that they could print on their banners. If, according to these critics, the "true" Nietzsche can only be found in these notes, we have to ask ourselves why Nietzsche bothered at all to produce, shape the works that he published from his notes. We have to ask ourselves what the difference is between a note in

Nietzsche's notebook and the same note included in one of his works.

For our analysis of Nietzsche's zerography we shall choose the most problematic text for such a reading, *Thus Spoke Zarathustra.* If we are able to demonstrate Nietzsche's zerography in this seemingly very coherent, seemingly all-too-serious text, then we shall be able to more easily recognize the deconstructive movement in most of Nietzsche's published texts.

Nietzsche repeatedly claimed that *Zarathustra* was his central text. He considered the works he wrote before *Zarathustra* as its preparation, the ones he wrote after *Zarathustra* as its commentary. Before 1945, Nietzsche scholars regarded *Zarathustra* as Nietzsche's greatest achievement, for they found in it his central philosophical ideas of the death of God, the overman, the will to power, and the eternal recurrence. Since the Second World War, most of the commentators have been embarrassed by this work. The embarrassment stems from its hymnic, biblical form and its teachings, which seem to produce the seriousness and claim to truth of a fifth gospel. Thomas Mann's attempt to discredit this "dangerous" and seductive work by pointing out its flaws in his essay, "Nietzsche's Philosophy in the Light of Our Experience," written in 1947, may serve as an example of the general shift away from *Zarathustra,* when he writes: "This faceless and shapeless fiend and winged man Zarathustra, with his rose-crown of laughter on his unrecognizable head, with his 'Become pitiless' and his dancing legs is not a creation, he is rhetoric, excited word play, tortured voice and doubtful prophecy in schemes of helpless grandezza, often moving and most always embarrassing—a non-figure staggering at the borderline of the ridiculous."[29] Hermann Wein's "Nietzsche ohne Zarathustra, Die Entkitschung Nietzsches: Der kritische Aufklärer" articulates this shift in Nietzsche criticism even more pointedly.[30] Nietzsche the psychologist and analyst of culture and religion is stressed at the expense of Nietzsche the creator of the "Zarathustra myth." Similarly Roland Barthes, whose later writings reflect Nietzsche's aphoristic style, could not bring himself to read *Zarathustra.*[31] One noticeable exception to the recent neglect of *Zarathustra* was Jean—Louis Barrault's theatrical performance of this work in 1973, which celebrated it as a "hymn to life" in the manner of the reception of *Zarathustra* during the period of German Jugendstil.[32]

Should we be embarrassed by Nietzsche's *Zarathustra?* Is it this blind, dangerous, "religious" book that evokes the pathos of truth? Our analysis of the signifying process in this work attempts to outline a movement that is central to most of Nietzsche's published texts: the sequential repetitive process of active forgetting and remembering, of seductive high seriousness, and of undercutting and mocking the performative and constative language.[33] Nietzsche outlined his insight into the necessarily metaphorical status of language in his earlier essays and in his notes on rhetoric. This critique of language is very much present in *Zarathustra,* but it rhythmically alternates with flights of forgetfulness, in which language is used "innocently," blindly. It is due to the presence of these two constantly recurring moments of creation and deconstruction, that diametrically opposed readings of *Zarathustra* are possible. If we choose to ignore the moments of reversal for the sake of achieving coherence and unity, we will end up creating a very serious, "pseudo-religious" book. In our analysis we shall primarily analyze Nietzsche's strategies through which he establishes this process of deconstruction, in which all of Zarathustra's teachings are caught.

Central to Nietzsche's view of artistic creation is his notion of active forgetfulness. Already in his essay on "The Use and Abuse of History for Life," he claims that "it is totally impossible to live without forgetting."[34] He calls the ability to forget a "divine ability,"[35] and in his Preface to *The Gay Science* he glorifies forgetting as the highest wisdom, which he primarily finds among the Greeks: "There are few things we now know too well, we knowing ones: oh, how we now learn to forget well, and to be good at *not* knowing as artists! " And he continues: "Oh these Greeks! They knew how to live. What is required for that is to stop courageously at the surface, the fold, the skin, to adore appearance, to believe in forms, tones, words, in the whole Olympus of appearance."[36] Nietzsche has to periodically forget his will to truth, his doubts, his critical insight into the nature of language, since "there could be no happiness, no cheerfulness, no hope, no pride, no *present,* without forgetting."[37] A reading of *Zarathustra* after a reading of Nietzsche's critique of language in his earlier "Philosophenbuch" may prompt us to regard *Zarathustra* as a sustained act of willed blindness and forgetting, as a work in which he relaxes his will to truth and adheres to a belief in "forms, tones, words." Nietzsche confirms this impression in one of his letters, when he writes: "My recommending Schopenhauer or Wagner to the German people, or creating Zarathustras in between [things of a dangerous kind] , are relaxations for me, but above all hiding places, in which I can again rest for a while."[38] It is precisely the aspect of the naive and of forgetting that Nietzsche stresses in the opening section of *Zarathustra,* where he glorifies the child as the highest metamorphosis: "The child is innocence and forgetting."[39] Indeed, Zarathustra himself is described as a naive believer in words, as a prophet who preaches his beliefs in the death of God, the overman, the will to power, and the eternal return in the archaic form of the biblical language. In his dithyrambic songs he praises his drunken forgetting which is produced by his love for sounds and words: "For me—how should there be any outside-myself? There is no outside. But all sounds make us forget this; how lovely it is that we forget" (*PN*, p. 329).

But Nietzsche creates the type Zarathustra in order to use him as a strategic device that allows him to parody the holy books by mimicking their form. In *Ecce Homo* he repeats his description of Zarathustra, which he already included in *The Gay Science:*

107

The ideal of a spirit who plays naively—that is, not deliberately but from overflowing power and abundance—
with all that was hitherto called holy, good, untouch-
able, divine: for whom those supreme things that the
people naturally accept as their value standards, signify
danger, decay, debasement, or at least recreation, blindness, and temporary self-oblivion; the ideal of a human,
superhuman well-being and benevolence that will often
appear *inhuman*—for example if it puts itself alongside
of all earthly seriousness so far, all solemnity in gesture,
word, tone, eye, morality, and taste so far, as if it were
their most incarnate and involuntary parody." (*BW,*
p. 755)[40]

The parodic nature of *Zarathustra* is certainly an obvious aspect which the
reader immediately notices, since it constantly puts into question the solemn, hymnic sayings of this work. In the Preface to the second edition of
The Gay Science, Nietzsche explicitly prepares his all-too-serious readers
for the parody in *Zarathustra:* " '*Incipit tragoedia*' we read at the end of
this awesomely aweless book. Beware! Something downright wicked and
malicious is announced here: *incipit parodia,* no doubt" (*GS,* p. 33).
Indeed, the deconstructive movement in *Zarathustra* can be described as a
"parodistic, ironic repetition of the books of tradition and Nietzsche's
own text."[41] The traditional book that is most obviously parodied is the
Bible. The parallels between these two texts have been well established.[42]
Zarathustra too begins at the age of thirty a new life; he gathers his disciples; he preaches as a prophet or Messiah; he is tempted and suffers. Even
the episode of "The Last Supper" is not missing. Zarathustra's and the narrator's use of formulaic expressions, archaisms, inversions in word position, syntactical peculiarities, and parables all mimic the biblical style.
The rhythm, musicality, and hymn-like quality of *Zarathustra* are primarily achieved through an imitation of the syntactic parallelism and repetitions of phrases that we find in the Psalms. The use of the biblical style
seems to serve two strategic purposes: Zarathustra's teachings are elevated
to the lofty level of the Bible, and thereby "authenticated." But since
Zarathustra's sayings are decidedly directed against Christianity, they effectively negate the biblical messages by imitating and parodying the
biblical style itself. Of the numerous examples we shall only quote a few:
"Blessed are the sleepy ones: for they shall soon drop off" (*PN,* p. 142), or
"Except we turn back and become as cows, we shall not enter the kingdom of heaven. . . . And verily, what would it profit a man if he gained the
whole world and did not learn this one thing: chewing the cud!" (*PN,*
p. 381). And in reference to the ass festival Zarathustra says: "And when
you celebrate it again, this ass festival, do it for your own sakes, and also
do it for my sake. And in remembrance of *me*" (*PN,* p. 429).

More significant than his parody of the style and teachings of the Bible is Nietzsche's parody of Zarathustra's own style and his own teachings. In Part Three, in the chapter entitled "On Passing By," Zarathustra encounters a parody of his own "phrasing and cadences" in the speech of the fool, also called "Zarathustra's Ape," who mimics and exaggerates Zarathustra's use of parallelism, word plays, and repetitions. But the major parody of Zarathustra's teaching occurs in Part Four, which Nietzsche attempted to keep out of public circulation. We can compare this Fourth Part with the ending of *The Gay Science,* where the spirits of that book suddenly attack the author and demand that he stop with his seriousness:

> But as I slowly, slowly paint this gloomy question mark [concerning "incipit tragoedia," in reference to *Zarathustra*] at the end and am still willing to remind my readers of the virtues of the right reader—what forgotten and unknown virtues they are!—it happens that I hear all around me the most malicious, cheerful, and koboldish laughter: the spirits of my own book are attacking me, pull my ears, and call me to order. "We can no longer stand it," they shout at me, "away, away with this raven-black music! Are we not surrounded by bright morning? And by soft green grass and grounds, the kingdom of dance? Has there ever been a better hour of gaiety? Who will sing a song for us. . . ? And even simple, rustic bagpipes would be better than such mysterious sounds, such swampy croaking, voices from the grave and marmot whistles as you have employed so far to regale us in your wilderness, Mr. Hermit and Musician of the Future! No! Not such tones! Let us strike up more agreeable, more joyous tones!" (*GS,* pp. 347-48)

The author of *The Gay Science* complies with the wishes of the spirits, and he sings the "Songs of Prince Vogelfrei." Similarly it seems, that the spirits or ideas of the first three parts of *Zarathustra* gather in the Fourth Part in Zarathustra's cave to parody the seriousness of the first three parts. Commentators of *Zarathustra* have had great difficulties with this Fourth Part. In order to save the seeming unity and seriousness of the first three parts, they have chosen to ignore the last part by claiming that its non-seriousness was due to Nietzsche's declining health. Eugen Fink, who sees the climax of *Zarathustra* in the Third Part, writes: "If Nietzsche had closed his work with the Third Part, it would have a strict stylistic unity: the form of conveying new philosophical ideas through parables. . . . In the Fourth Part embarrassing and awful derailments occur; the whole Fourth Part is a sudden fall. Somehow the poetic-philosophical vision seems to be exhausted. This Fourth Part hangs on to the work like an evil, malicious satyr play. . . ."[43] But Nietzsche seems to have carefully planned and calculated the change in tone and style. He wrote to his friend Peter Gast: "By the way I have to report to you not without grief, that now, with the Third Part, poor Zarathustra really falls into gloominess— . . . My plan demands it this way. . . . (At the end [Part Four] everything becomes bright again)." In a later letter to Gast he described the Fourth Part as "having been written with the frame of mind of a buffoon." And to his friend Gersdorff he wrote in 1888: "There exists a Fourth (and Last) Part of *Zarathustra,* a kind of sublime finale which is not at all meant for the public."[44] The narrative point of view, the tone and tempo radically shift in this Fourth Part. Whereas Zarathustra speaks to the crowd, his disciples, or to himself in the first three parts, he speaks very little in the last part. Most of the sections are taken up by the higher men and the ass, who parody Zarathustra's sayings, and Zarathustra himself seems to join this parody of his own teaching. His holy yes-saying to life, to the eternal recurrence of the same, is parodied in the Fourth Part by the ass's repeated braying "I-A" [J-A], which means "yes" in German. Not only does Zarathustra join the braying of the ass (*PN,* p. 425), but he is told that he could quite easily be an ass: "And whoever has too much wisdom might well grow foolishly fond of stupidity and folly itself. Think about yourself, O Zarathustra! You yourself—verily, over-abundance and wisdom could easily turn you too into an ass. Is not the perfect sage fond of walking on the most crooked ways? The evidence shows this, O Zarathustra—and *you* are the evidence" (*PN,* p. 427). Indeed Zarathustra surmises that these higher men are merry "at their host's expense." Viewed in this perspective, the litany in praise of the "adored and censed ass" can be read as a parody of Zarathustra's teachings, since the ass is without question the most yes-saying of all creatures. This whole section is also curiously entitled "The Awakening."[45]

Even the narrator who has been very unobtrusive and effacing in the first three parts, begins in the Fourth Part to question the veracity of his account by suggesting that there are several different versions of Zarathustra's life: "But the old soothsayer was dancing with joy; and even if, as some of the chroniclers think, he was full of sweet wine, he was certainly still fuller of the sweetness of life and he had renounced all weariness. There are even some who relate that the ass danced too. . . . Now it may have been so or otherwise. . . . In short, as the proverb of Zarathustra says: 'What does it matter' " (*PN,* p. 430).

But the most pervasive questioning of all of Zarathustra's teachings stems from the Magician's metalinguistic statements. He suggests that Zarathustra's sayings concerning the overman, the will to power, the death of God, and the eternal return are only rhetorical tropes, only lies. Zarathustra's speeches are "banished from all truth/Only fool! only poet!" (*PN,* p. 412). Zarathustra is exposed as a magician himself, as an actor, liar, counterfeiter, as a seducer who knows that he deceives. The Magician's song "Only Fool! Only Poet!" presents one of the most obvious moments of remembering the problematics of language in the rhythmical alternations between persuasive and constative language. In his introductory remarks to his song, the Magician leaves no doubt that he is singing of Zarathustra:

> "Suitor of truth?" They [the glowing glances of the sun]
>   mocked me; "you?
> No! Only poet!
> An animal, cunning, preying, prowling,
> That must lie,
> That must knowingly, willingly lie:
> Lusting for prey,
> Colorfully masked,
> A mask for itself,
> Prey for itself—
> *This,* the suitor of truth?
> No! Only fool! only poet!
> Only speaking colorfully,
> Only screaming colorfully out of fools' masks,
> Climbing around on mendacious word bridges,
> On colorful rainbows,
> Between false heavens
> And false earths,
> Roaming, hovering—
> Only fool! Only poet!"
>
> *(PN,* p. 410)

The Magician points out that any such insight into the nature of language makes any persuasive use of language impossible. He calls this awareness of rhetorical tropes the "adversary of this Zarathustra" (*PN,* p. 408). But true to the rhythmical alternation, the Magician's song is followed by the Wanderer's song about forgetting, about sitting like a date in the sun, without past or future.

Although the Magician's song is undoubtedly the most noticeable segment that puts Zarathustra's teachings into question on the grounds of Nietzsche's own insights into the nature of language, this passage is by no means an isolated moment. The Magician repeats in his song Zarathustra's own words from Part Three, where he uses the same images in order to praise words as a means of forgetting:

> "O my animals," replied Zarathustra, "chatter on like
> this and let me listen. It is so refreshing for me to hear
> you chattering: where there is chattering, there the
> world lies before me like a garden. How lovely it is that

111

there are words and sounds! Are not words and sounds rainbows and illusive bridges between things which are eternally apart? ... Precisely between what is most similar, illusion lies most beautifully; for the smallest cleft is the hardest to bridge. ... But all sounds make us forget this; how lovely it is that we forget. ... Speaking is a beautiful folly; with that man dances over all things. How lovely is all talking, and all the deception of sounds!" (*PN,* p. 329)

Zarathustra even describes his whole enterprise as one of writing poetry, of poetizing the overman by shaping into one that which is not equal: "And this is all my poetizing [*Dichten*] and striving, that I create and carry into One what is fragment and riddle and dreadful accident" (*PN,* p. 251). And in the section "On Poets" in Part Two, Zarathustra directly states that he himself is a poet, and that he has to lie:

But what was it that Zarathustra once said to you? That poets lie too much? But Zarathustra too is a poet ... *we* do lie too much. ... Alas, there are so many things between heaven and earth of which only the poets have dreamed. And especially *above* the heavens: For all gods are poets' parables, poets' frauds [*Dichter-Erschleichnis*]! Verily, it always pulls us higher, namely to the realm of the clouds: upon these we place our motley bastards and call them gods and overmen. For they are just light enough for these chairs—all these gods and overmen. (*PN,* pp. 239-40)

Zarathustra seems to be very much aware that his idea of the overman is only a poetic lie. He therefore repeatedly warns his readers of his poetic speeches, of his parables: "... that I speak in parables and limp and stammer like poets, and verily, I am ashamed that I must still be a poet" (*PN,* p. 309). Any concepts, any labels, be they traditional ones or "new" valorizations, are, according to Zarathustra, only parables. And he adds: "A fool is he who wants knowledge of them" (*PN,* p. 187). He similarly challenges any formulation of the eternal, hence permanent return of the same, since "all that is 'permanent' is also a mere parable" (*PN,* p. 238).[46]

Zarathustra's repeated awareness of the necessary falsity of all signs leads him at times to claim that all his speeches are mere noise that hides his silence: "It is my favorite malice and art that my silence has learned not to betray itself through silence. Rattling with discourse and dice, I outwit those who wait solemnly: my wit and purpose shall elude all these severe inspectors. That no one may discern my ground and ultimate will, for that I have invented my long bright silence" (*PN,* p. 286). Nietzsche himself seems to put his writings under erasure in the form of *Gedan-kenstriche.* [47]

We have been reading the passages on silence, the contradictions, negations, metalinguistic statements, the parodies and self-parodies as repeated moments in Nietzsche's process of signification. This process consists of the sequential rhythmical alternation between segments of forgetting and remembering. In positing his myths of the overman, the will to power, the death of God, and the eternal recurrence, Zarathustra uses almost every known ruse to authenticate his sayings and to persuade his readers. He claims having had a mythical, unmediated vision of truth ("and I have seen the truth naked" [*PN,* p. 242]), and he is directly spoken to by Life itself (*PN,* p. 338). He not only posits "new" tablets, but he presents himself as the one who can produce "new," "true" signs: "Here the words and word-shrines of all being open up before me: here all being wishes to become word, all becoming wishes to learn from me how to speak" (*PN,* p. 296). These are powerful strategies which Zarathustra uses in order to persuade his readers. But we have also noticed that these textual segments, in which Zarathustra posits his myths, are followed by segments that undermine the foundations of these myths. This play of building and destroying, of asserting and doubting, of riding old myths and parodying them, of lyrical flights and self-parody seems to form Nietzsche's zerography. This circular motion, which rhythmically passes through the moments of forgetting and remembering, puts everything into question: the metalinguistic statements, as well as the counter-myths of the overman, the will to power, the death of God, through which Zarathustra attempts to displace the Christian myths.

We again pose our initial question: What is the difference between a note in Nietzsche's notebook and the same one included in one of his works? Nietzsche composed *Zarathustra* from the numerous notes he wrote. But the notes included in *Zarathustra* are caught up in the flux, in the movement of deconstruction, whereas the note in the notebook is isolated and unambiguous, since its meaning has not been put into question. We may recognize now the danger and the problems involved in quoting not only from Nietzsche's notes, but from his works, since through quoting we "freeze" the sense of a passage, whose meaning is undecidable, since it is in a fluid state and caught within the movement of Nietzsche's zerography. Since we are interested in analyzing Nietzsche's signifying process, we primarily focus our attention on the works that were composed by Nietzsche, but which have been ignored by recent commentators. We regard Nietzsche's notebooks as almost any other writer's notebooks: they are normally filled with observations, thoughts, quotes from other books, plans, first drafts, etc. These notes are normally written at different times and different places. We do not tend to regard these notebooks as the writer's key work. If we make them the center of Nietzsche's work, we ig-

nore the movement of deconstruction, Nietzsche's zerography, which puts
all the assertions in these notes into question.

The University of Iowa

NOTES

1   Walter Kaufmann, "Jaspers' Relation to Nietzsche," in *The Philosophy of Karl Jaspers,* ed. Paul A. Schilpp (New York: Tudor, 1957), p. 428.

2   Arthur C. Danto, *Nietzsche as Philosopher* (New York: Macmillan, 1965), p. 13.

3   Karl Löwith, *Nietzsches Philosophie der ewigen Wiederkehr des Gleichen,* 2nd ed. (Stuttgart: Kohlhammer, 1956), p. 64.

4   Rudolf Steiner, "Die Philosophie Friedrich Nietzsches als psychopathologisches Problem," *Wiener Klinische Rundschau,* 14 (1900), 598-618; P. M. Möbius, *Über das Pathologische bei Nietzsche* (Wiesbaden: J. F. Bergmann, 1902).

5   Arthur Drews, *Nietzsches Philosophie* (Heidelberg: C. Winter, 1904); Eugen Fink, *Nietzsches Philosophie* (Stuttgart: Kohlhammer, 1960).

6   Walter Kaufmann, *Nietzsche, Philosopher, Psychologist, Antichrist,* 4th ed. (Princeton: Princeton Univ. Press, 1974), p. iii.

7   Kaufmann, *Nietzsche, Philosopher, Psychologist, Antichrist,* p. iii.

8   Kaufmann, "Jaspers' Relation to Nietzsche," p. 428.

9   Martin Heidegger, *Nietzsche* (Pfullingen: Neske, 1961), I, p. 481 (hereafter cited as *N*).

10   Philippe Lacoue-Labarthe, "L'oblitération," *Critique,* 313 (1973), 492.

11   François Laruelle, "Heidegger et Nietzsche," *Magazine Littéraire,* 117 (1976), 13. See the full development of his argument in his *Nietzsche contre Heidegger* (Paris: Payot, 1977).

12   Martin Heidegger, *What is Called Thinking?,* trans. J. Glenn Gray (New York: Harper and Row, 1968), p. 57.

13   "Spiegel-Gespräch mit Martin Heidegger," *Der Spiegel,* 23 (1976), 204.

14   Georges Bataille, *Sur Nietzsche* (Paris: Gallimard, 1945).

15   Pierre Klossowski, *Le cercle vicieux* (Paris: Mercure de France, 1969).

16   *Nietzsche Werke. Kritische Gesamtausgabe [KGW],* eds. Giorgio Colli and Mazzino Montinari (Berlin: de Gruyter, 1967-   ), III, 2, p. 383.

17   Maurice Blanchot, *Entretien Infini* (Paris: Gallimard, 1969), pp. 227, 231, 232.

18   Jacques Derrida, "La question du style," in *Nietzsche aujourd'hui?* (Paris: Union Générale d' Editions, 1973), I, 267. For a detailed analysis of Derrida's essay, see David B. Allison, "Destruction/Deconstruction in the Text of Nietzsche," *boundary 2,* VIII (Fall, 1979), 197-222.

19   Derrida, "La question du style," p. 280; *KGW,* V, 2, p. 480: " 'ich habe meinen Regenschirm vergessen.' "

20   Derrida, "La question du style," p. 267; "Tout cela à la fois, simultanément ou successivement, selon les lieux de son corps et les positions de son histoire."

21   Derrida, "La question du style," p. 287.

22   Derrida made this statement in his interview with Lucette Finas, which is published in *Ecarts,* ed. L. Finas, S. Kofman, R. Laporte, and J.—M. Rey (Paris: Fayard, 1973), p. 311.

23   Derrida recognizes Nietzsche as "having contributed a great deal to the liberation of the signifier from its dependence or derivation with respect to the logos, and the related concept of truth or the primary signified." See *De la grammatologie* (Paris: Editions de Minuit, 1967), pp. 31-32.

24   Bernard Pautrat, *Versions du soleil. Figures et système de Nietzsche* (Paris: Editions du Seuil, 1971), p. 266.

25   Jean-Michel Rey, *L'enjeu des signes. Lecture de Nietzsche* (Paris: Editions du Seuil, 1971), p. 7. Sarah Kofman's study is entitled *Nietzsche et la métaphore* (Paris: Payot, 1972).

26   A fuller discussion of these three studies on Nietzsche can be found in my essay, "Nietzsche und die Semiologie: Neue Ansätze in der französischen Nietzsche-Interpretation," *Nietzsche-Studien,* V (1976), 263-88.

27   Karl Jaspers, *Nietzsche: An Introduction to the Understanding of His Philosophical Activity,* trans. Charles F. Wallraff and Frederick J. Schmitz (Tucson: Univ. of Arizona Press, 1965), p. 10. Jaspers published his study on Nietzsche in 1936.

28   Jaspers, *Nietzsche,* p. 10.

29   Thomas Mann, "Nietzsches Philosophie im Lichte unserer Erfahrung," in *Schriften und Reden zur Literatur, Kunst und Philosophie* (Frankfurt: Fischer, 1968), III, p. 27.

30   In *Nietzsche-Studien,* 1 (1972), 359-79.

31   See *Prétexte: Roland Barthes,* ed. A. Compagnon (Paris: Union Générale d'Editions, 1978), p. 238. I am indebted to my colleague Steven Ungar for having elicited Barthes' statement concerning Nietzsche's texts.

32   See Jean-Louis Barrault, et al., *Nietzsche: A propos de 'Ainsi parlait Zarathustra'* (Paris: Gallimard, 1974), p. 10.

33   Paul de Man, "Rhetoric of Persuasion (Nietzsche)," in his *Allegories of Read-*

ing (New Haven: Yale Univ. Press, 1979), p. 131: "Considered as persuasion, rhetoric is performative, but when considered as system of tropes, it deconstructs its own performance." My own reading of *Zarathustra* is indebted to de Man's three essays on Nietzsche in *Allegories of Reading*.

34   See Friedrich Nietzsche, *Werke,* ed. Karl Schlecta (München, Hanser, 1956), I, p. 213.

35   *KGW,* VII, 1, p. 648.

36   *The Gay Science,* trans. Walter Kaufmann (New York: Vintage, 1974), pp. 37-38 (hereafter cited as *GS*).

37   *Genealogy of Morals,* quoted from *Basic Writings of Nietzsche,* trans. Walter Kaufmann (New York: Modern Library, 1968), p. 494 (hereafter cited as *BW*).

38   *Friedrich Nietzsches gesammelte Briefe* (Leipzig: Insel, 1903-   ), V, p. 617.

39   Quoted from *The Portable Nietzsche,* trans. Walter Kaufmann (New York: Viking, 1968), p. 139 (hereafter cited as *PN*).

40   See also *GS,* p. 347. Compare also the following statement of Nietzsche, in which he regards *The Gay Science* as a "Preparation to Zarathustra's naive-ironic position towards all holy things (new form of superiority: the playing with the saint) . . . Zarathustra who in a holy manner sets courage and mockery against anything holy" (In *Grossoktavausgabe* [Leipzig: Naumann, 1894-   ], XIV, p. 405).

41   See Gerhard Rupp, *Rhetorische Strukturen und kommunikative Determinanz* (Bern: Herbert Lang, 1976), p. 88.

42   See Siegfried Vitens, *Die Sprachkunst Friedrich Nietzsches in "Also sprach Zarathustra"* (Bremen-Horn: Dorn, 1951), pp. 31-43.

43   Eugen Fink, *Nietzsches Philosophie* (Stuttgart: Kohlhammer, 1960), p. 114. See also Anke Bennholdt-Thomson, *Nietzsches "Also sprach Zarathustra" als literarisches Phenomen* (Frankfurt: Athenäum, 1974). Her discussion of the Fourth Part seems to deconstruct her whole argument. Compare also Claude Lévesque's essay on *Zarathustra* entitled "Le puits d'éternité," in his L'Etrangeté du texte (Paris: Union Générale d' Editions, 1978). Lévesque only focuses on two sections of the Fourth Part, in order to maintain the coherence and unity of his argument concerning silence.

44   *Briefe an Peter Gast,* ed. Peter Gast (Leipzig, 1924), Nr. 145 and Nr. 164. The letter to Gersdorff is quoted from Friedrich Nietzsche, *Werke,* ed. Karl Schlechta (München: Hanser, 1956), III, p. 1228.

45   Walter Kaufmann suggestively compares this self-parody in *Zarathustra* with Nietzsche's remarks in *Ecce Homo,* where he states that he would rather be a buffoon than be pronounced holy: "I *want* no 'believers'; I think I am too mendacious to believe in myself. . . . I have a terrible fear that one day I will be pronounced *holy*. . . . I do not want to be a holy man; sooner even a buffoon. Perhaps I am a buffoon" (*BW,* p. 782). Walter Kaufmann's comments are in *PN,* p. 344.

46   This statement forms part of Nietzsche's parody of Goethe's "Chorus Mysticus" at the end of *Faust:* "Everything transient/ Is only a parable. . . ." Nietzsche parodied the whole chorus in the first poem of his collection, "Songs of Prince Vogelfrei," which forms the *finale* of *The Gay Science.* See Sander L. Gilman's study on *Nietzschean Parody. An Introduction to Reading Nietzsche* (Bonn: Bouvier, 1976) for a very useful discussion of Nietzsche's parodies of Goethe and Poe, and of Nietzsche's strategic use of parody in general.

47   See *Friedrich Nietzsches gesammelte Briefe* (Leipzig: Insel, 1903-), V, p. 617: ". . . für mich selber geht es immer erst mit den Gedankenstrichen los." I read here *Gedankenstriche* not as "dash," but as "crossing out ideas, thoughts." Otto Olzien's useful study on *Nietzsche und das Problem der dichterischen Sprache* (Berlin: Junker and Dünnhaupt, 1941) has as its main theme the tension between Zarathustra's wanting to express his ideas and his inability to express them in words. Bernard Pautrat also analyzes *Zarathustra* as being organized around Nietzsche's silence concerning his ideas and his inability to express them in words. Bernard Pautrat also analyzes *Zarathustra* as being organized around Nietzsche's silence concerning his idea of the eternal return. This absence of the center marks, according to Pautrat, the hole, Medusa's head, in the text of *Zarathustra.* See his "Nietzsche médusé," in *Nietzsche aujourd'hui?* (Paris: Union Générald d' Editions, 1973), I, pp. 9-30.

Nietzsche's Graffito: A Reading of *The Antichrist*

Gary Shapiro

Even those writers who have good things to say about Nietzsche usually do not have good things to say abut his penultimate book, *The Antichrist*. Like *Ecce Homo* it is often described as at least prefiguring Nietzsche's madness if not (as is sometimes the case) said to be part of that desperate glide itself. Those inclined to reject the book may be encouraged in this view by Nietzsche's statement to Brandes, in November 1888, that *The Antichrist* is the whole of *The Transvaluation of All Values* (originally announced as a series of four books) and that *Ecce Homo* is its necessary prelude. The reader will have already discerned my intention of retrieving this exorbitant text for the Nietzschean canon. Such operations of retrieval are standard enough moves within a certain kind of philological discourse which privileges the book as an expressive or cognitive totality. But Nietzsche, the arch philologist, is today often regarded as not only undercutting the grounds of such moves by challenging their hermeneutic presuppositions but as having exemplified in a paradigmatic fashion the discontinuous, fragmentary or porous text. The second view of Nietzsche's writings is a very traditional one; it is a commonplace with Nietzsche's earlier readers to regard all of his writing as distressingly wanting in order and style, despite their admiration for his thought. Such has continued to be the assumption of Anglo-American readers like Walter Kaufmann and Arthur Danto, who have aimed at articulating the internal order of Nietzsche's thought which the stylistic fireworks of the texts obscure. Recent French readers, most notably Jacques Derrida, have tried to show that fragmentation and undecidability are not merely secondary features of Nietzsche's writing but constitute its very element. Derrida outrageously suggests that the jotting "I forgot my umbrella" is typical of *all* Nietzsche's writing in its ambiguity and undecidability of meaning and in its systematic evasion of all contextual explication. One might wonder whether such a strategy of reading is indebted to Nietzsche's own hermeneutic strategy in *The Antichrist.* There Nietzsche anticipates Heidegger and Derrida by relying on the figure of *erasure* to designate his own relation to Christianity, its textual traditions, and its central figure, Jesus. Following the nineteenth century philological and historical methods to their extreme and thereby overturning and transvaluing (*umkehren* and *umwerten*) both the methods and Christianity, Nietzsche tries to restore the blank page which is Jesus' life to its pristine purity of white paper, *tabula rasa.* In this respect Nietzsche's project is very much like Robert Rauschenberg's erased De Kooning and like Derrida's attempt to shatter any determinate meaning in Nietzsche himself by revealing the irreducible plurality of woman in the apparent masculine ambitions of order and control in Nietzsche's style. All of these efforts nevertheless remain marked with the *signatures* of their authors; the negation of a negation cannot be negation itself. At the end there is Rauschenberg's art, Derrida's project of deconstruction, Nietzsche's graffito scrawled on the Christian text. This, however, is to anticipate the results of my project of retrieval.

Just as erasure is always an act which leaves its own mark, so retrieval is possible but need not produce that totalizing organic unity which has been the constant phantom of aesthetic thought. If retrieval is always partial it is also easier because the excesses of Nietzsche's readers here have been egregious. Consider, for example, Eugen Fink's Heideggerean book on Nietzsche which contains only a brief analysis of *The Antichrist,* dismissing its philosophical value:

> In the text *The Antichrist* (*Attempt at a Critique of Christianity*) Nietzsche battles against the Christian religion with an unparalleled fervor of hatred, and with a flood of invectives and accusations. Here the virtuosity of his attack, leaving no stone unturned, reverses itself. The lack of measure destroys the intended effect; one can't be convincing while foaming at the mouth. Essentially the text offers nothing new; Nietzsche collects what he has already said about the morality of pity and the psychology of the priest—but now he gives

his thoughts an exorbitant, violent edge and wants to insult, to strike the tradition in the face, to "transvalue" by valuing in an anti-Christian way.[1]

Fink's comment suggests that his reasons for thinking that "the text offers nothing new" may be just the stylistic excesses and rhetorical failings of which he accuses it. Certainly his judgment on the book follows well-established opinion about its place in the Nietzsche canon. Even when the book is regarded as a culminating work (applying a dubious schema of linear development), it is usually employed to demonstrate the tragedy of Nietzsche's career as author and thinker. Karl Löwith calls it the "logical conclusion" of the critique of Christianity begun in the untimely meditation on D. F. Strauss, author of the nineteenth century's first great life of Jesus. Yet according to Löwith even this late work shows that Nietzsche has not escaped his obsession with Christianity. From this perspective we would have to say that Nietzsche the philosopher is not free of the bad blood of German theology which he denounces so vehemently:

> Among Germans one will understand immediately when I say that philosophy has been corrupted by theologian blood. The Protestant pastor is the grandfather of German philosophy, Protestantism itself is *peccatum originale.* (A 10)[2]

It could then be argued that the growth and intensity of the obsession is part of the madness which prevented Nietzsche from seeing the book through to publication and which led him to consider it, alternatively as the first part of the *Transvaluation,* as the entire *Transvaluation,* and then as the *Curse on Christendom* which required *Ecce Homo* as a balance.[3] Yet even the last self-interpretation permits another construction: *Ecce Homo* balances *The Antichrist* by showing that the great curser and destroyer is one who lives in the halcyon element of the "perfect day, when everything is ripening and not only the grape turns brown" and asks *"How could I fail to be grateful to my whole life?"*[4]

What Arthur Danto calls the "unrelievedly vituperative" tone of the book is everywhere evident. At the conclusion of the book Nietzsche says of the Christian church that "to me, it is the extremest thinkable form of corruption, it has had the will to the ultimate corruption conceivably possible. The Christian church has left nothing untouched by its depravity . . ." (A 62). And Nietzsche pushes the rhetorical contrast to the extreme by defending the Roman Empire against Christianity, inverting the usual belief in the civilizing virtue or necessity of the latter's conversion of the former:

> Christianity was the vampire of the *Imperium Romanum* ... this most admirable of all works of art in the grand style was a beginning, its structure was calculated to *prove* itself by millennia. ... But it was not firm enough to endure the *corruptest* form of corruption, to endure the *Christian*. ... These stealthy vermin which, shrouded in night, fog and ambiguity crept up to every individual and sucked seriousness for *real* things, the instinct for *realities* of any kind, out of him, this cowardly, womanish and honeyed crew gradually alienated the "souls" of this tremendous structure ... (A 58)

It is this tone which might be taken to justify the reduction of Nietzsche's thought to the first-liner of a graffito sometimes found in modern cells and catacombs:

> God is dead—Nietzsche
> Nietzsche is dead—God

This reduction could appear to be the creative interpretation of a masterful will to power—if Nietzsche's thought and style are as uncontrolled as the critics suggest. Yet there are some signs at the beginning and end of the book which might lead us to pause. Nietzsche himself anticipates the strife of revengeful graffiti at the conclusion of his text:

> Wherever there are walls I shall inscribe this eternal accusation against Christianity upon them—I can write in letters which make even the blind see ... (A 62)

At the same time Nietzsche says in his preface that his readers must have a "predestination for the labyrinth" and "new ears for new music" if they are to understand this difficult writing. So like all of Nietzsche's books, *The Antichrist* is self-referential. It is concerned with those very questions of how it is to be read and how it exists as a piece of writing which we are disposed to think of as derivative and external interests of the critic and historian. The words which can be written on the wall are also directed by a powerful thought and a complex rhetorical strategy.

In *Ecce Homo* Nietzsche imagines "a perfect reader" who would be "a monster of courage and curiosity; moreover, supple, cunning, cautious; a born adventurer and discoverer" (EH 3). *The Antichrist* is in need of such readers and its need is compounded and complicated by the fact that it offers a Nietzschean account of what might variously be called interpretation, hermeneutics, or semiotics. To see this point it is necessary to contest an expressivist or emotivist reading of the text. That is we must question the assumption that because of the emotional intensity of its utterance we must read the book primarily as an outburst of rage or hostility. The rage and hostility are there in abundance; but we should not assume that their very presence excludes a significant structure of thought or that a writing with such a tone could not possibly contain any new thoughts of its own.

As both the inscription and the quotation from Nietzsche suggest, a graffito, whatever its peculiarly individual and private aspects, is inscribed in a public space, often in reply to others and inviting its own challenges and defacements. Like other texts, but in a self-conscious way, *The Antichrist* makes sense only in relation to other texts. It is a book which recalls a number of a similar genre (lives of Christ, polemical histories of religion) which were an important part of nineteenth century thought. Even its title is one which had been used, for somewhat different purposes (in 1873) by Ernest Renan, in a book which Nietzsche read a year before writing his own *Antichrist.* It is worth pointing out that Renan is a frequent antagonist both in *The Antichrist* and in other texts of the same period. In Renan's *Antichrist,* the Antichrist is Nero; not Nero merely as a savage persecutor but as the anxious parodic artist whose terrible and genuine aesthetic accomplishment is the theater of cruelty. Renan credits Nero with the discovery of a new form of beauty in which the defenseless virgin torn by the wild beast replaces the classic beauty of the integral and well-formed sculpture. Did Nietzsche, whose juxtaposition of Rome and Christianity is a constant theme of *The Antichrist* and *The Genealogy of Morals* identify himself with Nero? Perhaps only later when, mad, he entertains fantasies of imperial or divine power and writes "I am all the names of history"; Renan notes that Nero's histrionic ambitions led him to imitate or parody all of the great poetry of the classical world.[5]

These resonances are meant to suggest that *The Antichrist* is not immediate expression but a book which refers us back to other books and that the processes of writing, interpreting, reading, censoring and defacing are so far from being taken for granted that they form the chief means of elucidating Nietzsche's attack on Christianity. Nietzsche's *Antichrist* is full of references to the texts of the Old and New Testaments, to their textual histories, to the priestly fraudulence which produced them, to the texts of the liberal apologists for religion of the nineteenth century, to the textual sophistication of philologists and to the possible text, better and more accurate than all the others, which Dostoyesvsky or his like would have written if alive at the time of Jesus. Within this context *The Antichrist* offers, at its heart, one more narrative of the life of Jesus and one of the choicest examples of what Paul Ricouer has called the hermeneutics of suspicion.

All of the book either leads up to or proceeds from Nietzsche's concern with the textual politics of Judaism and Christianity. That Nietzsche should focus so much of his attention on the way in which the Bible was successively produced, edited, re-edited, interpreted and criticized could be justified simply in terms of the Jewish and Christian claims to be religions of the book. But Nietzsche has more specific reasons for this concern. All morality is a semiotic interpretation of the body and society; if there is to be a transvaluation of values it must proceed by offering a new reading of that which has been misread. So we find, as in *The Geneaology of Morals,* that the great hermeneutical conflict in *The Antichrist* is between the priest and the philologist. Nietzsche's great enemy is Paul, whom he credits with a genius for lying which was immediately taken up by the church; in doing so he and they declare war on the philologists:

> Paul *wants* to confound the "wisdom of the world": his enemies are the *good* philologists and physicians of the Alexandrian School—upon them he makes war. In fact, one is not philologist and physician without also being at the same time *anti-Christian.* For as philologist one sees *behind* the "sacred books", as physician *behind* the physiological depravity of the typical Christian. The physician says "incurable", the philologist "fraud"...
> (A 47)

The paradigm of priestly misreading and fraud is to be found in the editing of the Old Testament. Nietzsche accepts the general results of the higher criticism here, although his tone is completely different from the scholarly objectivity at which the professional philologists aimed. Just ten years before the writing of *The Antichrist,* Julius Wellhausen had written his *Prolegomena to the History of Ancient Israel* in which he argued that the Law could not be the basis of the histories and prophetic writings but must have been composed at a later date.[6] More specifically he attempted to show that it was only during the exile, following the Assyrian victory in the sixth century, that the shift occurred from Israel—a land of warriors, kings, and prophets—to Judaism, a religion of extensive law and ritual reserving a special place of power for the priests. It was the priests who attempted to preserve the life of their people even at the cost of exchanging a vital life for ritualistic constraint, and part of the price to be paid for this change would be a tremendous enhancement of the power of the priest within Judaism. In order to consolidate their power they edited the sacred writings which already existed and added new ones of their own which radically displaced priestly law and the political supremacy of the priest much further back into the past, providing them with divine and traditional sanction. The work of Wellhausen and others like him is not at all Nietzschean in tone; it is not only firmly grounded in contemporary philology but offers a brilliant example of how that philology could be employed with methodical precision in order to produce works of the greatest scope. Nietzsche alludes to this scholarly tradition although he never explicitly mentions Wellhausen. Certainly the five stage history which Nietzsche offers of Judaism and which he declares to be "invaluable as a typical history of the *denaturalizing* of natural values" is a radicalization of Wellhausen's segmentation of that history (A 25-7). Wellhausen's method of distinguishing exilic and pre-exilic Judaism is here filtered through the opposition of "good and bad," "good and evil" and the psychology of the priest. This capsule history may bear some comparison with that which Nietzsche had written concerning ontological inversion in his last book, *The Twilight of the Idols:* "How the True World Became An Error." According to Nietzsche the strata of Jewish history are: (1) "in the period of the Kingdom, Israel too stood in a *correct,* that is to say natural relationship to all things. Their Yahweh was the expression of their consciousness of power, of their delight in themselves, their hopes of themselves"; (2) After internal anarchy and external oppression have destroyed this natural state, it remains as an ideal—expressed by the prophets; (3) when the ideal fails as an ideal, Yahweh becomes *only* a god of justice "in the hands of priestly agitators" who establish that most mendacious mode of interpretation of a supposed "moral world-order"; (4) the priests, who have seized power within Judaism rewrite history in order to disparage the earlier great age in which the priest counted for nothing; (5) the rise of Christianity extends priestly *ressentiment* to all hierarchy and rank by attacking the conception of the Jewish people (the chosen people) as such. For Nietzsche this is not a new narrative analysis except insofar as it extends and intensifies his philological conception of history as a forceful reading and rereading of texts. When Nietzsche says that there are only interpretations he must be understood not as licensing all interpretations whatsoever but as indicating that all meaning and all change of meaning are exercises of power. To the extent that we accept this principle we are being prepared not only for the content of Nietzsche's erasure of Jesus but for an understanding of how such an operation is possible. What Nietzsche objects to in priestly reading is hardly forceful interpretation as such but that particular interpretation "the moral world-order" which is incapable of recognizing itself as interpretation.

Consider the following observation or priestly reading from Nietzsche's history of the five stages:

> the "will of God" (that is to say the conditions for preserving the power of the priest) has to be *known*—to this end a "revelation" is required. In plain words a great literary forgery becomes necessary, a "sacred book" is discovered—it is made public with all hieratic pomp,

> with days of repentance and with lamentation over the
> long years of "sinfulness" . . . the whole evil lay in the
> nation's having become estranged from the "sacred
> book". (A 26)

The passage is noteworthy for several reasons, and not the least of them is a typographical one. The extensive use of quotation marks is a philosophical device for quite literally *bracketing* the ideas and expressions with which Nietzsche is dealing. Unlike Husserlian bracketing, Nietzschean quotation is not so much designed to put the ontological status of its objects into doubt, but to suggest that we are dealing here with what has been said by specific people on specific occasions, perhaps gathering force through being repeated or reprinted. As opposed to conceptual analysis it refuses to grant that its objects are part of an impersonal world of ideas to be assessed on their own merits. Instead they are texts which issue from and are signs of power; to put them into quotation marks is to show that the method employed here is that of textual politics. In analyzing the Bible and the culture of the Bible this synthesis of philology and the hermeneutics of power finds its most important and most inexhaustible subject. That which is quoted is often provided with a translation: "sacrifice" is food for the priests, and " 'God forgives him who repents'—in German: *who subjects himself to the priest"* (A 26). Transvaluation is accomplished by translation. What gives the book its fevered pitch and shrill tone is this *duality,* its constant sense of turning one extreme into another. The duality is introduced by Nietzsche's own catechism of values defining good and bad in terms of power and weakness (A 2), is continued through a declaration of war on theology (A 9), and concludes with the antithetical translations of Biblical language and an anti-narrative of the life of Jesus. Within the Christian tradition itself the church has been constructed "out of the antithesis to the Gospel" (A 36) and Paul "embodied the antithetical type to the 'bringer of glad tidings' " (A 42). What seems at first like stylistic excess is simply a consistent carrying through of the polarity announced by the book's title. In a letter to Georg Brandes, Nietzsche himself indicates that such an analysis is appropriate when he calls the *Umwertung* a trope.[7] It is not just a deflection from the imagined normal path of thought but a movement of inversion and upending.

     In this sharp play of oppositions there are also some surprising continuities. Christianity is simply a continuation of Judaism and the New Testament employs a falsification similar to that of the Old. At the same time things which seemed to belong together turn out to be opposed: the real contrast is not Judaism and Christianity but early Israel, with its heroism and passion, and the later development of both religions; Jesus is not the origin of the church but its opposite. More radically Jesus is the antithesis of Christianity because the real " 'glad tidings' are precisely that there are not more opposites" (A 32), while Christianity is committed to the antithetical "good and evil" mode of valuation which Nietzsche analyzed in *The Genealogy of Morals.*

Jesus is the center of *The Antichrist,* but it is possible to reach him only by decoding and restoring the false oppositions of the gospels and the Church. The Church led by Paul is said to have practiced the same falsification on the life of Jesus as the priests of Judaism did on the early history of Israel. The more modern and more secular quest for the historical Jesus (Nietzsche refers explicitly to the work of D. F. Strauss and Renan and shows a familiarity with other toilers in this philological vineyard) does not arrive at its object for it is vitiated by the same assumption which structured the earliest accounts. That assumption is that the truth about Jesus must take the form of a story or narrative. Whether the principles are the miraculous history which begins with a remarkable birth and is punctuated by incursions of the supernatural or whether we are presented with a demythologized Jesus, there is a common presupposition that there is a significant temporal sequence of events which will illuminate the life of Jesus. Nietzsche proposes an ahistorical and non-narrative psychology of the redeemer, according to which Jesus was, in our everyday language "blissed out." Nietzsche's Jesus does not develop from a theological perspective because he is not a supernatural figure; no divine interventions mark off the different stages of his career. But neither does he develop in the secular and biographical sense because his whole life and teachings consist in the notion that the kingdom of heaven is a present condition of the heart to which we can all have instant access by becoming as children. All which seems to be fixed is melted down into its experiential import. "If I understand anything of this great symbolist," Nietzsche says, "it is that he took for realities, for 'truths,' only *inner* realities—that he understood the rest, everything pertaining to nature, time, space, history, only as signs, as occasion for metaphor" (A 39). In calling Jesus "a symbolist *par excellence*" Nietzsche suggests that Jesus is both the origin of the many interpretations which have accrued to him (or, more accurately, which have been *imposed* on him) and that he is also the refutation of all these interpretations. Jesus is a symbolist in the late nineteenth century sense of an artist who seeks to reveal a single great timeless insight through a variety of devices; like Jesus' parables none of these will be perfectly adequate to its subject matter, yet taken collectively they will all point to the ineffable experience which generates them. Symbolism is a non-narrative and nonrepresentational style; if it uses narrative or representational elements, as Jesus sometimes does, they are employed metaphorically in order to point beyond themselves. A true symbolist such as the one under analysis "stands outside of all religion, all conceptions of divine worship, all history, all natural science, all experience of the world, all acquirements, all psychology, all books, all art—his 'knowledge' is precisely the *pure folly* of the fact *that* anything of this kind exists" (A 32).

The history of Christianity is that of a complex series of signs and interpretations in which each sign points back to an earlier one and is susceptible of interpretation by later ones. Now Christian hermeneutics, from its beginnings in Paul to its sophisticated secular forms, supposes that this sign chain, if followed backwards, is not an infinite regress but terminates in an ultimate meaning which is the life of Jesus. Nietzsche perceives the chain of signs but sees them finally leading back to an absence rather than a fullness of meaning. Bruno Bauer, a young Hegelian whom Nietzsche referred to as one of his few genuine readers, had suggested the same view in a somewhat crude and material way by arguing that Jesus never lived and that the literature of the early church was all fabrication or delusion.[8] Nietzsche accepts a historical Jesus who is historically relevant only because his actual presence was that of a radically ambiguous sign capable of indefinite interpretation. As a philologist Nietzsche seems to have asked himself the Kantian question "how is a Christian semiotics possible? " and to have answered it by the transcendental deduction of a man who stands so far outside the usual processes of signification that everything is metaphor and symbol for him. Whereas later Christian semiotics assumes that there is some proper relationship between signs and their referents (or between signified and signifier), the semiotics of Jesus consists in a radical refusal of any such relationship. For Nietzsche, Jesus is an anti-sign or "floating signifier" who, if he incarnated anything, embodied the absence of meaning. The signs that Jesus uses are always *mere* signs or *only* signs: "Blessedness is not promised, it is not tied to any conditions: it is the only reality—the rest is signs for speaking of it" (A 33). In the beginning, then, there is not the word, but the enigmatic indication of the insufficiency of the word. The difference between Jesus and the Church is that Jesus' signs are used with a consciousness of their inadequacy to their subject while the Church believes that the gospels are divinely inspired and hence adequate signs. The growth of allegorical methods of interpretation within Christianity should not be cited as a counter-instance because its practitioners still tend to believe in a literal level along with the non-literal modes and because they suppose that the non-literal methods of interpretation are capable of elucidating their subject matter. Nietzsche's Jesus could be thought of as the metaphorical or symbolic principle itself; for him there is always such a large discrepancy between experience and its representation that he fails to establish any determinacy of meanings. It is just this indeterminateness which allows Paul and the Church to impose their own meanings on Jesus.

The same result follows from Jesus' lack of a history. If Jesus had a history then the tradition of text and commentary would have been under some constraint, such that even falsifications of Jesus' career would have contained internal evidence pointing back to their original. This is the case in the Old Testament, "that miracle of falsification the documentation of which lies before us in a good part of the Bible" (A 26). It is because there are historical narratives of a sort, based on the history of Israel, in the Old Testament, that scholars like Wellhausen are able to detect internal inconsistencies in the whole and reconstruct a *critical* history of Israel in which the formation of different historical accounts itself plays a role. In dealing with the Christian records philology has no such role to play because of the radical indeterminacy of its beginnings. Nietzsche throws up his arms in distress at the prospect of a philological study of the gospels. Here D. F. Strauss and others had expended enormous energy. But what was the point of it?

> I confess there are few books which present me with so many difficulties as the Gospels do. These difficulties are quite other than those which the learned curiosity of the German mind celebrated one of its most unforgettable triumphs in pointing out. The time is far distant when I too, like every young scholar and with the clever dullness of a refined philologist, savored the work of the incomparable Strauss. I was then twenty years old: now I am too serious for that. What do I care for the contradictions of "tradition? " How can legends of saints be called "tradition" at all! The stories of saints are the most ambiguous literature in existence: to apply to them scientific procedures *when no other records are extant* seems to me wrong in principle—mere learned idling (A 28).

The same holds for the more imaginative attempts to reconstruct the life of Jesus, such as the immensely popular and influential *Life of Jesus* by Ernest Renan; that book serves as a foil for Nietzsche to exhibit the more radical accomplishment of his own anti-biography. Renan was himself a philologist specializing in the Semitic languages. His *Life of Jesus* walks a thin line between the philological concerns of Strauss and the Germans and a tendency toward imaginative biography (incipient psychobiography) with a heavy dose of religious liberalism. Aware of the discrepancies in the sources, Renan explains the gospel narratives as the result of confusion, wishful thinking, and the tendency of the disciples and others to read their own idiosyncracies into Jesus' life. The gospels are neither biographies nor legends but "legendary biographies."[9] Renan's basic hermeneutic principle is borrowed, more or less consciously, from the well formed nineteenth century novel with its omniscient narrator:

> The essential condition of the creations of art is, that they shall form a living system of which all the parts are mutually dependent and related. In histories such as this,

> the great test that we have got the truth is, to have
> succeeded in combining the texts in such a manner that
> they shall constitute a logical, probable narrative,
> harmonious throughout. . . . Each trait which departs
> from the rules of classic narrative ought to warn us to be
> careful.[10]

The disordered paratactic form of the gospels is to be overcome for the sake of both art and history.[11] Accordingly Renan constructs a biography of Jesus as a child of nature who lived blissfully but briefly ("for some months, perhaps a year") with the consciousness that the Kingdom of God was within. Soon he becomes involved with John the Baptist and begins to preach a moral revolution to be produced by men. Meeting with opposition Jesus proclaims himself the son of God, alienates himself from nature, and preaches that the kingdom of heaven is at hand although it will be brought about through a divine rather than human agency. Yet this extreme tone, involving as it did a confrontation with established society and religion, could be maintained only briefly; at this point Jesus' death was a necessity, and Renan seems to mean that it was an aesthetic and narrative necessity.

It is worth noting that Renan encapsulates into Jesus' life that same distinction between a blissful inwardness and the spirit of opposition and revenge which is, from Nietzsche's perspective, the difference between Jesus and the early church. By this move Renan makes Jesus' more or less unconscious barbarization of his own message the pattern and the basis for the rancorous element within the whole Christian tradition. A continuous life serves as the model of an intelligible history. In this respect Renan, despite the Church's opposition to his book, is a reformer rather than a revolutionary; he just wants to purge the intelligible history of Jesus and the Church of legendary and supernatural elements. This motive of Renan's work appears even more clearly when it is realized that the *Life* is only one of seven parts of his comprehensive series, *The Origins of Christianity*. Nietzsche was acquainted with this ambitious historical project. A year before writing *The Antichrist* he wrote in a letter to Overbeck, himself a church historian:

> This winter I have also read Renan's *Origines,* with much
> spite and—little profit. . . . At root, my distrust goes so
> far as to question whether history is really *possible.*
> What is it that people want to establish—something
> which was not itself established at the moment it
> occurred? [12]

For Nietzsche, Renan represents the modern attempt to salvage the values of religion by means of history and science. He must have been particularly angered by Renan's use of his philological credentials to interpolate a continuity into discontinuous materials. In *The Antichrist,* Renan is mentioned repeatedly, and always as another example of one who has constructed a false narrative. There is too great a "contradiction between the mountain, lake and field preacher, whose appearance strikes one as that of a Buddha on a soil very little like that of India, and the aggressive fanatic, the mortal enemy of theologian and priest, which Renan has wickedly glorified as *'le grande maitre en ironie'* " (A 31). Given this discontinuity, Nietzsche argues that it more plausible to see it as the radical break between Jesus and those who invoke his name. This is also a critique of Renan in his own terms; for the attempt to impose a narrative form on his materials causes him to violate his own canons of organic unity.

Renan also errs in importing the narrative and character types of the hero and the genius into his story. But "to speak with the precision of the physiologist a quite different word would rather be in place here: the word idiot" (A 29). Such a character ought not to be portrayed as if he were the hero of a narrative; rather "one has to regret that no Dostoyevsky lived in the neighborhood of this most interesting *décadent;* I mean someone who could feel the thrilling fascination of such a combination of the sublime, the sick and the childish" (A 31). Nietzsche may very well have had *The Idiot* in mind as a literary model for his own analysis of Jesus.[13] That book exemplifies and solves the narrative problem which is essential to Nietzsche's account of Jesus. It has long been thought that the portrayal of a thoroughly good main character in the novel must be problematic, for one who is thoroughly good will not exhibit the tensions and contradictions which lend themselves to action and development. The problem goes back to Plato who objected to the traditional stories of the gods on the grounds that they represented that which was perfect as changing; such change was, strictly speaking, impossible, but to imagine it as occurring is to imagine the perfect becoming worse, or as having a defect which must be repaired through growth. Now Dostoyevsky's Prince Myshkin is the still point of a narrative which is constituted by the feverishly spiralling reactions of those around him to such a mixture of "the sublime, the sick and the childish." Just because he does not act and does not desire, he exists as a kind of empty space upon which the other characters can impose their own acts, desires, and fantasies. In citing these parallels and contrasts with the work of Renan and Dostoyevsky I mean to indicate more than influences and thematic correspondences. Nietzsche's polemic against Christianity is concerned with the falsifications of Christian narrative. Only by considering a variety of literary models can we begin to work our way back to the event at the heart of Christian semiotics. There is a kind of Platonic correspondence for Nietzsche between the large texts which are the body and the instincts and the smaller ones which are actual written documents; unlike Plato, however, he will use the smaller in order to read the larger. An even more striking difference, however, is that both texts stand in need of extensive emendation; like graffiti they do not have the permanent existence of the forms, but are always in danger of corruption and effacement by any who are powerful enough to wield an actual or a metaphorical pen.

To understand Christianity is to understand the blank wall which must be presupposed as the support of all of the inscriptions of history. In this respect Nietzsche's view of semiotic history, or at least of this portion of it, more closely resembles that of C. S. Peirce than it does that of Jacques Derrida. Derrida frequently cites Nietzsche in behalf of his idea that all writing refers back to an earlier writing and so on *ad infinitum;* he believes that an infinite regress of writings implies that in following back the chain of texts and interpretations we will never reach a point prior to the writing process itself.[14] Peirce on the other hand makes a crucial distinction between the continuity of the sign-process and its indefinite or infinite extension. According to him the sign process is continuous in that it has no absolute first or last term. But there are many cases of continuous series which are not indefinitely or infinitely extended—such as a line segment. We can consistently conceive of a sign-process beginning (or ending) at some point in time, even though it makes no sense to talk of the absolutely first (or last) sign in the series.[15]

The difference between Peirce and Derrida here is like that between Aristotle and Zeno on the possibility of motion. Aristotle showed that the infinite density and intensive continuity of the interval, however short, between Achilles and the tortoise ought not to be mistaken for the infinity of extensions. Motion is impossible, argues Zeno, because movement across any given interval requires an infinite number of steps, each taking a finite bit of time. Therefore, not even the first step is possible. But motion is a continuous process in which there is no unique first step or movement. Yet motion has a beginning despite its lack of a unique first or final term. Derrida is a skeptic about meaning who thinks that if there were any meaning it would require the inclusion of an infinite number of moments at the "beginning" and the "end" of the process of meaning. But all intervals here are too dense to be traversed, and all presumed ends or beginnings dissolve into endless ranges of prior and posterior nodes of meaning. Anything with such indeterminate boundaries can hardly be that full, present and defined thing which we are wont to think of as meaning. Therefore there is no meaning, although there is, in its place, an ultimately plural and diffuse web of *écriture.* From a Peircean point of view this is to confuse intensive and extensive infinity. It is to suppose that that which has an internal complexity of the highest degree must necessarily lack all definition and boundary. What Nietzsche adds to this account is an explanation of the setting and dissolution of bounds by acts of force. What is variously designated as will to power by Nietzsche, as Secondness by Peirce and as simply power by Foucault is what gives a contour and integrity to meaning. Such power is exercized variously in the different modes of writing, interpreting, rewriting, censoring, defacing, and erasing. Both Peirce and Derrida see the impossibility of a Cartesian account of meaning which would found all meaning on the intuitive presence of clear and distinct ideas, a first sign. Every sign is also an interpretation, as Nietzsche and Peirce would agree. But it does not follow that the process is without beginnings, ends, or limits.[16]

For Nietzsche, Jesus is not the first sign in the series (corresponding to a Cartesian intuition), as he is for Christian tradition, but neither is he caught up, as he would be on Derrida's reading, in a chain of signs which extends back indefinitely behind him. He is rather a break or rupture in semiotic history which is the ground of a new branch of that history; like the *tabula rasa* he is the empty presupposition of a history of signs, or like the wall on which the graffiti are inscribed he is the now invisible background of all that is visible. The significant difference between Nietzsche and Peirce here is that Nietzsche rejects the Peircean eschatology of the last sign as well as the first sign of Christianity. Peirce's vision of the "ultimate interpretant" has posed a major problem for his commentators, who should have noted earlier than they did that the "ultimate interpretant" can only be attained by the Christian virtues of faith, hope, and charity.[17]

At this point there may appear to be a tension between Nietzsche's psychological reconstruction of Jesus and his semiotic use of him. According to the latter the entire quest for the historical Jesus is misguided, whether carried out along orthodox, philological or Hegelian-aesthetic lines (the last being Renan's case). Yet Nietzsche does seem at times in *The Antichrist* to be writing one more life of Jesus to add to the pile he is simultaneously rejecting in principle. If Jesus is properly a blank page in semiotic history then why does Nietzsche provide us with his vivid sketch of a blissful naif? The case may appear even more difficult when it is noticed that despite Nietzsche's polemic against Renan, the two, read from a certain modern perspective and juxtaposed either with orthodox Christian predecessors, thorough philologists (such as Strauss and Wellhausen) or with the form criticism of the last fifty years, appear to share a number of distinctive theses concerning Jesus' life. Yet this would be a truncated reading of Nietzsche's argument. It is the semiotic rather than the biographical thematic which takes priority in *The Antichrist*. The blankness of the semiotic account, the project of erasure, is not one which can be accomplished by a simple pronouncement that "Jesus had no meaning, no life, no history"; the biographical obsession, the urge to find intelligible development and character, is not easily suppressed. In order to approximate a sense of semiotic blankness, erasure is an activity to be ever renewed. So to write of the blissed out Palestinian is to approximate such blankness within the framework of the biographical project. Like Socrates attempting to give his young men a sense of that

133

which is "beyond Being" by a series of analogies, Nietzsche suggests the series formed by accounts of the orthodox, the philologists, the historical aesthetes, his own reconstruction—all suggesting the erasure, the break, the unmotivated but powerfully instituted boundary.[18] When Nietzsche speaks of Jesus he is careful to suggest the many *different* narratives which *might* be written to replace the standard ones. The wish to have a Dostoyevskian novel of Jesus must not be understood on the assumption that *The Idiot* (or any narrative, in Nietzsche's view) is to be seen as mimetic or referential. This becomes clear when Nietzsche invokes the Amphitryon Story, the philologists and the aestheticians. Such methodological reflexivity distinguishes Nietzsche's approach from Renan's: Renan shows no awareness of the possible divergence between the demands of the *Bildungsroman* and those of historical truth.

Nietzsche undertakes to tell "the real history of Christianity" (A 39), by showing how the church's narrative distortions of Jesus are intertwined with the untold narrative of its own depredations of culture. Even where Jesus may plausibly be believed to have used narrative expressions himself, they must be construed in terms of his timeless experience; yet the church has not only misconstrued them as narrative but has written a poor and hackneyed story. Jesus speaks of himself as the Son in relation to the Father. What is the semiotic analysis of these expressions?

> it is patently obvious what is alluded to in the signs
> (*Zeichen*), "Father" and "Son"—not patently obvious to
> everyone, I grant: in the word "Son" is expressed the
> *entry* into the collective feeling of the transfiguration of
> all things (blessedness), in the word "Father" *this feeling
> itself,* the feeling of perfection and eternity. I am
> ashamed to recall what the church has made of this
> symbolism: has it not set an Amphitryon story at the
> threshold of Christian faith? (A 34)

As Giraudoux's title for his modern version of that story, *Amphitryon 38,* indicates, the story has been told many times of a god (Zeus), having impregnated a mortal woman (Alcmene) who then gives birth to an extraordinary son (Herakles). Surely one could have discovered a better model than this which is more suitable for comedy than sacred narrative; this is the sort of thing that Nietzsche may have intended in the remark that it was very strange of God to write Greek and then to write it so badly (BGE 121). "Dionysus vs. the crucified" (the last words of *Ecce Homo*) can refer to the opposition between the true and false gods of tragedy and comedy—among other things. Yet what is most appalling is not the generation of such stories, whose early believers, if not their fabricators, may be presumed to have been naive ("I take care not to make mankind responsible for its insanities"), but the modern man and the modern church who *know* the falsity of the tradition while continuing to reaffirm it. Now these signs are used and "recognized for what they are: the most malicious false-coinage there is for the purpose of disvaluing nature and natural values" (A 38). Like Hegel, Nietzsche believes that history has produced a self-consciousness about the irrelevance of the narrative and mythological forms in which religious doctrines are presented; but this self-consciousness has the effect of keeping the spirit entangled in ever more hypocritical deceptions rather than liberating it. To tell the "real history of Christianity" then is to tell it *critically* (in the sense of critical history developed in *The Use and Abuse of History*) in order to explode the ruling falsities of the day.

The plan of Nietzsche's critical history of Christianity has three stages. He begins *The Antichrist* by reiterating those theses about power and the distinction between a morality of self-affirmation and one of *ressentiment* which are familiar from his earlier writings. He proceeds to show how, in the case of Judaism, the priest's distortion of texts is both the product of *ressentiment* and a philological clue to its reconstruction. Given this general understanding of the politics of misreading and miswriting, Nietzsche analyzes the central case of Jesus himself, a man so opposed to the narrative mode that he had no defenses against those who would inscribe their own messages on his body. The final part of Nietzsche's book traces the history of these wicked writers whose imaginary narratives mask the real story of their own envy of the healthy and their subterranean pursuit of power. To reconstruct what they have done we need to know not only their own motives, instinct, and bodily condition, but something of the more or less instinctive hermeneutics and semiotics which such people will employ in constructing their narratives. Now an intelligible narrative will have as its skeleton a sequence of causes and effects. Because of its hostility to the healthy body, however, Christianity refuses to recognize the natural, physiological causes of human experience. Therefore it constructs a world of imaginary causes and effects (such as the soul and redemption) which is also populated by imaginary beings; consequently "this entire fictional world has its roots in hatred of the natural" (A 15, cf. A 49). Much of Nietzsche's semiotics, like Freud's, is based on the dream; it is a natural part of the dream-work to construct an imaginary narrative to explain some experience after the fact, as when being on the verge of awaking because of a loud noise we invent some dream story which culminates in a cannon-shot.[19] We do the same thing in waking life, however, in seeking reasons for feeling well or poorly; never satisfied with experiences by themselves we feel compelled to produce some narrative account of them. Ordinary narrative thus tends to be confused enough, but this confusion will be heightened immeasurably when the typical terms of the narrative are Christianity's sin and repentance, the flesh and the spirit, and so on.

Nietzsche's account of the history of the church after Jesus can be encapsulated rather briefly. Jesus' followers were in revolt against the Jewish establishment and so naturally sought even greater revenge upon that order; thus the early church shows itself to be a continuation of Judaism by other means, extending the Jewish attack on the "world" to institutional Judaism itself. Yet God permitted Jesus' death, so that must be interpreted as a sacrifice for the sake of sins. Paul, who sought power above all things, employed the instincts of *ressentiment* to shift attention away from this life by the fiction of the resurrected Christ. Only then are the Gospels written with their willful distortions and their "seduction by means of morality" (A 44). The text itself is dirty: "one does well to put gloves on when reading the New Testament" (A 46). These dirty graffiti are also symptoms of the defacing or rewriting of some of mankind's cleaner texts, the ancient world, Islam and the Renaissance (A 59-61). Nietzsche's account of these naughtiest writings on the cultural wall is always bound up with his analysis of the book which justifies them and reveals their psychological principles. The New Testament is a bad dream constructed on the principle of *ressentiment*. After giving an extensive account of its alleged falsifications of Jesus' sayings (A 45) Nietzsche says that "every book becomes clean if one has just read the New Testament: to give an example . . . Petronius" (A 46). This *Umwertung* of the idea of the dirty book is a characteristic strategy in *The Antichrist*. I suggest that we read the admittedly feverish imagery of dirt and cleanliness, body, blood and poison which becomes more and more pronounced as one reaches the end of the book as signs of deliberate authorship rather than as evidence of a loss of control. Nietzsche's transvaluation is meant to be an affirmation of the body in opposition to its denial in Christianity. Therefore it must openly be a text of the body and must describe its anti-text as a desecration of the body.

It is striking that Nietzsche invokes Zarathustra in the midst of this narrative (A 53-54), for what unites Zarathustra and Nietzsche's Jesus is a non-narrative view of the world. For both, the totality of experience is sufficient unto itself and stands in no need of external explanations. Jesus' opposition to narrative is instinctive and naive while Zarathustra's living of the eternal return is post-narrative and achieved only with great difficulty. The eternal recurrence is an anti-narrative thought because it knows no isolated agents in the sequence of events, but only the interconnection of all events; it knows no beginning, middle and end of the narrative but simply the continuous circle of becoming; and it tends to dissolve the mainstay of all narrative, the individual agent, into the ring of becoming. In carefully distinguishing himself from Zarathustra, Nietzsche indicates that he has not attained this anti-narrative stance himself, or if he did experience the eternal recurrence he also forgot it from time to time. In constructing his own narratives such as *The Geneaology of Morals* and *The Antichrist*, Nietzsche attempts to incorporate an awareness of the fallibility and perspectival character of all narrative which is rejected by dogmatic priestly narrative. We might think of the distinction between these two narratives as somewhat like the distinction which Marx would make between ideology and science. Ideological accounts of history are dogmatic and uncritical of their own principles of interpretation while scientific accounts are distinguished not only by knowing where to look for causes (in the relations of production or in the condition of the body) but by their knowledge that they too are products of these causes and therefore subject to explanation and correction from a more comprehensive standpoint. So it would be in the spirit of Marxism to regard Marxist science as itself tied to the material conditions of capitalism and subject to revision when capitalism is overcome. Of course Marx does not envision a non-historical science; Nietzsche's narratives are even more provisional in that they anticipate the abolition of the narrative principle itself. Or one might point out that just as the eternal recurrence will bring back the last man, so it will, even though opposed to the narrative principle, bring back that principle as well.

Nietzsche recalls Zarathustra in *The Antichrist* both for his opposition to priestly writing in blood and for his skepticism. As in the passage chosen for *Auslegung* in *The Genealogy of Morals*, Nietzsche chooses a section which explicitly has to do with reading and writing. Zarathustra speaks twice of the connection between blood and writing, once to announce "I love only that which is written in blood" (Z 67) and then, in the passage quoted in *The Antichrist* to criticize the priests for writing in blood:

> They wrote letters of blood on the path they followed,
> and their folly taught that truth is proved by blood.
> But blood is the worst witness of truth. (Z 116)

Both passages seem to apply to the *Antichrist* but only one of them is quoted. In part their difference has to do with the polyphonic or polytropic character of *Zarathustra.* But beyond that there is still the problem of the bloody tone of *The Antichrist* in addition to its bloody subject matter. In fact the conclusion of the passage makes a distinction between two sorts of bloody writing:

> And if someone goes through fire for his teaching—what
> does that prove? Truly, it is more when one's own
> teaching comes out of one's burning.

One kind of writing in blood is that of the ascetic; he deliberately spills his blood and then imagines that whatever he writes with it must be true. He has too much of an investment, through self-sacrifice, to allow him to question his own writing. The other sort is that which flows out of

137

powerful and healthy impulses which cannot be suppressed; it is thus that Nietzsche describes his own composition of *Zarathustra.* The *Antichrist* is, presumably, bloody in the second sense, not the first. Only this second kind of bloodiness is compatible with the skepticism which Nietzsche here attributes to Zarathustra and to Pilate, whose "What is truth? " makes him the *"one* solitary figure one is obliged to respect" in the New Testament (A 46). Writing in blood, like that in *The Antichrist* or *Zarathustra,* can be skeptical if it combines intensity with an awareness of the perspectival character of all discourse emanating from the body. The antithesis to the Christian set of sacred writings, beliefs, and values is not a new sacred text and alternative beliefs to be held with the same force; it is the genuine *Umwertung* of all those things, not simply a change in their content. *The Antichrist* aims at being the antithesis of Christian graffiti by opening up a space for playful writings like Nietzsche's own; it is meant to clear the walls for an exuberant position of inscriptions which will break out of the narrow circle of revenge in which writing under the sway of Christianity and morality has moved.[20]

University of Kansas

NOTES

1   Eugen Fink, *Nietzsches Philosophie* (Stuttgart: Kohlhammer, 1960), p. 34.

2   References are to *The Antichrist* by numbered section, usually following the translation of R. J. Hollingdale in *Twilight of the Idols and Antichrist* (Baltimore: Penguin Books, 1961).

3   *Antichrist* and *Ecce Homo* are often treated together in this respect. According to Kaufmann "The ending of *The Antichrist* and much of *Ecce Homo* show so strange a lack of inhibition and contain such extraordinary claims concerning Nietzsche's own importance that, knowing of his later insanity, one cannot help finding here the first signs of it." Walter Kaufmann, *Nietzsche,* 4th ed. (Princeton: Princeton Univ. Press, 1974), p. 66. Arthur Danto's judgment is a measured one: "The *Antichrist* is unrelievedly vituperative and would indeed sound insane were it not informed in its polemic by a structure of analysis and a theory of morality and religion worked out elsewhere and accessible even here to the informed reader." Arthur Danto, *Nietzsche as Philosopher* (New York: Macmillan, 1965), p. 182. Even in Danto's view the structure of thought which saves the *Antichrist* is one worked out elsewhere; he would apparently agree with Fink that the book offers nothing new.

4   *Ecce Homo,* page following Preface.

5   Nietzsche calls Renan his "antipodes" (*Beyond Good and Evil,* sec. 48); the sense of opposition made more precise a year later in a polemic on modern historiography in *The Genealogy of Morals* (III, 26): "I know of nothing that excites such disgust as this kind of 'objective' armchair scholar, this kind of scented voluptuary of history, half person, half satyr, perfume by Renan, who

betrays immediately with the high falsetto of his applause what he lacks, *where* he lacks it, *where* in this case the Fates have applied their cruel shears with, also, such surgical skill! '' Renan, then, is Nietzsche's anti-historian; it is notable that both *The Genealogy of Morals* and Renan's *Origins of Christianity* are philosophical histories which focus on the transition from Greek and Roman culture to Christianity. Nietzsche not only narrates the events differently but does so, to speak more precisely, in a genealogical rather than a historical manner. On genealogy as the alternative to history, see Michel Foucault ''Nietzsche, Genealogy, History,'' in *Language, Counter-Memory, Practice,* ed. Donald F. Bouchard and Sherry Simon (Ithaca, N.Y.: Cornell Univ. Press, 1977). For an anarcho-marxist assessment by a writer sometimes considered a Nietzschean, see Georges Sorel, *Le Systeme Historique de Renan* (Paris: G. Jacques, 1905).

6   Julius Wellhausen, *Prolegomena to the History of Ancient Israel* (New York: Meridian Books, 1957).

7   Georg Brandes, *Friedrich Nietzsche* (New York: Macmillan, n.d.) p. 85.

8   Nietzsche's admiring references to Bauer (e.g., *Ecce Homo,* V 2) indicate that he may have known Bauer's works on the history of Christianity. Albert Schweitzer's *The Quest of the Historical Jesus* is the most accessible account of Bauer's writing and of other nineteenth century works of this character.

9   Ernest Renan, *The Life of Jesus* (New York: Modern Library, 1927), pp. 45-54.

10   *The Life of Jesus,* pp. 62-63.

11   *The Life of Jesus,* p. 64.

12   Letter to Overbeck, February 23, 1887 in *Selected Letters to Friedrich Nietzsche,* ed. and trans. by Christopher Middleton (Chicago: Univ. of Chicago Press, 1969), p. 261.

13   For a scholarly account of Nietzsche's knowledge of Dostoeyevsky, see the articles by C. A. Miller in *Nietzsche-Studien,* 1973, 1975 and 1978.

14   Jacques Derrida, *Of Grammatology* Trans. G. Spivak (Baltimore, Md.: Johns Hopkins Univ. Press, 1974), and other writings. In saying that for Derrida all writing refers back to an earlier writing, the notion of ''referring back'' must not be understood as implying a linear temporal sequence but as suggesting that writing always occurs within an infinitely dense texture of writing. Derrida associates his view of writing with the Nietzschean and Heideggerian critique of the linear conception of time (*Of Grammatology,* pp. 86-87).

15   In his classical exposition of the theory of signs in 1868 Peirce argues for the impossibility of a ''first sign.'' See *Collected Papers,* (Cambridge, Mass.: Harvard Univ. Press), vol. 5, paragraphs 213-317 and especially 263 ff.

16   For Derrida's celebration of undecidability see *Spurs* trans. B. Harlow (Chicago: Univ. of Chicago Press, 1979); for the understanding of such celebrations as sacrificial religious rites see ''From Restricted to General Economy: A Hegelianism without Reserve'' in *Writing and Difference* trans. A. Bass (Chicago: Univ. of Chicago Press, 1978). There are discussions of

Spurs by David Allison and David Hoy in *boundary 2.* See also my review of *Spurs* in *Man and World,* 1981. In "The Rhetoric of Nietzsche's *Zarathustra"* (*boundary 2,* 1980), I have attempted to reconstruct the rhetorical strategy of a Nietzschean text. For Peirce on Zeno in a semiotic context, see *Collected Papers,* vol. 5, pars. 333-4.

17   For Peirce's claim that logic requires faith, hope, and charity see *Collected Papers* vol. 2, pars. 264-5 and Josiah Royce's Hegelian extension of Peirce in *The Problem of Christianity,* vol. 2.

18   Derrida explains the asymptotic conception of the deconstructive process in "Structure, Science and Play in the Discourse of the Human Sciences" in *The Structuralist Controversy,* ed. R. Macksey and E. Donato (Baltimore, Md.: Johns Hopkins Univ. Press, 1972). I am grateful to James Woelfel for incisive questions and comments about this and other parts of this paper.

19   *Human All Too Human,* par. 113.

20   Work on this paper was supported by the University of Kansas General Research Fund.

The Autobiographical Textuality of Nietzsche's *Ecce Homo*

Hugh J. Silverman

An autobiography is one's own life as written. Autobiographizing is writing one's own life. An autobiographical text is a particular written version, fragment, or account of one's own life. Autobiographical textuality is the feature of a text (autobiographical or otherwise) which characterizes the writing of a version, fragment, or account of one's own life. Although I am concerned with the autobiographical textuality of Nietzsche's *Ecce Homo,* I defer determination as to whether the text is, in fact, an autobiography since it has been argued that *Ecce Homo* is unsuccessful as autobiography.

This latter exclusion is occasioned by the introductory remarks of R. J. Hollingdale, the English translator for the Penguin edition: "It matters how you approach this book. If, under the guidance of the literature on the subject, you approach it as 'Nietzsche's autobiography' you will get very little out of it and probably won't even finish it, short though it is. As autobiography it is a plain failure. You cannot reconstruct Nietzsche's life even in its broad outlines from his 'autobiography'; it is in no way a narrative; it is not in the least 'objective.' "[1] Hollingdale is perhaps right: *Ecce Homo* is hardly Nietzsche's own life as written in any comprehensive sense. Of course, an autobiography need not provide a full account of one's own life. Sartre's *Words* recounts only the first twelve or so years of his life; Dante's *La Vita Nuova* is limited only to the early years during which he admired Beatrice; and Descartes' *Discourse on Method* is a severely restricted inquiry into the course and development of his own mind. On the other hand, if autobiographies are reserved for the large-scale enterprises which are announced by Benvenuto Cellini's *La Vita,* Rousseau's *Confessions,* Simone de Beauvoir's multiple volumes, and Russell's *Autobiography,* then perhaps Hollingdale has a point. But if *Ecce Homo* does not match up to these epic autobiographies, is it necessarily a "failure"? If we assume that one must be able to reconstruct the broad outlines of the autobiographer's life, then Hollingdale is probably correct. In subsection 3 of "Why I Am So Wise," Nietzsche offers a brief sketch of his Polish ancestry, his mother's and paternal grandmother's Germanness, his father's date of birth and death while Nietzsche was only five years old, and the date of his own birth along with the reason why he was named after King Friedrich Wilhelm the Fourth of Prussia. Yet all this is no more than a scant report—hardly sufficient material to qualify it as an autobiography in which his own life is written. With the exception of the dates and names Nietzsche offers, it has been argued that his other facts might even be spurious. For example, he may not be at all of Polish descent. For this reason, Hollingdale denies the "objective" character of the work.

By contrast, however, *Ecce Homo* is very much a narrative. It is not narrative in the sense of a nineteenth century novel, but neither is Thoreau's *Walden* or Roland Barthes' *Roland Barthes*—though they both would qualify as autobiographical narration. What Nietzsche narrates is why he is so wise, why he is so clever, and why he writes such excellent books. This is not chronological narration but it does recount Nietzsche's views about himself and his work. This specifically non-chronological yet thematic narration is one feature of the autobiographical textuality of the text.

Since some question has been raised as to whether *Ecce Homo* can be classified as autobiography, one might wonder whether the same holds for its status as an autobiographical text. Composed in the first person singular, it concerns the author and not some fictitious character—at least in name! *Ecce Homo* is fragmentary, but at the same time it is a written version of Nietzsche's own life. He does offer an account of "who he is." In these respects *Ecce Homo* is an autobiographical text even though it may not qualify specifically as autobiography. Since, furthermore, the text need not be autobiographical in order for it to demonstrate autobiographical textuality—Joyce's *Portrait of the Artist as a Young Man* is a case in point—I shall now restrict my examination to its autobiographical textuality, that is, the writing of features which characterize it as a version, fragment, or account of Nietzsche's own life. The text *Ecce Homo* introduces the problematic of writing one's own life as a persistent self-examination.

I. Self/Text

The autobiographical textuality of Nietzsche's *Ecce Homo* arises and operates at the intersection of self and text. A pure textless account of Nietzsche's life is no longer available. Nietzsche, the man, died in 1900. The text in which a first person singular appears is surely quite distant from the self who lived from 1844 to 1900. Hollingdale's report that the text (albeit largely autobiographical) makes poor autobiography indicates the inadequacy of *Ecce Homo* as an elaboration of the self. Yet this is not to say that there is not some correspondence between the self and the text. In fact, the correspondence as written is the place of the autobiographical textuality.

Ecce Homo is filled with remarks such as the one which opens the text: "Seeing that before long I must confront humanity with the most difficult demand ever made on it, it seems indispensable to me to say *who I am.*"[2] This "I" is situated somewhere between the self and the text. But how is the "I" (first person singular) the writing of Nietzsche's own life? He could be deceiving himself or his reader. The word could be a mask or impoverished version of the self. This debate could go on without end—with the possible conclusion falling on one side or the other, on the side of the subject or on the side of the object, on the side of the self or on the side of the text. Yet the writing of the "I" is the writing of a fragment—not as a representational unit, nor as a substitutional entity. The writing of the fragment is the trace or supplement at which the autobiographical textuality of Nietzsche's *Ecce Homo* is situated. Hence a textualized self announces its obligation to say who it is. This saying of a particular sort—one which links its own imperative with its own identity leaves something unthematized. In the transition from the imperative to the identity the autobiographical textuality is left over in the text. The remainder in the transition indicates a problematic: that a particular self, whom we can call Nietzsche, needs to account for itself. When realized, if realized, this need for the self to account for itself, to write itself as text, could result in an autobiography. If unsuccessful, it would at least leave the traces of an autobiographical textuality.

Continuing, the text reads: "This ought really to be known already: for I have not neglected to 'bear witness' about myself."[3] The remark would be curious if it were to be supposed that there is no connection between the author of the remark and its effect. By the remark a relationship between this written self and some reputation is affirmed. The text takes itself outside itself. It refers—or better still, establishes a connection—between this particular textualized self and the author of other works. The connection is not established as some sort of revelation to the reading public as in Kierkegaard's *The Point of View of My Work as an Author,* where he indicates that he is the author of all those pseudonymously published works. Whereas Kierkegaard announces an obligation to affirm an identity between himself as author of *The Point of View* and Constantine Constantius, Johannes de Silentio, Victor Ermita, and all the others, Nietzsche points out that the self in question in *Ecce Homo* already has a reputation. His identity is already known. There is already testimony of who he is. This textualized self is already on record as having an identity.

At bottom, one should know (*Im Grunde dürfte man's wissen. . .*) who this self is. But *who* should know who this self is? Can it be the same "one" who is specified in the subtitle of the work: "*Ecce Homo:* How One Becomes What One Is" (*Wie Man Wird—Was Man Ist*)? Surely the "one" who should have come across Nietzsche as a testimony will not always be identical with the "one" who becomes what one is if *Ecce Homo* is a successful demonstration. The "one" who should have encountered Nietzsche as a text can be called Nietzsche's "reader." This "one" who is his "reader" is different from Montaigne's reader mentioned at the outset of his *Essays* because Nietzsche, the author, does not name this "one" as a reader. *This* "one" is only the one who should already know. And what this "one" should know is something about Nietzsche's corpus. In the section entitled "Why I Write Such Excellent Books" there is some mention of his readers. If we take his claims to the letter, then he has readers everywhere except among Germans. His readers are "nothing but first-rate intellectuals and proven characters, trained in high positions and duties." He writes: "I even have real geniuses among my readers. In Vienna, in St. Petersburg, in Stockholm, in Copenhagen, in Paris, in New York—everywhere I have been discovered; but not in the shallows of Europe, Germany" (*EH*, p. 262). These non-Germans, then, could well satisfy the conditions of the "one" who is announced as having already some acquaintance with the self in question. But what of his non-readers—those who are mentioned in the passage which says: "And let me confess that my non-readers delight me even more—those who have never heard my name, nor the word 'philosophy' " (*EH*, p. 262). Although these non-readers are surely excluded from the "one" who is already witness to his textualized self, they are given credit for recognizing a lived self who meets them on the street and in the markets.

Yet it still must be asked whether any of these readers or non-readers qualify as the "one" who is announced in "How One Becomes—What One Is." If, as readers, they are restricted to those familiar with other books by Nietzsche, then surely they are excluded as are his non-readers who do not have *Ecce Homo* available to them. This exclusion, however, is operative only if these readers and non-readers can become who they are only by reading *Ecce Homo*. In a certain sense, this is indeed the condition announced, for the very title "How One Becomes What One Is" suggests that *Ecce Homo* is a manual, in the tradition of Ovid's *The Art* of Love, Capellanus' *The Art of Courtly Love*, Alberti's *The Art of Painting*, Erasmus' *The Education of a Christian Prince*, Machiavelli's *The Prince*, and so on to the many articles in *Popular Mechanics* where one learns how to build bookshelves, transformers, and woodsheds. Since Emily Post's and Amy Vanderbilt's volumes on etiquette, Alex Comfort's *The Joy of Sex*, and Hans Küng's *On Being a Christian* also qualify as "how to" books, they can be incorporated into the field in which "*Ecce Homo: How One Becomes What One Is*" is situated. But if *Ecce Homo* is simply a "how to" book, a manual on the art of living, then surely the "one" in question is realized only in the reading of it. If, however, the "one" in "How One Becomes What One Is" is only another way of saying "How I Have Become What I Am," then the substitution of the "I" for the "One" reverts even more directly to the textualized self who can be called Nietzsche. But is *Ecce Homo* simply an account of how Nietzsche has become what he is? If that were true in its strictest sense, then there could be no doubt that *Ecce Homo* is an autobiography, for it would thereby be Nietzsche's own life as written and not a manual at all. But doubt has already been placed upon *Ecce Homo* as autobiography in the narrowest sense. The third alternative is that "How One Becomes What One Is" constitutes a maxim according to which Nietzsche himself has or would like to have lived and according to which others might live—whether they be his readers or not.

Why, though, does Nietzsche write "How One Becomes What One Is" and not "How One Becomes Who One Is?" Why not: *Wie Man Wirt—Wer Man Ist?* In considering this self which is to become what it is, the question of *personal* identity is evaded. The question of identity remains, but the "who" is not at issue. In this respect, the problem as to whether the "one" is Nietzsche's non-readers, his readers, or himself is less pressing. The particular person—as a unity or a multiplicity—is not raised as a concern. The "what" rather than the "who" prevails.

Can one become what one is? Is this a task for the overman (der *Übermensch*)—a task which we all-too-human mortals could not achieve without great effort? Could even Nietzsche himself become what he is? Surely an element of the textuality of *Ecce Homo* is that Nietzsche sees himself as no longer announcing the eternal return and *amor fati* through his spokesman Zarathustra but that at last Nietzsche has placed himself in question. But Nietzsche is not in question as a person. He does not appear in person in the text. Rather what appears is a textualized self—the "what" is "how one becomes what one is."

This "what," this textualized self, is in a sense more real than the "I" which appears as a unit in *Ecce Homo* or the living Nietzsche whom we can read about in biographies such as the ones offered by Walter Kaufmann and Ronald Hayman. To become what one is is doubtless not an easy enterprise. Hence the passage: "I live on my own credit; it is perhaps a mere prejudice that I live" (*EH*, p. 217). The other books, each of which is assessed in a separate section of *Ecce Homo,* establish themselves as a kind of credit, an advance on Nietzsche's own life such that his own life is borrowed—not borrowed time, but borrowed autobiographical textuality. Without the writing of *Ecce Homo,* Nietzsche's autobiographical textuality would remain fragmentary, disjointed, and dismembered like Orpheus on the shores of Lesbos. But *Ecce Homo* inscribes itself as the account of Nietzsche's own life, as the identity which has been concealed behind so many clever and excellent books. Yet all those books are a kind of credit which has allowed Nietzsche to live. On the other hand, like a manuscript for which one is given an advance before it is submitted, like a car for which one is given credit before one has the money to pay for it, Nietzsche announces that he lives on the credit which he has given himself by writing his "other" books. For this reason, it could be doubted whether he lives at all, whether he is what he is, whether it is a pre-judgment that he lives, that there is an author who gives unity and identity to all those books. He must become what he is by writing *Ecce Homo.* But this claim is already the writing of *Ecce Homo,* is already the writing of his own life, is already the establishment of his autobiographical textuality.

In becoming what he is, Nietzsche also announces a duty. He must say: "Hear me! For I am such and such a person. Above all, do not mistake me for someone else" (*EH*, p. 217). There are specific character-istics to his identity. His autobiographical textuality could be given defi-nite descriptions. He does not give them, except as self-justification: why I am so wise, why I am so clever, why I write such excellent books. . . . What is important is that these features and characteristics of his identity could be given and if they were given then the textualized self would not be mistaken for someone else. The problem is that when one lives on credit, not only is there some question as to whether the bill will be paid, the manuscript submitted, the life lived, but also if not done appropriately someone else might supply the funds, the book, or the life. And since the goods are not already on hand, a mistake could be made. If someone else paid the bill, that would be fine. If someone else submitted the manu-script, that would be disconcerting. But if someone else lived the life, that would be intolerable. And mistaking someone else for what one is would leave one without an identity. For this reason, Nietzsche needs to say what he is or, even more significantly, he needs to become what he is by writing *Ecce Homo.* Hence the writing of *Ecce Homo* is the place of his autobio-graphical textuality. For in it, he can and does say what he is and what he is not. In the writing of *Ecce Homo* he becomes what he is and he distin-guishes himself from what he is not.

"I am a *Doppelgänger,*" he writes (*EH*, p. 225). A *Doppelgänger* comes and goes as a double. Sometimes it is regarded as a ghost after the person has died. Sometimes it is simply a double: a Dr. Jeckyl and

Mr. Hyde, a Golyadkin Sr. and Golyadkin Jr. in Dostoevsky's *The Double,* an alter ego in Conrad's *Secret Sharer,* an ego ideal in the Freudian account. In *Ecce Homo,* the *Doppelgänger* is the self and its text. The self is a kind of ghost which seeks its own form, its identity, its realization so that no one will mistake it for someone else. The autobiographical text is its form, identity, realization. The statement "I am a *Doppelgänger"* indicates that this dichotomy is not real, is not lived. What is lived is the textuality which announces itself as autobiographical, as writing one's own life, as appropriate to the authorship specifically at the intersection of the self and the text, at the stroke or slash between one and the other, between the "I" of the authorship and its textualization. At this juncture, Nietzsche's autobiographical textuality establishes its place.

II. Event/Writing

Ecce Homo is divided into a variety of sections. The "Foreword" introduces the text with four subsections. This "Foreword" is signed "Friedrich Nietzsche." Then there are a series of sections with a justificatory tone: "Why I Am So Wise," "Why I Am So Clever," "Why I Write Such Excellent Books." Following there are ten separate sections in which he discusses in turn ten of his books. The final section is entitled: "Why I Am A Destiny."

Apart from the title page, I have omitted one item in my accounting. Situated between the "Foreword" and the main body of the text which begins with the section entitled "Why I Am So Wise," one finds an inconspicuous half-page single paragraph text. This fragment has no title, no subsection number,—in short no regular place within the text as a whole. One might even say that it is out of place in the order of things. Since the "Foreword" is signed, we may be sure that Nietzsche names as his own the autobiographical textuality which arises at the intersection of self and text. This textuality then opens the space in which the remainder of *Ecce Homo* is situated. But what of the curiously placed fragment? Situated after the announcement of an autobiographical textuality in which the self/text is set as a pre-text, and before the main body of the text, the fragment occurs as an index of the juncture between the event and the writing of Nietzsche's own life.

A further remark is required concerning the placement of the fragment. Not only is it untitled, unnumbered, and unidentified, but in the German text, it is printed on a single page with nothing on the back. In both the Hollingdale and Kaufmann translations, this supplementary feature is lost, for on the back page is printed the beginning of "Why I Am So Clever." In the German text, then, the page could simply be torn out, and except for the gap in sequential page numbering, its absence would not be noticed! This tear-page, this interleaf is thus a marker of a textual difference established in the interstices of *Ecce Homo*. But it is an extremely important marker. It marks an event of Nietzsche's life written at the border of the "Foreword" on the one hand and at the beginning of the principal text on the other. It occurs at the limits of Nietzsche's signature and of the "I" which is so clever.

The event which the fragment marks is the moment of Nietzsche's writing of his own life. It is Nietzsche's appropriation of the gate of the moment (which he describes in *Thus Spoke Zarathustra*) as his own. The gate of the moment loses its status as a theory, as Zarathustra's proclamation, and, as an account of how one might live. In this event, the gate of the moment becomes proper to Nietzsche himself. It establishes an autobiographical textuality appropriate to Nietzsche as the self in question.

The fragment reads:

> On this perfect day, when everything is ripening and not only the grape turns brown, the eye of the sun just fell upon my life: I looked back, I looked forward, and never saw so many and such good things at once. It was not for nothing that I buried my forty-fourth year today; I had the *right* to bury it; whatever was life in it has been saved, is immortal. The first book of the *Revaluation of All Values,* the *Song of Zarathustra,* the *Twilight of the Idols,* my attempt to philosophize with a hammer —all presents of this year, indeed of its last quarter! *How could I fail to be grateful to my whole life?* and so I tell my life to myself. (*EH*, p. 221)

The perfect day is Nietzsche's forty-fourth birthday! Surely a momentous event in that—if he is accurate and the date is October 15, 1888—Nietzsche completes his last work: *Ecce Homo.* Thenceforth he no longer writes any more books. Thenceforth he goes mad and collapses in the piazza Carlo Alberto in Torino (on January 3rd, 1889). Although he continues to live until 1900—what could equally well be a momentous event—he no longer produces anything. Thus the momentous event is his birthday—forty-four. Christ is said to have been crucified at the age of thirty-three—for Nietzsche it is a factor of four instead of three. The day is "perfect"—the sun is at its height. Ripeness is a transitory time which will soon pass and on this perfect day, everything is ripening. Grapes turn brown as they tip from ripeness to over-ripeness. On this day, the eye of the sun falls upon Nietzsche's life. Just as the blazing sun beat down upon Van Gogh as he furiously painted whirling cypress trees and fields of bright yellow corn at the verge of his own insanity, so too the burning eye of the sun provided Nietzsche with the brilliance and luminosity which accompanied the pro-

duction of *Ecce Homo*. Thenceforth Nietzsche passed beyond sanity. In
the intensity of the sun, he became overripe. When the sun is at its height
there are no shadows, no lines on the map of one's life. As in the inter-
posed fragment, at a prior moment, the account is written as a Foreword,
a moment later it is the text of his writings. Since the sun casts no shadow
at its apex, it gives only the place where the self stands, it gives the self as
it is—what it is. It marks the place where one becomes what one is.

The self looks backward and forward. On each side, one finds
writing: the writing of a life as pre-text on the one hand, as main text on
the other. At the interface however the past and the future are entered as a
moment, as the present, as the place where the eternal return is realized
for the time being. Since the future would announce and affirm all that
Nietzsche had written—treating each of his already published books one by
one—and the past would announce the place of his autobiographical textuality as what is to be read as his own, the fragment itself is where Nietzsche returns eternally. Whatever is eternal or immortal about his life is
identified, preserved, saved. But *we* cannot save Nietzsche. We cannot
simply follow what he says and claim it to be eternal. He must save himself—just as he has the right to bury himself on this day. He has the right
to go mad, to stop writing, to become what he is. As he cites in the passage
from *Thus Spoke Zarathustra* just before he signs his "Foreword," "Now I
bid you lose me and find yourselves; and only *when you have all denied
me* will I return to you" (*EH*, p. 220). By losing him, we find ourselves.
We cannot find ourselves in him, in reading him, in seeking to make his
eternal return our own. And yet we can read his perfect day, we can find
his special event, we can see where he writes his own life as his own, as his
own choice, as his own right. Just as Christ told Peter that he would deny
him three times before the cock crows at dawn and that he would also
found Christ's Church on the rock. Similarly Nietzsche can only live, can
only become what he is if we deny him, let him be, and become our own.
In this sense, his autobiographical textuality belongs to him alone. He can
and must present to himself the four books which he completed in the last
quarter of 1888. As gifts, he must be grateful for them. But since he has
given them to himself—the delight is his own. He is of course grateful not
only for these presents, his gifts, but also for his whole life—a life which he
lives and makes his own—a life which he writes in *Ecce Homo* and which
he tells to himself. *Ecce Homo* is his narrative to himself and the place at
which the self enters the narrative as event is the limit-text or fragment in
which he announces a "perfect day."

III. Destiny/Understanding

In many of his writings, Nietzsche appeals to his notion of *amor
fati*—the love of fate which one must enact in order to go beyond and be-

come oneself. The last section of *Ecce Homo* is entitled "Why I Am A Destiny." Nietzsche begins by writing: "I know my fate" (*EH*, p. 126). He knows what lies before him—his testimony is clear as he writes it in his last testament. Yet he asks again and again: "Have I been understood?" He asks it three times at the outset of the last three subsections of "Why I Am A Destiny." Is there any doubt? For him to be understood would be for all the contradictions, reversals, and paradoxes to be resolved. For him to be understood, his destiny would have to be understood, his destiny would have to be clear to others. Yet his destiny is filled with misunderstandings. And if he is a destiny, then he must love, accept, and take on as his own whatever understanding ensues. Can he possess these consequences? Can he own them? To appropriate them as his own is itself his destiny. He has no other alternative. The effects of his writing returns him to his writing itself. He cannot deny these effects because he has written them as his own —they are as much his autobiographical textuality as the life he announces on that perfect day. To be true to his principles, he must will to live his destiny over and over again. But even if he were to deny his principles, he writes his own life as a destiny, as an autobiographical textuality which cannot be denied—only noted and remarked.

In becoming a destiny, he situates his textuality at the intersection between his self and his writings. At the opening of "Why I Write Such Excellent Books," we find the following passage: "I am one thing, my writings are another.—Here, before I speak of these writings themselves, I shall touch on the question of their being understood or *not* understood. I shall do so as perfunctorily as is fitting: for the time for this question has certainly not yet come. My time has not yet come, some are born posthumously."[4] The disjunction between his writings and his self is the place in which his autobiographical textuality inscribes itself—but it need not be accepted or even understood that a life is written in this interface. The disjunction itself however does establish the space for such an understanding to occur. The interface is the place of his birth (day) and as a "posthumous birth," it is his destiny.

He writes: "I do not want to be taken for what I am not—and that requires that I do not take myself for what I am not."[5] In order to avoid taking himself for what he is not he writes his own self-identity as an autobiographical textuality at the intersection of self/text, event/writing, destiny/understanding. He situates himself at the time of the apex of the sun where he marks himself without a trace of shadow. Yet along the way there are shadows. Looking backward, he writes that he is "a disciple of the philosopher Dionysus."[6] Looking forward, he presents his spokesman Zarathustra. Nietzsche stands somewhere between. But he also stands opposed to "the Crucified." The last words of the text are "Dionysus versus the Crucified. . ." His philosopher is opposed to Christ. Dionysus is therefore the anti-Christ. But Dionysus is not a philosopher, he is a Greek god. And Christ is not a philosopher any more than Dionysus. Yet in the *Birth of Tragedy,* Nietzsche claimed that a new god had entered the scene of classical Greek life—destroying the tragic beauty of works such as that of Aeschylus. This new god infected Greek tragedy (especially that of Euripides) with rationality. Socrates opposed himself to the Greek Dionysian which represented the harnessed passion of the Apollonian tendency and that of the barbarian Dionysian. This new god Socrates opposed Dionysus; he opposed Nietzsche's philosopher. Just as Socrates was an Anti-Dionysian, Nietzsche's Zarathustra announces the will to power which will take the overman beyond pity, beyond the herd morality, beyond good and evil—beyond Christian values in a revaluation of values. But where does Nietzsche stand if the one he follows is opposed by Socrates and the one he espouses opposes himself to Christian values? Nietzsche—as autobiographical textuality—stands between Dionysus and Zarathustra, but against the followers of Socrates and of Christ.

It will be remembered that the book is entitled *Ecce Homo*—the words uttered by Pontius Pilate as he had his soldiers bring Christ before the Jews. "Behold the man," Pilate said. In order to become his own destiny, Nietzsche applies this appellation to himself: behold the man. But the man does not appear. He is the anti-Christ and yet we have only the text of his position. The man is nowhere to be found. He is born posthumously. He cannot be understood except by being whatever his destiny may become. He must be the autobiographical textuality in which his own life is written as *Ecce Homo.* [7]

SUNY-Stony Brook

NOTES

1   R. J. Hollingdale, "Introduction," to Nietzsche: *Ecce Homo* (Harmondsworth: Penguin, 1979), p. 7.

2   F. Nietzsche, *Ecce Homo,* trans. Walter Kaufmann (New York: Vintage, 1967), p. 217 (hereafter cited as *EH*).

3   *Ecce Homo,* trans. Hollingdale, p. 33.

4   *Ecce Homo,* trans. Hollingdale, p. 69 and trans. Kaufmann, p. 259.

5   *Ecce Homo,* trans. Hollingdale, p. 69 and trans. Kaufmann, p. 259.

6   *Ecce Homo,* trans. Hollingdale, p. 33, and trans. Kaufmann, p. 217.

7   This essay was presented as an invited paper at the second annual meeting of the Nietzsche Society held in conjunction with the Society for Phenomenology and Existential Philosophy at the University of Ottawa (Canada) on November 6, 1980. An earlier version was given as a guest lecture for the University of Warwick Philosophy Department Weekend at St. Catherine's, Cumberland Lodge, Windsor Great Park (England) in February 1980. I am particularly grateful to David Wood, David Holdcroft, David Miller, and Richard Collier for their helpful comments and remarks, and to Daniel O'Hara for proposing that the essay be written in the first place.

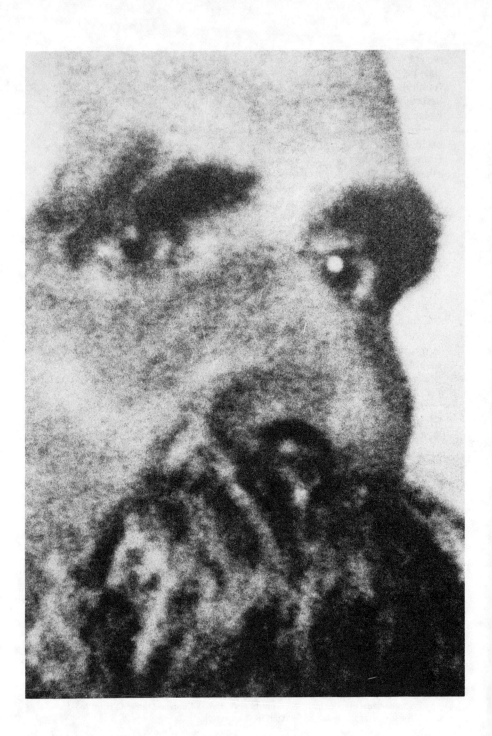

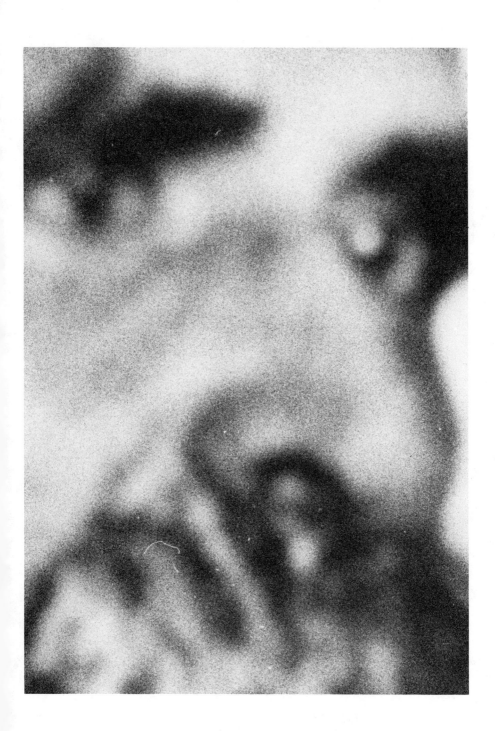

III Affinities and Differences

DER MAULWURF
Die philosophische Wühlarbeit
bei Kant, Hegel und Nietzsche

David Farrell Krell

*Für Helmbrecht Breinig, der jahrelang
wacker mitgewühlt hat.*

Auszüge §§§§§

Maulwurf, ahd. *muwërf,* "Haufenwerfer" (zu ags. *muwa,* engl.
mow, "Hügel"), dann volksetymologisch auf mhd. *molt,* mnd. *mul,*
"Staub," umgedeutet. . . .

Hermann Paul, *Deutsches Wörterbuch*

Djese sollen euch auch vnrein sein unter den Thieren/ die auff
erden kriechen/ . . . die Aydex/ der Blindschleich/ und der Maulworff.

III. Mose 11, 29-30

Wir erkennen unsern alten Freund, unsern alten Maulwurf, der so
gut unter der Erde zu arbeiten weiß, um plötzlich zu erscheinen.

Karl Marx

So ist es bis heute nicht gelungen, Maulwürfe zu züchten; sie entziehen sich den künstlichen Lebensbedingungen der Gefangenschaft durch Verzicht auf Fortpflanzung. . . . Ihre Anpassungsfähigkeit an den Terror menschlicher Naturbeherrschung ist minimal.

Opitz/Pinkert, *Der alte Maulwurf*

Man betrachte z.B. den Maulwurf, 'diesen unermüdlichen Arbeiter. Mit seinen Schaufelpfoten angestrengt zu graben—, ist die Beschäftigung seines ganzen Lebens: bleibende Nacht umgibt ihn: seine embryonischen Augen hat er bloß, um das Licht zu fliehen. . . . Was aber erlangt er durch diesen mühevollen und freudenleeren Lebenslauf? Futter und Begattung, also nur die Mittel, dieselbe traurige Bahn fortzusetzen und wieder anzufangen, im neuen Individuo. An solchen Beispielen wird es deutlich, daß zwischen den Mühen und Plagen des Lebens und dem Ertrag oder Gewinn desselben kein Verhältnis ist.

Arthur Schopenhauer

[Über die Skepsis als Schlaf- und Beruhigungsmittel] : . . . Und Hamlet selbst wird heute von den ärzten der Zeit gegen den 'Geist' und sein Rumoren unter dem Boden verordnet. "Hat man denn nicht alle Ohren schon voll von schlimmen Geräuschen? " sagt der Skeptiker, als ein Freund der Ruhe und beinahe als eine Art von Sicherheits-Polizei: "dies unterirdirsche Nein ist fürchterlich! Stille endlich, ihr pessimistischen Maulwürfe! "

Friedrich Nietzsche

. . . Ce monde hideux et bouleversant où les taupes elles-mêmes se mêlent d'espérer.

Albert Camus

Was ich schreibe, sind Maulwürfe. . . . Meine Maulwürfe sind schneller als man denkt. Wenn man meint, sie seien da, wo sie Mulm aufwerfen, rennen sie schon in ihren Gängen einem Gedanken nach. . . .

Günter Eich, *Maulwürfe*

Le sillage effacé de l'écriture par où la lecture fera surface, le cheminement souterrain d'une taupe. . . ; [*l'écriture*], cette activité frénétique, aveugle et Fouterraine. . . .

Hélène Cixous, *Neutre*

Schädlinge a Volksganzen jedoch, deren offenkundiger verbrecherischer Hang immer wieder strafbare Handlungen hervorrufen wird, werden unschädlich gemacht werden.

Hans Filbinger (CDU) im Jahr 1935

Maulwurffangprämie: Am Dienstagvormittag, 20.5. wird bei der Gemeindekasse die Maulwurffangprämie gegen Vorlage der Maulwurfschwänze ausgezahlt.

Amtliches Mitteilungsblatt der
Gemeinde Bollschweil-St. Ulrich,
Nr. 21, Jahrgang 1975

"¡Me falta algo, me falta algo!"

El Topo Gigio

Vorwurf §§§§§

Das Folgende als Versuch(ung) einer Nebeneinanderstellung von Textpassagen aus den Werken Kants, Hegels und Nietzsches, die ein merkwürdiges Bild dieser deutschen Philosophen entwerfen, das Bild nämlich des beinahe blinden, den Boden geschäftig durchwühlenden Schädlings, des Maulwurfs.[1] Das Bild entpuppt sich als mögliche Antwort auf die Frage: Wie verstehen sich die Philosophen Kant, Hegel und Nietzsche, wie schätzen sie ihre jeweilige Suche nach der Wahrheit ein? Denn—zumindest nach Kant—bietet die Metapher des Maulwurfs sich als passendes Selbstbildnis. Darüber hinaus ist zu fragen: Unterscheiden sich insbesondere bei Hegel und Nietzsche die Maulwurfsdeutungen derart, daß sich eine Kluft auftut, die zwei Epochen, die der Metaphysik und die einer "postmodernen," aber sonst kaum zu bezeichnenden Gegenwart, endgültig voneinander trennt?

I

Für Kant ist der Maulwurf gerade das, was er selber nicht ist, nämlich der Vertreter der Metaphysik, die über Jahrhunderte hinweg das Errichten von jedwedem wohlfundierten Gebäude einer wissenschaftlichen Philosophie verhindert hat. Wohl erwähnt Kant den Maulwurf selbst überhaupt nicht; es sind eher die bedauerlichen Ergebnisse von dessen intensiver Wühlarbeit, die die kritische Philosophie ins Auge fassen will. Nach einer Erörterung der platonischen Ideenlehre, die sich hauptsächlich mit dem Bereich der Moral und der Sittlichkeit beschäftigt, klagt Kant (KrV, A319/B375-76) wie folgt:

> Statt aller dieser Betrachtungen, deren gehörige Ausführung in der Tat die eigentümliche Würde der Philosophie ausmacht, beschäftigen wir uns jetzt mit einer nicht so glänzenden, aber doch auch nicht verdienstlosen Arbeit, nämlich: den Boden zu jenen majestätischen stattlichen Gebäuden eben und baufest zu machen, in welchem sich

allerlei Maulwurfsgänge einer vergeblich, aber mit guter Zuversicht, auf Schätze grabenden Vernunft vorfinden, und die jenes Bauwerk unsicher machen.

Nicht als Untergrabender, sondern als Ebnender versteht sich Kant: nicht als Maulwurf, sondern als Planierraupe. Um den Boden "eben und baufest zu machen," braucht sich der Philosoph angeblich gar nicht unter der Oberfläche der Erde zu bewegen, ja eine unterirdische Arbeit könnte das zukünftige Bauwerk nur gefährden. In der "Transzendentalen Deduktion" warnt Kant den Leser nichtsdestoweniger davor, daß er "über Dunkelheit klage, wo die Sache tief eingehüllt ist" (A88/B121), daß er die vielen Schwierigkeiten übersehe, die den Kritiker nötigen, "so tief in die ersten Gründe der Möglichkeit unserer Erkenntnis überhaupt einzudringen" (A98). Kritik der reinen Vernunft dürfe demgemäß keine Arbeit auf der Oberfläche sein. Es genüge nicht, die alten Maulwurfsgänge einfach von oben her zuzuschütten und auf diese Weise den Boden *scheinbar* eben und fest zu machen. Sowohl der Richter am Gerichtshof der kritischen Vernunft als auch der Architekt des Gebäudes der wissenschaftlichen Philosophie muß in die Tiefe eindringen; beide müssen also den Boden auf jeden Fall durchwühlen und untergraben, bis sie zum Grundgestein kommen. Damit werden diejenigen Fragen unumgänglich, die J. Sallis unlängst in seinem Aufsatz "Untergrabungen" gestellt hat: "Wie kann die Kritik den Boden bis zum Felsuntergrund erforschen, wenn nicht durch Bohrungen, die jenen Maulwurfswühlereien ähneln, deren Wirkungen die Kritik gerne auslöschen würde?" "Beraubt nicht auch der kritische Maulwurfsgang den Boden seiner Festigkeit, höhlt nicht auch er den Boden aus, bedroht also nicht auch er die Sicherheit aller Gebäude, die auf diesem Boden errichtet werden könnten?"[2]

Solche Fragen zeigen einen Riß auf, der die ganze Metaphorik von Kants Kritik zu sprengen und in eine sich widerstrebende Bewegung zu setzen droht. Hier liegt der Anfang einer neuen *Dialektik:* nicht die der transzendentalen Illusion, sondern die der eigentlichen, von der Geschichte der Metaphysik selbst her bestimmten Reflexion. Von Hegel bis Nietzsche führt jene Dialektik, die von einer zunehmenden und immer heftigeren Schwingung geprägt wird, in den Hinter- und Untergrund dieser Geschichte, deren Endstation als der Ab-Grund der Reflexion bezeichnet werden könnte. Ab-Grund der Reflexion heißt aber: ein gleichsam aus sich selbst entstehendes Bild und Selbstbildnis, eine nicht mehr auf die Kategorien einer Logik reduzierbare *imago.* Der Bewohner dieses Ab-Grunds ist *der Maulwurf.*

II

Über dem Schlußabschnitt von Hegels Vorlesungen über die Geschichte der Philosophie steht das Wort "Resultat." Diese Geschichte sei keine bloße Reihe von Ereignissen ohne *telos,* sie sei vielmehr die zweckgerichtete Offenbarung des Geistes, die sowohl Anstoß als auch Ziel hat. Dabei bestimmt die Geschichtlichkeit des Geistes die Wissenschaft seines Sichselbsterkennens, und zwar in solcher Weise, daß sich die Philosophie als "die wahre Theodizee" ergibt.[3] In seiner Berliner Antrittsvorlesung (Heidelberger Niederschrift) äußert sich Hegel im Rahmen seiner Einführung in die Philosophiegeschichte wie folgt:

> Der Besitz an selbstbewußter Vernünftigkeit, welcher uns, der jetzigen Welt angehört, ist nicht unmittelbar entstanden und nur aus dem Boden der Gegenwart gewachsen, sondern es ist dies wesentlich in ihm, eine Erbschaft und näher das *Resultat* der Arbeit, und zwar der Arbeit aller vorhergegangenen Generationen des Menschengeschlechts zu sein (XVIII, 21).

Erst im Laufe der Geschichte wird die Vernünftigkeit allmählich gewonnen und schrittweise zum festen Besitz gemacht, so daß die Vergangenheit wie der Gegenstand des Vergil'schen Epos sich als verehrungswürdig erweist, als die *"Reihe der edlen Geister,* die Galerie der Heroen der denkenden Vernunft" (XX, 465)—

"Tantae molis erat, se ipsam cognoscere mentem."

Verehrungswürdig allerdings vom jetzigen Standpunkt, d.h. von dem einer höheren, weiterentwickelten Welt her, deren Fortschrittsniveau knapp definiert wird: "Die Gegenwart ist das Höchste" (XX, 456).[4] Die Idee des Geistes anerkennt sich in dieser Gegenwart als sich erkennende, sich denkende Idee in ihrer Notwendigkeit, d.h. in ihrer Identität als Begriff. Im Besitz dieser an und für sich erkannten Vernünftigkeit schaut nun der Philosoph auf das ruhelos fortschreitende Streben des Geistes zurück. Da nimmt er wahr, wie der Geist sich geradlinig fortwühlt, bohrend, grabend, aber immer aufwärts steigend. Der Begriff eignet sich jetzt erstaunlicherweise ein Bild an. Das Bild des sich selbst erkennenden Geistes am Ende der Erinnerung, wie sie Hegel darstellt, ist: der Maulwurf. Die ererbte Botschaft des vernünftigen Denkens, das Resultat der Geschichte des Geistes als Begriff, ist: *Geist gleich Maulwurf.* Dazu sagt Hegel:

> Er schreitet immer vorwärts zu, weil nur der Geist ist Fortschreiten. Oft scheint er sich vergessen, verloren zu haben; aber innerlich sich entgegengesetzt, ist er innerliches Fortarbeiten—wie Hamlet vom Geiste seines Vaters sagt, "Brav gearbeitet, wackerer Maulwurf"—bis er, in sich erstarkt, jetzt die Erdrinde, die ihn von seiner

Sonne, seinem Begriffe, schied, aufstößt, daß sie zusammenfällt. In solcher Zeit hat er die Siebenmeilen- stiefel angelegt, wo sie, ein seelenloses, morschge- wordenes Gebäude, zusammenfällt und er in neuer Jugend sich gestaltet zeigt. Diese Arbeit des Geistes sich zu erkennen, sich zu finden, diese Tätigkeit ist der Geist, das Leben des Geistes selbst. Sein Resultat ist der Begriff, den er von sich erfaßt: die Geschichte der Philosophie die klare Einsicht, daß der Geist dies gewollt in seiner Geschichte (XX, 456).

Man ahnt hier die Spannung zwischen *Resultat* und *Tätigkeit:* Sich begreifen bedeutet, oder deutet zumindest an, sich ans Tageslicht bringen, sich erfassen, endgültig zu einer klaren Einsicht gelangen, d.h. auf Basis einer schon etablierten *claritas* zum Stillstand kommen. Begreift sich der Geist, erkennt sich das absolute Wesen als das Sichselbstdenkende, kommt der Geist vermutlich zur Ruhe. Alles Äußerliche, alles Gegenständliche, all das, was früher einmal fremd und unabhängig zu sein schien, ergibt sich jetzt als Moment des sich selbst erkennenden Geistes, erweist sich als mit dem Geist völlig identisch und von seiner Gewalt völlig abhängig. Somit gelingt dem Geist ein Blick ins Ewige: "Der Kampf des endlichen Selbstbewußtseins mit dem absoluten Selbstbewußtsein, das jenem außer ihm erschien, hört auf. Das endliche Selbstbewußtsein hat aufgehört, endliches zu sein . . ." (XX, 460). Damit ist die Geschichte der Philosophie so weit gelangt, daß der "auf seine Spitze getriebene" Geist das eigene Lebensprinzip, d.h. das eigentliche Geschehen seiner Geschichte, selbst enträtselt: das Leben des Geistes produziert den eigenen inneren Gegensatz immer aufs neue und versöhnt sich wieder mit ihm. Aber die Lebensweise des Geistes ist paradox: alles kämpferische Streben hört auf, es beruhigt sich im absoluten Wissen und Wollen seines wesenhaft ruhelos und nie aufhörenden Strebens. Resul*tat* ist und muß sein: *Tätig*keit. In der Berliner Antrittsvorlesung heißt es: "Der Geist der Welt aber versinkt nicht in diese gleichgültige *Ruhe.* Es beruht dies auf seinem einfachen Begriff. Sein *Leben* ist *Tat*" (XVIII, 22). "Resultat" (lateinisch *resultare: re + saltare*) ist das unermüdliche Sich-Wiederholen des Geistes, dessen Lebenslauf im Gedächtnis des Denkers immer wieder durchlaufen und durchlebt werden muß. Die Denkweise des auf seine Spitze getriebenen Geistes zeigt sich als Er-Innerung.[5] Er-Innerung ist das Anhören des Echos, welches in der imponierenden "Halle der heroischen Galerie der Denker" die Stille zerbricht, oder besser noch, das Betrachten der Bilder, die in dieser Galerie gezeigt werden.

Das in Hegels Vorlesungen immer wiederkehrende Bild (*imago* als Echo und Abbild zugleich) ist, wie wir wissen, das des Maulwurfs. Nach Hegels Ansicht gräbt sich der Maulwurf immer vor- und aufwärts; im Grunde geht in der Geschichte der Philosophie nichts verloren, wird nichts verschwendet. Nur der Geist schreitet fort und, von der Gegenwart her gesehen, besteht der Geist nur aus Fortschreiten. Weil die ihm entgegengesetzten Hindernisse rein innerlich sind, und weil sie also überwunden sind, sobald sie als innerlich, d.h. als identisch mit ihm selbst erkannt worden sind, kann sein Weg nur aufwärts führen. Eine solche Erkenntnis bekräftigt den philosophierenden Maulwurf. Sie bringt ihm das Vertrauen auf die Wissenschaft und auf sich selbst und verleiht ihm somit den Mut zur Wahrheit (XVIII, 13). Der Maulwurf arbeitet brav—wie der Geist des ermordeten Königs von Dänemark. Aber wie steht es mit einem solchen Vergleich? Wozu, am Ende der Geschichte der sich selbst denkenden Idee, die die Sprache des Begriffs und der Logik zum Mittel und Ziel hat, eine Sprache, in der Form und Inhalt identisch, d.h. gegenseitig vollkommen ausreichend sind (vgl. *Enzyklopädie,* § 236 ff), wozu überhaput eine *imago?* Wie war es möglich, daß damals, als das endliche Selbstbewußtsein aufhörte, endlich zu sein, ein Maulwurf dabei herauskam? Und warum ausgerechnet einer aus dem verfaulten Staate Dänemark? Denn wie seltsam in diesem Zusammenhang ist die Anspielung auf *Hamlet!* Der maulwurfsche Hamlet Senior wühlt sich eben nicht nur aufwärts zur Erdrinde und erst recht nicht zum Tageslicht. Im Gegenteil, er krabbelt nur nachts hinauf, um seinen Sohn in einen Racheplan zu verstricken. Sodann wühlt er sich wieder zurück zum Hades, abwärts in die höllische Finsternis, nicht von irgendwelcher Einsicht gestärkt, sondern geschwächt von der Darstellung seiner eigenen Geschichte, erschöpft von seiner Wiedererinnerung, erschreckt vom Morgenduft und der wachsenden Helle—

Der Glühwurm zeigt, daß sich die Frühe naht,
Und sein unwirksam Feu'r beginnt zu blassen.

Das Resultat der wühlerischen Tätigkeit dieses Geistes, das Ergebnis seines Rachewunsches, ist nicht Versöhnung, sondern Vernichtung, ist der Tod Hamlets Ophelias Gertrudes Claudius' Polonius' Rosenkrantz' und Guildensterns. Der siegreiche Fortinbras, der den Thron Dänemarks übernehmen soll, formuliert das Resultat so:

O stolzer Tod,
Welch Fest geht vor in deiner ew'gen Zelle,
Daß du auf Einen Schlag so viele Fürsten
So blutig trafst?

Brav gearbeitet, wackerer Maulwurf. Des Vaters Geist bleibt künftig in der Tiefe begraben, in der Stille von Lethes Ufer. "Ruh, ruh, verstörter Geist! " Ohne Sohn bleibt er jedoch unversöhnt, fern jeder Erinnerung. Das Resultat ist das alles auslöschende Vergessen, die ewige Untätigkeit, das Nichts eines endgültigen Aussterbens.

161

Hegel will aber ermutigend wirken. Er beschließt seine einleitende Betrachtung der Philosophiegeschichte mit einer Aufforderung an die Zuhörer. Die Studenten sollten nicht jener Täuschung zum Opfer fallen, die diese Geschichte als "eine blinde Sammlung" von Einzelfällen entstellt. Vom Standpunkt des Individuums her gesehen, erscheine sie zwar wie ein Meinungschaos oder wie bedeutungslose Haarspalterei; jedoch "wie Blinde in demselben," seien alle Einzelfälle vom gemeinsamen Geist, nämlich einem "Instinkt der Vernunft" getrieben, dessen "Gefühl oder Glauben" mit der Wendung "die Wahrheit ist *eine*" (XVIII, 36) umschrieben werden kann. Eine Randnotiz in der Heidelberger Niederschrift betont dies nochmals: "... fortschreitend; nichts Zufälliges ... das innere Beisichselbstbleiben des Geistes" (XVIII, 14). Solches Beisichsein darf andererseits nicht als eine Insichselbstversunkenheit verstanden werden. Irgendwie drängt der Geist gleichzeitig auf und ab, ein und aus. Das höchste Geheimnis, das diese seine Tätigkeit umgibt, wird am Ende der Vorlesung, etwa als ihr Resultat, so formuliert:

> Je tiefer der Geist in sich gegangen, desto stärker der Gegensatz: die Tiefe ist nach der Größe des Gegensatzes, des Bedürfnisses zu messen; je tiefer in sich, desto tiefer ist sein Bedürfnis, nach außen zu suchen, sich zu finden, desto breiter sein Reichtum nach außen (XX, 455).

Am Anfang seiner Vorlesung fordert Hegel seine Zuhörer auf, "*die Morgenröte einer schöneren Zeit*" zu begrüßen (XVIII, 13); am Ende malt er noch einmal die Tätigkeit des einen lebendigen Geistes aus:

> Auf sein Drängen—wenn der Maulwurf im Innern fortwühlt—haben wir zu hören und ihm Wirklichkeit zu verschaffen; sie sind ein schlechthin notwendiger Fortgang, der nichts als die Natur des Geistes selbst ausspricht und in uns allen lebt. Ich wünsche, daß diese Geschichte der Philosophie eine Aufforderung für Sie enthalten möge, den Geist der Zeit, der in uns natürlich ist, zu ergreifen und aus seiner Natürlichkeit, d.h. Verschlossenheit, Leblosigkeit hervor an den Tag zu ziehen und—jeder an seinem Orte—mit Bewußtsein an den Tag zu bringen. ... Ich wünsche Ihnen, recht wohl zu leben (XX, 462).

—Bis zur *Morgenröte* fehlt allerdings noch ein Siebenmeilenschritt. Und wenn der Maulwurf tatsächlich ans Tageslicht gezogen worden ist, wo endet dann die ganze Geschichte?

In der Tat wühlt sich der emsig philosophierende Maulwurf auf unvorhergesehenen Wegen noch tiefer. Er ahnt eine noch unsicher schimmernde Morgen- (oder Abend-?) röte, die über dem für den Unterirdischen natürlich ganz unsichtbaren Horizont schwebt. Im Herbst 1886 bereitet Friedrich Nietzsche in Ruta bei Genua eine zweite Ausgabe seiner 1881 erschienenen Schrift *Morgenröte: Gedanken über moralische Vorurteile* vor. Zu dieser Zeit ist Nietzsche mit seiner nächsten neinsagenden Abhandlung *Zur Genealogie der Moral* beschäftigt. Der jasagende Mittag seines schöpferischen Lebens, der Zenit des "Zarathustra," ist längst vorbei; es ist eigentlich Spätnachmittag, wenngleich noch nicht die Stunde der Dämmerung. Noch freut sich der Einsame auf den neuen Tag, dessen Morgenröte er schon irgendwie spürt. In der Vorrede zur zweiten Ausgabe schreibt Nietzsche:

> In diesem Buche findet man einen "Unterirdischen" an der Arbeit, einen Bohrenden, Grabenden, Untergrabenden. Man sieht ihn, vorausgesetzt, daß man Augen für solche Arbeit der Tiefe hat—, wie er langsam, besonnen, mit sanfter Unerbittlichkeit vorwärts kommt, ohne daß die Not sich allzusehr verriete, welche jede lange Entbehrung von Licht und Luft mit sich bringt: man könnte ihn selbst bei seiner dunklen Arbeit zufrieden nennen. Scheint es nicht, daß irgendein Glaube ihn führt, ein Trost entschädigt? Daß er vielleicht seine eigne lange Finsternis haben will, sein Unverständliches, Verborgenes, Rätselhaftes, weil er weiß, was er auch haben wird: seinen eignen Morgen, seine eigne Erlösung, seine eigne *Morgenröte?* ... Gewiß, er wird zurückkehren: fragt ihn nicht, was er da unten will, er wird es euch selbst schon sagen, dieser scheinbare Trophonios und Unterirdische, wenn er erst wieder "Mensch geworden" ist. Man verlernt gründlich das Schweigen, wenn man so lange, wie er, Maulwurf war, allein war—.[6]

Nietzsches Maulwurfsgang bohrt sich durch bis zu den moralischen Voraussetzungen, die alle bisherigen metaphysischen Systeme mehr oder weniger unbemerkt unterstützt bzw. durchzogen haben. "Ich stieg in die Tiefe, ich bohrte in den Grund," erklärt der sich erinnernde, zurückblickende Maulwurf, "ich begann ein altes *Vertrauen* zu untersuchen und anzugraben, ... ich begann *unser Vertrauen zur Moral* zu untergraben" (I, 1012). Somit hat Nietzsche genau die heikle Stelle der kritischen Philosophie Kants anvisiert, nämlich die der Sittlichkeit und der

Moral, wo Kant tatsächlich Maulwurfsgänge festgestellt hatte, die er dann von außen oder von oben her vergeblich zuzuschütten versuchte. Somit untersucht Nietzsche auch den großen Reichtum des Hegelschen Geistes, dessen "Bedürfnis," sich nach außen zu drängen, verdächtig geworden ist. Nietzsches Weg setzt sich im Untergrund fort, ohne jede Zuversicht einer einfältigen Panglossmetaphysik, auf der Spur eines tief verwurzelten Argwohns gegen alle Ausformungen eines heimlich auf der Moral aufgebauten Idealismus, dessen Grundstruktur seinerseits auf einer Mißachtung dieser Erde und dieses Lebens basiert. Nietzsche treibt seinen Tunnel gegen allen "Mut zur Wahrheit" voran, der sich für ihn eher als "Ohnmacht zur Macht" oder als der reine Wille zum Nichts entlarvt. Bei Nietzsche bleibt die Tätigkeit des Resultats ein Zurückspringen, ein resaltare ("... Gewiß, er wird zurückkehren ..."), welches nie zu irgendeinem Stillstand kommt, denn alles "was halt macht (bei einer angeblichen causa prima, bei einem Unbedingten usw.) ist die *Faulheit, die Ermüdung—"* (*Der Wille zur Macht,* Nr. 575, aus dem Jahr 1885-86). (Wenn Nietzsches genealogische Kritik überhaupt auf einer "Metaphysik" des Willens zur Macht beruht, so ist diese Kritik eine "Hyperkritik," diese Metaphysik eine "Hypophysik.") Bei Hegel wühlt sich der Maulwurf ausschließlich *fort* (im Sinne von *vorwärts* und *aufwärts*), auch wenn er in die Tiefe drängt; bei Nietzsche gräbt er sich hauptsächlich nach *unten* und *zurück.* Dieses Zurückkehren beruht auf keiner endgültig etablierten Einsicht, die aus dem Sicherinnern eine Geste des Fortschrittsoptimismus hätte machen können. Nietzsches Hamletlehre sieht nämlich ganz anders aus: "In der Bewußtheit der einmal geschauten Wahrheit sieht jetzt der Mensch überall nur das Entsetzliche oder Absurde des Seins ... : es ekelt ihn" (*Die Geburt der Tragödie,* I, 48). Andererseits zeigt sich auch bei Nietzsche die Geschichte der Philosophie als ein von einem "Gefühl oder Glauben" getriebenes Sichselbsthervorbringen, dieses wohlgemerkt nicht als Tätigkeit eines "Geistes"—auch wenn jene Tätigkeit als die Einsicht in das, was der Geist stets *gewollt* hat, interpretiert wird—sondern als die Gesetzgebung des Willens zur Macht. Der Geschichte der Philosophie liegt also nicht Hegels "Instinkt der Vernunft," sondern der Instinkt der Selbsterhaltung und -steigerung eines Lebewesens namens "Mensch" zugrunde. An die Stelle des Beisichseins des von der "Natürlichkeit" befreiten Geistes tritt jetzt die Selbsttäuschung des im Bereich des Sinnlichen verbleibenden Menschen; an die Stelle von Hegels "nichts Zufälliges" tritt die Unschuld des Werdens.

Wie steht es aber um jenen "Trost," welcher in der sichtbaren Welt der Oberfläche als Morgenröte erscheinen mag und welcher—selbst dem Untergründigen—eine "Erlösung" verspricht? Verharrt der Maulwurf da unten, oder kriecht er wieder hoch in Richtung der "ewigen Wiederkehr des Gleichen"? Der Gedanke der ewigen Wiederkunft "überfiel" Nietzsche 1881 (d.h. im Jahr der Veröffentlichung von *Morgenröte*) in Sils-Maria im

Oberengadin, "6000 Fuß jenseits von Mensch und Zeit" (*Ecce Homo*, II, 1128). Manchmal schien Nietzsche selber die Wiederkunftsidee nicht bloß der Probierstein bei der Auslese des Übermenschen zu sein, sondern auch ein "Trost."[7] Die Frage erhebt sich: Wird dann jene Lehre zur Rettung von und d.h. zur Rache an dieser Welt und ihrer *Zeit?* Wird sie zur "Erlösung" von der Vergänglichkeit und von dem für den Willen unerträglichen "es *war*"? Geht es hier im Endeffekt doch um ein weiteres Stückchen Heilsgeschichte (= *décadence*)? Nicht abzuleugnen ist die Gefahr, daß die Sehnsucht nach Erlösung das ganze Projekt des Nietzscheschen Denkens auf eine Abart Hegelscher Versöhnungsphiloso-phie reduziert, daß amor fati nicht mehr bedeutet als amor Vati (im Freudschen Sinne), daß Zarathustras mühevoll gewonnener Honig zum Süßen einer weiteren Tasse Beruhigungstee verwendet wird und daß das goldene Lachen das Übermenschen, das zu allem Werden und Sein J-A sagt, dem I-A des Eselgeschreis allzu ähnlich wird. Dagegen ist wohl zu betonen, daß die große Affirmation in der Wiederkunftslehre vor dem Mißtrauen der genealogischen Kritik nicht zu bewahren ist, daß der unersättliche Verdacht jene Lehre stets begleiten muß. Das Ja und das Nein sind also unzertrennliche Gefährten, der glühende Dionysos wandert an der Seite des grimmigen Silenos. Demzufolge bleibt der Wiederkunftsgedanke ein Weg nach unten, eine κατάβαδις oder ein "untergang," der "der Erde treu" bleibt. Hebt sich dieser Gedanke überhaupt je empor, so gelangt er nur bis an die Grenze zwischen Erde und Himmel—eine Grenze im Hochgebirge, da der Maulwurf (*talpa europaea*) nur bis in 2000 Meter Höhe überleben kann, d.h. bis zu jenen 6000 Fuß jenseits von Mensch und Zeit, die die Ferne der Geburtsstätte der Wiederkunftslehre anzeigen. Und es ist nach wie vor der Maulwurf, um den es hier geht. Der hochfliegende Adler und die sich um des Adlers Hals windende Schlange sind die Tiere *Zarathustras.* Auch das Kamel, der Löwe, der Esel und das Kind gehören zur Menagerie des bunten Persers. Was *Nietzsches* einziges Tierchen betrifft: er fliegt und zischt nicht, trägt keine Bürde, weder brüllt er noch kreischt er, und er spielt nur äußerst selten unbefangen ein Heraklitsches Brettspiel. Er krabbelt bloß, wühlt unerbittlich, aufwärts bis zur steinigen Erdoberfläche, dann bedächtig zurück. Als ein "Lehrer des langsamen Lesens" (I, 1016) trägt er grundsätzlich nie Siebenmeilenstiefel. Der Einsamkeit ständig ausgesetzt, erlernt er immer wieder das Schweigen. Um darüber reden zu können, muß er selbstverständlich "Mensch werden"—also nicht Zarathustra, nicht Übermensch, nicht Dionysos, sondern: Mensch. Er muß lernen, wie man wird, was man ist, muß hinunter zu Trophonios und dann der Pflicht nachkommen, darüber zu schreiben (vgl. Pausanias IX, 39, 4).

Dieses "Wie man wird, was man ist" als ein "Wie man ist, was man geworden ist": auf ein solches Leben hin, eines der unablässigen Wühlarbeit als Möglichkeit und Verhängnis, Geschick und Mißgeschick zugleich, ist das Sein des Maulwurfs in der (unserer) Zeit immer schon entworfen:

geworfener
Entwurf
des
Maulwurfs

entweder als ${\text{ζῷον}}$ λόγον ${\text{ἔχον}}$ das Lebewesen, das stets ein interpretierendes Wort im Maul hat, oder als Mulmwerfer und Erdfresser, der die frenetische Tätigkeit des Schreibens aufnimmt, deren ewiger Kreislauf des Vor- und Zurückwühlens ein Vorlaufen in den eigenen Tod ist (vgl. Heideggers *Sein und Zeit,* S. 264). Denn wohin (ver)führt letzten Endes diese *imago* des Maulwurfsphilosophen, von Kant über Hegel zu Nietzsche?

Aus Wilhelm Buschs *Dideldum! ,* vierter Abschnitt, "Der Maulwurf," hier einige abschließende Auszüge, eine Art

Nachwurf§§§§§

NOTES

1   Zur Maulwurfsliteratur aus einer linkspolitischen Perspektive s. Alfred Opitz und Ernst-Ullrich Pinkert, *Der alte Maulwurf: Die Verdammten (unter) dieser Erde, Geschichte einer revolutionären Symbolfigur,* Berlin, 1979. Die Auszüge aus Marx, Schopenhauer, Filbinger und Eich in dem vorliegenden Aufsatz stammen aus der Opitz/Pinkert'schen Sammlung. Die Rolle des Maulwurfs bei Kant, Hegel und Nietzsche wird in diesem Buch freilich nicht behandelt.

2   Dem Aufsatz von Professor Sallis, den ich im Manuskript lesen konnte, verdanke ich jede Menge Maulwurfsmulm. Auch den folgenden Mannheimer Mitwühlenden möchte ich hier herzlich danken: Ulrich Halfmann, Friederike Born, Burkhardt Allner, Elisabeth Hoffmann, Thomas Müller, Werner Reinhart, Margarete Seidenspinner, Jupp Schöpp und Jochen Barkhausen.

3   G. W. F. Hegel, *Werke in zwanzig Bänden,* Frankfurt/Main: Suhrkamp, 1971, XX, 455.

4   Selbstverständlich sind alle Zitate aus den *Vorlesungen über die Geschichte der Philosophie* nur vorläufig als Hegels Wortlaut zu akzeptieren. Man darf auf die verschiedenen kritischen Ausgaben, die zur Zeit in Frankreich, Italien und Deutschland in Vorbereitung sind, gespannt sein.

5   Vgl. die beiden letzten Seiten der *Phänomenologie des Geistes,* über "Er-Innerung."

6   F. Nietzsche, *Werke in drei Bänden,* Hrsg. Karl Schlechta, München: Hanser, 1956, I, 1011.

7   Vgl. *Der Wille zur Macht,* Nr. 1065 (November 1887-März 1888): "Jener Kaiser hielt sich beständig die Vergänglichkeit aller Dinge vor, um sie nicht zu *wichtig* zu nehmen und zwischen ihnen ruhig zu bleiben. Mir scheint umgekehrt alles vielzuviel wert zu sein, als daß es so flüchtig sein dürfte: ich

suche nach einer Ewigkeit für jegliches: dürfte man die kostbarsten Salben und Weine ins Meer gießen? —Mein Trost ist, daß alles, was war, ewig ist: —das Meer spült es wieder her."

THE MOLE
Philosophic Burrowings in Kant, Hegel, and Nietzsche

David Farrell Krell

*For Helm Breinig, burrowing bravely
over the years.*

Extracts §§§§§

Mole (cf. *mow, mould*): any one of the small mammals of the family *Talpidae*; esp. the common mole of the Old World, *Talpa europaea*, a small animal . . . having . . . exceedingly small but not blind eyes, and very short strong fassorial fore-limbs with which to burrow in the earth in search of earthworms and to excavate the galleried chambers in which it dwells.
Oxford English Dictionary

These also shalbe vncleane vnto you, . . . the Lyzard, and
the Snaile, and the Molle.
Leviticus xi, 30

We recognize our old friend, our old mole, who knows so well
how to work underground, then suddenly to emerge.
Karl Marx

Up to the present day it has proved impossible to breed moles; they withdraw from the artificial living conditions of captivity by refusing to propagate. . . . Their ability to adapt to the Terror of human dominion over nature is minimal.

Opitz/Pinkert, *The Old Mole*

Observe, for instance, the mole—that tireless worker. The occupation of his entire life is to dig laboriously with his shovel-like paws; ever-present night surrounds him; he has his embryonic eyes only that he may flee the light. . . . But what does he gain from his toilsome and joyless curriculum? Food and reproduction—in other words, nothing more than the means to continue on the selfsame miserable path, beginning again in a new individual. Such examples make it clear that an unfavorable ratio prevails between the toils and troubles of life and its outcome or gain.

Arthur Schopenhauer

[*On skepticism as a sedative*] : . . . And nothing less than *Hamlet* is prescribed today by the medicals of our time to settle the "spirit" and its subterranean rumblings. "Haven't we had enough dreadful noise?" says the skeptic, who is a friend of tranquillity, and almost an agent of the Security Police. "This underground negation is terrifying! Won't you *please* be quiet, you pessimistic moles!"

Friedrich Nietzsche

Does the Eagle know what is in the pit?
Or wilt thou go ask the Mole?
from William Blake, "Thel's Motto"

My instinct tells me that my head is an organ for burrowing, as some creatures use their snout and fore paws, and with it I would mine and burrow my way through these hills.

Henry David Thoreau

But parasitic pests on the body politic of the *Volk*, pests whose flagrant addiction to malfeasance will give rise again and again to criminal acts, will be neutralized.

Hans Filbinger (CDU), in 1935

Reward for the Capture of Moles: On Tuesday, May 20, bounties for the capture of moles will be paid out by the local treasurer upon receipt of the tails.

*Community Newsletter for the Town of
Bollschweil-St. Ulrich*, No. 21, May 16, 1975.

So then he scraped and scratched and scrabbled and scrooged, and then he scrooged again and scrabbled and scratched and scraped, working busily with his little paws and muttering to himself, "Up we go! Up we go!" till at last, pop! . . .

Kenneth Grahame, *The Wind in the Willows*

Prelude and Plaint §§§§§

What follows is an attemptation to juxtapose a series of texts from the works of Kant, Hegel, and Nietzsche. The texts project a curious image of these German philosophers, as that all-but-blind, busily burrowing rodent pest, the mole.[1] The image suggests something about the way these philosophers understand themselves, how they estimate their own search for truth. For, at least after Kant, the mole metaphor emerges as a fitting likeness of the philosopher. The question then arises: Do the various employments of the mole image, especially in Hegel and Nietzsche, differ in such a way that a gap opens up, a gap that divides once and for all two epochs, that of metaphysics from that of our "postmodern" present, to which we otherwise can scarcely lend a name?

I

The mole is precisely what Kant, in his own eyes, is not, namely, a representative of the metaphysical tradition. For metaphysics has for centuries obstructed the erection of every possible solidly founded structure for a scientific philosophy. Indeed, Kant does not mention the mole as such. What the Critical philosophy wishes to examine is the damage his intensive excavations have done. After a discussion of the Platonic Ideas, a discussion preoccupied mainly with the realm of morality and ethicality, Kant complains (*Critique of Pure Reason*, A319/B375-76):

> Although pursuit of these considerations is what lends
> philosophy its proper dignity, we must instead occupy
> ourselves now with a less resplendent yet still meritori-
> ous task, namely, we must level the ground and make it
> firm enough for those majestic edifices of ethicality. For
> in this ground we find all kinds of mole tunnels which
> reason has dug in its confident but futile search for treas-
> ure and which make such construction precarious.

Kant sees himself, not as excavator, but as leveler; not as "Mole," but as "Caterpillar." In order to "level the ground and make it firm enough" to build, the Critical philosopher ostensibly need not penetrate below the surface of the earth. Indeed, further subterranean work could only endanger future construction. Nevertheless, in the "Transcendental

Deduction" Kant warns his readers not to "complain about obscurity where the matter at issue is so profoundly veiled" (A88/B121) and not to overlook the many difficulties that compel the Critical philosopher to "penetrate so deep into the primary grounds of the possibility of our cognition in general" (A98). A critique of pure reason accordingly dare not be labor on the superficies. It would not be enough simply to cause the old mole tunnels to cave in by toiling away on the surface. In that way one would make the ground only *apparently* level and firm. The judge at the law court of pure reason and the architect who designs the buildings for a scientific philosophy—both of these must plunge into depths, they must at all events burrow and tunnel into the earth until they reach bedrock. But if that is so, certain questions inevitably arise, questions John Sallis has posed in his recent essay, "Tunnelings": "How can critique explore the ground all the way down to the bedrock except by tunneling down to it in a way not unlike that very mole-tunneling whose effects critique would expunge?" "Does not the critical mole-tunnel too deprive the ground of its firmness, tunnel it out, and threaten the security of any edifices that might be erected on that ground?"[2]

Such questions expose a crack that threatens to sunder the entire metaphorics of Kant's *Critique* and set it in motion against itself. Here a new *dialectic* begins. Not the dialectic of transcendental illusions but that of reflection proper, reflection as determined by the history of metaphysics itself. Such a dialectic, marked by an increasingly intense and violent oscillation, opens the path from Hegel to Nietzsche, a path into the background and underground of that history; the destination of the path might be designated as the "abyss," the vanishing of the ground and grounds where reflection is to take place. The "abyss" of reflection is described in an image that emerges under its own power, so to speak, an image that serves as a self-portrait which is no longer reducible to the categories of any logic. The one who dwells in the abyss is *the mole.*

II

The word "result" caps the final section of Hegel's lectures on the history of philosophy. That history is not merely a chronicle of events without *telos*; it is rather a purposeful revelation of and by spirit which has its motivation and its aim. The historicity of spirit thus defines the science of its knowledge of self, indeed in such a way that philosophy presents itself as "the true Theodicy."[3] In his inaugural lecture at Berlin (the following text being excerpted from the Heidelberg manuscript) Hegel says the following by way of an introduction to the history of philosophy:

> The possession of self-assured rationality, which is proper to us of the contemporary world, did not originate immediately, did not simply sprout from the soil of the

172

present; what is essential about it is that it is a heritage; more specifically, it is the *result* of the labor of all the past generations of mankind. (XVIII, 21)

Rationality is attained only in the course of history, becomes a permanent possession only step-by-step, so that the past proves to be venerable. For it manifests *"a column of noble spirits,* the gallery of the heroes of thinking reason," whose exploits are as august as the theme of Vergil's great epic—

So mighty the efforts that the mind might know itself.

Of course, the dignity of the past is perceived from the contemporary standpoint, which is one of a more highly developed world. Hegel formulates the status of its progress quite succinctly: "The present is supreme" (XX, 456).[4] The idea of spirit acknowledges itself as the idea that knows and thinks itself in its necessity, i.e., in its identity, as concept. In possession of such rationality, known in and for itself, the philosopher gazes back upon the incessantly progressive strivings of spirit. He ascertains that spirit burrows its way forward, digging and drilling, always on the ascent. Inexplicably and astonishingly, the concept now appropriates an image. The image of spirit that knows itself, the image that Hegel conjures at the very end of his recollection, is that of a mole. The heritage, the proclamation of rational thought, the result of the history of spirit as concept is the equation of spirit and mole. Hegel says:

It always comes forward and to the fore, because spirit alone is progression. Often it seems to have forgotten who it is, to have gotten lost. But, internally divided, it works its way internally forward—as Hamlet says of his father's spirit, "Well done, old mole"—until, having gathered strength, it pushes through the crust of earth that has separated it from its sun, its concept, and the crust collapses. When the crust collapses, like a rundown, abandoned building, spirit takes on new youthful form and dons seven-league boots. This labor of spirit to know itself, find itself, this activity *is* spirit, the life of spirit itself. Its result is the concept that it grasps of itself; the history of spirit yields the clear insight that spirit willed all of this in its history. (XX, 456).

We notice here a tension between "result" and "activity." To grasp oneself means, or at least suggests, bringing oneself to light, getting a view on oneself, achieving some ultimate and clear insight, and on the basis of such established clarity coming to rest. If spirit grasps itself, if the absolute essence becomes known as self-thinking, then spirit apparently achieves tranquillity. Everything external and objective, everything that once seemed to be foreign and independent, now turns out to be a moment of spirit which knows itself. It proves to be fully identical with spirit, fully subject to its sovereignty. At this point spirit can cast a glance into eternity: "The struggle of finite self-consciousness with absolute self-consciousness, in which the finite seemed to be excluded from the absolute, now ceases. Finite self-consciousness has ceased to be finite . . ." (XX 460). At this point the history of philosophy has reached a juncture where spirit, "driven to its very peak," responds to the riddle of its own existence, i.e., the riddle of the proper *happening* of its history. The life of spirit is a life that forever produces its own internal opposite, reconciling itself with that opposite. But spirit's existence is paradoxical: the relentless struggle ceases, and spirit rests on the absolute knowing and absolute willing of its essentially restless and ceaseless struggle. "Resul*tat*" does not imply mere "result," but an activity or deed, "*Tät*igkeit." In his inaugural lecture at Berlin Hegel notes: "But the spirit of the world does not submerge into indifferent *tranquillity*. For such is the nature of its simple concept, that its *life* is *deed*" (XVIII, 22). "Result" (cf. the Latin *resultare re + saltare*) is the ceaseless self-recapitulation of spirit, whose curriculum the thinker must preserve in memory, running through it, living through it, again and again. The mode of thought for spirit, driven to its peak, manifests itself as *remembrance.*[5] Remembrance heeds the echo that shatters the stillness in the imposing "hall of the gallery of thought's heroes"; better, it studies the images housed in that gallery.

As we have seen, the *imago* that recurs in Hegel's lectures, an *imago* that is both echo and visible object, is that of the mole. According to Hegel, the mole digs his way ever forward and upward; ultimately, nothing is lost or wasted in the history of philosophy. Only spirit is progressive, and, from the point of view of the present, spirit is only progression. Spirit burrows ever upward, for the obstacles that oppose it are overcome as soon as they are recognized as being internal, i.e., as being identical with it. Such knowledge invigorates the philosophizing mole, grants him confidence in science and in himself, and so nurtures courage in the truth (XVIII, 13). The mole works diligently—like the spirit of the murdered king of Denmark. But how do matters stand with that comparison? Why, at the end of the history of the self-thinking idea, which possesses the language of the concept and of logic as its medium and its end, a language in which form and content are identical, i.e., mutually fully adequate (cf. the *Encyclopedia* §§ 236 ff.), why an *imago* at all? How does it happen that when finite self-consciousness ceases to be finite the result is a mole? And why, of all things, a mole from the degenerate state of Denmark?

The allusion to *Hamlet*—how strange it is in the present context! The mole-like ghost of Hamlet's father does not dig his way merely upward to the surface of the earth, nor at all in order to reach the light of day. On the contrary, he scrabbles upward only at night, in order to engage his son in a plot of vengeance. And he soon burrows his way back to Hades, down to his murky limbo, not strengthened by any sort of insight but weakened by the telling of his own story, exhausted by the remembrance of it, blenching at the morning air and incipient light—

> The glowworm shows the maten to be near,
> And 'gins to pale his uneffectual fire—.

The result of the tunneling activity of this spirit, the outcome of his desire for revenge, is not reconciliation at all, but annihilation: the deaths of Hamlet Ophelia Gertrude Claudius Polonius Rosencrantz and Guildenstern. Victorious Fortinbras, about to accede to the Danish throne, formulates the "result" in the following way:

> O proud death,
> What feast is toward in thine eternal cell,
> That thou so many princes at a shot,
> So bloodily hast struck?

Well done, old mole. The spirit father now remains below, buried in the calm of Lethe's shore. "Rest, rest, perturbed Spirit!" But, bereft of child, unreconciled: there is no one to remember him. The result is all-extinguishing oblivion, eternal lethargy, the nothingness of ultimate undoing and demise.

But Hegel wishes to be encouraging. He closes his introductory observations on the history of philosophy by making a demand on his listeners. His students dare not fall prey to that deception which distorts the history of philosophy so that it seems to be "a blind conglomerate" of individual cases. Seen from the point of view of the individual, that history looks like a chaos of sheer opinions, like inane and endless hair-splitting. But, although "blind in themselves," all individual cases are quickened by a unitary spirit, as by an "instinct of reason," whose "feeling or belief" is that "the truth is *one*" (XVIII, 36). A marginal note in the Heidelberg manuscript emphasizes this once again: ". . . progressing; nothing accidental . . .; the inner remaining-at-one-with-itself of spirit" (XVIII, 14). Such being at one with oneself should not be understood as some sort of submergence in the self: spirit makes its way up and down, in and out, somehow simultaneously. The supreme mystery surrounding the activity of spirit is revealed at the very end of the lecture course, as its own result, so to speak. Hegel writes:

> The deeper spirit goes into itself, the stronger its opposite becomes: the depths are to be measured according to the magnitude of the opposite, i.e., of the need; the

deeper into itself, the more profound the need to seek
outwards in order to find itself, the greater its wealth on
the outside. (XX, 455)

At the outset of his lecture course Hegel invites his hearers to
greet *"the dawn of a more magnificent age"* (XVIII, 13); at the end he
limns once more the deeds of the one living spirit:

Whenever the mole burrows forth in the interior we
must heed his approach, we must assist him toward his
actuality. For it is an absolutely necessary process, expressing nothing less than the nature of spirit itself, the
spirit that lives in us all. I hope that this history of philosophy makes a demand upon you, the demand to grasp
the spirit of our age, which is natural to us; but you
must draw it out of its naturalness, i.e., concealment,
lifelessness, and into the light of day. Each one of you,
in his particular place, must consciously bring spirit into
daylight. . . . May you all fare well! (XX, 462)

It is a while yet to *Dawn*, a seven-league leap. And if indeed the
mole be dragged into daylight, where will his(s)tory end?

III

Deeper indeed, along routes no one could have charted, the philosopher mole is burrowing busily. He senses an uncertain, wavering dawn
(or is it dusk?), hovering on the horizon. For the subterrestrial one, of
course, the horizon is not visible. In autumn of 1886, in Ruta, near Genoa,
Friedrich Nietzsche prepares a second edition of his book, *The Dawn:
Thoughts Concerning Moral Prejudices*, which had first appeared in 1881.
During those same days he is occupied with his next no-saying treatise, entitled *Toward a Genealogy of Morals*. The yes-saying noontide of his creative life, the zenith of *Zarathustra*, is long past; it is actually late afternoon, although not yet the hour of twilight. The lonely one thrills to the
possibility of a new day, whose dawn already impinges somehow on his
awareness. In the Preface to the second edition of *The Dawn* Nietzsche
writes the following:

In this book you will find a "subterrestrial" creature at
work, burrowing, digging, subverting. You will see him,
presupposing that you have eyes for such work in the
depths, see how slowly, reflectively, with what gentle
implacability he moves forward. He scarcely betrays the

destitution that prolonged lack of light and air imply; one could even say that in his obscure toil he is satisfied. Does it not seem as though some sort of belief guides him, some sort of consolation grants him recompense? As though he perhaps wants to have his own long obscurity, his unintelligibility, his concealment and riddlesomeness, because he also knows what he *will* have: his own morning, his own redemption, his own *dawn*? ... Oh yes, he will turn back; do not ask him what he wants to do down there; he will tell you himself soon enough, this seeming Trophonios, this subterranean one, as soon as he has "become man" again. For one forgets silence altogether when one has been, like him, such a long time a mole, such a long time alone—.[6]

Nietzsche's mole-tunnels burrow through to those "moral" presuppositions that have undergirded or even pervaded all prior metaphysical systems in more or less subtle ways. "I descended into the depths, I burrowed into the ground," declares the mole, looking back and remembering, "I began to root about and investigate an ancient *confidence*, ... I began to subvert our *confidence in morality*" (I, 1012). Thus Nietzsche sets his sights on that particularly fragile spot in Kant's Critical philosophy, i.e., on the matter of morality and ethicality, the very place where Kant espied mole tunnels, which he then vainly sought to level from the outside, from above. Thus too Nietzsche examines the vast wealth of Hegelian spirit, whose "need" to propel itself to the outside has become suspect. Nietzsche's path proceeds underground, without the optimism of a naive metaphysics à la Pangloss. It follows the scent of suspicion, a deeply rooted distrust of all forms of idealism. For idealisms are secretly constructed upon a morality which is itself based on a deprecation of this earth and this life. His tunnel advances against all "courage in the truth," which he exposes as "impotence-to-power" or sheer "will-to-nothingness." In Nietzsche's case the resultant deed remains a leaping back, a *resaltare* ("Oh yes, he will turn back . . .") that never comes to a standstill. For everything "that comes to a stop (at an ostensible *causa prima*, an unconditioned, etc.) is *laziness*, weariness—" (*The Will to Power*, no. 575, dated 1885-86). (If Nietzsche's genealogical critique at all rests on a "metaphysics" of will to power, then the critique is "hypercriticism" and the metaphysics "hypophysics.") With Hegel, the mole burrows exclusively *forward* and *up*, even when it plunges into the depths; with Nietzsche, the mole mainly turns *back*, digs *down*. Such turning back does not rest on any securely established insight that could make of remembrance a gesture of optimism and belief in Progress. Nietzsche's interpretation of *Hamlet* is altogether different: "Conscious of the truth he has once perceived, man

177

now sees always and everywhere the terror or absurdity of Being . . .: it nauseates him" (*The Birth of Tragedy*, I, 48). For Nietzsche, too, however, the history of philosophy is a kind of self-production that is impelled by a "feeling or belief." It is not an activity of "spirit," even if that activity be interpreted as insight into spirit's having *willed* its history, but the legislation of and by will to power. At the origin of the history of philosophy lies, not Hegel's "instinct of reason," but the instinct of self-preservation and self-enhancement in a creature called "man." The being-at-one-with-itself of spirit which has been liberated from "naturalness" is now replaced by the self-deception of man who perdures in the realm of the sensuous. Instead of Hegel's "nothing accidental," the rubric now is: the innocence of Becoming.

But how is it with that "consolation" that seems to scintillate in the visible world of the superficies, a consolation that promises "redemption" even to the one who dwells underground? Does the mole hold out below, or does he creep upward once again—in the direction of the "eternal recurrence of the same"?

The thought of eternal return "ravished" Nietzsche in 1881 (the year that saw the publication of *The Dawn*). He was in Sils-Maria in the Oberengadin region of Switzerland, "6,000 feet beyond man and time" (*Ecce Homo*, II, 1128). Occasionally the idea of eternal recurrence seemed to Nietzsche himself to be not merely a touchstone by which the Overman would be selected but also a "consolation."[7]

The question arises: Does the doctrine of eternal recurrence become a matter of rescue from, and that means revenge against, the world and the *time* of this world? Is it a matter of "redemption" from transiency and from the "It *was*" of time, which the will cannot bear? Do we have here yet another minidrama in the history of salvation (read: decadence)? We cannot simply disregard the danger that the longing for redemption threatens to reduce the entire project of Nietzsche's thought to a hybrid form of the Hegelian philosophy of reconciliation. We dare not ignore the possibility that Nietzschean "love of fate" says nothing more than "love of father" in the Freudian sense; that Zarathustra's honey, gathered so laboriously, will be used to sweeten another cup of herbal tea relaxing to the nerves; that the Overman, whose golden laughter should be a *prayer* to Becoming, turns out to be a *brayer*, a jackass. In response to such questions and doubts we must emphasize that the grand affirmation found in eternal recurrence is not to be "rescued" from the distrust exercised by genealogical critique. Insatiable suspicion must always accompany that doctrine. "Yes" and "No" are inseparable companions, glowing Dionysos and glowering Silenos going together. Accordingly, the thought of eternal return remains a way down, a *katabasis* or down-going, which remains "true to the earth." If the thought ascends at all, it stops at the borderline between heaven and earth, at a boundary that winds through the mountains, since the mole (*talpa europaea*) can survive up to 2,000 meters of altitude, i.e., those 6,000 feet beyond man and time which measure the remoteness of the birthplace of eternal return. It remains, after all, a matter of the mole. The high-flying eagle with the snake wrapping himself about its throat—these are the animals of *Zarathustra*. The camel, too, and the lion, jackass, and child: they belong in the menagerie of the flamboyant Persian. *Nietzsche* has but one pet. He doesn't fly, doesn't hiss, bears no burdens, neither roars nor brays, and only very rarely plays innocently at Heraclitean games. He merely scrabbles and scrooges, burrowing relentlessly, up to the stony surface of earth, then back again, rapt in thought. As a "teacher of slow reading" (I, 1016), he refuses categorically to don seven-league boots. Perpetually exposed to loneliness, he learns silence over and over again. In order to talk about it he must of course "become man"—not Zarathustra, not the Overman, not Dionysos, but man. He must learn how to become what he is. He must go down to Trophonios and then fulfill his duty to write about it (cf. Pausanias's *Guide to Greece*, IX, 39, 4).

The "how to become what he is" as a "how to be what he has become": the life of ceaseless burrowing as possibility and fatality, dispensation and doom alike: this is how the mole's Being is projected in (our) Time right from the start, this is the:

> sole
> role
> of the
> mole

either as "the living creature that has speech," with a word of interpretation playing ever about the snout, or as the creature delving into mould and powdery earth, the being who takes up the frenetic life of writing, in which the eternal circuit of burrowings back and forth conducts him headlong to his own death (cf. Heidegger, *Being and Time*, p. 308). For where does it lead us, in the end, the seductive *imago* of the philosopher mole, from Kant, via Hegel, to Nietzsche?

By way of response, the following concluding extracts from Wilhelm Busch, *Dideldum!* , section four, "The Mole," as a kind of

Postlude and Threnody §§§§§

University of Mannheim

179

In seinem Garten freudevoll
Geht hier ein Gärtner namens Knoll.

A gardener by the name of Knoll
Surveys his garden on a stroll.

Doch seine Freudigkeit vergeht;
Ein Maulwurf wühlt im Pflanzenbeet.

Yet peace of mind will not be found;
A mole is burrowing in the ground.

Schnell eilt er fort und holt die Hacke,
Dass er den schwarzen Wühler packe.

So Knoll resolves to fetch a hoe,
To deal the beast a telling blow.

180

Jetzt ist vor allem an der Zeit
Die listige Verschwiegenheit.

He nears the burrow, hovers by it,
All absorbed in cunning, quiet.

Aha! Schon hebt sich was im Beet,
Und Knoll erhebt sein Jagdgerät.

Aha! A stirring in the ground:
Knoll wields the hoe without a sound.

Schwupp! Da—und Knoll verfehlt das Ziel.
Die Hacke trennt sich von dem Stiel.

Zip! But in vain the Knollic art,
For hoe and handle fly apart.

181

Die Hacke ärgert ihn doch sehr,
Drum holt er jetzt den Spaten her.

That irritates him just a shade;
He'll try his hand now with the spade.

Nun, Alter, sei gescheit und weise,
Und mache leise, leise, leise!

Prepare, old chap, to make the kill;
Compose yourself, be still, still, still!

. . . Schnupp' dringt die Schaufel, wie der Blitz,
Dem Maulwurf unter seinen Sitz.

. . . Crunch! goes the shovel, swift and straight,
Unseats the mole from his estate.

182

Und mit Hurra in einem Bogen
Wird er herauf ans Licht gezogen.

And hoopla-ho! with main and might
The vermin mole is brought to light.

Aujau! Man setzt sich in den Rechen
Voll spitzer Stacheln, welche stechen.

Ee-yow! Knoll plops down on the rake:
More than the mole is now at stake.

Und Knoll zieht für den Augenblick
Sich schmerzlich in sich selbst zurück.

A moment's pause, while Knoll withdraws
In pain from his impassioned cause.

183

Schon hat der Maulwurf sich derweil
Ein Loch gescharrt in Angst und Eil.

Meanwhile the mole, by terror struck,
Digs frantically, to change his luck.

Doch Knoll, der sich emporgerafft,
Beraubt ihn seiner Lebenskraft.

But goodly Knoll this time won't fail;
The mole's life hangs but by its tail.

Da liegt der schwarze Bösewicht.
Und wühlte gern und kann doch nicht;
Denn hinderlich, wie überall,
Ist hier der eigne Todesfall.

Here lies the nasty little pest,
Would burrow, but is laid to rest.
You gather from the way it lies:
A hindrance is one's own demise.

St. Ulrich im Hochschwarzwald, 1974-80

184

NOTES

1   For an account of the literature on the mole in Germany, especially from a leftist political stance, see Alfred Opitz and Ernst-Ullrich Pinkert, *The Old Mole: The Damned of/under This Earth: History of a Revolutionary Symbol*, Berlin, 1979. The extracts from Marx, Schopenhauer, and Filbinger printed above stem from the Opitz/Pinkert collection. Nevertheless, the monograph says nothing about the mole's role in Kant, Hegel, and Nietzsche.

2   I owe mountains of molehills to Professor Sallis, who generously sent me his "Tunnelings" in manuscript. And let me also thank the following among the milling moles of Mannheim: Ulrich Halfmann, Friederike Born, Burkhardt Allner, Elisabeth Hoffmann, Thomas Müller, Werner Reinhart, Margarete Seidenspinner, Jupp Schöpp und Jochen Barkhausen.

3   G. W. F. Hegel, *Werke in zwanzig Bänden* (Frankfurt am Main: Suhrkamp Verlag, 1971), XX, 455.

4   All references to Hegel's *Lectures on the History of Philosophy* must, however, remain provisional. Whether they represent Hegel's own words we simply do not know. The critical editions now being prepared in France, Italy, and Germany will, I trust, be of aid in this respect.

5   See the two final pages of Hegel's *Phenomenology of Spirit*, which treat *Er-Innerung*, self-internalizing remembrance.

6   Friedrich Nietzsche, *Werke in drei Bänden*, edited by Karl Schlechta (Munich: Carl Hanser Verlag, 1956), I, 1011.

7   Cf. *The Will to Power*, no. 1065 (November 1887-March 1888): "A certain emperor always kept in mind the transiency of all things, in order not to take them too much to heart and to remain tranquil in their midst. To me, on the contrary, everything seems much too valuable to be allowed to be so fleeting: I seek an eternity for everything. Ought one to pour the most precious unguents and wines into the sea? My consolation is that everything that was is eternal: the sea spews it forth again."

The Struggle Against Meta(Phantasma)-physics:
Nietzsche, Joyce and the "excess of history"

Joseph A. Buttigieg

I think that any modern hermeneutics is a hermeneutics
with a double edge and a double function. It is an effort
to struggle against idols, and, consequently, it is
destructive. It is a critique of ideologies in the sense of
Marx; it is a critique of all flights and evasions into
otherworlds in the sense of Nietzsche; a struggle against
childhood fables and against securing illusions in the
sense of psychoanalysis. In this sense, any hermeneutics
must be disalienating, aimed at disalienation, at
demystification.

Paul Ricoeur

STEPHEN

My centre of gravity is displaced. I have forgotten the
trick. Let us sit down somewhere and discuss. Struggle
for life is the law of existence but modern philirenists,
notably the tsar and the king of England, have invented

arbitration. (*He taps his brow*.) But in here it is I must kill the priest and the king.

Ulysses

By searching out origins, one becomes a crab. The historian looks backward; eventually he also *believes* backward.

Friedrich Nietzsche

Nietzsche's voluminous and diverse writings are, as much as anything else, "assaults against an obdurate wall of history and custom."[1] One of his earliest such assaults, the essay on *The Use and Abuse of History*,[2] provides Paul de Man with the means by which to unfold his ideas on the essential modernity of literature. It is de Man's contention that "literature has always been essentially modern"; hence, the notion of modernity presents the literary historian with a fundamental paradox. Modernity does not stand in simple opposition to and is most certainly not isolated from history; rather, "modernity and history seem condemned to being linked together in a self-destroying union that threatens the survival of both." De Man's insight (as well as his articulation of the paradox) is at once valuable and dangerous. For while it sheds light on the character of the literary enterprise and it helps to direct the way of the literary interpreter, it might also lead to a set of sterile critical procedures devoted to the perpetual affirmation of the paradox itself. The paradox articulated by de Man could turn out to be the very mode by which history is allowed, cynically perhaps, to effect the very paralysis or enchainment of modern man from which Nietzsche sought so vigorously to break loose. There is the genuine danger, in other words, that de Man's irony and bent for paradox might induce one to become enamoured of one's imprisonment, and thus remain locked in an endless reiteration of the inescapable predicament that "modernity cannot assert itself without being at once swallowed up and reintegrated into a regressive historical process."[3] The fact that this reiteration is capable of innumerable variations may be a source of joy to the aesthete, but it contributes little to and indeed might help undermine the struggle one *has* to wage against the hegemony of the phantasms bequeathed by the past.[4]

Nietzsche does not undertake the struggle against history naively, he is not unaware of his own entrapment. "For as we are merely the resultant of previous generations, we are also the resultant of their errors, passions and crimes; it is impossible to shake off this chain. Though we condemn the errors and think we have escaped them, we cannot escape the fact that we spring from them" (*UAH*, 21). Nor does Nietzsche entertain any illusions about the driving force which compels one to stand in opposition to history: it *is* will to power, and has nothing to do with "truth" and "justice":

188

Man must have the strength to break up the past, and apply it, too, in order to live. He must bring the past to the bar of judgment, interrogate it remorselessly, and finally condemn it. Every past is worth condemning; this is the rule of mortal affairs, which always contain a large measure of human power and human weakness. It is not justice that sits in judgment here, nor mercy that proclaims the verdict, but only life, the dim, driving force that insatiably desires—itself. Its sentence is always unmerciful, always unjust, as it never flows from a pure fountain of knowledge, though it would generally turn out the same if Justice herself delivered it. (*UAH*, 21)

The condemnation of history *is a necessity*, for history is a "disease," a "malady" which left unchecked destroys life by paralyzing its creative powers, depriving it of all vitality.[5]

The ideas expounded by Nietzsche in *The Use and Abuse of History* gain in complexity and significance when examined in the context provided by Nietzsche's further elaboration of his philosophy in his other (mostly subsequent) writings. It becomes clearer as one reads *Thus Spoke Zarathustra, Beyond Good and Evil, Joyful Wisdom, The Antichrist, Twilight of the Idols*, etc., what kind of dragons he enjoined youth to engage in mortal battle.[6] However, before turning to a discussion of the wider scope of Nietzsche's challenge to the foundations of the entire metaphysical tradition, it would be fruitful to direct attention to his insight into the debilitating power of history which manifests itself as memory. His ideas on the subject help illuminate and give depth to some of the most important literary creations of our century—particularly the works of James Joyce.[7] This is especially interesting since Joyce has often been offered as the prime example of modernism in literature, and Nietzsche is, for reasons that have become clearer with the emergence of "postmodern" criticism, the paradigmatic figure of the breakaway, or "turn," from the western humanistic tradition. Not coincidentally, both Joyce and Nietzsche were intensely preoccupied with the burden of history.

History, Nietzsche argues, is man's creation and imposition of order onto the chaos he inhabits. Man produces his own history so as to enable himself to live in a world which would otherwise overwhelm him. Furthermore, in producing history, which is to say in giving meaning to the surrounding cosmos, man affirms himself as creator of the world he lives in. However, when Nietzsche surveys the educational system and the socio-cultural establishment of his time, he notices that western man has abandoned his creativity, has ceased to mould and forge his own history, and is instead absorbed in the study and preservation of the history which has been handed down to him. History becomes a monument which conceals its own genealogy, so that modern man starts to regard it as sacrosanct and not merely as a fictional product of his own interpretative imagination. By doing this, man elevates the dead creation of a dead generation to the status of absolute sovereignty, he abandons the control he exercises over his own life, and allows his power to create his own past to wither. In effect, man thus unwittingly adopts the motto, "Let the dead bury—the living" (*UAH*, 17). There are, of course, certain advantages to be gained from according history such a privileged status: a sense of continuity, reality, origin, goal, and identity. More importantly, history becomes knowledge and evinces the need for its own destruction. Values are inherited and do not have to be repeatedly created anew, meaning is found ready made and need not be forged again, the constantly changing cosmos yields to a definitive text which is fixed and is not threatened by the vagaries of interpretation. In short, history ceases to be history and becomes, instead, a "monument of unaging intellect" which mocks in its fixity the shifting sands of the very same temporal world which gave birth to it in the first place.

The motto, "Let the dead bury—the living," would have been the most appropriate epigraph for James Joyce's *Dubliners*. In his collection of stories Joyce explores the ways in which history, manifesting itself as tradition, monument, habit, memory, etc., dominates the lives of various characters and paralyzes them into inaction. Eveline is turned to stone by her meditation on the past and by her evocation of her mother's ghost. In this short story, Joyce devotes five out of six pages to his character's recollections. The time has come for her to leave her family and her country, to truncate her connections with the past. She is about to escape with her lover, Frank. "He would give her life, perhaps love, too. But she wanted to live. . . . He would save her."[8] Yet, in the end, the chains of her past hold her back; she does not break through the gate of a dead past into the future but instead holds on to the barrier fiercely. Eveline, unable to forget and rendered immobile by the mnemonic ghosts she evokes, joins the company of the dead. In the final moments, when "all the seas of the world tumbled about her heart" (*D*, 41), and when she is on the verge of stepping into that world to seize it and fashion her life out of it, in those final moments when she needs to act determinedly in order to declare her commitment to life, she opts to look back and allows her will to be sapped of all power by insubstantial ghosts: the strains of an Italian song, her dead mother, and God. "Down far in the avenue she could hear a street organ playing. She knew the air. Strange that it should come that very night to remind her of the promise to her mother, her promise to keep the home together as long as she could. She remembered the last night of her mother's illness; she was again in the close dark room . . ." And, "she prayed to God to direct her, to show her what was her duty" (*D*, 40-41). Eveline does not even bring herself to reject positively the concrete, turbulent vital world that beckons her, she simply fails to embrace it or plunge into it. She does, however, cling to the security of what she "knows": a fabricated past which is rendered more real than her present urges. Eveline, in the dormancy of her will to freedom, becomes an empty husk, a paralytic, a victim of anemia induced by an excess of memory. "She set her white face to him, passive, like a helpless animal. Her eyes gave him no sign of love or farewell or recognition" (D, 41).[9]

"Excess of history," Nietzsche wrote, "has attacked the plastic power of life that no more understands how to use the past as a means of strength and nourishment" (UAH, 69). This is especially true of the Irish scene described by Joyce. In "Ivy Day in the Committee Room" history/memory emerges as the great pacifier, the convenient alternative to revolutionary action. Just when political differences threaten to lead to disagreement and shatter the lazy bonhomie of a group of undistinguished Dubliners, just when the situation calls for an assertion of principles and a commitment to a cause, the past is evoked; it is evoked precisely because it is dead and so that it could deaden any spark of passion. The Parnellites and the royalists bury their differences in an empty, nostalgic recollection of a ghost. They all approve of Hynes' verses on "The Death of Parnell" because Parnell no longer calls for a course of action, but has become a safe and convenient monument by virtue of his passage into history. Parnell is dead and gone, and the men in the committee room, like most other Dubliners, are also dead, buried under their heaps of history and memories.

The mastery exercised by the dead over the living is examined most poignantly by Joyce in the final and finest story of *Dubliners*. In "The Dead" memory functions as a palliative for a number of characters who are not willing to engage any of their energies to come to grips with their present lives. These characters ultimately invest the past with such power that the dead almost literally arise to govern their lives. Gretta Conroy wallows in her remembrance of Michael Furey, her youthful lover long dead. As she conjures up the ghost of Furey, whose presence becomes more immediate to her than that of Gabriel who is right beside her, Gretta withdraws from her concrete surroundings and indulges herself in a fit of sweet melancholy. Gabriel, angered initially by his wife's distance and indifference to his advances, finally achieves peace of mind by allowing himself similarly to escape into the world of the dead. Gretta and Gabriel, unable to achieve communion on the physical level and rendered impotent by their recollection of the dead, both head for the same netherworld of ghosts.

> The tears gathered more thickly in his eyes and in the partial darkness he imagined he saw the form of a young man standing under a dripping tree. Other forms were near. His soul had approached the region where dwell

the vast hosts of the dead. He was conscious of, but could not apprehend, their wayward and flickering existence. His own identity was fading out into a grey impalpable world: the solid world itself, which these dead had one time reared and lived in, was dissolving and dwindling. (*D*, 223)

The story concludes with Gretta and Gabriel and the whole of Ireland, the living-dead and the buried, all covered together by the same huge white winding sheet, "the snow falling faintly through the universe and faintly falling, like the descent of their last end, upon all the living and the dead" (*D*, 224).

It needs to be emphasized that Joyce's stories are not merely studies in the nature and effects of nostalgia. These stories are elaborations on the Nietzschean insight that "the historical sense makes its servants passive and retrospective" (*UAH*, 49). Joyce examines the ways in which life can be so debilitated by an excess of history as to cease to desire itself. Furthermore, if the stories in *Dubliners* are epiphanies, they are epiphanic in a most unusual way. Whereas a bright star guided the three legendary kings to the site of a birth that marked the end of an old dispensation and the inauguration of a new order, Joyce invites his reader to behold a series of mummified Dubliners, all victims of their complacency *vis-à-vis* the obduracy of their own dead legacies.

The earliest readers of *Dubliners* were struck by what they considered to be the morbidity of Joyce's vision. While uniform in their admiration of Joyce's stylistic mastery, the reviewers found the author wanting in another important respect: his stories contained no hint of a higher, or even merely better, order to which the characters could attain, nor did the stories offer the reader an alternative vision. "The book," according to the *Everyman* reviewer, "may be styled the records of an inferno in which neither pity nor remorse can enter. [Zarathustra believed, it will be recalled, that God died of pity.] [10] Wonderfully written, the power of genius is in every line, but it is a genius that, blind to the blue of the heavens, seeks inspiration in the hell of despair." The *Athenaeum* reviewer expressed the hope that Joyce might learn "to enlarge his outlook and eliminate such scenes and details as can only shock, without in any useful way impressing or elevating the reader." [11] What these and many other readers expected from fiction, Joyce could never provide. Indeed, how could Joyce offer the heavens as a consoling and uplifting counterforce while at the same time showing that those heavens were populated only by ghosts? Joyce's Dubliners, like Nietzsche's modern man, need to destroy the heavens, dispel the ghosts, stop looking upward, and start creating the very earth in which they were solidly anchored. First it is necessary to destroy and only then would it be possible to engage in a new creation—the new creation, however, would be so totally new, so manifestly a creation, so divested of any privilege that it could not be mistaken for yet another variation on what had been lost or destroyed.

The burial of the dead, though, is no easy task. It has been attempted on countless occasions in the course of western thought and each attempt proved futile. For, as Nietzsche understood quite well, the jettisoning of history means the abandonment of the "telos" which western man is least ready and able to give up—"the homeland to which metaphysicians promise a return," as Foucault puts it.[12] Moreover, there are so many guises under which the malady that is "an excess of history" takes hold of man that it frequently becomes impossible to identify it as such. One might entertain the conviction of having destroyed the preeminence of memory only to be invaded by the ghost of the dead God, or metaphysics, or tradition, or logocentrism, or moral order—these and many others are the ghosts by which the dead past continues to govern the living. Thus, while directing one's efforts against any of the ghosts, all too often one falls prey to the others.

In this regard, the efforts of George Eliot spring readily to mind since *Middlemarch* appeared at the same time that Nietzsche's earliest works were being published. With the death of Cassaubon, Eliot wished to signal the end of a failed inheritance. The whole history of belief in God and of confidence in an absolute centre which holds all myths together and gives them meaning had come to an end. Theology was dead, or so George Eliot thought. Guided largely by Feuerbachian thought, Eliot set out to create and describe a new order of which God was no longer the centre. But she failed (or refused) to recognize that the death of God means also the death of man, and therefore she proceeded to replace God with man while leaving the entire moral and cosmological structures she inherited intact. The language of George Eliot's new humanism differs none at all from the language of the theology which she thought she had buried with Cassaubon. One eternal verity, God, is replaced by another eternal verity, man. In other words, the inherited metaphysics which George Eliot presumed she could overthrow proved much too obdurate and it overtook her writing even while she thought she was laying it to rest.[13]

George Eliot's *Middlemarch* can, undoubtedly, be read as the embodiment of the paradox described by Paul de Man: in the attempt to conquer history the "modern" writer is swallowed up by history. George Eliot's novel, however, also provides a vivid example of what in Nietzsche's view stands between modern man and the freedom he must gain prior to creating a new order. The great stumbling block is the craving for certitude, or as Keats put it, the irritable reaching after fact and reason. Nietzsche offers several perspicacious accounts of this all too human yearning. In *Joyful Wisdom* he writes:

How much *faith* a person requires in order to flourish, how much "fixed opinion" he requires which he does not wish to have shaken, because he *holds* himself thereby—is a measure of his power (or more plainly speaking, of his weakness). Most people in old Europe, as it seems to me, still need Christianity at present, and on that account it still finds belief. . . . Some still have need of metaphysics; but also the impatient *longing for certainty* . . . the longing by all means to get at something stable . . . even this is still the longing for a hold, a support; in short, the *instinct of weakness*, which, while not actually creating religions, metaphysics, and convictions of all kinds, nevertheless—preserves them.[14]

And, in *Human, All-Too-Human*:

How strong the metaphysical need is and how difficult nature renders our departure from it may be seen from the fact that even in the free spirit, when he has cast off everything metaphysical, the loftiest effects of art can easily produce a resounding of the long silent, even broken, metaphysical string—it may be, for instance, that at a passage in Beethoven's Ninth Symphony he feels himself floating above the earth in a starry dome with the dream of *immortality* in his heart; all the stars seem to shine round him, and the earth to sink farther and farther away.—If he becomes conscious of this state, he feels a deep pain at his heart, and sighs for the man who will lead back to him his lost darling, be it called religion or metaphysics. In such moments his intellectual character is put to the test.[15]

I have quoted these two passages at considerable length because they are especially helpful for interpreting Joyce's portrayal of the progress of the artist in *A Portrait of the Artist as a Young Man* and in *Ulysses*.[16] These two novels make Joyce's affinity to Nietzsche quite clear. In both novels Joyce traces the progress of Stephen Dedalus as he moves wilfully towards fulfilling his self-imposed artistic vocation. Yet, it needs to be asseverated that Joyce never produces a picture of Stephen as creator but only of Stephen in the throes of becoming a creator. Whatever Stephen might think of himself, there should be little doubt that in *A Portrait* and in *Ulysses* he is still struggling against those forces which prevent him from attaining the status of a genuine, as opposed to a self-styled, artist. The forces which campaign against Stephen's emergence

194

as artist, in the full Nietzschean sense of creator, are the ghosts of history, the phantasms of his own past and the phantasms foisted upon him by his country and his religion—the two are hardly separable. Stephen himself is not unaware of these ghosts, nor is he blind to their pervasive influence. He knows he has to free himself from the excess of history in order to become the creator of a new order. "—History, Stephen said, is a nightmare from which I am trying to awake" (*U*, 34). Nevertheless, Stephen often fails to realise fully the extent to which he is enmeshed in that nightmare, and consequently his declarations of freedom are, with possibly one exception, premature. (The possible exception occurs when Stephen smashes the lamp with his ashplant in the phantasmagoric "Circe" chapter.)

In the process of growing up, Stephen Dedalus repeatedly oscillates in two directions: he moves up towards the "heavens" and then he heads back earthward from whence he springs upwards again. At all times he is trying to make sense out of the world he inhabits. He searches for meaning because the confusion he constantly faces brings him much suffering, and also because the "meaning" which has been handed down to him always proves inadequate. He realises before his adolescence that his family offers no refuge from the pains of strife and contradiction. Nor does he find a haven in the midst of the "common herd," that is he cannot simply bury himself among his peers. He must, then, embrace his loneliness and find for himself a world in which he can live, a world away from and above the one that tortures him. Yet, each time he escapes into fantasy he is brought down with a crash into the noisy, smelly world he abhors. Rather predictably he turns to religion. In religion he finds the peace he yearns for: by submitting himself to a transcendental order, he can still the insatiable desires of his body, ignore the contradictions of a vulgar and confused world, pacify his guilt, receive a meaning and goal for his life without having to create one for himself. No longer, for Stephen, the fear of mortality and the torture of incertitude:

> How simple and beautiful was life after all. And life lay
> all before him. . . .
> —*In vitam eternam. Amen.*
> Another life! A life of grace and virtue and happiness! It
> was true. It was not a dream from which he would wake.
> The past was past. (*P*, 146)

Zarathustra trod the same path on his way to becoming a true artist, a creator, "At one time Zarathustra too cast his delusion beyond man, like all the afterworldly. . . . It was suffering and incapacity that created all afterworlds—this and that brief madness of bliss which is experienced only by those who suffer most deeply."[17] Zarathustra, however, recognized the "afterworldly" (i.e. the world of metaphysics) for what it is: a convenient and treacherous fiction. Had he not rejected it, he would have been an aesthete and never would have become a creator.

The afterworldly, though, proves much harder for Stephen to overcome. He spurns the opportunity to pursue a religious vocation and in so doing he believes that he is forswearing the afterworldly in favour of the world itself. "He smiled to think that it was this disorder, the misrule and confusion of his father's house and the stagnation of vegetable life, which was to win the day in his soul" (*P*, 162). Stephen also misguidedly believes that he has liberated himself from the power and influence of those who governed his immediate past. He entertains the illusion that he is walking away free from his own history. Full of pride, he rejoices at the thought that he has conquered all those who sought to control his mind and is ecstatic about a future he thinks he will seize and fashion for himself. "So he had passed beyond the challenge of the sentries who had stood as guardians of his boyhood and had sought to keep him among them that he might be subject to them and serve their ends" (*P*, 165). But all too soon it becomes obvious that in his wild celebration of freedom Stephen unwittingly celebrates the metaphysics handed down to him by the tradition he claims to be renouncing. Stephen's "revolt against secondhand thought, secondhand learning, secondhand action" (*UAH*, 72) fails, and succeeds only in displaying itself as parody.

Stephen's thoughts on the beach have the character of a pastiche made up of clichés. These clichés are themselves the product of the long association of aesthetics with religion and metaphysics. "So timeless seemed the grey warm air, so fluid and impersonal his own mood, that all ages were as one to him . . . a new soaring impalpable imperishable being. . . . His soul was soaring in an air beyond the world and the body he knew was purified in a breath and delivered of incertitude and made radiant and commingled with the element of the spirit. An ecstasy of flight. . . . This was the call of life to his soul, not the dull gross voice of the world of duties and despair . . ." (*P*, 168-69). This is the scene and this is the language which countless Joycean explicators have taken to signal the emergence of Stephen as an artist. After all, Stephen declares at this point that his "soul has arisen from the grave of boyhood," and that henceforth he "would create proudly out of the freedom and power of his soul" (*P*, 170). But Stephen achieves no breakthrough here. He creates nothing new in his workshop; instead, his thoughts are supplied to him by an ancient tradition which although dead still exercises its stranglehold over the living.[18] The language that thinks Stephen's thoughts is the language of the priest he spurned; the wild flight of aesthetic ecstasy takes him to the same metaphysical realm he had reached on the wings of religious ecstasy. Whereas in his religious phase he was entranced by the mystery of eucharistic transubstantiation, in his aesthetic phase Stephen extols the analogous magic of transmuting the gross earth into eternal artifacts. Once he was delivered from incertitude by religion, now he is delivered by a talismanic symbol of the artist. In all this, Stephen feels he has come "near to the wild heart of life" (*P*, 171). Stephen, in fact, is very far from life and its sources; his aesthetic stance is as remote from life as the deadly theology of his teachers.

Stephen becomes an aesthete, *not* a creator, and his aesthetic creed confirms all of Nietzsche's dicta about the "instinct of weakness." Stephen emerges as the embodiment of the "need of metaphysics" and the "impatient longing for certainty" discussed by Nietzsche in the two passages quoted from *Joyful Wisdom* and *Human, All-Too-Human*. Stephen's phantasies of flight *away* from the earth are virtually a literal reiteration of Nietzsche's description of the seductive effects of religion and metaphysics. Nietzsche describes how the seduced thinker "feels himself floating above the earth in a starry dome . . . and the earth [seems] to sink farther and farther away." This is Joyce's rendition of Stephen's condition: "An instant of wild flight delivered him. . . . He felt above him the vast indifferent dome and the calm processes of the heavenly bodies; and the earth beneath him . . ." (*P*, 169, 172). The triumph of Stephen Dedalus, then, turns out to be only illusory. The "cerements, the linens of the grave" (*P*, 170) which constrain him have not been tossed aside, they cling to him more insidiously because less obviously than before. Once again, the ghosts of history prove too obdurate; they exercise their hegemony over the living in the most ironic manner. The best commentary on Stephen's failure is to be found in Nietzsche:

> It is not without deep pain that we acknowledge the fact
> that in their loftiest soarings, artists of all ages have
> exalted and divinely transfigured precisely those ideas
> which we now recognise as false; they are the glorifiers
> of humanity's religious and philosophical errors, and
> they could not have been this without belief in the
> absolute truth of these errors.[19]

Stephen's endeavours to loosen the grip that metaphysics has over him founder because he has not yet understood that his enemy is not outside him but resides within him. He cannot conquer the past by challenging its institutions without first exorcising the phantasm it has implanted in his mind. Stephen Dedalus rejects the world of his father by leaving it behind him, he will no longer acknowledge the demands made by his religion, his country, or even his family. He declares himself an exile. What he fails to perceive is that he carries the phantasm he inherited from the metaphysics of his forerunners with him. This phantasm consists of the notion of God: the God of Christianity and metaphysics. Stephen is so thoroughly possessed by this phantasm that his whole existence, as well as his mode of viewing existence, is governed by it. He cannot look at the world or at the work of art except from above, meta-physically, that is from the standpoint of God. The model he chooses for himself, Daedalus the artificer, is an analogue of God the father/creator. He places reality not in the world but in the impalpable atemporal realm of a higher reality. And he seats himself in the throne of the God of metaphysics so that he too can contemplate his creations with the cold indifference of one paring his fingernails. It is not hard to explain why Stephen often expresses great disdain towards the world, or why he expresses his disdain in the same fashion as the priests who repel him. Stephen Dedalus resists following Zarathustra's injunction: *"remain faithful to the earth*, and do not believe those who speak to you of otherworldly hopes! . . . Once the sin against God was the greatest sin; but God died, and these sinners died with him. To sin against the earth is now the most dreadful thing, and to esteem the entrails of the unknowable higher than the meaning of the earth."[20] Stephen's unreformed *contemptus mundi* reveals the degree to which the ghost of his dead religion still commands him. He is thoroughly preoccupied with his sin against God, so that when he utters the words of Lucifer, *"non serviam,"* he attests to the power of God's phantasm. If Stephen had truly dispelled God from his mind, he would have no need to take a stand against him.

In order for Stephen to become a creator he needs first to rid himself of the need to constantly negate the ghost that strangles his mind and affirm, instead, his own creative will. Stephen has to stop looking back and attend to Zarathustra's exhortation. "O my brothers, your nobility should not look backward but ahead! Exiles shall you be from all father-and-forefather-lands!"[21] Stephen, of course, opts for exile and at the end of *A Portrait* he bravely anticipates his departure from Ireland. Yet, his exile turns out largely to be only a physical separation from his land. When we encounter him again in *Ulysses*, he is still possessed by the ghost of the Christian God. He has still to separate himself from those whom Zarathustra calls "the swooners and head-hangers, whose hearts also hang limply, [who] preach, 'The world itself is a filthy monster.' For all these have an unclean spirit—but especially those who have neither rest nor repose except when they see the world from *abaft*, the afterworldly."[22] In *Ulysses*, Stephen Dedalus wages the final battle on his way to becoming a creator. This time he will struggle with the ghost inside him and not only with the institutions of power that block his way. He realises fully that he has to grapple above all with the phantasms of his mind. "*(He taps his brow.)* But in here it is I must kill the priest and the king" (*U*, 589).

Stephen Dedalus returns to Dublin from Paris to witness his mother's death, an event that reveals to Stephen in the most vivid way the extent to which he is still governed by the dead. "Dead breaths I living breathe, tread dead dust, devour a urinous offal from all dead" (*U*, 50). He had set out for Paris with surety, convinced of his emancipation from motherland and religion. Now, back in Dublin, he discovers himself to be

198

still a servant of two masters: "The Imperial British state . . . and the holy Roman Catholic and apostolic church" (*U, 20*)—hardly an example of free thought and most decidedly not his own master. Stephen had also left for Paris with the anticipation that he would create ambitious works in the smithy of his soul; but he returns carrying only a handful of curiosities:

> You were going to work wonders, what? Missionary to Europe after fiery Columbanus. Fiacre and Scotus on their creepy-stools in heaven spilt from their pintpots, loudlatinlaughing: *Euge! Euge!* Pretending to speak broken English as you dragged your valise, porter threepence, across the slimy pier at newhaven. *Comment?* Rich booty you brought back; *Le Tutu*, five tattered numbers of *Pantalon Blanc et Culotte Rouge*, a blue French telegram, curiosity to show:
> —Mother dying come home father. (*U, 42*)

The telegram Stephen brings back with him is more than a curiosity, it is the signal of his fall—a fall into the world which proves to be for Stephen, just as it was for his version of Shakespeare, the portal of discovery. It was Simon Dedalus who sent the telegram calling Stephen back from his deluded exile and leading him to his fall, but it was under the aegis of another father, Daedalus the artificer, that Stephen had attempted to escape the nets of his own past. Not even Daedalus the artificer, however, could have saved Stephen. Like Icarus's, Stephen's cry of "Father" procures him no salvation. "Fabulous artificer, the hawklike man. You flew. Whereto? Newhaven-Dieppe, steerage passenger. Paris and back. Lapwing. Icarus. *Pater, ait*. Seabedabbled, fallen, weltering. Lapwing you are. Lapwing he" (*U, 210*). There is yet another and much more potent father, or rather the ghost of a father, from whom Stephen still has to gain independence. He is the God of Christian metaphysics, the creator and the hangman. It is from this net that Stephen must fly in order that he may be able to arrogate for himself the power to create. The net Stephen has fallen into and from which he must shake loose is the "agenbite of inwit," what Nietzsche calls "the worm of conscience."[23]

In *Ulysses*, Stephen has no trouble identifying the ghost that haunts him. In the opening chapter when he is haunted on the first of many occasions by a vivid recollection of his mother, Stephen dismisses the phantasm by viciously apostrophising God: "Ghoul! Chewer of corpses!" (*U, 10*). Stephen understands, too, that the ghost within him which appears under the visage of his mother threatens his very life. "No mother. Let me be and let me live" (*U, 10*). Unless he succeeds in getting rid of this ghost, Stephen will, like the characters in *Dubliners*, join the company of the dead. God the hangman, "agenbite of inwit," memory—all these are the same enemy, the phantasm produced by metaphysics. There remains, however, another guise under which this phantasm haunts Stephen, namely that of God the father/creator.[24] Before Stephen can be free, therefore, he must also learn to identify this ghost and destroy it. This is particularly difficult for Stephen since his concept of the artist coincides with his concept of the metaphysical father/creator God. The issue is further complicated by Stephen's worry that his ambition to become a creator is thwarted by the fact that he owes his existence to a father who has always already preceded him as a creator. Stephen is consequently frustrated by his perceived status as parvenu, and as one who has been begotten, whereas God the father/creator is self-begotten and hence owes his origin to no one but himself.

The discussion of Shakespeare in the "Scylla and Charybdis" chapter brings to the surface the issues which lie at the very foundation of Stephen's problems as he strives towards becoming a creator. As he holds forth in the library, surrounded by some of Dublin's *literati*, Stephen also gives many indications as to how he will have to proceed in his struggle against the ghost that persecutes him. Quite appropriately, his entire presentation revolves around an interpretation of Shakespeare's ghost; not only the ghost that appears in *Hamlet*, but also, and more significantly, the ghost Shakespeare had to conquer in his own mind. What Stephen strives to establish, for his own sake rather than that of his skeptical audience, is that Shakespeare's triumph as superb creator resulted from his success in eschewing any need for a father and in establishing himself as both his own father and his own son. It may be argued that by being simultaneously father and son, Shakespeare managed to emulate the consubstantiality of God the Father and Son. Yet, Stephen's version of Shakespeare amounts to much more than a parody of orthodox trinitarian doctrine. Stephen's idiosyncratic portrayal of Shakespeare does not produce merely another analogue to God. Shakespeare, according to Stephen, is most unlike God in that he is most decidedly fallen. Shakespeare, the victim of Ann Hathaway's wiles, might recall Adam but can hardly be identified with either Christ or the almighty Father. Further, in his work, Shakespeare has to create his own history in order to free himself from the history into which he had fallen. *Hamlet*, at least as Stephen reads it, is anything but the work of a disinterested mind. Shakespeare was far too busy struggling with his ghost to have had time to pare his fingernails when creating *Hamlet*. Shakespeare was a creator inhabiting the world of the flesh and not an aesthete hovering in the beyond. *Hamlet* is the product of will to power (i.e. the will to create), and insofar as the play deals with metaphysics, Nietzsche's "afterworldly," it does so poorly. "—That model schoolboy, Stephen said, would find Hamlet's musings about the afterlife of his princely soul, the improbable, insignificant and undramatic monologue, as shallow as Plato's" (*U*, 186).

Stephen Dedalus's interpretation of Shakespeare's *Hamlet* marks a significant shift in his views about the nature of the work of art. In *A*

Portrait, Stephen develops an aesthetic theory firmly entrenched in the metaphysical tradition; so much so that W. K. Wimsatt discusses Stephen's position approvingly in the context of Thomas Aquinas's "apprehensio" and Kant's "disinterest."[25] Prior to his first voluntary exile Stephen frequently employed words like "impalpable," "radiance," "spiritual," "intangible," "mystery" in expounding his aesthetics. He imagined the work of art to be totally divorced from the world, something that can only be apprehended metaphysically. Now, in the public library, his disquisition on *Hamlet* depends very much on the assumption that the work of art is solidly anchored in temporality, the result of the creator's struggles with the phantasm of the absent father. It is left to Stephen's mockers to object to the irreverence of debasing a literary masterpiece by removing it from the mysterious, intangible, unreachable sphere of the aesthetic beyond. Stephen's listeners utter the sentiments that one would have expected from Stephen in *A Portrait*. A. E. Russell pontificates: "Art has to reveal to us ideas, formless spiritual essences. . . . The painting of Gustave Moreau is the painting of ideas. The deepest poetry of Shelley, the words of Hamlet bring our mind into contact with the eternal wisdom, Plato's world of ideas" (*U*, 185). A little later Russell reiterates his position in a manner that instantly brings to mind the orthodoxy that dominated literary criticism for the greater part of this century. "I mean, we have the plays. I mean when we read the poetry of *King Lear* what is it to us how the poet lived? As for living, our servants can do that for us, Villiers de l'Isle has said. Peeping and prying into greenroom gossip of the day, the poet's drinking, the poet's debts. We have *King Lear*: and it is immortal" (*U*, 189).

Russell's comments elicit in Stephen two lines of thought. In the first instance, Stephen mocks A. E.'s words and in the process of doing so he reveals the "afterworldly" mentality to which they attest. "Formless spiritual. Father, Word and Holy Breath. Allfather, the heavenly man. Hiesos Kristos, magician of the beautiful, the Logos who suffers in us at every moment. This verily is that. I am the fire upon the altar. I am the sacrificial butter" (*U*, 185). These thoughts differ significantly from those of Stephen the aesthete in *A Portrait*; they epitomize Stephen's new struggle against the phantasm that haunts him. The cynicism with which Stephen's mind responds to Russell's utterance simultaneously addresses Stephen's own lingering phantasmaphysics.

Subsequent to Russell's second intervention in the Shakespeare debate, Stephen's train of thought touches upon another aspect of his troublesome ghost: his conscience, the agenbite of inwit. There are actually three interrelated issues at play here: the persistent mordency of conscience, the yearning for a father, and the problem of individual consciousness. Stephen wonders why he should feel an obligation (and the corollary guilt) to pay A. E. Russell back the pound he had borrowed from him five months earlier. He realises that memory chains him to the obligation he incurred since memory is what provides him with his distinct individuality. "But I, entelechy, form of forms, am I by memory because under everchanging forms" (*U*, 189). Stephen on Bloomsday is the same Stephen who five months earlier had promised Russell the repayment of a one pound loan. Similarly, the Stephen who refused to kneel at his mother's deathbed is the same Stephen persecuted by the agenbite of inwit today. Stephen's entrapment in the whole moral system that constrains him stems from memory, from his inability to forget. But memory is also the touchstone for Stephen's ego. The issue of fatherhood is connected to this whole matter because what Stephen seeks in a father is a stable source, an origin to invest meaning upon his existence and purpose upon his work. A father would be for Stephen a "logos" and a "telos." Belief in God the Father supplies the foundation for the concept of history articulated by Mr. Deasy and rejected by Stephen. "All history moves towards one great goal, the manifestation of God" (*U*, 34). The same belief rests at the basis of a system of good and evil in which Stephen is still enmeshed.[26] Stephen dismisses God as a "shout in the street" (*U*, 34) with a shrug of his shoulders, but his concern with a stable ego and his powerlessness in the face of the agenbite of inwit betray the extent to which the ghost of the shrugged God still grips his intellect.

Stephen, it turns out, still needs to separate himself from the "common herd," otherwise he will remain paralyzed by guilt. He cannot be truly free to create unless he comprehends that good and evil do not derive from a privileged source in the beyond and that God the Father has been created by the "common herd" for the preservation of its system of values. Stephen must cease to think of his drive towards aloneness as deviate and sinful. He must also cast aside the traditional modes of conceiving of the "I." For as long as his self-assertions are directed *against* the homogenous "rest," Stephen will remain enclosed in the old structures of thought and will be prevented from creating by his overpowering resentments. Morality and religion, the sources of Stephen's incapacitating agenbite of inwit, are aspects of the same thing: the metaphysical tradition, or the belief in a superior reality. "Moral judgments," Nietzsche explains, "agree with religious ones in believing in realities which are no realities. Morality is merely an interpretation of certain phenomena—more precisely, a *mis*interpretation."[27] Stephen's tasks, then, are to recognize as no more than a human creation the morality which persecutes him, to abandon his quest for a new father or origin on which to ground his *raison d'être*, and to create his own good and evil, forge his own history and beginning, wean himself from the consuming desire for a stable self. In the end he will have to face a more terrible aloneness than he ever envisaged, but he will have opened the way to becoming a creator of what has been hitherto unknown. Stephen will be ready to fabricate the "uncreated conscience of his race" when he breaks through the slumber of mental habit and think with Zarathustra, ". . . what is good and evil *no one knows* *yet,* unless it be he who creates. He, however, creates man's goal and gives the earth its meaning and its future. That anything at all is good and evil—that is his creation."[28]

That Stephen understands, or at least intuits, the nature of his task is made evident in the course of his discussion of Shakespeare. Whether he ever succeeds remains necessarily doubtful because Joyce's art, unlike the modern art scoffed at by Nietzsche, is *not* "an art of tyrannizing—A coarse and strongly defined logic of delineation; motifs simplified to the point of formulas."[29] All we know about Stephen as we reach the end of the day in *Ulysses* is that he smashes the light in which the ghost that haunts him appears for the last time, and that he politely resists Bloom's paternal solicitations. He may well be on his way to becoming his own father, that is his own unprivileged beginning. It is possible that Stephen is now ready to start creating his own world, having cleared his mind at last of the gnawing phantasmaphysics that has until now barred him from genuine creativity.

The story of *Ulysses* is in large measure an account of the pitfalls awaiting the modern imagination after the death of metaphysics; it is an exploration into the persistence with which the ghost of a dead metaphysics haunts our age, preventing us from freely creating our own world. Joyce, like Nietzsche, makes quite clear why the condemnation of history is a necessity. He presents equally clearly the difficulties and frustration which attend such a condemnation. I am tempted to say that after Nietzsche and Joyce nobody is "at liberty to lie from 'innocence' and 'ignorance' " and that everyone knows "that there is no longer any 'God,' any 'sinner,' and 'Redeemer'—that 'free will' and 'moral world order' are *lies*: seriousness, the profound self-overcoming of the spirit, no longer permits anybody *not* to know about this."[30] But the history of Joyce criticism makes me hesitate. There have been numerous disagreements about the "proper" ways to interpret Joyce's works, but the vast majority of critics, whichever camp they belong to, have directed their efforts towards reinscribing Joyce back into the very metaphysical mould from which he struggled fiercely to free himself. Joyce's destruction (in the Nietzschean sense of the term) of the phantasms bequeathed him by a dead metaphysics has frequently supplied the excuse to revive the dead either under the guise of aestheticism or else in the bankrupt language of humanism. For some, Joyce remains a "sympathetic alien" from the belief in the God of Christian metaphysics; he leaves the mainstream only to assert his individuality.[31] For others, Joyce is "deeply aware of the Christian view of human life."[32] And perhaps most influential of all has been T. S. Eliot's view that Joyce has provided a confused age with a new myth, a paradigm by means of which order can be preserved in an anarchic and meaningless world. Hugh Kenner rightly insists that the "handy word 'myth,' as in Eliot's '*Ulysses*, Order and Myth,' is simply wrong, an uninspected legacy from the age of Matthew Arnold and Max Muller."[33]

What is most strikingly inappropriate about Eliot's use of the word "myth" is its application to the novel that best exemplifies the need to demythologize and demystify.

The reinscription of Joyce's works back into the metaphysical tradition is perhaps inevitable, not because Joyce's attempts to break loose from history prove the ultimate futility of all such attempts, but because it is easier to live with the ghosts of broken icons than to dwell with (not upon) the fragments. As the pope told Zarathustra: "Better to adore God in this form [i.e. of an ass] than in no form at all!"[34] The ghosts of meta(phantasma)-physics are exceedingly seductive and they cause such treacherous confusion that it is often not all clear what one is really seeking after: "I believe, O Lord, help my unbelief. That is, help me to believe or help me to unbelieve?" (*U*, 214). Part of the confusion arises from the need to renounce belief in the dead in order to believe in life, while at the same time belief in life is needed to dismiss the phantasms of the past. Is life a radical negation? Or is radical negation, the effective burial of the dead, a loud affirmation? Joyce's and Nietzsche's "Yes" resonates with the most conspicuous irony.

University of Notre Dame

NOTES

1   Edward W. Said, *Beginnings: Intention and Method* (New York: Basic Books, 1975), p. 323.

2   Friedrich Nietzsche, *The Use and Abuse of History*, trans. Adrian Collins (Indianapolis, Ind.: Bobbs-Merrill, 1957) (hereafter cited as *UAH*).

3   Paul de Man, "Literary History and Literary Modernity" in *Blindness and Insight* (New York: Oxford Univ. Press, 1971), p. 151. For a different treatment of Nietzsche's *Use and Abuse of History* in the context of literary history, see Paul A. Bové, "Nietzsche's *Use and Abuse of History* and the Problem of Revision," *boundary 2*, VII (Winter '79), pp. 1-15. Another essay on Nietzsche of special importance to literary studies is Paul de Man's "Nietzsche's Theory of Rhetoric," *Symposium*, 28 (1974), pp. 33-51.

4   A similar view is expressed by David Hoy, *The Critical Circle* (Berkeley, Cal.: Univ. of California Press, 1978), p. 135. "While de Man's analysis provides a valuable insight into the concept of modernity, the question remains whether affirming the tension to be a necessary state of affairs does not perpetuate metaphysical assumptions and an ironic cynicism that Nietzsche correctly attempted to undercut and overcome." This observation applies also, *mutatis mutandis*, to some of Jacques Derrida's most crucial assertions.

5   Thomas Mann, in an address delivered on April 29, 1947, devotes considerable attention to the Nietzschean idea that history "always underestimates what is growing into the future and paralyzes action." "Nietzsche's Philosophy in the Light of Contemporary Events," in *Nietzsche: A Collection of Critical Essays*, ed. Robert C. Solomon (Garden City, N.Y.: Anchor, 1973), pp. 358-370.

6 "And here I see the mission of youth that forms the first generation of fighters and dragon slayers; it will bring a more beautiful and blessed humanity and culture, but will have itself no more than a glimpse of the promised land of happiness and wondrous beauty" (*UAH*, 70). Daniel O'Hara and Paul Bové have drawn attention to Nietzsche's handling of the language and structures of romance. (See Paul A. Bové, "Nietzsche's *Use and Abuse of History* and the Problems of Revision," p. 13, n. 3). In "Literary History and Literary Modernity," Paul de Man finds that in passing on the task of overcoming history to youth Nietzsche is guilty of *mauvaise foi*. It is not entirely clear, however, that Nietzsche does not consider himself a participant in that youthful project.

7 Hardly anything of significance has been written critically about the great affinity between Joyce's literary endeavours and Nietzsche's philosophical explorations. There are a couple of passing references to the two writers in an essay written by William Blissett which is devoted primarily to Wagnerian elements in Joyce's works: "James Joyce in the Smithy of his Soul," *James Joyce Today*, ed. Thomas F. Staley (Bloomington, Ind.: Indiana Univ. Press, 1966), pp. 96-134. Suzette Henke writes of Stephen Dedalus that by the end of *Ulysses* "he becomes the *Ubermensch* who embodies 'the new, the unique, the incomparable, making laws for ourselves and creating ourselves.' Joyce's artist-hero is a Nietzschean overman, the messiah and priest of a new religion, who affirms the 'spirit of man in literature' and 'creates meaning for the earth.' " *Joyce's Moraculous Sindbook: A Study of ULYSSES* (Columbus, Ohio: Ohio State Univ. Press, 1978), p. 6. However, Professor Henke restricts her treatment of Nietzsche and Joyce to a few casual observations. For an extensive discussion of a novelistic study in the paralysing forces of memory and habit, see Samuel Beckett, *Proust* (New York: Grove Press, 1931).

8 James Joyce, *Dubliners* (New York: Viking, 1968), p. 40 (hereafter cited as *D*).

9 Hugh Kenner has argued quite convincingly that Frank was deceiving Eveline and that Frank "has skilfully shaped his yarn by the penny romances from which [Eveline] derives her sense of the plausible." *Joyce's Voices*, (Berkeley, Cal.: Univ. of California Press, 1978), p. 81. So Eveline is choosing between two fictions. Still, this does not alter the reasons why Eveline opts for one fiction rather than the other.

10 Friedrich Nietzsche, *Thus Spoke Zarathustra*, IV, "The Ugliest Man," in *The Portable Nietzsche*, ed. and trans. Walter Kaufmann (New York: Penguin, 1976). In my references to Nietzsche's works (except for *The Use and Abuse of History*) I indicate the section or aphorism rather than the page number, followed by the normal bibliographic information about the particular translation I elected to use.

11 *James Joyce: The Critical Heritage*, ed. Robert H. Deming (London: Routledge & Kegan Paul, 1970), I, pp. 64, 62.

12 Michel Foucault, "Nietzsche, Genealogy, History," *Language, Counter-Memory, Practice*, ed. Donald Bouchard, trans. Donald Bouchard and Sherry Simon (Ithaca, N.Y.: Cornell Univ. Press, 1977), p. 162.

13 For Nietzsche's comments on George Eliot, see *Twilight of the Idols*, "Skirmishes of an Untimely Man," 5. *The Portable Nietzsche*.

14   Friedrich Nietzsche, *Joyful Wisdom*, 347. *Joyful Wisdom*, trans. Thomas Common (New York: Frederick Ungar, 1960). This is the translation read by Joyce. Among the many books Joyce possessed until 1920, when he left Trieste for Paris, were three volumes by Nietzsche: *The Birth of Tragedy*, trans. W. A. Haussmann (Edinburgh and London: T. N. Foulis, 1911); *The Case of Wagner, Nietzsche Contra Wagner, Selected Aphorisms*, trans. A. M. Ludovici (Edinburgh and London: T. N. Foulis, 1911); *The Joyful Wisdom*, trans. Thomas Common (London: T. N. Foulis, 1910). The virtually complete catalogue of Joyce's library in 1920 has been compiled by Richard Ellmann, *The Consciousness of James Joyce* (New York: Oxford Univ. Press, 1977), pp. 97-134.

15   Friedrich Nietzsche, *Human, All-Too-Human*, 153. *The Complete Works of Nietzsche, Vol. VI*, ed. Oscar Levy (Edinburgh and London: T. N. Foulis, 1909).

16   James Joyce. *A Portrait of the Artist as a Young Man* (New York: Viking, 1964) and *Ulysses* (New York: Vintage, 1961) (hereafter cited as *P* and *U*, respectively).

17   *Thus Spoke Zarathustra* I, "On the Afterworldly."

18   William V. Spanos in an excellent discussion of Stephen Dedalus's aesthetic theory focuses on the passage in *A Portrait* where Stephen insists on the static quality of art (P. 205). He observes: "This famous passage constitutes a remarkably accurate *résumé* of New Critical poetic theory.... It is ironic . . . that in the face of persistent, if still unpopular, readings of *Portrait* as a satire on the angelism of *fin de siècle* aestheticism or as an exorcism of the angelic impulse that had a precarious hold on the young Joyce, that this at least ambivalent passage should serve with such scriptural authority as a primary source of New Critical doctrine." "Modern Literary Criticism and the Spatialization of Time," *The Journal of Aesthetics and Art Criticism*, XXIX (1970), pp. 96-97.

19   *Human, All-Too-Human*, 220.

20   *Thus Spoke Zarathustra*, I, "Prologue," 3.

21   *Thus Spoke Zarathustra*, III, "On Old and New Tablets," 12.

22   *Thus Spoke Zarathustra*, III, "On Old and New Tablets," 14.

23   *The Antichrist*, 25. *The Portable Nietzsche*.

24   For an extensive treatment of Stephen Dedalus's struggles with the concepts of God the creator and hangman, see William Schutte, *Joyce and Shakespeare: A Study in the Meaning of ULYSSES* (New Haven, Conn.: Yale Univ. Press, 1957), especially pp. 81-120.

25   W. K. Wimsatt, *The Verbal Icon* (Univ. of Kentucky Press, 1954), pp. 272 ff.

26   The obligation Stephen feels to adhere to the existing system of good and evil is itself evidence of his unadmitted belief in God. The inseparability of the two is established clearly and in numerous instances by Nietzsche. In a particularly relevant passage which is as applicable to the Irish Catholic Church as it is to

the priesthood of the Old Testament, Nietzsche writes: "With matchless scorn for every tradition, for every historical reality, they translated the past of their own people into religious terms, that is, they turned it into a stupid salvation mechanism of guilt before Yahweh, and punishment, of piety before Yahweh, and reward. We would experience this most disgraceful act of historical falsification as something much more painful if the *ecclesiastical* interpretation of history had not all but deafened us in the course of thousands of years to the demands of integrity *in historicis*. And the church was seconded by the philosophers: the *lie* of the 'moral world order' runs through the whole development of modern philosophy. What does 'moral world order' mean? That there is a will of God, once and for all, as to what man is to do and what he is not to do; that the value of a people, of an individual, is to be measured according to how much or how little the will of God is obeyed. . . ." *The Antichrist*, 26.

27 *Twilight of the Idols*, "The Improvers of Mankind," 1.

28 *Thus Spoke Zarathustra*, III, "On Old and New Tablets," 2.

29 *The Will to Power*, 827. *The Will to Power*, trans. Walter Kaufmann and R. J. Hollingdale (New York: Vintage, 1968).

30 *The Antichrist*, 38.

31 See J. Mitchell Morse, *The Sympathetic Alien: James Joyce and Catholicism* (New York: New York Univ. Press, 1959), especially pp. 4-5.

32 Helen Gardner, *The Art of T. S. Eliot* (London: Cresset Press, 1949), p. 86.

33 Hugh Kenner, *Joyce's Voices*, p. 64. Frank Kermode, likewise, finds *Ulysses* free from mythologizing. "We might ask whether one of the merits of the book is not its *lack* of mythologizing; compare Joyce on coincidence with the Jungians and their solemn concord-myth, the Principle of Synchronicity. From Joyce you cannot even extract a myth of Negative Concord . . ." *The Sense of an Ending* (New York: Oxford Univ. Press, 1966), p. 113.

34 *Thus Spoke Zarathustra*, IV, "The Ass Festival," 1.

"Neo-Nietzschean Clatter"—
Speculation and the Modernist Poetic Image

Joseph Riddel

Nietzsche in Basel studied the deep pool
Of these discolorations, mastering

The moving and the moving of their forms
In the much-mottled motion of blank time.

His revery was the deepness of the pool,
The very pool, his thoughts the colored forms,

The eccentric souvenirs of human shapes,
Wrapped in their seemings, crowd on curious crowd,

In a kind of total affluence, all first,
All final, colors subjected in revery

To an innate grandiose, an innate light,
The sun of Nietzsche gildering the pool,

Yes: gildering the swarm-like manias
In perpetual revolution, round and round . . .

(Stevens, "Description without Place")

I

There has never seemed to be a "question" of Nietzsche for
(modern) American literature. At least not in the sense of "question" of
problematic which Jacques Derrida has called the "Question du style" (or
"Eperons," in English, "Spurs"). Put another way, while there are admittedly thematic traces of Nietzsche woven throughout the text(ure)s of
modernist style, the question of Nietzsche as influence is generally identified in historical banalities, as a precursor of contemporary nihilism and
pessimisms. If Harold Bloom's appeals to Nietzsche's rhetoric of interpretation transcend this banality and transform it into a viable poetics, Bloom
nevertheless situates Nietzsche's "discolorations" in a history of influences
that transcribes the American scene of writing: Nietzsche being a "poet"
whose "father" is Emerson and whose influence in turn re-invents the
Romantic crisis poem in the style of modernism. Which is to say, Nietzsche intervenes in and breaks the illusion of philosophy's priority to poetic
vision, and retells in his own fictions of "perpetual revolution" the poetic
origins of the self/world.

Tracing Nietzsche's "traces" through modern literature would be
a formidable and not altogether rewarding task—a grand tour, as Bloom
might say, of the turnings of certain tropes, and of misreadings. On the
surface of it, Nietzsche is either the putative father of every pessimism or
the herald of every (fascistic) self-overcoming. This thematized Nietzsche,
of course, remains the philosopher indicting the modern (the Romantic),
and inditing in the margins of literature the radical critique of western intellectual entropy. This Nietzsche appears variously in Shaw and Mencken,
as well as in Proust and Spengler, and often in the most naive forms, as for
example in Scott Fitzgerald's youthful romances of the exiled and re-
pressed young artist. The nostalgia of this version of modernism is a commonplace and a somewhat irrelevant consequence of the very historicism
Nietzsche so vigorously deconstructed.

We do know that many of the most prominent American poets
had more than a passing interest in Nietzsche, though just what they ap-
propriated (and miscomprehended) is difficult to isolate. Perhaps the innocence of, if not antagonism toward, philosophy which characterizes so
much modernism (apparent at the same time in efforts to adapt philoso-
phemes to poetic truth-utterances) is the best index to the "question" of
Nietzsche's influence upon modernist poetry. Hart Crane's youthful reflection, "The Case against Nietzsche" (1918),[1] which defends the philosopher against the political insinuations of "Prussianism," does little more

than suggest the way Nietzsche was read (as an ethical thinker, even when an antagonist of predominant morals) by the poets—in Crane's case as a "mystery," like a voice of "Great Indra," a prophet of self-overcoming and recuperated wholeness. Wallace Stevens, who in the late 1930's and early 1940's collected Nietzsche's texts—and even read some of them, evidently —would deny any influence while reflecting it in both his themes and tropes.[2] And Ezra Pound, who is indigenously American in his rejection of philosophy and especially German metaphysics, very early recognized Nietzsche as one of those 19th century thinkers who "made a temporary commotion" and whose prose style was an intervention and disturbance in a world of received ideas.[3] One could perhaps trace Pound's interest in Nietzsche to A. R. Orage's little book on the philosopher's aesthetics,[4] but this is of little help in reading the tone of "neo-Nietzschean clatter" which surrounds his Mauberley. Is it the popularization and common gossip of intellectuals who threaten his fragile integrity or simply the image of an age in perilous change?[5] At least one can say that Pound seems to owe little of his right-wing politics or economics to Nietzsche, something that one cannot say with absolute surety about Stevens. But if these two very different poets—who serve our two most canonical critics, Hugh Kenner and Harold Bloom, as mutually exclusive titular fathers of the modernist "era"—seem to share only an admiration for Mussolini, it is necessary to look elsewhere than politics or economics, or to a history of ideas, for the modern problematic they share.

Indeed, to say that they share modernism, whether or not it is the contemporary scepticism derived from this or that philosophy, is to put the issue in terms of the same questionable historicism that permits canon formations of a "Pound era" or a "Stevens era," since it is the tendency of literary studies, according to Paul de Man, to describe the "structure of meaning" as preceding and standing outside the linguistic (and rhetorical) elements they necessarily inhabit.[6] More precisely, to pursue de Man's critique, which is directly related to the "question" of Nietzsche and the problematic of philosophy he locates in language, the poets do not so much follow Nietzsche as repeat him innocently, since neither poet nor philosopher can take the "detour or retreat from language"[7] into historiography or psychologism that is common among students of literature. Nietzsche, then, according to de Man, raises in the most acute and deconstructive way the "perennial question of the distinction between philosophy and literature"[8] which the poets cannot avoid, even though they must ask the question differently, or pose it, this question of where the one crosses the other, as it were, in-versely.

De Man's rhetorical analyses of Nietzsche's deconstructive rhetoric inaugurates a reversal of the "retreat from language" in critical discourse by turning to that almost forgotten moment in Nietzsche's canon in which the question of rhetoric is first raised. Not surprisingly, he finds that moment in the earliest texts, and not simply the early texts on rhetoric but even before that, in *The Birth of Tragedy*, which poses the question in terms of a narrative or genetic structure that both grounds and undermines its own argument. An argument that must be told as a story of literary origins and therefore an allegory which reveals the allegoricity of literary history. If it is not feasible to summarize, let alone repeat or amplify, de Man's exhaustive critique of Nietzsche here, it is no less impossible to double it in regard to the literature—or poetic theory—which Nietzsche putatively influenced. Nevertheless, the question de Man raises, in a most complex and sophisticated way, is anticipated in the modern poets' need to return (or simply turn) to questions of language: of referentiality, objectivity, precision, or adequation, and hence metaphor, of a language which resists its own ontological claims of being both medium and message. This is not to say that the return to language is unique or exclusive with what is called modernism, or that modernism employed in this way is a meaningful historical and metaphysical category. The apparent self-reflexivity of modern literature (which usually implies its particular inheritance from Romanticism) has been interpreted both as a sign of its weakness (of solipsism, of entropy) and its strength (its formal strength, its effort toward purifying language), even to the point that modernism's obsessive references to its own strategies are viewed as coherent poetic statements about its own coherence, statements that overcome their own figural status and stand as revelatory of "poetic" language in all its privilege or truth. On the other hand, a certain other notion of modernism, its putative return to concreteness or objectivity, has been interpreted as an overcoming of Romanticism and a recuperation of classical precision, a style of "attention" in which reference becomes not only sufficient to its object but synecdochal, a kind of "thing-itself" or "symbol," the "poem itself." This is another version of self-reflexivity, of both internal and external adequation of word and thing. These modernisms resolve the Romantic irony which de Man finds most poignantly elucidated in Nietzsche's aesthetic rhetoric, an irony which in de Man's reading resists every effort of resolution or overcoming.

It is inconceivable to de Man that literature can resolve what perplexes philosophy, especially when one marks the irreducible literariness (the figurality and rhetoricity) which inhabits all metalinguistic utterances and puts them in question. Similarly, an exploration of poetry, and particularly that poetry which appears to make metapoetic statements, must entertain the same ironic resistance to reductions of meaning or monological readings. It is this kind of "reading" which led Jacques Derrida to the unhistorical but remarkably salient statement (in *De la grammatologie*) that it was not only Nietzsche but Mallarmé, and more significantly for our purposes here, Ezra Pound and Ernest Fenollosa, who began, if began has any meaning here, the undoing of the western *épistémè* by disrupting its grammatological illusion of erasing writing (or in de Man's terms, of erasing rhetoricity).[9] Though appearing to give historical names and privilege to this belated beginning (again), Derrida like de Man after him resists the historical argument that would associate deconstruction with modernism (or post-modernism), but associates it instead with literature (or poetry) in which is (always already) inscribed the self-reflexive illusion and its undoing, or grammar (and its metapoetic statements) and rhetoric. If as Derrida suggests, Pound and Fenollosa, along with Mallarmé, recuperate an originary (graphic) poetics, they do not properly recuperate anything, but interrupt certain fictions of closure and offer a glimpse of the indeterminate demarcation between language and "reality," which rather than expelling the outside or otherness from language allow some indefinite element of the "other" *in* and thus disallow our coherent readings which are based on the precise demarcation, that fiction of the poem which depicts, expresses, or objectifies truth or "being."

Returning poetry to the linguistic problematic, a poet like Pound cannot be read as having completed the historical (traditional) model he seems everywhere to have privileged, if only as an eccentricity. No more than a poet like Stevens, who is variously read as continuing the Romantic tradition and providing a severe internal critique of it, can be read as a poet who completes the project of metaphor to erase or abyss the "abyss" that opens between "us and the object" and hence to provide, in the poem, the "thing itself" and not "ideas about" it.[10] If what follows seems thematic rather than rhetorical in its reading of the problematics of modernism, its insistence on the "neo-Nietzschean clatter" of modernist poetics does certainly reject the notion that Nietzsche's themes are modernism, in order to argue that the Nietzsche in-habiting modernism is a philosopher never yet "read" by the poets but one who has "read" the poets. That is, a Nietzsche which inhabits the rhetoric of poetry and disturbs its speculations, who *figures* in its illusions of self-reflexivity and at the same time *fractures* its self-reflective moments.

II

If any one term can be said to be a watchword of modernist (American) poetics, and especially of that strain most concerned with "tradition," it is "objectivity." For critics like Hugh Kenner it has become a valorized notion of a certain decorum of poetic style, most clearly exemplified by Ezra Pound and after him Louis Zukofsky, but also in a certain sense by Eliot as well as Williams and Marianne Moore. The ideal of objectivity, of an adequation of word to "thing" which produces a "precision" and even thing-ness of the word, has been fulfilled in modern literature in a tradition developing from Flaubert through the "Pound era" and thus never seemed in question to Kenner. On the contrary, it validates the "poetic" and "style" as synonyms to "truth," of "law." On the other hand, when a poet like Charles Olson, who is presumably in the "tradition," argues that one must finally substitute for the ideal of "objectivism" the idea of "objectism," because the former simply functions as a dialectical contrary to "subjectivism," far from affirming an ontological advance toward a purified "use" of language, he opens instead the question of "style" which Pound's Imagist/Vorticist theory had exacerbated. Which is to say, the inventive potential of Pound's theory of a return to objectivity in poetry lies not in his overcoming of linguistic mediation (a retreat, and *retrait*,[11] of/from language) but in his *turn* toward it, in his uncovering of a problematic of language that poetry has always entertained.

In two very different yet similar senses, the experiments of American modernist poets—whether ee cummings's typographical play or Hart Crane's Gnosticism—sought its origins in some ideal concreteness yet self-transcendence of the "word." The word, then was tied, onto-theologically, to the Biblical Word, fallen, as it were, or derived from some transcendental signified. Only Pound's theory seemed to divest itself, fundamentally, of metaphysics and theology, even if it argued that it was a critical as well as a stylistic movement. Imagism, in one way or another, however, infiltrates the poetry of Stevens as well as Eliot, Crane as well as Williams, and not necessarily as a prescription by which the poets learned to write. If I tend to argue here that in some curious way theory precedes and directs a practice that demolishes theory, I am arguing neither historically nor structurally. But I am questioning the curious procedure of a "method"—what Derrida has called the "Pas" of method,[12] the methodical *step* that is at the same time *no* method, or the undoing of method—which I believe Pound's Imagist revolution surreptitiously instigates.

Let me begin again, then, with the minimum prescription of the Imagist revolution, as Pound noted in a letter to Harriet Monroe concerning the irreducible element of style: "Objectivity and again objectivity, and expression: no hindside-beforeness—no straddled adjectives . . . Every literaryism, every book word fritters away a scrap of the reader's patience . . . Language is made out of concrete things" (*L*, 49).[13] "Go in fear of abstractions," he wrote in an early essay setting forth the tenets of Imagism, "the natural object is always the *adequate* symbol" (*LE*, 5; also 9). Moreover, the "natural object" is itself denominated most precisely in natural speech, so that the ideal of *adequation* is an ideal of language in its original, primordial, or poetic state. Pound here recounts a condensed but familiar history, of language's organic and cratylitic development which is contaminated by history and technology, by accumulating abstraction. Language is subject to usury, wearing out, but also to an usurious excess that leads to imprecision, to a multiplication of meanings which violate some ideal of a proper word for each thing or idea. Periodically, the poet or poets come to restore the economy of original adequation, which is not, however, the extravagant ideal of one word for one thing, but the economy of a word which inscribes the "law" of nature. What Pound calls the "tradition" in a sense anticipates a repetition, the periodic birth of an

214

original poet who comes to restore a general economy by exposing the usuriousness of an epoch which has grown exhausted, or en-tropic.

Along with Fenollosa, Pound sometimes tells this story of repeated intervention, of return and cure, in geological metaphors, and thus as a spatial rather than temporal history during which language has accrued layers of distancing abstraction, the word being effaced by accumulations and not substitutions; so that the poet, like the archeologist, must peel away or unlayer language back to its primordial inscription, which is to say its poetic nature: "Poetic language," according to Fenollosa, in that influential essay called *The Chinese Written Character as a Medium for Poetry*, "is always vibrant with fold on fold of overtones and with natural affinities" (*CWC*, 25).[14] The primordial, then, is not simple, but a manifold which has been distorted by the unfolding, or logical linearization, of western grammar. "The sentence form was forced upon primitive man by nature itself," he insists; yet, curiously enough, "Nature herself has no grammar" (*CWC*, 12, 16). In nature "there are no negations" (*CWC*, 14). The sentence form of a primitive or natural language, then, is not devoid of time. On the contrary, it is fundamentally temporal. But it cannot close. It can only be, purely if not simply, repetitional.

"Natural" language, then, is already poetic or irreducibly figural, and adequate to the "law" or "force" (mis-named nature) which engenders it only in the sense that the "law" is figuration or trope. Nature cannot, strictly speaking, be a proper name but only a principle of transition or transformation. Nature is not things—there are no copulas in nature, Fenollosa insisted—but the relation of things, of difference. Hence nature is a transference of power, or verbal, that is, metaphorical, and the metaphorical could only be defined as the reinscription of the verbal in the nominal, the irreducibility of the verbal to the nominal, or the temporal to the spatial. Western grammar had driven out the verbal and temporal in order to achieve its abstract categorical stabilities. It is this curious recovery of metaphor, or return to metaphor, the re-turn of metaphor in and into modernist poetics, which I want to explore in regard to what Ezra Pound called the "new method" of poetry.

From a relatively early series of essays, collectively titled "I Gather the Limbs of Osiris," to his publication of Fenollosa's essay, or for half a decade and even longer, Pound elaborated the paradoxes of a now-familiar modernism: that poetry is an instrument or method for recuperating an originary poetic language. This primordially poetic language is natural and objective only in the sense that it is originally rational or logical. Poetry, then, is at once original and repetitional: "A return to origins." he writes, "invigorates because it is a return to nature and reason. The man who returns to origins does so because he wishes to believe in the eternally sensible manner. That is to say, naturally, reasonable, intuitively" (*LE*, 92). Indeed, each of the previously mentioned essays posits within nature a more essential nature, or a language impounded, as it were, within language, a "force" or "process" like Hegel's Spirit, of which nature is the going-out-of-itself or exteriorization. In the "Osiris" essays he named this natural language, which is adequate to this "force," "Luminous Detail," and advocated a "new method of scholarship" based on the way this detail was identified, selected, and deployed in relation to other detail. This method demanded a genius for recognizing certain privileged facts among others, and a strategy for reinscribing this detail into "fields" or contexts where the luminous highlights all the rest: "Any fact is, in a sense, 'significant,' or 'symptomatic,' " he argued, "but certain facts give one a sudden insight into circumjacent conditions, into their causes, their effects, into *sequence*, and *law*" (*SP*, 22, my italics). That Pound confers upon this detail the valorized name of solar light, and defines it at once in metaphors of nature and metaphors of science (technology), is characteristic, as he says, of the modern.

The mixture of metaphors not only intimates that in any originary sense language is irreducibly a technic and instrumental, but that any notion of the natural already depends on a structure of language. Not simply a grammar, however. What Pound calls "luminous" or valorized detail (sometimes "fact") is already a metonymic substitution and a grammatical dislocation, so that one cannot think of his redeployment of this detail as simply a re-grammatization—for example, as the notion of parataxis substituting for or displacing hypotatic order. When Pound accepts Fenollosa's view of poetic language as a weave of verbal and nominal, the one irreducible to the other in the "abstraction" of ideogrammatic writing —and a writing, moreover, which like nature can have no strict grammar— he promotes a "method" which at the same time suspends and undoes method. The reinscription of the verbal into the nominal undoes the grammatico-logical order and suggests the priority of the figural, which is also the trope. Pound's Image is a trope of trope. To speak of his "style" as metonymic rather than metaphoric, in Jakobson's sense, is to misplace the thrust of his "method," then, since it is precisely the undecidability of the Image (as a medium of transference or a substitution) that confirms its irreducible linguistic, graphic, and rhetorical nature. In this sense, Pound's new method surreptitiously recovers the rhetoricity of poetry which in other contexts he so aggressively denounces, though here rhetoricity must be understood in de Man's and Nietzsche's sense and not as the ab-use (in the moral sense) of language for psychological deception. The same Pound who vigorously denounces rhetoric in poetry is most assertive of the pedagogical and persuasive function of poetry.

Though committed to an orderly, and even classical, terminology, Pound struggled toward redefinitions that demanded he break or disrupt the very decorums of his discourse as if from the inside of that discourse. We might say now that his recognition, along with Fenollosa's, that nature has no grammar is a recognition that every epistemological moment is a linguistic moment, which de Man describes as the figural or rhetorical in-

216

tervention (or reinscription) into the grammatical and logical order. Thus nature's symmetries are inhabited or disturbed by the anamorphic, the verbal "law" which Pound calls, somewhat in the sense of Nietzsche, "force" and energy.

Pound therefore defines "Luminous Detail" as "interpreting detail"; and in the Fenollosa essay, at a point where its author is arguing that "Metaphor, [poetry's] chief device, is at once the substance of nature and language," Pound adds his own footnote, distinguishing true from false metaphor: "true metaphor" is "interpretative metaphor or image," and its function, in contrast to "untrue, or ornamental metaphor," is transformative. Poetry and nature, then, can only be thought on the model of language, and language is a transformational (or translational) field of energies. Nature is not only a field of analogies, but an alogical resistance to any effort to understand it grammatically and logically. In Pound's proposed "new method," which links poetry to scholarship, thereby indicating the critical thrust of poetry, luminous or interpretative detail cannot be some creative, unitary presence or singular energy which it is the poet's genius to recover from language or through language. On the contrary, the originary is metaphor itself, and metaphor maintains relations by multiplying analogies, therefore resisting any reduction of analogy to a unified field theory. When introduced or reinscribed into a field of detail, luminous detail at the same time organizes and disturbs that field, like the return of some devalorized and unabsorable entity. The interpretative does not function like Eliot's catalyst, which ideally promotes a reaction without becoming a part of it. On the contrary, the interpretative interferes and agitates, setting off a translative or substitutive movement. The "luminous detail" functions at the same time as a center and an excess.

Pound read Ovidian metamorphosis as an irrepressible de-positioning or de-grammatization, as an overthrowing of the morphic or structural rigidity from the inside. Metamorphosis could be identified with nature, then, and most clearly understood as a certain model of a language or metaphor. Metaphor not only transports or carries over from one structure to another, but, like nature, branches and multiplies. It is a *law* of fecundity or super-abundance, an economy of excess. The organic metaphor, then, cannot be read in a sentimental or theological way, as the circle of determined return. Metamorphosis breaches and overflows its boundaries. It is marked by violence and excess. Art, therefore, is metaphor and metamorphic, hence, as he argued in his first book, *The Spirit of Romance*, "interpretative" (*SR*, 87). Pound's "Credo" for Imagism insisted that the Image, itself a figure for the poem, was a play between the visual and the abstract, and thus between the figural and the grammatical, the one resisting a reduction to the fixture of the other. To produce poetry, the poet introduces that which interferes or disturbs, but that which in itself does not totalize or order. For example, the Ovidian Dionysus in Canto Two, a translation and appropriation of Dionysus, out of Golding's translation, becomes not only a figure of literary interference, but a figure of figure, Dionysus being that which inhabits any grammar or system (the ship on which he is transported) but cannot be reduced to it. Dionysus entangles and becalms the ideal of a completion of the voyage, and by his delay produces by resistance the most vigorous transformations of meaning while at the same time permitting an excess of metamorphic possibilities, all those Protean expansions of story and trope. Thus, in the "Credo" of Imagism: "A man's rhythm must be interpretative" (*LE*, 9). And in *Gaudier-Brzeska*, which remains the programmatic text for Imagism, Pound calls poetry the "language of exploration," employing once again his favorite metaphor for metaphor: interpretive or explorative metaphor functions like an electric circuit, by transformations, leaps, reversals, and resistances, a figure he had earlier employed in *The Spirit of Romance*, where poetry is compared to "an electric current" which "gives light where it meets resistance" (*SR*, 97); and in the "Osiris" essays, interpreting detail is said to "govern knowledge as a switchboard governs an electric circuit" (*SP*, 23, also 24).

In the same spirit, he both praises modern scientists for achieving precision of definition and damns them for having reduced nature or "energy" to "unbounded undistinguished abstraction" (*LE*, 154). The scientist, he argues in an essay on Cavalcanti, where he is also promoting his theory of "interpretative translation," fails to understand "energy" as other than a "shapeless 'mass' of force," and insists that if scientific language could come to "visualize that force as floral and extant (ex stara)" or in "botanical terms," it would be able to give "shape" and "loci" to its thought (*LE*, 154). Visualization, the exteriorization of force into form, is not simply a movement from invisible to visible, but is ex-pli-cative, an unfolding. At which point he offers as example an early version of a figure that will recur in the *Cantos* as the primary figure for poetic ordering—the "rose in the steel dust," the figure of the floral pattern generated by an iron magnet held under a glass on which iron filings are sprinkled. The language of nature must be reinscribed into the abstract language of science; but at the same time, a language of nature becomes sentimental unless the precisions of scientific abstraction are in turn reinscribed into botanic figures: "We might come to believe that the thing that matters in art is a sort of energy, something more or less like electricity or radioactivity, a force transfusing, welding, and unifying. A force rather like water when it spurts up through very bright sand and sets it in swift motion. You may make what image you like" (*LE*, 49). Whatever the image, it is a double inscription, of the figural (at the same time confused with the natural or organic) into the grammatical. The Image, then, is irreducible to a singular notion of language, or to univocity. Nature is "interpretative metaphor" and metaphor is natural only if both are thought of in terms of a violence or a resistance, a repetition that intervenes upon itself. Thus what Aristotle meant by the "apt use of metaphor," says Pound, in perhaps his only favorable reference to the philosopher, was that it provided a "swift perception of relations" and that "use" must be understood as a "swiftness, almost a violence, and certainly a vividness. This does not mean elaboration and complication" (*LE*, 52). "As language becomes the most powerful instrument of perfidy," Pound writes elsewhere, "so language alone can riddle and cut through the meshes" (*LE*, 77).

As we might expect, Pound's formulations of the new poetics of Imagism, of "making it new," is less radical in conception than in its strategy of attack. In this respect, the celebrated theorist of "tradition"—he used the notion earlier and more provocatively than Eliot—can be read as undermining the way criticism today seems to understand it: as the valorization of the cultural continuity of the west. If language is to be used to cut through the "meshes" and "perfidy" that language has constructed, then it is necessary for us to explore Pound's argument in terms quite incompatible with his own concise simplifications. To repeat, it is Pound's strategy, never directly spelled out, that is the clue to "making it new." The very notion of periodicity that characterizes his sense of tradition is a notion of repeated discontinuity and a discontinuous repetition, the style of a creative period being the sign of a resistance to the style of a previous period. If every major style, as Paul de Man has argued in another context, is in a sense a "modernism,"[15] the modernism of the ideogrammatic method would be an *always already* modernism. The nonlinguistic inhabits language from any conceivable beginning and disturbs its illusions of self-presence.

But Pound's strategy needs to be defined more exactly than his broader cultural generalizations allow, and to this end I want to turn to a short essay which has not attracted much critical attention. In 1922, he published a translation of Remy de Gourmont's *Physique de l'Amour*, under the title *The Natural Philosophy of Love*, to which he added a translator's "Postscript." A longtime admirer of Gourmont's prose (though not necessarily the letter of his thought), Pound had published a year earlier, in a text called *Instigations*, an essay on that part of Gourmont's work which he found most crucial for the modern writer: Gourmont's concern with "modality and resonance in emotion" which distinguishes man from all other biological species, the "right of individuals to *feel* differently" (*LE*, 340). Pound was particularly attracted to a cluster of Gourmont's non-fictional texts on biology, love, and aesthetics, which Pound lauded as instigations or provocations, as the "dissociation" rather than syntheses of ideas. A decade later, in an introduction to the second edition of Pound's translation, Burton Rascoe would also discount the intellectual rigor of Gourmont's biologism as bad science or research, but celebrate his "defense of sensuality" which Rascoe called an "extenuation of Nietzsche's 'Transvaluation of Values' " (*NPL*, xvii). Gourmont's "principle philosophical concept," according to Rascoe, maintained that "intelligence is antinatural and the result of a long process in defeating the elementary purpose of nature which is the 'perpetual return to unity' through fecundation and birth" (*NPL*, xi-xii).

Pound has little to say of this "philosophy" of the ever-deflected return in his translator's postscript except to remark at one point that the biological theory was consistent with the great geological speculation of the 19th century upon the "rapidity of the earth's cooling, if one accepts the geologists's interpretation of that thermometric cyclone" (*NPL*, 303). Pound, indeed, found in Gourmont an "instigation" or a resistance to the nihilism of this unidirectional and levelling theory, without however denying the larger truth that everything was indeed cooling or moving toward random dispersal. In Pound's formulation, as a "body approaches the temperature of its surroundings," its cooling speed decreases, just as the larger body it inhabits, the earth, remains warmer still than its surroundings. Pound is playing with a notion of resistance and prolongation which would be elaborated decades later by cybernetics to explain that, while man lived within the inevitability of the general theory, because he was not an isolated but an open system he composed a resistance to the very entropy to which he was at the same time subject. And Pound, as if to anticipate Norbert Wiener, found man's resistance to lie in the efficiency of the machines, the tools which were almost literally projections of his body and which made possible an efficiency and economy of delay: "The invention of the first tool turned his mind," Pound says of man; "turned, let us say, his 'brain' from his own body" (*NPL*, 304).

The "Postscript" refines a theory of poetic invention, as resistance, out of this "turn" of mind—this trope which produces trope. Pound's opening sentence modulates Gourmont's biological theory into a theory of language; or at least, of the Image: "it is more than likely," he writes, speculating upon a passage from Gourmont's text, that "the brain itself is, in origin and development, only a sort of clot of genital fluid held in suspense or reserve" (*NPL*, 295). Perhaps it is more than coincidental that this passage owes less to Gourmont's physiological intuitions than to a section of Nietzsche's *The Will to Power* which bears the indexical heading, section 805, "On the genesis of art": "That making perfect, seeing as perfect, which characterizes the cerebral system bursting with sexual energy . . . : on the other hand, everything perfect and beautiful works as an unconscious reminder of that enamoured condition and its way of seeing —every perfection, all the beauty of things, revives through contiguity this aphrodisiac bliss. (Physiologically: the creative instinct of the artist and the distribution of semen in his blood—) The demand for art and beauty is an indirect demand for the ecstasies of sexuality communicated to the brain."[16]

Like Nietzsche, as we will see in a moment, Pound's deconstruction of a genetic theory of poetic making begins in a double displacement: if the image is an "ejaculation" of nature, nature is a play of images, the "power of the spermatozoide": or in other words, language is a metaphor for physiology, and physiology for language. Again, of the play between the figural and the grammatical. And if the "turn" of mind is poetry, and poetry an "upspurt of sperm," we hardly have to appeal to the double sense (or non-sense) of the *seme* irrupting at the inside of semen which we have learned to call, in a word which belongs to no one language, *dissémination*.[17] Pound accentuates, then, the discontinuity of origin and image: "I am perfectly willing to grant that the thought once born, separated, in regard to itself, not in relation to the brain that begat it, does lead an independent life . . ." (*NPL*, 301). But if this discontinuity suggests, on the one hand, a pattern of thermodynamic dispersal, and perhaps an entropy, it also suggests the economy of a "suspense or reserve." Pound's metaphor of the seminal "brain" is a figure for the poetic "reserve" he elsewhere calls "tradition," of the always already play of images. Thus, when Pound turns to the figure of dreams or dreaming to project his notion of poetic making, we must recognize the "reserve" of dream images not as archetypes of some poetic universal unconscious, but as a "textual" reserve.

If the poet dreams, it is because he nods, or by a chance that is also a strategy, disturbs the orderly and coherent structure of literature's great house so that new and unexpected affiliations or rhymes occur or are produced: "Do they [dreams] not happen precisely at the moments when one's head is tipped; are they not, with their incoherent mixing of known and familiar images, like the pouring of a complicated honeycomb tilted from its perpendicular? Does this not give precisely the needed mixture of familiar forms in nonsequence, the jumble of fragments each coherent within its own limit?" (*NPL*, 299-300). "We have the form-making and the form-destroying 'thought,' " he continues, and while he wishes to think of poetry as the first, as constructive, it is precisely this disorienting dreaming, this "turn" of mind from itself, that he celebrates as the "interpretative" or deconstructive process of poetry. Poetic construction involves a deconstructive intervention, a re-turn of metaphor, as it were, but a return which may also appear as a withdrawal. The "ideogrammic method," as we will see, involves more than the appropriation and re-articulation of other texts, but puts a new stress on the strategies of allusion, reference, quotation, citation and re-citation, translation, incorporation and inscription, in which the re-turn of figure, or the re-inscription of figure into figure produces the effect of metaphoric withdrawal, of the effacement of figure; so that for a moment, at the moment the non-linguistic re-invades language, one senses the return of the "object," in Pound's terms, a coherent field of relations, or an Image. Thus when Pound finds what Kenner calls "subject rhymes" running through widely disparate texts and fragments of texts, and rearticulates not only different literary texts but different orders of texts (literary, historical, mythical), he does not so much reveal an underlying order or cultural law affiliating all texts to the poetic impulse, as he reveals the disturbing metamorphic work (form-making and form-destroying) of language. Pound's Image, then, is what I have called elsewhere a "machine" of repetition; and its very name, as we will see, signifies the return of metaphor. But first I want to swerve from poetic theory to philosophy, or to the breach in philosophy where Pound situates literature.

III

Derrida's linkage of the "names" of Pound and Fenollosa with Nietzsche and Mallarmé was made, as I suggested earlier, necessarily in a language of historical priority and influence that denies or undermines such conceptions. Even the suggestion that what Pound and Fenollosa retrieve, in their return to an ideogrammic method, is an "irreducibly graphic poetics," and that one could never think of an original or primary poetics as purified of writing, the graphic, that poetic language cannot be idealized as natural and immediate—all such suggestions must employ, even as they deny and undermine, an historicist rhetoric, which Derrida identifies with the "dominant category of the *épistémè*: being." It is this *épistémè* of being as "transcendental authority," Derrida argues, which modernist poetry, along with philosophy and even before it, "at first destroyed and caused to vacillate."[18] To "destroy" takes on a radically different, Nietzschean, implication from annihilate, so that in contemplating an "irreducibly graphic poetics" one has to think the oxymoron of a *structure of destructions* or *field* (open) *of force*. Such structures are inseparable from language, or more precisely, from writing understood in the doubles sense of metaphor and rhetoric.

Still, Pound's own assaults upon 19th century idealism and metaphysics notwithstanding, one must recognize in his somewhat belated rediscovery of the Chinese ideogram the familiar rhetoric of one hoping to recuperate an original or primordial poetic language. But it is just this irreducible double face of a "graphic" poetics that intervenes and disrupts any nostalgia for origins and makes traditionalist poetics subject to a diacritical reading. Following de Man, as well as Derrida, it is therefore necessary to recognize that the "neo-Nietzschean clatter" of modernism resides in a "linguistic predicament" that is inextricable from the discourse of either philosophy or poetry, and which Nietzsche's most recent commentators—who also have uncovered a "new Nietzsche"—have located in his deconstructed notion of "Art." Of art which is associated with, at the same time, a constructionist and a genetic notion, of the "impulse" toward metaphor, sometimes called the "will to power," which itself is allied with a certain, disoriented notion of "repetition."

Sarah Kofman, one of the best "new" readers of the "new" Nietzsche, has in a number of books explored the philosopher's so-called linguistic nihilism in terms contrary to the ethical and descriptive approach common to those who "apply" philosophy rather than "read" it.[19] And like de Man, she discovers already in his Nietzsche's first book, *The Birth of Tragedy*, the linguistic problematic most readers defer to later texts. As Kofman reads him—and I am being overly schematic here—Nietzsche's privileging of music assumes from the outset the inadequacy or irreducible metaphoricity of language, and therefore ascribes to music the same condition of broken immediacy he ascribes to language. The privilege of music, then, cannot lie in its natural origin or transcendental authority. On the contrary, music is already a part of the realm of representation, or the symbolic language of feeling, of pleasure and pain. The privilege of the language of music to other, and not necessarily subsequent or more fallen, languages, Kofman goes on, is the result of a hierarchy which Nietzsche establishes to distinguish between the different levels of symbolic language.

Music can only be privileged over percept and/or concept, as one metaphor over another, because its intensity makes it the more general language or best representation of the "primordial melody of pleasure and pain"; so that, for example, the lyric (with its images) stands as a metaphorical expression of music and is therefore a less privileged language of metaphor, and so on down the scale of displacements to opera which makes sound the metaphor of the lyric image or text. Thus Nietzsche's hierarchy make an uneasy distinction only between good metaphor (music) and bad metaphor, and not between ontological levels. And despite the insistence that music already belongs to metaphor and not presence, Nietzsche, according to Kofman, has to recognize that he has rebuilt the very metaphysical structure that he had begun by reversing. The problem led almost immediately, as Kofman reads it, to a questioning of the hierarchy. If Nietzsche's first maneuver had been to reverse the Aristotelian priority of thought to image or idea to representation, he had by his reversal reproduced a system in which metaphor was progressively devalued. Even good music or good metaphor is a devaluation, of which the image is a further figurative devaluation. Nietzsche's need to rehabilitate metaphor, in Kofman's readings, takes the form in subsequent texts, and most problematically in the fragmentary and incomplete *Book of Philosophy* (*Philosophenbuch*), of a strategic reinscription. Metaphor re-turns but under another name, as the idea of *text* or *interpretation*, of the "will to power" signified as the irruption of force, but an "artistic" and not a natural force: "The notion of metaphor now becomes entirely 'improper' because it is no longer referred to a proper or natural term, but to an interpretation."[20] If Nietzsche abandons the privileged name of metaphor at this point, however, he reprivileges it under the name of interpretation and ascribes to it a function of intervention rather than a function of representation or recuperation.

Though she does not in this context address directly that particular section, the only completed one, of the *Book of Philosophy* which has become the touchstone of recent criticism, she is without question referring to the significance of that philosophical fable we know as (in translation) "Truth and Falsity in an Ultramoral Sense."[21] Despite its recent currency as the basic text for deconstruction readings, with certain exceptions the essay continues to be employed rather than "read"—as a categorical statement of the inadequacy of language to reality or to the presence of the "Thing-in-Itself." Despite such warnings as de Man's concerning the problematic inscribed in any philosophical fable which must employ the very devices and concepts of metaphysics it is in the process of undoing, or despite Eugenio Donato's observations on the inevitable narrativity and hence belatedness of a form which can only tell the story of its own "incapacity" to make its story adequate to the truth it espouses, there remains the tendency (at least for literary criticism) to read the "fable" as a series of conceptual remarks.[22]

The first section of the "fable," then, has generally been considered a philosophical truism denouncing or murdering "truth," or relegating it to the vertigo of an endless recession of forgettings. But this reading in a sense elevates the aphoristic to an illusory if not sufficient substitute for "truth." We can recall the economy and aphoristic condensation of Nietzsche's definitions undoing definition: words are recognized as the expressions of a "nerve stimulus in sounds," and everything after, percept or concept, consists of metaphors of metaphors deriving, though deriving no longer makes sense here, from that "First metaphor." There is no natural or "proper" link, the fable asserts, between the "First metaphor" which cannot be natural because it already belongs to the realm of sense (or the symbolic) and any presence of "Thing-in-Itself" (*TF*, 506-07). Both nature and the "Thing-in-Itself" are already and irreducibly metaphorical. This allows Nietzsche's famous and much-quoted conclusion: "What therefore is truth? A mobile army of metaphors, metonymies, anthropomorphisms," and so on, including the figure of "truth" as like effaced coins or "illusions which one has forgotten that they are illusions" (*TF*, 508), a sentence which silently undermines the propriety of the copulative. (There is no nature in the copulative.) But the fable has not yet passed the midpoint of its first half, and continues to pile metaphor upon metaphor as if to mock the very history of philosophy, building (as Nietzsche says) its own "pyramidal order with castes and grades" (*TF*, 509) out of the very devalued figures it has forgotten to be illusions or metaphors. What the fable substitutes for the necessary "laws" of causality and adequation is a concept or metaphor of "*aesthetical* relation," a "suggestive metamorphosis" which is also a "stammering translation into a quite distinct foreign language," a force which undoes the stabilizing concept of "phenomena" as a necessary intermediary dialectically conjoining symbolic or figural levels. Not only has Nietzsche undone the ontological or natural origin of figure, he has disrupted the notion of rational and economical transfer between levels of metaphor. But even the "aesthetical" is one of those laborious constructions at which language has worked, the very metaphor of a genetic myth which must also be undone. The aesthetical has always grounded philosophy, in language *habits* and not natural laws.

But when Nietzsche turns to the second part of his fable, he must tell, or repeat, a slightly different story; or perhaps one could say he must repeat a story of repetition. If, as he asserts, the history which the fable narrates can be condensed into two general phases—"it is *language* which worked originally at the construction of ideas; in later times it is *science*" (*TF*, 512)—this compressed history is at once vindicated and undone by the very narrative structure in which it has to be told. It is not at all improbable that Nietzsche's history of, first, language's and, then, science's construction allegorizes a general history of philosophy, developing from a logic which draws its metaphors from nature (and thus from a forgotten figurality) to a science or logic which builds paradigmatically (and categorically) like Kant's or syntagmatically (and dialectically) like Hegel's by attempting to efface and overcome the metaphoricity of its means. If the scientific phase imitates and repeats by forgetting the symbolic or linguistic epoch—in the way, to follow Nietzsche's metaphors, that the builders of the "great columbrarium of ideas, the cemetery of perceptions" imitate the working of bees at building cells and then filling them with honey—the original builders and those who build their huts, like worshippers, beside the "towering edifice of science" have only forgotten that they are condemned to repetition, and to metaphors of metaphors (*TF*, 512-13). It is Kant's columbrarium and Hegel's pyramidal tomb that already contain not the truth or honey but only embodied signs of it. The "honey"—and one might evoke here Wallace Stevens' paradoxical line, "The honey of heaven may or may not come, / But that of earth both comes and goes at once"—is not a natural presence but a product, even a by-product. The image or form is not derived from presence, but presence (as the sign or body) is produced in the image or form. Yet not in imitation of the form, nor derived from it. It is because form and content have no natural affinity that a generative repetition seems to take place:

> That impulse toward the formation of meta-
> phors, that fundamental impulse of man, which we
> cannot reason away for one moment . . . is in truth not
> defeated nor even subdued by the fact that out of its
> evaporated products, the ideas, a regular and rigid new
> world has been built as a stronghold for it. This impulse
> seeks for itself a new realm of action and another
> river-bed, and finds it in *Mythos* and more generally in
> *Art*. This impulse constantly confuses the rubrics and
> cells of the ideas by putting up new figures of speech,
> metaphors, metonymies; it constantly shows its
> passionate longing for shaping the existing world of
> waking man as motley, irregular, inconsequently

incoherent, attractive, and eternally new as the world of dreams is. For indeed, waking man per se is only clear about his being awake through the rigid and orderly woof of ideas, and it is for this very reason that he sometimes comes to believe that he was dreaming when that woof of ideas has for a moment been torn by Art. (*TF*, 513)

Art is one of the names of that "impulse" or repetition earlier called "aesthetical"; or better, it is the intervention or re-turn of this force upon itself. This impulse has always inhabited language, and not simply as its negative or counterforce. Art does not simply reverse the construction impulse, but disrupts it from the inside, since *Art* and *Mythos* are already archaic forms ("another river-bed") to which the "impulse" returns, structures once constructed by the "impulse." Art, then, is not primordial, but the scene of reinscription, and the artistic "impulse" was never constructive or generative but primordially deconstructive. Nietzsche has reversed the privilege of metaphor by first devaluing it, and then in the same gesture re-privileging the devalued. Metaphor becomes irresistible. This reinscription of Art—another name for interpretation's will to power—is a double inscription of the heterogeneous, best described in Derrida's phrase as the "primordial structure of repetition," which, as Rodolphe Gasché has recently observed, borrows the name primordial while cancelling the metaphysical implications of its deriving from presence.[23] Art or interpretation, in Derrida's terms, obeys the "strange structure of the supplement": that which is added on, or is reinscribed, both reverses and intervenes, tearing at the very structure which has been constructed out of it. Art is originary figure, a combat—a *war*—and in de Man's sense, a tropic dis-figuring.

Now, I have been arguing all along that something of this kind is already implicated in Pound's efforts to describe how poetry "makes it new," which means something quite different from making poetry new or recuperating an original self-presence of language called poetry. What Pound calls the Image, or "interpretative metaphor," may be said to follow the movement of double inscription or the "strange structure of the supplement." Indeed, Pound's very choice of names for this structure takes a devalued concept of the image (as imagery, or ornamental metaphor, or representation), and reprivileges it. His Image, with a capital "I," of Imagisme, with its French suffix, is another figure for the poem, a figure of figurality or "interpretative metaphor." One cannot think of the Image, whether as the name for a single poem or as a generic concept, without thinking its irreducible double nature, or without thinking of it as a reinscription. And Pound's definition of the "one image poem" as a "form of super-positions," as "one idea set on top of another," as "cinematographical," almost literally details a reinscriptive logic: "In a poem of this sort one is trying to record the precise instant when a thing outward and objective transforms itself, or darts into a thing inward and subjective" (*G-B*, 89). Therefore, he can speak of the Image as "analytical," and call upon the analogy of analytical geometry in contrast to other mathematical models which are descriptive. The analytical Image is productive rather than representative, in the sense, as Pound argues, that it transcribes and erases the *re*, producing a presentational or re-petitional effect, a figure instead of some *res* itself. The Image proposes a reinscriptive logic, a "phantasikon," which Pound once said was the right name for Imagination.

We have already seen how Fenollosa's remarkable essay has equated nature with poetry or metaphor, and how Pound understands this return to the verbal, or the reinscription of the visual into the verbal in ideogrammic writing, as a critical or interpretative figure. A close reading of that essay, which I have attempted elsewhere,[24] has to recognize, as Pound explicitly remarked, that Fenollosa chose to tell the story of language's origin, its historical dispersal or de-orientation, and its recuperation of power through the reintroduction or reinscription of graphic writing into phonetic writing, in a "narrative" mode. So that one should be as cautious of reading it is a descriptive history as in reading Nietzsche's "fable" as a decisive ontological argument. That the story he tells both follows Hegel's and reverses it is self-evident, but also deceiving, since Fenollosa in his other writings interpreted the return to the Chinese character in terms of a curious historical reversal, or retreat, of poetry.

It was Fenollosa's contention that American thought, or Transcendentalism, was not only compatible with Oriental thought or Zen doctrine, but that it had been a virtual recuperation of the Oriental—the result of a very strange double movement. On the one hand, he argued, the Zen "book of nature," which had already derived the "categories of thought" from the "basis of nature's organization," was an "independent discovery of Hegelian categories that lie behind the two worlds of subject and object."[25] On the other, American thought had been touched by Oriental thought in a manner more direct than the Hegelian or historical mediation of the West; that is, in a way contrary to any thinking of the western movement (grammatical) of thought. Fenollosa hypothesized a Pacific "stage" for this interaction of American and Oriental thought, a "pacific School of Art," he called it, generated by "actual dispersion and control throughout the vast basin of the Pacific." Pacific art accentuated the Eastern "centre of dispersion" in contrast to the Western centering—while Chinese art was the only "large form of world art that combine[d] both impulses." The Chinese ideograph, therefore, is not Idealistic or synthetic: "It thus becomes a great school of poetic interpretation," though interpretation here for Fenollosa meant reading nature as a "storehouse of spiritual laws."

The freshness of Emersonian thought, or Transcendentalism, he appeared to conclude, was the result of its more direct apprehension of the originary interpretative thought of the Chinese, though Transcendental thought necessarily inscribed its intuitions in what Whitman had called "Hegelian formulas." However bizarre the historical formulation, and despite the incoherence or blindness that permits him to find the origins of western humanism in the forgotten nature of oriental graphism, and to forget that his own reading of the ideogram is a purely western idealization, Fenollosa may be said to *radical*ize the thinking of the Chinese grapheme in a way he could not have understood. His view of the historical "retreat" of Chinese poetry, a retreat or withdrawal which in its way returns to meet or intervene upon the advance and historical decline of western thought, is indirectly recounted in "The Chinese Written Character . . . ." as Pound noted, as a completed history of language. Yet, this history will not end or close. Fenollosa's narrative disrupts its own advance. The keynote of all Fenollosa's teaching of the meeting between East and West lies, according to Van Wyck Brooks, in his notion of "spacing." Spacing and dispersal—and while we have come to think of spacing in a sense quite different from Fenollosa's definition that "all art is harmonious spacing," his notion of Oriental dispersion and decentering as preceding western centering has critical implications which explode the idea of cyclical history. Therefore the Chinese ideograph was the sign that there could be no unitary style, or no pure cultural style but only a curious interweaving of the heterogeneous: "just as it is true that the alien influence lies at the very core of the national." The return to the "method" of Chinese writing, prophesied at the very conclusion of "The Chinese Written Character," would not be the culmination or closure of a western poetics, nor a recuperation of some primordial method, but a sign of another poetic "beginning," of return or inaugural repetition.

It is no accident, then, as I have suggested elsewhere, that the ideographs Fenollosa chooses to exemplify this return to a natural writing, which is to say, to metaphor, are ideographs of the sun-rising, or more accurately, ideographs retranscribing the English sentence, "Sun rises (in the) East," back into a language which the western grammar had murdered, or stabilized. The return of the sun is enabled by the intervention, or reinscription of the "visible hieroglyphics" of Chinese radicals, so that the sign of the Orient is the sign of the "sun entangled in the branches of a tree," a sun that rises by passing over and erasing the "horizon" which it projects in its turning. Here is the curious figure of metaphor returning upon itself, of metaphor withdrawing into metaphor advancing, and re-drawing a *radical* horizon: "the sun is above the horizon, but beyond that the single upright line is like the growing trunk of the tree sign" (*CWC*, p. 33). Recall Williams in *Paterson*, where the poem is "the ignorant sun / rising in the slot of / hollow suns risen . . ."; "When the sun rises, it rises in the poem / and when it sets darkness comes down / and the poem is dark."[26]

228

And Fenollosa: "Thus in all poetry a word is like a sun, with its corona and chromosphere; words crowd upon words, and enwrap each other in their luminous envelopes until sentences become clear, continuous light bands" (*CWC*, p. 32). This figure of the innate harmony and natural affinity of things discovered and "enveloped" in a horizon ordered and centered upon the poetic word is, in its way, an euphoric affirmation of Hegel's "symbol." But if the "poetic word" is only "like" a sun, Fenollosa can only recur to the tautology implicit in his circular definition. The sun never appears except in its sign, which can rise only in the text it presumably illuminates and envelopes. It rises only in its corona. The sun—which projects horizons and erases them at the same time, breaching the very boundaries it produces—is a figure for all the other figures which are its "light bands." This sun never properly arrives or re-orients itself. Rather, its turning is dis-orienting. Fenollosa ascribes to poetic words not only luminosity but excess, "overtones," which are like nature's excess. The clarity of poetry, its luminosity, lies in the "delicate balance of overtones" or the plurisignificance of radical relations which are repeatedly re-drawn. The sun does not close upon itself, or return, but re-turns.

IV

This figure of the "horizon," composed by the double movement of repetition or re-turn and displacement, has become in a sense the "scene" of modern American poetry, of "making it new." More appropriate, because more undecidable, than the frontier, the horizon is inexhaustible and ever moving, advancing and receding at the same time, the sign of a sun which projects it and follows it, never arriving. The product of a sun which is a "poetic word." Wallace Stevens, indeed, allegorized or thematized that scene of writing in a late poem which he called "A Primitive Like an Orb,"[27] emphasizing in the titular metaphor the paradox of an original which is only an image or particle of that perfection from which it is supposed to have evolved by falling; and yet by which alone, as figure, we not only know but produce the absent idea of perfection. Thus the primitive is figural, the "giant on the horizon" or "centre on the horizon, concentrum, grave / And prodigious person, patron," an ex-centric and double notion of the originary power of writing, a "giant of nothingness" which is at once the father and death ("grave"). Thus Stevens on this "fated eccentricity" of modern writing:

> That's it. The lover writes, the believer hears,
> The poet mumbles and the painter sees,
> Each one, his fated eccentricity,
> As part, but part, but tenacious particle,
> Of the skeleton of the ether, the total

Of letters, prophecies, perceptions, clods
Of color, the giant of nothingness, each one
And the giant ever-changing, living in change.

(PEM, 320)

This figural horizon, this figure on the horizon, is figure itself. The center, projected "on" the horizon, is the "nothingness" of language which Stevens everywhere relates to "change." Poetry resides in the self-effacing horizon of language, in this metaphorical impulse which, as Nietzsche indicates, repeatedly re-inhabits the old structures and tears at their illusory order.

However different Stevens' style from Pound's—the differences that tempt critics to privilege one or the other, and to extend this privilege into an attack on subjectivist or prophetic imprecision (for example, Hart Crane's) or into a celebration of objectivist accuracies (for example, Williams')—these poets obsessively retell a story of writing in and at the margin. It is a story not simply of the anxiety of influence or belatedness, but of the irony or paradox of repetition. Whether they tell it gravely, like Crane, as a gnostic account of failure to retrieve or recuperate some historically dispersed Word (the myth of *logos* separated from *lexis*) or ironically (though some might say, dandiacally) like Stevens, as a "never-ending meditation" of "And yet(s)" and "as ifs," of delay and deferral between "desire" and the "object" or between "word" and the "thing itself" it must become—however it is told, it is a story of reinscriptive logic, of poetry re-turning to interfere, disrupt, or break what Nietzsche called the "regular and rigid new world" of "ideas" which have taken up residence, like "evaporated products," in the houses of forgotten metaphors.

Crane, indeed, tells this story in the form of pseudo-epic, as the belated reconstruction of *The Bridge*, even when he projects the figure of the poet (as a modern technocrat, an airman) who seeks to derive his vision directly from the transcendental—the poet who wears on his wrist a "Sanskrit charge / To conjugate infinity's dim marge—Anew" (*CP*, 92). To conjugate "Anew" is to conjugate belatedly, and to derive one's myth not from the *logos* but from the sign of its absence, the "dim marge" or shadow figuration. But Crane's poet far from piercing or transcending this margin is revolved within it. His plane (language) tropes and returns. Conjugation does not decline an infinitive into temporal debris, but is the loop of language upon itself:

> But first, here at this height receive
> The benediction of the shell's deep, sure reprieve!
> Lead-perforated fuselage, escutcheoned wings
> Lift agonized quittance, tilting from the invisible brink
> Now eagle-bright, now

```
                    quarry-hid, twist-
                                        -ing, sink with
Enormous repercussive list-
                    -ings down
Giddily spiralled
                    gauntlets, upturned, unlooping
In guerilla sleights, trapped in combustion gyr-
Ing, dance the curdled depth
                                        down whizzing
Zodiacs, dashed
                    (now nearing fast the Cape!)
                    down gravitation's
                                        vortex into crashed
    . . .dispersion . . . into mashed and shapeless debris . . .
                                        (CP, 92-93)
```

      Space does not permit anything like an exhaustive reading of the problematics that infiltrate Crane's long poem, which explores thematically the difficulties of reconstructing a "bridge" between the "broken world" of time and the "Word," while at the same time insisting that the means are lent to the poet by the Word so that he in turn can construct a form (an "Unfractioned idiom") that will "lend a myth to God" ("Proem" to *The Bridge*). Any reading of *The Bridge* must come to the question of its epical or pseudo-narrative structure and its assumption of a cyclic and teleological history of loss and promised recuperation. That is, a structure which repeats a veritable cliché of history, of exile and promised, if thwarted, return, of history as loss and fall. In this instance, the fall of history occurred in a moment when history was separated off from vision or when history was deprived of the economy of myth. The poem as bridge would rejoin myth and history and therefore rejuvenate history as "Paradigm," "Verb," "intrinsic Myth," or "Vision-of-the-Voyage," that is, as pure form or *logos*. The poem, therefore, would be a construct or sign transformed into symbol ("synergy"), but a symbol, as Hegel noted, which because it is *of* time can never be purified of its signifying and mediating function—that is, the symbol must remain a sign, however valorized as "intrinsic" myth.

      The epical structure, then, is entangled in the irreducible graphic doubleness of language, like the cables and derricks of the suspension bridge or the "cordage-tree" (the cross-like mast) of Columbus's ship in the "Ave Maria" section, delayed at sea, its message of a discovery threatened by the very medium upon which it must return (*CP*, 50-51). "Language," Crane wrote, in a phrase that may very well prefigure his theme, "has built towers and bridges, but itself is inevitably as fluid as always" (*CP*, 223). Poetry, which tries to overcome this incessant double reflection of language, or erase its own impediments, can only reproduce the figural margin it breaches or effaces. In *The Bridge*, history is the figure of the margin or horizon that the poem must overcome, but which it can overcome only by reinscribing, like a symbol that is inextricable from a sign. If the poem therefore appropriates the narrative form of epic, and projects itself toward a triumphal ending or vision wherein everything is gathered into "One Song, one Bridge of Fire! Is it Cathay? '' (*CP*, 117) or toward a re-orientation, it can only portend that "Song" overcoming song as a supplication and a question projected beyond "antiphonal" whispers of words. "Cathay" remains within history, a name and a place, however much it is a mythical or visionary promise. The poem, that is, can never arrive at its destination, "beyond time," because it cannot extricate itself from the time of language—*time* being that name, as de Man has said, of "truth's inability to coincide with itself":[28] as in a poem's graphic mark, "Always through spiring cordage, pyramids / Of silver sequel" (*CP*, 116).

Just as the poem can neither transcend nor suppress the irreducible "cipher-script of time" or of sound and figure (song and cordage), or just as the bridge defines the river and the river the bridge, each one being a form of the other, each irreducible to the other, so does the poem defer necessarily any synthetic reduction of opposites to one. Thus the recurring metaphor of the "serpent" and the "eagle" (derived very likely from Nietzsche, out of Hegel) is resolvable only in the "margin grass" of some textual moment ("the serpent with the eagle in the leaves" in one phrase; "in the boughs" elsewhere [*CP*, 117; 75]); figures of time and space respectively constituting the "body," the lady, of a continent which would be the last link in a circle, a bridge or poem completing the return of myth into history. The textual weave resolves nothing, however, since it cannot erase its own mark of artifice. Like the dance of Maquokeeta, the serpent or American Dionysus, the poem re-marks its own "lie"—"Lie to us,—dance us back to tribal morn" (*CP*, 73)—which is to say, the poem marks its own scene as language, as dance, which cannot transcend to pure song. Dionysus' frantic dance, weaving serpent and eagle, cannot efface their incoherence (they are not opposites) or erase the inadequation of myth and history. It can only stage, therefore, the return or reinscription of poetry into its own metaphoric structure, of poetry's "impulse," the impulse toward metaphor as Nietzsche called it, which reinvades the solidified structures (the "slumbering pyramid") it has worked at constructing.

Poetry, then, cannot be a vision or prophecy of construction; it is rather a scene of deconstruction. It becomes an ironic commentary on the belatedness of vision, of the laborious invention of idealism which has had to be forgotten. The poem derives its theme of historical decadence and entropy from the very epical or narrative mode it must employ in attempting to overcome entropy, in troping en-tropy. That is, it borrows its theme from language, and more exactly, from language's inability to

232

close the distance between figurality and meaning. Language, time, and death are therefore wound in the "boughs" and "leaves," in the "labyrinthine mouths of history" which can only give their "reply" to a question which is derived from a ready-made (metaphoric) answer. *The Bridge*, which is a tautological title, a title referring only to the poem, or to an ideal poem for which the poem is only a sign—*The Bridge*, far from lending a "myth to God," can only lend a myth to Poetry, a myth to which the poetic image is never adequate. The bridge as metaphor of metaphor marks the unbridgeable distance between myth and history, and signifies poetry as that uncertain and indeterminate margin which precludes our clear demarcation of the two.

I wish to conclude with a somewhat less complex thematization of this poetics of re-turn or reinscription, though one which is likely to provoke more resistance from readers who like to believe that poetic or metapoetic statements are sufficient to some "truth" they evoke. I am referring to Stevens' short, programmatic verse entitled "Not Ideas about the Thing but the Thing Itself" which critics commonly read not only as the asseveration but the achievement of poetic self-overcoming, not simply an effacement of that scepticism he calls the "mortal no" but a fulfillment of the "passion for yes."[29] There is no questioning the fact that Stevens' affirmations, rhetorical as they are, whether comic or sentimental, almost always follow close upon his doubts, with a dialectical inevitability that seems to affirm poetry's recuperative powers. There is less of Crane's pathos in Stevens, Harold Bloom's readings notwithstanding; so that when we come upon such assertions as the "desire" for a metaphor to bridge the "dumbfoundering abyss / Between us and the object" (*PEM*, 329) it is easy enough to read the explicit statement of a desire as the efficient cause of its satisfaction—to read the imperative "must(s)" of a "supreme fiction" as the efficient cause of a fully articulated "supreme fiction." The strategic placement of "Not Ideas . . ." at the end of his Collected Poems could not help but confirm his desire to achieve some "total book," or on first reading to overcome every threatening mediation he had so tentatively and cautiously worked around in poem after poem exploring "The Motive for Metaphor." But "What is, uncertainly, / Desire prolongs its adventure to create / Forms of farewell" (*PEM*, 346). "Not Ideas . . ." seemed, as he wrote in another poem, to "defy / The metaphor that murders metaphor" (*PEM*, 296) and to posit a poetic moment of perfection, of transparent self-reflexion, that he had once posited in his "Adagia": "Perhaps there is a degree of perception of which what is real and what is imagined are one: a state of clairvoyant observation, accessible or possibly accessible to the poet or, say, the acutest poet."[30] As usual, Stevens' aphoristic commentary is cautious and qualified, and like his poetry, deferential of its own perfections: a poetry of the "perhaps," "possibly," and "as if." "Not Ideas about the Thing," however, seems aggressively affirmative, and not cautionary or delaying:

At the earliest ending of winter,
In March, a scrawny cry from outside
Seemed like a sound in his mind.

He knew that he heard it,
A bird's cry, at daylight or before,
In the early March wind.

The sun was rising at six,
No longer a battered panache above snow . . .
It would have been outside,

It was not from the vast ventriloquism
Of sleep's faded papier-mâche . . .
The sun was coming from outside.

That scrawny cry—It was
A chorister whose c preceded the choir.
It was part of the colossal sun,

Surrounded by its choral rings,
Still far away. It was like
A new knowledge of reality.

(PEM, 387-88)

The poem proposes a basic and simplified poetic ideal—as Stevens writes elsewhere, to "Trace the gold sun about the whitened sky / Without evasion by a single metaphor" (*PEM*, 288) or to seek an "Image certain as meaning is // To sound" (*PEM*, 296). But this would only be a perfection of metaphor, a metaphor of metaphor which would for a moment efface what Stevens called the "prolific ellipses" (*PEM*, 299) of our knowledge. Here, in "Not Ideas . . . ," it is a desire to overcome the mediations of thought, to "know" the "outside," or for the moment, in poetry, to precipitate the inside into the outside, to erase the difference that mediates the old knowledge, and to allow to stand forth, in the poetic moment, a metaphor that is the thing-itself. At first, this way to the outside can only be through metaphor, the "cry," a figure stripped and devalued to its minimum utterance, a simile for remembrance. Now he wants to know that "cry" not as some recollection, but a "cry" of immediacy (as in another verse he called the poem the "cry of its occasion, / Part of the res itself and not about it" (*PEM*, 338)—not as metaphor, not something "from the vast ventriloquism / Of sleep's faded papier-mâche." Yet, the more this "scrawny cry" is stripped of metaphor and precipitated "outside," the more it is conceived not as image but as voice, the more emphatically it is secured to that which is returning: "It was part of the colossal sun," and, moreover, a sun whose return is announced by "choral rings" or images which precede and obscure its return. This returning "cry," this voice, can only be the sign of "choral rings" which precede the sun, a metaphor whose metaphoricity is at once forgotten and re-marked. If we are tempted to relate this "sun" to that at the beginning of "Notes toward a Supreme Fiction," as that which will "bear no names" or which undoes repeatedly all the names ascribed to it (*PEM*, 207-08), we must still recognize that the "outside" is figural, and that the "new knowledge" is not immediate but *like / A new knowledge of reality.*"

We do not have to appeal to the *nouvelle critique* to recognize the irreducible figurality of the sun as the metaphor for metaphor, but we do need to recognize that this figure can only be thought of as "reality" or the "outside" at the very moment of its return or reinscription into metaphor, its undoing or tearing of the stable structure of ideas which it has worked at building. If the sun has a "project," as Stevens writes in "Notes toward a Supreme Fiction," that project is supplementary. As the figure of figure, the sun is repetition, a "merely going round" (*PEM*, 232). It returns or rises from a certain outside that is never outside, and breaches those apparently clear and distinct demarcations, like inside/outside, that at once give us the stability and security of "ideas" and threaten poets with mediation and belatedness. Only in the moment of metaphorical re-turn or reinscription is the veil apparently torn and the poet able to indulge the fiction, or supreme fiction, of unmediated vision.

But the effect, or as Nietzsche would emphasize, the "illusion" of a "new knowledge" is produced only in the moment of metaphor's return, and not in a poem that is a story of that return. For "Not Ideas . . ." is a thematization of writing, and of a pure return of meaning that in the same gesture is delayed and deflected. Could we say that Stevens' "sun" here is Nietzsche's, to recall the epigraph with which I began? Nietzsche likens the return, or the repetition of the impulse toward metaphor, to a "Saturnalia" of the intellect, and I will leave it to you whether we might now imagine, in the spirit of Borges, that Nietzsche, reader of Emerson, was also a reader of Stevens and Pound—*that* Nietzsche who, at the conclusion of "Truth and Falsity," saw the revolution of art not as a modernist theme but as an irruption, what Stevens called the "perpetual revolution," of and at the margin we misname origin:

> Man himself . . . has an invincible tendency to let himself be deceived, and he is like one enchanted with happiness when the rhapsodist narrates to him epic romances in such a way that they appear real or when the actor on the stage makes the king appear more kingly than reality shows him. Intellect, that master of dissimulation, is free and dismissed from his service as slave, so long as It is

able to deceive without *Injuring*, and then It celebrates Its Saturnalia . . . . Whatever It now does, compared with Its former doings, bears within itself dissimulation, just as its former doings bore the character of distortion. It copies human life, but takes it for a good thing and seems to rest quite satisfied with it. That enormous framework and hoarding of ideas, by clinging to which needy man saves himself through life, is to the freed intellect only a scaffolding and a toy for Its most daring feats, and when It smashes it to pieces, throws it into confusion, and then puts it together ironically, pairing the strangest, separating the nearest items, then It manifests that It has no use for those makeshifts of misery, and that It is now no longer led by ideas but by intuitions. From these intuitions no regular road leads into the land of the spectral schemata, the abstractions; for them the word is not made, when man sees them he is dumb, or speaks in forbidden metaphors and in unheard-of combinations of ideas, in order to correspond creatively with the impression of the powerful present intuition at least by destroying and jeering at the old barriers of ideas.[31] (*TF*, 514)

UCLA

NOTES

1 "The Case against Nietzsche," *The Complete Poems and Selected Letters and Prose of Hart Crane* (Garden City, N. Y.: Doubleday Anchor, 1966), pp. 197-98 (hereafter cited as *CP*).

2 See *The Letters of Wallace Stevens*, sel. and ed. by Holly Stevens (New York: Knopf, 1966), pp. 409, 431-32, 461-62, 486, 532.

3 *The Literary Essays of Ezra Pound*, ed. with introd. by T. S. Eliot (Norfolk, Conn.: New Directions, 1954), p. 32.

4 A. R. Orage, *Friedrich Nietzsche, the Dionysian Spirit of the Age* (London: Fouks, 1906). See also Orage, *Nietzsche in Outline and Aphorism* (Chicago: McClurg, 1910).

5 The question refers to the following lines, from "Hugh Selwyn Mauberley," *Personae, Collected Shorter Poems* (New York: New Directions, 1971), p. 199:

Mildness, amid the neo-Nietzschean clatter,
His sense of graduations,
Quite out of place amid
Resistance to current exacerbations,

Invitation, mere invitation to perceptivity
Gradually led him to the isolation
Which these presents place
Under a more tolerant, perhaps, examination.

6   De Man, *Allegories of Reading* (New Haven, Conn.: Yale Univ. Press, 1979), p. 79.

7   *Allegories of Reading*, p. 79.

8   *Allegories of Reading*, p. 119.

9   See Derrida, *Of Grammatology*, trans. by Gayatri Spivak (Baltimore, Md.: Johns Hopkins Univ. Press, 1976), p. 92.

10   These tropes are taken respectively from the poems "Saint John and the Back-Ache" and "Not Ideas about the Thing but the Thing Itself," *The Palm at the End of the Mind, Selected Poems and a Play*, ed. by Holly Stevens (New York: Random House, Vintage, 1972), pp. 329 and 387-88. "Not Ideas . . ." will be discussed at some length later in this essay.

11   I am referring to Derrida's essay, in part on Heidegger's notion of metaphor, entitled (in "literal" English translation) "The *Retrait* of Metaphor," *Enclitic*, 2 (Fall 1978), 4-33. The translation retains the untranslatable (non-)word *retrait* which "bears" the various senses of retreat, re-drawing, withdrawal, recess, re-marking, retirement, as they touch upon notions of *trait* and trait, mark, line, etc.

12   "Pas," *Gramma*, nos. 3/4 (1976), 111-215.

13   Subsequent quotations from Pound's writings (and including Fenollosa's essay) will be noted in the text, as follows:
     G-B: *Gaudier-Brzeska, A Memoir* (New York: New Directions, 1970)
     L: *The Letters of Ezra Pound, 1907-1941*, ed. by D. D. Paige (New York: Harcourt, Brace, 1950)
     LE: *The Literary Essays of Ezra Pound* (see note 3)
     SP: *Ezra Pound, Selected Prose, 1909-1965* (New York: New Directions, 1973)
     SR: *The Spirit of Romance* (New York: New Directions, n.d.—first pub. in 1909)
     NPL: "Postscript" to Pound's translation of Remy de Gourmont, *The Natural Philosophy of Love* (New York: Liveright, 1932—first pub. in 1922)
     CWC: Ernest Fenollosa, *The Chinese Written Character as a Medium for Poetry*, ed. by E. Pound (San Francisco: City Lights, 1969)

14   See Fenollosa, *CWC*: "The wealth of European speech grew, following slowly the intricate maze of nature's suggestions and affinities. Metaphor piled upon metaphor in quasi-geological strata" (23). Nature, then, which "furnishes her own clues," in "homologies, sympathies, and identities" (22), can never appear outside of metaphor. It can never be other than its clues or signs. And if all one can know of nature is metaphor—that is, of the process passing from unseen to seen, from visible to invisible, the classical metaphysical definition

of metaphor—all we can know is already "figure": "is it not enough to show that Chinese poetry gets back *near* to the processes of nature by means of its vivid figure, its wealth of such figure? " (31, my italics). To say that poetry reveals nature as "relations" can only mean that poetry reveals only metaphor, a tautology. Except that by revealing metaphor it reveals the undoing of grammar and logic and their accompanying systems of taxonomy: "This was probably why the conception of evolution came so late in Europe. *It could not make way until it was prepared to destroy the inveterate logic of classification*" (27, F's italics? or P's?).

15 See the last two chapters of *Blindness and Insight* (New York: Oxford Univ. Press, 1971), pp. 142-86.

16 *The Will to Power*, ed. by Walter Kaufmann (New York: Vintage, 1968), p. 424.

17 See Jacques Derrida. *La dissémination* (Paris: Seuil, 1972). Like other Derridean terms, *dissémination* functions to defamiliarize conceptual notions of orderly (organic) dispersal, the concept of a broken but recuperable unity. Dissemination, he once remarked, in a non-definition, is that which does "not return to the father"; it is an irreducibly doubled term, and, as he says, includes by semantic accident not only two incompatible and etymologically unconnected meanings, but meanings which are often, by linguistic habit, elided in an organic figure. It is not simply that *seme* and *semen* accidentally inhabit the same phonemic structure, but that, in a metaphor which has become a cliché, we have been accustomed to think of the naturalness of language in terms of the word as seed or vice versa. Derrida's coinage resists our either discarding the metaphor as false or forgetting its accidental, irrational, and non-ontological status.

18 *Of Grammatology*, p. 92.

19 Kofman, *Nietzsche et la métaphor* (Paris: Payot, 1972), a chapter of which appears in *The New Nietzsche, Contemporary Styles of Interpretation*, ed. David Allison (New York: Delta, 1977), pp. 201-14.

20 *The New Nietzsche*, p. 208.

21 For "Truth and Falsity . . .," see *The Philosophy of Nietzsche*, ed. with an introd. by Geoffrey Clive (New York: Mentor, 1965), pp. 503-15. Clive's selections are taken from the Oscar Levy translation of Nietzsche's Works (hereafter cited as *TF*).

22 See de Man, *Allegories of Reading*, pp. 111-13; and Donato, "Divine Agonies: Of Representation and Narrative in Romantic Poetics," *Glyph 6* (Baltimore, Md.: Johns Hopkins Univ. Press, 1979), pp. 98-100.

23 See "Destruction as Criticism," *Glyph 6,* pp. 175-215, esp. p. 193. Gasché's important essay elaborates the "deconstructive" strategy of reversal and displacement (or intervention) in terms of the devaluation and then reinscription of the devalued term into the discourse, much in the way Nietzsche devalues and then reinscribes metaphor.

24 See "Decentering the Image: The 'Project' of 'American' Poetics? " *Textual Strategies*, ed. with introd. by Josué V. Harari (Ithaca, N. Y.: Cornell Univ.

Press, 1979), pp. 322-58, esp. pp. 332-40. Also published in *boundary 2*, VIII (Fall 1979), 159-88.

25 The quotations from Fenollosa in the following paragraphs are from his *Epochs of Chinese and Japanese Art*, new and rev. ed. with copious notes by Prof. Petrucci, 2 vols. (New York: Dover, 1963), an unabridged publication of a 1913 text. The remarks by Van Wyck Brooks are from his essay, "Fenollosa and His Circle," *Fenollosa and His Circle* (New York: Dutton, 1962), pp. 1-68, esp. p. 62.

26 W. C. Williams, *Paterson* (New York: New Directions, 1963), pp. 4, 99.

27 Stevens, *The Palm at the End of the Mind*, pp. 317-20 (hereafter cited as *PEM*).

28 *Allegories of Reading*, p. 78.

29 For example, Roy Harvey Pearce, in "Toward Decreation," *Wallace Stevens, A Celebration*, ed. by Frank Doggett and Robert Buttel (Princeton, N. J.: Princeton Univ. Press, 1980), p. 299, remarks rather plaintively of critics who follow Stevens' *via negativa* and yet do not honor his affirmative recovery: "I cannot understand the resistance of some of Stevens' exegetes to the fact of this dialectic [which overcomes the negative and 'proclaim(s)' it has found the 'hard prize' of the 'yes' or truth] and to the demands it put upon him, not to say them, to take with all seriousness poetry as 'the act of the mind.' " In this rhetoric, in which dialectic becomes a "fact" assuring its self-overcoming, rhetoric seems to be effaced and a high "seriousness" to triumph. I am apparently one of those critics Pearce cannot "understand," and though it is not an essay of mine he had yet read, my piece in the same volume (entitled "Metaphoric Staging: Stevens' Beginning Again of the 'End of the Book,' " pp. 308-38, 354-58n) would stand as such a "resistance" to taking poetic declarations as self-evident ontological triumphs. Perhaps poetic rhetoric is only a "seizure" of truth in two contrary senses of that word.

30 Wallace Stevens, *Opus Posthumous*, ed. Samuel French Morse (New York: Alfred A. Knopf, 1957), p. 166.

31 In *Allegories of Reading*, pp. 114-15, Paul de Man submits this passage, as the culmination of his reading of the essay/fable, to close scrutiny, emphasizing the nebulous and uneasy place of the artistic "self" who far from controlling, let alone triumphing through, this intuitional power, remains vulnerable to the very rhetorical trap that literature has exposed as the error of philosophy.

Nietzsche's Prefiguration of Postmodern American Philosophy

Cornel West

You ask me about the idiosyncracies of philosophers? . . . There is their lack of historical sense, their
hatred of even the idea of becoming, their Egyptianism.
They think they are doing a thing *honour* when they
dehistoricize it, *sub specie aeterni*— when they make a
mummy of it. All the philosophers have handled for
millennia has been conceptual mummies; nothing actual
has escaped from their hands alive. They kill, they stuff,
when they worship, these conceptual idolaters—they
become a mortal danger to everything when they
worship. Death, change, age, as well as procreation and
growth, are for them objections—refutations even. What
is, does not *become;* what becomes, *is* not. . .
Nietzsche, Twilight of the Idols

What I relate is the history of the next two
centuries. I describe what is coming, what can no longer
come differently: *the advent of nihilism.* This history

241

can be related even now; for necessity itself is at work here. This future speaks even now in a hundred signs, this destiny announces itself everywhere; for this music of the future all ears are cocked even now. For some time now, our whole European culture has been moving as toward a catastrophe, with a tortured tension that is growing from decade to decade: restlessly, violently, headlong, like a river that wants to reach the end, that no longer reflects, that is afraid to reflect.

Nietzsche, *The Will To Power*

Nietzsche is the central figure in postmodern thought in the West. His aphoristic style—the epigram as style—governs the elusive texts of postmodern philosophers such as Ludwig Wittgenstein and E.M. Cioran. His anti-hermeneutical perspectivism underlies the deconstructive stance of postmodern critics such as Jacques Derrida and Paul de Man. His genealogical approach, especially regarding the link between knowledge and power, regulates the neo-Marxist textual practice of postmodern critic-historians such as Michel Foucault and Edward Said. And his gallant attempt to overcome traditional metaphysics is a major preoccupation of postmodern thinkers such as Martin Heidegger, Hans-Georg Gadamer and Jean-Paul Sartre.

In this paper, I will try to show the ways in which Nietzsche prefigures the crucial moves made recently in postmodern American philosophy. I will confine my remarks to two of Nietzsche's texts: *Twilight of the Idols* and *The Will To Power*.[1] The postmodern American philosophers I will examine are W.V. Quine, Nelson Goodman, Wilfred Sellars, Thomas Kuhn and Richard Rorty. The three moves I shall portray are: the move toward anti-realism or conventionalism in ontology; the move toward the demythologization of the Myth of the Given or anti-foundationalism in epistemology; and the move toward the detranscendentalization of the subject or the dismissal of the mind as a sphere of inquiry. I then shall claim that Nietzsche believed such moves lead to a paralyzing nihilism and ironic skepticism unless they are supplemented with a new world view, a new "countermovement" to overcome such nihilism and skepticism. Lastly, I will suggest that postmodern American philosophy has not provided such a "countermovement," settling instead for either updated versions of scientism (Quine and Sellars), an aristocratic resurrection of pluralistic stylism (Goodman), a glib ideology of professionalism (Kuhn), or a nostalgic appeal to enlightened conversation (Rorty). Such weak candidates for a "countermovement" seem to indicate the extent to which postmodern American philosophy—similar to much of postmodern thought in the West—constitutes a dead, impotent rhetoric of a declining and decaying civilization.

Anti-Realism

The originary figures of modern analytic philosophy—Gottlob Frege, Alexius Meinong, Bertrand Russell and G.E. Moore—are the acknowledged ancestors of postmodern American philosophers. These figures constituted a formidable realist revolt against psychologism, conventionalism and idealism.[2] Frege revolted against J.S. Mill's psychologism and J. Venn's conventionalism in logic; Meinong, against Franz Brentano's psychologism in object theory; Russell and Moore, against F.H. Bradley's Hegelian idealism in metaphysics and epistemology. Each separate attack shares a common theme: an attempt to resurrect realism.

There are many forms of realism in modern analytic philosophy, including naive realism, Platonic realism, critical realism and internal realism.[3] The basic claims of any form of realism are that objects, things, states of affairs or the world exist externally to us and independently of our sense experience; and that these objects, things, states of affairs or this world, in some fundamental way, determine what is true, objective and real.

This two-prong definition of realism suggests two important elements of any realist position. First, it links any realist position to some notion of correspondence (or re-presenting) between either ideas and objects, words and things, sentences and states of affairs, or theories and the world. Second, this definition proposes something other than human social practice to serve as the final court of appeal which determines what is and what we ought to believe. To put it crudely, realism is preoccupied with assuring us that there is an external world and with obtaining the true (accurate, objective, valid) copy of this world.

Postmodern American philosophers affirm the first-prong of the definition of realism—thus bypassing idealism—but see no need to build the notion of correspondence into the way the claim is stated. In short, they are highly critical of the subject-object problematic embodied in the first-prong of the definition such that grasping reality consists of crossing the subject-object hiatus, leaving one's inner world in order to get in contact with the external world, and of one's ideas copying or corresponding to the world.

Postmodern American philosophers reject the second-prong of the definition of realism—thus promoting conventionalism in ontology. They refuse to accept the view that the world determines truth or that the world is the final court of appeal which compels us to accept what is or believe as we ought.

This rejection is based on two major insights of postmodern American philosophers: the conventional character of constructing (reductionist or nonreductionist) logical systems of the world and the theory-laden character of observations. The first insight crystallized after

Rudolf Carnap's highly acclaimed yet unsuccessful attempt in his *Logical Construction of The World* (1928) (and better known as his *Aufbau*) to rationally reconstruct the process of acquiring knowledge by reducing (or translating) statements about the world to those of immediate experience. The second insight was gained from A.J. Ayer's popular yet no less unsuccessful attempt in his *Language, Truth and Logic* (1936) to defend the verificationist theory of meaning (or roughly promoting the primacy of observational evidence for determining the meaningfulness of a sentence).

Almost a decade after his painstaking study of Carnap's *Aufbau* in his masterful work, *The Structure of Appearance* (1951), Goodman concluded in his renown essay, "The Way The World Is,"

> What we must face is the fact that even the truest description comes nowhere near faithfully reproducing the way the world is . . . for it has explicit primitives, routes of construction, etc., none of them features of the world described. Some philosophers contend, therefore, that if systematic descriptions introduce an arbitrary artificial order, then we should make our descriptions unsystematic to bring them more into accord with the world. Now the tacit assumption here is that the respects in which a description is unsatisfactory are *just those respects in which it falls short of being a faithful picture;* and the tacit *goal* is to achieve a description that as nearly as possible gives a living likeness. But the goal is a delusive one. For we have seen that even the most realistic way of picturing amounts merely to one kind of conventionalization. In painting, the selection, the emphasis, the conventions are different from but no less peculiar to the vehicle, and no less variable, than those of language. The idea of making verbal descriptions approximate pictorial depiction loses its point when we understand that to turn a description into the most faithful possible picture would amount to nothing more than exchanging some conventions for others.[4]

After his search for a criterion of adequacy for constructionaı systems, such as Carnap's phenomenalistic one, or for scientific theories, such as Einstein's special theory of relativity, Goodman held that the choice is not based primarily on mere agreement with the facts, i.e., observational data, but rather on, among other things, structural simplicity. In his influential essay, "The Test of Simplicity", he writes,

Thus selection of a theory must always be made in advance of the determination of some of the facts it covers; and, accordingly, some criterion other than conformity with such facts must be applied in making the selection. After as many points as we like have been plotted by experiment concerning the correlation of two factors (for example, of time and deterioration of radioactivity), we predict the remaining points by choosing one among all the infinitely many curves that cover the plotted points. Obviously, simplicity of some sort is a cardinal factor in making this choice (we pick the "smoothest" curve). The very validity of the choice depends upon whether the choice is properly made according to such criteria. Thus simplicity here is not a consideration applicable after truth is determined but is one of the standards of validity that are applied in the effort to discover truth.[5]

In a later essay, "Art and Inquiry" and in his most recent work, *Ways of Worldmaking* (1978), Goodman advances the notion of fitness as appropriate to (and as replacement for) talk about truth.

Truth of a hypothesis after all is a matter of fit—fit with a body of theory, and fit of hypothesis and theory to the data at hand and the facts to be encountered.[6]

Briefly, then, truth of statements and rightness of descriptions, representations, exemplifications, expressions—of design, drawing, diction, rhythm—is primarily a matter of fit: fit to what is referred to in one way or another, or to other renderings, or to modes and manners of organization. The differences between fitting a version to a world, a world to a version, and a version together or to other versions fade when the role of versions in making the worlds they fit is recognized. And knowing or understanding is seen as ranging beyond the acquiring of true beliefs to the discovering and devising of fit of all sorts.[7]

In his famous essay, "Two Dogmas of Empiricism," Quine observed that in Ayer's attempt to correlate each meaningful sentence with observational evidence, i.e., empirical confirmation, Ayer remained tied to Carnap's reductionist project by trying to reduce the meaningfulness of a sentence to its empirical import.

But the dogma of reductionism has, in a subtler and more tenuous form, continued to influence the thought of empiricists. The notion lingers that to each statement, or each synthetic statement, there is associated a unique range of possible sensory events such that the occurrence of any of them would add to the likelihood of truth of the statement, and that there is associated also another unique range of possible sensory events whose occurrence would detract from that likelihood. This notion is of course implicit in the verification theory of meaning.

The dogma of reductionism survives in the supposition that each statement, taken in isolation from its fellows, can admit of confirmation or infirmation at all. My countersuggestion, issuing essentially from Carnap's doctrine of the physical world in the *Aufbau,* is that our statements about the external world face the tribunal of sense experience not individually but only as a corporate body.[8]

Quine extended his critique of updated empiricism to the most cherished notion of modern analytic philosophers—the notion of analyticity, the idea that a statement is true by virtue of meanings and independently of fact. Given his Duhemian holism, the idea of an isolated statement being true without empirical confirmation is as unacceptable as the idea of an isolated statement being true with empirical confirmation. His main point is that the basic "unit of empirical significance is the whole of science,"[9] namely, competing theories (versions or descriptions) of the world, not isolated statements, since the truth-value of such statements can change relative to one's theory of the world.

If this view is right, it is misleading to speak of the empirical content of an individual statement—especially if it is a statement at all remote from the experiential periphery of the field. Furthermore it becomes folly to seek a boundary between synthetic statements, which hold contingently on experience, and analytic statements, which hold come what may. Any statement can be held true come what may, if we make drastic enough adjustments elsewhere in the system. Even a statement very close to the periphery can be held true in the face of recalcitrant experience by pleading hallucination or by amending certain statements of the kind called logical laws. Conversely, by the same token, no statement is immune to revision.[10]

Goodman and Quine are the (retired, Harvard) patriarchs of postmodern American philosophy. Their respective holistic critiques of Carnap and, to a lesser degree, Ayer, constitute the emergence of postmodernity in American philosophy and mark the Americanization of analytic philosophy.[11] If Goodman and Quine are the patriarchs, then Richard Rorty and Thomas Kuhn are the renegade stepchildren. Rorty and Kuhn have followed through most thoroughly on the anti-realist, historicist and conventionalist implications of the views of Goodman and the early Quine.

In his celebrated article, "The World Well Lost," Rorty concludes that the theory-laden character of observations relativizes talk about the world such that appeals to "the world" as a final court of appeal to determine what is true or what we should believe is viciously circular. We cannot isolate "the world" from theories of the world, then compare these theories of the world with a theory-free world. We cannot compare theories with anything that is not a product of another theory. So any talk about "the world" is relative to the alternative theories available. In response to the second prong of the definition of realism—to the notion that the world determines truth—Rorty states,

> Now, to put my cards on the table, I think that the realistic true believer's notion of the world is an obsession rather than an intuition. I also think that Dewey was right in thinking that the only intuition we have of the world as determining truth is just the intuition that we must make our new beliefs conform with a vast body of platitudes, unquestioned perceptual reports, and the like.[12]

Kuhn, the other stepchild of Goodman and Quine, has received more attention than any postmodern American philosopher of science primarily because he has provided a new descriptive vocabulary which gives a new perspective on a sacrosanct institution, i.e., natural science, in our culture in light of the early Quine's pragmatism and Goodman's conventionalism. His controversial yet highly-acclaimed book, *The Structure of Scientific Revolutions* (1962) serves as a rallying point for anti-realists owing to statements such as the following:

> A scientific theory is usually felt to be better than its predecessors not only in the sense that it is a better instrument for discovering and solving puzzles but also because it is somehow a better representation of what nature is really like. One often hears that successive theories grow ever closer to, or approximate more and more closely to, the truth. Apparently generalizations

247

like that refer not to the puzzle-solutions and the concrete predictions derived from a theory but rather to its ontology, to the match, that is, between the entities with which the theory populates nature and what is "really there."

Perhaps there is some other way of salvaging the notion of 'truth' for application to whole theories, but this one will not do. There is, I think, no theory-independent way to reconstruct phrases like 'really there'; the notion of a match between the ontology of a theory and its "real" counterpart in nature now seems to me illusive in principle.[13]

If I am right, then 'truth' may, like 'proof', be a term with only intra-theoretic applications.[14]

There surely have been anti-realists (such as Hegel), conventionalist philosophers of science (such as Pierre Duhem) and pragmatists (such as John Dewey) prior to the rise of postmodern American philosophy. But I claim that it is Nietzsche who most openly and unequivocally prefigures the anti-realist, conventionalist move made by postmodern American philosophers.

For example, in the section entitled, "How The 'Real World' At Last Became A Myth" in *Twilight of The Idols,* Nietzsche comically mocks the notion of a theory-free world, a "world" that can be appealed to in adjudicating between competing theories of the world.

4. The real world—unattainable? Unattained, at any rate. And if unattained also *unknown.* Consequently also no consolation, no redemption, no duty: how could we have a duty towards something unknown?

(The grey of dawn. First yawning of reason. Cockcrow of positivism.)

5. The 'real world'—an idea no longer of any use, not even a duty any longer—an idea grown useless, superfluous, *consequently* a refuted idea: let us abolish it!

(Broad daylight; breakfast; return of cheerfulness and *bon sens;* Plato blushes for shame; all free spirits run riot.)

6. We have abolished the real world: what world is left? the apparent world perhaps? . . . But no! *with the real world we have also abolished the apparent world!*

(Mid-day; moment of the shortest shadow; end of the longest error; zenith of mankind;

INCIPIT ZARATHUSTRA.) (*TI*, pp. 40-41)

Nietzsche clearly subscribes to the insight of postmodern American philosophers which holds that facts are theory-laden. He writes in *The Will To Power,*

> Against positivism, which halts at phenomena—"There are only *facts*"—I would say: No, facts are precisely what there is not, only interpretations. We cannot establish any fact "in itself": perhaps it is folly to want to do such a thing. (*WP,* p. 267)

> There are no facts, everything is in flux, incomprehensible, elusive; what is relatively most enduring is—our opinions. (*WP,* p. 327)

Goodman's pleas for a pluralism of versions of the world as manifest in the following passages:

> The movement is from unique truth and a world fixed and found to a diversity of right and even conflicting versions or worlds in the making.[15]

> There are very many different equally true descriptions of the world, and their truth is the only standard of their faithfulness. And when we say of them that they all involve conventionalizations, we are saying that no one of these different descriptions is *exclusively* true, since the others are also true. None of them tells us *the* way the world is, but each of them tells us *a* way the world is.[16]

echoes Nietzsche's quip,

> No limit to the ways in which the world can be interpreted; every interpretation a symptom of growth or of decline.
> Inertia needs unity (monism); plurality of interpretations a sign of strength. Not to desire to deprive the world of its disturbing and enigmatic character! (*WP,* p. 326)

As we saw earlier, for Goodman, this pluralism suggests multiple criteria for accepting versions of the world—in science and art.

Truth is not enough; it is at most a necessary condition. But even this concedes too much; the noblest scientific laws are seldom quite true. Minor discrepancies are overridden in the interest of breadth or power or simplicity. Science denies its data as the statesman denies his constituents—within the limits of prudence ... Truth and its aesthetic counterpart amount to appropriateness under different names. If we speak of hypotheses but not works of art as true, that is because we reserve the terms "true" and "false" for symbols in sentential form. I do not say this difference is negligible, but it is specific rather than generic, a difference in field of application rather than in formula, and marks no schism between the scientific and the aesthetic.[17]

Similarly for Nietzsche, seeking after 'truth' is essentially a matter of positing a goal and achieving that goal.

The ascertaining of "truth" and "untruth," the ascertaining of facts in general, is fundamentally different from creative positing, from forming, shaping, overcoming, willing, such as is of the essence of philosophy. To introduce a meaning—this task still remains to be done, assuming there is no meaning yet. Thus it is with sounds, but also with the fate of peoples: they are capable of the most different interpretations and direction toward different goals.

On a yet higher level is to *posit a goal* and mold facts according to it; that is, active interpretation and not merely conceptual translation. (*WP,* p. 327)

Note the way in which Nietzsche's perspectivism, most clearly stated in the following passage,

That the value of the world lies in our interpretation (—that other interpretations than merely human ones are perhaps somewhere possible—); that previous interpretations have been perspective valuations by virtue of which we can survive in life, i.e., in the will to power, for the growth of power; that every elevation of man brings with it the overcoming of narrower interpretations; that every strengthening and increase of power opens up new perspectives and means believing in new horizons—this idea permeates my writings. The world with which we are concerned is false, i.e., is not a fact but a fable and approximation on the basis of a meager sum of observations; it is "in flux," as something in a state of becoming, as a falsehood always changing but never getting near the truth: for—there is no "truth." (*WP,* p. 330)

anticipates the early Quine's pragmatism, best articulated in this famous paragraph,

> As an empiricist I continue to think of the conceptual scheme of science as a tool, ultimately, for predicting future experience in the light of past experience. Physical objects are conceptually imported into the situation as convenient intermediaries—not by definition in terms of experience, but simply as irreducible posits comparable, epistemologically, to the gods of Homer. For my part I do, qua lay physicist, believe in physical objects and not in Homer's Gods; and I consider it a scientific error to believe otherwise. But in point of epistemological footing the physical objects and the gods differ only in degree and not in kind. Both sorts of entities enter our conception only as cultural posits. The myth of physical objects is epistemologically superior to most in that it has proved more efficacious than other myths as a device for working a manageable structure into the flux of experience.[18]

Note also the crucial role of utility and human interests in the early Quine's pragmatism and Nietzsche's perspectivism.

> The quality of myth, however, is relative; relative, in this case, to the epistemological point of view. This point of view is one among various, corresponding to one among our various interests and purposes.[19]

> The apparent world, i.e., a world viewed according to values; ordered, selected according to values, i.e., in this case according to the viewpoint of utility in regard to the preservation and enhancement of the power of a certain species of animal.
> The perspective therefore decides the character of the "appearance"! (*WP,* p. 305)

Postmodern American philosophers, unconsciously prefigured by

Nietzsche, are aptly described by Rorty, when in the process of delineating what he calls 'edifying' philosophers such as Dewey, Kierkegaard and the later Heidegger, he writes,

> These writers have kept alive the suggestion that, even when we have justified true belief about everything we want to know, we may have no more than conformity to the norms of the day. They have kept alive the historicist sense that this century's "superstition" was the last century's triumph of reason, as well as the relativist sense that the latest vocabulary, borrowed from the latest scientific achievement, may not express privileged representations of essences, but be just another of the potential infinity of vocabularies in which the world can be described.[20]

Nietzsche catches the flavor of this passage when he writes,

> That the destruction of an illusion does not produce truth but only one more piece of ignorance, an extension of our "empty space," an increase of our "desert" (*WP,*p. 327)

Demythologizing the Myth of the Given

The Myth of the Given is an attempt to secure solid foundations for knowledge-claims; it is a quest for certainty in epistemology.[21] The Myth of the Given roughly holds that there is a given element—a self-justifying, intrinsically credible, theory-neutral, noninferential element—in experience which provides the foundations for other knowledge-claims and serves as the final terminating points for chains of epistemic justification. Therefore the attempt of postmodern American philosophers to demythologize the Myth of the Given is a move toward anti-foundationalism in epistemology. It is not surprising that such anti-foundationalism is akin to the anti-realism, holism and conventionalism we examined earlier.

The two major proponents of the Myth of the Given in modern analytic philosophy are C. I. Lewis, a beloved teacher of Quine and Goodman and H. H. Price, an appreciative student of Russell.[22] For both philosophers, the given element and its interpretation constitute the basic characteristics of knowledge and experience. As Lewis states:

> There are in our cognitive experience, two elements, the immediate data such as those of sense, which are presented or given to the mind, and a form,

construction, or interpretation, which represents the
activity of thought.[23]

Price also notes after acknowledging the data of the historian, general and
detective,

> But it is obvious that these are only data relatively and
> for the purpose of answering a certain question. They
> are really themselves the results of inference, often of a
> very complicated kind. We may call them data *secundum
> quid.* But eventually we must get back to something
> which is a datum *simpliciter,* which is not the result of
> any previous intellectual process.[24]

As we said earlier, for Lewis and Price, the very foundations of
knowledge are at stake in this distinction. Lewis is quite candid about this,

> If there be no datum given to the mind, then knowledge
> must be altogether contentless and arbitrary; there
> would be nothing which it must be true to. And if there
> be no interpretation which the mind imposes, then
> thought is rendered superfluous, the possibility of error
> becomes inexplicable, and the distinction of true and
> false is in danger of becoming meaningless.[25]

Similarly for Price, the phenomenological investigation of the particular
modes of perception (which lies outside of science) provides the
foundations for science. "Empirical Science can never be more
trustworthy than perception, upon which it is based."[26]

We are fortunate to have Goodman's direct response to Lewis's
two component view of knowledge owing to a symposium in which they
both (along with Hans Reichenbach) took part at an American
Philosophical Association meeting at Byrn Mawr in 1951. Needless to say,
Goodman is critical of Lewis's view. He replies not by denying the notion
of the given but by severing any links of a given element with notions of
the true, false or certain.

> But this all seems to me to point to, or at least to be
> compatible with, the conclusion that while something is
> given, nothing given is true; that while some things may
> be indubitable, nothing is certain. What we have been
> urged to grant amounts at most to this: materials for or
> particles of experience are given, sensory qualities or
> events or other elements are not created at will but
> presented, experience has some content even though our

description of it may be artificial or wrong and even though the precise differentiation between what is given and what is not given may be virtually impossible. But to such content or materials or particles or elements, the terms "true", or "false", and "certain" are quite inapplicable. These elements are simply there or not there. To grant that some are there is not to grant that anything is certain. Such elements may be indubitable in the vacuous sense that doubt is irrelevant to them, as it is to a desk; but they, like the desk, are equally devoid of certainty. They may be before us, but they are neither true nor false. For truth and falsity and certainty pertain to statements or judgments and not to mere particles or materials or elements. Thus, to deny that there are empirical certainties does not imply that experience is a pure fiction, that it is without content, or even that there is no given element.[27]

Five years later in his essay on Carnap, "The Revision of Philosophy", Goodman picks up the given-interpretation issue again and this time he rejects the distinction outright.

Any such view rests on the premise that the question "What are the original elements in knowledge?" is a clear and answerable one. And the assumption remains uncontested so long as we are dominated by the tradition that there is a sharp dichotomy between the given and the interpretation put upon it—so long as we picture the knower as a machine that is fed experience in certain lumps and proceeds to grind these up and reunite them in various ways. But I do not think this view of the matter will stand very close scrutiny.[28]

And in his latest book, the very notion of epistemological foundations and the given element in experience are dismissed and dispensed with.

With false hope of a firm foundation gone, with the world displaced by worlds that are but versions, with substance dissolved into function, and with the given acknowledged as taken, we face the questions how worlds are made, tested, and known.[29]

The most explicit attempts in postmodern American philosophy to demythologize the Myth of the Given are those of Wilfred Sellars and Richard Rorty. For Sellars, the Myth of the Given results from a confusion between the acquisition of knowledge and the justification of knowledge, between empirical causal accounts of how one comes to have a belief and philosophical investigations into how one justifies a belief one has. This confusion dissolves when one realizes that knowledge begins with the ability to justify, the capacity to use words. Everything else, he holds, is a non-cognitive causal antecedent. Sellars' psychological nominalism claims that there is no such thing as pre-linguistic awareness; or, to put it positively, that all awareness—of abstract and particular entities—is a linguistic affair. According to his view, ". . . not even the awareness of such sorts, resemblances, and facts as pertain to so-called immediate experience is presupposed by the process of acquiring the use of a language."[30]

Sellars's view precludes the possibility of any form of the Myth of the Given because it rules out any self-justifying, intrinsically credible, theory-neutral, noninferential epistemic element in experience. This is so because if knowledge begins with the ability to justify, then its beginnings (or "foundations") are public and intersubjective, matters of social practice.

For example, one of the forms of the Myth of the Given subscribed to by traditional empiricist philosophers,

> . . . is the idea that there is, indeed must be, a structure of particular matter of fact such that (a) each fact can not only be noninferentially known to be the case, but presupposes no other knowledge either of particular matter of fact, or of general truths; and (b) such that the noninferential knowledge of facts belonging to this structure constitutes the ultimate court of appeals for all factual claims—particular and general—about the world.[31]

This privileged stratum of fact is justified by appeals to prelinguistic awareness of self-authenticating, 'phenomenal' qualities. Price tries to defend this view by characterizing a normal perceptual situation—of a tomato under regular circumstances of light—in which he arrives at certain indubitable beliefs.

> One thing however I cannot doubt: that there exists a red patch of a round and somewhat bulgy shape, standing out from a background of other colour-patches, and having a certain visual depth, and that this whole field of colour is directly present to my consciousness. . . . This peculiar manner of being present to consciousness is called *being given* and that which is thus present is called a *datum*. The corresponding mental

attitude is called *acquaintance, intuitive apprehension,* or sometimes *having.*[32]

Sellars then replies,

> ... that one couldn't have observational knowledge of any fact unless one knew many other things as well. ... For the point is specifically that observational knowledge of any particular fact, e.g., that this is green, presupposes that one knows general facts of the form X is a *reliable symptom* of Y. ... The essential point is that in characterizing an episode or a state as that of *knowing,* we are not giving an empirical description of that episode or state; we are placing it in the logical space of reasons, of justifying and being able to justify what one says.[33]

Sellars concludes that the conception of knowledge based on the Myth of the Given, along with its concomitant picture of epistemology,

> ... is misleading because of its static character. One seems forced to choose between the picture of an elephant which rests on a tortoise (What supports the tortoise?) and the picture of a great Hegelian serpent of knowledge with its tail in its mouth (Where does it begin?). Neither will do. For empirical knowledge, like its sophisticated extension, science, is rational, not because it has a *foundation* but because it is a self-correcting enterprise which can put any claim in jeopardy, though not *all* at once.[34]

Rorty's epistemological behaviorism extends Sellars's psychological nominalism, accenting even more the intersubjective, i.e., social character, of the "foundations" of knowledge.

> Explaining rationality and epistemic authority by reference to what society lets us say, rather than the latter by the former, is the essence of what I shall call "epistemological behaviorism," an attitude common to Dewey and Wittgenstein. This sort of behaviorism can best be seen as a species of holism—but one which requires no idealist metaphysical underpinnings.[35]

Following Sellars's attack on the Myth of the Given and linking this attack to Quine's holism, Rorty claims,

A holistic approach to knowledge is not a matter of antifoundationalist polemic, but a distrust of the whole epistemological enterprise. A behavioristic approach to episodes of "direct awareness" is not a matter of antimentalistic polemic, but a distrust of the Platonic quest for that special sort of certainty associated with visual perception.[36]

By combining the insights of Sellars and Quine, Rorty arrives at his own radical conclusion.

When Sellars's and Quine's doctrines are purified, they appear as complementary expressions of a single claim: that no "account of the nature of knowledge" can rely on a theory of representations which stand in privileged relations to reality. The work of these two philosophers enables us . . . to make clear why an "account of the nature of knowledge" can be, at most, a description of human behavior.[37]

In *Twilight of the Idols,* Nietzsche acknowledges that fundamental quest in Western philosophy for self-authenticating, self-justifying, intrinsically credible beliefs and concepts must rest, to use Stanley Cavell's Wittgensteinian phrase, "outside language games."[38] For Nietzsche, as for Sellars, such beliefs and concepts must presuppose some other kind of knowledge rather than serve as the foundation of our knowledge; they are grounded on what we already know rather than serve as the grounds for all that we know. He writes in section 4 of his Chapter entitled " 'Reason' in Philosophy,"

The *other* idiosyncrasy of philosophers is no less perilous: it consists in mistaking the last for the first. They put that which comes at the end—unfortunately! for it ought not to come at all!—the 'highest concepts', that is to say the most general, the emptiest concepts, the last fumes of evaporating reality, at the beginning *as* the beginning. It is again only the expression of their way of doing reverence: the higher must not be *allowed* to grow out of the lower, must not be *allowed* to have grown at all. . . . Moral: everything of the first rank must be *causa sui.* Origin in something else counts as an objection, as casting doubt on value. (*TI*, p. 37)

Nietzsche considers the quest for certainty and the search for foundations in epistemology—any forms of the Myth of the Given—

unattainable and ultimately self-deceptive. Any such quest and search must be subordinate to an inquiry as to why the will to power takes the form of such a quest and search.

> It might seem as though I had evaded the question of "certainty." The opposite is true; but by inquiring after the criterion of certainty I tested the scales upon which men have weighed in general hitherto—and that the question of certainty itself is a dependent question, a question of second rank. (*WP,* p. 322)

Any attempt to ground knowledge-claims must be demystified such that the practical aims and goals concealed by such an attempt are disclosed.

> Theory and practice.—*Fateful distinction, as if there were an actual* drive for knowledge that, without regard to questions of usefulness and harm, went blindly for the truth; and then, separate from this, the whole world of *practical* interests—
>
> I tried to show, on the other hand, what instincts have been active behind all these *pure* theoreticians—how they have all, under the spell of their instincts, gone fatalistically for something that was "truth" *for them*—for them and only for them. The conflict between different systems, including that between epistemological scruples, is a conflict between quite definite instincts (forms of vitality, decline, classes, races, etc.).
>
> The so-called drive for knowledge can be traced back to a drive to appropriate and conquer. . . (*WP,* p. 227)

Nietzsche's rejection of foundationalism in epistemology results from his acceptance of the Heraclitean flux, of the world of becoming which forever slips out of the arbitrary conceptual schemas through which humans come to "know" the self and world.

> The character of the world in a state of becoming as incapable of formulation, as "false", as "self-contradictory." Knowledge and becoming exclude one another. Consequently, "knowledge" must be something else: there must first of all be a will to make knowable, a kind of becoming must itself create the deception of beings. (*WP,* p. 280)

258

A world in a state of becoming could not, in a strict sense, be "comprehended" or "known"; only to the extent that the "comprehending" and "knowing" intellect encounters a coarse, already-created world, fabricated out of mere appearances but become firm to the extent that this kind of appearance has preserved life—only to this extent is there anything like "knowledge"; i.e., a measuring of earlier and later errors by one another. (*WP,* p. 281)

For Nietzsche, as for Quine, Goodman, Sellars and Rorty (and against Plato, Aristotle, Descartes, Kant, Kripke and Levi-Strauss), knowledge is not a matter of grasping fixed forms, static essences or permanent substances and structures. Rather knowledge is a matter of perceiving phenomena under a description, within a theory or in light of a version in order to, to use a Wittgensteinian phrase, "help us get about." On this point, the early Quine's pragmatism and Nietzsche's perspectivism again converge.

Each man is given a scientific heritage plus a continuing barrage of sensory stimulation; and the considerations which guide him in warping his scientific heritage to fit his continuing sensory promptings are, where rational, pragmatic.[39]

Not "to know" but to schematize—to impose upon chaos as much regularity and form as our practical needs require.
In the formation of reason, logic, the categories, it was *need* that was authoritative: the need, not to "know", but to subsume, to schematize, for the purpose of intelligibility and calculation. . . (*WP,* p. 278)

Nietzsche's conception of knowledge as elastic in character and creative in content is echoed in Goodman.

Furthermore, if worlds are as much made as found, so also knowing is as much remaking as reporting. All the processes of worldmaking I have discussed enter into knowing. Perceiving motion, we have seen, often consists in producing it. Discovering laws involves drafting them. Recognizing patterns is very much a matter of inventing and imposing them. Comprehension and creation go on together.[40]

> Coming to know means "to place oneself in a
> conditional relation to something"; to feel oneself
> conditioned by something and oneself to condition it—it
> is therefore under all circumstances establishing,
> denoting, and making-conscious of conditions...
> (*WP*, p. 301)

Nietzsche debunks the Myth of the Given because, for him, knowledge is not a set of beliefs to be "grounded", but rather a series of linguistic signs which designate and describe the world in light of our evolving needs, interests and purposes.

> It is an illusion that something is *known* when we
> possess a mathematical formula for an event: it is only
> designated, described; nothing more! (*WP*, p. 335)

He surely would agree with Rorty that demythologizing the Myth of the Given—and promoting anti-foundationalism in epistemology—results in, "... preventing man from deluding himself with the notion that he knows himself, or anything else, except under optional descriptions."[41]

Detranscendentalizing the Subject

The last crucial move of postmodern American philosophy I will examine is the detranscendentalizing of the subject—the dismissing of the mind as a self-contained sphere of inquiry. This move is a natural consequence of the anti-realism, holism, conventionalism, and anti-foundationalism we examined earler.

It is important to note that notions such as the subject, self-consciousness, ego, and "I" were under attack by modern analytic philosophers. Therefore this last move of postmodern American philosophers is part of the general trend of modern analytic philosophy.

For example, Quine's treatment of this matter follows, in many ways, the logical behaviorist position put forward in Gilbert Ryle's classic work, *The Concept of Mind* (1949). This position, largely intended to debunk the Cartesian myth of the "ghosts in machines", roughly holds that talk about mental states, i.e., an intentional idiom, is but a clumsy and confusing way of talking about dispositions to behave in certain ways under specific circumstances, i.e., a behavioristic idiom. Quine's well-known passage in his *Word and Object* (1960) summarizes his own behavioristic position,

> One may accept the Brentano thesis either as showing
> the indispensability of intentional idioms and the
> importance of an autonomous science of intention, or as

showing the baselessness of intentional idioms and the emptiness of a science of intention. My attitude, unlike Brentano's, is the second. To accept intentional usage at face value is, we saw, to postulate translation relations as somehow objectively valid though indeterminate in principle relative to the totality of speech dispositions. Such postulation promises little gain in scientific insight if there is no better ground for it than that the supposed translation relations are presupposed by the vernacular of semantics and intention.[42]

Underlying this viewpoint is Quine's eliminative materialist position, namely, the view that there simply are no mental states, but rather neural events. In this way, Quine detranscendentalizes any notion of the subject.

Rorty deepens this version of detranscendentalizing the subject by abandoning the very notion of mind-body identity. On his view, the social practice of speaking in neural events (by those who know neurology) and the social practice of speaking in mental states (by those who do not know neurology) "are just two ways of talking about the same thing."[43] And the "thing" being talked about in each case is that which is posited within one's theory. As Sellers points out, such thing-talk, be it neurological or common-sensical, occurs in,

> a framework of "unobserved," "nonempirical" "inner" episodes. For we can point out immediately that in these respects they are no worse off than the particles and episodes in physical theory. For these episodes are "in" language-using animals as molecular impacts are "in" gases, not as "ghosts" are in "machines." They are "nonempirical" in the simple sense that they are *theoretical*—not definable in observational terms . . . Their "purity" is not a *metaphysical* purity, but, so to speak, a *methodological* purity . . . the fact that they are not introduced as physiological entities does not preclude the possibility that at a later methodological stage, they may, so to speak, "turn out" to be such.[44]

Sellars's methodological behaviorism—his way of detranscendentalizing the subject—permits him to be a behaviorist (like Quine) without thinking that all one's theoretical concepts in relation to "mental events" will turn out to refer to neurological phenomena (unlike Quine)—though, of course, they may.

> The behavioristic requirement that all concepts should be introduced in terms of a basic vocabulary pertaining

to overt behavior is compatible with the idea that some behavioristic concepts are to be introduced as theoretical concepts.[45]

Nietzsche's dismissal of the mind as a self-contained sphere of inquiry is illustrated in section 3 of his Chapter entitled, "The Four Great Errors" in *Twilight of The Idols.*

> ... the conception of a consciousness ('mind') as cause and later still that of the ego (the 'subject') as cause are merely after-products after causality had, on the basis of will, been firmly established as a given fact, as *empiricism.* . . Meanwhile we have thought better. Today we do not believe a word of it. The 'inner world' is full of phantoms and false lights: the will is one of them. The will no longer moves anything, consequently no longer explains anything—it merely accompanies events, it can also be absent. The so-called 'motive': another error. Merely a surface phenomenon of consciousness, an accompaniment to an act, which conceals rather than exposes the *antecedentia* of the act. And as for the ego! It has become a fable, a fiction, a play on words: it has totally ceased to think, to feel and to will! . . . What follows from this? There are no spiritual causes at all! The whole of the alleged empiricism which affirmed them has gone to the devil! (*TI,* p. 49)

Like Ryle, Nietzsche's detranscendentalizing of the subject begins with a critique of Descartes.

> "There is thinking: therefore there is something that thinks": this is the upshot of all Descartes' argumentation. But that means positing as "true a priori" our belief in the concept of substance—that when there is thought there has to be something "that thinks" is simply a formulation of our grammatical custom that adds a doer to every deed. In short, this is not merely the substantiation of a fact but a logical-metaphysical postulate. (*WP,* p. 268)

Similar to Rorty and Sellars, Nietzsche views subject-talk as mere convention, a matter of social practice rooted in our needs, interests and purposes.

> "Everything is subjective," you say; but even this is

interpretation. The "subject" is not something given, it is something, added and invented and projected behind what there is. (*WP,* p. 267)

However habitual and indispensable this fiction may have become by now—that in itself proves nothing against its imaginary origin: a belief can be a condition of life and nonetheless be false. (*WP,* p. 268)

He concludes that subject-talk is a linguistic social practice derived from our grammar, namely, the subject-predicate structure of our judgments.

In every judgment there resides the entire, full, profound belief in subject and attribute, or in cause and effect (that is, as the assertion that every effect is an activity and that every activity presupposes an agent); and this latter belief is only a special case of the former, so there remains as the fundamental belief that there are subjects, that everything that happens is related attributively to some subject. (*WP,* p. 294)

Nihilism

If Nietzsche prefigures certain important developments in postmodern American philosophy, then it is appropriate to note briefly that he believed such developments ultimately lead to nihilism unless they are supplemented with a new world view. He makes this point clearly in his Preface to *The Will To Power.*

For one should make no mistake about the meaning of the title that this gospel of the future wants to bear. *"The Will to Power:* Attempt at a Revaluation of All Values"—in this formulation a countermovement finds expression, regarding both principle and task; a movement that in some future will take the place of this perfect nihilism—but presupposes it, logically and psychologically, and certainly can come only after and out of it. For why has the advent of nihilism become *necessary?* Because the values we have had hitherto thus draw their final consequence; because nihilism represents the ultimate logical conclusion of our great values and ideals—because we must experience nihilism before we can find out what value these "values" really had.—We require, sometime, *new values.* (*WP,* pp. 3-4)

For Nietzsche, this nihilism results from certain ideals of modern Europe, especially those ideals which presuppose belief in the categories of "aim", "unity", and "truth". Nihilism is a natural consequence of a culture (or civilization) ruled and regulated by categories which mask manipulation, mastery and domination of peoples and nature.

> Suppose we realize how the world may no longer be interpreted in terms of these three categories, and that the world begins to become valueless for us after this insight: then we have to ask about the sources of our faith in these three categories. . .
> Conclusion: The faith in the categories of reason is the cause of nihilism. We have measured the value of the world according to categories *that refer to a fictitious world.*
> Final conclusion: All the values by means of which we have tried so far to render the world estimable for ourselves and which then proved inapplicable and therefore devaluated the world—all these values are, psychologically considered, the results of certain perspectives of utility, designed to maintain and increase human constructs of domination—and they have been falsely *projected* into the essence of things. (*WP*, pp. 13-14)

Nihilism ushers in an era in which science—the great pride of modern Europe—provides greater and greater instrumentalities for world domination. As Maurice Blanchot observes,

> The moment Nihilism outlines the world for us, its counterpart, science, creates the tools to dominate it. The era of universal mastery is opened. But there are some consequences: first, science can only be nihilistic; it is the meaning of a world deprived of meaning, a knowledge that ultimately has ignorance as its foundation. To which the response will be that this reservation is only theoretical; but we must not hasten to disregard this objection, for science is essentially productive. Knowing it need not interpret the world, science transforms it, and by this transformation science conveys its own nihilistic demands—the negative power that science has made into the most useful of tools, but with which it dangerously plays. Knowledge is fundamentally dangerous . . . for a universe cannot be constructed without having the possibility of its being

destroyed . . . by making science possible, Nihilism becomes the possibility of science—which means that the human world can be destroyed by it.[46]

Nietzsche considers nihilism to be "partly destructive, partly ironic". (*WP*, p. 14) It is marked by philosophical positions of anti-realism, conventionalism, relativism and anti-foundationalism. We have seen that postmodern American philosophers support such positions. Quine describes himself as a "relativist,"[47] yet warns against associating him with the "epistemological nihilism"[48] of Kuhn. Goodman labels his position "as a radical relativism under rigorous restraints, that eventuates in something akin to irrealism."[49] Rorty calls himself an "historicist"[50] and Kuhn admits to subscribing to a form of relativism.[51]

The crucial moves made by postmodern American philosophers are highly significant in that these moves disclose the unwarranted philosophical assumptions and antiquated theoretical distinctions upon which rests much of modern analytic philosophy. Yet—and in this regard they resemble their counterparts in postmodern literary criticism— postmodern American philosophers have failed to project a new world view, a countermovement, "a new gospel of the future". Quine's and Sellars's updated versions of scientism not only reflect their positivist heritage, but, more importantly, reveal their homage to an outmoded cultural mode of thought. Goodman's attempt to infuse the idea of style with new life is intriguing yet ultimately resorts to an old aristocratic preoccupation. Kuhn's unequivocal promotion of the proliferation of learned societies (or groups) engaged in puzzle-solving under converging paradigms amounts to an unimaginative ideology of professionalism. And Rorty's ingenious conception of philosophy as cultured conversation rests upon a nostalgic appeal to the world of men (and women) of letters of decades past. These viewpoints do not constitute visions, world views or, to use Gilles Deleuze's phrase, "discourses as counter-philosophies"[52] to the nihilism to which their positions seem to lead. Instead their viewpoints leave postmodern American philosophy hanging in limbo, as a philosophically critical yet culturally lifeless rhetoric mirroring a culture (or civilization) permeated by the scientific ethos, regulated by racist, patriarchal, capitalist norms, and pervaded by debris of decay.

Union Theological Seminary, New York City

NOTES

1 The English translations I shall refer to throughout this essay are: *Twilight of the Idols,* trans. R. J. Hollingdale (Middlessex, U.K.: Penguin, 1968), and *The Will to Power,* trans. W. Kaufman and R. J. Hollingdale (New York: Vintage, 1968). References to these editions, designated *TI* and *WP* respectively, will be incorporated in the text. The first work, written in 1888, was one of

Nietzsche's last and best texts; the second, is a selection from Nietzsche's notebooks, 1883-1888. Nietzsche's philosophical (and metaphilosophical) views have not been examined in relation to the latest developments in postmodern American philosophy primarily because of the distance between his work and Anglo-American philosophy. This distance exists owing to two basic reasons. First, Nietzsche and Anglo-American philosophers radically disagree on the appropriate mode of philosophizing, on how philosophy should be done, pursued and codified. For Nietzsche, philosophy is a consuming passion, a gay vocation—hence more adequately pursued in a literary mode for a general intelligent audience; whereas, for most Anglo-American philosophers, philosophy is a pedagogical activity, a serious profession—hence more adequately pursued in a technical mode for a highly specialized audience. Second, Anglo-American philosophers are noted (and notorious) for "their lack of historical sense." Therefore, their interest in and attention to philosophical figures preoccupied with history, e.g., Hegel, Kierkegaard, Marx, Nietzsche, is minimal. It is not surprising that of the five major books on Nietzsche in English—Walter Kaufman's *Nietzsche: Philosopher, Psychologist, Antichrist* (Princeton: Princeton Univ. Press, 1975), R. J. Hollingdale's *Nietzsche* (London: Routledge & Kegan, 1973), Arthur Donto's *Nietzsche as Philosopher* (New York: Macmillan, 1965), Crane Brinton's *Nietzsche* (Cambridge, MA: Harvard Univ. Press, 1941), and J. P. Stern's *Friedrich Nietzsche* (New York: Penguin, 1979)—only one is written by an Anglo-American philosopher, namely, Arthur Danto. And Danto is an atypical Anglo-American (or analytic) philosopher, with diverse interests and publications ranging from Croce, philosophy of history and Sartre to Nietzsche and Schopenhauer.

2   It comes as no surprise that analytic philosophy, with its "lack of historical sense," has produced little historical reflection and interpretation of itself. Besides Richard Rorty's early introductory essay in *The Linguistic Turn* (Chicago: Univ. of Chicago Press, 1967) and his recent book, *Philosophy and the Mirror of Nature* (Princeton: Princeton Univ. Press, 1979), there is only John Passmore's *A Hundred Years of Philosophy* (Middlesex, U.K.: Penguin, 1970) which is pedantic reportage and straightforward exposition—neither historical reflection nor interpretation—of late 19th and 20th century developments in European philosophy. The pertinent works of Frege, Meinong, Russell and Moore I have in mind are Frege's classic "On Sense and Reference," in Peter Geach and Max Black, eds., *Translations from the Philosophical Writings of Gottlob Frege* (Oxford: Oxford Univ. Press, 1952); Meinong's "The Theory of Objects," in Roderick Chisholm, ed., *Realism and the Background of Phenomenology* (California: Glencoe, 1960); Russell's "Meinong's Theory of Complexes and Assumptions," *Mind,* Vol. 13 (1904), 204-219, 336-354, 509-524; and Moore's "The Refutation of Idealism," in *Philosophical Studies* (London, 1922).

3   For noteworthy examples of naive (or common-sensical) realism, see G. E. Moore's "A Defense of Common Sense" and "Proof of an External World," in his *Philosophical Papers* (London, 1959); for Platonic realism, see Bertrand Russell's *Principles of Mathematics* (Cambridge, 1903) and to a lesser extent his *Problems of Philosophy* (New York, 1912); for critical realism, see Roy W. Sellars's *Critical Realism* (Chicago, 1916) and his "A Statement of Critical Realism," *Revue internationale de philosophie,* Vol. I (1938-1939), 472-498; and for internal realism, see Hilary Putnam's recent work, *Meaning and the Moral Sciences* (London: Routledge & Kegan Paul, 1978), Part Four entitled "Realism and Reason."

4   Nelson Goodman, *Problems and Projects* (New York: Bobbs-Merrill, 1972), pp. 29-30.

5   Goodman, *Problems and Projects*, pp. 279-80.

6   Goodman, *Problems and Projects*, p. 118.

7   Nelson Goodman, *Ways of Worldmaking* (Indianapolis: Hackett, 1978), p. 138.

8   Willard Van Orman Quine, *From A Logical Point of View* (New York, 1963), pp. 40-41.

9   Quine, *From A Logical Point of View*, p. 42.

10   Quine, *From A Logical Point of View*, p. 43.

11   Wilfred Sellars, son of the aforementioned Roy Sellars, deserves a similar place, alongside Quine and Goodman. But his highly technical style of writing as well as his position at the University of Pittsburgh (slightly removed from the center of fashionable intellectual activity and notoriety) unfortunately has rendered his writings less accessible and influential.

12   Richard Rorty, "The World Well Lost," *The Journal of Philosophy,* Vol. LXIX, No. 19 (1972), p. 661.

13   Thomas S. Kuhn, *The Structure of Scientific Revolutions,* 2nd ed. (Chicago: Univ. of Chicago Press, 1970), p. 206.

14   Thomas S. Kuhn, "Reflections on My Critics", *Criticism and the Growth of Knowledge,* ed. Imre Lakatos and Alan Musgrave (Cambridge: Cambridge Univ. Press, 1970), p. 266.

15   Goodman, *Ways of Worldmaking*, p. x.

16   Goodman, *Problems and Projects*, pp. 30-31.

17   Goodman, *Problems and Projects*, pp. 117, 118.

18   Quine, *From A Logical Point of View*, p. 44.

19   Quine, *From a Logical Point of View*, p. 19.

20   Rorty, *Philosophy and the Mirror of Nature*, p. 367.

21   This phrase was popularized by Wilfred Sellars's influential University of London lectures originally entitled "The Myth of the Given: Three Lectures on Empiricism and the Philosophy of Mind" and now known simply as "Empiricism and the Philosophy of Mind," *Minnesota Studies in the Philosophy of Science,* Vol. I, Herbert Feigl and Michael Scriven, eds. (Univ. of Minnesota Press, 1956). For a brief, cogent and sympathetic elaboration on this Myth, see Michael William's *Groundless Belief: An Essay on the Possibility of Epistemology* (New Yaven: Yale Univ. Press, 1977), Chapter 2 and for the only treatment I know of how this Myth functions in traditional philosophical hermeneutics, see my essay, "Schleiermacher's Hermeneutics and The Myth of

the Given," Special Hermeneutics Issue, *Union Seminary Quarterly Review,* Vol. XXXIV, No. 2 (Winter 1979), pp. 71-84.

22   For C. I. Lewis's pertinent work, see his *Mind and the World Order* (New York: Dover, 1956) and "The Given Element in Empirical Knowledge," *The Philosophical Review,* Vol. 61, 2 (April 1952), pp. 168-73. For H. H. Price's relevant work, see his classic *Perception* (London: Methuen & Co., ltd., 1964). Lewis's book was first published in 1929, Price's in 1932. More recent defenders of the Myth of the Given include A. J. Ayer, *The Foundations of Empirical Knowledge* (London: Macmillan & Co., ltd., New York: St. Martin's Press, 1958), R. M. Chisholm, *Theory of Knowledge,* 2nd ed. (Englewood Cliffs, N.J.: Prentice Hall, 1977), Jonathan Bennett, *Locke, Berkeley, Hume: Central Themes* (Oxford: Oxford Univ. Press, 1971), and John L. Pollack, *Knowledge and Justification* (Princeton: Princeton Univ. Press, 1975). For a survey of the variety of versions of the Myth of the Given, see J. J. Ross, *The Appeal to the Given* (London: Macmillan, 1970). Lastly, for a fascinating and original attempt to reject the Myth and Quine's holism (at the same time!), see Clark Glymour's *Theory and Evidence* (Princeton: Princeton Univ. Press, 1980).

23   Lewis, *Mind and the World Order,* p. 38.

24   Price, *Perception,* p. 4.

25   Lewis, *Mind and the World Order,* p. 39.

26   Price, *Perception,* p. 1.

27   Goodman, *Problems and Projects,* pp. 61-62.

28   Goodman, *Problems and Projects,* p. 9.

29   Goodman, *Ways of Worldmaking,* p. 7.

30   Sellars, "Empiricism and the Philosophy of Mind," p. 289.

31   Sellars, "Empiricism and the Philosophy of Mind,"p. 293.

32   Price, *Perception,* p. 3.

33   Sellars, "Empiricism and the Philosophy of Mind," pp. 298-99.

34   Sellars, "Empiricism and the Philosophy of Mind," p. 300.

35   Rorty, *Philosophy and the Mirror of Nature,* p. 174.

36   Rorty, *Philosophy and the Mirror of Nature,* p. 181.

37   Rorty, *Philosophy and the Mirror of Nature,* p. 182.

38   Stanley Cavell, *The Claim of Reason* (Oxford, 1979), p. 226.

39   Quine, *From A Logical Point of View,* p. 46.

40   Goodman, *Ways of Worldmaking,* p. 22.

41 Rorty, *Philosophy and the Mirror of Nature,* p. 379.

42 Willard Van Orman Quine, *Word and Object* (Cambridge, 1960), p. 221.

43 Rorty, *Philosophy and the Mirror of Nature,* p. 122.

44 Sellars, "Empiricism and the Philosophy of Mind," p. 319.

45 Sellars, "Empiricism and the Philosophy of Mind," p. 316.

46 Maurice Blanchot, "The Limits of Experience: Nihilism," *The New Nietzsche: Contemporary Styles of Interpretation,* ed. and intro. David B. Allison (New York, 1977), pp. 122-23.

47 W.V. Quine, *Ontological Relativity and Other Essays* (New York, 1969), pp. 50ff.

48 Quine, *Ontological Relativity,* p. 87.

49 Goodman, *Ways of Worldmaking,* p. x.

50 Rorty, *Philosophy and the Mirror of Nature,* pp. 9, 10.

51 Kuhn, "Reflections on my Critics," p. 264.

52 Gilles Deleuze, "Nomad Thought," *The New Nietzsche,* p. 149.

Autobiography as *Gestalt*:
Nietzsche's *Ecce Homo*

Rodolphe Gasché

> Joining one heading to another, not
> completing one path of discourse.
> —Empedocles

> Upward, downward, the way is one
> and the same.
> —Heraclitus

Nietzsche's autobiography, his self-presentation in *Ecce Homo*,[1] has until now been subjected to no other treatment than that inflicted by philosophy. In other words, this text has been considered either as literature or as an essentially philosophical writing disguised under the appearances of a literary genre. According to the second of these two genuinely philosophical alternatives, *Ecce Homo* has to be stripped of all of its esthetic magic, of what belongs to Nietzsche's great style and his art of poetry, in order to reveal the authentic experience of being hidden beneath its delusive exteriority. Martin Heidegger, undoubtedly the first to promote a philosophical reading of *Ecce Homo*, escapes as little as anybody else this kind of logic. Indeed, the few remarks on *Ecce Homo* interspersed in his *Nietzsche* have no other purpose than to demonstrate that Nietzsche's self-presentation is "neither concerned with the biography of Nietzsche nor with the personality of Mr. Nietzsche," so that "being and world, which both ground the work" may finally come into view. Indeed, the work as work remains concealed to us as long as we leer at that which is the object of historical and psychological reporting: the "life" of the man.[2] A way in which truth grounds itself, Nietzsche's self-reflection represents for Heidegger a sort of appendix to his intrinsically philosophical work, an appendix by means of which he "continuously prepares himself for the sacrifice demanded by his task."[3] As Nietzsche's self-presentation is an essential sacrifice in which truth becomes, *Ecce Homo* no longer pertains to literature or to the genre of subjective and idle self-mirroring. On the contrary, *Ecce Homo* appears to be the thinker's questioning of his destiny. Yet, paradoxically enough, the distinction between the individual and destiny that intersects with the opposition of literature and philosophy, of self-reflection and the task of thinking, allows for another approach to this work that no longer simply yields to the preceding dyads. Heidegger will lend us the conceptual tools to approach *Ecce Homo* in a different way, in a way which he partially paved himself, but which for reasons too lengthy to develop here, he refused to pursue.[4] My question then is the following: What if, like the systems of the presocratics represented in *Philosophy in the Tragic Age of the Greeks*, *Ecce Homo* was a similar effort to use one's personality to think the essence of Being? What Eugen Fink all too hastily misinterprets as an anthropological reduction and deformation,[5] that is to say Nietzsche's attempt to understand the presocratics' systems as forms in which strong personalities manifest themselves, a manifestation that names Being in its question-worthiness, may well be the way in which *Ecce Homo* is to be read.

   At first, such an enterprise of determining the essence of being in terms of greatness or grandeur (*Grösse*), or, more precisely, as *Typus*, has to be retraced historically back to the romantic ideal of a synthesis of poetry and philosophy in the form of a "new mythology," or art of poetry (*Dichtkunst*), as formulated in *Das älteste Systemfragment des deutschen Idealismus* (1876), as well as to Friedrich Schlegel's *Charakteristik*; but above all it has to be retraced to Friedrich W. J. Schelling's draft of a narrative philosophy (*erzählende Philosophie*) in *The Ages of the World* (1911-13). Yet what the romanticism of Jena aspired to is only a more sophisticated and more conscious attempt to think being as *Gestalt*, which is the modern version of the Platonic *idea*, as Heidegger has shown. Indeed, partaking of that monumental history discussed by Nietzsche in *The Use and Misuse of History*, a history which represents the continuum of all immortal figures (*Gestalten*) through which being articulates itself typologically or as Nietzsche also puts it, monographically,[6] *Ecce Homo* has to be understood as a continuation not only of the project of romanticism, but also of that project which as *Gestalt* determines modern thought, and of which romanticism is but one, however important, variation.

What, then, is a *Gestalt?* The *Gestalt* is not simply identical to the Hegelian notion of figure or shape (*Gestalten des Bewusstseins*) that according to the *Phenomenology of Spirit* represent the living incarnations of the concept, the "actualized essentiality" in a history.[7] Nor is it the *Gestalt* of Gestaltpsychology, that is to say, a whole that encompasses more than the total sum of its parts and that is the source of all *Sinngebung*. If, in *The Origin of the Work of Art* (1935-36), as he explains himself in the Addendum from 1956, Heidegger determines the notion of *Gestalt* as the Greek sense of *morphe* (and the notion of the *Ge-stell* as the gathering of the bringing-forth into the rift-design as bounding outline, or *peras*) then *Gestalt* designates here the truth's being fixed in place (*Festgestelltsein*), that is to say, the way in which truth is established (*eingerichtet*) in being itself.[8] Heidegger's later use of this notion, for instance in *What are Poets For?* (1946) and in *The Question of Being* (1955), differs considerably from this seemingly very general, but in fact originary, meaning of the word. Indeed, if *Gestalt* initially translates the Greek experience of the coming forth into the limits of a form, Heidegger's later and more narrow use of this notion, its modern meaning, so to speak, bends, as he explains, to the Western destiny of being. While in the case of the Greeks the notion of *Gestalt* is linked to the notion of *idea,* that is to say to the way in which Being comes forth into its presence (*An-Wesen*), its appearance, its aspect (*Ansehen, Aussehen*), Heidegger's later use of *Gestalt* is restricted to modernity's representation (*Vorstellung*) of what it conceives of as Being. In this manner *Gestalt* appears to be the modern version of the Greek *idea*, which it stems from but which it also displaces. Yet what is the modern concept of being which the *Gestalt* serves only to represent (*vorstellt*), that is to say, which it only lets take up a position opposite to the subject, as an object? Being of being is "the incipient power gathering everything to itself, which in this manner releases every being to its own self. Being of being is the will. The will is the self-concentrating gathering of every *ens* unto itself."[9] This modern definition of Being implies, as Heidegger has shown in *The Question of Being,*[10] that a type of humanity characterized by extreme subjectivity grounds all being as subject. This type of humanity not only represents (*vorstellen*) being as rooted in a self-reflexive subjectivity of Being as such; it also represents itself in order to set itself forth (*herstellen*). Characterized as a challenging-forth, the *Stellen* of the *Vorstellen* of being (as well as the *Stellen* of the *Herstellen* of mankind) links the modern notion of Being as well as the type of humanity it presupposes to the fate of technology as a challenging revealing. Now this unconditional and therefore complete unity of the attitude of representation, of producing, and the objective character of the world,[11] this unity of the will as a self-concentration, the unity of

Being, consequently, is represented in modern metaphysics as *Gestalt*. *Gestalt* then, in short, is the specific way in which the modern concept of a self-concentrating and self-reflexive Being, a Being congenital to a type of humanity that as *subjectum* fathers on all being, is being *vorgestellt*.[12]

In other words: if modern metaphysics, since Descartes at least, conceives of the absolute presence of being as self-consciousness, self-presence and subjectivity, and if the *Gestalt* is the manner in which this presence is represented (*vorgestellt*), it is indeed no surprise if, historically speaking, the "genre" of autobiography and self-presentation becomes, as *Gestalt*, the form par excellence for the exposition of the modern concept of being. Inaugurated by Saint Augustine and Montaigne, autobiography will rapidly manifest its relation to the Platonic determinations of being as *eidos/idea*. But it will soon become obvious as well that autobiography, despite its origin in the Greek notion of *idea*, does not coincide with it: it is this difference which constitutes it as a *Gestalt*, as a form in which the self-reflexivity of being is *vorgestellt*, whereas the idea is the way in which being comes into its *Aussehen*. Let us briefly emphasize the complex links between autobiography and the Greek notion of *idea*. Such a link can easily be shown in the case of Descartes, for example, at the beginning of the second part of the *Discourse on Method*, where the subject of meditation constitutes itself according to what is called the four horizons of being. Held up by the winter in southern Germany, "the whole day shut up in a room heated by an enclosed stove," the *subject* Descartes, turning away from the book of the world in order to study himself, discovers that only *one single* person will be able to make all his thoughts tend toward the *same ethical end* and, consequently, approach *truth*.[13] Thus, *on, hen, agathon*, and *aletheia* govern the constitution of the subject Descartes, who by representing himself in the horizon of these four determinations, reinterprets being as the subjectivity of the thinking subject: *ego cogito*. One could also make the same point in the case of Rousseau, where the obsession with transparency and sincerity, after some scrutiny, appears to depend on the idea of a *self-affection* of light, and where the desire for *uprightedness* can be shown to depend on the Greek notion of *stasis* as an essential determination of being as presence.

This being established, I will try to argue in what follows that not only is the figure of Zarathustra, as Heidegger has demonstrated, a *Gestalt*, but Nietzsche's self-representation in *Ecce Homo* as well. Yet if in a first moment Nietzsche obeys the logic of the *Gestalt* to elaborate a conception of being as *Typus*, as great personality, in a second he also subverts this same representation of being, and with it the notion of subjectivity and self-reflexivity. With this second movement, Nietzsche not only breaks away from the romantic heritage, but, more radically, from the modern representation of being, from the form of autobiography in which being is represented, and from representation itself, i.e., from representation as *Vorstellung*.

274

The duality of Nietzsche's enterprise becomes evident at the start of *Ecce Homo*, in its subtitle borrowed from Pindar: *How to become, what one is.*[14] Indeed, if this subtitle can be read as a Parmenidean interpretation of being as something lasting, as something standing in itself, this same subtitle also calls for a Heraclitean reading of being as becoming. If this is true, however, then it is possible that in his "autobiography" Nietzsche may not be concerned with either one of these metaphysical concepts of being and becoming.[15] What I hope to show, on the contrary, is that Nietzsche *already* operates in the *interval* of these two complementary metaphysical determinations of being in order to elaborate the time and space of what he calls the eternal return of the same, which as Nietzsche's *great thought* does not break away from Platonism in order to remain caught within a simple reversal of it, as Heidegger forcefully tried to argue, but which stages an *other* notion of history, of time and space, beyond what governs the metaphysical duality of being and becoming. As we will see, it is precisely the great thought of the eternal return of the same that undermines the very notion of *Gestalt* and of the genre of autobiography, and that also calls for a re-thinking of self-presentation.

I

In order not to be mistaken for his own work, and in particular for some of its Hegelian overtones, and thus perhaps for Hegel himself,[16] Nietzsche decides to narrate his life, to tell *himself* his life.[17] This self-revelation or revelation to oneself clearly continues and repeats the autobiographical motive of Descartes's second meditation.[18] Yet this enterprise that grew to maturity at a very particular moment of Nietzsche's life, and that is expressed at a most singular point in the text of *Ecce Homo*,[19] soon enough appears as the result of conflicting forces, and as an undertaking which is contradictory in itself. Indeed, seeing himself compelled to say who he is, Nietzsche experiences this need as a necessary condenscension, as a fatal descent (*Niedergang*) opposed by the instincts of distance. This interplay between necessity and the pride of the instincts, instead of assuring a contemporaneity with himself and his fellowmen, causes Nietzsche's attempt to reappropriate his former work and to make up his life through self-presentation to produce an even greater unequality, and an even greater distance in regard to his own self. This fatal failure of autobiography, however, this catastrophe due to Nietzsche's *Gegensatz-Natur*, is not simply an unsuccessfulness. Indeed, what Nietzsche achieves through the impossibility of reappropriating himself, of recognizing himself all by himself, and thus by the failure to become a self-consciousness, is an *untimely* (*unzeitgemässe*) relation to himself. The different possible readings of *Ecce Homo*'s subtitle—*How one becomes, what one is*—will furnish evidence of this.

On the one hand, this subtitle demands, as aphorism 263 of *Human, All-Too-Human* intimates, that one should become what one already is. Yet Nietzsche does not leave us any doubt about the fact that "to become what one is, one must not have the faintest notion of *what one is*" (*EH*, p. 254). To become what one is, consequently, precludes all forms of self-knowledge from such a becoming. Indeed, instead of being the model of becoming oneself, *nosce te ipsum* is for Nietzsche rather the ruin of self. Thus: "Nosce te ipsum would be the recipe for ruin, forgetting oneself, making oneself smaller, narrower, mediocre, become reason itself" (*EH*, p. 254). The "Know thyself" is dangerous not only because it represents a *contradictio in adjecto*, and this is why Nietzsche in *Beyond Good and Evil* can express his "unconquerable distrust of the *possibility* of self-knowledge,"[20] but also because such knowing would drain the *what*, i.e. one's lasting essence.[21] The reason for this is that such an objective knowledge would require, as the telos of one's becoming, one's becoming different from oneself. The "Know thyself" clearly expresses the desire to become an other, to become different from oneself. Yet it is precisely this that is to be avoided if one wants to become what one is: "I do not want in the least that anything should become different than it is: I myself do not want to become different" (*EH*, p. 255). To become what one is is to become the *same*. What is, *returns* through its becoming. As it is a becoming that excludes the process of self-consciousness and of all reflexive movements, what one is can only occur as a sudden erruption of "the organizing idea" into "the whole of consciousness" (*EH*, p. 254), interrupting the continuity of its surface and of the flow of subjective time. What erupts into the self in this *untimely* manner, is the self*same*. The return of the same, its re-petition, is thus the non-reflexive, yet not immediate, mode of becoming what one is. The Parmenidean reading of the subtitle, a reading that privileges being over becoming, consequently turns into a determination of being as a *same* that is not identical to itself, but that relates to itself in the mode of repetition, of an unreflexively mediated relation to itself. The idea of being gives way to the repetition or return of the same.

On the other hand, our subtitle allows a Heraclitean reading which instead of emphasizing the idea of being, shows being only to be a modification, a modality even, of becoming. When Nietzsche urges us not simply to comprehend the word "Dionysian," but to comprehend *oneself* in this word (*EH*, pp. 272-73), and when, moreover, such a comprehension is not without the touch of the "genius of the heart"—"from whose touch every one walks away richer, . . . richer in himself, newer to himself than before, broken open, blown at and sounded out by a thawing wind, perhaps more unsure, tenderer, more fragile, more broken, but full of hopes that as yet have no name, full of new will and currents, full of new dissatisfaction and undertows . . ." (*EH*, pp. 268-69)—then it follows from this that the phenomenon of the Dionysian puts an end to the immobility of being. Indeed, to read the subtitle *How to become, what one is* in a Heraclitean fashion implies an "affirmation of passing away *and destroying*, which is the decisive feature of a Dionysian philosophy; saying Yes to opposition and war; *becoming*, along with a radical repudiation of the very concept of *being*" (*EH*, p. 273). What, then, does our subtitle mean? Besides bringing into question all possible freezing of becoming into individual beings and into motionless being in general,[22] the subtitle indicates the way of one's becoming "the eternal joy of becoming, beyond all terror and pity—that joy which includes even joy in destroying" (*EH*, p. 273). Consequently, the subtitle *How to become, what one is* questions the ways of liquefying all petrified individual forms, of dissolving being as frozen and immobilized becoming, and finally of becoming becoming itself. It is the eternal joy of becoming that one is to become as what one always already is. With this second reading of the subtitle, the *same* that one is to become, and that one can only become in a process that excludes all self-consciousness, appears to be becoming itself. Becoming is the *same* that proceeds from repetition or return. As it excludes all self-reflexivity, it is no longer a *self*same, but a self*same* which as becoming relates to itself in the mode of repetition.

Both the Parmenidean (or Platonic) and Heraclitean readings of *what* one is to become thus appear to be incorrect. Indeed, if the same that one is to become must be free from all becoming, as a Parmenidean interpretation requires, the fact that the ideality of such a selfsame is linked in Nietzsche to a necessary absence of all self-knowledge, and to a movement of return or repetition, already undercuts the very possibility of such a selfsame as a self-identical ideality.[23] A Heraclitean reading of this selfsame, on the other hand, a reading that would sustain Heidegger's critique that Nietzsche raises becoming to the status of everlasting being and that would thus remain within the limits of a simple inversion of platonism, is equally problematical. As Aristotle already knew, there is no such a thing as an essence of becoming. But, more importantly, it is the very determination of becoming as return or repetition that does not allow its transformation into something self-identical like being or ideality. The *same* that one is to become does not have the structure of an ideality or of being: excluding all forms of self-consciousness, self-reflection or self-affection, the *same* is no longer a presence, a self-presence. With this the two alternative readings collapse. *How to become, what one is*, or *Ecce Homo*, is on the contrary, the exposition or the notion of a *same* that is characterized by an absence of all self-referring and self-reference. Nietzsche, unable to avoid the pleonasm, calls this same (which is a becoming in the mode of a return) the eternal return of the same.[24] It represents a no longer speculative or reflexive relation to oneself, of the selfsame to itself, but a self-reference that can only be a relation of return or repetition.

Such a definition of the *same*, or of the notion of a non-reflexive self-reference, encounters formidable problems as to its conceptualization. Nothing seems to be more reluctant to the habits of language than to express such a relation. The immemorial self-reference of such a non-identical same, however, occurs on the level of the *mise-en-scène* of texts, of a text such as *Ecce Homo*, for instance. Yet, as spatiality has always been a way of illustrating the category of time, the text's spatial arrangements reveal the specific temporality not only of the text, but also of its "object": the non-reflexive *same*. It can easily be shown that *Ecce Homo* stages the two traditional concepts of time: its representation as "the unconditional and infinitely repeated circular course of all things" which originates in Heraclitus (*EH*, pp. 273-74), as well as its representation as linear and continuous historical time. Yet the becoming characteristic of the *same* obeys neither its circular representation[25] nor the time of historicism. Nor does it obey the dialectical matrix; it is rather to be understood as the affirmation of chance, as the repeated casting of a die which forever shows the figure six.[26] As such, and as opposed to the Hegelian synthetic notion of time, the temporality of the non-identical *same* will take place in the interval of its linear and circular representation—as a sort of *Un-time* (*Unzeit-*) that defies all representation. Unable to conceptualize this *Un-time*, and unable to represent it as such, *Ecce Homo* will *stage* the space of this unheard of time as the interval of Nietzsche's double origin. Indeed, in order to write his "innermost history, [his] . . . *becoming*," (*EH*, p. 280), and in order to mark this history off from all linear narration of events, Nietzsche writes *Ecce Homo* in the space where his "own practical and theoretical skill in interpreting and arranging events has now reached its high point,"[27] to quote the aphorism entitled *Personal Providence* from *The Gay Science*. The first sentence of the first chapter of *Ecce Homo* opens with the riddle of Nietzsche's double origin which we will now have to analyze in some depth:

> The good fortune of my existence, its uniqueness perhaps, lies in its fatality: I am, to express it in the form of a riddle, already dead as my father, while as my mother I am still living and becoming old. This dual descent, as it were, both from the highest and the lowest rung on the ladder of life, at the same time a *decadent* and a *beginning*—this, if anything, explains that neutrality, that freedom from all partiality in relation to the total problem of life, that perhaps distinguishes me. (*EH*, p. 222)

Nietzsche starts recording his history as having its source in this kind of double origin from the moment he becomes aware that recovery from his sickness will only be possible by means of a return to his "nethermost self" (*EH*, p. 287). This return is coupled to an interest in medicine, physiology and natural sciences (*EH*, p. 286). This interest at the expense of the (in fact decadent) preoccupation with history is supposed to further an active "ignorance *in physiologicis*," through which a rearrangement of his personal history at the benefit of his nethermost self could be achieved.[28] Let us then try to follow Nietzsche in the exploration of his buried nethermost self.

First we will have to recall the unusual beginning of Nietzsche's career as a writer:

> This beginning is exceedingly strange. I had discovered the only parable and parallel in history for my own inmost experience—and thus became the first to comprehend the wonderful phenomenon of the Dionysian. (*EH*, pp. 271-72)

This beginning is indeed strange, for a moment in the past coincides with the actuality of Nietzsche's life. It is the similarity of these two moments, as much as the identity between Nietzsche's experience and the Dionysian, that triggers his insights into the phenomenon of the Dionysian itself. In this way, moreover, history turns out to be double: on the one hand, you have a repetition or a return of the past: Dionysian or Heraclitean history; on the other, history properly speaking as the Apollonian and Socratic fall away from Dionysian history. But this latter is itself a double phenomenon. It cannot be overlooked that besides his determination as becoming *and* destruction, Dionysos has a double origin: twice born, once from the womb of the princess Semele, once from the leg of Zeus. Nietzsche's origin, parallel to the Dionysian parable (*Gleichnis*), is equally double.

In chapter 3 of *Why I am so wise*, Nietzsche comes to speak of "this *dual* series of experiences" that proceeds from his double origin. In this particular context, Nietzsche explains their double nature by his descent, which involves a double nationality. "My ancestors were Polish noblemen: I have many racial instincts in my body from that source . . . . Yet my mother, Franziska Oehler, is at any rate something very German" (*EH*, p. 225). Nietzsche's father, Karl Ludwig Nietzsche, "was full of deep reverence for the Prussian king Frederick William IV . . . . I myself, born on the birthday of the above named king, on the fifteenth of October, received, as fitting, the Hohenzollern name *Friedrich* Wilhelm" (*EH*, p. 226). Thus German because of his name—"perhaps more German than present-day Germans"—but Polish because of his descent and according to his instincts,[29] Nietzsche possesses "a 'second' face in addition to the first." He is, in every respect, a *Doppelgänger* (*EH*, p. 225). This double descent, however, does not yet exhaust Nietzsche's duplicity. In order to thoroughly examine the enigma of Nietzsche's fatality, let's consider what he tells us about his father:

> My father, born in 1813, died in 1849. (*EH*, p. 226)

> My father died at the age of thirty-six: he was delicate, kind, and morbid, as a being that is destined merely to pass by—more a gracious memory of life than life itself. (*EH*, p. 222)

> I consider it a great privilege to have had such a father: it even seems to me that this explains whatever else I have of privileges—*not* including life, the great Yes to life. (*EH*, p. 226)

Nothing but a reminiscence of the future, of Nietzsche's future *life*, the father withers away as soon as he has engendered his son. Yet the legacy of this dearly beloved father is double: Nietzsche not only inherits life, but also a *"wicked* heritage . . . at bottom, [a] predestination to an early death" (*EH*, p. 287). At the moment when "selflessness" and "sense of duty" pave the way for Nietzsche's decadence, however, this wicked heritage turns into a remedy: his sickness detaches him from decadent life and allows him to come to his own aid. With this, a tentative reading of the enigma of the double origin becomes possible. Indeed, to die as one's own father is to give birth to oneself. As the wicked heritage, "a predestination to an early death," is transformed into a lifegiving remedy, Nietzsche gives *life* to himself by dying as his own father.[30] And yet, what does it mean, when he writes that as his mother he is still living and becoming old? The mother's function consists of carrying a child for the full term. But not yet due to be born, his time not yet having come, he will remain as his own mother indefinitely pregnant with himself: "I live on my own credit: it is perhaps a mere prejudice that I live" (*EH*, p. 217). Being also the highest rung on the ladder of life, its endpoint, the role of the father is to take life away as well. The wicked heritage, and death as one's own father, impedes all possible becoming from the outset. But this misfortune is precisely what allows Nietzsche to short-circuit the process of decadence. Deprived of the possibility of a continuous climbing from the lowest to the highest rung on the ladder of life, Nietzsche can altogether escape the time of decadence, i.e. linear historical time. As his mother endlessly carries him for the full term, he grows old "at the same time a *decadent* and a *beginning*." More succinctly put, since Nietzsche is already dead as a beginning that would develop into an end, Nietzsche remains an eternal beginning that is already its *end*. Congenitally deprived of all becoming,

Nietzsche enjoys the eventuality and privilege of *repeating* himself *eternally* as the *same*, as a beginning which is its end.

As if he were meditating a certain fragment of Heraclitus in which birth is said to be an adversity,[31] this repetition or return of oneself as a stillborn beginning and as a selfsame that does not want to become different, by taking place *in* and *as* the interval of *beginning* and *decadence*, opens up a third space. This is the space of the eternal return of the same. Before further exploring this space, let us remark that Nietzsche determines this space to be neutral. Although this interface of Nietzsche's *Doppelnatur*—opened up (for instance) through an interruption of the flow of time by sickness—represents a state of "fullness and self-assurance of a *rich* life," as well as a space of perspectives "toward *healthier* concepts and values" (*EH*, p. 223), it is *not* a dialectical space. It is just as little a place where complementary or self-contradictory doubles resolve into nullity, into abstract nothingness. Rather Nietzsche's dual descent, which provides him with his most subtle smell for the "signs of ascent and descent"—"I know both, I am both" (*EH*, p. 222)— characterizes this intermediary space of the return of the same as a space of neutrality and impartiality toward "the total problem of life."

To better understand this remarkable space, let us focus on a figure which, at first, may be mistaken for a sublation of the *Doppelblick*. Having stressed that he is at the same time a decadent and its opposite, Nietzsche writes:

> This dual series of experiences, this access to apparently separate worlds, is repeated in my nature in every respect: I am a *Doppelgänger*, I have a "second" face in addition to the first. *And* perhaps also a third. (*EH*, p. 255)

The *Doppelgänger* possesses a "second" face: his insights into the world are "fruitful and terrible at the same time" (*EH*, p. 289). In *Ecce Homo* this double face is also linked to Nietzsche's homage to the month of January. During this month—in Roman chronology it was dedicated to the god Janus who as *Ianus bifrons* is a deity of beginnings (and endings)—Nietzsche conceived of his *Gaya Scienza*. Janus as a guardian of doors and gates, and as presiding over the beginning of things, looks simultaneously forward and backward. In the interface of his two-faced figure, he then possesses what Nietzsche in *Dawn* calls the third eye: it is this which is the theatrical or tragic eye.[32] Regarded as a door-keeper and a guardian of gates, his statue stood where two roads met. But does the *Doppelgänger* not also walk on a double road? Or rather is his place not at the intersection of two roads, there where a third road begins? In *Ecce Homo*, Nietzsche, indeed, suggests such an interpretation when he recalls the very conception of his *Zarathustra*:

Mornings I would walk in a southernly direction on the splendid road to Zoagli, going up past pines with a magnificent view of the sea; in the afternoon, whenever my health permitted it, I walked around the whole bay from Santa Margherita all the way to Portofino. This place and this scenery came even closer to my heart because of the great love that Emperor Frederick III felt for them; by chance, I was in this coastal region again in the fall of 1886 when he visited this small forgotten world of bliss for the last time.—It was on these two walks that the whole *Zarathustra I* occurred to me, and especially Zarathustra himself as a type: rather he *overtook* me. (*EH*, pp. 297-98)

At the intersection of two ways, so to speak, of the way which leads upward and the way which leads downward and around the bay, as well as in the interval of the times of the rising and the setting sun, Nietzsche is overtaken by Zarathustra. The time of Zarathustra coincides with what Nietzsche calls the "great noon." In *Ecce Homo* he defines his task as follows:

My task of preparing a moment of the highest self-examination for humanity, a *great noon* when it looks back and far forward, when it emerges from the dominion of accidents and priests and for the first time poses, *as a whole*, the question of Why? And For What? —This task follows of necessity from the insight that humanity is *not* all by itself on the right way. (*EH*, p. 291)

Similar to illness, which as a suspension of the necessary decadent flow of time allows for a *Wiederholung* (a repetition, a renewing and a bringing back) of what Nietzsche calls the nethermost self, the *great noon* (*grosser Mittag*) and the "right way" represent a break of the continuum of space and time, during which the *type* of Zarathustra is impressed on Nietzsche. This fork in the road, this momentary caesura of the way upward and the way downward which are one and the same, leads us back to the initial riddle of Nietzsche's double origin. Indeed, on a solution of that riddle at the beginning of the text depends not only our entrance of the text but also our understanding of what it may mean to find oneself (*Selbstfindung*) through repetition.

A first transcription of the riddle's solution reads as follows: I have killed myself as my own father so that I can commit incest with myself as my mother while as my father I am preventing myself from being born. As we proceed in our analysis of the status of this riddle and of its solution, it becomes inevitable that we recall a series of events following the death of Nietzsche's father. We already know that he died at the age of 36.

> In the same year in which his life went downward, mine too, went downward: at thirty-six, I reached the lowest point of my vitality—I still lived, but without being able to see three steps ahead. (*EH*, p. 222)

If Nietzsche's father died in 1849, and if Nietzsche reached the lowest point of his life before renouncing his professorship at Basel in 1879, exactly thirty years lie between his father's death and his temporary blindness. This low in his life, incidentally, is not without relation to reading:

> I have seen this with my own eyes: gifted natures with a generous and free disposition, "read to ruin" in their thirties. (*EH*, p. 253)

For that very reason, turning from reading will lead Nietzsche out of decadence:

> My eyes alone put an end to all bookwormishness—in brief: philology: I was delivered from the "book"; for years I did not read a thing—the greatest benefit I ever conferred on myself. (*EH*, p. 287)

Now, this blindness during which Nietzsche is unable to see three steps ahead, and which he experiences thirty years after his father's death, at the moment when he reaches his father's age—36, this blindness is precisely a self-punishment for having slain himself as his own father and for having committed incest with himself as his own mother. At the fork of the road, consequently, in the interface of the way upward and the way downward, as well as the moment when he looks both forward and backward, that is to say when finding himself as the same, Nietzsche *repeats* all the moments of the triangular oedipal configuration. The oedipal triangulation, necessary in the becoming of the subject in a genealogy calling for a continuous and accumulative time, appears here equally vital to one's becoming a type. What does this repetition and its inevitability stand for? Does it mean that there is no difference between a self-conscious subject encrusted in a genealogy and a type who dismisses all apology? [33] Is the moment of mediation in both cases the same? Will the third space, the unusual space of the interval, be absorbed in this triangulation? These are some of the questions to be raised at this point. But before we can begin answering them, we have to further investigate Nietzsche's temporary blindness.

This loss of sight, which prevents Nietzsche from seeing more than three steps ahead, is connected to three days of migraines during which he excels in dialectics:

> In the midst of the torments that go with an uninterrupted three-day migraine, accompanied by laborious vomiting of phlegm, I possessed a dialectician's clarity *par excellence* and thought through with very cold blood matters for which under healthier circumstances I am not mountain-climber, not subtle, not *cold* enough. (*EH*, pp. 222-23)

If Nietzsche reminds us immediately afterwards that he considers "dialectic as a symptom of decadence—for example in the most famous case, the case of Socrates" (*EH*, p. 223), similar indeed with its three operative steps to the three-day migraine, to the vision reduced to three steps, to the triangular oedipal configuration—then the book *Dawn* to which Nietzsche gives birth under these circumstances, necessarily announces a *new* beginning. A beginning of what? What is this new beginning as it appears (only) *as* a repetition of triangular figures?

Paradoxically enough, the figure three, as a figure of closure and presiding over the movement of speculative thought in its totalizing perspective, the figure three is made to turn upon itself and becomes a sign of liberation. Take for instance Heinrich von Stein, who came to visit Nietzsche for three days:

> This excellent human being, who had walked into the Wagnerian morass with all the impetuous simplicity of a Prussian Junker, . . . acted during these three days like one transformed by a tempest of freedom, like one who has suddenly been lifted to his own weight and acquired wings. (*EH*, p. 227)

Nor should we forget the following:

> With a dithyramb like the last one in the third part of *Zarathustra*, entitled "The Seven Seals," I soared a thousand miles beyond what has been called poetry hitherto. (*EH*, pp. 265-66)

The threefold figures being simultaneously symptomatic of decline *and* ascent, the new beginning springs forth from the *superiority* and exceeding *excellence* of the repetition of precisely those threefold figures. Does Nietzsche not write that he "possessed a dialectician's clarity *par excellence*?" It is *as* a repetition of the totally mediated and speculative

284

closure of the tertiary figures that a new beginning is inaugurated. The third space and the new beginning come into effect only through the repetition of those totalizing tertiary figures which, on the other hand, presuppose the space of the interval without which they could not come forth.

But as totalizing figures, both the number three and the threefold or triangular movements are blind to the eventuality of their superior repetition in this intermediary space (whence their possibility originates). Such a blindness can be witnessed, for instance, in the case of Eugen Fink, one of Nietzsche's critics, for whom the third part of *Zarathustra* represents the core (*Herzstück*), the mean, the middle (*die "Mitte"*), the center of the whole work. To him this third part is necessarily the "natural end of the work," and concludes "the step-by-step development of Nietzsche's central thought"; thus, returning a third time, Zarathustra-Nietzsche is said to "find himself as the essential middle (*wesentliche Mitte*) of his thinking." Compared to this third part, then, the fourth part of the *Zarathustra* is naturally derogatory.[34] But is this indeed so? Is this essential middle not rather a beginning of something else instead of the endpoint of a quest for self-identity, self-appropriation and self-reflection? If this third part were in fact the superior *repetition* of all of the speculative movements that culminate in the parousia of the self, then this third part would be the beginning of a resolutely non-totalizing repetition of those very same tertiary figures, staging by this repetition the very space where those totalizing movements spring forth. Yet, what Fink called the essential middle—the moment and the space of mediation—will then, as a result of repetition, have to be made dependent on the possibility of repetition itself. The repetition of the threefold figures in the third space, repeated for their own sake in order to open the space of their possibility, shows mediation consequently to be dependent on repetition itself. With this, repetition as a non-reflexive mode of self-reference of the same appears to be the condition of possibility, the degree zero of all mediation and reflection. The third space and the new beginning *is*, as the space in which all mediation and reflection is engendered, also the place of re-turn of what it gives birth to.

Is it not in such a light that not only the third part of *Zarathustra* but also the fourth part has to be judged? A dithyramb, that is to say a hymn to Dionysos, concludes the third part of *Zarathustra*. With this dithyramb, Oedipus takes off his mask, so to speak, and steps forward as Dionysos. Needless then to look for a fourth way, for a way out of the essential middle, oedipal genealogy, self-conscious subjectivity. It is indeed already present *as* difference of the third way. But then, the fourth part of Zarathustra cannot be derogatory: instead of following a successful exposition of Nietzsche's central thought, it is *the* repetition of that very beginning achieved in part III, it is the same.

No doubt, what is repeated and its repetition are in *relation* to one another. They share a mutual sphere of *mediation* whereby the repetition of the same is not *immediate* (*unmittelbar*). Yet, the fact that the recurrence of a same presupposes a common medium does not necessarily entail that the repeated and its repetition would relate to one another in terms of *differences*. On the contrary, we know that what is repeated is affirmed in its totality. It is not repeated as a negative determination, that is to say as a moment of a whole, of a system, of a concept (*Begriff*). Despite the sphere of mediation of which they partake, despite the lack of all immediacy that characterizes them, the repeated and its repetition do not stand in a reciprocal relation of reflexive determination, of what Hegel named *Reflexionsbestimmung*. The relation between the repeated and its repetition as well as the relation between mediation and reflection on the one hand, and repetition on the other hand, are divested of all specular properties.

Thus, instead of initiating a process in view of an end which would also as a result represent the speculative ground of the point of departure, the affirmation through repetition of the threefold figures constitutive of self-identical entities, of the oedipal triad and the dialectical triad, leads to a collapse of the difference between beginning and end. What is repeated in its totality, without determining it as a moment in regard to another, thus negatively, *is* an aborted beginning, stillborn so to speak as the starting point of a possible development. Beginning and end are here the *same*. In the absence of all reflexive determination between the repeated and its repetition, between beginning and end, *mediation* boils down to repetition, to the recurrence or return of the same. With it we reach the end of all development, of all exposition (*Ausführung*).

What is at stake here then is more than a quest for the transcendental possibility of mediation and reflection. Indeed, by showing on the one hand how both presuppose repetition as a non-reflexive relation, and while demonstrating on the other that the affirmation of the repeated as the same also breaks down the process of mediation, Nietzsche literally practices a non-reflexive discourse. Indeed, the new beginning will not be a beginning of philosophy, as determined for instance at the outset of Hegel's *Science of Logic*.[35]

On the contrary. As a non-reflexive, non-specular relation between affirmed self*sames*, as a degree-zero mediation that excludes all mirroring, all specular reflection through one's negative or other, the notion of repetition leaves the horizon of the determinations of consciousness and history. A same, a selfsame, as well as a discourse that relates to itself in the mode of a return, can no longer be mistaken for the "identical" or be constitutive of being as presence. These were, however, the presuppositions, the beginning and end, of philosophy.

A selfsame that excludes all reflexive mediation is a type. In elaborating such a notion, Nietzsche must undercut all possibility of self-appropriation. The mode of specular self-appropriation is the *Gestalt* of autobiography. As we saw, it is the medium of exposition of the modern concept of being as self-present subjectivity. Nietzsche, then, using the discourse of self-presentation in *Ecce Homo* to elaborate the notion of a non-reflexive selfsame as *Typus*, simultaneously overcomes the form of autobiography and its concept of being. In addition, if the function of the *Gestalt* as *Selbstdarstellung* consists in erecting the self as self-present being, in bringing it forth in order to reappropriate it, the derogation from such specularity through the repetition of a non-reflexive selfsame or type also announces the limits of representation as *Vorstellung*, and the opening up of the problem of *Darstellung* as such.

Unable to recognize this, the humanist critic is reduced to accusing Nietzsche of "exorbitant subjectivity" as well as of "endless and tormented selfmirroring."[36] What Nietzsche undertook in *Ecce Homo* while imitating the traditional genre of autobiography, is on the contrary the end of subjectivity, and of its correlative notion of being.

SUNY—Buffalo

NOTES

1   On October 30, 1888, Nietzsche writes to Peter Gast: "On my birthday, I began again with something that seems to be going well and has already made considerable progress. It is called *Ecce Homo*, or *How One Becomes What One Is*. It concerns, with great audacity, myself and my writings." *Selected Letters of Friedrich Nietzsche*, ed. and trans. Christopher Middleton (Chicago, Univ. of Chicago Press, 1969), p. 319. See also the letter from November 14, 1888, to Meta von Salis: "This *Homo*, you will understand, is myself, including the *Ecce*" (p. 324).

2   Martin Heidegger, *Nietzsche* (Pfullingen: Neske, 1961), I, 474-75.

3   Heidegger, *Nietzsche*, I, 260.

4   On Heidegger's reading of Nietzsche, see Philippe Lacove-Labarthe, "L'obliteration," in *Le sujet de la philosophie*, Typographies I (Paris: Aubier-Flammarion, 1979), pp. 113-84.

5   Eugen Fink, *Nietzsches Philosophie* (Stuttgart: Kohlhammer, 1973), p. 43.

6   "One thing will live, the sign-manual (*Monogramm*) of their inmost being, the rare flash of light, the deed, the creation." *The Use and Abuse of History*, in *The Complete Works of Friedrich Nietzsche*, ed. O. Levy (New York: Russell, 1964) V, 18-19.

7   Hegel, *Phenomenology of Spirit*, trans. A. V. Miller (Oxford: Oxford Univ. Press, 1977) p. 160. On Hegel's use of the notion of *Gestalt*, see also Heidegger, *Hegel's Concept of Experience*, trans. Kenley Dove (New York: Harper, 1970).

8   Heidegger, "The Origin of the Work of Art," in *Poetry, Language, Thought*, trans. Albert Hofstadter (New York: Harper, 1971), pp. 64, 77, 84.

9   Heidegger, "What are Poets For?" in *Poetry, Language, Thought*, pp. 100-101.

10   M. Heidegger, *The Question of Being*, trans. William Kluback and Jean T. Wilde (New Haven: College and University Press, 1958).

11   Heidegger, "What are Poets For? ," p. 111.

12   For Heidegger's use of the notion of *Gestalt*, see the remarkable article of Philippe Lacove-Labarthe, "Typographie," in *Mimesis, Des articulations* (Paris: Aubier-Flammarion, 1975).

13   Descartes, *Discourse on Method and the Meditations*, trans. (Penguin Books, 1968), pp. 35-36.

14   To Lou Salomé he writes on June 10, 1882: "Pindar says somewhere, 'Become the being you are'! " (*Selected Letters*, p. 183).

15   As to the *fictitious* nature of the notions of becoming and being in Nietzsche, see Paul de Man, "Action and Identity in Nietzsche," *Yale French Studies*, no. 52 (1975), p. 24.

16   "It smells offensively Hegelian," writes Nietzsche about *The Birth of Tragedy* in *Ecce Homo*, in Friedrich Nietzsche, *On the Genealogy of Morals* and *Ecce Homo*, trans. Walter Kaufmann (New York: Random, 1967), p. 270 (hereafter cited as *EH*).

17   *EH*, p. 221. See also the following passage from a letter to Georg Brandes on November 20, 1888: "I have now told my own story with a cynicism that will make history." (*Selected Letters*, p. 326.)

18   "But I, who am certain that I am, do not yet clearly know enough what I am; so that henceforth I must take great care not imprudently to take some other object for myself, and thus avoid going astray in this knowledge which I maintain to be more certain and evident than all I have had hitherto." (Descartes, *Meditations*, p. 103.)

19   On the intercalated leaf between the preface and *Ecce Homo* "properly" speaking:

      On this perfect day, when everything is ripening and not only the grape turns brown, the eye of the sun just fell upon my life: I looked back, I looked forward, and never saw so many and such things at once. It was not for nothing that I buried my forty-fourth year today; I had the *right* to bury it; whatever was life in it has been saved, is immortal. The first book of the *Revaluation of All Values*, the *Songs of Zarathustra*, and *Twilight of Idols*, my attempt to philosophize with a hammer—all presents of this year, indeed of its last quarter! *How could I fail to be grateful to my whole life?* —and so I tell my life to myself. (*EH*, p. 221)

This intermediary space in the text on *Ecce Homo*—a space, according to Heidegger, which is exemplary of the poet himself insofar as he is being born in the bridal encounter (*Brautfest, Brauttag*) of men and gods as the one who "stands between men and the gods and endures this 'inbetween' " (Heidegger, *Erläuterungen zu Hölderlins Dichtung* [Frankfurt/Main: Klostermann, 1963], p. 98)—has recently been the object of a yet unpublished study: "L'Otobiographie de Nietzsche" by Jacques Derrida.

20   Nietzsche, *Beyond Good and Evil*, trans. in *The Philosophy of Nietzsche*, ed. (New York: Modern Library, 1954), p. 601.

21   "A thing that is explained ceases to concern us.—What did the God mean who gave the advice, 'Know thyself!'? Did it perhaps imply 'Cease to be concerned about thyself! become objective!'—And Socrates?—And the 'scientific man'?" (*Beyond Good and Evil*, p. 454).

22   This subversion of all individuality at the benefit of *what one is* considerably limits the scope of Gilles Deleuze's revaluation of the question *Who one is* in his *Nietzsche et la philosophie* (Paris: Presses Universitaires de France, 1967), pp. 86-88.

23   Jacques Derrida, *Speech and Phenomena: And other essays on Husserl's Theory of Signs*, trans. D. Allison (Evanston: Northwestern Univ. Press, 1973), pp. 52-53.

24   "It is out of the unfolding of the 'same' as differance that the sameness of difference and of repetition is presented in the eternal return." Derrida, "Differance," in *Speech and Phenomena*, p. 149.

25   See Bernard Pautrat, "Nietzsche medusé," in *Nietzsche aujourd'hui* (Paris: Coll. 10.18, 1973).

26   See Deleuze, *Nietzsche*, pp. 29-33; as to the image of the die, see for example *The Use and Abuse of History*, p. 20, where Nietzsche speaks of the real historical nexus of cause and effect, which, rightly understood, would only prove that nothing quite similar could ever be cast again from the dice-boxes of fate and the future.

27   Nietzsche, *The Gay Science*, trans. Walter Kaufmann, (New York: Vintage, 1974), p. 224.

28   See Rodolphe Gasché, *Ecce Homo ou Du Corps Ecrit* (Urbino: International Center of Semiotics and Linguistics, 1976).

29   On December 29, 1888, Nietzsche writes to Meta von Salis: "and thank heaven that in all my instincts I am a Pole and nothing else." (*Selected Letters*, p. 343.)

30   Pierre Klossowski strangely enough concludes his analysis of this passage as follows: "Donc, Nietzsche n'est jamais le père de lui-même puisqu'*il est mort en tant que son père*," (Pierre Klossowski, *Nietzsche et le cercle vicieux*, [Paris: Mercure de France, 1969], p. 275).

31   The fragment goes as follows: "Being born they wish to live and have their fate; or rather to rest; and they leave behind children, who in turn will meet

their fate" (*Selections from Early Greek Philosophy*, 4th ed., ed. M. C. Nahm [New York: Appleton-Century-Crofts, 1964], p. 73).

32   See aphorism 509: "THE THIRD EYE.—What! You are still in need of the theatre! are you still so young? Be wise, and seek tragedy and comedy where they are better acted, and where the incidents are more interesting, and the actors more eager. It is indeed by no means easy to be merely a spectator in these cases—but learn! and then, amid all difficult or painful situations, you will have a little gate leading to joy and refuge, even when your passions attack you. Open your stage eye, that big third eye of yours, which looks out into the world through the other two." (*The Day of Dawn*, trans. in *The Complete Works of Friedrich Nietzsche* [New York: Russell, 1964], IX, 353.)

33   "For an individual to posit his own ideal and to derive from it his own law, joys, and rights—that may well have been considered hitherto as the most outrageous human aberration and as idolatry itself. The few who dared as much always felt the need to apologize to themselves, usually by saying: 'It wasn't I! Not I! But a *god* through me'." (Nietzsche, *The Gay Science*, p. 191.)

34   Fink, *Nietzsches Philosophie*, pp. 65, 82, 114, 118.

35   As well as Heidegger's notion of "the unmediated character of a beginning": "A genuine beginning, as a leap, is always a head start, in which everything to come is already leaped over, even if as something disguised. The beginning already contains the end latent with itself." ("The Origin of the Work of Art," p. 76.)

36   Fink, *Nietzsches philosophie*, p. 14. Compare to Heidegger's *Nietzsche*, I, 260, where Heidegger understands Nietzsche's self-reflection (*Selbstbesinnung*) as precisely the contrary of an idle self-mirroring (*Selbstbespiegelung*).

IV Critiques

Nietzsche Knows no Noumenon

David B. Allison

It has become a virtual postulate in recent criticism that any competent reading of Nietzsche must attend to a perceived loss of sense, of semantic evacuation, incompleteness, and inconsistency in the Nietzschean text. Some critics even insist on an axiomatic void at the very heart of his texts. In the most general terms, it would appear that two considerations compel this caution: a renewed awareness of Nietzsche's rhetorical resources—certainly, his almost profligate use of irony, metaphor, metonomy, and repetition—and a perplexity concerning his various epistemological formulations. To compound matters, Nietzsche's epistemological accounts often seem to confuse two traditionally distinct spheres, that of a proper knowledge claim and the language through which the claim may be articulated. Acutely aware of the constraints governing the possibility of comprehension, Paul de Man, for example, concludes his analysis on a note of obdurate pessimism; namely, that the reader is condemned by a war of rhetoric to "an apparently endless process of deconstruction," a veritable cancellation or destruction of the Nietzschean text itself.[1] Less eristically, perhaps, Carol Jacobs claims that the Nietzschean text is nonetheless defeated and rendered dumb by the defect of a congenital stammering, a rhetorical agency which "menaces the definitive distinction between identity and discrepancy, between repetition and contradiction, distinctions without which the concepts of history, signifier, and signification are meaningless."[2] Likewise, Paul Bové finds Nietzsche's texts to be fully equivocal and paradoxical. Not only are their assertions continually subverted by a duplicitous rhetoric, but the conceptual formations which might somehow escape this subversion are "already coopted" and "epistemologically entrapped" by an additional agency, "the revisionist power structure" of the Hegelian dialectic.[3] The same holds true, in turn, he argues, for any critical operation which seeks to enjoin the Nietzschean text. The threat to both the intelligibility of the text and its critical articulation is, in every case, dramatically stated. For de Man, the threat is to reason itself. For Jacobs, it arrives unannounced as the "incomprehensible." For Bové, it operates as "the limits of epistemological understanding." By each account, the judgment rendered would be silence, and its effect would be to transform Nietzsche's text into a book of the dead.

While these critics understandably represent a variety of approaches, there is a striking similarity between their analyses and the most traditional readings of Nietzsche, which reflect the by now practically unquestioned thesis that Nietzsche—particularly, in *The Birth of Tragedy* and the collateral writings of his early period—was fully committed to the idealist doctrines of Schopenhauer and Kant, and that the "deeper" reality about which he wrote so inadequately was the "world will" of the former or the "in-itself" of the latter. De Man, for example, restates this entirely conventional view and uses it as the initial premise for his own analysis: "He [Nietzsche] uses and remains faithful to the Kantian element in Schopenhauer's terminology and this allegiance is itself epistemologically founded." "Such an element," he continues, "is not just what we usually call reality, but *Ding an sich,* the entity as substance in its identity with itself."[4]

Given these profoundly binding metaphysical tenets ("the ontological cards have been stacked from the beginning," de Man remarks), it was only plausible that Nietzsche's use of language, especially rhetoric, would be found to have been severely compromised. In the end, as de Man succinctly expresses this position,

> There is little difficulty in matching the two mythological poles, Dionysus and Apollo, with the categories of appearance [i.e., "phenomena"] and its antithesis [the "noumenal" realm], or with the relationship between metaphorical and proper language. From its first characterization as dream, Apollo exists entirely within the world of appearances. The dream . . . is mere surface. . . . This state of illusion happens to coincide with what is usually called 'reality' in everyday speech, the empirical reality in which we live. . . . All appearance, as the con-

cept implies, is appearance of something that, in the last analysis, no longer seems to be but actually is. This "something" can only be Dionysus . . . the origin of things. As such, the Dionysian condition is an insight into things as they are. . . . The Apollonian appearance is the metaphorical statement of this truth.[5]

Briefly stated, we seem confronted by the closure of an absolute and double bind: language is restricted *ab initio* to metaphorical expression, and that in turn is said to "represent" what is itself only an illusory order, a fictive "reality," so called. Such a formulation—at once entirely conventional and distinctively postmodern—does more than to condemn Nietzsche's texts to the far side of reason's sleep; at the same time it ironically acknowledges its own fragility in the face of such a closure. Text and critique are quite simply sundered and cast adrift, no longer even homologous; a prospect de Man and others find regrettable indeed, but apparently unavoidable.

The drift or freeplay between two kinds of texts, between Nietzsche's text and its critique (or, a common variant of this: the discontinuity between his published works and the unpublished notes, drafts, outlines, jottings, and letters) thus serves to displace a prior opposition, one which occurs within a single text: the ecstatic rhetoric of Dionysus and its articulate counterpart, the voice of Apollo. Finally, this rhetorical set conventionally expresses two orders of being, the Dionysian "reality" (specifically equated with the Schopenhauerian world will or the Kantian noumenal reality) and the phenomenal order, the world as "representation," "idea," or "appearance." Innumerable strategies disport themselves along this axis of filiation (most notably, those of representation, truth, signification, and power), each of which has at one time or another guided the analysis of *The Birth of Tragedy.*

It is no accident, furthermore, that such recent criticism has tended to view this most important early text of Nietzsche from the vantage point of "On Truth and Lie in an Extra-Moral Sense," for these two early works share common concerns and appear to express a common structure of genesis, that of the doubly productive metaphor. Nietzsche's well-known formulation from "Truth and Lie," i.e., that language is the metaphor of metaphor, could be said to prescribe the very itinerary of rhetorical genesis and drift. The parallel between these two texts, each of which employs a genealogical structure of production or displacement, could be drawn even more strongly: each narrative advance in either of the two accounts seems to be one of reflection or reproduction, and each entails a subsequent deformation, which in turn leads one further away from the respective origins of the genealogical train. With each transformation or deformation, the origins themselves become progressively irrecuperable.

In the absence of a governed discourse, one which effectively repeats or invokes a verifiable origin, one might well follow de Man's perplexity and insist on the epistemological necessity of what would *ground* such a discourse, namely, a conventional metaphysics of representation. Such a non-figurative ground would serve—however inadequately—to establish a prime term or primary analogate for the (dis-) figurative rhetoric of metaphor. Yet even if this insistence yielded an adequate account of rhetorical tropes (and this would only repeat the Aristotelian model), it would not be sufficient to deal with the discourse of Dionysus and the purportedly noumenal reality (the "really real") to which it testifies, as set forth in *The Birth of Tragedy.*

I wish to show: (1) that this recourse to the noumenal realm is inadmissible, even within the terms of objective idealism; (2) that, in fact, Nietzsche maintained no such necessity for a noumenal realm; (3) that "the Dionysian" corresponds to a fully empirical order; (4) that Nietzsche at least attempted to establish a discourse adequate to the Dionysian during the period of *The Birth of Tragedy;* (5) that his account of the Dionysian provokes a re-examination of the status of subjectivity itself. Certain implications which stem from this position may be anticipated briefly, although space prohibits me from developing them in the present paper: (1) the conventional belief in an "epistemological break" between "the early Nietzsche" and "the late Nietzsche" must be abandoned. (2) The distinction between a figurative and disfigurative rhetoric operating concomitantly within the text of Nietzsche must be seriously re-examined. (3) The supposition that Nietzsche maintained a strict correspondence theory of truth, at the time of his early writings must likewise and correlatively be re-examined, if not replaced, by a mixed theory, one incorporating elements from coherence and contextualist accounts. Such a view is stated clearly by the period of *The Genealogy of Morals,* even though it is most apparently operative in the early essay, "Truth and Lie." Such an analysis in turn must question the usually univocal status of the term "representation." (4) The semantic weight of such performative aspects as are embraced by his account of music and sentiment or mood must be seriously investigated and rethought in view of (a) grammatical closure and (b) the social and political dimensions of intersubjective life.

Dionysian discourse and the immense domain it bespeaks, remains necessarily opaque, indeed immune, to the kind of analysis traditionally directed toward it by a representationalist theory of ideas. What is demanded by such an analysis is both the fact and the adequacy of representational thought itself, of categorial reason to master its object and to represent it as conceptually articulable. The adequacy of the critical judgment, fully rationalistic, however, is in all cases unquestioned. But if the "Dionysian element" escapes the representational discourse of a totalizing rationality, in no way can it be said to follow *a fortiori* that this element remains beyond a coherent empirical order, or that it should be understood as a noumenal ground or metaphysical world will, terms which by definition would preclude its very experience. Indeed, within such a noumenal order—the unconditioned itself—neither subjectivity nor objectivity could even arise, nor the very possibility of their agency, truth, or consequence. The initial distinction of such an unconditioned order is, moreover, an hieratic one: by a presumed *ordo essendi,* it claims an absolute metaphysical priority over any empirical or conditioned world whatsoever. This is a sorely disquieting claim, since to be made, it requires articulation and confirmation through an *ordo cognoscendi;* its claim *to be* must somehow be attested by a capacity of human knowledge.

Doubtless, it was for just these reasons that Kant could only *postulate* a noumenal order. He did so to satisfy the regulative demand of understanding that whatever appeared *must be* the appearance of something else, a demand which recoiled at the irrational prospect of a causally infinite regress: "Everything that exists, exists as substance, or as a determination inherent in it; or, everything contingent exists as an effect of some other thing, namely, of its cause."[6] This necessity, for Kant, paralleled the critical imperative itself: "Understanding and sensibility, with us, can determine objects *only when they are employed in conjunction.*"[7] Any object of possible experience, excluded from subsumption by the categories of the understanding was thus held to be inadmissible, since this exclusion would amount to a transcendental, and thus, illegitimate employment of reason. Ultimately, Kant argued, sensibility is fully governed by the "proper" employment of the categories, which employment serves to *define* objective representation; namely, discursively articulate formations (strictly speaking, experiences which could be represented in turn by assertoric judgments): "For we cannot in the least represent to ourselves the possibility of an understanding which should not know its object discursively through categories."[8]

For Kant, it was quite enough to assume that sensible intuition occurs only by means of categorial representation. This is why the concept of the noumenon is merely a "limiting concept," one which "must be understood as being such only in a negative sense." In fact, the noumenon serves as a doubly negative limit:

(1) It is postulated to *subtend* the order of sensibility and serve as a metaphysical "substrate." Thus, the noumenal order could, without logical contradiction, effectively ground the phenomenal order. As such it would serve as an antidote both to dogmatic idealism (the Berkelian variety) and to reason's horror at the prospect of an infinite causal regress.

(2) The noumenon also stands as an *antithesis* to the sensible order, namely, as a possibility which lies *beyond* it. In this case, it could, without logical contradiction, constitute the *intelligible* order. Yet in both cases, the noumenon would typically exceed the categorially ordered manifold: in the former, because sensibility is governed by the categories of the understanding; in the latter, because no sensible intuition corresponds to the bare logical possibility of such an intelligible order. The noumenon

299

would thus be either unintelligible or suprasensible. It would be as Kant described it, a wholly "problematic" concept, one which is positively excluded from human experience in any case.

Like Kant, Schopenhauer also maintained that the empirical order is strictly determined by the forms of intuition (space and time) and by the categories of the understanding, terms he designated collectively as "the principle of sufficient reason." Objective experience, for Schopenhauer, was thereby assimilated—and fully equivalent—to the rational, causal modes of subjective "representation" or "idea." But while he adopted the concept of noumenon from Kant ("Thing-in-itself signifies the existent independently of our perception, in short, that which properly is. . . . For Kant it was = X; for me it is Will"), Schopenhauer nonetheless affirmed it as a positive order, one framed precisely to counter the negative character of Kant's limit case.[9] If the empirical world is thus the representation of a totally unconditioned ground, then such a (metaphysically prior) ground must itself stand as the point by point antithesis to the causally conditioned, rational order of nature. The concept of a noumenal realm, therefore, was dictated by the principle of sufficient reason and stood as its exact opposite: the rechristened "world will" was, by Schopenhauer's definition, beyond space, time, form, matter, objectivity, motion, causality, and hence, beyond all individuation, differentiation, or multiplicity; it was necessarily *other* than reason, and therefore, positively irrational. Indeed, he argued, it was without origin, purpose, or surcease.

Despite all appearances, Schopenhauer nonetheless claimed—at least, initially—that one could have an immediate knowledge of the will. This would be a "most direct knowledge," one of a "special" or "exceptional" kind: an "inner" consciousness or awareness. Directed back upon the datum of its own animate body, this intuition would immediately show the subject's real being as will, his "subjective essence" or noumenal reality. By this privileged *inner intuition* Schopenhauer hoped to avoid the mediating and distorting character of spatial representation, the Kantian form of external, objective intuition. The full presence of the in-itself would thereby be given to the for-itself in the immediacy of self-consciousness. With this assurance (what Descartes called "the Archimedean point" and what Hegel located in "the self-knowing subject"), Schopenhauer would extend the intuition to its broadest conceivable application; from the self as will to the world as will:

> We are not merely the *knowing subject,* but in another
> aspect, we ourselves also belong to the inner nature that
> is to be known, *we ourselves are the thing in itself;* that
> therefore *a way from within* stands open for us to that
> inner nature belonging to things themselves, to which we
> cannot penetrate from without. . . . The thing in itself

can, as such, only come into consciousness quite directly, in this way, that *it is itself conscious of itself*. . . . In
fact, our *willing* is the one opportunity which we have of
understanding from within any event which exhibits itself without, consequently the one thing which is known
to us *immediately,* and not, like all the rest, merely given
in the idea. Here then, lies the datum which alone is able
to become the key to everything else, or, as I have said,
the single narrow door to the truth. Accordingly we
must learn to understand nature from ourselves, not conversely ourselves from nature. What is known to us immediately must give us the explanation of what we only
know indirectly, not conversely.[10]

So far, at least, went the positive claim. Upon reflection, Schopenhauer
realized that his case for the *via affirmativa* was far less sanguine, if not
finally unattainable. Having determined the character of the noumenon by
its postulated exclusion from the principle of sufficient reason, Schopenhauer found his assertions dramatically curtailed by the epistemological
paradox of representation; i.e., by his making a claim about the nature of
transcendent being from the standpoint of what is at best a transcendental
possibility of knowing—precisely the illicit transfer he found so risible in
Kant's notion of noumenal freedom. More importantly, his claim that inner intuition was in fact capable of grasping this noumenal reality supposed that intuition itself operated outside the second *a priori* form of
sensibility, namely, temporality. When put to the test, however (in
Ch. XVII, Supplement to Book II, "On the Possibility of Knowing the
Thing in Itself"), this supposition was surprisingly, if not prudently, with-
drawn:

> Accordingly, we have to refer the whole world of
> phenomena to that one in which the thing in itself ap-
> pears *in the very thinnest of veils,* and only *still remains
> phenomenon* insofar as my intellect . . . does not even in
> *inner* perception put off the form of . . . time.(*WWI*,
> Vol. II, p. 408)

With the failure to transcend empirical intuition, whatever is given to inner
reflection remains an *object* to the intuiting *subject;* hence, it remains
mere "idea" or "representation."
     In the end, there can be no effective recuperation of the noume-
non. There must in all cases of knowing, be a "residuum"—"an unfathomable something" of *qualitates occultae*—which cannot be explained:

> In all that we know there remains hidden from us a

certain something, as quite inscrutable, and we are obliged to confess that we cannot thoroughly understand
even the commonest and simplest phenomena. (*WWI*,
Vol. II, p. 303)

More strongly still, "the more necessity any knowledge carries with
it, . . . the less reality, properly so called, is given in it" (*WWI*, Vol. I,
pp. 158-59). Quite simply, Schopenhauer was forced to acknowledge that
the will can be given neither to the senses nor to the intellect: "It is therefore related to them," he lamented, "as our sensibility is related to the
possible properties of bodies for which we have no senses" (*WWI*, Vol. I,
p. 468).

Since the individual (or, individuated) will can only be given empirically, Schopenhauer conceded that his speculative discourse was per-
force analogical. Yet like the scholastic formulations of St. Thomas and
Cajetan, the real analogy in question is that which is framed to secure the
noumenal *ground* of the empirical order: the human body stands to the individual will (i.e., as its objective manifestation) as the phenomenal world
stands to its noumenal ground (of "world will"). This four-termed analogy
(of proper proportionality) is insoluble, however, unless the component
terms are themselves clarified. The primary analogate—world will—is itself
in question, and thus, cannot help resolve the analogy (between the two
sets of relations) which it in part constitutes. Likewise, the primary analogue—the individual will—remains especially problematic, since individuation does not pertain to the noumenal order. The relation which each part
of the analogy advanced (i.e., the relation of manifestation), as well as the
relation between these two relations (the extensional relation) is in every
case impossible to discern or to confirm. Schopenhauer's final recourse, in
defense of the *via analogia,* is to *abstract* the individual's phenomenal will
from its several acts (i.e., from its specific motives and occasions in space
and time), and with "this conviction," designate what is thereby removed
from the phenomenal subject his "real inner nature." He then "transfers it
to all these phenomena which are not [immediately] given to him."[11]

This last defense of analogical discourse is itself exposed as a discursive strategy of power. Abstraction and generalization, terms which are
synonymous with the Western tradition of metaphysical mastery, are the
proper instruments of this defense:

We must borrow for it [the subject's noumenal will] the
name and concept of an object, or something in some
way *objectively given,* consequently one of its own *manifestations.* But in order to serve as a *clue* for the understanding, this can be no other than the most complete of
all its manifestations. . . . Now, this is the human will
[the phenomenally objective order of volitions, urges,

stimuli, etc.] . It is, however, well to observe that here, at any rate, we only make use of a *denominatio a potiori*, through which, therefore, the concept of will receives a greater extension than it has hitherto had. . . . I therefore name the genus after its most important species . . . and then transfer it to all the weaker, less distinct manifestations of the same nature, and thus we shall accomplish the desired extension of the concept of the will. (*WWI*, Vol. I, pp. 143-44)

The attempt to define a metaphysical "world will" by the rhetorical expedient of synechdoche or metonymy, according to the terms of what is "assumed" to subtend the discrete subjective act, and yet be the "groundless" antithesis of the latter—admittedly "incomprehensible" and "nonsensible," quite beyond all space, time, and individuation—was, for Nietzsche, no less than arrant hyperbole. If *World as Will and Idea* was Schopenhauer's response to the question *"What is* this world of perception besides being my own idea?"*, Nietzsche's later epithet concerning this labored project seems almost generous in retrospect: "Never have so few dug so deep and come up with so little."

According to the terms of objective idealism, the noumenon remains at best a speculative postulate: since it cannot be intuited, it cannot be discursively articulated. Likewise, and conversely, since it cannot be categorially represented, it exceeds all sensible experience. Oddly, however, it is just this initial postulate that seems to pass without question among Nietzsche's critics, namely, that he maintained the metaphysical reality of such a noumenal order, and that he termed it "the Dionysian." Of course, there is ample evidence in *The Birth of Tragedy* to attest to this. Indeed. Every reader knows that Nietzsche wrote tirelessly and at length of "the will," the "world will," endless, boundless, etc. What could be more obvious than this patently idealist vocabulary of the noumenon? Yet it was precisely the appearance of indebtedness to Schopenhauer and Kant on this question that Nietzsche himself wished to correct in his later preface to *The Birth of Tragedy,* the "Attempt at a Self-Criticism."

How I regret now that in those days I still lacked the courage (or immodesty?) to permit myself in every way an individual language of my own for such individual views and hazards—and that instead I tried laboriously to express by means of Schopenhauerian and Kantian formulas strange and new valuations which were basically at odds with Kant's and Schopenhauer's spirit and taste! . . . I observed and spoiled Dionysian premonitions with Schopenhauerian formulations.[12]

What was at issue, then, in the later preface was to show that his earlier analysis was only *nominally* defective; despite the borrowed vocabulary, Nietzsche argued that his account in *The Birth of Tragedy* remained consistent and valid, that it in no way committed him to the metaphysical tenets of Schopenhauer and Kant, and thus it entailed neither the hopelessly optimistic moral world order of Kant nor the resignation and despair of Schopenhauerian pessimism. On the contrary, and precisely *because* the Dionysian was *not* to be understood as a noumenal reality, he could present an analysis which laid claim to some degree of historical and psychological objectivity, the very qualities he found so lacking in the romantic-idealist tradition of 18th- and 19th-century scholarship.

"The Dionysian" was indeed all-too-humanly empirical. It was the affective register of ecstasy, of intense delight and suffering, everywhere experienced throughout the ancient world. From the initial discussion of this term in *The Birth of Tragedy,* Nietzsche consistently referred to it (and to the Apollonian as well) as an instinct, drive, pulsion, power, or force, i.e., principally as a *Trieb,* often as an *Instinkt* or *Macht.* In fact, he was careful to distinguish two general expressions of this instinctual element at the outset, the specifically "Greek" formation (which would correspond to the ritualized activity of the Dionysian cults), and the "barbarian" or "bestial" variety, a distinction which broadly anticipates the later Freudian models of secondary and primary process activity.[13]

Even by the time Nietzsche composed *The Birth of Tragedy,* his use of conventionally metaphysical language was strained to the point of breaking, in order to accommodate this experiential order of affectivity and passion. Not only would the borrowed vocabulary of "will" soon pass over into the antimetaphysical vocabulary of "will to power," with its "multiplicities of forces," its "perspectival" coherences, and the prospect of its "eternal recurrence," but the collective formations of what he still termed "will" were already defined empirically as "phenomena" and "sensations" (which, he noted, are not possible without objects), i.e., as substantial, bodily, and material unities.[14] The transition to his own vocabulary was perhaps assisted by his substitution of such terms as "the primordial one" or "the original process" for the Schopenhauerian "world will." Moreover, it is repeatedly established in his notes of the period that these substitutions were held to be synonyms for "the world" and "existence," generally: specifically, for a world of becoming—of generation and strife, attraction, discord, and plurality. If anything, his language became ever more influenced by his reading of the presocratics during this period (especially, Heraclitus), and already by the end of 1870, he characterized his own emergent philosophy as an "inverted Platonism."

Since the Dionysian was thus an instinctual component of empirical reality, Nietzsche's most difficult task was to characterize it in positive terms. On the one hand, it had to be articulated in a vocabulary which would correspond to a dynamically conceived empirical order, thereby acknowledging its ontological parity with the latter. To this end, of course, Nietzsche most often discussed both orders (i.e., instincts and their objects, or, the affective individual and his world) in terms of their common dynamic or energetic properties. Unlike the recourse of Schopenhauer, this move was neither meant to be metonymic nor synechdotal, nor, in any way a *denominatio a potiori.* Alternatively, and because the Dionysian had to do with affective behavior generally (most specifically, pathos), Nietzsche was loath to consider it in simply objective, or discretely representational terms. What was at issue was one of the most striking elements of subjective life, yet, at the same time, a dimension of subjectivity which seemed to enjoy a public, intersubjective existence as well. Indeed, it was the cultural depth and historical universality of the Dionysian which commanded his attention in the first place. If the categorial language of particular entities—the tradition of Aristotelian metaphysics, which extends through Kant and Schopenhauer—seemed inadequate to this task, so did the restriction to entirely subjective mental states.

Perhaps Nietzsche's most successful early attempt to form a positive discourse for the Dionysian resulted from his reflections on Schiller's theories of poetry and drama.[15] It was Schiller who first emphasized the intentional and relational properties of sentiment, and understood the affective register of feelings or moods (*Stimmungen*) according to the notion, borrowed from music, of tone, tonality, or better, of attunement (*Stimmung*): i.e., according to an external and pervasive field, one accessible to a plurality of subjects and which embraced a collateral space. Affectivity, in this sense, was not to be thought of as a strictly immanent datum of subjectivity, entirely self-enclosed and discrete. Such a view, for Schiller, testified more to a considered solipsism than to one's ordinary experience. The reflection on Schiller's understanding of sentiment enabled Nietzsche to resolve two closely related problems which seemed to stand in the way of a positive discourse about the Dionysian: the first concerned the curious status of Archilochus in relation to the evolution of poetry and, ultimately, to tragic drama. The second was to account for the striking fact of ecstasy, which in part defines the very occurrence of Dionysian states.

According to what was said of him in ancient times, and by the few remaining fragments of his work, we know that Archilochus, the traditional originator of lyric poetry, was of a singularly Dionysian temperament. He both composed and led Dionysian choruses, and his work was unique in its passionate intensity, especially in its extremely coarse eroticism. Doubtless these uniquely un-Homeric qualities explained why his contemporaries denounced him. Heraclitus, Critias, and Pindar in particular excoriated him for his rejection of the aristocratic-Homeric ideals, ideals Archilochus himself remarked were of little interest, save perhaps, for those who preferred to die pointlessly in battle. Nevertheless, Nietzsche observed, this bastard son of a Parian slave woman—ever intoxicated and often savage—was given a status equal to that of the Apollonian Homer:

> The ancients . . . place the faces of Homer and Archilo-
> chus, as the forefathers and torchbearers of Greek
> poetry, side by side on gems, sculptures, etc., with a sure
> feeling that consideration should be given only to these
> two, equally completely original, from whom a stream
> of fire flows over the whole of later Greek history.[16]

Why this should have been the case is problematic. If traditionally Archilochus was seen as merely a "subjective" poet, why should this one individual's rather sordid testimony be of any consequence at all? Nietzsche's response was that in lyric poetry (especially in view of its association with music), the important consideration was not so much the communication of a personal or subjective experience as such—for however intriguing that might have been, no one is entirely incapable of it—but, rather, the creation of a "musical mood."

When Nietzsche introduced the term in Chapter 5 of *The Birth of Tragedy,* he recalled his indebtedness to Schiller's analysis of the complex character of mood, and went on to say that the *Stimmung* or the *musikalische Stimmung* is not simply the objective re-presentation of an internal mental state: "The sphere of poetry does not lie outside the world as a fantastic impossibility spawned by a poet's brain."[17] If it were only this, the musical mood would be merely a particular image produced by the individual poet. In that case, the mood character of lyric poetry—itself tonal, musical—would be but another example of Apollonian "objective" art, the art of discrete representational images and concepts. But if the "musical mood" of lyric poetry was neither Apollonian (as the objective image series of epic poetry) nor simply a subjective testament, what then was it, and why should it have been capable of igniting the world of tragic drama? But if mood is understood, following Nietzsche's reading of Schiller, as relational attunement, it follows that the mood state is *all pervasive* for one's own experience: it is neither simply "within" nor "without," neither "subjective" nor "objective" in the strict sense. Rather, and because of its uniquely experienced status, it appears suffusive, elemental, nonlocalizable, or as Nietzsche remarked, "indecomposable"—as the fog inhabits the night, as the presence of anxiety. Understood from this perspective, mood lends a tonality to all things in its field, including the poet himself. Thus, the lyrical experience and the lyrical re-creation of the mood, were quite literally ecstatic: as such the mood dispossessed the poet of his "own" subjectivity, his own "I" or ego. What was given to and by the lyric poet, then, was the uniquely Dionysian state of disindividuation. As Nietzsche remarked, "The artist has already surrendered his subjectivity in the Dionysian process," and he now feels an "identity with the heart of the world"—he experiences the world as his "primordial home" (*Urheimat*).

By providing the direct and indirect sources of affective excitation, by providing the somatic and psychological grounds of this elevated mood, by providing an object for it as well—the world under the image of the god Dionysus—and by investing it with the aim of an ecstatic instinctual satisfaction, Archilochus effectively recreated this heightened mood in his audience. And by this accomplishment, by becoming what Nietzsche termed a "world poet," Archilochus inaugurated the tradition of tragic drama itself.

Nietzsche devoted a large part of his early writings to analyzing these constitutive elements of mood (most notably, perhaps, the background phenomena of pain and what he termed musical "dissonance"), of the poetic and tragic re-creation of heightened affectivity; his analysis was nonetheless meant to be historically accurate, since the deployment of affective states formed the very "subsoil" of Greek cultural and political life.[18] The entire question of the Dionysian, then, was also a historical issue. And, again, it was the appearance of Archilochus which at once broadened the issue and suggested its resolution. For Nietzsche, the obvious fact was that the ecstatic states initially supposed a repressive order—"a military encampment of the Apollonian, . . . encompassed with bulwarks"—which, in turn, was dynamically bound to the conditions of distress, poverty, and warfare that characterized the emergence of Doric culture from the late Archaic period. Foreshadowing the demise of the *kaloi kagathoi,* as Nietzsche would later describe it in *The Genealogy of Morals,* Archilochus (himself the progeny of an Ionian slave) demonstrated a vital truth to the disaffected *hoi polloi:* that the Apollonian individual was *only* a pretense, an aristocratic construct of Homeric culture. Moreover, when enacted as a regulated and regulative form of life, this pretense led nowhere but to the grave, an unhappy one at that. Thus, the generation of the heightened mood ultimately produced an entirely new *subject.*[19] Again, this was effectively realized in the Dionysian cult ritual by (1) intensifying the source and variety of instinctual excitation; (2) transferring the instinctual object to the world of Dionysian intensities and images; (3) fundamentally altering the aim of these long-governed and strictly codified instincts: the rather austere and fearful stability of a long-forgotten Ilium was replaced by the prospect of a veritably orgiastic fulfillment.[20] Through the expediency of intensification and decodification, one would be *literally*—if only briefly—reborn, as had the mythological Dionysus. Nietzsche went on to argue (in Chapter 23 of *The Birth of Tragedy*) that the seemingly magical properties of this *ecstasis* or *dispossession* would be retained in classical tragedy itself, and be governed in turn, by the effective orchestration of audience transferrence: i.e., the audience's ability to transfer the general mythological content onto the specific figure of the masked actor. This process was aided and intensified, of course, by the chants of the dithyrambic chorus and by the accompanying instrumentation.[21] Likewise, this ecstatic state would be further enhanced by the dramatist's use of rhetorical condensation, his capacity to portray convincingly the actor's epic pronouncements as "image sparks" of a reality more expansive than that of his own subjectivity.

Dionysian discourse ultimately concerns this state of dispossession or what Nietzsche generally termed, the "collapse" or "destruction" of individuation: disindividuation. If this discourse often appears inadequate to its subject matter, as Nietzsche frequently acknowledged, this was in part due to the generality of his thematic concerns in *The Birth of Tragedy*, and in part to the novelty of his own analysis—in addition to the infusion of a borrowed vocabulary. Since the Dionysian state of ecstasy is the disruption of ego identity, of *individual* existence *per se*, to speak of it in positive terms at all is exceedingly problematic. Yet when Nietzsche attempted to articulate it, to address it descriptively, he often referred to it as *primal*, as prior to the state of individuation, or even, as more *natural* than the Apollonian state. If such terms seem paradoxically romantic or Schopenhauerian, we should recall that the issue for Nietzsche was the very constitution of the subject *as* an individual, as well as the intensely experienced world given *to* the individual. In the Dionysian state, one is dispossessed of all that renders the individual a singular and distinctive subject in the first place: the specific concatenation of character, personality, tastes, fears, expectations, reflection, and values. The Apollonian *begins* here, with the ordering, selection, and elevation of certain dispositions, with the idealization of particular values and judgments, and casts these forth as unified and exemplary images for the purpose of defining and preserving the individual *as* a discrete individual. In this sense, the Apollonian analogy of the "dream state" corresponds to the idealized elements of a prescriptive code, one that constitutes the individual and preserves him as such within a society. The Dionysian state, aptly described as "intoxication," would thus correspond to a suspension, a "decodification" of these individually and socially sanctioned codes.

Dionysian priority, finally, is neither metaphysical (noumenal), nor representational (*eikastic*), nor productive (*poieic*). Rather, it is an analytical priority: it testifies to the always present instinctual sources of human behavior which, in the absence of particular, individual, and categorial determination, can but weakly be termed polymorphous, undirected, and nonspecific. This state carries with it, Nietzsche insisted, the element of *alogia*, what is unmeasured or unproportioned, what escapes form and determination.[22] By the same account, the Dionysian *world* is said to be more *natural*, but only in the sense that nature as a whole is more extensive than the individuating and possessive dream image would have us believe: it has to do with that undiminished state of existence upon which forms are enacted, codes imposed, and specific goals wrought. As the intentional correlate to the Dionysian state of ecstasy, it is a world of proximate surfaces, of cathected intensities and forces—everywhere immediate, experienced without restraint, proportion, or prescription. This is why the Dionysian voice, which spoke through tragic drama, was perhaps more of a cry, a lament, a song of joy or praise, than a discourse—properly speaking. Consequently, it was never simply "true," nor simply opposed to a "false" discourse of Apollo.

SUNY-Stony Brook

NOTES

1   Paul de Man, "Genesis and Genealogy in Nietzsche's *The Birth of Tragedy*," *Diacritics,* Winter 1972, p. 52. See also his "Nietzsche's Theory of Rhetoric," *Symposium,* Spring 1974, and "Action and Identity," *Yale French Studies,* No. 52, 1975.

2   Carol Jacobs, *The Dissimulating Harmony* (Baltimore: The Johns Hopkins Univ. Press, 1978), pp. 21-22.

3   Paul Bové, "Introduction: Nietzsche's *Use and Abuse of History* and the Problems of Revision," *boundary 2,* VII, No. 2 (Winter 1979), pp. 1-15.

4   De Man, "Genesis and Genealogy," pp. 47-48.

5   De Man, "Genesis and Genealogy," p. 49.

6   Kant, *Critique of Pure Reason,* tr. Norman Kemp Smith (New York: St. Martins Press, 1965), A 259/B 315. Note that, in the passage quoted above from "Genesis and Genealogy," de Man makes exactly the same kind of representationalist demand: "All appearance, as the concept implies, is appearance of something that, in the last analysis, no longer seems to be but actually is. This 'something' can only be Dionysus," i.e., the "antithesis" of all appearance, the noumenal realm.

7   Kant, *Critique of Pure Reason,* A 268/B 314.

8   Kant, *Critique of Pure Reason,* A 256/B 311.

9   "Some Reflections on the Antithesis of Thing-in-Itself and Phenomenon," in *Philosophy of Schopenhauer,* tr. B. Bax and B. Saunders, (New York: Tudor, 1936), p. 255.

10   A. Schopenhauer, *The World as Will and Idea,* III Vols., tr. R. B. Haldane and J. Kemp (London: Routledge & Kegan Paul, 1883), Vol. II, pp. 404-5 (hereafter cited as *WWI*).

11   *The World as Will and Idea,* I, p. 142. See also, p. 136: "We shall judge of all objects which are not our bodies . . . according to the analogy of our own bodies, and shall therefore *assume* that as in one aspect they are idea . . . so in another aspect, *what remains of objects when we set aside their existence as idea* of the subject, *must* in its inner nature *be the same* as that in us which we call *will.* For what other kind of existence or reality would we *attribute* to the rest of the material world?" (emphasis added).

12   Nietzsche, *The Birth of Tragedy,* tr. W. Kaufmann (New York: Vintage, 1967), p. 24. *Werke: Kritische Gesamtausgabe,* ed. G. Colli and M. Montinari (Berlin: De Gruyter, 1967ff.), *Abt.* III, *Bd.* I, pp. 13-14 (hereafter cited as *BT* and KGW respectively).

13   For a discussion of the "popular" and "epidemic" aspects of these expressions, see his "Dionysian Worldview," *KGW,* III / 2, 43-69, and the drafts from Autumn 1869—Spring 1870, esp. P I 15.

14   Shortly after the publication of BT, in 1872, Nietzsche would admonish himself for still retaining this technical vocabulary. See, e.g., "The Philosopher: Reflections on the Struggle between Art and Knowledge," in *Philosophy and Truth,* tr. D. Breazeale (New Jersey: Humanities Press, 1979), pp. 1-58. H.J. Mette, *"Sachlicher Vorbericht"* to Vol. I of *KGW,* pp. xxi-cxxvi, esp. # 163. See also, *KGW,* III / 3, pp. 206-214. (7[135-173]).

15   *KGW,* III / 3, pp. 230-31 (8[7]).

16   *BT,* 5, p. 46; *KGW,* III / 1, p. 38.

17   *BT,* 8, p. 61; *KGW,* III / 1, p. 54.

18   See esp., "The Greek State," *KGW,* III / 2, pp. 258-71, and "Homer's Contest," *KGW,* pp. 277-86.

19   *KGW,* III / 3, pp. 230-31 (8[7]).

20   On the Dionysian veneration of Sexuality, see *Twilight of the Idols,* "What I Owe to the Ancients," section 4.

21   The intoxicating effects of these instruments on the Greek populace is sufficiently witnessed by Aristotle's strenuous rejection of them in the *Politics.* For Aristotle, the flute especially (as well as the zither, sackbut, heptagon, etc.), serves only the "vulgar pleasure" of the audience. "It does not express a state of character, but rather a mood of religious excitement; and it should therefore be used on those occasions when the effect to be produced on the audience is the release of emotion, and not instruction." Significantly, "flute playing prevents the player from using the voice." He continued, citing an ancient myth: "Athena, it tells us, invented the flute—and then threw it away." Aristotle's explanation? "She threw it away because the study of flute playing has nothing to do with the mind." *The Politics of Aristotle,* Book VIII, Ch. 6, Eng. tr. by E. Barker (New York: Oxford Univ. Press, 1962), pp. 348-49.

22   *KGW,* III / 3, p. 145 (7[2]).

Oedipus as Hero:
Family and Family Metaphors in Nietzsche

Tracy B. Strong

> The past is a nightmare from which I am trying to awake.
>
> James Joyce, *Ulysses,* Chap. 2

> If one does not have a good father,
> one must provide oneself with one.
>
> *Human-all-too-human,* Vol. I, ¶381

It is only a slight exaggeration to characterize political and social thought since Hegel as a series of attempts to come to terms with the manner in which the past impressed itself on the present. The past was a nightmare: it restricted autonomy, relativized moral choice, blinded the will. For most liberal thought, the hope of progress required that one live only in the present and future, never in what one had been. Marx hoped that praxis would sift historical reality and determine what would remain actual and what would be confined to the ash heap. For John Stuart Mill, freedom of choice itself encouraged the development of man "as a progressive social being" and made it possible to escape the threats to authenticity by which the modern world bound humans to the historical. Burckhardt held up the ahistorical vision of an historical period; the civilizations of the Renaissance and of Greece were at least dreams that things did not have to be as they were.

Clearly this list can go on; redemption from time past, whether by denial or acquiescence, was a central concern of those who thought seriously about the world. Clearly, also, there are a number of different ways to endeavor to avoid being time's fool. In this paper I am concerned, in particular, with that understanding of the past made in metaphors drawn from the family. A number of writers share this view: I shall be concerned here with Nietzsche, but obviously Freud, Wittgenstein, possibly Spengler, share this position. For all of these men, human beings are, so to speak, inevitably and forever the children of their parents; their past lives on in them without dynamics which might enable them to escape from it. In this understanding, human beings, indeed societies also, are the embodiment, a making-flesh, of that which has not died but continues to live on and grow as who they are. All that still was, now is: the adverbial paradox points at the implicit despair in the possibility of overcoming time. From this perspective, no matter what shape our lives may take, individually or collectively, we are still caught in and partake of who we were, of our genealogy.

Clearly there are other metaphors available: those who, with Marx, take courage from history find that the bourgeois world contains contradictions which, at the proper and appointed historical moment, will sunder the integument which holds that world together. From contradictions, a new world will emerge. However, for those to whom the family remains a fundamental metaphor of social existence, nothing radically new can result: no matter what one does, one will always be the child of one's parents.[1]

For Nietzsche, we are caught in a great and given historical family. The genealogy of slave morality informs us that a particular way of structuring existence has come to dominate in the West over the last twenty-five hundred years, to the extent that there is now simply no other alternative. As he remarks in the end of *On the Genealogy of Morals,* the "ascetic ideal," itself the last stage of slave morality, has triumphed "out of lack of opposition."[2] As is known, Nietzsche contends that there is something radically and inalterably wrong with our genealogy and that that error will not in and of itself lead to a deep alteration of existence. In this he differs from Marx: it is not in the nature of flies to find the way out of the fly bottle.

II

The year 1888 marks the last year of Nietzsche's sanity. Its conclusion accomplishes the last of the six-year cycles which he sees making important changes in his life.[3] He has now, he indicates, completed the preliminaries necessary for his philosophy; with the ground sufficiently cleared, he will proceed to those writings which will "revolutionize the world." Accordingly, at the beginning of 1888, he writes to many friends that he is finally ready to begin his major work.[4] By the end of the year, he sends a postcard to Peter Gast proclaiming a good news: "The world is transfigured: sing me a new song." The theme of most of the letters from this last year is of a final break with his past: now he is himself and has accomplished his own person. Thus, to Paul Deussen, on the third of January: "Basically, as concerns me, all is now epochmaking; my entire past (*Bisher*) crumbles away from me and when I add up what I have done in the last two years it appears to me now as always one and the same piece of work: to isolate myself from my past, to cut the umbilical cord between me and it." The theme is of a new birth or a re-birth, of separation from his parents, a theme repeated in a letter to the Danish critic Brandes on February 19th, where Nietzsche indicates that he has "survived himself." All this is further linked to the repeated claim, such as the one he had made a week earlier to von Seydlitz, that he was the "first philosopher of this era" and stood "ominously between two millenia."[5] That which he was is dead; that which he is lives on.

Yet this claim is clearly a problem.[6] To Nietzsche it does not appear that one should be able to get rid of one's past, to be self-engendered. For, if one *is* because of one's past,[7] then everything one does to break the chains of that past must itself be subject to that past and must thus merely reinforce it in increasingly subtle and powerful ways. Kant establishes in the *Critique of Pure Reason* that no matter what one thinks, being human, one always thinks in the same structure. For Kant, there is no choice but to accept the limitations of reason as the sign of the value of one's humanity, rather than of its failings. But since for Nietzsche humanity itself is profoundly flawed in its universal slave morality, there is no solace to be gained from the mere acknowledgement of one's past. How then can Nietzsche claim to have broken the hold of his past? How can he claim to inaugurate a new philosophical era? This is, one might say, a question about the possibility of revolutionary politics; what would it mean to be made new?

Nietzsche's judgment of a philosophy is also always a judgment of the philosopher. Any form of thought which excludes itself from its own critique is automatically suspect. To such thinkers, Nietzsche's first question is what one might call therapeutic: why is it that the philosopher in question seeks to protect himself in an uncriticized redoubt? Hence we find Nietzsche's well-known attacks on Socrates' physiognomy, as if he had to compensate for his ugliness; the accusation that Kant was morally deficient and the attacks on Descartes's cowardice. Nietzsche will even profess a preference for thinkers with "small ears" rather than "large" ones.[8] All of this should seem strange, but it is not. If one cannot separate the doer from the deed, as Nietzsche argues in the *Genealogy of Morals,* then the judgment about one is the judgment about the other. No acts are immaculate.

313

I should note here that Nietzsche's position is not a kind of ideological reductionism: Nietzsche is not saying that it all comes *down* to a matter of physiology. He is rather saying something which we have known well at least since Freud. The deep meaning of the Socratic imperative to self-knowledge is that what a person says and does has something to do with who a person is. This is not immediately a judgment on the value of the act or person, but any such judgment will be a judgment about both.

With this in mind, it is only natural to turn the focus of Nietzsche's understanding of the past on Nietzsche himself, and to investigate Nietzsche's thought by investigating Nietzsche. Nietzsche himself does this. I am here in part merely explicating his own self-critique, for his self-critiques are an integral part of his thought. In these terms, who Nietzsche *is* becomes important, for it has something to do with what Nietzsche *says*. And it is all the more important in that the central investigatory concepts in Nietzsche are clearly those which relate to the general problem of identity, self, and family.

Consider for a moment "genealogy," the most basic conceptual tool of his general investigations into morality and Western culture. The approach is derived from Kantian premises, especially the use of the transcendental deduction. Like Kant, Nietzsche is trying to figure out how a given act or configuration of acts is (historically) possible. His claim is that Western morality forms a coherent structure which, through a set of comprehensible transformations, has assumed various forms (*ressentiment,* bad conscience, etc.). As with Freud's understanding of neurosis, the idea is that various facets of a person's behavior can be understood in terms of a common structure, itself implanted at an early age.

I have discussed the notion of genealogy in more detail elsewhere.[9] Such an understanding necessarily implies that radical change will not, in and of itself, come from willful human action, at least not as long as that action is *itself* a manifestation of the structure which had previously governed.[10] Nietzsche speaks, for instance, of "the strange family resemblance of all Indian, German and Greek philosophizing" and attributes this to the "unconscious domination by and orientation to similar grammatical functions."[11] We are caught, one might say, in a family portrait: to do anything, we must do something which we can do, yet everything we can do is structured by who we are and what we have been. Our actions will then reflect and make manifest that structure of ourselves.

Put it another way: one is always the child of one's parents. In *The Gay Science,* Nietzsche is involved in a discussion of attitudes and approaches to knowledge. He speaks of the sons of registrars and clerks. Should they turn to scholarship, they would be philosophers "who in the end are only systematizing minds—in them the form of the fathers' work has become content. One is not without retribution (*ungestraft*) the child of one's parents."[12] Nietzsche goes on to speak of other sons, of which

314

the following is of importance here: "One recognizes the sons of protestant ministers and teachers by their naive assurance; as scholars, they already take their subject matter as proven, if only it is given from the heart and with warmth: at bottom, they are thereby convinced that they are believed." In other words, insofar as Nietzsche is a scholar (*ein Gelehrter*), he remains the child of his parents. We know that he was a scholar and that he wished to leave that life. The scholar in fact "always has something of the old maid," in that (s)he is "conversant with neither of the two most valuable functions" of a human being, "to procreate and to give birth."[13] As Nietzsche develops this section of *Beyond Good and Evil,* we find that scholarship, even philosophy which is "scholarly," will be only a "mirror," at most a great act of criticism. Nietzsche sees the creative alternative as a form of political change, "a compulsion to great politics."[14] Nietzsche is clear that not *any* politics will do; but some sort of "political" change will be required to overcome the "naivete" which he inherits as his father's son. The first thing that Zarathustra comes to realize on his return from the mountains is that speaking from the heart, even to a willing audience, will not be effective.[15]

"One is not without retribution the child of one's parents." We know that Nietzsche was the son of a Protestant minister and that his father died during his fourth year. We know also that Nietzsche spent much of his life proclaiming the futility of thinking that one might escape from one's genealogy. *Zarathustra* is filled with passages that praise those who would "go under," that is, who accept their genealogy for what it is, understand it to be flawed and thereby wish only to perish. As early as 1862, in an essay on "Freedom of the Will and Fate," Nietzsche writes that "The doings of a person (*Tätigkeit des Menschen*) . . . do not start with birth, but already in the embryo—who can know here—already in parents and ancestors."[16] In *Beyond Good and Evil* he describes as "the problem of race" that "One cannot wipe away from the soul of a man that which his ancestors liked most to do and did constantly. . . . It is simply not possible that a man would *not* have the qualities and preferences of his parents and ancestors in his body."[17] We know finally that at the end of his life, pressing time and in haste, Nietzsche wrote as his last work an autobiography, which he entitled with the shout by which Pilate had presented Christ to the crowd, *Ecce Homo.* Family metaphors and concern with how his own family affects his self in his vocation run throughout Nietzsche's work. By an examination of these metaphors and their use, it is possible to cast light only on what Nietzsche thought of the power and strength and effect of the family structure. Unpacking these metaphors will illuminate how Nietzsche thinks that he himself has at least partially escaped family and, in becoming who he is, has finally become his own person, able to be a *true* philosopher for the modern world.

In 1888 Nietzsche publishes six books. This output is much greater than that of the previous years, itself already impressive. Furthermore, Nietzsche projects a number of major works, which he says will in two years revolutionize the world. He writes to Brandes, as well as to some others, that he is making arrangements to have his new works translated into six languages with a first edition of "c/ one million copies." Nietzsche, of course, did not accomplish this task; in Turin, in early January 1889, he becomes insane: nothing of what is recorded of what he said in the last ten years of his life, either under treatment or under the supervision of his sister, appears to have more than clinical interest.[18] The works of 1888 look in two directions. Some of them look to the past. They come to terms with Wagner, the man he claims most to have loved, or with his own past and influences on him, especially in *The Twilight of the Idols.* Others look to the future: the *Antichrist* is subtitled the "First book of the revaluation of all values" and through its "destruction" of Christianity is held to lay the way for a philosophy of the future. Lastly, looking to the present in this year of summing up and anticipation, he writes *Ecce Homo,* an autobiography subtitled "How one becomes who one is." This remains unpublished until 1905. It is to the autobiography that I first turn to investigate Nietzsche's understanding of the family and of his family in relation to his work.

Ecce Homo represents for Nietzsche an account of what one might call his life project until that point. It is an explicit claim to have accomplished the task he had set out for himself some twenty-six years earlier. He wrote then: "If we wish to contemplate Christian teaching and church history with a free and impartial glance, then we must completely articulate many positions contrary to usual ideas. However, as we are restricted from our youngest days by the yoke of conventionality and prejudice and constrained by the impression our childhood makes on the natural development of our self (*Geistes*), we believe it almost to be an indecency (*Vergehen*) to have to consider if we have chosen a freer position, so as then to be able to pronounce an impartial and appropriate judgment on religion and Christianity. Such a task is not the work of a few weeks, but of a life."[19] This is, even though in youthful formulation here, the task to which he set himself. Already at eighteen, his understanding of his vocation was complex. The endeavor that is his life turns out perhaps to be more complicated than he understood then; but *Ecce Homo* must be read as the *comte rendu* of what he sees himself as having accomplished, not "just" in terms of his writing, but also in terms of his self. He is ready to move beyond the scholar and the critic, "to become who he is," to be the person whom he calls "the first philosopher of the modern age."

I propose then that one should read *Ecce Homo* precisely as what Nietzsche says it to be, as an autobiography. As always, as I hope to show, if one takes Nietzsche on his own terms, one sees him both more clearly and more interestingly.

The discussion in the "Preface" to *Ecce Homo* focuses around two themes: the achievement of who one is and the loss of what we might call the parental or authority image. The self achieved is to stand immediately in the present; it is sufficient unto itself, not shaped by its ancestors. To achieve this involves, Nietzsche continues on, selectivity from what one has done. The formal epigraph to *Ecce Homo* is an exceptionally beautiful formulation:

> On this perfected day, when everything ripens and not only the grape turns brown, a look of the sun just fell on my life: I looked backwards, I looked forwards, I never saw so many and so good things at once. It was not in vain that I buried my forty-fourth year today: I had the right to bury it—what was life in it is saved, is immortal.[20]

Nietzsche then lists three books, "presents of this last quarter" of 1888 and concludes the epigraph:

> How could I not be thankful to my entire life? And so I tell myself my life.

He is, now, immortal; his life is in recurrence, like a story told again for the first time. What follows then, one might say, must be the account of a sort of rebirth: whatever in "himself" is preserved and made eternal, reborn, as are gods; the rest has perished. The obvious question is how this extraordinary process has come to be; it is precisely to that consideration that Nietzsche turns in the opening section of the book.

> The good fortune of my existence (*Daseins*), perhaps its uniqueness, lies in its frailty: to express it in the form of a riddle, as my father I have already died, as my mother I still live and become old. This double descent, at once from the highest and the lowest rung on the ladder of life, at the same time *decadent* and beginning—this, if anything at all, explains the neutrality, that freedom from partiality in relation to the general problem (*Gesammtproblem*) of life, that characterizes me. For signs of rise and decline I have perhaps a better scent than any one has had until now; for this I am the teacher *par excellence*—I know both, I am both.

The passage proceeds immediately to a discussion of the death of his father.

The section is perhaps purposively dark with mystery, but one should not lose sense of its conventionality. This is, after all, his autobiography, in which he should tell us who he is. The usual way of beginning an autobiography would be with a description of one's birth and of one's parents. In fact, this is precisely what Nietzsche does and proceeds from there to a discussion of his childhood, the death of his father, and on to most of the events that mark the generality of any life.

There is, of course, more. In this opening section he also claims to know and be both his (dead) father and (alive) mother. He links decadence and death to the father and beginning and growth to the mother. The whole passage in fact seems to be self-consciously written to call Oedipus to mind. Oedipus, too, had a most ambiguous relation to his father; indeed, it is the fact that he was *not* his father which stood as the source to all of his problems. The question of identity by which Nietzsche introduces himself here is posed as a riddle, as was that of the Sphinx to Oedipus. However, though we cannot help but think of Oedipus here, there is an important difference. The Sphinx had by its riddle queried Oedipus only about the truth of man's relation to nature and not about man's relation to himself. In *Ecce Homo* Nietzsche plays his own Sphinx to himself,[21] no longer confronting the differentiation of man from nature, but of himself from men. This paragraph then can be seen as representing the step which Nietzsche takes "beyond" the Greeks, responding here to his oft expressed imperative to surpass even them.

Nietzsche associates himself with the classic birth of the hero.[22] Heroes are generally without parents, or at least without normal parents. Furthermore, they must die, in order to be reborn. Thus, in his autobiography, like a hero Nietzsche sees himself as already dead. He is reborn autochthonically without parentage, or as his own parent. Such a person could truly be the beginning of a world, since he would share nothing with the past.

In a preliminary way, let us notice here that the hero is then a person who is not subject to the classical Oedipal situation as described by (say) Freud. The hero has no known father, and generally no mother, or at least none of the usual sort. Thus he simply never encounters what the child with parents, with a past, must do to achieve a resolution of the psychological situation in which he finds himself. The hero constitutes an annihilation of the entire Oedipal situation; somehow, if he were subject to it, he would not be able to accomplish his task. At the writing of *Ecce Homo,* Nietzsche thinks himself the person who can accomplish his (own) task. But he has already gone the hero one better. He is not simply in the position of not having a father, as is the hero, but he is already dead *as* his father. Like Tiresias he has had both sexes.

Thus the deeper significance of the epigraph cited above is that by this day, his forty-fourth birthday, he marks the achievement of a self which is purely his and is no longer part of his family. He claims to have annihilated his genealogy. It is worth noting here the "decree against Christianity" which he appends to the *Druckmanuscript* of *Der Antichrist* is dated to mark the inauguration of a new era; it is "promulgated on the day of salvation, on the first day of year One."[23] Furthermore, in one of the last pieces of work—a poem appended to *Nietzsche Contra Wagner* on January 2, 1889, we find:

> Who is father and mother to me?
> Is not Prince Abundance father
> To me and quiet laughter mother?[24]

Here and elsewhere Nietzsche refers to himself as born posthumously.[25] He has died to his self and is reborn as himself.

One is wrongly tempted here to begin by making an appeal to mythology and metaphor. It is more important to see precisely that Nietzsche is discussing relations to parents and why it was so important that he deal with them in the manner which he claims to have. Only then will we be able to arrive at an explanation of precisely what it means to escape one's genealogy, of how it was possible and why it was necessary to get rid of and annihilate one's family. Why is the family, or the family situation, such a problem for Nietzsche? Why does it provide the metaphor for that which he sought to escape and from which he hoped to show the way out for others?

III

If there is validity to Freud's claim about the universality of the Oedipal situation, it comes preliminarily not in the fact that every son wishes his father dead and his mother his, but in the fact that the male child, and in fact all children, generally spend most of their early years in a given sociopsychological structure. There is (almost) always the trio father--mother-child. Inevitably, we are all children of our parents. Who we are, therefore, is formed in relation to the particular *structure* which we call the family. Freud's claim about the Oedipal situation was that the male child is put into an impossible position: he must both get rid of (the) father and be (the) father. Yet, if it was important to get rid of (the) father, then becoming (the) father must in itself be threatening. The vocabulary was not available to Freud, but we might call this now a schizophrenicgenic situation: the child is called by his sociopsychological environment to act in two incompatible yet equally necessary ways. The central recognition of Freud's late work, such as *Civilization and its Discontents* and the essay "Analysis Terminable and Interminable,"[26] is that the neurotic resolution of the above situation appears as the only alternative to schizophrenia. Better unhappiness than madness, one might say.[27]

The *Genealogy of Morals* is Nietzsche's account of this situation.[28] Nietzsche argues that slave morality requires that one produce a source of suffering in order to make possible a conclusion as to who one is.

Thus, though one tries to account for and escape from suffering, since the structure of one's self is dependent on that suffering, one finally arrives at a situation where one generates one's own suffering. In Freudian terms, while remaining the son, one takes on the father too: at this point, the dynamic is both self-sustaining and self-destructive. Such, according to Nietzsche and to Freud, is the moving logic of civilization, which appears universally necessary to Freud and historically inevitable to Nietzsche.

I am here pointing to a structural similarity between the diagnoses in the *Genealogy of Morals* and the Oedipal situation. What does it, in fact, mean to "resolve" the Oedipal situation? The son, confronted with his mother and father is faced with an apparently irresolvable situation. If, on the one hand, he achieves the object of his desire—cathexis on the mother—he must kill the father. Yet, this must result in a death of the self, or at least a strong threat to self, since to obtain the mother he must be (like the) father.[29] Yet, if the (male) child were to "win" the Oedipal conflict, he would be maintained in a permanent stage of childhood and schizophrenia. Thus, for Freud, as I have indicated above, the price for avoiding schizophrenia was neurosis—civilization *must* have its discontents. Freud implies, though never completely explicitly argues, that we *should* pay the price for avoiding schizophrenia. Faced with irreconcilable objects of desire, individuals cannot resolve the situation directly; therefore they postpone and repress their desires, and the energy which was originally parentally directed comes out in other areas. Eventually, as they have children, the whole process starts over again in relation to those children. The alternative of neurosis and schizophrenia is again proposed and again resolved in favor of the former.[30]

I do not want to be taken here to be giving a "Freudian" analysis of Nietzsche's childhood. I am arguing that the categories by which Freud analyzed the Oedipal situation are useful clarifications of the dynamics of genealogy. They cast light on the riddle which opens Nietzsche's autobiography. Nietzsche does intend to call our attention to Oedipus and to the figure of the hero: Nietzsche is a man who began his public career by trying to figure out the true identity of the hero in Greek tragedy. If we now turn to a reading of the *Oedipus Tyrannus,* additional clarifications may be found. In the *Tyrannus,* when Oedipus has his first suspicions that it may have been Laius whom he killed at the crossroads, he worries aloud to Jocasta, still, of course, without the suspicion that Laius was his father. Jocasta hastens to assure him and perhaps herself that even if the one guard who escaped changes his story from "many bandits" to "one bandit":

> He cannot make the death of Laius
> Accord with the saying of the oracle.
> For Loxias expressedly said that Laius
> Was doomed to die by my child; that child
> However shed no blood, *since he first perished himself.*[31]

What she is telling Oedipus is that he is already dead. Tiresias, in his first appearance, has already told Oedipus that this day he would be born and die. But if Oedipus is dramatically and ironically dead, who is he? Or more precisely, *who will he be?* The central fact about Oedipus' story is that it puts together the problem of self (who am I?) with the problem of parents (of whom am I the son?), and permits only *one* answer to those two questions.[32] And the answer is terrifying and clear. If Oedipus is to be *anyone* at all, he must be his own father (and therefore also his own patricide).

Being one's own father is recognized by the chorus as a terrible fate and productive only of unhappiness and suffering. The *Tyrannus* and the *Colonnus* study how men come to deal with unhappiness. At the end of the *Tyrannus,* "no man can be counted happy"—presumably no man who is what Oedipus is; but at the end of the *Colonnus* "all is ordered for the best" and the chorus glorifies the polis. We may take the ending of the *Colonnus* to be the claim that the *polis* is the solution to the problems of family.

Central here are the relations between self and polity. Over the developments of Sophocles' writing, there is a noticeable shift from the paternal tyranny of the beginning of the *Tyrannus* to the full polis of Athens in the *Colonnus.* Hannah Arendt has brilliantly argued that these plays show us that the only escape from the suffering of existence is to pay the price for politics, for the life with others as reciprocating individuals.[33] For this to be possible, Oedipus has both to give up his paternity of himself and his paternalistic rule of Thebes. The sufferers from the plague came to Oedipus explicitly as children. Politics, we might then say, as did Aristotle some years later, depends on being released from the family.

The problem, to put it crudely and enigmatically, is to avoid becoming your own father. If you become (the) father, you remain caught in the family tree. This may not be too bad if you have a good genealogy, but even then it will remain a vicious circle and merely a supportable compulsive repetition of the past. Oedipus shows us the curse and the suffering of genealogy; he is redeemed in the transformation of the world from the tyranny of Thebes to the polis of Athens. Indeed, we might remember also that Theseus too killed his own father. With this we return to Nietzsche. He argues in the *Birth of Tragedy* that it is precisely in the drama that the Greeks understand what it means to renew oneself as oneself and not as a mere repetition of the past. Tragedy, with its focus on the hero ensured by the chorus, is a natural subject for Nietzsche from his earliest writing. The *Birth of Tragedy* is, he writes in *Ecce Homo,* an "exceedingly strange" beginning. "I had *discovered* the only metaphor and equivalent for my experience which history had. . . ."[34] Nietzsche's concern in the *Birth* is a concrete formulation of the experience which he knows himself to be going or to have gone through. It is thus central that he turns to Greece rather than to Christianity, for in the latter one dies for the father in order to be reborn *in* the father, but not as oneself.

IV

Look then at Nietzsche's family and his understanding of it. He is born in 1844, on the 15th of October. He is the first child of a Lutheran pastor; both Nietzsche's parents are themselves children of pastors. In 1846 a sister is born, and in 1848 a brother; in 1849 his father dies. In 1850 his brother dies suddenly, and the family moves from the small Saxon village of Röcken to the town of Naumburg. At age twelve he suffers from headaches and eyestrain; two years later, he obtains a scholarship to a first-rate boarding school at Pforta.

We see in Nietzsche's life the occurrence of a situation not unlike the claim at the beginning of his autobiography to be dead as his father and to live on and grow as his mother. Certainly, his father died no later than the first beginnings of the Oedipal period, during that time when the identification with the father figure may not yet have resulted in any conflict which required resolution. It is also clear that Nietzsche was raised by women; an aunt joined his mother after the move to Naumburg. This, however, has somewhat different significance for him than one might have otherwise thought. He makes a particular identification with his father in the first part of *Ecce Homo:* His father "dies at 36," the age which Nietzsche identifies as his own lowest point. It is at this age that Nietzsche writes "The Wanderer and his Shadow," the first part of the second volume of *Human-all-too-human.* He refers to himself there as but a shadow; he has given up his Basel professorship, feels abandoned by the Wagners (and is), and writes to Malwida von Meyensburg that he "thirsts after the end" (January 14, 1880) and to Overbeck that he contemplates "the solution of a pistol."

Presumably, this is a death for Nietzsche: he does not expect to survive. At the lowest point in 1880 he begins anew: *Dawn of Day* is his next book. As his father, he sees himself as having died at the end of the decade; the years following are a slow, often painful, rebirth. Here his comments on his father's character are importantly revelatory of the sort of relationship which Nietzsche felt he had to resolve. His father was "delicate, kind, and morbid, as a being destined to merely pass by—more a gracious memory of life than life itself." Later on in the original section 3 of *Ecce Homo* (about which see below) he claims that he holds it "a great privilege to have had such a father; the farmers before whom he preached . . . said that an angel must have looked as he did." In sum, the general picture which Nietzsche gives us of his father is of a perfect being, not really of this earth and destined to move rapidly away from it. At age twelve, Nietzsche remembers his father as living a Christian life, "quietly, simply, but happily, . . . loved and respected" by all who knew him.[35] There is nowhere in his youthful writings (which date from age twelve on) anything which presents his father as other than wonderful and perfect, nor his home then as other than quiet, interesting and pleasant.

According to Nietzsche, his father becomes melancholic or mentally unwell (*gemütskrank*) in September 1848; this is diagnosed by a "famous physician" (Opolcer) as a "weakening of the brain."[36] His father suffers greatly, goes blind and eventually dies ten months later on the 27th of July, 1849. In his description of the burial, Nietzsche pays much attention to the music, the bells, and the sound of the organ. The death of his father is the subject of several descriptions in Nietzsche's early writings. Again and again, he returns to his *Lebenslauf,* as if to get clear the nature of his earliest days. By 1861 (he is 17) he is comparing his father's disease to that which afflicted the king.[37] He repeats again that year his claim that his father took suddenly sick and adds that there were no known causes.

Nietzsche gives two extended versions of the importance of his father's death. Associated with both of these accounts of that death is a dream which Nietzsche characterizes as "extraordinary." In the months following the death of his father, Nietzsche's younger brother takes sick—his mother claims from "pains in the teeth"—and dies suddenly. Shortly before, Nietzsche has a dream of which he gives later two extended versions, one at age fourteen and another at seventeen. In each account, he claims the dream to have been a premonition of the death of his brother. The dream, however, is clearly connected with the death of his father and may serve to illuminate what Nietzsche makes of his relation to that death. The first version:

> When one carries away the top of a tree, it becomes withered and bare and the birds leave the branches. Our family was bereft of its head, all joy flowed out of our hearts and deep sadness reigned in us. The wound was barely slightly healed, however, when new pain tore at us once more. At this time, I dreamed that I heard organ music in the church as if for a funeral. As I looked to see what the reason for it was, suddenly a grave stone lifted itself up and my father clad in burial dress stepped out of it. He hurried in to the church and soon returned with a small child in his arms. The tumulus opened, he stepped in and the top sank once more down on to the opening. Immediately, the organ sound ceased and I awoke.
>
> The day after that night young Joseph suddenly took sick with cramps and died in a few hours. Our pain was immense. My dream was entirely realized. The little body was lain in the arms of my father.[38]

Three years later Nietzsche takes up the dream again. He has in the interim several times picked up the theme of the loss of the top of the tree, and clearly associates the transfiguration of home, joy and peace into sorrow and pain with the death of his father. Though he confounds the two events, he also associates the loss of home with the loss of his father. (They did not in fact move to Naumburg until 1850, about a year after the death of his father.) Along these lines, Nietzsche's youthful poems are filled with references to the loss of *Heimat* (home).[39] From this time forth, he thinks of himself as *"ohne Heimat."*

In the second version of the dream, a number of details become more precise; they concern especially those of his activity in the dream and those of music. The change in focus is significant. I am concerned here, as is Pierre Klossowski,[40] not with the actual occurrence of this dream at age six, nor with its reality as a premonition. Rather, the elaborations of the dream over the two versions give an indication of the dream-work involved. We can learn what the dream was to Nietzsche's psyche. In the second version, Nietzsche repeats in a paragraph those characteristics of his father now familiar to us. He then proceeds to a couplet:

Ah, they have buried a good man
And he was more than that to me.

Some months after, a second unhappiness hit me of which I had a premonition in a dream. It seemed to me that I heard muffled organ sounds from the nearby church. Surprised, *I opened the window* which gave onto the church and the cemetery. The grave of my father opened, a white form climbed out and disappeared into the church. The dismal and disquieting sounds continued to ring out; the white shape reappeared, carrying something under the arm which I did not clearly recognize. The cover raised itself, the form sank into it, the organ was quiet—I awoke. The next morning my younger brother, a vivacious and gifted child, was overtaken with cramps and died in half an hour. He was buried directly *beside* the grave of my father.[41]

A number of things appear noteworthy. First, the second version seems clearly to benefit from details which Nietzsche must have gathered from his mother. The half-hour death time and the giftedness of the child are not likely to be part of the dream or the knowledge of a six-year-old. Secondly, the emphasis on the child is downplayed in the second version. The emphasis is more on Nietzsche himself. Though other details are much less distinct, the music is much more important in the second. (Here it is worth remembering that Nietzsche associated the sound of organ most centrally with the death of his father.) In both, the child is not in the

324

house but in the church. Lastly, the catalyst for the whole dream in both versions is the sound of the organ. It does not seem to me too much to conclude that the dream is more about Nietzsche than it is about a premonition of the death of his younger brother. Given that in the second version there is a parallel between the opening of the window and the opening of the grave, one suspects two things: first, that Nietzsche is trying to see his dead father; secondly, that because he is trying to see his father, his father carries him off. One should not seek to see one's father; if one does, one dies with him.

The death of the father is associated with music which in turn leads one to join the father. Thus Nietzsche is already dead in his father, but he has also joined his father and has in a certain sense become one with his father. *Therefore he does not need to replace his father with his mother,* which would be the standard resolution of the Oedipal situation. Instead, he becomes, as it were, his mother beside the father: It is thus, as both mother and himself, that he lives on and needs no parents other than himself to become who he is.[42]

This is the claim: the standard resolution of the Oedipal situation consists in adopting the paternal principle for oneself. This necessarily entraps one in a neurotic dilemma which Nietzsche, much as Freud, sees at the source of the discontents of civilization. One cannot be rid of what one has been. For Nietzsche, this discontent is somewhat more dangerous and less endurable than it is for Freud. The escape from the ascetic ideal which has no adversaries requires that one become one's own parents and that one die to one's own father and mother and engender oneself. That this is prompted by music gives us some insight into the initial attraction of the young scholar Nietzsche to the *Birth of Tragedy from the Spirit of Music.*

The dynamic which Nietzsche poses as a riddle at the beginning of his autobiography thus finds itself biographically explicated in the account which Nietzsche gives of his childhood dream. One way of expressing the significance of this dream is to say that it points to a radical rejection on Nietzsche's part of the psychological structures that characterize the most prevalent experience of the formation of the self. The self that Nietzsche becomes has escaped from the tyranny of the Oedipalized past.[43] Jacques Derrida, in his recent book on Nietzsche, argues that the originality of Nietzsche's philosophy lies precisely in the fact that Nietzsche's work is beholden to no source of meaning. "There is . . . no truth in itself, but only a surfeit of truth; even for me, about me (*pour moi, de moi*) truth is plural."[44] For Derrida, that Nietzsche can write like this makes him the voice to which modernity can respond. It is because Nietzsche has overcome the parentage of two sexes, because he is both male and female, writer and written, that he is able to be the voice for a time which can no longer acknowledge God, nature or reason. Derrida shows us, I think, that to have escaped from the past implies that Nietzsche and his writings have no (one) meaning, or rather that they have more meanings than readers.[45]

An important question remains, however, which with the publication of a new edition of Nietzsche's works, we are for the first time able to answer. If the dynamics of the family situation are in fact what I claim them to be above, what are we to make of Nietzsche's mother and sister? As mentioned above, Nietzsche was brought up by his mother and by an aunt; but his was not a happy childhood. At twelve he begins to suffer from a set of headaches which plague him intermittently through the rest of his life. He is afflicted by the loss of home in the leaving of Röcken. He writes a poem upon his departure for Pforta which portrays his first sight of that place almost as a paradisical city.[46] Friendships occupy a central and almost desperately important place in his life from a very early age on, often more to him than to the other person involved.[47] Further, we know of the struggle that surrounded his relations with his sister, whom he repeatedly and in increasingly clear terms rejects for her vision of him, for her presumptions to greatness, for her antisemitic husband, and for the nature of her encouragements to him. In fact, one suspects that if Nietzsche has taken his mother's place next to his father and has become his own mother, then his own mother and mothering relations would pose precisely the most important threat to his sense of self. They constitute a reminder that he may not be who he is, since his mother is there to prove it.

In early September 1882, Nietzsche writes to Overbeck that during an argument with his mother about Lou Salomé she "said something so rash that I had my trunks packed and left Leipzig early the next morning." In another letter to Overbeck, Nietzsche indicates his mother has accused him of defiling the tomb of his father by his writing; given the above dynamics, that would be the psychologically most threatening thing that she might have said.[48] In fact, Nietzsche's letters are from an early age onwards full of comments about the difficulty of the relation with his mother and sister. At times it becomes quite violent, as in the draft of a letter dated Autumn 1882 during the height of the "Lou Crisis": "I have known for a long time that beings such as my mother and sister must be my natural enemies—The air for me is spoiled, to have to remain with such people."[49]

In the fall of 1888, Nietzsche prepares the manuscript of *Ecce Homo* and sends it off to the publishers. At that time he receives a letter from his sister, then in Paraguay, which Nietzsche quotes indirectly to Overbeck in a letter dated Christmas 1888: she says that she supposes that he now "wants to be famous too" and makes disparaging remarks about the Jewish Danish critic Georg Brandes who had recently, to Nietzsche's great pride and delight, been giving lectures on Nietzsche in Copenhagen. Nietzsche is clearly furious—"seven years it has been going on," he exclaims, as he had earlier in the year to other correspondents after similar

326

provocations. On reception of his sister's letter, he sends off to a printer a new version of section 3 of the first chapter of *Ecce Homo*. *Ecce Homo* remains unprinted until 1905 and then comes out with an *art-nouveau* frontispiece by a printer who had not published Nietzsche before. Mazzino Montinari has well detailed the adventures of this new insert and of how it was rescued surreptitiously by Peter Gast from the destructive intentions of Nietzsche's sister.[50] In his new critical edition of Nietzsche, it is now published in its rightful place for the first time. I give it here in its entirety, partly because it has not been rendered into English before to my knowledge, and partly because it reveals a lot about the relation of Nietzsche to the dangerous figure of (his) mother.

> I hold it to be a great privilege to have had such a father. The farmers before whom he preached—for he was, after he had lived several years at the Altenburger Court, for the last years a preacher—said that an angel would have looked the way he did.
>
> And with this I touch upon the question of race. I am a Polish nobleman, *pur sang,* in whom there is not mixed a drop of bad blood, least of all of German. Were I to look for the deepest contradiction to me, I would always find my mother and my sister—to believe myself related to such *canaille* would be a blasphemy on my godliness. The treatment which I have experienced from the side of my mother and sister, up until this moment, infuses me with an unspeakable horror: here is at work a perfect infernal machine, with an unfailing certainty as to the moment at when I can be bloodily wounded—in my highest instances . . . for then one lacks all strength to protect oneself against the poisonous worm. . . . The physiological contiguity makes possible such a *disharmonia praestabilita.* . . . But I recognize that the deepest objections to the "eternal return," my own most abysmal thought, are always mother and sister.
>
> But as a Pole, I am also a monstrous atavism. One would have to go back centuries to find this race, the most noble there is on earth, as generally pure as I am. Against all that is today called *noblesse,* I have a superior feeling, one of distinction—I would not do the young Kaiser the honor to act as my coachman. There is only one particular case where I recognize my equal— and I do so with deepest gratitude. Frau Cosima Wagner is easily the noblest nature; and so that I do not say with this one word too much, I say that Richard Wagner is for me easily the noblest man . . . the rest is silence. . . . All

ruling concepts about affinities are physiological nonsense, which cannot be outdone. The pope himself had commerce today with this nonsense. One is least related to one's parents: it would be the surest sign of commonness, to be related to one's parents. Higher natures have their origin much further back: it is with them that the most has been accumulated, saved and increased. The greatest individuals are the oldest: I don't understand it, but Julius Caesar could have been my father—or Alexander, this embodied Dionysos. . . . In this moment, at which I write, the mail brings me a Dionysos head.[51]

This is a strange and difficult passage, perhaps obviously touched by the onset of insanity. (In his last letter to Burckhardt, Nietzsche will identify himself in a schizophrenic fashion as "all names in history.") But the letter is not at all out of control. He shows care in his relation to the Wagners: in an earlier draft he had written that their (Cosima and Richard's) relation was adulterous, probably in relation to himself (i.e., that Cosima should have been—was—his wife); now this is "a word too much." Even the Dionysos head which he receives in the mail is conceivably a photograph of such a head which he might have gotten from one Rosalie Nielsen.[52]

Most central here is that Nietzsche denies the importance of the biological family; he claims to be a throwback at first to an ancient race of noble Poles, then finds a father in Caesar or Alexander. What is important is not that he is claiming paternity from some unknown or impossible source, but that he thinks that his relationship with his biological father to be now so attenuated that he (Nietzsche) now exists as a person, *as if* Caesar had been his father. The very next section in *Ecce Homo* starts with a discussion of another character trait he owes to his "incomparable father." Clearly this passage does not constitute a rejection of the father, but a rejection of taking his father's place, especially in relation to the mother.

The mother and sister, on the other hand, are the most single threats to his selfhood: indeed, they constitute the "deepest possible objection to the doctrine of eternal return." It is not possible to fully explicate in this essay what might be meant by that. I have elsewhere elaborated my understanding of eternal return,[53] and will simply assert here the conclusion of that argument: eternal return for Nietzsche stands as an understanding of the world which if practiced—a praxis, we might now say—will permit a change in *who* an individual is. To change who one is, however, means to change what one's past has been. Eternal return is thus a way of dealing with the past such that a particular past (still alive in one's present) is eliminated and replaced by another past. Thus "we plant a new form, a life, a new instinct, a second nature which withers the first."[54] With this we can now understand still better Nietzsche's epigraph to *Ecce Homo*. We also see why his mother and sister are such threats: they are embodiments of the genealogy which he is annihilating and serve as reminders of at least the difficulty if not the impossibility of escaping from a particular form of life.[55] They are one of the reasons he writes *Ecce Homo*—so that he be not mistaken. It is probably not incorrect to see the book as Nietzsche's attempt to avoid precisely what happened to him after his insanity and death, namely, that his mother and sister become the official (and dangerously incorrect) interpreters of his writings. For Nietzsche, to be his own mother and to live on and grow as himself, he must necessarily eliminate his parental mother and her minion Elizabeth. Thus only will it be true that "one is least of all related to one's parents": to the degree that one is so related, one has not become who one is.[56]

Nietzsche appears then as someone who has broken the hold of Oedipus, at least of the paternal Oedipus of the *Tyrannus*. He has broken the neurotic repetition—the *circulus vitiosus* as he calls it elsewhere—which would have kept him in bondage to the past and can now stand free before the world. He announces that he will in two months confront the world as it never before has been. Karl Jaspers thinks that Nietzsche was jealous of Christ and there is a grain of truth there. But Nietzsche also thinks now that he has overcome Christ: he has not joined his father in heaven, but become his own progenitor on earth.

In the discussion of Nietzsche's dream above, I noted that his dream was a spectacle in which he was himself cast as the tragic hero: he dies and is reborn; music is at the origin of the whole vision. With the above discussion in mind, we have an understanding of precisely what attracted Nietzsche to the topic of the *Birth of Tragedy* and can now gain a better understanding of his interpretation of Greek sacred drama.

In the *Birth of Tragedy*, Nietzsche gives a portrait of Greek tragedy in what one might call its sociopolitical function. The great tragedians are able, as hopefully later also will be Wagner, to make "art seem natural," namely, to give to the polis a secure and unquestioned foundation inside which individual greatness becomes possible. The artistic foundation of the state is necessary because, Nietzsche argues, there is no natural basis to any culture. This is what the "dionysian" means: a profound insight and understanding into the basic unjustifiability of any given configuration of events. Two moves compose the tragic process; these moves find their happy conjoining in the creative act of tragedy, which requires both the dionysian insight and the apollonian form-giving. Their union is the creation of tragedy and the foundation of the state. "We will have gained much for aesthetic science," writes Nietzsche, "when we have arrived, not by logical insights, but by unmediated certainty, at the understanding that the development of further art is bound up with the duality (*Duplicitaet*) of the apollonian and the dionysian—much as procreation from the doubleness (*Zweiheit*) of the sexes depends on incessant quarrels and only periodic reconciliations." The aim of the book therefore is to produce the immediacy of insight, an insight which cannot be questioned and is not traceable to its origins.[57] The coming together of these two different drives produces a new birth which is Attic tragedy.

Attic tragedy produces a certainty of what is, and of who we—here as audience—citizens are.[58] The great achievement for Greece is thereby a "self" which is authentically its own and not dependent on what comes before or on the empires which surround Greece. In Nietzsche's reading, tragedy forms the social and political means for a constant renewal of that which is properly Greek and in Greek. The Dionysian hero, Oedipus for instance, is for Nietzsche the key addition to the earliest Greek drama. It is when the illusion of the figure of Dionysos is added to the "Urdrama" that tragedy can accomplish a vision in which the world is once again brought back to completion.

Here one is tempted to ask, what is complete? To answer this it is necessary to investigate the nature of the God which appears to make the tragedy whole and operative. Nietzsche indicates that the name Dionysos is a name given almost at random to the general drive or artistic principle which he is discussing; Prometheus, Orestes and Oedipus serve as exemplars of this figure. In the Birth of Tragedy, Nietzsche takes over much from an earlier privately printed essay on "Socrates and Greek tragedy."[59] Among the longer passages which remain unchanged we find a discussion of Oedipus as a tragic hero. Nietzsche argues that the image of Oedipus which the dramatist gives us is only a "Lichtbild," a photographic slide seen only when projected. One can go even deeper into the myth. Here Nietzsche is claiming an understanding of the Oedipus myth even more profound than is the image immediately apparent in the plays.

> Oedipus, the murderer of his father, the husband of his mother, the riddle solver of the Sphinx! What does this mysterious triad of these fateful deeds tell us? There is an age long (uralt) folk belief, especially Persian, that a wise magician can only be born from incest. Looking back on the mother marrying and riddle solving Oedipus, we immediately interpret this to ourselves to mean that where the spell of present future . . . has been broken by prophetic and magical powers, a monstrous unnaturalness—as there, incest—must have already occurred as cause. How else might one constrain nature to give up her secrets, if not through a triumphant resistance, that is, by means of something unnatural? This insight, I find expressed in the horrid triad of Oedipus' destiny: the same man who solves the riddle of nature—the Sphinx of double nature—must also as murderer of his father and husband of his mother break the most sacred natural

orders. Indeed the myth seems to wish to whisper to us, that wisdom and particularly *dionysian wisdom is an unnatural abomination,* such that he who by means of his knowledge plunges nature into the abyss of annihilation, *must also experience in himself* the dissolution of nature.[60]

Here Nietzsche describes the dionysian magician in terms very close to those which he uses to describe himself in his autobiography. The unnatural birth of this figure is the precondition of its ability to resolve the tragedy. The tragedy can only perform its sociopolitical functions when it is resolved by the appearance of the figure of Dionysos. Therefore, for Nietzsche to perform for Europe the role that the spectacle of Oedipus performed for Athens, he, too, will have to die to his old identity to be reborn as his self. Only in this way can the "Dionysian phenomenon" be achieved for Europe. Of Nietzsche's last seven letters, three are signed "The Crucified" and three "Dionysos," each a figure who died and was reborn. The seventh one, his final letter to Burckhardt,[61] is signed first "*Astu*" (Greek: home city), then "Nietzsche," and contains the claim that he is "all names in history." These letters constitute the sign that Nietzsche has lost himself as he was and has now found himself newly at home. As befits a god or a hero, he is chthonically reborn, this time of himself only. The family he was in is no more. It is only properly Pirandellian to note that after visiting Nietzsche in the asylum in 1890, Peter Gast subsequently wrote to Fuchs that at times "Nietzsche almost seemed as if he were faking madness, as if he were happy to have ended in this manner."[62]

I do not want to say what we would conclude on all this. Nietzsche is claiming that there is a mode of existence radically different from that in which human beings have been living for the last twenty-five hundred years. Nietzsche clearly identifies his ability to ground this new personality structure—one which is not human-all-too-human but *übermenschlich*—in his own heroic ability to overcome the lure and temptations of the neurotic slavely moral stance of the ascetic ideal.[61] He claims that, freed from entrapment in what has been, he will no longer be driven by his own past. But *we* do not know what to say. The discovery of his new self, nonfamilial in character, coincides, and perhaps not only coincides, with the advent of his insanity. Certainly nothing in his loss of self, nor even more in his preliminary concern at that point to "rule the world" (letter to Fuchs, December 18, 1888) and have his own new identity publically fixed once and for all, "for eternity" (to Fuchs again, December 27, 1888), necessarily leads us to the conviction that the new self is preferable to the old. The price of the family may be the *Unbehagen* which Freud saw and the neuroses that define it. To live without *Heimat,* as Nietzsche knew himself to be doing, is to live in the end in a dangerous and world historical gamble. Nietzsche's wager is that one can go through the abyss of selflessness in order to build a transfigured world from the destruction of the old. The "polar night of icy darkness" lay ahead for Nietzsche much as it did also for Max Weber. We admire Nietzsche that he dared to go into it with a full sense of what lay behind. We do not say if the possible outcomes are endurable. If not, however, then we will have to revise the wisdom of Marsyas: it will be a far better thing not to have been born, than to have been born of oneself.[64]

University of California, San Diego

NOTES

1   The dynamic of rebellion against parental authority is at the center of Carl Schorske's important book, *Fin de Siecle Vienna. Politics and Culture* (New York: Knopf; distributed by Random House, 1980). See my review in *Worldview,* 1980.

2   *Genealogy of Morals,* III, ¶ 25-26. Citations from Nietzsche are my translations, which, however, have been constantly informed by those of Walter Kaufmann, when available.

3   He writes to Overbeck, February 11, 1883, of his "eerie, deliberated, secluded secret life, which takes a step every six years, and actually wants nothing but the taking of this step." Letters are cited from Friedrich Nietzsche, *Werke in drei Baenden* (München, 1955); an English translation may be found in Christopher Middleton, ed. and trans., *Selected Letters of Friedrich Nietzsche* (Chicago: Univ. of Chicago Press, 1969). Any letters not found in these editions will receive specific citation.

4   See letter to Gast, December 1889.

5   These last two citations from Carl A. Bernouilli, *Franz Overbeck und Friedrich Nietzsche. Ein Freundschaft* (Iena, 1908), II. Band, pp. 221-22.

6   This is recognized well in J. P. Stern, *A Study of Nietzsche* (New York: Cambridge Univ. Press, 1979). See my review in *Ethics* (Jan., 1981).

7   The best extensive coverage of this question is in Alexander Nehamas, "The Eternal Recurrence," *The Philosophical Review* (Jan., 1981).

8   See Werner Dannhauser's anguished discussion of this preference of Nietzsche's in his *Nietzsche's View of Socrates* (Ithaca, N.Y.: Cornell Univ. Press, 1976).

9   See my *Friedrich Nietzsche and the Politics of Transfiguration* (Berkeley and Los Angeles: Univ. of California Press, 1975), pp. 29-49.

10   This theme is at the basis of Hannah Arendt's important discussion of Nietzsche in *The Life of the Mind: Willing* (New York: Harcourt Brace, 1978), pp. 158-71. See also Strong, *Friedrich Nietzsche and the Politics of Transfiguration,* Chap. VIII.

11   *Beyond Good and Evil,* ¶ 20.

12   *The Gay Science,* ¶ 348.

13   *Beyond Good and Evil,* ¶ 206.

14   *Beyond Good and Evil,* ¶ 208.

15   *Thus Spoke Zarathustra,* Prologue. See the discussion in Strong, *Friedrich Nietzsche and the Politics of Transfiguration,* p. 174.

16   Friedrich Nietzsche, *Jugendschriften* (München, 1923), p. 68.

17   *Beyond Good and Evil,* ¶ 264.

18   For accounts of this material, see E. F. Podach, *Nietzsches Werk der Zusammenbruch* (Heidelberg, 1961), as well as Schechta's account at the end of the third volume of his edition, and especially Curt Paul Janz, *Friedrich Nietzsche. Biographie* (München, 1979), Vol. III, p. 9-226.

19   *Jugendschriften,* p. 60.

20   *Ecce Homo,* Epigraph.

21   If I read him correctly, this is what J. P. Vernant would have us see in his "Ambiguité et renversement" in *Mythe et tragédie en grèce ancienne* (Paris, 1972), p. 114 ff.

22   See, classically, Otto Rank, *The Myth of the Birth of the Hero* (1914).

23   For this see the edition of *Antichrist* in *Werke. Kritische Gesamtausgabe.* Hrg v. G. Colli und M. Montinari (Berlin, 1967 ff), Vol. VI, ¶ 3, p. 252. The passage is not in Kaufmann's edition, nor in Schlechta's. This edition is hereafter cited as *WKG.*

24   *WKG, Nietzsche Contra Wagner,* p. 442.

25   See *Antichrist* and *Ecce Homo.*

26   Freud's essay may be found in *Collected Papers* (London, 1953), Vol. V, pp. 316-57.

27   See here G. Deleuze et F. Guatarri, *L'anti-Oedipe. Capitalisme et schizophrénie* (Paris, 1972); M. Foucault, *Madness and Civilization* (New York: Random House, 1973); and Gerard Mendel, *Le révolte contre le père* (Payot, 1968).

28   It is worth pointing out that both the *Genealogy* and *Civilization and its Discontents* have approximately the same structure. They proceed from a rejection of religion, through an analysis of the palliatives to the resulting unhappiness to the major problems, and conclude on a note of world historical pessimism.

29   Anthropological evidence for, if not analysis of, this may be found in Sir James Frazer, *The Golden Bough,* as well as in Mendel, *Le révolte contre le père.*

30   See the end of *Civilization and its Discontents.*

31   Lines 851 ff.

32   See here André Green, *Un Oeil en trop. Le complexe d'Oedipe dans la tragédie* (Paris, 1969), especially pp. 219-88.

33   Hannah Arendt, *On Revolution* (New York, 1963). See George Kateb, "Freedom and Worldliness in the Thought of Hannah Arendt," *Political Theory,* 5:2 (May 1977). Much of this essay is a disguised discussion with Kateb and Arendt.

34   *Ecce Homo,* "The Birth of Tragedy 2."

35   All of this material is cited unless otherwise indicated from Vol. III of Schlechta. I have also learned additional details from Janz, *Fredrich Nietzsche,* Vol. I.

36   See the discussion in Janz, *Friedrich Nietzsche,* I, p. 44.

37   Schlechta, III, p. 91. See Janz, *Friedrich Nietzsche,* I, p. 43.

38   Schlechta III, p. 17.

39   See *Jugendschriften,* pp. 7, 10, 12, etc.

40   I owe much in this essay to the strange and brilliant work by Pierre Klossowski, *Nietzsche et le cercle vicieux* (Paris, 1969).

41   Schlechta III, p. 93.

42   See Klossowski, *Nietzsche et le cercle vicieux,* pp. 255-60.

43   Some contemporary writers such as Deleuze and Guattari argue that the price in neurosis which one pays for capitalist civilization is too great and that the schizophrenia and polymorphous sexuality corresponding to the non-resolution of the oedipal situation is a preferable alternative. See Dusan Makavejev's wonderfully knowing view of this position in *Sweet Movie.*

44   Jacques Derrida, *Spurs/Eperons. Nietzsche's Styles* (Chicago: Univ. of Chicago Press, 1979), p. 102.

45   *Spurs,* p. 138. See my review in *Ethics* (Jan., 1981).

46   *Jugendschriften,* p. 3.

47   See here H. Roeschl, "Nietzsche et la solitude," *Bulletin de la société française des études nietzschéenes,* 1958.

48   The second letter is February 1883. It is discussed in E. F. Podach, *The Madness of Nietzsche* (New York, 1931), p. 85.

49   See the seminal article by M. Montinari, "Ein neuer Abschnitt in Nietzsches 'Ecce Homo,' " *Nietzsche Studien* (Berlin, 1972), I, pp. 382-418. Passage cited is p. 391. See also p. 392 and letter to von Seydlitz, June 11, 1878.

50   See Montinari, "Ein never Abschnitt in Nietzsches 'Ecce Homo,' " and especially Bernouilli, *Franz Overbeck und Friedrich Nietzsche,* pp. 304 ff. for a long and pained discussion of the politics of the Nachlass.

51   Punctuation is Nietzsche's original. The text is in *WKG,* Vol. I, ¶ 3, pp. 265-67.

52   So speculates Montinari, p. 382.

53   Strong, *Friedrich Nietzsche and the Politics of Transfiguration,* Chap. IX.

54   *The Use and Misuse of History for Life,* ¶ 3.

55   See Derrida, *Spurs,* pp. 88-96.

56   Janz, *Friedrich Nietzsche,* III, p. 82, notes that one of the few traits Nietzsche displayed during his stay in the asylums was an occasional violent hostility to the presence of his mother.

57   *Birth of Tragedy,* ¶ 1 (first sentence).

58   See Strong, *Friedrich Nietzsche and the Politics of Transfiguration,* pp. 161-68.

59   *WKG,* III, ¶ 2, pp. 95-132.

60   *WKG,* p. 106; *Birth of Tragedy,* ¶ 9.

61   See the discussion in G. Deleuze, *Logique du sens* (Paris, 1968), p. 75.

62   See the short discussion in R. J. Hollingdale, *Nietzsche. The Man and his Philosophy* (Baton Rouge, Louisiana State Univ. Press, 1965), p. 291.

63   It is worth noting that Nietzsche uses the term *übermenschlich* from his early adolescence on. See Schlechta III, p. 60.

64   Thanks to Helene Keyssar for a sensitive reading.

Nietzschean Values in Comic Writing

George McFadden

1. Tragic and Comic in Nietzsche

Among Nietzsche's transvaluations of value, one of the most prophetic was his overturning of Aristotle's original dictum that the comic avoided the "harmful." Nietzsche coupled delight and destruction; he found them inextricably mingled in the creative behavior of the human who is a producer and a product of modern culture. Written at the start of the whole movement toward black humor, a passage like this stands as a manifesto:

> Man no longer needs a "justification of ills"; "justification" is precisely what he abhors: he enjoys ills *pur, cru;* he finds senseless ills the most interesting. If he formerly had need of a god, he now takes delight in a world disorder without God, a world of chance, to whose essence belong the terrible, the ambiguous, the seductive.
>
> In such a state it is precisely the *good* that needs "justifying," i.e., it must be founded in evil and danger, or involve some great stupidity: then it still pleases. Animality no longer arouses horror: *esprit* and

c 1980, Princeton University Press

happy exuberance in favor of the animal in man
is . . . the most triumphant form of spirituality.[1]

The "justification of ills" Nietzsche rejects here is the formulation of evil
as a mystery, with perhaps a divine but certainly not a human solution. He
tells us that it is useless to make evil into a problem soluble only by God,
for evil is a part of existence itself; existence is ambiguous, both good and
evil by its nature, and necessarily so. Instead of accepting the ambiguity of
existence, in the past human beings onesidedly rejected it, and produced
their concept of God so as to give him the responsibility of coping with
evil. The "world of chance" which follows upon the rejection of this God
ought to suffuse humanity with a sense of new and vastly increased power,
enough to encourage us to take upon ourselves the evils as our own responsibility. Perhaps they are subject to our control—if not through science and
technology, then through human wisdom and endurance. In such a mood,
the "good," in its former sense of grace shining forth in the actions or
character of a human as a touch of the divine, would no longer have God
as a ground. The good would seem adventitious, unnecessary, not to be
relied on as a steady thing. Thus, as Nietzsche says, it would need to seem
out of keeping with its environment ("founded in evil and danger"), or it
would appear self-contradictory and weak ("involve some great stupidity"). Good, not evil, would then need to be justified, for even to detect
its existence would be no easy matter. When it appears as "happy exuberance in favor of the animal in man," however, good strikes many people as
evil, and then they notice it. Though Nietzsche does not make the application, this bit of irony helps to explain how outrageous sensuality, ob-
scenity, and pornography came to be so heavily emphasized in black
comedy.

  Some of Nietzsche's most fundamental ideas had been anticipated
by Schiller, who stressed the importance of freedom and its immediate relationship to mere chance, especially in the comic. Schiller also accepted
destructiveness, at least in satire, and he recognized the coexistence in
Lucian and Swift of a destructive as well as a playful vein of writing that
had qualities of the comic besides the purely satirical. But he differed from
Nietzsche in stressing "the beautiful soul" or "the beautiful heart" of a
free spirit like Lucian. When this ordinarily "playful" satirist deals with
the corrupt life of Rome, Schiller says, he reaches sublime heights of condemnation and repudiation. Nietzsche on the contrary, only scoffed at
"beautiful souls."[2]

  Though Nietzsche never appeared concerned to distinguish tragic
joy from comic joy, he firmly denied that the modern age was capable of
the tragic. He rejected, not only Wagner's *Parsifal,* but all modern tragedy.
In the "Self-Criticism" of *The Birth of Tragedy* which he wrote in 1886,
while he failed to make clear his own notion of stage or literary comedy,
Nietzsche did quite definitely exclude "the tragic view of life" in favor of

a comic—or at least a laughing—one. In section 18 of *The Birth of Tragedy* fifteen years earlier, he had credited Kant and Schopenhauer with an insight that inaugurated a new culture, which he then ventured to call "a tragic culture." He had followed that tribute with an enthusiastic paragraph, written with Wagner in mind:

> Let us imagine a coming generation with such intrepidity of vision, with such a heroic penchant for the tremendous; let us imagine the bold stride of these dragon-slayers, the proud audacity with which they turn their back on all the weaklings' doctrines of optimism in order to "live resolutely" in wholeness and fullness: would it not be necessary for the tragic man of such a culture, in view of his self-education for seriousness and terror, to desire a new art, the art of metaphysical comfort, to desire tragedy as his own. . . .[3]

In 1886, making fun of "metaphysical comfort," Nietzsche answered his own question: "No! you ought to learn the art of *this-worldly* comfort first; you ought to learn to laugh, my young friends, if you are hellbent on remaining pessimists."[4] And he repeated the passage from Book IV of *Thus Spoke Zarathustra* which ends, "Laughter I have pronounced holy: you higher men, *learn*—to laugh! " (Section 20). Nietzsche's reasons, in denying that European man in the nineteenth century was capable of expressing in life or in art anything like the tragic sense of terror or of joy that the Greeks once knew, are the same reasons that black and absurd comedy used to establish its condemnation of inanity, banality, mechanization and meaninglessness in modern society. His critique of the modern world and modern man, in its negative aspects, has been so widely accepted that it has for some time now lain under the same curse of banality, over-acceptance and over-internalization, as those humanitarian pieties that he attacked. Alienation, over-education, over-conceptualization, museum culture, denial of the body, destruction of real communities and substitution of "lonely crowds," *ressentiment,* and in general a decline of whatever is excellent toward its least common denominator—Nietzsche pilloried all of these. But he found a joy in his destructions, a joy he knew how to express.

"Laughter I have pronounced holy: you higher men, *learn*—to laugh! " This command of Zarathustra's is aimed at freeing his disciples from his own Devil, his worst enemy, whom he repeatedly calls "The Spirit of Gravity": "I found him serious, thorough, profound, and solemn: it was the spirit of gravity—through him all things fall. Not by wrath does one kill but by laughter. Come, let us kill the spirit of gravity."[5] This command strikes down all those who have embraced "the tragic vision" and "the tragic view of life" as their religion; clutched as "a solace and a stay," to use Matthew Arnold's phrase, the tragic view of life hardly seems the affirmation, the "Saying Yes to life" which Zarathustra stood for. When the Sixth Seal is broken, his word is, "my sarcasm is a laughing sarcasm . . . for in laughter all that is evil comes together, but is pronounced holy and absolved by its own bliss. . .,." And the Seventh Seal reveals the light of antinomianism: "Are not all words lies to those who are light? Sing! Speak no more! "[6] Nietzsche's celebration of joy in destruction has attracted many more artists than Arnold's "culture." Paradoxically, Nietzsche's attitude seems acceptably mystical to them and Arnold's too pragmatic.

It is not immediately obvious that Nietzsche's thought should be applied to the comic on stage or in fiction; few critics have tried to do so. Not formulated rules, but Nietzsche's own example, especially in *Thus Spoke Zarathustra,* will give us the clue. As a beginning, we can establish a conceptual basis by taking up some of his remarks on beauty.

In *The Will to Power* we find a passage (§§416-17) written during 1883-1888, in which Nietzsche gives a quick resume of the steps he took in reaching his ultimate insight: the eternal recurrence of the same. His first solution, he says, had been the perception of "Dionysian wisdom," which he defines as "Joy in the destruction of the most noble and at the sight of its progressive ruin: in reality joy in what is coming and lies in the future, which triumphs over existing things, however good. Dionysian: temporary identification with the principle of life (including the voluptuousness of the martyr)."[7] This early awareness Nietzsche must have had before he wrote *The Birth of Tragedy,* along with his conviction that the proper pursuit for man was not happiness. Already in that first book he had subordinated beauty to the orgiastic delight in the agon that tragedy then was to him: a mingling of pleasure and pain. Beauty is only a temporary form, a delay. "I took the will to beauty (i.e., to persist in like forms) for a temporary means of preservation and recuperation," he continues. "Fundamentally, however, the eternally-creative (like the eternal compulsion to destroy) appeared to me to be associated with pain."[8] This pain that is a part both of the creative and the destructive forces must be a sign that an expenditure of ourselves is required; according to Nietzsche, man's basic urge is not to pursue happiness but to expend himself. Beauty cannot overcome or permanently keep at bay this pain of existence, but it can be a means of temporary delight in allowing us to enjoy forms which appear, by some perfection in them, to persist as themselves. Such forms, however, call for kinds of participatory giving of oneself that involve some individual sense of struggle.[9]

The complement (and more than just the complement) of beauty is "the ugly," which has a remarkable genesis. "The ugly is the form things assume when we view them with the will to implant a meaning, a new meaning, into what has become meaningless: the accumulated force which compels the creator to consider all that has been created hitherto as unacceptable, ill-considered, worthy of being denied, ugly."[10] The character of

Nietzsche's thought comes out in these "definitions" that really do not define entities but the ways in which we might regard our experience, emotionally as well as intellectually, as falling under aspects of the whole process of becoming, so that nothing would stand as permanent being. Beauty stabilizes certain forms (or rather "the will to beauty" does) in that they continue to give delight. The nature of the ugly appears to be more complex: there is no "will to the ugly," but rather a will to meaning that leads us first to see as ugly that to which we already feel a need to give some new meaning. The ugly is something that is perceived to be in need of change and that cries out to be changed. The strength and pathos of this appeal prevents the ugly from being a mere contradiction or absence of beauty. The ugly had indeed been viewed as the partial content of a certain powerful aesthetic quality, the sublime, as defined by Burke, Kant, and Schiller; to Nietzsche the sublime is the cloak of the ugly.

While Nietzsche's thought presents pain as a broader, more ambiguous and complex aspect of experience than pleasure, he refuses to allow either pleasure or pain an ultimate place in his scheme of human values. Joy, however, is truly fundamental. It mingles pleasure and pain; happiness is subordinate to one's sense of fulfilling the general will to power, with its simultaneously destructive and creative aspects and therefore its joy.

This thought expressly mingles, if it does not totally confound, the tragic with the comic view of life. Since, as we can no longer doubt, Nietzsche's thought was second to none both in its prophetic insight and actual influence over new movements in literature, we should not be surprised by what we find today: not old-fashioned tragicomedy, a combination of two distinct and contrasted moods, one expressed in the main plot and the other in the subplot, but instead black comedy; not nineteenth-century "drama," but a mingling of the ugly to-be-destroyed-for-now and the beautiful to-be-preserved-for-awhile. The question that is so difficult to answer with regard to this thought, whether the new meanings come first and reduce the old to ugliness, or are brought into being only as the outcome of desire or need and prompted by the insufficiency of the presently-existing, is just as hard to answer with regard to the art of the twentieth century. Destruction of forms seemed to come first, and many traditionally-minded people still cannot see that any meanings have arrived.

Still, criticism has clarified many new attitudes and in their light has described new "genres" (fiction without plot or character, ritual drama, absurd or asocial theater, particularist verse, minimal art, and perhaps too many others). Critics have helped us to realize that parody, not a genre in itself, but a reflective way of playing with genres that exploits a sure but critical sense of their generic characteristics, is the most prevalent formal principle in the comic writing of the modern age. Joyce, for example, parodied the Homeric archetype of all Western epic, using prose and a very unheroic hero; and then he wrote *Finnegans Wake,* a parody not only of the forms of fiction but of literary language itself. Eliot's *Waste Land* might be considered a parody of the Juvenalian satire, mixing in elements of the pastoral as Schiller predicted would be done. One might even risk the speculation that *Madame Bovary* (hardly a tragic book) is a parody of the novel of romantic fulfillment, a black comic equivalent for the nineteenth century of *Don Quixote*.

In all of this destructive activity, at first tragedy was the "ugliest" form, in being the most in need of change. Its terror was swallowed up in solace—in pity, which Nietzsche feared and detested; its meaning ended in a stoic pose or in making excuses founded on the myth of progress. To Nietzsche terror was basic to existence, pity only degrading to pitied and pitier. The reason he put so high a value on Greek tragedy and such a low one on the tragic writing of his own era appears in the entry already quoted in part, where he continues the account of the genesis of his own thought thus:

> 1. My endeavor to oppose decay and increasing weakness of personality. I sought a new *center*.
> 2. Impossibility of this endeavor recognized.
> 3. Thereupon I advanced further down the road of disintegration—where I found new sources of strength for individuals. We have to be destroyers! —I perceived that the state of disintegration, in which individual natures can perfect themselves as never before—is an image and isolated example of existence in general. To the paralyzing sense of general disintegration and incompleteness, I opposed the *eternal recurrence*.[11]

The point of this development for us is that, while Greek tragedy was born out of strength and integration, nineteenth-century tragedy maintained itself only as an expression of weakness in an age of disintegration, where the absence of limit precluded the tragic while it freed individuals to seek a perfection of their own. Once he realized that this absence of limit and this struggle for perfection are an image of all existence, Nietzsche received his mysterious impulsion to act always knowing it was not even the first of many times, much less once for all time: in other words, to act comically and not tragically. Better, then, to take up the tone of laughter and to avoid the "serious, thorough, profound, and solemn." Better, most of all, to avoid the comforting, and rather to shock, offend, terrify, ridicule, madden, intoxicate oneself and one's audience. Nietzsche however, never suggested it was possible for art to use these means exclusively, and his own practice in *Thus Spoke Zarathustra* indicates he was aware of definite limitations on the use of the offensive and the terrible in art.

Laughter itself is a limit, in that it is a release. Especially when one laughs at himself, he sets a limit to his self-importance and to the importance of his claims or his sufferings. At least, this is true of sane laughter. Nietzsche's most important image by far is Zarathustra, and his laughter is the most striking thing about him; this laughter is always eminently sane. Zarathustra is gentle rather than terrible. His madness and intoxication are under the signs of hospitality and conviviality. He shocks us in the formally destructive, but to us delightfully recognizable, disguises of literary parody.

As a total structure, *Thus Spoke Zarathustra* parodies the form of the "life and sayings of a holy man," as we find it in the Gospels, the *Life of Buddha,* or the *Little Flowers of St. Francis.* Zarathustra, of course, is Nietzsche's own invention. He is presented as a dancer, jester, and comedian, specifically in order to do away with the aura of seriousness that might otherwise surround so great a prophet. The language throughout, Walter Kaufmann tells us, "abounds in allusions to the Bible, most of them highly irreverent."[12] It also abounds in puns and coinages—Nietzsche ridiculed and parodied not only Luther's German Bible but the German language itself. He also parodied the Sermon on the Mount, the Last Supper, and the mass. Today this parody seems more playful than vindictive. Though we must allow for a greater shock value when these irreverences first appeared in the 1880s, yet parodies of a much more ribald and outrageous sort were rife in the middle ages and were actually granted academic and ecclesiastical sanction. Of course, Nietzsche disbelieved in the texts he parodied, and therein lies a great difference. But while Nietzsche's parodies effectively present his anti-Christian ideas, they are constructively fictional and unpolemic to an outstanding degree. Kaufmann's comparisons to Joyce's *Ulysses* and the second part of Goethe's *Faust* are therefore well taken.

It would be too hasty to say at this point in the argument that Nietzsche's practice in *Thus Spoke Zarathustra* illustrates something like a comic theory. Only let us repeat then that the book is anything but tragic. It is reasonable to assume that the comic form of this work might turn out to be the obverse of what the youthful author raved over in *The Birth of Tragedy.* It is a work of art throughout, obviously intended as such. Nietzsche meant it to achieve beauty in forms that persist in their own likeness (to use his own language), for the sake of the preservative and recuperative power that such forms possess. He thought of Greek tragic art as all the more joyous because Greek experience was full of pain. The depth of pain is measurable not by expressions of anguish, but reciprocally by the degree of sublimation of pain in the joy of the whole Dionysian celebration, of which tragedy was only a part, and comedy too. Nietzsche's paradox about laughter, that it was invented by the most suffering of animals, man, extends this reciprocal character of artistic expression in the direction of the comic.[13] Because man is strong he turns sorrow into laughter. According to Nietzsche, he does not laugh at the sorrows of other, weaker men, nor did human beings invent laughter as a way of expressing superiority over the rest of creation, as if they were gods rather than mortals. "Learn to laugh at yourselves,"[14] is the word of Zarathustra to his convalescing higher men. Laughter is a sign of strength in *Thus Spoke Zarathustra,* and also a way of becoming strong.

The laughter of Zarathustra, besides being the most important trait of his fictional character, is a highly effective image in itself. It is a revealing sign of his sunny outlook on all of life, more frequent even than his singing, dancing, or jesting. Perhaps Nietzsche wished to accentuate this difference between his Zarathustra and Aristotle's magnanimous man, who smiled a bit but never laughed out loud. Zarathustra is as courteous and generous as Aristotle's model man, and in a more delicate and psychologically inner way. Indeed, Zarathustra may be a bit exposed to the charge of over-complexity and refinement. He is too indulgent to the "human, all too human" to be quite comic all the time, too given to sudden fears, questionings, emotional affirmations, even sermonizing. At other times he is too inhumanly strong, superior, reliable. If he were meant to stand on his own feet as a comic character, Zarathustra would have to be purged of these qualities. The whole structure of *Thus Spoke Zarathustra,* however, indicates that he is not meant to stand by his own inner force alone, but that he may be taken as a parody of the figure of Jesus in the Gospels.

Thus Spoke Zarathustra consists of four books, like the four canonical Gospels. Nietzsche intended to write more, but the story of Zarathustra is complete in the four books that he finished, and in them the parallel to the earthly life of Jesus is rounded off. After a period of obscurity Zarathustra enters upon his public life, preaches to the people, travels away from his chosen town into the countryside, attracts twelve disciples (of whom one is "loved"), performs works of power, rebukes a great city, goes away into the desert, is tempted, returns, upbraids the lukewarm, the hypocritical, and the pharasaical, is transfigured before his disciples, holds a final festival supper with them, which he commands them to observe in his memory as a ceremony of mystical communion in the (earthly) good, and finally leaves them to go off into a new phase, where he is to find companions more akin to himself. The style of *Thus Spoke Zarathustra,* besides being similar in diction to the Bible, offers many quotations, allusions, and parodies of Bible materials, especially from the New Testament. As for Zarathustra's own speeches, they have a rather strong similarity to the psalms in their more lyrical passages. There are further similarities (no doubt intentional) to other holy books, especially the *Life of Buddha.*

Nevertheless, Zarathustra never loses the force of authority—of the non-authoritarian type, that is, required by Nietzschean thought. He is a living model, an image invented to present Nietzsche's ideas without recourse to a merely conceptual and systematic framework. His new "psychological" thought was aimed to transcend the horizon of science and the rules of logic. He created a figure capable of presenting philosophy as personal behavior, with an ambiguity suited to reality. The interrelationship of the ideas and image is neither irrational nor arbitrary; it is personal.

344

Ideas are never presented as intellectual judgments, but as modes of action in a context of subtly controlled feeling and with the strong flavor of aesthetic promotion or rejection.

As Nietzsche invokes laughing Zarathustra to overcome the Spirit of Gravity, the image of the agon now becomes a comic one. For Zarathustra, "Whatever in me has feeling suffers and is in prison; but my will always comes to me as my liberator and joy-bringer."[15] Suffering and frustrated (i.e., "in prison"), the self is more recognizably the self; its imprisonment only calls attention to its individuality. According to Nietzsche, one must keep in mind, "self" is the body, first of all and most importantly; only secondarily is it the "ego." His view was not unlike Freud's in some ways, and in so far as Nietzsche tended to value actions performed unconsciously or spontaneously as the only "perfect" activity,[16] his romantic view of the unconscious has tended to supplant Freud's more rigorously defined one in the outlook and writing of modern artists and critics. Nietzsche's "self" was unscientific, anti-Darwinian, and undetermined except that, as Zarathustra laments, "Alas, much ignorance and error have become body within us."[17] Nietzsche would not look for systematic explanations of change, like evolution; it was necessary to him that the changes become subject to human aspiration and will.

2. The Black Comic Technique

The comic possibilities of the Nietzschean self arise out of his image of willing. As if he were reversing the old apologue of the body and its members, Nietzsche took the fable out of political philosophy and internalized it. It then serves as a psychological account of what happens within us, to explain our feeling-states and our behavior from moment to moment. Nietzsche's image is that of a little political community, rather like a Greek city state, with a public spirited elite and a well-integrated *demos.* Power would normally flow through such a body politic without inhibitions. Mutual confidence, common aims, and the familiar expectations of command and obedience would guarantee an easy continuity of intention and execution. Willing would not seem to originate at any one point in the power process, or within any single segment of the community; it would spring from the whole body. Those who actually gave the orders would rejoice in the beneficial execution of plans for the common good as well as in their own exercise of command as individuals. The pleasure of superiority is not by any means the issue, either; rather it is the sense of expenditure in a willing participation. The sense of having shared in willing what one saw being fulfilled would undoubtedly heighten one's delight in the entire process.

Delight Nietzsche finds to be our response to the overcoming of obstacles when our willing is effective and not frustrated. In his playful vein, he suggests that our "will" is a good deal of a fiction, a way of looking (after the event) at the total psychosomatic process which occurs when a human being acts. Indeed, the Will to Power is not my will, or even Caesar's, but a force working through all of life. When I have the sense of guiding this force, I am elated, just as the governing elite of a community might take pleasure in seeing social programs carried out successfully. This sense would be the more perfect the more the community was a perfect one, because of the greater degree of identification between commander and commanded. "In this way the person exercising volition adds the feelings of delight of his successful executive instruments, the useful 'under-wills' or under-souls, to his feeling of delight as commander. *L'effect c'est moi.*"[18] Although Nietzsche is not talking about art in this passage, it is impossible not to apply these words to participation in artistic experience. It is as if he were unfolding the meaning of Shakespeare's symbolic presentation of power and the power of art in *The Tempest.*

The analysis suggests two possible kinds of comedy, based either on the Will to Power or on its frustration. The first would be outright magical fantasy (Kafka's Oklahoma Nature Theater perhaps seems to have been intended so, in the unfinished *Amerika*); the second would deal with the infinitesimals of the comic calculus, directing our attention to that dumb delight which accompanies our good health like a friendly shadow—but, by showing it often frustrated and unsuccessful, it would remind us of how lucky we are most of the time.

In Kafka's only expressly comic work, *Amerika,* one can open the book just about at random and find passages that illustrate Nietzsche's account of the inner experience of the sensation, thought, and emotion of willing, together with the notion of the commander "I" and the obeyers. Very rarely is the passage one of wish fulfillment, as it is in the excerpt which follows, where Karl is seeking to make contact with the recruiting team of the Nature Theater:

> "You all play very badly," said Karl, "let me have a turn."
> "Why, certainly," said Fanny, handing him the trumpet, "but don't spoil the show, or else I'll get the sack." Karl began to blow into the trumpet; he had imagined it was a roughly-fashioned trumpet intended merely to make a noise, but now he discovered that it was an instrument capable of almost any refinement of expression. If all the instruments were of the same quality, they were being very ill-used. Paying no attention to the blaring of the others he played with all the power of his lungs an air which he had once heard in some tavern or other. He felt happy at having found an old friend, and at being allowed to play a trumpet as a special privilege, and at the thought that he might likely get a good post very soon. Many of the women stopped playing to

listen; when he suddenly broke off scarcely half of the trumpets were in action; and it took a little while for the general din to work up to full power again.

"But you are an artist," said Fanny, when Karl handed her the trumpet again. "Ask to be taken on as a trumpeter."[19]

This passage of wish fulfillment is set in an episode of comic anagnorisis replete with the imagery of sex fantasy; nothing of this, though, would serve to account for the sense of freedom which, more than anything else, generates a comic effect in the passage. The two *termini* are there—Karl's aloneness and joblessness at one end, a "good post" at the other, with an old friend, among admiring women. The sense of motion between the two points is made actual by his blowing the horn. The thought is threefold: finding an old friend, the privilege of playing the trumpet, the likelihood of a good job. The singleness of intention and the emotion are what the artist feels when he succeeds in stilling the usual quotidian din long enough to gain a hearing, and gives expression to the music within him, what he makes of his experience, however random, with the instrument at his disposal. Much more might be said about this recognition scene, but the main point is that its comic quality depends upon the fulfillment of the Will to Power, as Nietzsche describes it, and not simply upon the fulfillment of a fantasy.

More typical of *Amerika* is one of the numerous passages recounting Karl's frustration. This one, near the beginning of the story, is actually in close coincidence with Nietzsche's analysis of the complex state and process of willing. It comes when Karl has been enticed away from his uncle's New York apartment to the estate of a Mr. Pollunder, vaguely placed on Long Island. Karl is anxious to get back to his uncle's:

> But Karl had felt more and more restless the more clearly he became aware of his relation to his uncle during his speech, and involuntarily he struggled to free himself from Pollunder's arm. Everything cramped him here; the road leading to his uncle through that glass door, down the steps, through the avenue, along the country roads, through the suburbs to the great main street where his uncle's house was, seemed to him a strictly ordered whole, which lay there empty, smooth and prepared for him, and called to him with a strong voice. Mr. Pollunder's kindness and Mr. Green's loathsomeness ran into a blur together, and all that he asked from that smoky room was permission to leave. He felt cut off from Mr. Pollunder, prepared to do battle against Mr. Green, and yet all round him was a vague fear, whose impact troub-

led his sight. He took a step back and now stood equally
distant from Mr. Pollunder and Mr. Green.[20]

This passage, above all else, deals with Karl's emotion. Freedom is presented with considerable emotional force in Karl's image of the "strictly ordered whole" which will take him so smoothly to his uncle's house; and
the impact of the emotion is heightened, in Kafka's way, by its actual
damming up. Since Karl cannot execute the command his "I" is giving
him, he becomes frustrated and anxious. The people around him, both
apparent friend and apparent enemy, blur together, and the room itself
darkens. All of his "powers" seem to desert him, like routed troops. So it
is not simply that Karl cannot leave Mr. Pollunder's, but rather that Kafka
wants us to partake of the full experience of the frustrated will to power.
Karl is not free—this is what it is like not to be free, in a commonplace
human situation, without the melodrama of a Bonivard and his dungeon
by Lake Leman. Note that it is precisely what Nietzsche specifies as the
signs of willing that are missing here: "the straining of the attention, the
straight look which fixes itself exclusively on one thing"—Karl is power-
less, his attention equally divided between Mr. Pollunder and Mr. Green;
there is no "inward certainty that obedience will be rendered"—what Karl
feels inwardly is "a vague fear"; and far from identifying himself with the
others present, Karl takes a step back from them and from the path which
he so desires to follow. Nor can Karl escape the sense of self-division,
above all because of the powerlessness of his "I," split in two between Mr.
Pollunder and Mr. Green.

Kafka's exploitation of the complex state of willing and its frustration may plausibly be associated with the will to power. Yet I am concerned even more with the question of what, if anything, makes this passage comic. Many critics, first among them Edwin Muir (Kafka's translator) have insisted upon Kafka's humor throughout the whole of his fiction.
Furthermore, there is ample theoretical justification for regarding such
writing as ridiculous, provided we are willing to invoke the old-fashioned
but once dominant superiority theory. Reading Kafka's analysis of Karl's
experiences, we take a perhaps malicious, perhaps pitying pleasure (which
harms no one, for what we are concerned with is only fiction) in the boy's
continual frustration, because it enhances by contrast our own sense of
power. The scenes of Karl's frustration are sometimes remindful of our
own misadventures (for example, some remarkable pages dealing with the
functioning of a hotel information desk), but even these universal cases
still allow us to feel masterful by comparison to the inept Karl, whose inadequacy is pervasive and compulsive. Most of the time, also, one can regard Karl's hesitations and anxieties as grotesquely exaggerated and therefore ridiculous. That many readers still relish this simplistic response might
seem to be proved by the prevalence of such "heroes" as Karl in recent
plays, films, and novels.

Yet something very like Kafka's technique is described by Nietzsche in such a way as to throw the sufferings of Karl in *Amerika* into a new light for us: "It seems, a little hindrance that is overcome and immediately followed by another little hindrance that is again overcome—this game of resistance and victory arouses most strongly that general feeling of superabundant, excessive power that constitutes the essence of pleasure. . . . Pleasure and pain are not opposites."[21] In the unfinished *Amerika,* Karl, of course, does not so much overcome his inhibitions as merely survive them. Perhaps the reader who identifies himself with Karl is amused because his sense of sympathetic frustration tenses and relaxes in a pleasurable rhythm; perhaps other readers, refusing to identify with him, laugh at him instead because they find him ridiculous.

Nietzsche, in substituting his communal model of will in place of old notions, like that of will as a faculty of the soul directly opposed to the body and its animal instincts, opened up the microexperience of human existence to observation and commentary, and thus helped to discover a new world to writers of fiction. It is an interior life of the soul rivalling the one so carefully mapped out over the centuries by the moralists and mystics. Self as body, above all, rather than as spirit, is a more intransigent subject for a writer, but a better one by present notions, because it is more dense and more opaque. Rather obviously, its possibilities seem to lie in the comic rather than the tragic direction. Moreover, the threat of interest is still freedom: in Nietzsche's transvalued ethos, "liberation" from "imprisonment," for the feelings, is as important as enhanced freedom for the spirit was to Schiller.

The more traditional writers of modern comedy (who are unwilling or unable to work in the area of these micro-experiences) deal with our sense of experience as it is externally affected in one of two ways: either psychologically, in the form of aggressive neurotic forces presented as type characters involved in some strongly-patterned combination of inhibitions (Pinter), or much more allusively by presenting a "society" that is schematized to the point of absurdity (most "absurd" comedy). The society (in Ionesco, for example) does not differ much from the characteristics Nietzsche attributed to his "last men," or even from this description written with tongue in cheek by Kierkegaard almost a century and a half ago:

> the whole romantic school related or thought they related to an age in which men had become ossified, as it were, within the finite social situation. Everything had become perfected and consummated in a divine Chinese optimism that allowed no rational longing to go unsatisfied, no rational wish unfulfilled. Those glorious assumptions and maxims drawn from custom and convention had been made objects of a pious

idolatry. . . . One married, one lived for domesticity, one filled his position in the state. One had children and family cares. . . . One meant everything to his own, year in and year out with a certainty and precision always correct to the very minute. The world was becoming childish, it had to be rejuvenated.[22]

3. Liberation from The Spirit of Gravity

Black, absurd, and "sick" comedy aim at the special kind of Dionysian joy that revels in the destruction of such a society of Philistine automata. But there is a more genuine Dionysian joy that is only to be found in the destruction of forms that are noble and good rather than ugly. One might be inclined to feel that this latter joy is far more likely to infuse successful works of art. In his own account, Nietzsche presented a kind of foolery as liberating—forms of lightheartedness, gaiety, prankishness—everything in fact that contravened the spirit of gravity. It does not always provoke laughter, nor is there an insistence on cynical or malicious ridicule. Certainly there is no suggestion anywhere in Nietzsche that we laugh at anyone's weakness of will in a spirit of hostility or even rivalry. The spirit of gravity itself is to be mocked, laughed at, and killed, not its unhappy victims. Freedom thus emerges in Zarathustrian comedy as something like the interplay of feeling and volition, proceeding so as to release our feelings from a sense of imprisonment. Free play would thereby achieve the moment of permanence that beauty maintains and would offer beauty's recuperative power. None of the opposed terms—Dionysian/Apollonian, Zarathustra/Spirit of Gravity—would be annulled, abrogated, or transcended in any final way. Their contest would be structured so as to achieve a series of moments of recuperative power, overcoming, or sublimation. The impulses in which we share, and are most made aware of, must seem to be given the freest play, and thereby to fulfill the Nietzschean notion of a simultaneously active communal will involving writer and reader. Nietzsche will thus appear as a thinker in the mainstream of the Romantic epoch in that he assigns a central role to freedom.

4. The Nietzschean Image of Art

I shall now try to explain how a Nietzschean image for the mechanism of self-becoming has pervaded thought about the activity of the artist since his time, and still provides us with our picture of the relationship of art to nature today. To clarify the process of selving and sublimation, Nietzsche invented a little parable: a lake "one day ceased to permit itself to flow off; it formed a dam . . . this lake is rising higher and higher . . . perhaps man will rise ever higher as soon as he ceases to *flow out* into a god."[23]

The image from hydrostatics was used previously for economics, to present the idea of capital accumulation; and it has since served as a metaphor to codify the terms of financial functioning in general. Even before Adam Smith it was already a very potent central image, having served to present the circulation of the blood (as Smith used it to present the circulation of wealth), and long before that the flow of the four humours within the body. Also, as tidal ebb and flow it connected the human "temperament" with the waters of the earth and the gravitational pull of the moon, and thus with the universe as a whole. It was not until Nietzsche's lifetime, however, that the image received its most richly significative development. It was applied to the behavior of electricity in circuits, making detailed use of every metaphorical possibility: inflow, collection, tension, discharge, gap, open circuit, closed circuit, short circuit, high and low pressure (voltage), strong and weak current, wave formation, cyclical rise and fall, and so on *ad infinitum*. Moreover, the notions associating electronic circuitry with work and therefore with economics continued to be strong: capacity, energy, output, resistance, consumption, efficiency of production, storage, and transmission of energy. When one adds the phenomena of radio, there is no end to such images, new ones are being made every day.

Nevertheless, the parametric form of the image for the arts was the psychological one originated by Nietzsche and developed by Freud. What is stored up are aeons of human experience, extended still further back into the animal past. Our collective experience exists today as if gathered in a vast lake, whose unfathomed depths are charged with every profound instinct and source of emotional energy known or yet unknown to us. The race as a whole and every individual member of it draws upon powers latent in this reservoir, but by far the deepest draughts are drawn by the great genius, and particularly the great artist.

Bergson used the lake image, and extended it to a picture of the stormy ocean. He also added a different version of his own, the deep, fluid, fiery core of life encrusted all over with its pellicule of social use and wont. Freud, as we all know, developed it into a well-mapped psychic world. His interior world picture is ours today more effectively than similar images furnished by Galileo or Newton in their time ever were. In Freud, who clung to the hydrostatic version, Nietzsche's "power to flow" became cathexis and his "damming up" became the censor mechanism or the superego. The deepening lake became the unconscious, its primal state the libido. Also, the primary energies stored up became "capital," just as a "head of water" is a source of profitable energy when used to do work. Freud's imagery is highly convertible with economic coding, but for the discussion of art the most effective conversion was into electric, and now into electronic terms. Thus libidinal drives are given a much higher energy potential as a result of inhibitory mechanisms which we perceive acting like resisters and condensers in an electical circuit. The result in art is imagined as a high voltage discharge across the gap between the unconscious and the conscious mind. This spark, linking one to one's unconscious, is what the genius artist communicates to the spectator or reader.

The notion of a "gap" suffused with electric tension, that then acts as a carrier or bridge from a high potential source through a low potential medium, is by now an omnipresent, if usually submerged, metaphor in the minds of all of us. Without it, twentieth century literary theory (particularly in New Criticism) would shrink to half its compass. Recently, however, we have learned to redeem the image from a threat of elitism. When it ceased to be satisfactory to view the modern artist as the Promethean fire-bringer, the picture of the electromagnetic field in space came into play. The "gap" ceased to exist as involving a high energy and a low energy polar opposition between poetic and ordinary language, or genius and consumer; in its place we have a free play of forces intersecting in a text which has no author as origin of significance but whose unfolding, or undulation, is the carrier wave for meanings given it (as well as taken from it) in an energy exchange of an open sort which we call "writing." This version of the image is not, however, a transformation denoting a break with Freud, Bergson, and Nietzsche. The new image is actually more faithful to Nietzsche's original version than either Bergson or Freud dared to be, for they both had a lively interest in the maintenance of European civilization, even though they were dismayed at its actual state of unsuccess. Like Nietzsche, the French critics, who gave this theory and submerged image its present currency, aim at dispersing Western authority beyond recovery.

5. Nietzsche's Nostalgia for the Naive

The persistence of the romantic movement in Western culture has been due in significant measure to the German fascination with idealized Greek antiquity, part of what Nietzsche saw was the Teutonic yearning for the south. The Germans, I should say, colored the first romantic wave through Winckelmann's and Goethe's Hellenism, the second through Nietzsche's Dionysian, the third through Heidegger's concern for the original Greek thought and mode of being. Each involved a special kind of *Heimweh* or nostalgia, and always for the naive. The first was for the genuine Greek taste, purified of the crass, utilitarian, and vulgar Roman accretions. The second was for the Greek nature, at one with the world in a union of *physis* and *cosmos*. The third has been, and still is, a nostalgia for the naive, where the almost unorganized simplicities of existence are sought in art because they allow human imagination its most untrammeled scope. The special longing for freedom that characterizes these three different phases of one movement is a persistent mark which helps to unify them. Whatever the terms used, the essential is self-determination: the self locates itself by seeking out its proper home. It finds its "limit" in the Hegelian sense, in a community, either immediate and political, or else in an ideally humane society. In either case the home is longed for as an alternative kind of life that permits substantive values to come into being and to endure. From the first, beginning with the thinkers and artists who looked to Greek antiquity as a uniquely privileged alternative, an original, primal home, all romantics have desired a setting such as the Greeks had for values especially opposed to actual bourgeois conditions as they have been from the later eighteenth century until now.

The Romantic escaped the imprisonment of "time and its 'it was'" by turning feelings of "revenge" against the past into acceptance of whole alternative worlds,[24] fictional worlds created by a succession of great innovators in the arts. The first wave began to move in the last quarter of the eighteenth century, with the idealized recovery of "Hellas" and "the Gothic." Goethe's *Götz von Berlichtigen,* Schiller's *The Robbers,* the novels of Walter Scott conjured up past ages; Goethe's first and second parts of *Faust* seemed to equilibrate the Gothic and the ancient Greek worlds in order to afford a magical perspective on the modern one. These works provided acceptable versions of a past redeemed of its burden, while serving to free artist and audience, imaginatively at least, from the bondage of a bourgeois civilization that threatened to tie everyone down to the petty and the mean. By the mid-seventies of the nineteenth century, Richard Wagner had composed a more singleminded mythic alternative world and established it at Bayreuth. Half a century later still, the solitary writing of James Joyce in *Ulysses* created an entirely different sort of alternative world, in which the recurrence of the past takes place in Nietzschean style as the present of the fictional dream, parodically the same as in the Greek past of Homer. Then, by means of a seemingly infinite control over the entire reservoir of language, Joyce in *Finnegans Wake* distanced the petty and the mean of individual experience by giving it universal forms.

With regard to our own inquiry, we may recall that Nietzsche first welcomed Wagner's innovation as a new "Birth of Tragedy," only to reject it fifteen years later in favor of laughter. Nietzsche repudiated Wagner, along with Baudelaire, as a decadent. He recognized clearly in them certain symptoms of a peculiar bourgeois unhealthiness, and he sometimes managed even to recognize the extent to which he shared the disease himself. Nietzsche's real problem was the one already recognized by Goethe, bourgeois meanness. In its place he created an illusion: the tyrant instincts —pitiless and dreadful passions—which call resistance into being and thereby generate power.[25] Thus he turned his own small need, as a means of successfully controlling it and freeing himself for self-direction, into a great need which he did not encounter at any time in his life except in his thinking and writing. His methods (adopted recently by French structuralism and the *Tel Quel* group) are suited to the magnification of the individual *pensuer* into a worldshaker. Nietzsche himself went further, and identified himself with a timeless aristocracy, for which he had almost no personal or family qualifications. Like the true *parvenu,* he usurped aristocracy and was as loyal to his ideal as the greatest snob. This foible is comically apparent even in his early writing; in his decline into insanity it might easily provide a source of the cruel laughter he wrote about so often. Nietzsche's value as a critic of this kind of pettiness in himself and others, however, is enormous.

He is certainly correct in observing that, like Baudelaire, Wagner was among the first to reinterpret in vastly distanced myths the psychology of neurotic modern individuals living in an urbanized culture. His accusations of decadence, whether justified or not in their tone of prophetic denunciation, outline the profile of bourgeois art since 1850. He charged it, and its spokesman Wagner in particular, with coupling perfect sexual union and death in a kind of androgynous sterility that prevents its heroines from having any children. Instead of working toward redemption, the decadent hero is content to fall into some form of annihilation. There are no plans made for the future, for this world is soon to pass away. Freedom is defined falsely as closeness to the void. Past centuries are not borne as heavy burdens to be abnegated, but reappear sentimentally as escapes from the overpowering meanness and complexity of modern life. Hence the preference for ready-made myth rather than history, for the turgid rather than the unambiguous style, for extreme emotions rather than clear feelings: all three forms of excess are meant to blunt the impact of actual existence. In the place of desire for life there is a yearning to be carried away into some form of extinction. "Tragic" suffering then becomes a suffering from the unbearableness of life itself, instead of a glorious contest in which the human agonist lives the fullest possible life. Modern heroes are found willing their own destruction. The death of desire and the extirpation of passion, like thy imperatives of an exotic and sterile religion, take hold of all "serious" and "profound" art. The Spirit of Gravity is the god of the decadents.

Against this kind of "tragic" outlook and its "metaphysical solace" Nietzsche finally set up the laughter of Zarathustra as the laughter of freedom from all this, and—as we have been arguing—established the foundation for almost all of the modern black comedy that needs to be taken seriously. This form of humor, as he said, is based on instincts that are *"pur"* and *"cru"* that is, primitively and puritanically destructive of the accretion of conventional modes of behavior; and it can be both crudely and cruelly ridiculous. In terms drawn from the history of the comic, the Nietzschean doctrine calls for a recurrence of the *sauvage* spirit of Archilochus. One then seems to desire the humiliation, degradation, painful suffering, and indeed the death of one's hated butt; and only the force of life inherent in the essential comic prevents the last of these desires from being accomplished.

In beginning with the early Greeks, Nietzsche was giving free rein to his own particular nostalgia. He longed for the naive in its pure Attic form, before the decadence of Socratic reasoning had set in with the tradition of Plato. He never changed the conviction stated in one of his earliest essays, "Homer's Contest," that "Man, in his highest and noblest capacities, is wholly nature and embodies its uncanny dual character. . . . The Greeks, the most humane men of ancient times, have a trait of cruelty, a tigerish lust to annihilate."[26] This "dual character" of Greek nature gives rise to the twofold mythic figure of Eris. The first is the goddess of discord; she is cruel and promotes feuds and open warfare, things necessary as ways to honor; the second or better Eris rouses men to deeds of contest rather than armed hostility; one might call her the goddess of competition. The better Eris, however, does not inspire people with laudable ambition only, but with envy, jealousy, and spite as well. "The whole of Greek antiquity," Nietzsche assures us, "thinks differently from us about hatred and envy."[27] Here, of course, he is quite mistaken, for he has actually drawn an accurate portrait of the cutthroat competitor who was the typical nineteenth century capitalist tycoon.

Nietzsche insisted on incorporating the twofold Eris in his description of the Greek naive: Wherever we find the 'naive' in Greek art (e.g., the 'naiveté of Homer'), he said in Section Three of *The Birth of Tragedy,* we encounter the most powerful effect of culture as a two-fold triumph over a terrible insight into the depths of reality and an intense experience of suffering.

He defined culture as unity of artistic style in all the expressions of the life of a people. The Attic smile on the visage of an antique statue of a warrior, therefore, indicated to Nietzsche an Apollonian triumph over horrors of war that both the living soldier and the living artist first tasted to the full. This naive is by no means innocent and Edenic, quite the opposite; it is a total life style, founded in dreadful insight and intense suffering, and overcoming these tyrants by means of illusions of power and joy.

In the unphilosophical sense of the term, we might say that Nietzsche idealized the Greeks, as Goethe and Schiller had done in the first wave of romanticism and Heidegger was to do in the third. We should realize, however, that Nietzsche was a leader in revolutionizing the present mode of thinking as it conceives of "idea" and "nature." He rejected the dualisms of ideality and reality, soul and body, form and matter, nurture and nature. He tells us that the Greeks originated the "idea" of unifying their culture and their natural environment. But they originated it by doing it; it is only we moderns in the Platonic tradition who must make an idea of it. For the early Greeks it was a naive matter of everyday concern for their real needs. This argument appears in an early, almost programmatic essay, "On the Use and Abuse of History." It is prophetic not only for Nietzsche's own work, but for the characteristic outlook of the modern artist.

He began by setting up his favorite concept of the past as a burden, a burden that needs to be first assumed and then abrogated, by one means or another so long as one gives full weight to the life-and-death importance of the task. And finally he brings a long, richly suggestive argument to its culmination by citing the example of the Greeks. They "did not long remain the overburdened heirs of the entire Orient" (that is, of "Asiatic vague immensities" in Yeats's words). The ancient Greeks "learned to *organize the chaos*," says Nietzsche, by "thinking back to themselves, that is, to their own true necessities."[28] The outcome of their thinking was the idea of culture as a new and better nature.[29] The Greeks and the Asiatics inhabited the same geographical world, but the Greeks went on to create a world of their own and to live in it fully. Out of a totality of need (i.e., chaos) they summoned the strength to give expression to themselves as a community organized by human will so as to respond to human desire. They lived humanly, even in the nature they gave to the gods whom they envisioned in order to manage the universe they themselves brought forth.

Nietzsche's personal culture and life style was aimed at exactly the same naiveté as he attributed to the early Greeks. That which is most personal of all, his style of writing, has been called "talking to himself," and "heightened conversation." In Nietzsche's own words, his goal was the "cheerful and benevolent" overcoming of "any trace of suffering or depression"—Suffering that he continually describes in his letters as infinite and intense, and depression verging on the suicidal. The cheerfulness he cultivated was rather to be called joy, joy as deep as the depths of pain he endured so willingly, despite all his complaints. Joy was his defense in the agon with the "weakness and weariness which those who dislike me will look for."[30] Quite evidently, the naiveté Nietzsche saw as the chief mark of the early Greek style in art and life was the mask he sought to present to the world in his own activity as an artist and a man. It became the style of his own self-creation. The discursive and still academic structure of the *Untimely Meditations* from which we have just been quoting soon gave way to the series of aphorisms and paragraphs in which his later books took shape. The style was an innovation in German that he himself put on a par with Luther's Bible and the prose of Goethe. Its ease and apparent informality were achieved at great cost to the artist. These qualities are thus the equivalent of the "Attic smile" and they constitute a rebirth of the naive in an epoch of decadence. At last they became the strongest evidence for Nietzsche's doctrine, centered as it was on joy, power, self-mastery, and genius as self-creation. No wonder that the thought of Nietzsche and his practice as a writer remained powerful throughout two successive waves of romantic nostalgia for the naive.

Temple University

NOTES

1   Friedrich Nietzsche, *The Will to Power,* translated by Walter Kaufmann and R. J. Hollingdale (London: Weidenfield and Nicolson, 1968), § 1019, p. 57. Most of the translations used in this article are so widely accepted it seems adequate to cite originals by section only.

2   *The Will to Power,* § 100, pp. 63f., where Nietzsche attacks Rousseau, the spokesman for the *bel âme,* for his moralizing and his need of God.

3   *The Birth of Tragedy and The Case of Wagner,* translated by Walter Kaufmann (New York: Vintage, 1967), § 18, pp. 112f.

4   "Attempt at a Self-Criticism," *The Birth of Tragedy,* § 7, p. 26f.

5   *Thus Spoke Zarathustra,* translated by Walter Kaufmann, in *The Portable Nietzsche* (New York: Viking, 1954), "On Reading and Writing," Part One, p. 153.

6   *Thus Spoke Zarathustra,* Part Three, "The Seven Seals," § § 6, 7, pp. 342f.

7   *The Will To Power,* § 417, p. 224.

8   *The Will To Power,* § 416, p. 224.

9   *Thus Spoke Zarathustra,* Second Part, "On the Tarantulas," pp. 312f.

10   *The Will To Power,* § 416, p. 224.

11   *The Will to Power,* § 417, p. 224.

12   *The Portable Nietzsche,* p. 108.

13   *The Will to Power,* § 990, p. 517.

14   *Thus Spoke Zarathustra,* Fourth Part, "On the Higher Man," § 15, p. 404.

15   *Thus Spoke Zarathustra*, Part Two, "Upon the Blessed Isles," p. 199.

16   *The Will to Power,* § 289, p. 163.

17   First Part, "On the Gift-Giving Virtue," § 2, p. 189.

18   *Beyond Good and Evil,* translated by Helen Zimmern, in *The European Philosophers From Descartes to Nietzsche,* edited by Monroe C. Beardsley (New York: *Modern Library,* 1960), § 19, pp. 816f.

19   Franz Kafka, *Amerika,* translated by Willa and Edwin Muir (New York: Schocken, 1962), pp. 277-79; *Gesammelte Schriften,* edited by Max Brod (New York: Schocken, 1946), II, 269f.

20   *Amerika,* p. 82; cf. the key phrases in the German text, p. 84: "der Weg . . . erschein ihm als etwas streng Zusammengehöriges, das leer, glatt, und für ihn vorbereitet dalag, und mit einer starken Stimme nach ihm verlangte."

21   *The Will to Power,* §699, p. 371.

22   *The Concept of Irony,* trans. L. M. Capel (Bloomington, Ind.: Indiana Univ. Press, 1968), p. 318f.

23   *The Gay Science,* translated by Walter Kaufmann (New York: Vintage, 1974), §285, p. 232.

24   The terms are Nietzsche's; see *Thus Spoke Zarathustra,* Second Part, "On Redemption," p. 252; Martin Heidegger, *What Is Called Thinking,* translated by J. Glenn Gray (New York: Harper, 1972), pp. 92ff., deals with their modern significance.

25   *Twilight of the Idols,* in *Portable Nietzsche,* "Skirmishes of an Untimely Man," §38, p. 542. Cf. *Will to Power,* §§704, 705; also R. J. Hollingdale, *Nietzsche* (Baton Rouge: Louisiana State Press, 1965), pp. 242f.

26   *Portable Nietzsche,* p. 32.

27   *Portable Nietzsche,* p. 35.

28   In *The Complete Works of Friedrich Nietzsche,* edited by Oscar Levy (London: T. N. Foulis, 1915), II (titled *Thoughts Out of Season*), 3-100; see p. 99. For the German, see *Werke,* edited by Giorgio Colli and Mazzino Montinari (Berlin: deGruyter, 1972), Third Part, Vol. I, 329, where *das Chaos zu organisiren* is given emphasis.

29   Cf. R. J. Hollingdale, *Nietzsche,* pp. 122-25.

30   R. J. Hollingdale, *Nietzsche,* pp. 140, 144, 185.

Mendacious Innocents, or, The Modern
Genealogist as Conscientious Intellectual:
Nietzsche, Foucault, Said

Paul A. Bové

For Daniel O'Hara

> We have never sought ourselves—
> how could it happen that we
> should ever find ourselves?

> —Nietzsche, The Genealogy
> of Morals

> And I am not a demigod,
> I cannot make it cohere.
> If love be not in the house
> there is nothing.

> —Ezra Pound, Canto 116

I

So many poets, philosophers, and critics have dealt with genealogical figures in their writing, that one must doubt seriously if another essay on the subject can hope either to contribute, even modestly, to the subject or to represent adequately the range and complexity of the issues already developed with such subtlety by so many others.[1] Indeed, one cannot even hope to present a descriptive chronicle of the archive on genealogy let alone a serious, developed, and demonstrative critique of its various subdivisions and crosslistings. For it is the peculiar nature of the most sophisticated writing on genealogy that it is always, as Jacques Derrida might say, a double-writing: supremely self-reflexive and self-aware, always simultaneously keeping two eyes both on its subject matter and on the irony of following on in a tradition of speculation about following-on. It seems as if writing about genealogy and writing which is the recording of genealogical research are unique sites for the detailed enactment of the sublime epistemological self-consciousness of the most avant-garde humanist intellectuals. And how wonderfully seductive are the attractions of doubling these sublime stakes in a discourse exponentially more playful and self-aware in its re-presentation of the dilemma of influence! In the hands of a sufficiently talented *Ecrivant,* such as Derrida in *Glas* or, perhaps more to the point, Geoffrey Hartman in his lovingly mad review of *Glas,* "Monsieur Texte,"[2] such a performance could be entertaining, productive of new versions of old figures, informative about the difficult problems of "theft," "inter-textuality," and "influence," and potentially liberating from the deadening, anti-aesthetic life of the everyday world.

Such performances would seem to have peculiar limits for their production depending upon not only the inventiveness of the writer, but also upon the writer's landscape of scholarly memory. Skeptical, destabilizing wit (is this not a redundancy; for Kierkegaard, irony is a riddle and its solution possessed simultaneously[3]) combined with immense learning, research skills, and a hypertrophied memory would reserve the energy for such potentially limitless play. One cannot, of course, say that it is limitless play of the "same kind" without indulging in metaphysics—which must, honestly, be announced as such. And, quite obviously, such a gesture would round the writer back to the initial moment of critical self-consciousness. However, such a gesture, in closing this circle represents its self-consciousness in its own closure and marks a further peculiarity: infinite play in a finite series, i.e., the ambiguity of the eternal repetition of the same. But, it is, if you will, only a *formal* closure inversely akin to the New Critics' Hegelian desire to apotheosize the Idea in the complex mosaic of the poem as image.[4] One might object that such a formal closure is an emptying out of "life" and "meaning"—this Derrida mockingly calls "Rousseauistic nostalgia"[5]—yet one can also see this formalization as the final, not-so-troubling encircling of the shaded space of cultural production. But, the central point is this: each of these alternatives taken separately and both taken together represent one important aspect of the Modern scholar's cultural location and intellectual conscience. Whether it goes by the name *écriture, aporia,* "anxiety of influence," or "worldliness," this closure, by its own tenets, does no more than represent the Modern intellectual's sense of place and power.

II

Canto XIII is a montage of Ezra Pound's figures of history, writing, influence, and creativity.[6] It is organized primarily by a subterranean figure of power which underlies the poem's superimposed fragments of knowing, love, music, civic order, character, and scholarship. Specifically, Canto XIII is Pound's meditation on the aesthetic urge to wholeness, completeness, and closure. It is also a representation of the imaginative attitude of much of Modern and Postmodern poetry to the burdens of history and the rage to order.

Canto XIII opens with the hieroglyphic foregrounding of the self-aware revisionist Kung against a historically burdened background of cultural and natural precursors:

> Kung walked
> > by the dynastic temple
> > > and into the cedar grove
> > > > and then out by the lower river

> (p. 58)

This image represents the intuition of all Modern poets and of all Modern intellectuals concerned with matters of genealogy. It indicates the permanent, inescapable relationship between the revisionist and the tradition he revises. Kung's walk marks the choreography of the "Modern" mind defining itself in a dance of difference from the "dynastic" authorities already "there" in the culture. It marks the bonded alterity of this binary relation which paradoxically compels the Modern revisionist to project his own identity in a symbiotic trope of the predecessor.

Canto XIII, however, escapes the melancholy, Bloomian consequences of this allegory of genealogy.[7] Simply and reductively put, Canto XIII palliates the potential anxiety of influence by refusing the central configuration of power as competition upon which contemporary theories of anxiety rest. Power and authority emerge, rather, as the resignation of the imagination to incompletion—which is not the same as secondariness—and to the knowledge of the loss of sublimity in the Modern World. Yet, these privatives enable the production of a major poem for they themselves represent an attitude toward the past which does not, from anxious exhaustion, put an end to poetry itself. For the motive underlying the anxiety of imaginative response is not only an Oedipal fear of castration—this is too broad—but also, in the Modern world, the desire for wholeness, for completion—the aesthetic remnant of the theological and metaphysical will to power in synthesis.

Kung raises and dismisses this spectre of a filial competition to displace dynastic power; the issue, of course, is how the poet should represent himself publicly, that is, whether he should pursue authority and, having announced his own incarnation, become "representative":

> And "we are unknown," said Kung,
> "You will take up charioteering?
>   Then you will become known,
> "Or perhaps I should take up charioteering,
>   or archery?
> "Or the practice of public speaking?
>
> (p. 58)

How to become known. Alternative possibilities spring up in response to this trope of self-identity; they appear in the voices of Kung's ephebes, as the peaks and valleys of Kung's own psyche: for Tseu-lou, " 'I would put the defenses in order;' " for Khieu, to put the province "in better order than this;" for Tchi, in "a small mountain temple" to maintain " 'order in the observances,/with a suitable performance of the ritual;' " and, finally, for Tian the lute-player, to sing Haiku-like painted images. These are all turns on being known: the military, i.e., the defensive or anxious; the domestic, i.e., political or economic; the religious, i.e., the conservative and mythic; and the aesthetic, i.e., the apprehensive and fragile:

> And Thseng-sie desired to know:
>   "Which had answered correctly? "
> And Kung said, "They have all answered correctly,
> "That is to say, each in his nature."
>
> (p. 58)

In their ambition and their innocent need for approval, each ephebe, each trope on the problem of self-annunciation and self-becoming, competes not only against the predecessors' authority—which keeps them "unknown—but each trope competes for survival with the others: the sons' struggle with each other in their battle against "the dynastic temple." And they demand of the father-poet, Kung, assurance that their own individual schemes, their own central metaphors for their self-identity, are "correct," that is, legitimate, named, and empowered in the violent battle of cultural transformation.

That Kung refuses to judge among the competitors is of utmost significance: "And Kung smiles upon all of them equally" (p. 58). He seems to accept the relative value of each trope as the essential and correct expression of a particular role, thereby authorizing each "son" to announce himself along the lines of the centrally empowered figure by which each desires to make himself known. Yet, Kung is *not* justifying and authorizing this near chaotic, individualistic intergenerational and internecine warfare. Rather his statement and gesture, his smile, express another ethos than that of competition.

For the ephebes, order and self-creation, that is, becoming "known," emerge only in conflict with the predecessor, a conflict enabled by a central metaphoric ideal—defense, economy, myth, or art—represented as a beneficial displacement of the predecessor and the dynastic. In this model, the power and authority of the dynasty block the ephebes' birth in public by dominating cultural and imaginative space. Kung not only does not choose among the various central metaphors which are transumptive responses to his original question about being "known," but he refuses to enter the domain of competition with the dynastic or among the ephebes and thereby steps aside from the entire network of cultural or imaginative activity conceived as competition. His smile marks both an understanding of how such competition makes of the ephebe merely a replica of the dynasty which beckons him to authority, to enter and seize the temple, and a recognition of how men themselves perpetuate their bondage to a system of maddening repetition. For each of the ephebes cultivate merely the newest substitution for an earlier dynastic metaphor represented by the ephebes as bankrupt and infertile just so that it can be "legitimately" displaced by their own self-annunciations. Kung, the metaphor of Pound's openness to the pressures and possibilities of the tradition, tolerates and develops all of the competitive alternatives, but without choosing any as a weapon in this dynastic struggle.

Instead, Canto XIII suggests that domestic and political order can be supported only by "character," that is, a power strong enough to cultivate the potentially warring tropes of self-annunciation without choosing one as even a temporary master trope:

> If a man have not order within him
> He cannot spread order about him;
> And if a man not have order within him
> His family will not act with due order;
> And if the prince have not order within
> him
> He can not put order in his dominions.

(p. 59)

Each ephebe's trope is not only one part of a larger whole, but each is also a hypertrophy of one metaphor or trope as a self-definition. Such unilinear

363

development of an insignia-like designation is unlike Kung's gentle attitude represented by his "walking" and "smiling":

> "Anyone can run to excess,
> It is easy to shoot past the mark,
> It is hard to stand firm in the middle."
>
> (p. 59)

"To stand firm in the middle" is for a man to have "order within him." Taking a stand in the middle means avoiding the central problem of all self-production: excess consists in a competitive *imposition* of a totalizing order based on a guiding and privileged metaphor—an equally dangerous excess for the imagination despite the metaphor's primary sphere of value: military, political, mythic, or aesthetic.

The order Kung suggests a ruler must have to avoid excess depends upon refusing the seduction of authority inherent in the hypertrophy of a trope. His order depends not only upon such a refusal, which implies an openness to all the different tropes present, at least potentially, to the imagination, but also upon the recognition of the important role ignorance, forgetting, privacy, and incompleteness play in sustaining imaginative life. Put another, simpler way, Kung figures power not as competitive displacement, but as a refusal of closure, that is, he transforms the dynastic figuration of power as productive authority into a trope of discontinuous historical narration:

> "And even I can remember
> A day when the historians left blanks in their writings,
> I mean for things they didn't know,
> But that time seems to be passing."
>
> (p. 60)

The point here is that the ephebe's self-annunciation in and through a central figure is always a dynastic, or canonical, revision of the canon which, thereby, sustains the dynasty somewhat on the model of the family romance. Kung's smiling and refusing to make a selective judgment to authorize a trope for his own and his followers' identity is akin to the last historians' strength to have gaps in their revisions or reconstructions. Their unwillingness to impose a master trope through interpretation, their hesitancy to extend the dynastic organization of power through well-made retelling, suggests an alternative figure of power. They do not merely, as it were, reorganize "the relations of production" by changing the guard in control of power; in other words, by letting the ephebe gain authority in identity, by creating, supposedly, an individual voice and hence, an identity. But, rather, they change the means of production and what is produced.

364

To gain authority, to achieve identity, that is, a voice and control, the ephebe creates two hypostases, or accepts the already given: the canonical self-interpretation of the tradition in the hegemonic present, that represented by "the dynastic temple" and the world of publicity; and, a cohesive self-identity named by and produced by the central trope of his identity. In the contemporary critical sphere, one might consider Harold Bloom to be the paradigm of this type of production. The past is always remade and reified in these transformations of the dynastic and the authority of the remaking depends, of course, upon its cogency and completeness, upon knowledge and continuity. Legitimacy occurs when counter-versions of the late are excluded by the newly dominant interpretation. Yet, the ongoing pursuit of such displacement gives legitimacy above all to this competitive mode of displacement. Changing the mode and product of these productive forms would suspend this competitive model and result in a configuration of power which leaves space for the different interpretations of an imperfectly known and highly mediated past. Moreover, in the spaces of reconstruction, power persists as a surplus freed from competitive patterns. It allows not only for aesthetic activity that has the strength to stand without melancholy in the face of natural change and priority, but also the honest imagination strong enough *not* to reify the moment in pursuit of a mythic Paterean quest for the sublime:[8]

> And Kung said, "Without character you will be unable to
>   play on that instrument
> Or to execute the music fit for the Odes.
> The blossoms of the apricot
>   blow from the east to the west,
> And I have tried to keep them from falling."

(p. 60)

III

I have begun what is essentially a discussion of the figure of the genealogist in Nietzsche's *Genealogy of Morals*, Michel Foucault's *Discipline and Punish*, and, to a lesser extent, Edward W. Said's *Orientalism*,[9] with this allegory of Canto XIII because it poses richly and directly two important issues: can the genealogical revisionist escape the filial problem of the Modern world, i.e., avoid reproducing the structure of that he revises; can genealogy clarify the central issue of much of contemporary scholarly activity: to struggle against power itself or to attempt a new mode of organization of power.

Given what is now common knowledge of Pound's politics, it would seem that as a revisionist he opted for a fascist reorganization of power. Yet, the Kung Canto suggests that, even prior to the defeat of the

Axis in WWII and prior to the appearance of quietistic figures like Francis of Assisi in the later cantos, Pound conceived of the Modern struggle as one against power figured as competition and continuity. That Pound could reinvent his own trope to see in fascism the concrete manifestitations of "character" does not deny the sensibility of Canto XIII. It poignantly begs a harder question: how can the imagination deny its own openness in fantasizing Mussolini as the figure of "character." The political answer to this question is available in Pound's individualistic project and period. For the figure of Kung does not represent, among its various echoes, the positive possibility of a community except as an extension of a hierarchical elite, a pseudo-oriental, medieval emanation of order from within the self-aware, balanced, and imaginative leader—a leader whose generosity and tolerance cannot prevent the decline of the state into competition, who can only *try* to prevent the apricot blossoms from falling.

If Pound's poem, and his life, too, pose the difficult question of the Modern intellectual's figure of himself, Nietzsche, Foucault, and Said project certain varied and more or less tentative images of the intellectual conceived as self-conscious, politically aware genealogist. There are certain stable features to this characterization over one hundred years as well as interesting debts and differences in the three versions of this literary figure I intend to examine.

IV

Beginning a consideration of Nietzsche's *Genealogy* with the ending of the text allows us, appropriately, to tell the story of his work in a flashback, as it were. It lets the entire agon of Nietzsche's project stand out clearly and places the final stroke on his portrait of the genealogist, of the modern critical intellectual:

> We can no longer conceal from ourselves *what* is expressed by all that willing which has taken its direction from the ascetic ideal: this hatred of the human, and even more of the animal, and more still of the practical, this horror of the senses, of reason itself, this fear of happiness and beauty, this longing to get away from all appearance, change, becoming, death, wishing, from longing itself—all this means—let us dare to grasp it—*a will to nothingness,* an aversion (*Widerwillen*) to life, a rebellion against the most fundamental presuppositions of life; but it is and remains a *will!* ... And, to repeat in conclusion what I said at the beginning: man would rather will *nothingness* than *not* will.—
>
> (*GM,* pp. 162-63)

Genealogical research is, then, essentially a revealing of something begun in the past and continuing into the present. Moreover, it is a revealing which clarifies the "what-ness" of something always present, but unnoticed in its "what-ness." Indeed the genealogist exposes what it is about men's own societal creations which, although essential to self-preservation and self-understanding, they "conceal" from themselves. When such concealment is no longer possible, the genealogist demystifies the "natural" qualities of the omnipresent, unexamined groundings of the fading dynastic organization and, by naming it, furthers its emergence from concealment. In place of the interpretation which declared the "what-ness" off-limits, the genealogist produces a counter-interpretation which, not only discloses this "what-ness" as man-made and treacherous, but also explains its existence and, often, offers an alternative.

Put differently, the genealogist re-reads the surface of cultural activity to find a meaning in it different from that which it seems, itself, to offer and approve. Realignment of the cultural phenomena available publicly discloses the lines of force in a culture organized toward certain ends and proceeding through certain transformations. And genealogical redistribution of surface fragments, not only demystifies the veiling, legitimating ideologies of a system, but produces a new reading which is a more convincing asymptotic approximation of the truth of the matter.

In this essay, however, I am not primarily concerned with these issues, but with the way in which Nietzsche represents himself, or the genealogical intellectual generally. The passage from the conclusion of the *Genealogy* quoted above suggests that, above all, the genealogist concerns himself with the cultural configurations of power, of the possibility and legitimacy of certain tropes and interpretations, and with the concrete human effects of such power structures. Moreover, this same passage suggests the heroic nature of the genealogist who, as it were, alone and for the first time risks or dares a confrontation with the powers of the hegemonic culture in order to demystify them: "let us dare to grasp it. . ." And, furthermore, the powerful daring of the genealogist's demystification renders the previously authoritative hegemonic interpretation inoperative or impotent: "We can no longer conceal from ourselves. . ." Not, that is to say, after Nietzsche's performance in *On the Genealogy of Morals.*

I am not concerned with the *truth* of Nietzsche's claim—even though it does seem impossible to resist his analysis. What concerns me is the composite trope of the genealogical intellectual emergent in Nietzsche's text and, partially through it and its successors, disseminated and empowered in the discourse of Modernity. Of course, the truth or irresistibility of Nietzsche's analysis of the ascetic ideal wonderfully validates the image of the isolated, struggling, heroic, oppositional figure rising above and against the treacheries of the past and present. But is it not one of the ironies of Nietzsche's text that his analysis itself is convincing because the marginal role of the oppositional intellectual in a society in which he is ever more irrelevant is itself attractive and powerful? This is said, not to deny the efficacy of the image as a reactivation of critical intelligence; it is rather to question if this intelligence does not itself belong to an easily defined "counter-tradition" whose own diversion of militant tropes doesn't, in anticipation, proleptically, code the activities of the self-proclaimed, critical heroes whose seductive claims to privilege, courage, and authority we discover conform to an already-given niche in cultural production.

For the essential facet of all Nietzschean activity is its competitive or agonistic character. Nietzsche's rediscovery of the agon's centrality in Western culture is itself achieved in a series of struggles against a metaphysics, theology, and science which deny or conceal the role of conflict in cultural creation:

> The two *opposing* values "good and bad," "good and evil" have long been engaged in a fearful struggle on earth for thousands of years; and though the latter value has certainly been on top for a long time, there are still places where the struggle is as yet undecided. One might even say that it has risen even higher and thus become more and more profound and spiritual: so that today there is perhaps no more decisive mark of a *"higher nature,"* a more spiritual nature, than that of being divided in this sense and a genuine battleground of these opposed values. (*GM,* p. 52)

Despite the complex defensive ironies involved in this stance toward Darwin, i.e., Nietzsche's troping on Darwin's evolution *toward* the unity of a species as an "evolution" toward ongoing battle, it is clear that the "mark" of a "higher nature," including Nietzsche's own, is the degree of struggle waged in and by that individual against the hegemonic forces of ascetic nihilism. Nietzsche makes clear that one of his goals in this text is to reactivate this struggle so that the temporary victory of Judea ("Good and Evil") can be upset by the next coming of Rome ("Good and Bad") (*GM,* pp. 54-55).

It must be made clear that, in the Modern world, Nietzsche's struggle against the deadening effects of an ascetic, humanistic culture capable of using all productive knowledge for its own nihilistic ends must be supported. Indeed, effective intellectual opposition demands precisely the complex historical research and sophisticated rhetorical demystifications Nietzsche performs under the heading "genealogy." The only way we can come to understand who we are and how we have come to be ourselves is through such self-conscious genealogical research. For such analysis alone reveals how we have made ourselves—as Marx would put it, made ourselves not as we might have liked, but made ourselves nonetheless.[10] And, moreover, such research suggests that we might remake ourselves, not according to any definite pre-given plan as higher men or overmen, but by realizing that, since all of our societal codes are man-made mediations of nature, experience, and mind—and, hence, are not "natural"—the future, although burdened by the past, is open and not an ever-declining echo of the past.

Genealogical research, for Nietzsche, reactivates the struggle for the future; its reading of the past is potentially liberating in the knowledge, the self-consciousness it produces and makes possible. However, genealogy also exists within a range of epistemological and grammatological problems which taken together as complex irony form a radical skepticism. Such skepticism sometimes threatens paralysis. A limited example in Nietzsche's *Genealogy* of such a potentially paralytic gesture can be found in the third essay, section 25. Nietzsche argues that Modern science is the completion of ascetic nihilism because it destroys man's "former respect for himself." That is, the demystifying knowledge produced by science functions as an extension of the priests' contempt for the world by demonstrating that man, despite his ambitions for the transcendent and pure, operates in his culture from the basest of motives and ignorance. In other words, science now compels man into nihilism. Nietzsche, thus, problematizes the value of knowledge as well as the value of modern disciplines which produce it: "Presuming that everything man 'knows' does not merely fail to satisfy his desires but rather contradicts them and produces a sense of horror, what a divine way out to have the right to seek the responsibility for this not in 'desire' but in 'knowledge'! " (*GM,* p. 156).

The paralytic possibility lies in reading this as a self-reflexive passage which inscribes genealogical knowledge in the same nihilistic framework of science. Or, more complexly to see the "desire" which grounds the "interest" of genealogical research as a neutralization of its status as "knowledge" in a battle waged against science from a perspective simultaneously within and outside that framework.

Of course, Nietzsche denies these possibilities any efficacy by putting these abysmal reflexivities or contradictions to work for him. For only in the comic representations of the will to truth resident in the production of knowledge can the genealogist damage that modern asceticism: "the ascetic ideal has at present only *one* kind of real enemy capable of *harming* it: the comedians of this ideal—for they arouse mistrust of it" (*GM,* p. 160). Telling more truth will not damage asceticism or science; only adopting a comic stance toward it can have that effect. Genealogy not only produces a new type of knowledge, but it adopts a parodic, extreme attitude toward other knowledge, the means and desires of its production, and its value. How best to problematize knowledge? By destabilizing the very text which produces "knowledge about knowledge." That is, by exploding the assumed status of scientific text, truth, and criticism. In a comedy of duplications, genealogy is not paralyzed but enabled in its goal: to wage a winning battle against the hidden ascetic "behind" previous organizations of knowledge and society:

> All great things bring about their own destruction through an act of self-overcoming. . . . And here I again touch on my problem, on our problem, my *unknown* friends (for as yet I *know* of no friend): what meaning would *our* whole being possess if it were not this, that in us the will to truth becomes conscious of itself as a problem? (*GM,* p. 161)

The attractiveness of this gesture lies in its openness toward the future, its revelations regarding past mystifications, its promise of successful battles against Modernity's nihilism and oppression, its positive contribution to new self-consciousness about "science," and, above all, in its promise as a means of transferring or reorganizing power away from the ascetics toward those who have an "intellectual conscience." In fact, *On the Genealogy of Morals* is a central text, perhaps even the initiatory one, in a tradition of oppositional criticism. Even though Nietzsche's figures in this text are by no means original in the sense of having no history, they authorize an image of the conscientious intellectual. And, indeed, intellectuals and critics from Nietzsche to Foucault and Said have drawn on, or been inscribed within, this figure of the antagonist of the hegemonic culture's primary means of interpreting and representing itself. Nietzsche lends authority to a certain representation of the intellectual and helps, in this way, to sustain a literary tradition containing the figures necessary for the critic to represent himself, to find his own voice. This is not to imply, perniciously, that such oppositional figures are, as a result, no different in kind or value from those of intellectuals operating within the dynastic canon of hegemony. Such an argument would itself be nihilistic. It might more appropriately be observed that, in this context, it is inappropriate to speak of *one* hegemonic culture since the "counter-culture" of the genealogical intellectual exists—albeit, marginally—"alongside" or "within" the dominant scientific mind.

It is, however, important to realize that the oppositional work done by the genealogists is itself possible only because a well-made tradition of authorized figures representing the legitimacy, importance, and attractiveness of such work exists. That is to say, genealogical activity not only provides knowledge about the history of the present to open the future; but, almost by definition, it puts into play, empowers, a certain set of representations of the value and importance of intellectual work which not only contradicts nihilistic science, but attempts to replace it. Nietzsche's central insight into the agonistic nature of cultural production is central to all genealogical research, that is, genealogy as a practice and representation of intellectuals and their work gains power as an institution only as it replicates itself in more genealogical production. Although the value of each text depends upon its subject—morals, prisons, Orientalism—much of the effectiveness of these texts lies in the way they realign the intellectual's image, reorganize critical production, and provide an alternative, non-nihilistic cultural institution as a support for self-consciousness. Moreover, these texts are themselves different, i.e., they organize themselves in non-linear, analogical fashion to avoid the reifying tendencies of much "scientific" discourse.

On the Genealogy of Morals offers, as we have seen, a complex representation of the genealogist. What must be stressed, parodoxically, in light of the institutional possibilities just discussed, is the isolation of the genealogist. In the "Preface" of 1887, Nietzsche almost immediately identifies his difference from his age as the enabling factor of his insight and practice:

> Because of the scruple peculiar to me that I am loathe to admit to—for it is concerned with *morality,* with all that has hitherto been celebrated on earth as morality—a scruple so entered my life so early, so uninvited, so irresistibly, so much in conflict with my environment, age, precedents, and descent that I might almost have the right to call it my *"a priori"*—my curiosity as well as my suspicions were bound to halt quite soon at the question of where our good and evil really originated. (*GM,* p. 16)

Nietzsche gives us in this passage the scene of instruction of the conscientious intellectual. The violent penetration of consciousness by a "scruple" antagonistic to the shell of public sentiment is the initial weighing of Nietzsche's peculiarity. The cutting edge of this uninvited guest frees the intellectual's curiosity to examine a common phenomenon, morality, in an uncommon light, free of societal preconceptions. In fact, this irresistible scruple guides this curiosity in a struggle against family, nation, and religion—evils which must be overflown. The genealogist is "born" in a revolt against the given; the sharp edge of the liberating scruple which tears the obscuring veil of the hegemonic figures of morality becomes a pointed weapon not only goading the conscientious intellectual along in his process of research and individuation, but also fracturing the dynastic edifice against which the genealogist defines himself. This originary scruple, this *"a priori"* which enables genealogical research and individuation, is also a measure of success. It is a standard to weigh the value of the self achieved by the single-minded pursuit of the goal set for curiosity. A stable point of reference for the self and its project, it appears over and again as the central metaphor of the genealogist's texts.

371

But this scruple exists nowhere but in the system of research, individuation, and liberation. It "enters," but from no "outside." Its "entrance" is merely a penetration pricking consciousness, announcing a "choice" of "identity" to be struggled for in the rhetorical and research struggle of the conscientious intellectual against the hegemonic mediation of meaning and value in his culture. No causal or scientific description explains the origin of this type of intellectual: Nietzsche's image suggests a mysterious, precarious, and heroic calling more akin to the deflowering of a virgin than a blissful call from God to the priesthood. But even this metaphor is inadequate unless the engaged couple becomes a hermaphroditic figure capable of self-penetration. For the men of a "higher nature" (*GM*, p. 52), the scene of instruction is self-generated. While Nietzsche's biographies suggest the importance of his father, Pastor Nietzsche, and his early reading, along with visits to his maternal grandfather as moments in his awakening, the *Genealogy* suggests that intellectual conscience is the victory of the critical mode of the psyche over the power of given representations to interpret the world and shape the self. Not the public system for organizing language, but the exact otherness of the psyche's tropes designate the heroic genealogist for his struggle.

While the scruple deposited in the critical mind from the psyche's plethora of tropes is a small thing, like all healthy zygotes it exists to grow. This "*a priori*" becomes a self only if the intellectual allows nothing to escape, for all matters may be relevant to his project and cannot be artifically cut-off from him for disciplinary or other reasons. Hence, Nietzsche's insistence on the relation between philosophy, poetry, music, philology, psychology, and politics. The persistent growth of the zygote means ideas do not change fundamentally: "the ideas themselves are older . . . they have become riper, clearer, stronger, more perfect! " But, Nietzsche is pleased by more than the persistence of a complex of isolated ideas. The intellectual conscience of the genealogist requires that all ideas intersect with each other and, above all, grow out of the integrated life of a philosopher, of the man who lives the scruple of his project. Nietzsche reflects the importance of representing the peculiarity of the conscientious intellectual as just such a harmony of life and thought in the following euphoric version of a Schopenhaurian idea:

> *That* I still cling to them today, however, that they have
> become in the meantime more and more firmly attached
> to one another, indeed entwined and interlaced with one
> another, strengthens my joyful assurance that they
> might have arisen in me from a common root, from a
> *fundamental will* of knowledge, pointing imperiously
> into the depths, speaking more and more precisely,
> demanding greater and greater precision. For this alone

is fitting for a philosopher. We have no right to *isolated* acts of any kind: we may not make isolated errors or hit upon isolated truths. Rather do our ideas, our values, our yeas and nays, our ifs and buts, grow out of us with the necessity with which a tree bears fruit—related and each with an affinity to each, and evidence of *one* will, *one* health, *one* soil, *one* seen.—Whether *you* like them, these fruits of ours? —But what is that to the trees! What is that to *us,* to us philosophers! (*GM,* p. 16)

The work's apparent unity strengthens the intuition that the work reflects a unified will generating texts and an identity.

Nietzsche produces a figure of an intellectual with the privilege of responsibility for what Eliot would call "the unified sensibility," in other words, for Nietzsche, a responsibility for culture. It is no accident that genealogical research, as we see it, for example, in Foucault and Said, violates the traditional Modern division of disciplines and is often valuable for precisely this reason. The "fundamental will of knowledge" refuses the limits of the disciplines in its research. One of the more problematic implications of this Nietzschean emphasis on a privileged responsibility is a charge of elitism. He is empowering a representation of the intellectual as a higher being, precisely a self-productive, reproductive, balanced, oppositional figure most accurately designated by the still privileged organic metaphor of wholeness and life.

In this 1887 "Preface," Nietzsche is offering an interpretive strategy. The intellectual's recapitulation of his work finds the "affinity" between "fruits" which "prove" the "common root." Such a strategy is, if nothing else, an expression of a desire to find wholeness. But as the "completion" of an allegory of the intellectual's power and individuation —from scruple to common root—finding the beginning and the end are one—it is an authoritative and attractive figure with which to represent the value and romance of the oppositional figure:

Thereupon I discovered and ventured diverse answers; I distinguished between ages, peoples, degrees of rank among individuals; I departmentalized my problem; out of my answers there grew new questions, inquiries, conjectures, probabilities—until at length I had a country of my own, a soil of my own, an entire discrete, thriving, flourishing world, like a secret garden the existence of which no one suspected.—Oh how *fortunate* we are, we men of knowledge, providing only that we know how to keep silent long enough! (*GM,* p. 17)

The genealogist's creative powers rival those of any poet in this image.

Indeed, it calls to mind not only Sidney's description of the poet as a producer of an alternative nature, but Pater's version of the Wordsworthean sublime as well. This is, as it were, the alternative face of the tedious, non-heroic image genealogical research often presents. A genealogist of morals, Nietzsche tells us, must not gaze into the blue sky for essentialist answers to the problem of the origin of morality. He should turn toward another color: "namely *gray,* that is, what is documented, what can actually be confirmed and has actually existed, in short, the entire long hieroglyphic record, so hard to decipher, of the moral past of mankind! " (*GM,* p. 21).

This is the anonymous, dark commitment of the genealogist to the library and to the endless decoding of texts long covered-over by the "official" history of events. It is often a painful process bringing the researcher too often into contact with the "repellent sight of the ill-constituted, dwarfed, atrophid, and poisoned" (*GM,* p. 43). This Nietzsche can bear only if granted an occasional glance at the perfect, the beautiful. But, fundamentally, the strength and responsibility of the genealogist is to bear much: "distress, want, bad weather, sickness, toil, solitude." Nietzsche offers a paean to the heroism of the sublime conscientious intellectual: "Fundamentally, one can cope with every-thing . . . born as one is to a subterranean life of struggle; one emerges again and again into the light, one experiences again and again one's golden hour of victory—and then one stands forth as one was born, unbreakable, tensed, ready for new, even harder, remoter things, like a bow that distresses only serves to draw tighter" (*GM,* p. 44). The conscientious intellectual is born in a struggle when "scruple" pierces public perception and lives and grows in battle as well. Each genealogical struggle is more difficult, but each promises the reward of greater strength to commit to new, more trying battles. Self-definition is not only renewal, but extension. For, although the battle is "subterranean," that is, waged out of the public eye as a way of undermining the city's fortifications, it is also "private" or "psychological," that is, waged between the internal aspects of the psyche for the spoils of individuation and self-knowledge. The genealogist's great strength consists not only in being a "higher nature," but in winning the battle of morality for Rome against Judea. This means that knowledge does not master or "produce" the individual, but that through the battles of the library there emerges a man of a different type, oriented toward the remote things of the future with a strength and confidence which promises a victory over the library-record of all that is ugly and poisonous in man.

The genealogist is one version of that Zarathustran figure whose very existence transcends, justifies, and redeems human inadequacy. Even though he achieves no final apotheosis, for he must emerge "again and again into the light," his every victory incarnates and approximates that apotheosis. Indeed, Nietzsche's figure makes clear we have only one "golden hour of victory" which echoes and repeats itself in each momentary overcoming of struggle. Each rebirth spirals toward perfection; each victory tightens and increases the sinew-like tensile strength of this genealogist who takes aim at more distant goals.

In a curious retelling of the myth of the Fall and of the Odyssean legend of a visit to the underworld, Nietzsche has the Modern hero struggle not only out of the public eye, subversively, if you will, but concretely in a library, in a maze of gray documents where he finds, in language worthy of Jonson's "Excoriation Upon Vulcan" or Pope's *Dunciad,* the culmination of the "ill-constituted, dwarfed, atrophied, and poisoned" in "maggot man." The genealogist returns armed with the knowledge of the future and, in an image surely echoing Odysseus' battle with the suitors in Ithaca, with the bow of his own victory turned against those who would further sap the cultural strength of man with their ascetic nihilism. One must only recall Athena's constant aid to Odysseus to recognize the tradition underlying Nietzsche's representation of the redeeming figure which follows upon the tensed bow image:

> But grant me from time to time—if there are divine
> goddesses in the realm beyond good and evil—grant me
> the sight, but *one* glance of something perfect, wholly
> achieved, happy, mighty, triumphant, something still
> capable of arousing fear! Of a man who justified *man,*
> of a complementary and redeeming lucky hit on the part
> of man for the sake of which one may still *believe in
> man!* (*GM,* p. 44)

This is the Nietzschean response to nihilism which, of course, has its fullest expression in Zarathustra and the Eternal Return: "The sight of man now makes us weary—what is nihilism today if it is not *that? —*We are weary *of man"* (*GM,* p. 44).

While it is true, of course, that Nietzsche promulgates a transvaluation of all values as the response to ascetic nihilism, I have chosen to give less attention to this project in *On the Genealogy of Morals* than to the figure of the genealogist, himself. For this very transvaluation can only be carried out by those Zarathrustran redeemers who appear in Nietzsche's writings as a variable composite figure of "artist-philosopher-saint." The genealogist is, as it were, a powerful synechdoche of this composite trope—powerful because he represents the sublime victory of the marginal intellectual over nihilism. That is, the genealogist is a domestic figure in Modernity. Akin in training and values to the leaders of the authorized disciplines of the hegemonic culture, the genealogist is a transformation of his enemy: he problematizes knowledge in a carnival of "truths." He is not outlandish, but subversive and different. Most importantly, his strength depends on his vision of himself as a predecessor of the perfect man. The genealogist promises that culture shall be formed once again by the intellectual warfare of ideas which will determine the "evolutionary" course of history. Like John crying in the wilderness, the genealogist pronounces a redeemer whose figure he himself is. If the redeemer is late in arriving and different from him, the point is made only more clearly: for the incarnation "emerges again and again." In Nietzsche's vision, the incarnation occurs *not* in an annunciation of the Word, but in a carnival staged repeatedly as a comic battle against knowledge and truth, and so, against nihilism. The genealogist does not make himself god in his agonistic research; but, in each work's victory over ascetic nihilism, he appears as an emanation of the perfect man—whose intuition fuels the genealogist's warfare to redeem man himself.

For Nietzsche, the genealogist is a central synechdoche and prolepsis of the perfect man, perhaps even his midwife. Certainly, the Nietzschean genealogist has been of maieutic service to later conscientious intellectuals, like Foucault and Said. *On the Genealogy of Morals* has securely encoded a complex composite figure of the oppositional figure in Western Modernity and has provided, not a model to follow, but an etching whose chief features are strong, sharp, and purposeful. It presents a face whose key aspects are like those of the scientist, of the defender of the Modernist ideal of nihilistic asceticism but crinkled with a wise, deadly smile which marks it as a "comedian of this ideal." Seriousness, anger, personal interest—all of these are sublineated to produce this comedy. For without the comedy, "genealogy" becomes "science" or pointless hysteria. Only the genealogist's conviction that he is the avatar or emanation of the perfect man authorized this comedy. The success of the comedy in liberating him from a mere repetition of science or self-betraying impotence alone legitimates the "glow" or "intuition" of the "perfect man." Comedy arises in those moments of well-being after illness and danger.

V

Nietzsche's sense of the comedy of science can be illustrated by a brief discussion of his separation of "origin" and "purpose" in the "*Second Essay,* 'Guilt,' 'Bad Conscience,' and the Like." Nietzsche takes up the question of how man can be made responsible for the future, that is, how he can remember and forget.

Asceticism is essentially a forced training of the central nervous system which creates memory by darkening the mind and senses to most phenomena and by so indelibly inscribing a "few ideas" that they become "natural" and "omnipresent"—and, thus, perfect targets of the genealogist's subversion. "In a certain sense," Nietzsche writes,

the whole of asceticism belongs here: a few ideas are to

be rendered indistinguishable, ever-present, unforgettable, "fixed," with the aim of hypnotising the entire
nervous and intellectual system with these "fixed
ideas"—and ascetic procedures and modes of life are
means of freeing these ideas from the competition of all
other ideas, so as to make them "unforgettable."
(*GM,* p. 61)

This is a privileged introduction to Nietzsche's discussion of the
difference between "origin" and "purpose." For Nietzsche shows that
these "fixed ideas" are inculcated through a politico-legal-biology of the
nervous system; in this, he, of course, anticipates Foucault. Most
significantly, however, Nietzsche's text not only reminds us of the
"purpose" of punishment in the ascetic West, but points out as well the
forceful mystification of "origin" and "purpose" which obscures the
workings of the penal institution itself. That is, the institutions of
punishment compel the intellectual error which prohibits one from seeing
the effects of punishment in their central role in culture: identifying
"purpose" and "origin" is a "fixed idea" which itself prohibits the
perception of how "fixed ideas" "originate." For so long as one confuses
the purpose and origin of punishment as the one project, "to correct
criminal acts," then one will make no progress in understanding and
demystifying "fixed ideas" or "punishment."

Once a thinker enters into this cyclic, parodic "truth-saying"
about the relation of punishment, memory, forgetting, and central ideas,
one enters, in fact, the comedy of asceticism. One laughs at one's close
escape from the nihilistic ambush asceticism sets for the will in the
idealization of the origin. Nietzsche expresses the painful human cost of
learning these few ideas in a passage which suggests Foucault's "Docile
Bodies":

The worse man's memory has been, the more fearful has
been the appearance of his customs; the severity of the
penal code provides an especially significant measure of
the degree of effort needed to overcome forgetfulness
and to impose a few primitive demands of social
existence as *present realities* upon these slaves of
momentary affect and desire. (*GM,* p. 61)

For Nietzsche the "origin" of reason lies in breaking bodies to induce
memory and reflection: the wheel, the stake, boiling oil, and stoning shape
all remembering:

With the aid of such images and procedures one finally
remembers five or six "I will not's," in regard to which

377

one had given one's *promise* so as to participate in the advantage of society—and it was indeed with the aid of this kind of memory that one at least come "to reason"! Ah, reason, seriousness, mastery over the affects, the whole somber thing called reflection, all these prerogatives and showpieces of man: How dearly they have been bought! How much blood and cruelty lie at the bottom of all "good things! " (*GM,* p. 62)

To protect its own coercive, minimalist, nihilistic tendencies, Western asceticism obscures the origin of reason in violence by idealizing the origin and by claiming the over-coming of all violence as its own "purpose." Here we are close to one of the motives of Nietzsche's comic stance. For asceticism *will* bring all violence to an end since it is a disguised form of racial suicide, of willing self-destructiveness rather than not willing at all. Arresting the ascesis and glancing toward the perfect man requires a heroic laughter which raucously reclaims the violence of origins and all interpretations—a reclamation of violence away from ascesis and for the future, a lynching of reason in a noose of passion, and a rupturing of the linear chain of causal, or even dialectical, explanation.

Nietzsche makes clear that explaining the origin of punishment or of the law by its "purpose" is a theological imposition upon the origin of an interpretation privileged and needed by the dynastic claims of the hegemonic culture. Breaking the circle of identity formed by that imposition reveals its violence under the guise of idealism, restores the violence of the origin, of the difference between interpretations, and of the crucial difference between "origin" and "purpose," themselves. In this, Nietzsche offers an entire carnival of unmaskings which reveal not the "truth," but the forgotten mechanisms of struggle by which we remember and forget, take and claim responsibility for our history—which reveal, in short, how painfully we have made, and still can make, our own culture:

there is for historiography of any kind no more important position . . . the cause of the origin of a thing and its eventual utility, its actual employment and place in a system of purposes, lie worlds apart; whatever exists, having somehow come into being, is again and again reinterpreted to new ends, taken over, trans- formed, and redirected by some power superior to it; all events in the organic world are a subduing, a *becoming master,* and all subduing and becoming master involves a fresh interpretation, an adaptation through which any previous "meaning" and "purpose" are necessarily obscured or even obliterated. . . . But purposes and utilities are only *signs* that a will to power has become master of something less powerful and imposed upon it the character of a function; and the entire history of a "thing," an organ, a custom can in this way be a continuous sign-chain of ever new interpretations and adaptations whose causes do not even have to be related to one another but, on the contrary, in some cases succeed and alternate with one another in a purely chance fashion. The "evolution" of a thing, a custom, an organ is thus by no means its *progressus* toward a goal, even less a logical *progressus* ... but a succession of more or less profound, more or less mutually independent processes of subduing, plus the resistances they encounter, the attempts at transformation for the purpose of defense and reaction, and the results of successful counteractions. The form is fluid, but the "meaning" is even more so. (*GM,* pp. 77-78)

Culture survives only through such transformations. The very complex process Nietzsche describes has reached a crisis for the victory of the ascetic interpretation spells an end to the entire process. And the grip of the ascetic on the will to power, itself, can be loosened only by the genealogist's heteroclite knowledge and mockery of asceticism's idealizing mask. The ideological justification of all asceticism is that it puts an end to strife and warfare. While behind this humanstic mask, it sacrifices life to its own mean perpetuation and, thereby, consumes life, itself:

A legal order thought of as sovereign and universal, not as a means in the struggle between power-complexes but as a means of *preventing* all struggle in general ... would be a principle *hostile to life,* an agent of the dissolution and destruction of man, an attempt to assassinate the future, a sign of weariness, a secret path to nothingness.— (*GM,* p. 76)

Such a powerful catachresis—peace assassinates life—is the *locus classicus* of the comedy of all ideals. Taken with the previous quotation, it forms the central, authorized product and process of Modern genealogy. The "creation" of "things" in interpretation, the subduing of people by representatives, the complicity of causality and reason with nihilism, the role of chance in the transformational events of history, the conflicts of interpretations, the denial of "proper meaning" to the event as a sign—all these and more, in a Nietzschean sense, make possible Foucault and Said. For their work in *Discipline and Punishment* and *Orientalism* is a revised continuation of the reinterpretation of power-complexes to new ends, and, as such, is, to a degree, a filial extension of the Nietzschean genealogical carnival.

Nietzsche's importance to Foucault and Said is a commonplace of Post-structuralism and so requires no elaborate explanation.[12] Indeed, a good deal of contemporary Nietzsche scholarship owes its perceptions to their genealogical work on power.[13] The nature of the hermeneutical paradox is such that the work of the successor often illuminates that of the authorizing predecessor.

This is not the place to elaborate the detailed distinctions between Nietzsche, Foucault, and Said; for they are many and valuable. Nor do I intend to suggest that, although Nietzsche predates a good deal of Foucault's and Said's meditations on the power of systems of representation, he in any way preempts them. I do, however, want to make two points, one following from the other: that genealogy is itself a systematic representation of the intellectual and of "objects" of knowledge—even if an ironic subversion of all other systems—and, as a result, that the relation of the individual subject to systems of representation must be reconsidered. On this latter point, there is an apparently important difference between Nietzsche and Foucault, on the one hand, and Said, on the other.

Although Heidegger insists that Nietzsche's reliance on the will to power is a metaphysics,[14] it is nonetheless true that Nietzsche's own antimetaphysical stand led him to reject all permanent "substrata" behind surface appearance, including the subject, itself:

> A quantum of force is equivalent to a quantum of desire, will, effect—more, it is nothing other than precisely this very driving, willing, effecting, and only owing to the seduction of language (and of the fundamental errors of reason that are petrified in it) which conceives and misconceives all effects as conditioned by something that causes effects, by a "subject," can it appear otherwise . . . as if there were a neutral substratum behind the strong man, which was *free* to express strength or not to do so. But there is no such substratum; there is no "being" behind doing, effecting, becoming; "the doer" is merely a fiction added to the deed—the deed is everything. (*GM*, p. 45)

It is interesting to note here Nietzsche's translation of David Hume's objections to causality from the sphere of associational psychology to language.[15] This change effectively removes the psyche as a stable entity-in-itself from the account of causality and so not only admits endless change to the system, but removes all analysis of "depths" from an essentialist explanation. Rather than the nature of the mind, knowable by psychology in its recesses, the historical surface record of language becomes the operative "mis-reading" of "events" in causal sequence. The "subject" is merely one fiction among many resident in metaphysical language.

Nietzsche does not "eliminate" the subject. He refuses the "subject" as an adequate explanation of events because it nihilistically turns consciousness away from "surface" happenings, from the configuration of actions, and toward fruitless preoccupations with other language games which conceal the operations of power. "The deed is everything" means that power creates reason, judgment, individual will, causality—in short, the subject. Foucault's various studies of clinics, prisons, and sex have shown how this has happened. For Nietzsche, then, the "subject" is no more than a sign for a series of events which can be represented and analyzed by means of intellectual history—means of which Said avails himself in *Orientalism,* especially in his brilliant readings of Renan, Massignon, and Gibb. From this it would follow that these three Orientalists are re-creations of *Orientalism* to the degree to which this book subverts the authorized representations of them. This, of course, Said would not deny since his avowed intent is to begin a counter-archive struggling with the dynastic power of the Orientalist disciplines.

Nietzsche's denunciation of the subject leaves room too for Foucault's famous project, announced in *The Order of Things* and continued to *The History of Sexuality:*

> Can one speak of science and its history (and therefore of its conditions of existence, its changes, the errors it has perpetrated, the sudden advances that have sent it off on a new course) without reference to the scientist himself—and I am speaking not merely of the concrete individual represented by a proper name, but of his work and the particular form of his thought? Can a valid history of science be attempted that would retrace from beginning to end the whole spontaneous movement of an anonymous body of knowledge? ... I do not wish to deny the validity of intellectual biographies, or the possibility of a history of theories, concepts, or themes. It is simply that I wonder whether such descriptions are themselves enough, whether they do justice to the immense destiny of scientific discourse, whether there do not exist, outside their customary boundaries, systems of regularities that have a decisive role in the history of the sciences. I should like to know whether the subjects responsible for scientific discourse are not determined in their situation, their function, their perceptive capacity, and their practical possibilities by

conditions that dominate and even overwhelm them.[16]

Foucault attempts to develop a mode of research and of writing which reflects and reinforces the death of the subject, of all metaphysical substrata such as "organicism," "causality," and "geneticism." If power-knowledge is anonymous, if as Nietzsche says, "there is no 'being' behind doing, effecting, becoming," then a new research practice not itself involved in the discourse of the subject must develop to provide access to it. For it is in the nature of hermeneutic activity that a metaphysical research mode, no matter how demystifying, provides access only to what is already known, that is, to the realm of metaphysics thereby strengthening its dynasty—this no matter how "successful" such a project may be in polemical terms.

If the anonymity and ubiquity of power depends, as Nietzsche and Foucault insist, on the dominance of causal (or organic/genetic) and subject-based hermeneutics, then what does an analytic which resists these terms (successfully or not is another matter) look like? Foucault's general project and style have been commented on at length by Edward Said, Hayden White, Jonathan Arac, and Michael Sprinker.[17] I would like to stress merely one or two points already well-known about Foucault to complete my general argument.

In *Discipline and Punish,* Foucault willfully refuses to provide causal explanations for change or organic models of growth. The text also studiously depersonalizes itself avoiding all opportunities to represent the figure of the genealogist directly as Nietzsche does in *On the Genealogy of Morals.* In place of causal explanations or organic models, Foucault offers careful descriptions of differences suggesting, rather concretely, the material truth of Nietzsche's claim that a "thing" or "custom," such as penal judgment, is "a continuous sign-chain of ever new interpretations and adaptations whose causes do not even have to be related to one another but, on the contrary, in some cases succeed and alternate with one another in a purely chance fashion" (*GM,* p. 77). This process of adaptation appears in Foucault's text on the level of style as "catachresis," as Hayden White points out, and on the level of "content" as a series of transformations of a custom or thing each of whose appearances can be marked off as an event. In *Discipline and Punish,* this is not an organic or genetic process, but nearly a structuralist one in which no "original" exists, but only a succession of indeterminate transformations of other already-given transformations.

For example, in "The Body of the Condemned," Foucault describes how "a different question of truth is inscribed in the course of the penal judgment" in the eighteenth and nineteenth centuries. Instead of ascertaining guilt and the appropriate law under which to punish the criminal, questions of therapy and rehabilitation become important:

> A whole set of assessing, diagnostic, prognostic, narrative judgements concerning the criminal have become lodged in the framework of penal judgment. Another truth has penetrated the truth that was required by the legal machinery; a truth which, entangled with the first, has turned the assertion of guilt into a strange scientifico-juridical complex. (*DP,* p. 19)

Foucault's text dramatically refuses to suggest "how" or "why" such a penetration occurs. He looks into neither the depths nor the blue sky. Instead of speculating on a cause—which might be found in the subject, capitalism, or evolution—he offers an elaboration on a sub-case, on an adjacent issue: "A significant fact is the way in which the question of madness has evolved in penal practice" (*DP,* p. 19). The genealogist moves over the surface of events laterally as well as successively. This is in keeping with the Nietzschean value of the "deed" and of the ubiquity, complexity, and anonymity of power which Foucault repeatedly images in terms of webs, relays, and networks. He is never so happy as when he can present a previously unnoticed "entanglement."

The depersonalization of the figure of the genealogist which Foucault attempts goes hand in hand with the refusal of metaphysical groundings. It also reflects Foucault's clinamen away from one aspect of Nietzsche: that apocalyptic redemptive stress placed on the genealogist as the midwife of the perfect man, as the surety of the future. It is the heroic artistic individual become Zarathustra upon whom Nietzsche rests all his joy and work. The *amor fati* of the heroic man in his solitude, the genealogist in his descent into the "library," returning as guarantor of the future, who can say "yes" to the eternal return of the same—it is this which is absent from Foucault. In its place, he offers a research strategy, a point of view on the history of the modern soul (*DP,* p. 23). The problem is to adopt a strategy not already metaphysical, i.e., not itself produced by the disciplinary society Nietzsche and Foucault both probe: "By studying only the general social forms, as Durkheim did . . . one runs the risk of positing as the principle of greater leniency in punishment processes of individualization that are rather one of the effects of the new tactics of power. . . " (*DP,* p. 23). Does Foucault refuse the sublime figure of the genealogist in Nietzsche because, as a result of an admittedly complex process of psychological, stylistic struggle, it is itself one of the "products" of the disciplinary society's individualization? Is Nietzsche the figure behind Durkheim here? In any case, Foucault presents a strategy of mapping rather than a heroic struggle as his approach to understanding power: "I simply intend to map on a series of examples some of the essential techniques that most easily spread from one (disciplinary institution) to another. These were always meticulous, often minute, techniques, but they had their importance: because they defined a certain mode of detailed political investment of the body, a 'new micro-physics' of power. . ." (*DP,* p. 139).

Like Nietzsche and Foucault, and unlike all historians of ideas, Said insists on the materiality of the power of representation; there is nothing "so innocent as an 'idea' of the Orient." Also like Foucault, Said insists on the importance of a point of view on his material which allows the familiar to be seen in a new way: "my hybrid perspective is broadly historical and 'anthropological,' given that I believe all texts to be worldly and circumstantial in (of course) ways that vary from genre to genre, and from historical period to historical period." Yet, Said goes on to say that, unlike Foucault, and largely for empirical reasons, he does "believe in the determining imprint of individual writers upon the otherwise anonymous collective body of texts constituting a discursive formation like Orientalism" (*O,* p. 23).

Said's reversal of Foucault on this point is, rather obviously, more than a merely empirical matter. Said's sympathy with Gramsci leads him to quote significantly from *Prison Notebooks* at precisely the moment when he articulates the unavoidable subject of the "personal dimension" of his project: " 'The starting-point of critical elaboration is the consciousness of what one really is, and is "knowing thyself" as a product of the historical process to date, which has deposited in you an infinity of traces without leaving an inventory . . . therefore it is imperative at the outset to compile such an inventory' " (*O,* p. 25). Said is explaining his own stake in doing an inventory of the disciplines which have done much to shape him as an Arab in the West as well as, of course, the West and the Middle-East themselves.

As the quotation from Gramsci makes clear, Said does not reactivate the subject to extend the Nietzschean figure of the perfect man as an apocalyptic or redemptive device. Nor is he reestablishing some metaphysics Foucault hopes to avoid. Rather, by producing an inventory of Orientalism he is cataloguing the history of the humanistic Western intellectual and demystifying its idealistic tendencies. More: he is also demonstrating that the skills of the literary intellectual can be adopted to a confrontation with the worldliness of texts as systems of representation. *Orientalism* is an inventory of how the Western intellectual has come to be in the service of the hegemonic culture and an example of an alternative role. One need only see (*O,* p. 273) how useful T. S. Eliot's notion of tradition and the individual talent and I. A. Richards' metaphor of balanced compasses can be in explaining the role of the intellectual in relation to his discipline to understand Said's stress on the determining influence of the subject. For to the degree that *Orientalism* successfully disseminates a new practice for the literary intellectual Said himself will become such a determining influence on Modern humanistic studies. Of course, such an interpretation suggests that Said's image of the intellectual is not so distant from the heroic Nietzschean figure of the genealogist. For it is Said's attempt to re-legitimate humanistic intellectuals in the contemporary world which most reminds one of the self-exiled, isolated Nietzsche. Interestingly, both are renegades from a discipline they try to redeem by transcending. Both employ the philological and critical techniques of their own disciplines combined with essential borrowings from related fields to organize an oppositional figure of the intellectual in the West.

Yet, the differences between Nietzsche's and Said's version of this figure are important. While it is crucial, of course, that unlike Nietzsche, but like Foucault, Said remains a member in good standing of his profession—no matter how unappreciatively in certain quarters—perhaps the chief difference between them for my purposes is a discursive one. While Nietzsche's catachretical style and philosophy always turns away from the proximate and authorized figures of his discipline and culture, Said readily adapts them to his own ends. This is an important point and one related to Foucault's stylistic experiments. It becomes an issue precisely because Said makes so telling a case for the need of literary critics to become oppositional rather than remain mandarin figures. Moreover, it becomes a problem because Said makes such a brilliant and powerful case against Orientalism as it existed until quite recently.

The question is a simple one: how complete an oppositional practice does Said represent when he employs the central metaphor of Modern criticism to demystify Orientalism *without,* at the same time, destroying those devices he employs? Are these devices not themselves part of, supports for, the general bankruptcy and nihilism of the West captured so brilliantly by Said? I do not believe this is a point which can be dismissed as jesuitical or refined away by broader "political" considerations. For as Nietzsche makes all too clear, ascetic nihilism constantly extends its hegemony under the guise of respectability, of morality.

Put differently, the question is this: can *Orientalism* be a seriously oppositional text when many of the major devices it unquestioningly employs belong to one of the essential ideological instruments of the hegemonic culture under question? Is this not to reestablish that culture by extending its techniques, its "cultural-psychological" map, as it were? I pose these questions *not* to deny the significance and, at times, the beauty of *Orientalism,* but to confront an inescapable methodological problem and choice: how obliged is the critic to be subversive, or ironical, about the weaponry which makes his project possible? Is it not true that the paradoxically conservative nature of Said's project emerges not in his admiration of Auerbach (*O,* pp. 258-9), but in his attempt to redeem the critical intellectual discipline from the mandarins of refinement by putting to use some of their central tools:[18]

Within this field, which no single scholar can create but

> which each scholar receives and in which he then finds a
> place for himself, the individual researcher makes his
> contribution. . . . Thus each individual contribution first
> causes changes within the field and then promotes a new
> stability, in the way that on a surface covered with
> twenty compasses the introduction of a twenty-first will
> cause all the others to quiver, then to settle into a new
> accommodating configuration. (*O*, p. 273)

Said here is arguing that there can be no true representation of anything and that, consequently, discursive fields are formed by this type of unsettling and accommodation.

This is, of course, self-reflexive, i.e., in criticism and Orientalism, Said is like the twenty-first compass. But there is a special type of double irony here too, for the oppositional critic makes a seemingly anti-hegemonic point by utilizing two of the most powerful tropes of two of the most hegemonic figures—Eliot and Richards—and concludes, in so doing, that all disruptions of the unified discursive field can be "accommodated." In the figure, the critic marks the limits and possibilities of the oppositional intellectual loyal to the procedures of his discipline. It is significant that in this most powerful of revisionist texts, the inability to mark a more than incremental distance, a true difference from the dynastic becomes clear. Said's text reveals the need and difficulty of thinking through how we are all organized—authorized and molested, as he might put it—by the history of our being, by our "inventory"—especially if we hope to emulate Said in attempting critical projects to reorganize the power structures of our culture.

Some reviewers of *Orientalism* have suggested too simplistically that Said does to Orientalism what Orientalists do to the "Orient," that is, produce an undifferentiated "object" about which one can unjustifiably generalize.[19] It seems to me that this is an unfair charge as long as it does not recognize two things: the consistency of Orientalism as a discipline and the cultural/epistemological difficulties I have just described. For employing the techniques of criticism against an adjacent discourse, Orientalism, (indeed, they are at times the same!), will reveal precisely the family resemblance these reviews object to. But it is not a resemblance which can be effaced, only qualified, twisted, parodied.

One understands, of course, why Said cannot accept the Nietzschean injunction that comedy is the only enemy of nihilism. The immediate pressures of our historical reality suggest that such comedy is itself mandarin self-indulgence. Said turns the weapons of the West against its own machinery for self-representation and exposes a good deal of the ugliness masked by that machinery. He engages in open warfare for high stakes and is seemingly successful. Yet, one must wonder if *Orientalism* does not generate a degree of contempt for Western man's sexually driven need to subjugate the "Other" in the form of the "Orient" and if this contempt does not mark another entanglement of Orientalism with nihilism. "All science," to quote Nietzsche again, "has at present the object of dissuading man from his former respect for himself, as if this had been nothing but a piece of bizarre conceit" (*GM,* pp. 155-56). Not only does Said make clear that the West's self-representation is such a bizarre conceit, but *Orientalism* suggests, in its successes and failures, that the figure of the oppositional critic may be as well. In other words, we arrive at the parodic moment of Nietzschean comedy in any case. Nietzsche would, one must presume, laugh with relief at having escaped the hidden dangers of such an oppositional figure which would assassinate him by drawing him treacherously into the ubiquitous web of a Western tradition of nihilism.

Nietzsche saw fit to end *On the Genealogy of Morals* by repeating his insight that science is nihilistic because it destroys humanity. He was briefly repeating his warning regarding the seductive illusions dangerously buried in intellectual activity. Foucault and Said have been sensitive to the same possibilities and dangers as Nietzsche and in the complex judgments which must be made of their work we see that they are his true heirs. For in the genealogies of all of these intellectuals, life wrestles with and against death. In their various commitments to man and science, one sees the truth of Nietzsche's fundamental paradox: "the ascetic ideal is an artifice for the *preservation* of life" (*GM,* p. 120).

University of Pittsburgh

NOTES

1   See, for example, Paul De Man, "Genesis and Genealogy in Nietzsche's *Birth of Tragedy," Allegories of Reading* (New Haven: Yale Univ. Press, 1979), 79-102; Michel Foucault, "Nietzsche, Genealogy, History," *Language, Counter-Memory, Practice,* ed. Donald F. Bouchard (Ithaca: Cornell Univ. Press, 1977), 139-64; Edward W. Said, *Beginnings* (N. Y.: Basic Books, 1976), 158 f; Jacques Derrida," 'Genesis and Structure' and Phenomenology," *Writing and Difference,* trans. Alan Bass (Chicago: Univ. of Chicago Press, 1978), 154-68.

2   "Monsieur Texte: On Jacques Derrida, His *Glas," Georgia Review,* 29 (1975), 759-97, and *Saving the Text* (Baltimore: The Johns Hopkins Univ. Press, 1981), pp. 1-32.

3   *The Concept of Irony,* trans. Lee M. Capel (Bloomington: Indiana Univ. Press, 1965), p. 265.

4   See Paul A. Bové, *Destructive Poetics* (New York: Columbia Univ. Press, 1980), 93-130.

5   *Writing and Difference,* p. 292.

6   *The Cantos of Ezra Pound* (N. Y.: New Directions, 1979), 58-60, hereafter cited by page number in my text.

7   On this, see, of course, Harold Bloom, *The Anxiety of Influence* (N. Y.: Oxford Univ. Press, 1973) and Bové, *Destructive Poetics,* pp. 7-31.

8   See *Selected Writings of Walter Pater,* ed. Harold Bloom (N. Y.: Signet Books, 1974), p. 135.

9   Friedrich Nietzsche, *On the Genealogy of Morals,* trans. Walter Kaufman (N. Y.: Vintage Books, 1969), hereafter cited as *GM;* Michel Foucault, *Discipline and Punish,* trans. Alan Sheridan (N. Y.: Pantheon Books, 1977), hereafter cited as *DP;* Edward W. Said, *Orientalism* (N. Y.: Pantheon Books, 1978), hereafter cited as *O.*

10   *The Eighteenth Brumaire of Louis Bonaparte,* trans. anon. (N. Y.: International Publishers, 1975), p. 15.

11   It is true that in the later writings, the "saint" is demoted from this trinity.

12   See Foucault, "Nietzsche, Genealogy, History" and Said, *Orientalism,* pp. 131-32, 203-04, 337, 343.

13   See, as one example, David B. Allison, ed. *The New Nietzsche: Contemporary Styles of Interpretation* (N. Y.: Delta Books, 1977). Note also Derrida's central role in this new "style" of interpretation: Jacques Derrida, *Spurs: Nietzsche's Styles,* trans. Barbara Harlow (Chicago: Univ. of Chicago Press, 1979).

14   See Martin Heidegger, *Nietzsche: The Will to Power as Art,* trans. David Krell (N. Y.: Harper and Row, 1979), esp. pp. 3-6 and 59-66.

15   This is, of course, an effective transformation of the Kantian model as well.

16   "Foreword to the English Edition," trans. anon. (N. Y.: Vintage, 1973), pp. xviii-xiv.

17   Said, "The Problem of Textuality: Two Exemplary Positions," *Crit. Inq.,* 4 (1978), 673-714; White, "Michel Foucault," *Structuralism and Since,* ed. John Sturrock (Oxford: Oxford Univ. Press, 1979), pp. 81-115; Arac, "The Function of Foucault at the Present Time," *Humanities in Society,* 3 (1980), 73-86; Sprinker, "The Use and Abuse of Foucault," *Humanities in Society,* 3 (1980), 1-22.

18   For Said's articulation of precisely this project, see "Reflections on Recent American 'Left' Literary Criticism," *boundary 2,* 8 (1979), 11-30.

19   See Daniel O'Hara, "The Romance of Interpretation," *boundary 2,* 8 (1980), 259-84 for a discussion of this and other questionable charges made against *Orientalism* by its initial reviewers.

Ecce Homo: Narcissism, Power, Pathos, and the Status of Autobiographical Representations

Charles Altieri

The rhetoric of crisis for contemporary criticism contains within itself a basic source of criticism's problems. On the one hand the critic expects and is expected to spell out the contradictions, failures, and achievements of a culture. But each of his or her assessments depends on invoking standards that are usually problematic—partially because of the difficulty of securing authority but even more perniciously because of the inevitable self-staging and self-idealizing that go into positing standards of judgment. Thus to describe conditions of crisis is usually to stage oneself as ennobled both by one's perceptions and by one's courage to live with those perceptions. Critical ideals then can easily appear as primarily disguised statements of need and mirrors not of the society but of the critic's self-regard. Nietzsche once said that if one wants to dwell very long over an abyss one had better be an eagle. Even Nietzsche did not see how we invent abysses in order to convince ourselves we can take on the eagle's powers of sight and of flight.

My subject in this essay is the imperative in Nietzsche's anti-idealizing strategies for rendering autobiography and the problems it produces. But I shall proceed somewhat slowly and indirectly because I think that a central element in our lack of confidence in traditional humanistic values consists of the fact that the imperative for self-knowledge has produced an inescapable suspicion that all our critical ideals, including that one, lose their external power as we come to see the internal, essentially narcissistic needs they serve.[1] I want to show first, the need for such self-consciousness by briefly looking at a contemporary social critic who, in my view, comes to appear somewhat ridiculous by its conspicuous absence. Then we shall examine Nietzsche's grappling with the existential and conceptual implications of admitting these fantasized expressive impulses into the sphere of philosophical thinking. This will provide us a way of analyzing some of the remarkable artistry informing *Ecce Homo*. But my ultimate purpose is to create a stage where I can perform a moralistic troping of Nietzsche. I shall argue that Nietzsche's shifting the emphases in philosophy from proposition to expression returns us to criteria of ethos and to a need for a version of traditional Humanism's concern to stage motives in relation to historical models for making and judging visions of a best self.[2]

The *alazon* of this essay is Christopher Lasch, or at least the Christopher Lasch revealed in an exchange on his book, *The Culture of Narcissism*. One cannot construct an effective *alazon* without some reduction and simplification, but I think I can deal fairly with the features of Lasch's work which indicate relevant forms of blindness. Lasch argues that contemporary capitalist America has become an essentially narcissistic culture in which deep forms for establishing identity—through work, personal attachments, and accepting time and traditions—have been supplanted by insecure forms of self-esteem achieved by immediate gratifications available if one manipulates appearances and interpersonal relationships. Political protest becomes self-promotion, politics spectacle, and literary mimesis only self-performance seeking attention in order to grasp a momentary sense of worth. It would be difficult to deny that Lasch describes significant contemporary phenomena. But the crucial issue is whether his descriptions can take the form of true criticisms, and thus justify their lack of sympathy for, say, what writers think they are trying to do. As criticisms, Lasch's terms require some kind of moral authority and some decent evidence that real alternatives to the present state of affairs are possible. Were people ever really "better," and if they were can one be fairly sure that the virtue stemmed from strength and not from scarcity or weakness? As Nietzsche might say, the versions of work ethic and personal attachments Lasch praises might well be compromises with social conditions where one had to ennoble a repressive life with very few gratifications available. I find it hard to imagine a culture with a great deal of wealth and freedom where many of the powerful do not exhibit the traits Lasch condemns.[3] Certainly actors in the Socratic theater like Alcibiades and Phaedrus needed similar, if more trenchant, psychological, and philosophical criticisms.

My main purpose is less to quarrel with Lasch than to analyze his own unwillingness and inability to face up fully to criticisms like these in the *Salmagundi* exchange. The critic is responsible for stating where he gets his ideals. And if one's analytic case is weak, we tend to shift our sense of origin from concepts to psychic needs; we view the ideals as supplements for the self more than as potentially objective norms a society can embrace. Lasch is doubly vulnerable to such a shift in perspective: the scope of his criticism requires large scale alternatives which easily appear essentially ways of staging his own identity, and the content of his work, a critique of narcissism, is most vulnerable to contamination by the critic's unconscious participation in something very close to what he condemns. Molière seems ready to pounce.

These claims require evidence. And the evidence carries with it sad images of how vulnerable any social critic becomes because he is likely to base his own identity on the ideals he employs for his critical acts. This vulnerability is clearest in Lasch's response to an essay accusing him of narcissism. ("Mirror on mirror mirrored is all the show.") The authors, Janice Doane and Devon Hodges, offer a somewhat ornately overgeneralized but very intelligent version of what can be best summarized as Lacanian feminism. They argue that Lasch asserts the unreality or fantasy of others' modes of discourse while denying the desire and artifice informing his own position. Fortified by nostalgia and self-righteousness, Lasch uses a critique of public life in America in order to justify his own claim to be beyond politics because he so clearly sees the flaws of those in all political camps. Ironically, then, this social critic unreflectively ends up producing for himself precisely the alienation he condemns, while authenticating his role of lonely and disillusioned seer as not infantile regression but a comprehensive grasp of truth.

I do not like this form of genealogical analysis. It participates in the genetic fallacy of reducing descriptions to states of mind. But how hard it is to avoid such reduction becomes clear in Lasch's response to his critics. Here critical discourse collapses almost entirely into the claims of the ego, but since the mask of rational critic is never dropped, the ego does not take responsibility for its own performance. So, expression cannot here complement proposition but becomes its unmasking supplement. First, Lasch's response to the three essays in the Symposium devotes three pages to a point only one makes, and then in an offhand way—that many of his critics have placed his work in the category of self-help books that make fortunes for their author by diagnosing maladies. This need for the critic to avoid the contamination of other critics is itself a moving social commentary. But the psychology is even more interesting. For Lasch's defense of his attack on Narcissism begins with a careful, and probably unnecessary, effort both to stage his response as necessitated by a wide audience and to make clear the proper image one is to have of the author's purposes. The denial of self-promotion protests and promotes too much. This would be unfair quibbling if Lasch ever accepted the imperatives of critical discourse and actually took on his critics. But his response to Doane and Hodges is largely a series of *ad feminas* attacks on the seriousness of their position and its reliance on fashionable Structuralist models. How could woman tell truth from fashion without these admonitory words:

> But then Doane and Hodges aren't interested in serious social and political analysis and don't know what to make of it when they come up against it. Like many critics of *The Culture of Narcissism*, they rely not on arguments but on accusations of "nostalgia," "belief in an ideal past." . . . I have answered such pseudo-criticism before, but their persistence suggests a level of uneasiness impermeable to rational argument . . . . The recognition of decline does not entail idealization of the past, merely a willingness to look facts in the face. Unlike Doane and Hodges, I don't believe that gratuitous attribution of unworthy motives to one's opponents can take the place of argument, but I begin to wonder if my critics' inability to distinguish an analysis of cultural decline from "nostalgia" doesn't betray a simple failure of nerve —an inability to admit that many things are in fact getting worse and may get a good deal worse than they are now. Doane and Hodges, like many other intellectuals, can't seem to see what is readily apparent to ordinary men and women.[4]

Although Doane and Hodges do use unspeakably "fashionable" figures, their case is not the radical praise of subject-object unity Lasch accuses them of taking from texts like *Anti-Oedipe*. Instead they address the "serious" problem of correlating desire, fantasy, truth, and power—a problem with a long history in Western thought. Their case queries precisely the standards or grounds on which Lasch's arguments depend. So theirs is no simple contrast of reason and madness—although Lasch may think that any attack on his control of the meaning of reason must be a mad charge of madness. Instead Doane and Hodges use Lacan in order to propose in contrast to Lasch's serious rationality an equally serious version of a Baroque dance of desires in an endless, self-conscious play of masks. Hegel saw exactly this form of life as a necessary response to the limits of overgeneralized Enlightenment reason. But Lasch has neither the self-consciousness nor the patience to try out masks. So when argument collapses we are left only with a terribly vulnerable exposure of need underlying reason and of the fantasy roles one can play by imagining oneself as a hard-nosed, accurate, unblinking refuser of all nonsense—that is of almost all otherness. As Lasch's content collapses we begin to look at the language of the last quotation and its connections with the following passage:

> Aware of the intricate, convoluted character of the links between culture and personality, painfully conscious of the pitfalls in studying them, . . . I have relied heavily on the work of my predecessors in the sociology of culture. Risking the predictable rebuke that I look at American society "behind a barricade of books," I have tried to carry on a dialogue . . . with a long line of sociologists, anthropologists, psychoanalysts, and social critics. (*S*, p. 196)

These passages are almost unreflective versions of Rousseau at his blindest. The rebuke, for example, is an actual one, by Andrew Hacker, here introduced by a reminder that our hero knew what fools he addressed and therefore could dismiss the charge. This display of the ethos of the author is more radically and painfully present in the syntax of these sentences. Notice how the introductory modifying phrases in consecutive sentences suspend any dynamic sense of argument so that the author can bask in staging the nobility and seriousness of his enterprise. These suspending clauses are close to literal repetitions of Narcissus' mirror—timeless moments of self-absorption only reluctantly yielding up personal justification and a network of alliances for the work of analysis. This kind of observation, again, would be cavilling, were Lasch not so vulnerable to it and his actual argument against Doane and Hodge not conducted in the same, essentially adjectival, substitutes for actual argument.

II

What has all this suspension by Altieri to do with Nietzsche? Compare to Lasch's self-reflections some opening remarks from *Ecce Homo:*

> Seeing that I must shortly approach mankind with the heaviest demand that has ever been made on it, it seems to me indispensable to say who I am. This ought really to be known already: for I have not neglected to "bear witness" about myself. But the disparity between the greatness of my task and the smallness of my contemporaries has found expression in the fact that I have been neither heard nor even so much as seen. . . . Under these circumstances there exists a duty against which habit, even more than the pride of my instincts revolts, namely to say: *Listen to me! for I am thus and thus. Do not above all, confound me with what I am not.* . . . I am

> even an antithetical nature to the species of man hither-
> to announced as virtuous. . . . I erect no new idols. . . .
> *To overthrow idols* (my word for ideals)—that rather is
> my business. Reality has been deprived of its value, its
> meaning, its veracity to the same degree as an ideal
> world has been *fabricated*. . . . The *lie* of the ideal has
> hitherto been the curse on reality.[5]

In many respects the beleaguered tones are similar. But in turning his plight into a denunciation of ideals, Nietzsche suggests a highly self-conscious dimension to those tones. *Ecce Homo*, after all, is most coher-ently read as an autobiography seeking simultaneously to be an anti-autobiography—that is, to deny all the decorums and reticences that accompany an agent's presentation of himself as worthy of the time and attention he asks of an audience or of himself as audience. There seems no other way to explain why Nietzsche links an attack on ideals with a level of assertion that borders on self-parody without ceasing to be serious asser-tion. The self's demand to be seen in its uniqueness is continually being flaunted: the self claims to be a world-historical agent, an anti-Christ who writes chapters entitled "why I am so wise" and "why I write such great books," and a figure whose most mundane habits of bodily care repay at-tention.

My thesis is that the more fully we recognize the lies and hidden self-theatricalizing in Lasch, the more we can recognize and appreciate what is involved in Nietzsche's self-consciously flaunting the same theater. If Lasch's ideals of truth and seriousness begin to appear as pretexts for fantasy, Nietzsche will demand that any philosophical self be based on and take account of the psychic theatrics on the margins of philosophical argu-ment. Nietzsche insists on maintaining the expressionist or performative grounds of philosophizing so that one can in that immediate context meas-ure the claims philosophy has to capture and to extend real experience. If philosophy is to deny ideals, then its authority can come neither from dreams of propositional truth nor rigorous logic, because both of these are ideals whose relation to experience is posited by philosophy and not tested by more immediate dramatic standards. Thus traditional philosophy can be seen as a willful attempt to posit a principle of authority which one then appears to discover as an objective principle for controlling the will. If this situation is to be even partially changed, the philosopher must turn from truth to truthfulness (*EH*, p. 128). Truthfulness provides an immedi-ate state of personal expression.[6] Thus it affords a measure of the relation between thinking and existential conditions because it tests the powers ideas confer for living a certain kind of life. Philosophy, and autobiog-raphy, must prove their worth as forms of power. And one basic index of power is how fully one can consciously "become what one is"—Nietzsche's subtitle—precisely by avoiding the delusions of ideal truths and noble rational selves in pursuit of those truths. To the extent that fantasies of power go unacknowledged or get denied on unspecified methodological grounds, ideas of reason are the most pernicious enemy to true thinking and to the possibility of people taking responsibility for themselves. By pursuing ideals one stages oneself as what one is not. Thus Nietzsche's refusal of decorum can be seen as a self-absorbed attempt to evade the traps of narcissism. First, he continually warns his reader not to be seduced, not to idealize the will to power that linguistically dances an attempt to fascinate him. And more important, aware that "idealism—is the real fatality in my life, the superfluous and stupid in it" (*EH*, p. 55), Nietzsche tries to break all the mirrors to his dance. His dream is to have self-assertion which is so authenticated in the doing, in the truthfulness and courage of radical action, that there is no need to take pleasure in static reflection on one's deeds. One tries to keep becoming where one is rather than turn back in suspended phrases to revel in the intention or the meaning or the value of what one did.[7] Autobiography becomes a precondition for revaluing the hierarchy between deeds and the terms of self-knowledge and self-approval which are the subject matter of philosophy.

It is this resistance to unselfconscious idealizing and empty assertions of the authority of seriousness and of truth that makes Nietzsche so central a figure in contemporary French thought. The necessity for this movement I think I have demonstrated; its adequacy must now become the focus of attention. In order to do this, I want to analyze the nature of Nietzsche's counter-ideal as a version of the expressionist tradition in nineteenth-century thought and then I want to show how the autobiographical form leads that position into traps which not even Nietzsche's self-consciousness can fully avoid.

Nietzsche's alternative to idealizing philosophy and forms of autobiographical representation consists largely of several overlapping images for a form of authentic behavior measurable in terms of health and power rather than reference to some abstract standard. Nietzsche's truthfulness is a condition of presence or plenitude where multiplicities coexist and are expressed in terms of courageous deeds. The performative conditions of discourse are the immediate contexts, complements, and tests of any propositional content. Any propositions are, to restate Whitehead, not means to picturing some independent truth but lures for the full articulation of personal powers.[8] I call this an expressionist position because it participates in a wide-spread intellectual movement, descending in different strands from Rousseau, Romantic aesthetics, and Idealist thought. This movement is best defined by opposition to all mimetic standards which insist that representations achieve their truth by manifesting accurate copies of some original—either empirical or ideal (as in Reynolds). In Nietzsche's terms, this mimetic standard requires idealization because it poses a test of validity and of adequacy independent of the energies manifested in the active agent: in art the reflection is a copy; in philosophy it is a proposition referring to some independent state of affairs; and in moral thinking the reflection constitutes a realm of moral models or abstract ideas which allow one to evaluate actions.

Once we recognize the overlapping issues connected to notions of mimesis and idealization, it is easy to see how Nietzsche's thought is expressionist. Like his predecessors he demands a philosophy not reducible thoughts as pictures but capable of reflecting upon the nature and force of acts of thinking; he insists on a dramatic test of the value of such acts of reflection through forms of autobiographical thinking (of a relation between thinking and doing); and he sees that once one challenges the authority of philosophical ideals and universals, one creates enormous problems of interpretability. Without trusted models and with action as a norm of power, the agent to some extent creates the very conditions by which he can be interpreted. It becomes virtually a sign of power to resist interpretation because this demonstrates one's overcoming fidelity to any abstract idea.

Nietzsche may be distinguished from his expressionist predecessors by the way he synthesized themes from Rousseau and from Hegelian idealism. With Rousseau, he breaks entirely from teleological versions of expression which measure value by its dialectical place in an unfolding life of Spirit. But he deepens Rousseau's version of an uninterpretable immanence of the self by adapting to his purposes a secularized version of idealist accounts of the fullness of Spirit. This articulation of spirit retains Rousseau's sense of autobiography as a measure of value, but it enables Nietzsche to project himself as much more than a psychological individual. *Ecce Homo* denies the adequacy of virtue—it has an antithetical philosophical role which Rousseau did not assume—and thus it must find ways of deepening the claims on the life of spirit which an "antithetical" immoralist can demonstrate. One can apply to this work Nietzsche's remark on *Beyond Good and Evil*: "The book is a *school for gentlemen*, that concept taken more spiritually and radically than it has ever been taken" (*EH*, p. 112).

Developing new terms and tests for spirit is the conceptual and rhetorical core of Nietzsche's attempt to alter the nature of autobiographical self-assertion. The key, as I have suggested, is to overthrow specular, reflective means for positing identity and giving it value in relation to models. For under such models the self is divided and refracted through a complex chain of reflections between self and model, between model and the society that controls it, and between parts of the self that must be exaggerated or displaced in order to produce a sense of correspondence to ideals. In order to break out of this circle, the fundamental condition is an assertion of freedom through accepting impulses which have no validation beyond one's desire:

The power for the mightiest reality of vision is not only

396

compatible with the mightiest power for action, for the monstrous in action, for crime—it even presupposes it. . . . We do not know nearly enough about Lord Bacon, the first realist in every great sense of the word, to know what he did, what he wanted, what he experienced within himself. (*EH*, p. 59; ellipses Nietzsche's)

The challenge to autobiography is to dramatize the nature and consequences of these transgressions while projecting a character whose excesses have a claim on our lives. What this enterprise involves for Nietzsche is clear in his subtitle, "How One Becomes What One Is." "What" replaces "who" because agency is a condition of physical being not of abstract identity. And, more important, the emphasis on the "how" of becoming integrates all the themes of truthfulness and power. Attention to how one becomes what one is calls attention first of all to the process of writing the autobiography. Identity is not in a model but in a process, not in a mirror—where, like Lasch, one is tempted to become what one is not so that one can appear to be what one desires—but in the activity of building and destroying multiple mirrors. This activity measures the value of a life in several ways. It is a sign that one cares enough about one's energies to devote attention to them simply for their unfolding, without any need to conceal them by idealizing them through some moral purpose or claim to be representative. To tell a life, without external justification, is to prove that one wills and accepts one's own necessities. And the quality of energies released in the how of the telling is a sign of the powers conferred by the way the life has been lived and the free play of consciousness directed. Expressive energies give truthfulness presence and power that simply make propositional models of truth pale in significance. The expressive agent need not refute ideals; he need merely "draw on gloves in their presence" (*EH*, p. 34). This leads to a final attribute of Nietzsche's autobiographical style. Nietzsche dramatizes his freedom from canons of interpretation, canons which virtually require idealizing and altering individual experience. Nietzsche's text is intended to fascinate and to provoke, without resolving itself by subordination to descriptive, ethical, or literary criteria. To ask whether Nietzsche's autobiographical claims are true will provoke the same kind of madness as asking whether statements of desire or literary compositions are true. Nietzsche appropriates for a life versions of internal self-reference and powers to confer form (the attribute of genius according to Kant) which had at best been claimed for works of art, and thus carefully separated from an order of truths. His autobiography simply is the writing: "One has above all to hear correctly the tone that proceeds from his mouth, this halcyon tone, if one is not to do pitiable injustice to the meaning of its wisdom. . . . Here *faith* is not demanded: out of an infinite abundance of light and depth of happiness there falls drop after drop, word after word" (*EH*, p. 35). The test and achievement of Nietzsche's freedom from ideals consists largely in this freedom of tone to dictate how we read: we do not search out the truth of propositions but observe Nietzsche absorb the propositional into his own medley of tones and metamorphizing of roles. How one becomes what one is depends on criteria of power, not those of truth, for the question the term poses calls attention to the ways one articulates or fills out immediate potentials.[9]

Nietzsche's emphasis on how one becomes also directs us to basic aspects of the content of autobiography (e.g., *EH*, p. 64). Here the correlate of the freedom, power, and form-creating attributes of the telling is the agent's capacity to give voice to multiple features of its potential, with no hierarchic exclusions. The "how" serves as a concrete measure of existential powers. A capacity to realize one's potential for becoming is manifest as the panoply of properties that resist the negations of idealism, the imperative to fix oneself as what one is not. For Nietzsche the master ideas are plenitude, health, courage, and multiplicity. Each of these properties is directly manifest in physical terms, in a Nietzschean version of Hegel's dictum that quantity becomes quality as multiplicity leads one out to dance a range of powers and roles which do not become chaotic because there is no abstract unity, no need, and no self-division by which to define something as a lack or a chaos:

> The entire surface of consciousness—consciousness is a surface—has to be kept clear of any of the great imperatives. . . . In the meantime the organizing idea destined to rule grows and grows in the depths. . . . Regarded from this side my life is simply wonderful. . . . Order of rank among capacities; distance; the art of dividing without making inimical; mixing up nothing, "reconciling" nothing; a tremendous multiplicity which is nonetheless the opposite of chaos—this has been the precondition, the protracted secret labor and artistic working of my instinct. The magnitude of its *higher protection* was shown in the fact that I have at no time had the remotest idea what was growing within me—that all my abilities one day *leapt forth* suddenly ripe, in their final perfection. . . . No trace of *struggle* can be discovered in my life, I am the opposite of a heroic nature. To want something, to "strive" after something, to have a "goal," a "wish" in view—I know none of this from experience. (*EH*, p. 65)

The correlate of this plenitude, of course, is precisely the dual success achieved by the autobiography—the satisfaction in the writing and the emergence of a coherent character and world-historical type in a work arbitrarily structured of disjunctive sections and mere chronological succes-

398

sion of writings. Despite this disjunction, the power of personality, of the natural grace Nietzsche proclaims above, enables the text's language itself to become the same kind of integrated multiplicity as the personality.[10] Plenitude stems from a physical ground of form whose power is simply the energy to ride every image to every truth (*EH*, p. 103): "The involuntary nature of images, of metaphor is the most remarkable thing of all; one no longer has any idea what is image, what metaphor, everything presents itself as the readiest, the truest, the simplest means of expression" (*EH*, p. 103).

The ultimate paradox of Nietzsche's book is that the rejection of narcissism occurs precisely in the successful ways his autobiographical form authenticates the range of powers we have been discussing. This success in deforming and reforming autobiographical logic goes a long way towards sustaining its own most indecorous assertions of the book's world-historical importance. Consider the ways in which Nietzsche reverses Augustine's *Confessions*. Augustine's conversion depends on his fixing his identity through a complicated series of models and stories within stories, all testifying to his capacity to imitate Christ and saintly imitators of Christ. Imitation is, for Augustine, the principle for grounding a community and for achieving transcendence. And the climactic moment in his Christian logic of growing down in order to grow up, of rejecting culture in order to find true identity, comes when one can make oneself symbolically regress to childhood and obey a command whose only authority is the book that contains it. For Nietzsche, on the other hand, autobiography testifies to the development of a power to create and to impose meanings. *Ecce Homo* exists, in effect, in order to demonstrate the development, the meaning, and the power of the panoply of terms Nietzsche invents or redefines—"immoralist," "Zarathustra," and "anti-Christ."[11]

By reversing Augustine, Nietzsche reinforces his own power to control meanings. Structurally and thematically he reinterprets the idea of conversion so that it is not finding some other to ground the self but finding one's individual health in one's sickness. (Part of Nietzsche's world-historical quality is the irony that his vision is now as contaminated by versions of *I'm OK, You're OK* as Christ's is by pietistic dogmatisms.) This reversal is then fulfilled by his complex rhetorical and philosophical war on Christianity precisely in terms of the power to create values:

> The third essay [of *Genealogy of Morals*] gives the answer to the question where the tremendous power of the ascetic ideal, the priestly ideal, comes from.... Answer: not because God is active behind the priests ... but ... because hitherto it has been the only ideal.... What was lacking above all was a counter-ideal until the Advent of Zarathustra. (*EH*, pp. 114-15)
>
> I contradict as has never been contradicted and

am nonetheless the opposite of a negative spirit. I am a bringer of good tidings such as there never has been; only after me is it possible to hope again. With all that I am a man of fatality. (*EH*, pp. 126-27)

The unmasking of Christian morality is an event without equal, a real catastrophe. He who explores it is a *force majeure*, a destiny—he breaks the history of mankind into two parts. One lives before him, one lives after him. (*EH*, p. 133)

Refusal of decorum makes such claims possible. But Nietzsche's real genius lies in coming fairly close to making good on their logic and appropriation of metaphoric contexts, so that he creates an effect of monstrosity justified—Nietzsche's mad logic unravels distinctions between madness and truth. For, viewed empirically, what is it that justifies Christ's claim to divinity but a power to effect world history? Nietzsche claims exactly the same power by projecting himself as the advent of a new order, the birth of a new law reducing the old to a blind reductiveness. By tying his values closely to Christ, he can insist that the anti-Christ addresses the same needs and is authorized by the world-historical failure of what only Nietzsche has the audacity to oppose on the same level of generality and psychological appeal. It is almost as if the refusal of decorum is itself a sign that history has finally produced someone assertive enough to take on Christ. Thus Nietzsche's script poses as its measure of the poverty of Christ's word the loss of nerve it imposes on men. To have the nerve to assert one's antithetical being is in effect to prove both one's freedom from Christ and one's capacity to inaugurate a new world-historical order.

It is only in this contrastive relation to Christ that we can fully appreciate the intelligence and perversity of Nietzschean rhetoric. In effect he erases the distinction between religion and rhetoric because he seems to recognize that his contrasts with Christ are at once religious arguments and pure rhetorical strategies for magnification. Again we must think that simply the audacity to take on Christ is almost proof of the claim. The conquest is not by depth of argument, but historical opportunity, a pure surface contingency. Yet to understand the co-presence of historical contingency, a form of selection by destiny, and the reversal of humanist and Christian ideals of depth and justification is a remarkably deep conceptual achievement. But there is still more to Nietzsche's plays with contrastive rhetorics. For in order to fully take on the stage Christianity built as means to project and characterize divinity, Nietzsche must provide an alternative to its metaphysics, preferably an alternative that itself compounds claims about states of affairs and self-conscious rhetorical strategies for magnification. The ideas of eternal recurrence and *amor fati* beautifully serve both functions. Both are self-consciously theatrical backdrops for projecting the self as a tragic hero because they demand a full psychic responsibility for

400

one's life. But they also comprise something close to a genuine metaphysical order that extends and deepens both the world perceived and the state of the knower. Eternal recurrence and *amor fati* give the hero a content, a ground for knowing and willing himself which allows images of transformation, for example, into the pure sweetness or gaiety of tragic joy. Without his rhetorical metaphysics, that is without his staged conflict with Christ, Nietzsche would be only a belated Enlightenment figure subordinating the lyrical, Dionysian spirit to a dream of rational lucidity, and blurring human dignity by the vulgar dependent stance of viewing history as progress. But by highlighting personal conflict, and thus by using autobiography not as an alternative to history but as a test of one's historicity, Nietzsche shifts from a discursive to an expressionist model in which lucidity can be felt and danced as a form of power. The essence of that power is at once to create and to understand the claim and the responsibility of being a world-historical necessity: "To accept oneself as a fate, not to desire oneself 'different'—in such conditions this is great rationality itself" (*EH*, p. 47). Part of this fatality, we must remember, is to create fictions of fatality. The will is not a moral agency but an energy for becoming what one is in such a way that the becoming and the knowing are correlative, then Nietzsche can put in personal terms powers that Heidegger would neutralize as impersonal thinking and being. In the act of becoming articulate as the fact and fiction that one is through this conjunction of rhetoric and metaphysic, the anti-Christ posits a self-conscious, solitary reversal of the Christian salvation drama: "To redeem the past and to transform every 'it was' into an 'I wanted it thus'—that alone would I call redemption" (*EH*, p. 110).

III

It seems that the more fully we attend to Nietzsche's art, the more we are seduced by the power of his autobiographical alternative to idealization. But I cannot quite convince myself of the success of his ironies or the adequacy of his tonal complexity to dance among contradictory attitudes. There remains a sense of the pathos of his lucidity, a sense that his very freedom from ordinary illusions tempts him to stage a self profoundly trapped by and dependent on forms of rhetorical idealization basic to an autobiographical logic. Creating a counter-ideal (*EH*, p. 115) will almost inevitably trap one in a version of the idealism he opposes. This may be only a subjective reaction on my part. There is no way I can prove my views, since even if one acknowledges the pathos, there remains the plausible alternative that Nietzsche flaunts the pathos as one more feature of his complex anti-autobiographical act.[12] I want to try to show, nonetheless, that the pathos of Nietzsche's attitude is very hard to dismiss by celebrating his ironic powers. For those who agree with the sense of pathos, I shall then propose an account of it which leads us beyond Nietzsche's intentions to matters of criteria that one buys when one shifts from propositional to expressive models of truth. Self-dramatizing expressive acts cannot always choose or control the rhetorics they depend on for valuing the expression. My case will be circular: I need to claim that certain attributes of the text create impressions Nietzsche can't control, and I need to presuppose a community sharing the background which produces such associations. But I will know if we in fact dwell within this circle only if I spell out my assumptions. If they hold up, it is possible to perform a moral troping on the immoralist, to describe or situate the somewhat strange status of Nietzsche's anti-decorous discourse, and ultimately to argue for a conventional humanist way to handle the inevitable pathos of narcissism.

My argument depends on showing how in Nietzsche's anti-idealist use of autobiographical structures there are some contradictions which are not readily subsumed into his ironic celebration of multiple tones and personae. It is these that suggest Nietzsche's dependence on received cultural values in both conceiving and projecting his self-image. And this unconscious but inescapable dependency in turn generates two aspects of the pathos I have been claiming: Nietzsche's apparent inability to control fully the very terms of his self assertion is duplicated by the way in which his mastery is not powerful enough to prevent the reader from feeling pathos at some of the ways Nietzsche makes himself vulnerable. We find Nietzsche in an ironic play where the desire to deny ideals produces dependencies which deepen one's desire for independence. This in turn demands even more dependence on rhetorical structures for manifesting and supporting the desired independence. It takes some extensive quotation in order to capture the complexity of these issues:

> Now when I compare myself with the men who have
> hitherto been honored as *pre-eminent* men the distinction is palpable. I do not count these supposed "pre-eminent men" as belonging to mankind at all. . . . They
> are nothing but pernicious, fundamentally incurable
> monsters who take revenge on life. . . . I want to be the
> antithesis of this. Every morbid trait is lacking in me. . . .
> At no moment of my life can I be shown to have adopted any kind of arrogant or pathetic posture. The pathos
> of attitudes does not belong to greatness; whoever needs
> attitudes at all is false. . . . I know of no other way of
> dealing with great tasks than that of play. (*EH*, p. 67)

> It is even a part of my ambition to count as the
> despiser of the German par excellence. . . . I cannot endure this race, with which one is always in bad company,
> which has no finger for nuances—woe is me I am a
> nuance. . . . In the end the Germans have no idea whatever how common they are. . . . I tell each of my friends

to his face that he never thinks it worth the trouble to study any of my writings. . . . Ten years: and no one in Germany has made it a question of conscience to defend my name against the abused silence under which it has lain buried. . . . I myself have never suffered from any of this; I am not injured by what is necessary; *amor fati* is my innermost nature. This does not mean, however, that I do not enjoy the irony, even the world-historic irony. (*EH*, pp. 123-25)

It would be foolhardy to moralize too quickly. Nietzsche is right here about many things, not the least of which is his initially preposterous claim that ignoring his work was a world-historic irony. Along with this intimidatingly indecorous prescience, Nietzsche gives us several reminders not to take any of his assertions or seeming contradictions literally. *But how far can irony go before its play with multiple contradictions begins itself to appear as an attitude not chosen in freedom but desperately grasped as a way of reducing vulnerability and allowing one to wallow in self-justifying contradictions?* Attitude begins to function as a sustenance of personal myths. Nietzsche resists evasiveness; he flaunts the needs which might underlie his claims to independence as if he had mastered them. But for those trained by Nietzsche to become psychologists, the intensity of his pursuit of immediacy seems somewhat overdetermined and thus possibly evasive. Assertion may be revenge of self-defense, and the insistence that one is not uneasy or suffering may be a supplementary evasion of the danger of disgust and pity at mankind (*EH*, p. 131). To come close to getting away with such assertions of freedom is a sign of Nietzsche's power. But his claims to difference leave him all too close to our typical self-evasive ways. If we would use similar self-defensive devices or fall into similar contradictions, Nietzsche's likeness to us makes his difference less a difference in kind than a difference in skill at doing what we would like to do. Nietzsche protests so well and so clearly that he makes the needs served by his claims too pronounced to be conquerable by irony or self-conscious acknowledgement. A playful attitude remains an attitude, and a highly articulate distance from those whose attention one desires is not ironic enough to hold off the inevitable sense of the pathos involved in needing the ironic stance. Thus even when Nietzsche is right in moments like these, he so badly needs to be right that we find it hard to avoid attending more to the emotional conditions of the utterance than to its possible validity.

Nietzsche invites this kind of reading through his insistence on expressive rather than propositional values. What he appears not to have seen fully is that in changing models of philosophical discourse one alters criteria but one never escapes at least some background which dictates some terms on which one will be assessed—whatever the personal intentions and force of style. Expressive discourse invokes what I have described else-where as a grammar of expectations.[13] This grammar is essentially the frame of tacit knowledge described when rhetoricians talk about manipulating ethos. Ethos is to expression what logical structures and rules of induction are to propositions, although conditions for determining ethos are looser. Now what creates the pathos in Nietzsche is his inability to succeed completely in establishing or manipulating the very conditions of ethos demanded by both his expressionist ideals and his autobiographical mode. Expression is "expression of" some properties, and the "of" vacillates between subjective and objective genitive. The agent then both controls some features of expression and is symptomatically expressed or revealed by others. Power and pathos then are virtually constant corollaries, perhaps most closely interwoven in texts that try to evade or master one's dependency on ethos.

I have to some extent demonstrated specific elements of Nietzschean pathos. But the strongest, and most generally significant, aspect of my case involves features of pathos that derive from the nature of the autobiographical form as it resists Nietzsche's attempts to transform it for his ironic, anti-idealistic purposes. I want to show four ways in which Nietzsche gets caught up in contradictions he cannot fully control because he partially succumbs to idealizing features of autobiographical rhetoric. Nietzsche tries to assume power over contradictions, indeed to make contradiction a sign of his power to perpetrate transgressions. But the wish is not necessarily sufficient to produce success—that will depend on how we read the ethos of the specific actions. And how we read the ethos will depend in part on how we see Nietzsche's relation to tensions virtually inherent in expressionist versions of autobiographical form.

The first two contradictory aspects of autobiographical form consist in the problem of giving value to claims about unique personal powers or experiences. The idealist finds value in what an individual life instantiates. But if one wants to dramatize a "supreme virtue of truthfulness" (*EH*, pp. 128-29) as projected in an individual's becoming what he is, one enters upon a difficult task of using, subverting, and being subverted by the evaluative assumptions of one's society. This problem should be clear in the passages we have just analyzed, where Nietzsche must try ironically to distance himself from evaluative terms which he nonetheless wants to take on—for example, freedom from need or vengeance. And once the seeds of irony about Nietzsche's irony are planted, a subversive effect comes to color all the terms for plenitude. Irony appears as partly only another strategy for idealizing oneself in attitudes one need take no responsibility for. Nietzsche's superman merges with Kierkegaard's aesthetic man and seducer. Consider, here, as an example, Nietzsche's brilliant appropriation of the logic of conversion and use of conflict as a self-consciously rhetorical construction. Despite the achievement, it seems to me that he still remains dependent on a logic of conversion that dictates his rhetoric of health and heroism without conflict. The terms for positing conversion, health, and self-control are not self-generated. Similarly the ironizing of conflict does not evade Nietzsche's need to rely on contrastive terms for establishing his value and significance. And these terms belie the claims to self-sufficiency and make the assertions seem not triumphant conquests but supplementary evasions of needs and fears. The antithetical man who protests too much seems to be insisting on little more than a rhetorical state, and rhetoric laid bare calls out for genealogical analysis, for attention to where the assertions come from.

Where the first contradiction involves rhetoric for the self, the second involves relating claims for the self's uniqueness or authority to some coherent image of his audience. The problem here is that the self will vacillate between stressing similarity to his audience and stressing difference. Each role, moreover, can be a sign of weakness or of strength, since at times Nietzsche views the noblest audience as one that can resist being fascinated by him. Like God, the unique individual must be validated simultaneously by being understood and by being not understood. But unlike God, a man is likely to express need and to rage against the need at each pole, needing and hating both his dependencies and his drive to independence. For an audience is both a confirmation of merit and a contamination of it because of its blindness. The conflicts here permeate *Ecce Homo* and are very difficult to take as triumphant contradictions, because even if deliberate they will appear as means for evading contradictory needs. On the one hand Nietzsche insists on his difference—"to have understood, that is to say experienced, six sentences of" *Zarathustra* "would raise one to a higher level of mortals than modern man could attain to" (*EH*, p. 69). But two pages later he recognizes the need to limit his case for the ignorance of his audience so that at least some ideal readers will exist to confirm his world-historic role (*EH*, p. 91). At other points in the book, these conflicting attitudes, and the probable underlying emotional conflict of need, dependency, and desire for revenge, coexist in a single passage. "Whoever does not agree with me on this point I consider infected. . . . But the whole world does not agree with me. . . . The physiologist demands excision of the degenerate part, he denies any solidarity with it, he is far from pitying it. But the priest wants precisely the degeneration of the whole, of mankind: that is why he conserves the degenerate part" (*EH*, p. 97; the first ellipsis is Nietzsche's).

My final two contradictions are more philosophical and representative of problems in measuring the possible truth or value of a form of truthfulness. Nietzsche takes on philosophically a tension I have tried to show is basic to Victorian and modern poetry—one between stances of illusionless, value-free, essentially suspicious lucidity and one authorizing or grounding forms of lyrical or emotional intensity traditionally based upon beliefs and experiences now rejected by the lucidity stance.[14] Nietzsche chooses an autobiographical form in order to reconcile a mind which has mastered enlightenment lucidity and one aware of the Dionysiac roots and consequences of a fully tragic emotional relation to one's thinking. Nietzsche's form of philosophical expressionism, with its dance between critical irony and tragic gaiety earned by that irony, comes as close as any stance I know to successfully achieving this resolution. But there remain edges that threaten to unravel the whole cloth. The hermeneutics of suspicion central to his version of lucidity does not connect easily to the claims for health and plenitude, except as an extreme tragic pose. And that pose can't fully suspect itself because that would undermine the full self-possession of tragic gaiety. Moreover, suspicion, like irony in Frye's system, corrodes everything it touches, leaving the mind necessarily divided against itself. One sees, for example, that the act of framing a call for a revaluation of values depends on belief in or use of the myth of truth (*EH*, p. 126)—in either case the lucidity claim remains dependent on a not-self in order to authorize a full emotional reaction. Finally it becomes impossible to tell power from pathos: does Nietzsche's triumphant artifice signify an expressive power that validates truthfulness over truth or is it precisely the power over artifice that allows him to make suspicion a mask for self-evasion and to manipulate idealizing postures for resisting idealism?

I have been speaking as if there were no way to decide on these suspicions. To seek truth where truthfulness is at play is to risk going mad. Yet instead of accepting Nietzsche's achievement in breaking the hold of "truth" standards, I have imposed on him standards I claim to derive from a sense of ethos. But these are no more definitive than a sense of truth that puts the concept under erasure. They do, however, shift the focus of vacillation from the semantic sphere emphasized by deconstruction to an emotive tension between power and pathos involving issues of self-constitution and communal judgment. The last field for contradiction I shall discuss is created by the ways expressive agents try to shore up their work against this kind of vacillation. They try to invent within a text forms for valuing the intensity and scope of the powers dramatized. But the very need to locate terms for authorizing power reveals dependencies and lacks which bring back all the potential pathos the author is warding off. In Nietzsche's case, contradictions arise because the expansive stage he needs for the power he claims seems to require two incompatible forms of justification. (That it requires justification at all is, of course, a problem for Nietzsche.) Consider again the passage above where Nietzsche asserts, "Only after me is it possible to hope again," and "with all that I am necessarily a man of fatality" (*EH*, p. 127). Here he wants to act on two world-historical stages at once: his truthfulness matters both because it overthrows Christianity, making possible a new future, and because it articulates a way of dealing with fatality and eternal recurrence. He needs a dream of the future for at least two reasons. He must posit a time when he can be read, since part of his authority in the present is based on his difference, and his biological realism demands something like empirical Darwinian measures of power. But these frameworks measure quantity not quality. They do not indicate the nature of depth or aspects of consciousness that in Nietzsche's eyes allow him to propose a new version of Hegelian *Geist*. For this version of nobility he needs the qualitative test of depths of awareness and strength of will provided by unblinking *amor fati*. But as soon as one can hold out hope in change or vindication occurring some time in the future, he has a means for evading the necessities of return and the pure fatality of one's need to justify oneself. If history justifies one, then he has only replaced one impersonal ideal by another, and only move from Jesus to Marx or Darwin. He has found something outside himself to justify his energies. He has gained authority by losing what it was he wanted to authorize: "All idealism is untruthfulness in the face of necessity" (*EH*, p. 68). Yet not to claim historical justification is almost as destructive of authority, since the full tragic hero burns up his energy rather than passing it on to others. He thus manifests his historical irrelevance as part of the fatality he affirms. Art and power like Nietzsche's deserve a better fate, but to get that fate they have to theatricalize their own theatricality. And then one becomes what one is not because every how requires a what, every hero a valet, and every power some impersonal basis for rhetorical justification. The autobiographical hero is also, inevitably, a seducer. And the seducer is, almost as inevitably, his own most constant victim.

IV

I want now to ask whether there is some significant truth to be drawn forth from this account of the vacillations of truthfulness. Or, what may be the same thing, it is time to see whether the moral troping of Nietzsche I have been deferring will hold up under scrutiny. In order to do this we need to recapitulate the several kinds of irony one can elicit from a reading that does not seek only to recover Nietzsche's intended meaning but inquires into the problems inherent in his project. This leads us to the questions of what status we can give Nietzsche's text, or what kinds of predicates we can coherently project onto it. For we are dealing with an object that revels in contradictions and yet fails to master some basic contradictions needed to give value and significance to the festive spirit. My response to this question should be obvious to anyone aware of the Lacanian echoes in my description of Nietzsche's succumbing to idealism. It seems to me that both the power and the pathos of Nietzsche's text can be explained if we view it as a radical or pure adult version of something like the Lacanian "imaginary."[15] Nietzsche's aim is representation of the self in its uniqueness; his strategies entail seducing an audience away from the impersonal standards of a symbolic order; and his mode is an affirmation of contraries which suspends any standard form of reality testing—to the extent that its fundamental terms of value remain contradictory but are accepted because of the specular needs they fill. In this autobiography the act of narrating and the life narrated cannot be at variance. Thus the text has its deepest affinities with forms of self-projection like the daydream which are free of reality-testing. Nietzsche's power, then, is the intensity of his fidelity to fantasies of power and the illusion he creates that desire composed as art can create truth. His pathos stems from the signs of the power of forces outside the dream reminding us of the dependencies and determinations which cannot be incorporated within a unique seamless will to power.

It is precisely this identification with the imaginary they find in Nietzsche which leads Deleuze and Guattari to pose a psychology and social theory opposed to values associated with reality-testing. They would insist that I have no authority to impose external reality standards as my way of reducing Nietzsche to pathos. Nietzsche's power is his ability to suspend these reductive and neurotic norms for a higher gaiety. This line of thinking is very difficult to refute in abstract terms. For whether or not norms exist depends in large part on whether one does or must subscribe to some cultural values. Once one accepts a culture one accepts a grammar of norms. I offer, then, two partial ways of avoiding the claims of Deleuze and Guattari. First, Nietzsche chose autobiography and thus asked to be judged by his success in manipulating norms associated with this form. Whether or not he thought he had transformed it, his success depends on the judgments of his readers. Second, no one needs to acknowledge norms. There remains, however, the question of how they in fact live their lives and the kinds of interpersonal relations they can establish. I cannot imagine a social life without some accepted forms of ethos by which to attribute meanings to actions. One can certainly gain power by denying these norms, but one cannot also expect to be recognized and valued for what one is, nor can one attribute much value to other people. I may be wrong, of course, but even caring that I am wrong suggests one's dependence on structures of value independent of one's transforming powers. Refutation requires even more social terms—they are the price of discourse—whether one's arguments be based on propositional or expressive criteria.

There is a somewhat strange, yet appropriate, test for my claims about ethos. Consider how one might argue against Nietzsche. To do so in terms of propositions seems a hopeless enterprise, since Nietzsche's propositions will not stand still to fight. Instead, one must grant Nietzsche's truthfulness and take him on where he is most vulnerable, where he asserts the power of his ideas to produce autobiographical consequences. Here we have imaginative standards for at least focusing discussion on the values in and possible consequences of Nietzsche's performance.

In my view the most problematic or ironic feature of Nietzsche's autobiographical stance is its claim to uniqueness. For uniqueness claims are as perversely idealistic as are willful claims to possess truth and seriousness. In the theatre produced by either type of claim one is never quite the

408

self one proclaims one is. Where Lasch's "truth" leads to a "serious" rejection of politics, Nietzsche's truthfulness leads to a concluding section based on the refrain "Have I been understood?" This refrain is in part an assertion of authority, of the right to teach, and it is in part an ironic assertion that even asking about understanding is in a way a mistaking of Nietzsche's independence. But no irony quite muffles the pathetic cry for compassion as the autobiographical "I" concludes by claiming identifications only partially realized and partially belied by the pressure of need, with its evocation of a contingent historical being: "Have I been understood—Dionysos against the Crucified" (*EH*, p. 134). The pathos here is deep enough to make me wonder if Nietzsche was aware of an identification with the crucified victim as well as the pagan God. Nietzsche's ultimate autobiographical assertion is of being another. But he appears as two others—victim and conqueror, and as two, not quite either the one desired or the one doing the desiring.

If the ending of *Ecce Homo* is the climax for the pathos of Nietzsche's version of truth, a second irony brings us around to the truth of his pathos. Nietzsche constructs and maintains a powerful imaginary world in his pursuit of his uniqueness. But our capacity to identify with that demand for uniqueness indicates that the bonds between Nietzsche and his reader lead to a very different conclusion about the nature of the imaginary. The claim to uniqueness may have some truth or be capable of being sustained by a dramatization of truthfulness. Yet the most obvious truth about it is its commonness: we all share imaginary dreams of uniqueness—the *Ubermensch* is everyman in the contradictory space of the imaginary. We are all, like Lasch, "serious" about our rejection of others as not quite able to grasp the magnitude of our achievements.

When the *Ubermensch* loses his uniqueness, we can make morals of the immoralist. First, Nietzsche's attack on philosophy is, ironically, almost too successful for its own good. For he reminds us how to appreciate positivistic movements. These movements are not necessarily blind to all the complexities of the imaginary. Rather it is precisely in deference to our capacity to delude and to stage ourselves that they try to mark out criteria that for specific purposes allow interpersonal verification. Positivism often produces its own temptations to idealizing its role, but at least it contains a partial corrective to these psychological limitations. If one extends this line of argument, one can go from positivism to Hegel and to the basic differences between his and Nietzsche's views of Spirit. Because Spirit is continually self-negating and taking on new identifications in Hegel, it prepares a way for acknowledging likeness and thus going beyond solitary tragic gaiety. At several points in the *Phenomenology*'s *Bildungsroman*, moments of Nietzschean irony at the collapse of universals give way to a universal recognition that men share both the recognition of the collapse and the imaginary (or undetermined) projections of spirit that cause the *anomie*. This leads to a final secular stage characterized by a comic state of community based on a mutual sense of pathos and a corresponding willingness to grant one another forgiveness. Here Lasch's truth and Nietzsche's power both fail, but within a level of discourse that allows us to recognize our shared need for staging both truth and power. We begin to accept the partial, tentative nature of both propositional and expressive criteria.

Once we accept our common plight as beings caught up in the imaginary, it appears ridiculous to trade insults about one another's narcissism. We can forgive ourselves at least that. But we still need to control self-love, or, less morally, to find a shared stage for assessing what it leads us to produce. And given both the commonness of the phenomenon and the need for qualitative distinctions, I do not think that psychology or social history are the most relevant disciplines for making critical claims about narcissism. What matters is not what society has been like, since that is so much a function of deprivation and repression, but what society can be like. This realm of inquiry demands that we base our critical discourse on those aspects of ethos that give us a common vocabulary for describing and assessing performances, whatever their motive. Once we stress likeness rather than difference, we recognize how people have capacities to try on different images. What controls narcissism, then, is the quality of a community's discourse about images. For while we cannot deny our need for mirrors, we can provide intelligent and complex conditions for the images to which we will grant respect. The problem is not narcissism but the banal terms people use for representing themselves to themselves when they are content with reflections of their empirical selves. Nietzsche's dream was to erase all but self-controlled, playful differences between the stage and existential conditions of judgment in order to achieve a radical sense of the plenitude of momentary states of being. Yet this plenitude proves as evanescent and evasive as any dream of an unmediated relation to God. If one is to achieve as lucid a self-consciousness as possible, it is probably that instead of escaping ideals one must try to live out ideals which can bear the scrutiny of self-reflective life. Ideals must be articulated as reasons in a context of communal norms. This is by no means an original position, but it is required by contrast to what results from the pursuit of originality. In order to bear this scrutiny one has two choices—the blindness of a Lasch in which scrutiny serves one's fantasy of seriousness or the acceptance of terms of public life in which one's delusions can at least be tempered by a history of judgments and caricatures. Quotation from a traditional humanist is perhaps the only way my own identifications in this argument can be justified. Here, then, is Diderot to Rousseau: "I know that, whatever you do, the testimony of your conscience will always speak in your favor. But is that testimony alone sufficient?" For some readers Rousseau's response is perhaps all too appropriate: "I trembled with such rage and was so utterly astounded as I read this letter that I could hardly get to the end. But this did not prevent me from observing the skill with which Diderot affected a milder, more affectionate and franker tone than in any of his other letters."[16]

University of Washington

NOTES

1   I am using the idea of narcissism in the same logical slot normally occupied by the more general concept of genealogical analysis. I do not intend to collapse all genealogical analysis into themes associated with narcissism, but rather to show how the issue of narcissism raises in a concrete way problems and strategies of reasoning ultimately applicable to broader concerns. In doing this I shall proceed without a firm definition of narcissism. Instead I shall remain largely with an Ovidian image of the narcissist as one who suspends practical interactions with the world and ordinary communal practices because he is fixated on an image reflecting himself to himself in an idealized way that seems to demand narrowing the world to that single, static theater. As one sees in the analyses in Christopher Lasch, *The Culture of Narcissism* (New York: W. W. Norton, 1979), this Ovidian image holds for many cases where there is an appearance of ordinary practices, but the basic motivation is a form of suspended, self-staging self-regard.

2   It should be obvious by now that my troping will be an implicit argument against Jacques Derrida, *Spurs: Nietzsche's Styles*, trans. Barbara Harlow (Chicago: Univ. of Chicago Press, 1979) and especially Paul de Man, "Rhetoric and Persuasion," in *Allegories of Reading* (New Haven: Yale Univ. Press, 1979), pp. 119-31. I accept de Man's suspicions about the adequacy of propositional criteria, but I argue that terms for ethos are reasonably determinate and bring to bear another set of criteria. De Man tries to deconstruct the idea of a coherent performative by holding performatives responsible to conditions of reference (p. 125) and by basing his case on a forced reading of a passage in Nietzsche on thinking as an act. Nietzsche seems in that passage concerned more with thinking than with acts. And, whatever Nietzsche's intentions, thinking is a terrible example of an action since it lacks the dimensions of selection, physical behavior, and public responsibility we usually associate with actions or performatives.

3   Larry D. Nachman offers a version of this argument in his very intelligent contribution to the symposium on Lasch in *Salmagundi*, No. 46 (1979), pp. 180 ff. (This Symposium is hereafter cited as *S*.) Nachman argues that the evils Lasch attacks may not stem from any particular form of modern society but from modernity itself and the nature of the demands for psychic satisfaction inherent in secularization. (Yet the Greeks, I suggest below, had the same problem.)

4   *S*, pp. 198-99. It is interesting that Nachman also levels the charge of nostalgia, but his seriousness is not impugned. Nor does Lasch answer his interesting claim that nostalgia is a powerful source of totalitarianism (*S*, p. 182). Lasch's one specific criticism of Doane and Hodges is that they do not even know the difference between primary and secondary narcissism. He is correct (cf. their comment on the bottom of p. 190), but the mistake is largely irrelevant since only secondary narcissism is relevant for social analysis. Doane and Hodges make nothing depend on their use of "primary narcissism."

411

5   Nietzsche, *Ecce Homo*, trans. R. J. Hollingdale (Harmondsworth: Penguin, 1979), Foreword, sects 1 and 2, pp. 33-34 (hereafter cited as *EH*).

6   Jackie Wilferd first showed me the importance of the concept "truthfulness" for dealing with Nietzsche. Jim Swan did the same with ideas of dependency. And on ironies of power I learned a good deal from Lucille Kerr, "The Paradox of Power and Mystery: Carlos Fuentes' *Terra nostra*," *PMLA*, 95 (1980), 91-102. And on *Ecce Homo*, I first saw its radical attack on identity because of a talk presented by Rudolphe Gasché at the International Association for the Study of Philosophy and Literature, 1979.

7   Nietzsche does not deny narcissism, but he does deny that narcissism is a problem, for it too can be lived as a form of power. The difference is that a Nietzschean hero would not take the terms for self-reflection from some ground in an other that authorizes the ideal. Thus narcissism, or self-regarding self-consciousness, can be an extension of a flexible play among masks. How this works is the theme of Derrida's *Spurs*. I will return to this issue when I try to criticize the self-sufficiency of Nietzschean irony.

8   If one pushes de Man's deconstruction of performance to its logical (?) conclusion, one would have to say that Nietzsche deconstructs even the power of self manifest in his ironic achievement. I consider my description of *Ecce Homo* as an attempt to save the energetic Nietzsche from the deconstructionist consequences of the epistemologist Nietzsche. It is in this respect, moreover, that I see my work as adding a dimension of dramatistic analysis largely absent in Gilles Deleuze's brilliant reconstructions of the coherence in Nietzsche's thought.

9   For Nietzsche's power as based on his capacity to integrate roles, see Albert Cook, "The Moment of Nietzsche," *Carleton Germanic Papers*, 7 (1979), 8-10. This, in turn, indicates how and why Nietzsche at once repeats and extends the blend of vulnerability and ironic distance that characterizes Rousseau's insistence on the non-interpretability of his work. By "non-interpretability" I mean a text's refusal to acknowledge interpretive hierarchies produced by generic or social codes. Extreme versions of this mode will deliberately (?) render intention a problematic or undecipherable aspect of meaning.

10   I am not sure whether it matters when one deals with Nietzsche, or whether I am primarily being rhetorical, but I feel I must mention one passage in *Ecce Homo* which contradicts my discussion here: "I am one thing, my writings are another" (*EH*, p. 69). If one takes this literally, the structure of this autobiography as a relation between the condition of Nietzsche's "health" and a chronology of texts make little sense.

11   "The self-overcoming of morality through truthfullness, the self-overcoming of the moralist into his opposite—into me—that is what the name Zarathustra means in my mouth" (*EH*, p. 128).

12   In other words, every time one wants to hold Nietzsche responsible for a position, Nietzsche wants to have the possibility of saying that he staged that illusion so that his responsibility lies somewhere else—in the making of discourses or moving of discourse rather than in the illusion of content. This seductive evasion is Nietzsche's "feminine" style or what Deleuze calls a "nomad thinking" which resists all codification. See "Nomad Thought" in ed. David Allison (New York: Delta Books, 1977), pp. 142-49. My argument in the following

pages is largely an indirect quarrel with the consequences Deleuze and Derrida derive from Nietzsche's claims to be free from consequences imposed by codes.

13   The outlines of my case are clear in "Presence and Reference in a Literary Text: The Example of Williams's 'This Is Just to Say,' " *Critical Inquiry* 5 (1979), 489-510 and "Expressive Implicature: An Extension of Grice's Views," forthcoming in *Centrum*. I give a fairly full account of "grammar" in my *Act and Quality* (Univ. of Massachusetts, 1981). And my case on ethos and autobiographical power stems largely from the arguments of Charles Taylor, "Responsibility for Self," in *The Identities of Persons,* ed. Amélie Rorty (Berkeley: Univ. of California Press, 1976), pp. 281-300. I must confess to some very free adaptations of this work, but I think I preserve his central argument.

14   "The Plight of Victorian Lyricism as Context of Modernism," *Criticism,* 20 (1978), 281-306.

15   I say "like the Lacanian imaginary" because I am by no means sure I understand Lacan. As Herb Schneidau says of Derrida, "One misses too much reading him in the original." And with Lacan I am not sure even what the original language is. Also I want to use the idea of "imaginary" only for its difference from the symbolic and the empirical (a term I prefer to "real"), with no dependence on Freud, however transformed into semiotics or mathematics. Thus for me the "imaginary" is a state of demand consisting of a sense of possible immediacy and support for a specular version of one's uniqueness derived from a fantasy of a nurturing other. This nurture is the opposite of an impersonal order where the self is essentially a function of symbolic structures. If truth is figurative castration, the imaginary is best figured in an image of the King's power to make demands on women. The King wields a force of presence or phallic power which fascinates women into surrendering and affirming his image of himself as unique.

16   Rousseau, *Confessions,* trans. J. M. Cohen (Baltimore: Penguin, 1953), pp. 442-43. I am aware that these invocations of the past and images of ethos bring contaminations with them—in my case the ghost of Irving Babbitt. But recognizing analogues for one's projections of desire can allow making specific one's differences—the criteria for ethos are flexible and allow many levels. Thus my grounds are Hegel and Wittgenstein, not Arnold, and I think, at least, that a rhetorical attack on Lasch purges also the most offensive features of Babbitt's "seriousness." For a fuller conceptual case on how judgments take place, see my essays "Going On and Going Nowhere: Wittgenstein and Literary Theory" and "The Ends of Criticism," both of which remain dependent on some kindly journal.

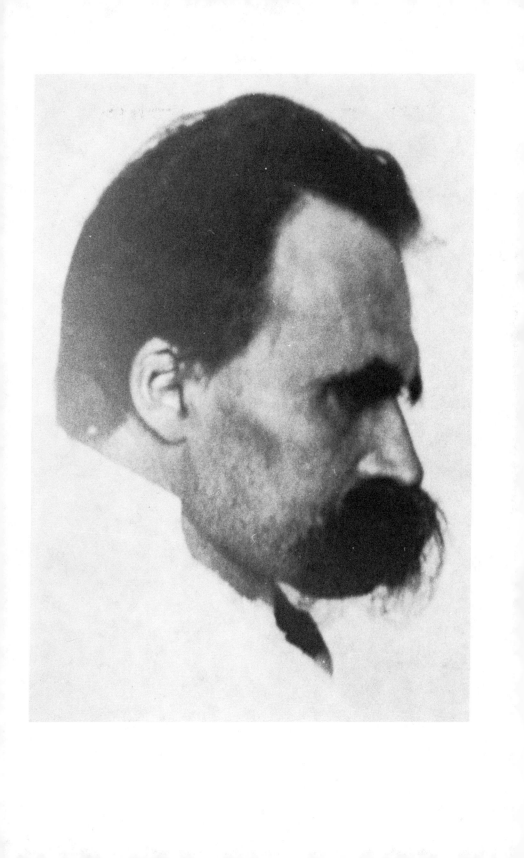

Aesthetics, Rhetoric, History:
Paul de Man and the American Use of Nietzsche

Jonathan Arac

For some fifteen years before his death in 1983, Paul de Man's writing and teaching led the American intellectual movement, focused in academic departments of literature, known as "deconstructive criticism." The fixity of death by no means assures that we can now understand his work with greater rigor.[1] Influence may swell when its specific circumstances pass from consciousness under repression. So de Man argued from Nietzsche in "Literary History and Literary Modernity" (1970), the best brief elaboration of his theoretical starting-point.[2] Nonetheless, there is some use in trying to forestall myth by history, and here I essay this through a deliberately reductive strategy: setting de Man's major book *Allegories of Reading* (1979) alongside the little-known first book of a younger critic, *Nietzsche, Henry James, and the Artistic Will* (1978) by Stephen Donadio.[3] Donadio is more ambitious than most, placing himself in the lines of Lionel Trilling and Walter Kaufmann, yet compared to de Man, he exemplifies recent "normal" American critical practice. The differences between de Man's position and Donadio's clarify the beginnings of de Man's work in counter-commentary, more an intervention within criticism than a direct response to works of literature. Without the normal errors such as one may find in Donadio, it seems that de Man might never have written, for his criticism is parasitic, belated,

417

revisionary in presupposing a primary pattern of reading to work from. Often in de Man's essays, however, the primary pattern is assumed, merely alluded to or worked through so briefly that unaware readers may not grasp the point or may take it as a straw man. Donadio's book offers a usefully generous example. The contrast with Donadio, then, helps define the novelty of de Man's work in the arena of American criticism. Any similarities that remain between them will emphasize all the more strikingly the defining traits of our current critical practice.

Nietzsche continues to puzzle us; reading him produces such divergent effects that even the limited discipline of literary criticism contains interpretations of Nietzsche which suggest wholly different ways of our living in the world. Stephen Donadio makes art and the self his interlocked master term; reading and rhetoric are the key words for Paul de Man. The reality of literature for one is aesthetic, for the other linguistic. They agree only in denigrating history. Nietzsche, however, does not compel us to consider writing as only a psychic event or only a verbal event. Writing is an event within a culture, among people, working from and toward social relations, between a past and a future.[4] Yet after some attention to the cultural "air" of the later nineteenth century, Donadio leaves us stranded in the imagination, while de Man—for instance—finds only "pseudo-historical arguments" (*AR*, 117) in Nietzsche's specification of difference between Greek and German audiences.

The chapters on Nietzsche in *Allegories of Reading* follow initial chapters on great moderns—Yeats, Rilke, Proust—and precede six chapters on Rousseau. In relating Nietzsche and his contemporary Henry James, Donadio looks forward to Yeats and modernism and backward to Emerson. The seriousness with which we take Nietzsche and his recognized extremity of mind and language allows Donadio to treat James as the major figure he is, not as a provincial obsessed with "manners." These books thus suggest that literary studies today share a canon. Both agree on the appropriate context for Nietzsche: Yeats—who took so much from him and who still so defines our way of thinking about modern literary greatness; Rousseau, James, Proust—novelists of frustrated passion and passionate self-constructors. Beyond this canon, however, there seems no common ground. De Man attacks almost everything that Donadio relies on, for Donadio's book exemplifies the situation within American literary criticism that has made deconstruction flourish.

I

From his preliminary remarks on Yeats to his concluding remarks on *The Golden Bowl,* Donadio's language strives to define a unity that reconciles opposites. Yeats writes of two "pictures" in his memory. First, "I have climbed to the top of a tree by the edge of a playing field, and am looking at my school-fellows and am as proud of myself as a March cock when it crows to its first sunrise." But then he recalls "a hotel sitting-room in the Strand, where a man is hunched up over a fire . . . a cousin who has speculated with another cousin's money and has fled from Ireland in danger of arrest." Each image "represents a fragment of the artist's experience," argues Donadio, but together in "juxtaposition" they offer "simultaneously and in a single plane" nothing less than "a complete account of the significance of the artistic enterprise" (NJ, vii-viii).[5] Donadio identifies his juxtaposition of Nietzsche and James with the intention he discerns in Yeats. This is no modest gesture toward the necessary fictionalizing and wishfulness that accompany any critical project, for Donadio believes that such paradoxical totalizing actually works. Witness his concluding observations on Maggie Verver: Her ultimate triumph depends on "a fusion of contradictory qualities of personality" (NJ, 244) that allows her to live successfully through the "moral paradox" of the book and achieve within herself "aggressiveness" that is "reconciled" with "renunciation," bringing these "antithetical feelings" into a "tense equilibrium." Finally "self-interest and selflessness have fused, and the currency of worldly success has become interchangeable with that of spiritual nobility" (NJ, 251).

This rhetoric is both critical and philosophical. It echoes phrases from Coleridge's Biographia Literaria that resound in T.S. Eliot, I.A. Richards, Cleanth Brooks, and M.H. Abrams, while it also alludes to a key moment in Heraclitus.[6] The modulation within western philosophy that helped make new criticism possible and that accounts for the proper specificity of Donadio's project is "aesthetics." His work is continuously concerned with the "artistic will." To this end, he situates Nietzsche and James amidst passages from Schiller's Letters on the Aesthetic Education of Mankind, Hegel's Aesthetic, and Oscar Wilde. A passage he cites from Wilde gives Donadio's sense of this tradition: "From the high tower of Thought we can look out at the world. Calm, and self-centered, and complete, the aesthetic critic contemplates life." He "is safe" (NJ, 55).[7] Such distanced, secure overview Donadio defines as the goal both Nietzsche and James sought in the "central belief held increasingly by both" that "art" is "the sole means of ordering and justifying the chaos of our experience in the world . . . a means for the continual reassertion of personality and the mastery of experience" (NJ, 16).

James demonstrates his mastery in the relation that he established to the "restless, chaotic, random world of experience." To that world, "he would have to yield . . . that portion of his life that was its due if only, ironically, to ensure that that area existing beyond his direct control would always remain available as the unfailing source of sustenance for his all-consuming art" (NJ, 61). The only irony I find here is that of a sharp bargain. Yield a little to life, and you can make it yours to use forever.

Nietzsche's project is presented as much the same. He tries "to rescue values from the rush of time and to reestablish them—as Plato and his Christian followers also sought to do—on some secure, unchanging ground accessible to persons capable of detaching themselves from their immediate historical circumstances" (*NJ*, 99). This reads Nietzsche from the point of view of a humanities course surveying the western tradition, for which Nietzsche has not even "reversed" let alone broken with metaphysics; he has merely recollected it.

To make up for thus diminishing Nietzsche's philosophical interest, Donadio does well to insist that James's concern with "point of view" requires serious philosophical attention.[8] Early in his analysis, Donadio finds the Jamesian "lucid reflector" a "simultaneous embodiment of ends and means" (*NJ*, 125). This incarnation of reconciled opposites returns, at the climax of Donadio's analysis, as the figure demanded both by James's theories and by Nietzsche's "Use and Abuse of History": "an observer who stands at an ideal aesthetic distance from the experience he describes . . . [who] somehow remains above the experience without being altogether detached from it, a profoundly interested observer whose imagination is engaged" (*NJ*, 141-142). Meditation on that "somehow" which makes contradictories co-possible leads Donadio to recognize "religious implications" (*NJ*, 144),[9] resulting in his final formulation: "To the extent that he succeeds, in James's terms, the novelist presents us with a complete and unobstructed vision of nothing less than the world as it is, the world as it would be perceived by the ultimate perceiver, God" (*NJ*, 154). I should make clear that "God" is not one of "James's terms." It has emerged from the logic, or rhetoric, of Donadio's inquiry.

This creation of God as a necessary consequence of an aesthetic position poses extremely serious questions. Where does Donadio stand? Is he showing James up by demonstrating that his position requires an entity that it never acknowledges, just as Nietzsche too only echoes the religious "Platonism of the masses" that he thought he had seen through? Or is Donadio co-opting James and Nietzsche for a reconstruction of God to which he subscribes? Regardless of his stand, it is striking that Donadio has arrived, quite independently, at Derrida's claim that there is a systematically coherent relation among art, the self, the symbol, the dialectic, and theology. If one cannot accept this package, if we think that there must be some other way to grasp our lives, must we discard Nietzsche and James?

II

I find much to suggest that on his own terms Donadio has not won his case. He idealizes into a "center" what James calls only the "effect of a center" (*NJ*, 166) and ignores James's attention to the slippery "displacement" his makeshift centers undergo.[10] I want to focus, however, on Donadio's assertion that Nietzsche and James find the transcendence of history necessary, lest the self be merely a passive product of its times.

420

Donadio clinches his claim with a long quotation from Leo Strauss on the function of "Jerusalem" and "Athens" in Nietzsche and then goes on to summarize: "The distinction here between Jerusalem and Athens would seem to correspond in essence to James's distinction between 'Europe' and 'America'—if that distinction is seen as reflecting the contrast between 'historical' and 'inner' culture which we have already considered, and if it is noted that for James the transcendence of 'historical' culture and the attainment of 'inner' culture functions [sic] . . . as moral imperatives" (*NJ*, 93). This analogical argument depends on a hall of mirrors, of "seem" and "is seen," correspondence and reflection. Even while emphasizing distinctions, it depends upon assimilation—as in the use of a singular verb for plural subjects. It parallels Athens and Jerusalem—which Strauss claims Nietzsche aims to unite—with America and Europe—which Donadio claims James aims to separate.

The earlier links of the chain offer equally significant problems. The contrast of "inner" and "historical" culture comes from Thomas Sergeant Perry's reading of Nietzsche (there is no evidence offered either that James knew his friend's distinction or that it is a good reading of Nietzsche), and Donadio finds in it a "resemblance" to James's "distinction between the culture of Europe and that of America." American culture "consists essentially in the cultivation of the self . . . while for the European [culture] suggests nothing so much as a passive relation—a veritable bondage—to the past." The European "is nothing in himself, but, like Madame Merle in *The Portrait of a Lady,* exists entirely in his 'relations' " (*NJ,* 18-19). Madame Merle is the only reference here to any work of James's, but she is an American,[11] not a European by birth, and had to acquire her culture with all the avid self-fashioning of Isabel Archer or Henry James himself. So the opposition of Europe and America collapses into a split within "America." Moreover, this description of the European who "is nothing in himself" curiously echoes a great moment of American literature that Donadio later makes much of. Emerson's revelation in *Nature,* "crossing a bare common, in snow puddles, at twilight, under a clouded sky," leads him into a "passive relation": "I become a transparent eyeball; I am nothing; I see all; the currents of the Universal Being circulate through me" (*NJ,* 163).

This is one indication that the problem of the self is more tangled than Donadio's argument will allow; another indication emerges in a passage from *The Portrait of a Lady* cited later. Madame Merle asks, "What shall we call our 'self'? Where does it begin? where does it end? It overflows into everything that belongs to us—and then it flows back again. . . . One's self—for other people—is one's expression of one's self" (*NJ,* 80). Although Isabel Archer cannot effectively answer Madame Merle, Donadio warns that "it is important not to be misled by James's irony," by which he means not that we must recognize things are complicated, but that we must recognize Madame Merle is wrong. Yet Madame Merle sees the self as questionable, not as easily defined by conventional boundaries. She insists only that external expression makes one's self *for other people.*

Whatever may remain hidden inside is not what we live in the world with. Yet only if we trust to some relation between that external expression and the inside can we know anything at all of anyone.

Donadio rests his whole critical project upon a wager like Madame Merle's that by reading expression one may discover a self. For he describes his book as entailing "what Nietzsche once described as 'those most difficult and captious of all deductions . . . the deduction which makes one infer something concerning the author from his work' " (*NJ*, x). I find that James also underwrites Madame Merle's stance, and not only in his own descriptive practice. When Isabel thinks through her errors in judging Osmond, she regrets having "mistaken a part for the whole," a synecdochic misinterpretation, but she neither wishes nor judges that she could have avoided interpretation and gained immediate intuition of another self. Fully to explore this would involve the relation of James and Balzac, about which Donadio has nothing to say. Balzac was as important to Yeats as was Nietzsche, was as involved as Emerson in responding at once to Swedenborg and Cuvier, was for James the defining figure in the history of the novelistic enterprise to which he committed himself, and is the exemplary writer of the self within what Madame Merle called "the whole envelope of circumstances."

Consider further a letter of James's cited to show that his ambition far exceeded merely writing "novels of manners." Donadio claims the letter bases Americanness on "the assumption that it is possible to free oneself from the past" (*NJ*, 75). Yet in the letter James hopes someday to "do for our dear old English letters and writers *something* of what Ste.-Beuve and the best French critics have done for theirs." To do something for old writers, to emulate great elders, is certainly not bondage, but it is hardly to be "free . . . from the past." The reference to Sainte-Beuve comes early in the sequence, and Donadio hints that it is left behind when James really gets launched. In quoting about a page, Donadio omits a few lines, including this sentence: "I feel that my only chance for success as a critic is to let all the breezes of the west blow through me at their will."[12] James has high ambitions, but they are attached to *critical* writing, including the critically self-conscious play with hyperbolic literary geography, the "western breezes" that had already for decades figured in American literary manifestoes. James's freedom is not in a vacuum, but in refashioning a culture.

Donadio represses James's wish to be a critic in order to emphasize the story of his creativeness; he emphasizes Nietzsche's quest for transcendence but never mentions the concern with "interpretation" so crucial to Nietzsche whether as philologist, genealogist, or Antichrist. To ignore criticism and interpretation is to ignore that attention both writers paid to reading, to language—both matters of relation to the past as well. One could not tell from Donadio's book that language was a major topic in Nietzsche's writing, nor could one guess the importance James places in the Preface to *The Golden Bowl* (the one novel Donadio reads at all) on re-reading as an activity continuously productive of differences.[13] The

New York Edition is James's greatest creation, and it is an historical act of revision.

III

De Man's work is an antidote if we are unhappy with the James and Nietzsche produced by Donadio; it would be even more useful for anyone happy with those figures, but happy people shun strong medicine. Just as Donadio expounds what de Man attacks, so he ignores what de Man expounds. Although neither author refers to the other,[14] de Man often seems directly in dialogue with Donadio. Donadio began with the explication of a passage from Yeats, and the first work de Man reads is "Among School Children." At the poem's end, de Man notes the modulation from the image of the chestnut-tree to that of dancing and finds that "synecdoche . . . the most seductive of metaphors" (AR, 11) tempts us to answer with a happy totalization the question, "How can we know the dancer from the dance?" De Man, however, wants us to take that question very seriously, to feel dismay at the impossibility of separating what are nonetheless importantly distinct elements and thus of achieving knowledge. The problems that complicate the relation of knowledge and action, of any agent and action, are Nietzschean concerns that guide much of de Man's book and that first appear here. Donadio took two disparate images from Yeats and claimed a unity for the totality they build; de Man takes two closely related images, analyzes the temptation to unite them, and concludes that they must be placed firmly apart. In the rhetorical terminology so crucial in his book, and for which Nietzsche is the major explicit theoretical authority, de Man resists the "seduction" of metaphor (including synecdoche) in order to create metonymies, reducing what had seemed necessarily related to relations that are merely contingent.[15]

De Man examines this pattern of metonymic reduction as it operates through all the texts he reads, but one particular aspect of his inquiry opposes Donadio's most directly. De Man challenges the common judgment that after his early work on rhetoric as a professor, Nietzsche as philosopher "turned away from the problems of language to questions of the self" (AR, 106). Donadio's book corresponds exactly to this commonplace in its lack of attention to language and its constant emphasis on the self as the supreme object of interest for Nietzsche and James.

De Man scrutinizes writers' language, but he also shows the scrutiny to which writers' texts have already put language. He insists that "discursive texts," those that we call nonfictional or philosophical, must be read just as attentively as we read fictional or literary texts. Both kinds of texts are difficult because "dialogical."[16] Such a text "puts the truth or falsehood of its own statement in question." "Dialogical" texts are responsible in their assertions not by maintaining an inhibited equipoise, but, as in good dialogue, by making strong statements that are answered back, either explicitly in argument or implicitly through narrative or figure. As a result, we must interpret the whole text before we can know what to make of any part of it—that is, such texts "cannot be *quoted* without first having been *read*" (*AR*, 226). This remark hits Donadio. Too often he quotes long passages as if their bearing were self-evident; too often the observations made on such quoted passages have no clear relation to what has been quoted and are clarified by no argument elucidating their relation to the work as a whole.

Because rhetorical language complicates the simple regularities of logic or grammar, because of the problematic relation between language in use and language as a tool of theory, de Man warns repeatedly against expecting to find a smooth continuity between a writer's "poetry and poetics" (*AR*, 25). "Deconstruction" itself depends on discrepancies in this realm, for it does not work through a relation "between statements" as in logic or dialectic. Rather it "happens" between "metalinguistic statements about the rhetorical nature of language" and a "rhetorical praxis that puts these statements into question" (*AR*, 98).[17] Yet Donadio treats James for a whole book before finally offering a brief reading of one novel. There is no hint that the practice of James's fiction ever jars with the theoretical statements about point of view in the Prefaces to the New York Edition.

Donadio and de Man stand opposed on four issues then: should critics define unities, or expose the absence of unity? does language have priority over the self? may we quote without reading? can we trust that a writer's works embody his or her poetics? Taking de Man's side will give us a Nietzsche and James who do not aim to be God. But perhaps de Man is just the latest whitewash for literature, attempting to make it seem more responsible and harmless than it really is.

IV

Such a suspicion is hard to avoid, and it can never be removed, for de Man's own position may mistake the effect of his readings. Yet the comparison with Donadio highlights those elements within de Man that most subdue this suspicion.

Allegories of Reading is a sustained polemic against the "aesthetic" as a category for criticism, however unavoidable it may be in life.[18] Crucial to Donadio is Nietzsche's famous early statement that life finds its justification only as an "*aesthetic phenomenon*" (*NJ*, 196, 200). De Man remarks that for Nietzsche this was "an indictment of existence rather than a panegyric of art" (*AR*, 93). Proust's writing, finds de Man, exposes "the metaphysical system that allows for the aesthetic to come into being as a category" (*AR*, 14). When de Man notes our neglect of the "dialogic" character of philosophic writing, he lays blame on "ideologies derived from the misuse of aesthetic categories" (*AR*, 226). Is there any proper use of the aesthetic? De Man's essay on Rilke strips away all the reasons aesthetics has ever offered for admiring great poetry, and Rousseau "never allows for a 'purely' aesthetic reading" of his novel *Julie*, for he finds in "suspended meaning" not "disinterested play" but instead "always a threat or a challenge" (*AR,* 207-208). Rousseau therefore always acknowledges a referential dimension to his novel, as to the rest of his writings.

De Man follows Rousseau in elaborating this point. For Kant to "ground aesthetic judgment in nonreferentiality," de Man charges, was to make possible "semiological insight" but only "at the cost of a repression" with decisive consequences for literary criticism. For it turned "theoretical poetics," which is a "branch of applied linguistics," into "aesthetics," which is a "branch of applied psychology" (*AR,* 208). This is de Man's challenge: our critical task is linguistic analysis, shunning aesthetics and the self, which are bound to each other in a metaphysical system of totalization that makes every writer and reader struggle to be God.

We can escape this temptation, this "seduction," only by recognizing the necessary referentiality of language, argues de Man. He does not, however, thereby return literature to the world. For referentiality is a function of language quite independent of the real existence of its referents. Indeed, rhetorical analysis can show reference to be impossible. The nature of language is such, however, that, as my previous sentence exemplifies, "deconstruction states the fallacy of reference in a necessarily referential mode" (*AR,* 125). A fuller formulation of this principle summarizes de Man's exploration of aesthetics and the self in Rousseau: "The discourse by which the figural structure of the self is asserted fails to escape from the categories it claims to deconstruct, and this remains true, of course, of any discourse which pretends to reinscribe in its turn the figure of this aporia. There can be no escape from the dialectical movement that produces the text" (*AR,* 187).

"Text" is de Man's most specific concern. In quiet polemic against the emphasis of the late Roland Barthes on the pleasurable "liberation of the signifier" (*AR,* 114) and against the exhilaration that Derrida finds warranted by Nietzsche, de Man insists that textuality is terribly frustrating rather than gratifying. How *can* we know the dancer? He dwells on, and in, this cognitive impasse. So he defines a *"text"* as a double-bind, as "any entity that can be considered from [this] double perspective: as a generative, open-ended, non-referential grammatical system and as a figural system closed off by a transcendental signification that subverts the grammatical code to which the text owes its existence" (*AR,* 270).

A text can never "know" what it is doing; it has lost the privilege de Man once accorded to literature. *Blindness and Insight* argued that critics were caught in the strange logic of the title but that literary writing was free from it. In contrast to his interpreters, Rousseau had no blind spots.[19] Now, every text by definition has blind spots. Moreover, de Man abandons the new-critical and aesthetic terminology of "literary language," a crucially repeated term even in the latest essays of *Blindness and Insight* but virtually absent from

Allegories of Reading. This trajectory of de Man's work hardly makes him a defender of literature.

He stands rather with Rousseau and Plato, occupying and challenging the border between literature and philosophy by their willingness to name literature as "lie." Plato and Rousseau attacked literature by taking seriously its claims to truth—perhaps, readers have felt, because their own extreme susceptibility to literature kept them from heeding disclaimers that it need not be taken so seriously, no one believes it anyway. De Man writes from the stance of one who has been betrayed by literature and is trying, gingerly, to discover what it is that has done this to him. His most common term for the effect of literature is "seduction."[20] This is no happy eroticism, but a dangerous temptation that deconstruction exists to combat.

The function of this figure in de Man gains important illumination from the "Diary of the Seducer" in Kierkegaard's anatomy of the "aesthetic," *Either/Or.* The character A comments on the seducer, who may be himself:

> He knew how to excite a girl to the highest pitch, so . . . that she was ready to sacrifice everything. When the affair reached this point, he broke off without himself having made the slightest advances and without having let fall a single word of love, let alone a declaration, a promise. And still it had happened, and the consciousness of it was doubly bitter for the unhappy girl because there was not the slightest thing to which she could appeal . . . since the relationship had had reality only in the figurative sense. . . . It was real, and yet, when she wished to speak of it, there was nothing to tell.[21]

In this model of the aesthetic text, its nonreferential, purely contemplative status produces a situation in which it seems that the victims seduce themselves. This for de Man is what we do in reading through the category of the aesthetic. Yet even to see that a text is referential, that it does make "promises" (*AR,* 275-276), may lessen our guilt but in no way protects us from other pain. Such is our humanity that even when we have reduced the text to a "machine," its power remains and "seduces [us] into dangerously close contact" (*AR,* 298). Like Nietzsche, Rousseau, Proust, and James, de Man constantly rewrites a story of impossible, destructive passion.

V

In de Man's reading, Julie's insight into the blindness of her love for Saint-Preux cannot save her from repeating the error of love, with God as its object. In de Man's writing, his insight into the errors of metaphorical assimilaton cannot prevent him from repeating that gesture throughout his work. To write of rhetorical deconstruction necessitates de Man's stretching the senses of such rhetorical terms as chiasmus and anacoluthon, carrying them over from matters of word order and grammatical construction into semantics, thus himself leaping the gap he had so labored to establish between grammar and meaning. His most constant trope transfers consciousness and agency, such as we usually attribute to people, to language itself. We have already noticed "seduction"; "knowledge" also figures in this play.[22] De Man's practice undoes his theoretical attempt to disrupt the categories of inner and outer (which allow for a transfer of properties leading to a synecdochic totalization). For to describe the process of deconstruction, he constructs metaphysical dualisms, the revelation of what was hidden, the discovery of reality beneath appearance.[23] Even to raise the question of "truth and error" and thus challenge the aesthetic, he must appeal to a sense of "epistemology" that would offer philosophic "foundation" (AR, 245) for our beliefs. Yet Richard Rorty has argued at persuasive length, and de Man following Derrida has elsewhere briefly suggested, that such a foundational epistemology is itself untenable.[24]

All this is no more than de Man has already allowed; he claims no freedom from the textual problematic that he elucidates. In his essay on Rousseau's *Narcissus,* for instance, he depicts a figure that many readers would take for his own ideal self-image: "No longer the dupe of his own wishes . . . he is as far beyond pleasure and pain as he is beyond good and evil. . . . His consciousness is neither happy nor unhappy, nor does he possess any power. He remains, however, a center of authority to the extent that the very destructiveness of his ascetic reading testifies to the validity of his interpretation" (AR, 173-174). The essay proceeds to dismantle this figure. The question remains, however, whether de Man's text can avoid establishing this "center of authority" and setting it to work. For in recent American criticism this figure, although an error, has had an extremely powerful effect. This mask walks among us, gives talks, writes dissertations, publishes, and its name is legion.

De Man's work has entered history, solving in practice the theoretical impasse from which *Allegories of Reading* began, when de Man found himself "unable to progress" (AR, ix) from local reading to a broader history. His theory projects this case outward: history exists only as a repetition of that inability to progress, only in allegorizing the self-consuming tangle of textuality. If "necessity" is a mark of history, then history will always be a metaphorical fiction, but contrary to de Man's suggestion (AR, 289-90), there is no incompatibility between causality and contingency.[25] It would benefit us if de Man had read his own figures of history as attentively as he read the metaphorical seductions of the texts he scrutinizes. For when de Man claims that rhetoric has only the "appearance of a history" (AR, 131) or that "temporal sequence" is only a "semblance,"[26] these disjunctions, in abjuring history, reconstruct metaphysical duality.

Nietzsche, just where he most lends himself to de Man, offers also the possibility of another reading that enables genealogical history. De Man quotes Nietzsche's famous answer to "What is truth?": "A moving army of metaphors [sic], metonymies and anthropomorphisms, in short a summa of human relationships that are being poetically and rhetorically sublimated, transposed, and beautified until, after long and repeated use, a people considers them as solid, canonical, and unavoidable" (AR, 110-111; quoting from "On Truth and Lies in a Nonmoral Sense"). The "human relationships," the "people," and the "long use," however, de Man ignores.[27] Yet these are the elements, no less than the figures, from which to construct a history of the contingencies that have put us in the odd place that we are.

VI

I conclude with the rhetoric of several Jamesian topics that Donadio has addressed. My own interest is in using such analysis to move toward a renewed sense of history, of "realism" even, rather than as an end in itself or in the service of Donadio's expressive aestheticism.

I have noted Donadio's reliance upon a rhetoric of reconciled opposites, which in anglo-american criticism derives from Coleridge. Recall, for instance, Coleridge on the symbol as characterized "above all by the translucence of the Eternal in and through the Temporal. It always partakes of the Reality which it renders intelligible; and while it enunciates the whole, abides itself as a living part in that Unity, of which it is the representative."[28]

A moment from the grand party at Milly's Palazzo in The Wings of the Dove demonstrates James's wary scrutiny of such rhetoric. Donadio takes the novel as defined by Milly's point of view (NJ, 130-131), but James lets us see Milly, and her effect, through others, displacing his center. Densher first sees Milly in romantic, symbolist terms, as "embodied poetry,"[29] but the scene moves toward acknowledging an arbitrary process of semiological construction rather than crediting a natural transparency that gives symbols their representative power.

The phrase "embodied poetry" suggests the inherence of Milly's spiritual value within her physical body and echoes the infatuation of symbolist critics from Coleridge to the present with Donne's phrase, "her body thought." But the passage dismembers that embodied poetry. Kate fixes Densher's attention on Milly's pearls, separating a part from the whole, destroying the totality, revealing that Milly's embodied poetry owes its appeal to these jewels—unlikely as that is for a "dove." Densher departs from Coleridgean unity in seeing the pearls as the "symbol of differences," and then comes a further shift. A moment later, Milly herself "symbolise[s] . . . the great difference." She now stands for her pearls, rather than their being part of a spiritual totality that she embodies. The thing has taken over the person.

Pearls, moreover, are not unique to Milly: "They suit every one." They are detachable; Kate could wear them. They are arbitrarily placed on Milly, like allegorical identifications, rather than inhering naturally in her like symbols. The differences they symbolize are not necessary to the nature of things but are contingent differences that money produces within human life-histories in society. Ordinarily we see the effects of money as if they were natural, but at moments we recall that human activities are responsible for the arbitrary distribution of wealth and its consequences, just as they are for the rhetorical assignment of meanings to figures. Thus in reducing the claims of symbol in this passage, James accomplishes a realistic function. In exposing the conventions of literature and society alike, he reminds us that we might make things different. The "will to power" is a Nietzschean concept, relevant here, that de Man and Donadio ignore.

Consider in this context the metamorphoses of the figure of the Dove in the party-scene. First the appropriateness of "dove" as a figure for Milly is questioned: doves aren't usually bejewelled. Then the symbolic force of the figure is recuperated through the natural qualities of the dove, which has the power of flight and therefore may properly represent the soaring splendor Milly manifests. The figure is no sooner naturalized, however, than it grotesquely exceeds nature. No dove is so large as to nestle in its wings a whole company of people, only a dove taken out of nature into an arbitrary system of signification. The other characters make Milly a dove, and her final triumph is to make their own figure return to haunt them.

The end of the book offers more specification of James's rhetorical concern. The dying Milly has sent Densher a note from Venice to London, which seems clearly intended to arrive on Christmas. Densher surmises that it must therefore inform him that he will inherit Milly's wealth. Profoundly moved by this act of generous forgiveness, he nonetheless brings the note unopened to Kate. Kate and Densher scrutinize the envelope. They marvel over its beautiful handwriting. Kate then takes the "sacred script" and throws it in the fire. They are sure of its intention. Why worry about how it is said? But as Densher later ponders the event, he reckons that in Milly's letter "the intention . . . would have been . . . the least part of it. The part of it missed forever was the turn she would have given" (*WD*, 2:10, 6).

This "turn" that would have made all the difference translates Greek *tropos*, the general rhetorical term for figure of speech. Densher recognizes that a turn—a trope—is not just a means of expression; it is not necessarily at one with intention. The turn changes intention, for trope is interpretation, not transparency. So in *Pride and Prejudice* Bingley tells Lizzie Bennett that she has mis-taken Darcy's comment: "You are giving it a turn which that gentlemen did by no means intend," and thereby "converting" a sarcasm "into a compliment" (ch. 10).

"Converting," by its Latin etymology, involves the same semantic area as English "turn" and Greek *tropos,* and it operates powerfully within James's critical vocabulary. Donadio recognizes the importance of the term, but he characteristically accords it only psychological significance: "alternating aspects of James's personality find their imaginative expression in his work, and . . . this book . . . attempts to trace that process of transformation (or 'conversion') by which one state of feeling reverses itself and becomes its opposite" (*NJ,* 6-7). James uses the term quite differently. In the early "Art of Fiction," the key term of "experience" is not a matter of feeling but an activity, an interpretive "power" that "converts the very pulses of the air into revelation."[30] The late "Lesson of Balzac" praises him for "converting into history" so much.[31]

"Conversion," this differential turning, is James's word for how an individual contributes to the making of culture, both works of art and the total human disposition toward society. It is not a smooth process of transmission. It produces a substitution, a difference made at some cost and loss, for the original is gone. As a writer, James's conversions involve the criticism of earlier modes of writing and their replacement by his own, and they involve equally the loss of any direct connection to a world outside his books. Representation is not transparent.

This position is elaborately articulated in a prefatory passage that itself transforms the "chemical" process of conversion into a "mystical" cooking: "We can surely account for nothing in the novelist's work that hasn't passed through the crucible of his imagination, hasn't in that perpetually simmering cauldron his intellectual *pot-au-feu* been reduced to savoury fusion. . . . It has entered . . . into new relations. . . . Its final savour has been constituted but its prime identity destroyed."[32] James's figure makes clear that the process is not so reversible as Donadio wishes.

The value of conversions comes explicitly into question later in *The Wings of the Dove.* Densher has long been resisting any "turn"; he values his "straightness," and both as a matter of male sexuality and of general morality refuses to be "bent" by Kate's will. He seeks the straight path toward their sexual union and marriage and resents every "dodge" Kate finds to put him off (echoing a word James uses in the Preface for his own compositional practice). Her "readiness" to love him is "the woman herself" (*WD,* 2:8, 3), but the dodge, the turn, violates nature and its desirable straightness. Finally, however, at the book's end Densher tries to deny the natural passage of time and its consequences. He tries to re-establish his life with Kate "as we were" (*WD,* 2:10, 6), bending time to his will through the rhetorical figure of metalepsis that replaces the present with the past, wishfully substituting a far-distant cause for its no longer existent effect. If anything can protect against time, trope can, but nothing does: "We shall never be again as we were," the book ends.

The book's figures enact the transformation of "straightness" in Densher's awareness, and the turning point occurs in his reflections as the physician departs to confer with Milly about her disease. With a "cry" and a "swerve," the gondola suddenly vanishes from sight on its "short cut," and this "difference" suddenly evokes "the truth that was truest about Milly," that "great smudge of mortality" which speech refuses to "reflect." The passage makes us

430

question with Densher: what is the value of "beautiful fictions," of the "aesthetic instinct" to avoid "outrage"? The line of feeling resonates with the traditional values of our culture. We believe in truth, disinterest, revelation, and not in "suppressions," and we therefore register deeply the difference between the two states evoked. Densher is facing the worst in the relation of art and life. Like Plato, Rousseau, de Man, he sees the baselessness of the aesthetic. But as he does so, the "fool's paradise" of art begins to turn to something else. In revising the first edition for the New York Edition, James made two crucial alterations at this point. For "had now come in," he rewrote "had now crossed the threshold," and for "space," he rewrote "precinct."[33] These changes suggest ritually sacred space, appropriately cut off (the etymological sense of "temple" and "precinct") from the rest of the world, and the physician becomes a mediating figure between the two realms. Like the "artist *in triumph*" James summons up in his prefaces,[34] all we finally glimpse of the physician is his back, as he interposes his shoulders between us and the vision we are grateful to be spared. Through Densher, James here has posed the fundamental critical question about his work: how do we appraise (or "appreciate") the losses exacted in making his kind of "beautiful fiction"?

Donadio makes vivid to us the power of the aesthetic for James, for Nietzsche, and for himself. De Man places the aesthetic in the "appearance" of history engendered by Kant's misreading of Rousseau.[35] But human history is real enough for our purposes, even if it is a history of error. If truth is not God's but a "mobile army of metaphors," their "long use" still makes one "people" different from another, or from itself over time. During the same years that de Man was working through his rhetorical alternative to the use of Nietzsche for American humanism, Michel Foucault turned Nietzsche's genealogical inquiries to use for anti-humanist historiography.[36] In the practice of Foucault's *Discipline and Punish* (*Surveiller et Punir,* 1975) and *History of Sexuality* (*La Volonté de Savoir,* 1976), genealogical history has shown the creation and long use of the "delinquent," the "hysterical woman," the "pervert" in the war of "human relationships." Drawing upon the very passage from "On Truth and Lies in a Nonmoral Sense" that I have been discussing with regard to de Man and that Hillis Miller analyzes in this volume, Edward Said in *Orientalism* (1978) has shown the creation and long use of the "oriental" as some peoples' weapon against others. Without explicit reference to Nietzsche, the genealogical history of *The American Jeremiad* (1978) by Sacvan Bercovitch has demonstrated the coercive power of the "American" to differentiate and mold a people. Forthcoming books by contributors to this volume—Cornel West on racism, Daniel O'Hara's *Romance of Interpretation,* Paul Bové's *Masterful Opponents*—carry this genealogical project farther. The "aesthetic," then, is a lie that James and Nietzsche both dismantle, as Donadio overlooks, and a truth that both yield to, as he sees and does likewise. Their struggle with the "aesthetic" forms part of the historical specificity of their writing, which de Man denies on behalf of a general theory of textuality. De Man's vigilance preserves us from Donadio's error, but to preserve ourselves from de Man's, we must look elsewhere.

University of Illinois at Chicago

NOTES

1   On this issue, see de Man, "Shelley Disfigured," in Harold Bloom et al., *Deconstruction and Criticism* (New York: Seabury, 1979); and Jonathan Arac, "To Regress from the Rigor of Shelley: Figures of History in American Deconstructive Criticism," *boundary 2* 8:3 (1980).

2   Collected in *Blindness and Insight: Essays in the Rhetoric of Contemporary Criticism* (1971; enlarged ed. Minneapolis: Univ. of Minnesota Press, 1983).

3   Paul de Man, *Allegories of Reading: Figural Language in Rousseau, Nietzsche, Rilke, and Proust* (New Haven: Yale Univ. Press, 1979); Stephen Donadio, *Nietzsche, Henry James, and the Artistic Will* (New York: Oxford Univ. Press, 1978). Future parenthetical references abbreviate de Man as *AR* and Donadio as *NJ*.

4   No less than Donadio's aestheticism or de Man's deconstruction, Fredric Jameson's Marxism refuses this understanding of Nietzsche, as I argue in "Nietzsche, Theology, the Political Unconscious," *Union Seminary Quarterly Review* 37 (1983). See, however, the conjunction of Marx and Nietzsche in Marshall Berman, *All That is Solid Melts into Air* (New York: Simon and Schuster, 1982), esp. pp. 19-23.

5   For a different understanding of Yeats's autobiography, see Daniel T. O'Hara, *Tragic Knowledge* (New York: Columbia Univ. Press., 1981).

6   See fragment 90 of Heraclitus, "All things are an Exchange for Fire, and Fire for all things, just as goods for gold and gold for goods," cited in *NJ,* 199.

7   On English aestheticism, see Daniel T. O'Hara, *The Romance of Interpretation: Visionary Criticism—Pater through de Man* (New York: Columbia Univ. Press, forthcoming).

8   Donadio ignores Sartre's famous statement of the need for metaphysical definition of fictional techniques in his essay on *The Sound and the Fury* (1939; much reprinted in translation).

9   Donadio ignores the work of J. Hillis Miller on the religious implications of fictional techniques in *The Disappearance of God* (1963), and *The Form of Victorian Fiction* (1968).

10   Henry James, Preface to *The Wings of the Dove,* in *The Art of the Novel* (New York: Scribner, 1934), p. 302.

11   Henry James, *The Portrait of a Lady,* Modern Library reprint of New York Edition, I, 246. "Rarer even than to be French seemed it to be American on such interesting terms," thinks Isabel Archer of Madame Merle.

12   Henry James, *Letters,* ed. Leon Edel (Cambridge: Harvard Univ. Press, 1974), I, 77.

13   *Art of the Novel,* pp. 338-39.

14   Donadio lists in his Bibliography de Man's three essays on Nietzsche that go into *Allegories of Reading,* but in 43 pages of Notes they are not cited, nor are they mentioned in the text.

15   De Man developed this basic argument as early as a dissertation chapter on "Image and Emblem in Yeats," now first published in his posthumous collection, *The Rhetoric of Romanticism* (New York: Columbia Univ. Press, 1984). Several times there de Man cites Yeats's "How can we *know* the dancer from the dance?" as "How can we *tell* the dancer from the dance?" (both emphases mine), thereby emphasizing the metonymic process of reduction and separation over metaphoric (synecdochic) expression and identity.

16   In current critical discussion, the "dialogical" evokes the work of Mikhail Bakhtin, which de Man addressed in "Dialogue and Dialogism," *Poetics Today* IV (1983).

17   I have emended the text, which reads, "puts these statements into a question."

18   In his last years de Man continued to question the "aesthetic." See especially the essay on Kleist in *The Rhetoric of Romanticism* and essays on Kant and Hegel in another posthumous collection, *Aesthetic Ideology,* to be published by University of Minnesota Press.

19   *Blindness and Insight,* p. 139. My awareness of de Man's shift was heightened by the critique of his earlier position in Paul A. Bové, *Destructive Poetics* (New York: Columbia Univ. Press, 1980), pp. 46-48. Rodolphe Gasché also argues for such a shift in " 'Setzung' and 'Übersetzung': Notes on Paul de Man," *Diacritics* 11:4 (Winter 1981), while Suzanne Gearhart argues otherwise in a challenging response, "Philosophy *before* Literature: Deconstruction, Historicity, and the Work of Paul de Man," *Diacritics* 13:4 (Winter 1983).

20   Since the Index lists only proper names, I offer some instances of this figure in *AR:* pp. ix, 11, 14, 15, 20-22, 24, 26, 35, 42, 45, 48, 53, 55, 66, 67, 71, 93, 110, 114, 115, 119, 159, 169, 181, 184, 200, 205, 210, 262, 298.

21   Søren Kierkegaard, *Either/Or,* trans. David F. Swenson and Lillian Marvin Swenson, rev. Howard A. Johnson (Princeton: Princeton Univ. Press, 1959), I, 303.

22   For example, "Any speech act produces an excess of cognition, but it can never hope to know the process of its own production (the only thing worth knowing)" (*AR,* 300).

23   For example, "A vast . . . network is revealed . . . that remained invisible to a reader caught in naive metaphorical mystification" (*AR,* 16). See also pp. ix, 67, 72, 124, 212, 249; and Stanley Corngold, "Error in Paul de Man," in *The Yale Critics,* ed. Jonathan Arac, Wlad Godzich, and Wallace Martin (Minneapolis: Univ. of Minnesota Press, 1983).

24   Richard Rorty, *Philosophy and the Mirror of Nature* (Princeton: Princeton Univ. Press, 1979); and Paul de Man, "The Epistemology of Metaphor," *Critical Inquiry,* 5 (1978).

25   See *AR,* 288: "The use of a vocabulary of contingency . . . within an argument of causality is arresting and disruptive." But it is perfectly normal to say, "I was late because [causality] there happened [contingency] to be an accident blocking the way." Moreover, de Man links contingency to metonymy, which most rhetorics link to causality. He derives metonymy as contingency from its accepted sense as "contiguity," and here too confusions arise, for at times he takes contiguity as the "isolation" of one thing from another (*AR,* 145), at times as connection, continuity—or "continguity" (*AR,* 14, 66).

26   *AR,* 162. The link of sequence and semblance echoes the final lyric from *Faust,* "Alles Vergängliche / Ist nur ein Gleichnis," which in "Linguistics and Poetics" Roman Jakobson had glossed as "anything sequent is a simile."

433

27   For de Man's fullest reading of this passage, see "Anthropomorphism and Trope in the Lyric," in *The Rhetoric of Romanticism.*

28   *Collected Works of Samuel Taylor Coleridge* (Princeton: Princeton Univ. Press, 1969-), VI, 30. My argument on symbol and allegory is indebted to "The Rhetoric of Temporality" (1969), now collected in *Blindness and Insight.*

29   References to *The Wings of the Dove* follow the text of the New York Edition, giving volume, book, and section numbers. The whole passage under discussion occupies about a page in II:8, 3. Future references abbreviate the novel as *WD.*

30   Henry James, *The House of Fiction,* ed. Leon Edel (1957: rpt. London: Heinemann, 1962), pp. 31-32.

31   *House of Fiction,* p. 69.

32   Preface to "The Lesson of the Master," in *Art of the Novel,* p. 230.

33   See the text of the first edition as reprinted by the Modern Library, II, 325. This whole passage under discussion occupies about a page in the New York Edition, II:9, 4.

34   Preface to *The Tragic Muse,* in *Art of the Novel,* p. 96.

35   For the figure of "engender," see *AR,* 205, 272, 274, and especially 162: "Texts engender texts" and "consist of a series of repetitive reversals that engenders the semblance of a temporal sequence." I take this sexual allegory as a reading of Yeats: The Swan "engenders . . . the broken wall, the burning roof and tower" through Leda's inevitable failure to gain Zeus's "knowledge with his power."

36   See "Nietzsche, Genealogy, History" (1971), trans. Donald F. Bouchard and Sherry Simon in *Language, Counter-Memory, Practice,* ed. Donald Bouchard (Ithaca: Cornell Univ. Press, 1977).

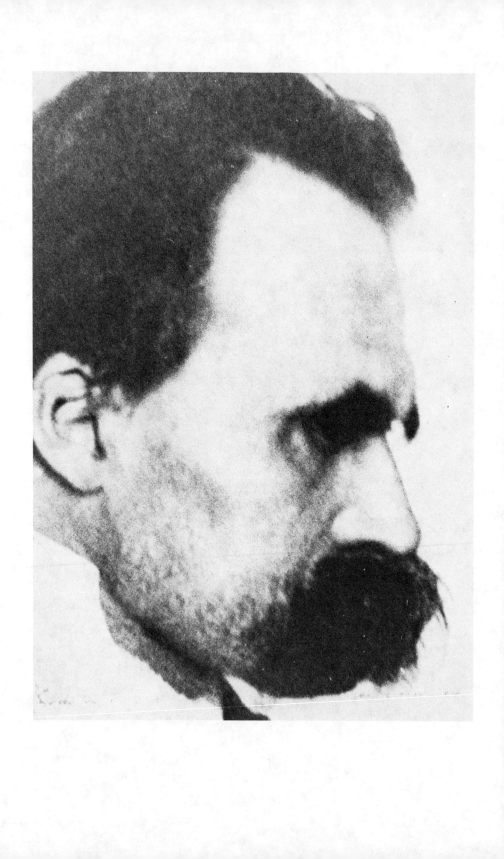

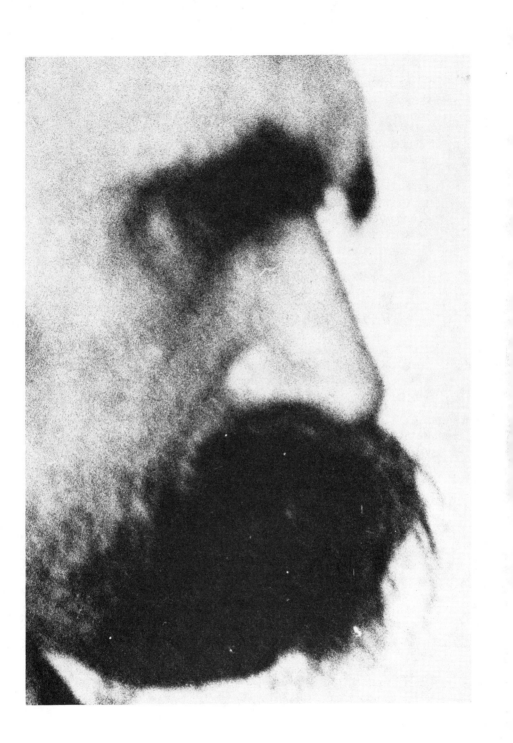

CONTRIBUTORS

David B. Allison teaches at the Stony Brook campus of the State University of New York. He is Translator of Jacques Derrida's *Speech and Phenomena,* editor of Derrida's *Edmund Husserl's 'Origin of Geometry,'* editor and translator of *The New Nietzsche,* and has written articles on Nietzsche, Heidegger, Derrida, Levi-Strauss, and Wittgenstein. He is presently working on a Nietzsche book and one on Descartes.

Charles Altieri, formerly at SUNY-Buffalo and now teaching at the University of Washington, is a member of the Editorial Board of *boundary 2.* He has recently published *Act and Quality: A Theory of Literary Meaning and Humanistic Understanding.*

Jonathan Arac, Associate Professor of English at the University of Illinois at Chicago Circle, is author of *Commissioned Spirits: The Shaping of Social Motion in Dickens, Carlyle, Melville, and Hawthorne* (Rutgers University Press, 1979) and in 1978-79 held an ACLS Fellowship to work on *Rhetoric and Realism in Nineteenth-Century Fiction.*

Paul Bové is an Associate Editor of *boundary 2* and author of *Destructive Poetics* (Columbia University Press). He is currently writing a book on the cultural and theoretical implications of the academic study of English Literature.

Joseph A. Buttigieg is an Assistant Professor of English at the University of Notre Dame. His essays on modern literature and criticism have appeared in *boundary 2, Christianity and Literature, Union Seminary Quarterly Review,* and *American Book Review.* He is currently completing a book on *A Portrait.*

Stanley Corngold teaches in the Departments of Germanic Literatures and Languages and Comparative Literature at Princeton University. He is the author of *The Commentator's Despair*—a study of Kafka's "Metamorphosis"—and recent essays on Rilke, Dilthey, and Nietzsche. *New Directions* will bring out his studies of seven German writers in 1982.

Rudolphe Gasché is an Associate Professor of Comparative Literature at the State University of New York at Buffalo. Recently he published his second book, *System und Mataphork in der Philosophie von Georges Bataille,* and is currently working on a book-length critique of the philosophy of reflexivity.

David Farrell Krell is an Associate Professor on the Faculty of Languages and Literature of the University of Mannheim, West Germany. Born in

438

Pittsburgh, Pennsylvania, he received his Ph.D. in philosophy from Duquesne University. The author of *The Logos of Logic* and of numerous articles in scholarly journals, Dr. Krell is the editor and co-translator of Martin Heidegger's *Basic Writings, Early Greek Thinking,* and *Nietzsche* for the Harper and Row Heidegger Series. He is also on the editorial board of *boundary 2.*

Rudolf E. Kuenzli, Associate Professor of English and Comparative Literature, and Director of the Dada Archive and Research Center at the University of Iowa, has written on Dada, Derrida, Nietzsche, and contemporary literary theories. He is currently working on a study of Nietzsche's style.

George McFadden, Professor of English at Temple University, is author of *Dryden the Public Writer: 1660-1685,* and the forthcoming *Discovering the Comic* (Princeton University Press), from which the essay appearing in this issue is taken.

J. Hillis Miller is Frederick W. Hilles Professor of English and Professor of Comparative Literature at Yale University where he is also currently the Director of the Literature Major. He is the author of *The Disappearance of God, Poets of Reality, Thomas Hardy: Distance and Desire,* and other books and essays. His *Fiction and Repetition: Seven English Novels* is forthcoming from Harvard Press. The essay in this issue of *boundary 2* is drawn from a chapter of a book in progress to be called "The Linguistic Moment."

Dan O'Hara, an Assistant Professor at Temple University and an Assistant Editor of *boundary 2,* is the author of *Tragic Knowledge: Yeats' Autobiography and Hermeneutics* and many essays on the aesthetic tradition in modern and post-modern criticism.

Joseph N. Riddel, Professor of English at UCLA, is the author of books on Wallace Stevens, William Carlos Williams, and C. Day Lewis, and is at work on a study of American poetics.

Gary Shapiro, Assistant Professor of Philosophy, University of Kansas, has published papers on Hegel, Peirce, Sartre, and Heidegger and is currently completing a book on the philosophical significance of Nietzsche's writing.

Hugh J. Silverman is Associate Professor of Philosophy and Comparative Literature at State University of New York at Stony Brook. He is co-editor of *Jean-Paul Sartre: Contemporary Approaches to his Philosophy,* editor of *Piaget, Philosophy and the Human Sciences,* and translator of Maurice Merleau-Ponty. Author of over thirty articles in recent continental

439

thought, he is preparing a book entitled *Between Phenomenology and Structuralism,* and another on Sartre and the Structuralists.

Tracy B. Strong is presently Associate Professor of Political Science at the University of California, San Diego. He has previously taught at Amherst College, Smith College, the University of Pittsburgh, and Harvard University. At present he is working on the relation between aesthetics and political theory during the generation which follows Nietzsche as well as on a biography of a member of his family. He is the author of *Friedrich Nietzsche and the Politics of Transfiguration* (University of California Press), as well as several articles in political theory.

Cornel West is Assistant Professor of Philosophy of Religion at Union Theological Seminary, New York City. He has published essays dealing with Schleiermacher, Heidegger, Wittgenstein, Derrida, Marxist theory, liberation theology and Afro-American thought. He is presently revising his dissertation on the Marxist conception of ethics and initiating a study on the genealogy of modern racism.

ACKNOWLEDGEMENTS AND ILLUSTRATIONS

boundary 2 wishes to thank the following for their permission to publish certain portions of this issue:

David Farrell Krell, for the excerpts from Martin Heidegger, *Nietzsche, Vol. II: The Eternal Recurrence of the Same,* trans. with Notes and an Analysis by David Farrell Krell, to be published by Harper and Row, Inc., and copyrighted (c) 1982 by Harper and Row, Inc.

David Farrell Krell, for the pictures of Nietzsche featured in the issue. They were originally taken by Hans Olde (a painter) as part of his commission to paint a heroic portrait of the dying philosopher in Summer 1899. These pictures were originally published in the 1930s in a now defunct Swiss *Zeitschrift, Du.* As such, they are in the public domain.

J. Hillis Miller, for those portions of *boundary 2* ("Dismembering and Disremembering in Nietzsche's 'On Truth and Lies in a Nonmoral Sense' ") taken from the section on *Nietzsche* in the chapter on *Yeats* of *The Linguistic Moment,* to be published by Princeton University Press, and are copyrighted (c) 1981 by Princeton University Press.

Publication of this issue has been made possible by a grant from the Coordinating Council of Literary Magazines, through funds received from the New York State Council of Arts.